MARKET GRID FOR REFRIGERATION 15¢

East	Midwest	South	Mountain	Pacific	Region Place of Use
					Home
X					Food Stores
					Wholesalers
					Restaurants
					Hospitals
					Schools
					Military Reservations
					Business Offices
					Other Institutions
					Trailers
					Picnics
					Planes
					Trains
					Ships

Marketing strategy planning requires judgmer
every "market" can be conceived of as a gri

Basic Marketing:
A
Managerial
Approach

Basic Marketing:
A Managerial Approach

E. Jerome McCarthy, Ph.D.
Professor of Marketing
Michigan State University

Third Edition, 1968  **Richard D. Irwin, Inc.**
Homewood, Illinois
Irwin-Dorsey Limited, Nobleton, Ontario

Third Edition

First Printing, April, 1968

Library of Congress Catalog Card No. 68–19500

Printed in the United States of America

Preface

This text is designed for use in an introductory course in marketing, either in schools with one or two marketing courses or in the larger business schools with a full complement of marketing courses.

All business students should be introduced to the basic problems and practices in marketing management. At the same time, it is clearly wishful thinking to assume that a student can be taught all there is to know about marketing in one or two courses. And it is just as clear that, even in larger schools with a range of marketing courses, less than one third of all business students become marketing majors.

This text, then, is an attempt to meet the needs of the majority of beginning marketing students who are taking their first and perhaps only course in marketing. It tries to give the student an understanding and a feel for the marketing manager's job, and the world in which he operates.

Admittedly, this text does not offer a complete and detailed description of all possible problems or solutions in the marketing area. But it does offer a broad and necessary understanding of marketing problems, giving the student a foundation for investigating more comprehensive references. A student must see the whole picture before he can appreciate the details.

As a basic introductory text, *Basic Marketing: A Managerial Approach* differs considerably from similar works. It takes a *managerial approach* to marketing problems. While the text material, of course, is similar to that found in the traditional texts, the approach definitely is not. We will see marketing situations through the manager's eyes.

Marketing strategy and designing a marketing mix (but not day-to-day implementation) are stressed to give the student the big picture. This planning takes place in *a dynamic social and political environment*, however, and the effect of the economy on marketing (and vice versa) is given extensive treatment.

The first chapter, therefore, takes a broad historical and social point of view to set the stage for the managerial material which follows. This social viewpoint is alluded to throughout the material and then returned to at the end of the text when the social efficiency of marketing management and marketing is treated.

Following the introductory chapter, the role of marketing and marketing management in the operation of an economic system is stressed. The focus upon satisfying varying target markets on a market grid is emphasized especially. Then, the framework within which the marketing manager must operate and the tools with which he works are discussed. These include marketing research and sales forecasting.

The characteristics and buying habits of target customers—both final consumers in the United States and world markets, and intermediate customers, such as businesses, farmers, and governments—are described.

Based on the behavior of target markets and the company's own objectives, a marketing mix is developed next out of four ingredients, called the four P's: Product, Place (that is, channels and institutions), Promotion, and Price. These sections comprise the bulk of the text and are concerned with developing the "right" product and making it available at the "right" place with the "right" promotion and the "right" price, to satisfy target customers and still meet the objectives of the business.

After a final discussion on integrating the four P's and controlling the marketing process, we return to a consideration of how efficient the marketing process is and especially to the question, "Does marketing cost too much?" At that time, many of the criticisms of marketing are presented and discussed. This approach is used because, while students are concerned with the efficient organization and management of the marketing process, they also are interested in how marketing as an institution helps our economy operate and grow.

An international flavor is included not only in Chapter 7 but throughout the text in recognition of American businesses' growing interest and involvement in the world market. Technical details are not emphasized. The international material merely provides perspective and shows the universal applicability of the principles and approaches presented throughout the text.

It is hoped that, in this framework, marketing will be looked upon by more students as a useful, fascinating, and very necessary function in our American economy.

This material can be studied in a number of ways. *One,* the reading material can be supplemented with lectures and class discussion of the text material. *Two,* understanding of the text material can be enhanced by conventional questions and problems. *Three,* thought-provoking questions can be used to encourage the student to investigate the marketing process and organize his own way of thinking about it.

The text is organized so that any of the methods or any combination of them can be used. All are compatible with the management orientation. However, at least experimentation with the third approach is highly recommended.

I reevaluated my approach to teaching beginning marketing when some educators made some interesting observations. Dr. J. S. Bruner, at Harvard, found that a child learned more geography when given a map and asked to predict where the biggest cities *should be,* rather than by straight memorization of where they actually are. Other educators had success using similar methods, such as asking children to "invent" multiplication as a short cut to addition.

Trying to apply these ideas using conventional marketing texts was difficult, however, since most of the "answers" were given early—sometimes in the first chapter or two. Thus it was not possible to have the student read the text and still develop his own ideas as the text moved along.

This text works differently. It assumes that the student comes to the beginning marketing course with some experience—if nothing else, as a consumer—and that he is able to project what "should be" or "probably will be" on the basis of this prior knowledge. Certainly the student's vocabulary, in the sense of conventional marketing terms and definitions, will be lacking. But he can anticipate the nature of these terms and especially the functions which are provided by the various firms.

It is for this reason—that the student should be encouraged to "think ahead"—that this text deliberately avoids introducing certain concepts and definitions before they are needed. Precise definitions of wholesaling and retailing, for example, are delayed until midway in the book, when the entire area of where and how goods should be made available is considered.

When all the details are not presented early, then creative thought can be encouraged by the questions following each chapter. These questions encourage the student to think ahead and develop what "ought to be," and then subsequent chapters present commonly accepted definitions and methods of operation. For example, following the introductory management chapters, customers—both intermediate customers and final consumers—are analyzed. The questions here encourage the student to think about the kind of products these customers *might like,* the kinds of shopping behavior they *would exhibit,* where the goods *should be made available,* and how they *should be priced and promoted.*

In the Product area, after the student has had a chance to roughly categorize the products which will be available, the conventional terms are introduced and his past experience is organized for him.

The questions at the end of the Product chapters ask him how these products should be made available. After he has had a try at this, the conventional definitions and institutional material on wholesaling and retailing are introduced in the Place area; and so on.

This approach follows in sequence four basic steps in psychological learning theory:

1. Motivation.
2. Investigation.
3. Organization.
4. Utilization.

The first few chapters attempt to motivate the student by encouraging his interest in the subject and indicating how important marketing and marketing management are to the operation of a whole economy. The questions at the end of the early chapters encourage him to do his own investigation. Then subsequent chapters provide the commonly accepted organization.

In the middle chapters, the approach is to alternate between Steps 2 and 3—from investigation to organization and then to further investigation, building upon the material previously organized. Finally, at the end of the book, a number of cases of various types are included. They can be used to encourage the student to utilize the thinking he has done in the investigation and organization stages. If there is time, a few of these cases (or cases from other sources) should be tried during and at the end of the course to "set" the material and give the student a chance to utilize the fruits of his own thinking. This completes the learning cycle.

As indicated earlier, this third approach need not be used. The first two can be used quite satisfactorily. I highly recommend the third approach, however, as I have thoroughly enjoyed teaching the course since experimenting with its use. Most students feel they know quite a bit about marketing when they come into this course. When the entire course is "high spotted" in the first few chapters, it becomes difficult to maintain interest in "old stuff." If, instead, the instructor and text encourage the student to organizie and use his experience and common sense to almost "write" the book, he becomes involved. Many even enjoy the course.

Leads for further reading are provided in many comprehensive footnotes, but the literature of marketing and related fields is so voluminous that selection for others is difficult. With the background provided by this text, the student should be able to locate useful material through his library's card catalog, the *Industrial Arts Index,* and the *Reader's Guide to Periodical Literature.* For leads to books and articles published through 1949, he should see: David A. Revzan, *A Comprehensive Classified Marketing Bibliography,* Parts I and II (Berkeley: University of California Press, 1951). For more recent references he should see the fine bibliographical series published by the American Marketing Association.

This book is a result of the blending of my experiences in business, at Northwestern University, Michigan State University, and the Universities of Minnesota, Oregon, and Notre Dame. Many people, too numerous to mention, have had an influence on this text. My colleagues at the University of Notre Dame had a profound effect on my thinking during the years we were developing a beginning course emphasizing marketing management. The original edition of this text grew out of this work. To all of them, and especially the many students who suggested case materials and have criticized and made comments about both the original edition and the revised editions, I am most grateful.

Helpful criticisms and comments were made on either the original edition or the revised editions by the following professors: Harry Lipson of the University of Alabama, William Stanton of the University of Colorado, Phillip McVey of the University of Nebraska, Edwin H. Lewis of the University of Minnesota, William T. Kelley of the Wharton School of Finance and Commerce, Fred Kniffin of Pennsylvania State University, and Louis Stern of Wayne State University. I am especially indebted to Professor Yusaku Furuhashi of the University of Notre Dame for reading several versions of both revised editions and counseling on the international marketing emphasis. Also, Professor Henry Gomez and his colleagues at New York University provided especially detailed comments and suggestions.

Others who have been especially helpful include Professors Ferdinand Mauser at Wayne State University, Gerald Albaum at the University of Arizona, Joseph Siebert at Miami University, Karl Reyer at Southern State College, George Schwartz at the University of Massachusetts, Eric S. Stein of Chicago City Junior College, James D. Taylor of State University of South Dakota, G. J. Eberhart of Indiana State College, William G. Panschar of Indiana University, and Mr. Alan Kelman at Michigan State University.

Mr. and Mrs. Durward Humes and Mr. Kenneth Wylie provided invaluable editorial assistance and many fresh ideas. Esther Knoblock took many hours of dictation and typed the manuscript.

Last, but not least, I must thank my wife, Joanne, for considerable patience, advice, and assistance, and finally for proofreading under typically chaotic conditions.

To all of these persons as well as the many publishers who graciously granted permission to use their material, I am deeply grateful. Responsibility for any errors or omissions are certainly mine, but the book would not have been possible without the assistance of many others.

East Lansing, Michigan   E. Jerome McCarthy
March, 1968

Contents

Chapter

5

Page

6

7

8

Consumers: A Behavioral Science View   151

9

Intermediate Customers and Their Buying Behavior   177

Chapter

27

28

29

ation. *Keeping competitors down may push prices up. But the customer is coming into view.* Marketing as an economic institution does *not* cost too much: *Give customers complete freedom and no freedom. Is pure competition the welfare ideal? Creating demand does not misallocate resources. "False" standards according to whom? Sometimes it's the little things that count. Marketing expands output through innovation. Marketing men get their fair share of income. Does marketing cost enough? Market system is automatic and effective. Consumers ask for it, consumers pay for it. Social planners wonder if consumer should be king.* Marketing must keep satisfying customers.

Appendix: Marketing Arithmetic   669

The operating statement: *Only three basic components. Time period covered may vary. Management uses of operating statements. A skeleton statement gets down to essential details. Meaning of "sales." Meaning of "cost of goods sold." Meaning of "gross margin" and "expenses."* Detailed analysis of sections of operating statement: *Cost of goods sold for a wholesale or retail concern. Cost of goods sold for a manufacturing concern. Expenses. Summary on operating statements.* Computing the stockturn rate. Operating ratios help analyze the business. Markups: *Markup conversions.* Markdown ratios help control retail operations.

Cases

Marketing management: a vital topic

Marketing, some people will be glad to tell you, need not be very complicated or costly. In fact, they feel that entirely too much has been made of it. Their argument is summarized in Emerson's old adage: "If a man . . . make a better mousetrap . . . the world will beat a path to his door!" Such persons are sure that a good product is all one needs for success in business. Build it, and you've got it made, they insist.

The mousetrap adage probably wasn't true when it was first expressed, and it certainly is not true today. In modern, well-developed economies, the grass might well grow high on the path to the Better Mousetrap factory—if that new product is *not* properly marketed.

Today, the design and production of a good product is only one step. A producer must continually study his customers' needs and preferences. He may have to advertise his product and arrange for transportation and warehousing. And, of course, he must sell it, perhaps with the aid of wholesalers and retailers. Broadly speaking, he must design a production and marketing system—a *total system*—which satisfies someone. This whole process can be complex, and sometimes is very expensive.

Why study marketing?

In our economy of abundance, businesses *must* cater to their customers. They cannot simply wait until customers "beat a path" to their doors, because most of us can get along quite well without the product of any particular manufacturer, wholesaler, or retailer. We need clothing, for example, but we do not need a particular clothing manufac-

Modern economies are "customer-oriented"

1

turer's product. The same is true of food, house furnishings, automobiles, sports equipment, and most other consumer goods. Likewise, manufacturers usually have several sources of supply for the components incorporated into their products.

The fact that customers do not depend on any one firm's product is partly responsible for our complex marketing structure. Bread is a good example. It is normally available in bakeries, grocery stores, delicatessens, and sometimes even in drugstores. Since bread is bulky and perishable, several competing bakeries are usually located in or close to our cities. These factories handle their own distribution with their own drivers and trucks. This is a relatively expensive process, since only a few loaves are delivered to each store. But as long as prices are reasonable, it is unlikely that there will be much competition from bakeries out of the area.

Bread by air. Sometimes, however, customer demands may create new opportunities and change the market situation. Certain customers may desire special products—in this case, special kinds of bread—not being supplied by existing sources. To meet such demands, bread may be transported a much greater distance, at a correspondingly greater cost.

Such a situation did exist for some time when a New England baker flew bread products daily to the Chicago market. A number of Chicago consumers, not satisfied with existing products, were willing to pay considerably higher prices for the products of this particular baker. Eventually this market expanded to the point that the baker built a plant in Chicago. But other specialty breads are still shipped great distances. Breads made in Los Angeles and Washington State move all over the West Coast and to Hawaii.

The axiom, "The customer is always right," applies in these instances. It is, in fact, a guide to most marketing activities. The many and varied consumer demands often necessitate a more complex marketing structure. These varied demands also lead to marketing problems for individual businesses. But whatever the problems or (from another standpoint) opportunities, the customers' needs must be served because, without sales, there would be no need for a firm to exist.

Almost half the consumer's dollar for marketing

A good share of the consumer's dollar goes for marketing activities. Professor R. Cox estimated that 41.7 percent of final buyers' dollars for *goods* went for distribution activities. Other analysts, using other methods, have calculated figures up to 58.9 percent. Professor P. D. Converse estimated that the cost of marketing for 1929 through 1948 varied from 48 to 50.5 percent of the consumer's dollar.[1]

An activity of this size and importance certainly requires study. If almost half the consumer's dollar is spent on marketing, it is probable that a similar percentage of the nation's workers is engaged in marketing activities. While the exact number of people employed in market-

[1] *Business Week,* January 12, 1952, p. 122; Reavis Cox, *Distribution in a High-Level Economy* (Englewood Cliffs, N.J.: Prentice-Hall, Inc., 1965), p. 149; and Paul W. Stewart and J. Frederic Dewhurst, *Does Distribution Cost Too Much?* (New York: The 20th Century Fund, 1939), pp. 117–18.

ing has not been determined, it was estimated in 1950 that 407 persons were engaged in *commodity distribution* for each 1,000 engaged in *commodity production.* To this distribution group must be added the large number of people engaged in marketing services. Comparative figures from the late 1800's show the immense growth of U.S. marketing during less than 10 decades. In 1870, there were only 88 persons working in *commodity distribution* for every 1,000 in *commodity production.*[2]

An equally important reason for a college student to study marketing is the availability of many starting jobs in this area. Even more important, marketing offers opportunities for rapid growth and advancement. **Greater opportunity for youth**

A few years ago, an American Management Association official predicted: "Every company president elected from 1965 on will be a marketing man."[3] This was perhaps overstated, but it is true that young people are welcomed and can move upward fast in this dynamic and growing field. And perhaps as a sign of what is coming, General Electric, the company that has pioneered the acceptance of a marketing orientation, appointed a marketing man as its chief executive officer as early as 1963.[4]

In marketing, the compensation on the way to the top is very attractive. Although some marketing jobs offer lower starting salaries than other jobs, after 5 years the average earnings of those who started in marketing have about matched or bettered other business groups—and after 10 years they are ahead of all of them. One study showed the following average monthly salaries:[5]

Field	5 years after Graduation	10 years after Graduation
Engineering	$856	$1,016
Accounting	782	1,014
Sales—marketing	853	1,027
General business	787	995

A careful study of marketing will give the student a better idea about business and where the best opportunities lie for a career.

Marketing is a vital regulating force in our economy. It allocates resources as needed to meet consumer demand. It affects the distribution and size of income. A firm's basic source of income is sales. If a **Marketing, the great regulator**

---

[2] Harold Barger, *Distribution's Place in the American Economy Since 1869* (Princeton, N.J.: Princeton University Press, 1955), pp. 7–8.

[3] "Marketing Sold to the Company," *Business Week,* July 27, 1959, pp. 78–83.

[4] "G. E. Shifts Herald Harder Consumer Sell," *Business Week,* October 12, 1963, p. 88.

[5] Frank S. Endicott, "Trends in Employment of College and University Graduates in Business and Industry," (Evanston, Ill.: Northwestern University, 1967).

3

firm can't sell enough of its products and/or services to make a profit, it probably will go out of business.

This process can be seen at work in the soft-coal, hat, leather, textile, and many agricultural and mining industries. These industries receive a relatively small share of national income, in part because consumers have not been willing to pay more for the relatively undifferentiated products and services offered by these industries. Consumers have wants and needs that are as varied as their patterns of living and as numerous as their special interests. They want products that have a clear identity and a specific utility. Quite naturally, they shift their spending to industries and firms that try to satisfy their needs.

Basic economic functions done by marketing

Marketing also performs some basic economic functions. Three of the four basic utilities isolated by economists are part of the marketing job. *Time, place, and possession* utility are definitely created by marketing, and it could be argued that the creation of *form* utility, usually considered a production activity, should be directed by marketing. Having goods available *when* and *where* they are wanted, and then completing the sales transaction to provide *possession* utility, is the very essence of marketing. The provision of these utilities adds to the consumer welfare and is a very significant part of any economic system.

Marketing encourages innovation and growth

There is, however, an even more fundamental reason for studying marketing. Without sales, there can be no business. Marketing is a stimulus that encourages innovation. Research effort and investment money are attracted when customers are willing to pay for a new product or service. When sales and profits justify it, companies press on to further innovations and improvements. In recent years, industries that have followed this pattern include business machines and electronics.

In general, where a well-organized market economy is operating, there are opportunities for new investment, and the level of business activity, employment, etc., is high. But when marketing activities are neglected, the result is often slower growth or even stagnation. According to one management expert, marketing holds the key to the growth of "underdeveloped" countries. His philosophy is stated succinctly as follows:

Marketing occupies a critical role in respect to the development of such "growth areas." Indeed, marketing is the most important "multiplier" of such developments. It is in itself in every one of these areas, the least developed, the most backward part of the economic system. Its development, above all others, makes possible economic integration and the fullest utilization of whatever assets and productive capacity an economy already possesses. It mobilizes latent economic energy. It contributes to the greatest needs: that for the rapid development of entrepreneurs and managers, and at the same time it may be the easiest area of managerial work to get going.[6]

---

[6] Peter F. Drucker, "Marketing and Economic Development," *Journal of Marketing,* Vol. XXII (January, 1958), p. 253. Reprinted from the *Journal of Marketing,* national quarterly publication of the American Marketing Association.

In summary, marketing is vital for the development of a flourishing industrial society—the aspiration of most people in this world.

Development of customer-oriented economies and companies

Marketing has not always been so important or complex. If we define marketing as a process of getting goods from producers to consumers (an extremely simplified definition), it is obvious that relatively little marketing was done in ancient Egypt, for example, or in feudal Europe. Even today, a marketing structure far less complex than that in the United States operates in many parts of Asia, Africa, and Latin America.

To begin to understand why marketing is so important to modern societies, it will be fruitful to look at the development of economic systems, with primary emphasis on Western civilization.

The life of early man, scratching for an existence, could be truly described as *subsistence living*. Yet there are still many parts of the world that have not advanced much beyond this level of living. Such peoples still raise and consume almost everything they produce, living without money and sharing both the output and the work of their communities. In India, for example, approximately 85 percent of the population lives in villages that still operate on a partially communal basis. There is little place there for selling.[7] **From subsistence living to money economies**

In some economies, specialization in production took place at an early stage. About 2100 b.c., the Code of Hammurabi was set down to help regulate the highly developed society that had grown up on the fertile river valleys of the Tigris and the Euphrates. Trade flourished, and these communities rose above the subsistence level because of (1) specialization in production and distribution and (2) an assurance that this specialization would work. That is, artisans were willing to leave the self-sufficient farm economy when they were fairly sure of being fed out of the food production of others. Trade continued to grow whenever there was political stability—especially during the long period when the Romans ruled the Mediterranean area and controlled its commerce.[8]

Trade dried up when Rome's power was broken. Western Europe moved into feudalism. Basically, feudalism was a return to an almost self-sufficient economy in which each family or manor grew and made what it needed. Eventually, however, the feudal manors began to come out of their isolation. At first, small weekly markets were developed. These markets—from perhaps 5 to 15 miles apart—were close enough to travel to and from in one day.

Slowly, as towns grew, these marketing meetings became more frequent until they became daily events. Eventually a town would

---

[7] Ralph Westfall and Harper W. Boyd, Jr., "Marketing in India," *Journal of Marketing,* October, 1960, pp. 11–15.

[8] Herbert Heaton, *Economic History of Europe* (New York: Harper & Bros., 1948).

build a market hall to protect the sellers and buyers from the weather. Retail shops and warehouses developed so that the produce and wares did not have to be hauled back and forth to the farms each day.

This was a natural evolution of retail markets in the interior of Western Europe. The Middle East and the Mediterranean Sea Coast cities had gone through these stages many centuries before. As soon as there was a sufficient surplus for trading beyond the town boundaries, wholesale markets in nonperishable commodites went through an evolution similar to that of the retail markets.

Industrialization forces more emphasis on marketing

During the Middle Ages, the roots of organized industry and specialization of labor were implanted. With the greater demand for goods, the old retail-handicraft method was no longer adequate. In the small village, journeymen and apprentices could produce goods that satisfied local preferences. But the great variety in design and quality was not satisfactory for large-scale trading in other areas. More standardized products were needed, and in larger quantities.

These needs were met by wholesale handicraftsmen who supplied specifications and materials to workers who were paid by the piece. They were similar to some of our present subcontractors or small independent manufacturers, although their work usually was done in the homes of the workers.

In this system of production, workers became more dependent on production for the market. This work was profitable to the workers *as long as the goods were sold*. When the system did not function because of wars, famine, or other reasons, there was a natural reversion to village self-sufficiency.

Starting about 1700, the Industrial Revolution and the growth of the factory system increased productivity. Both new and old commodities were produced at lower prices. This offered new opportunities for trade, but it also meant that markets had to be found to absorb the greater output.

Adam Smith's *Wealth of Nations,* published in 1776, encouraged the development of free and unrestricted trade. Yet, in spite of the revived interest in trade, much of Europe's trading of this period took place—and, in fact, still takes place—in the original markets developed in the Middle Ages.

Development in the United States

The development of trade in the United States parallels that of the Middle East and Europe. Some of the very early trade in America, especially in the southern colonies, was conducted by European trading companies operating under charters from their governments. Some of the early colonies were actually trading settlements established to gain a foothold in the New World. These colonies were supposed to provide a market for Europe's finished products and a source of raw materials for the mother country.

As settlers moved west, however, there was less and less dependence on England. As long as the majority of finished products came from Europe, the import-export firms pretty much controlled trading. But finished-goods production in the United States began to increase after the Revolutionary War and during and after the War of 1812, when

6

imports declined. The canning industry, for example, developed during this period, and the meat packing industry was started in 1818 in Cincinnati.

The ports, the railroads, the discount houses

Even before the development of a substantial American finished-goods industry, many of the larger retailers in the seacoast cities began buying from importers in large lots and servicing the smaller retailers, especially inland. Many of these large retailers switched entirely to wholesaling in the early 1800's.

These early wholesale centers usually were in waterfront towns, since transportation was still tied to the rivers, lakes, and oceans. By 1850, most of the major wholesale centers were well-established centers that have maintained their importance through the years, such as New York, Philadelphia, Baltimore, Boston, New Orleans, Detroit, Chicago, and the river towns of Pittsburgh, Cincinnati, Louisville, and St. Louis.[9]

The growth of railroads opened new markets. After the Civil War, the number of manufacturing establishments grew rapidly, and the established wholesalers and retailers providing outlets for the many small manufacturers easily dominated distribution. But in the late 1800's, many manufacturers became dissatisfied with their distribution arrangements because they found that they could produce more goods than retailers and wholesalers wanted. Some manufacturers, discovering the value of aggressive sales and advertising efforts, began sending out their own salesmen and branding and advertising their products.

Retailers also responded to this outpouring of goods. Abandoning the general store approach of that day, they began to specialize in various types of goods. Retail stores grew larger and larger. Today, we find a great variety of speicalists in retailing, all the way from small shops catering to special tastes to large discount houses offering lower prices to the masses.

The productivity of the American economy continued to grow at the rate of about 3 percent compounded annually. Many aggressive manufacturers sensed that more and more consumers were able to satisfy their basic needs and have something left for luxuries. They began to cater to the mass market rather than just the "carriage trade." In the early 1900's, for example, automobiles were already an important part of the American economy. The mass production of many thousands of "luxury" goods has led to many dynamic and competitive changes in our economy. Mass advertising, personal selling, and newer and more complex forms of wholesaling and retailing have developed to adjust to a changing market.

From the production era to the marketing era

In recent years, an increasing number of producers, wholesalers, and retailers have recognized the importance of marketing. These companies have traveled the long evolutionary road from the days when the overwhelming consideration was producing or stocking products. Now

---

[9] T. N. Beckman and N. H. Engle, *Wholesaling—Principles and Practices* (rev. ed.; New York: Ronald Press Co., 1951), chap. v.

they focus their attention on the customer and try to integrate the total company's effort toward satisfying him.

Identifying the following three orientations helps clarify the evolution: (1) production or product, (2) sales, and (3) marketing.

Seldom has the story of this evolution been put so clearly and candidly as by R. T. Keith, the top executive of Pillsbury, Inc., reciting the "philosophic history" of this manufacturer of flour, cake mixes, and animal feeds.

Keith admitted that the marketing concept has been a long time coming in his company. Pillsbury was formed in 1869. It continued until about 1930 in what Keith calls "the production era." This was a period when products were relatively scarce, and the most important job of the company was production. Beginning in 1930, the company went into the "sales era." It became conscious of the fact that it had to cater to customers and that its dealers had other sources of supply. Promotion of the available products became extremely important, both to middlemen and to customers.

The sales era continued until about 1950. By then, Pillsbury had developed new cake mixes. The sales of these products were growing so rapidly that there was need for a coordinator to organize the efforts of production, research, procurement, and sales. As Pillsbury faced up to this task, Keith points out, the sales era was replaced by the "marketing department era." This meant a heavy emphasis on short-run policy planning.

The advertising department and the sales promotion department were dissolved in an effort to have one coordinating policy-making body. Obtaining people who were effective at short-run marketing policy making was difficult. Such experienced men were relatively scarce. The consequence was a three- to four-year development period during which some of the marketing department's short-range planning was not fully effective. These marketing men were maturing, however, learning how to translate ideas into products and products into profits.

In a relatively few years, Pillsbury had developed men with a marketing management approach, and in 1958, according to Keith, the company went into a new era—the "marketing company era." Now, in addition to short-run marketing planning, the *total company effort* is guided by the marketing concept, that is, service to customers. Long-range, as well as short-range, planning is involved. Pillsbury's marketing specialists now look and plan 3 to 10 years ahead.

Much more is said about the marketing concept in the next chapter, but it is important to note here that the marketing concept is gaining enthusiastic acceptance in progressive companies.

What is marketing?

We have deliberately avoided defining "marketing" until now, to allow you to develop some tentative definitions of your own.

From the historical discussion, for example, you may have developed a definition built upon the exchange of surplus commodities. This certainly would have been appropriate for past times.

Or your tentative definition may have stressed the exchange of goods in a production-oriented economy. Such a definition would emphasize the production of the goods at which the family or plant were most efficient, and exchange of those goods for other goods they were less able to produce themselves.

A more modern definition, in tune with greatly expanded productive capacity, might emphasize the adaptation of production facilities to the market. Specifically, marketing might be defined as the response of businessmen to consumer demands through adjustments in production capabilities. Adjusting production capabilities would refer to the coordination of production, accounting, finance, and marketing in the light of the changing needs of consumers who are affluent enough to have varied buying choices.

To arrive at a more active concept of marketing, however, we are going to look at it from the marketing manager's viewpoint.

As the marketing manager knows, marketing directs!

The marketing manager is concerned with the direction of specific functions and activities (which encompass several functions). In this sense, the definition that emphasizes the need to adjust production capabilities might be too general. The marketing manager is concerned with specific activities, and he works toward specific results.

Within this framework we may define marketing in the following way: *Marketing is the performance of business activities which direct the flow of goods and services from producer to consumer or user in order to satisfy customers and accomplish the company's objectives.*

So that the student will realize the full importance and scope of marketing, let us clearly specify the meaning of this definition by discussing its components.

Are the activities of product development, product design, packaging, credit and collection, transportation, warehousing, and price setting included in "marketing?"

There is little doubt that personal selling and advertising are marketing activities, but many business executives would limit the scope of marketing to them. They feel that the job of marketing is to "get rid of" the product which has been produced and priced by the production, accounting, and financial executives. We must reject this narrow view of marketing.

When we define marketing as the performance of the activities which *direct* the flow of goods and services, we mean just that: direct.

Marketing should begin with the customer, not the plant. Marketing and not production should determine what products are to be made—including decisions about product development, design, and packaging; what prices are to be charged—including decisions about credit, collection, and pricing policies; and where and how the products are to be advertised and sold.

This does not mean that marketing should take over the traditional production, accounting, and financial activities, but merely that it will "direct" these activities. After all, the purpose of business is to sell products, not to make products that *might* sell.

A factory can make products, but it takes coordination of all the activities of the business to make sales, especially at a profit. In other

9

words, we should see marketing as the coordinating force of the "total system" which is the business itself.[10]

Marketing management aims at customers

The marketing concept

Modern management has evolved from a production-oriented to a sales-oriented and finally to a marketing-oriented view of business.[11] General Electric was the leader in the development of the marketing concept. This really should be considered a new philosophy of business, rather than just a method of operation.

The marketing concept provides a systematic approach that G.E. feels is a practical, sound way to manage marketing in any business, large or small. This approach (1) makes sure the manager knows what and where his markets are, (2) provides effective customer and product service, (3) sees that he has the right product at the right place at the right price, (4) sells to the greatest possible number of customers through the most efficient sales and distribution channels, and (5) supports the product adequately with advertising and sales promotion.[12] This approach emphasizes the customer but also requires that all marketing activities focus on specific company objectives—profit, sales volume, and market share targets.

Obviously the marketing concept requires a "total system of action."[13] All of this planning, done with selected target markets in mind, shows that the total business sytem must be integrated to work well. This is why our definition of marketing emphasized the word, *direct*. Someone must integrate the total business effort. Marketing management is the logical choice, since it is the link between the business firm and the customer.

Many other companies, agreeing with G.E., have emphasized marketing management and the central role marketing plays in the operation of a business. Among those companies are Scott Paper Co., W. A. Sheaffer Pen Co., Purex Corp., Max Factor & Co., Chesebrough-Pond's, B. T. Babbitt, Corning Glass Co., Pillsbury Company, Philco Corp., U.S. Steel Corp., and the Linde Products Division of Union Carbide Corp. Many small companies also realize the importance of interrelating basic company decisions so that they will be able to meet cus-

---

[10] There are various approaches to the study of marketing, including the commodity, institutional, and functional approaches. In our study, however, all of these will be incorporated into the management approach, i.e., we will take the business manager's viewpoint and use the other approaches where they contribute to our understanding.

[11] For further discussion on this, see Robert L. King, "The Marketing Concept," in George Schwartz (ed.), *Science in Marketing* (New York: John Wiley & Sons, Inc., 1965), pp. 70–97; Bernard J. Lalonde and Edward J. Morrison, "Marketing Management Concepts Yesterday and Today," *Journal of Marketing*, January, 1967, pp. 9–13; and Richard T. Hise, "Have Manufacturing Firms Adopted the Marketing Concept?" *Journal of Marketing*, July, 1965, pp. 9–12.

[12] Adapted from Edward S. McKay, "How to Plan and Set Up Your Marketing Program," *A Blueprint for an Effective Marketing Program* (Marketing Series No. 91 [New York: American Management Association, Inc., 1954]), p. 15.

[13] The need for tying all the parts of a business together is presented in a new light in James W. Culliton, "Age of Synthesis," *Harvard Business Review*, September–October, 1962, p. 36 ff.

tomer preferences.[14] In fact, it is hard to find business success stories in which a customer orientation has been ignored or flouted.

To illustrate, we can contrast a very successful application of the marketing concept to an unsuccessful one. The Ford Motor Co. Mustang "sports" car *was* designed according to the marketing concept. Considerable marketing research was done *before* the product was designed or the whole marketing strategy developed. Then the strategy was selected in the light of consumer research and company resources and objectives.[15] The outstanding success of the Mustang is well known.

Ford's earlier experience with the ill-fated Edsel is another story. While there was considerable consumer research on the Edsel, it tended to focus on promotional possibilities, because the automobile design itself and the basic marketing plan were already fixed. Even though consumers expressed little enthusiasm for those parts of the plan to which they were exposed, their attitudes were not permitted to affect the basic plan. The research had come too late and was not used to help direct the whole effort.[16]

Marketing aims at particular customers

In our free economy, no consumer is forced to buy any goods or services, except those which society insists are essential. Schools, police, national defense, public health, and food inspection are considered essential services. They are provided by the community, where members are taxed to pay for them. If the state required the consumption of certain commodities, then the marketing job would be relatively simple, concerning chiefly the transport of goods to convenient locations and their sale there.

Freedom of consumer choice, however, has a great deal to do with the management of marketing. In a free society, customers buy from whomever they feel makes the most attractive offer. The overwhelming importance of the customer is suggested by the following quotation, *taken from a booklet distributed to production employees* by a large industrial organization. Trite and obvious as it may seem, it is important to note the emphasis some producers place on the customer and the educational job they are doing *within their own companies*.

WHAT IS A CUSTOMER?

A customer is a person who brings us his wants. Our job is to fill them profitably—to him and to ourselves.

A customer expects value in what he buys from us. If we do not give him value, he will go elsewhere to find it.

A customer's good opinion of our company is the most valuable asset in the world. Whatever we can do to build that good opinion will eventually be to our advantage.

A customer's good opinion cannot be bought or stolen. However, it can be freely given in response to our gift of value.

A customer is never too far away to affect our jobs, no matter how remote

---

[14] Robert J. Holloway, "Marketing Decisions in the Small Firm," *Business News Notes,* School of Business Administration, University of Minnesota, No. 40 (September, 1958).

[15] Talk by George Brown, Director of Marketing Research, Ford Motor Co., at Tri-State Marketing Teachers Meeting, May 8, 1965.

[16] Talk given by Paul Lazarsfeld at the University of Notre Dame in 1964.

from him our work may seem. One small slip or flaw in any department can lessen the value of our product or service in the customer's eyes.

A customer is the boss behind our boss. By serving him well, we serve ourselves as well.[17]

It might be said that customers have a "veto power" over the operations of any company trying to sell products to them. More correctly, this is a veto by abstention. To be effective, many customers must simultaneously reject the product. This veto power obviously belongs only to the group of customers the marketing manager is trying to reach—his target customers. If, for example, a manufacturer has intended to attract only a small, elite group, the rejection of his product by most other customers is of no consequence. But should this target group reject the product, all effort has been wasted.

Marketing takes global view

A modern, marketing-oriented firm is not limited to satisfying customers merely in one region or even in one country. Increasingly, marketing-oriented companies are taking a broader view of potential markets. People all over the world are viewed as potential customers, and multi-national companies are being formed to serve them better. Throughout this text we will continue to take this global view of business and marketing.

Universal functions: marketing has many facets

In both domestic and international marketing, we find the same basic marketing functions—buying, selling, transporting, storing, grading, financing, risk-taking, and market information. It will be valuable to explain these basic functions and how they serve as a foundation for our managerial approach to marketing.

The first two, *buying* and *selling,* are concerned with the exchange process. The *buying* function is concerned with the search for, and evaluation of, product and services. For middlemen, this means a search for the products they will offer to their customers. The *selling* function involves promoting the product and would include the use of personal salesmen and advertising. This is the best known, and some people feel the only, function of marketing.

The functions of *transporting* and *storing* involve the handling and movement of goods. These are the major activities of many marketing institutions, especially warehouses, transportation agencies, wholesalers, and some retailers.

The function of *grading, financing, risk-taking,* and *market information* assist other functions. *Grading* is dividing the product into the most attractive quantities and by the most useful quantities, thus aiding the storing and selling functions. *Financing* facilitates the exchange of money for goods and provides the credit necessary for storing. The *risk-taking* function is inherent in any business activity and is the reason why good management is so valued and consequently so well

---

[17] *It Pays to Be Customer-Minded* (New York: Alumni Publications, Inc., 1955), p. 12.

compensated. One of management's jobs is to measure and control the risk.

The *market information* function, including collecting, analyzing, and disseminating data, provides the feedback activity that is needed in any system. Without current information, the manager will probably rely on old information—and it is very possible that last year's facts may prove the basis of this year's error.

No matter how simple or how complex the marketing process is, all the functions of marketing must be performed. If the marketing manager were trying to improve the efficiency of the "total system," he would attempt to provide these functions with maximum efficiency. In some cases, this might require combining various middlemen into a "total system." In such a system a farmer, for example, may permit a wholesaler to pick up his products at the farm, haul them into town, grade them according to recognized standards, carry the financial burden until they are sold, and through this period, take the risk that they can be sold. If this job is complicated, one wholesaler may not be willing to handle all these activities, and two or more wholesalers may become involved.

Functions can't be eliminated

The important fact is that even if the farmer were to do all of this himself, *none* of the functions would be skipped. He would still have to grade the products on his own farm, store them until they are needed, and transport them into town. During this time, he would have to finance his own activities and bear any risk of price fluctuations or quality deterioration. In either situation, he would watch the newspaper or listen to the radio for market information on prices, supplies, and weather conditions.

Providing these functions underlies much of the activity of marketing. We will discuss them frequently in this text.

Marketing means systems of action

Marketing is concerned with the flow of goods and services from producers to final consumers. It is concerned with the total process or system, not just one level in the marketing system and the buyers and sellers directly above and below it. A manufacturer of grocery products, for example, cannot be concerned only about whether he can "dump" some goods on some wholesalers. He must know whether they will move through those wholesalers to retailers and finally be accepted by final consumers. If they will not move smoothly to consumers, then inventories will back up and all of his efforts will be wasted.

Although individual firms are concerned primarily with their own affairs, and understandably so, in a very real sense we can think of competing "total systems" composed of cooperating producers and middlemen. Sears, Roebuck and associated producers, for instance, compete with General Electric and associated middlemen in the sale of radios. In this text, we will be concerned both with a "total system" which is the whole firm itself, and also "total systems" which tie together producers and middlemen.

13

Marketing and help for underdeveloped nations

Our primary emphasis will be on marketing systems in modern societies and on the effectiveness of competing marketing systems. But marketing also is necessary if a subsistence economy is to rise above that level. Without an effective marketing system, the underdeveloped countries may be doomed to what Professor Nurkse has called "a vicious circle of poverty."[18] By this, he means that no one will leave his subsistence way of life to produce for the market because there is no market for any goods he might produce. And there are no buyers because everyone else is engaged in producing for his own needs. Marketing institutions may provide the dynamic element for breaking this vicious circle.

In this sense, a study of marketing systems will not only improve our understanding of our present and future institutions but will also illuminate the problems of the underdeveloped economies. A knowledge of these economies will be increasingly important as our interest in the world market grows.

An important goal of this text is to prepare you, the student, to evaluate *future marketing systems* and to understand the marketing management problems of distributing *products that are not yet even on the market*. In other words, we will try to develop your ability to analyze future marketing problems and systems, not merely to analyze and describe present or past systems.

Marketing serves customers, profits, society— and customers

The interesting thing about marketing is that when all the various business and marketing activities are coordinated, the whole is greater than the sum of the parts. Marketing acts as the link between customers and the production side of business. Through careful blending of the needs of customers with the capabilities of production, marketing management attempts to satisfy its customers.

This is not done just to be nice, it should be emphasized. Generally speaking, customers are willing to pay higher prices for, or buy more of, those goods which best satisfy them. Thus efficient marketing can increase profits, which are required to attract investment and provide jobs and to pay for research to develop new or better products. Profits are not only the goal of most businesses, but they can be used as a rough measure of a firm's efficiency in satisfying customers. In this sense, business and customer goals are not at odds.

There is little question that marketing is vital to modern economies. It probably will become even more important in the future. In this text, we will consider the viewpoint and techniques of marketing management, to give you a better understanding of marketing systems and processes, and the point of view in a marketing-oriented firm.

---

[18] Ragnar Nurkse, *Problems of Capital Formation in Underdeveloped Countries* (Oxford: Basil Blackwell, 1953), p. 4.

As we move along through the following chapters, management will be emphasized, but running a strong second in emphasis will be customer reactions and welfare and the impact of consumer behavior and the firm on the economy. For it is only through long-run satisfaction of consumers that marketing management can justify its role in a free enterprise system.

Questions and problems

1 It is fairly easy to see why people do not beat a path to the mousetrap manufacturer's door, but would they be similarly indifferent if some food processor developed a revolutionary new food product which would provide all necessary nutrients in small pills for about $100 a year per person?

2 What costs are included in marketing costs? Which of these do you feel might be eliminated? How would our economy be changed if it were illegal to incur any marketing costs?

3 Discuss the nature of marketing in a socialist economy. Would the development of wholesaling and retailing systems be any different? Discuss the kinds of marketing decisions that a socialist planner and a free enterprise entrepreneur have to make.

4 Identify marketing functions being provided or eliminated when a farmer sells tomatoes, corn, or other home-produced products at a stand in front of his house.

5 Why is the satisfaction of consumers apparently considered of equal importance with satisfying the firm's objectives in the text's definition of marketing?

6 Describe a recent purchase you have made and indicate why that particular product was available at a store, and, in particular, at that store.

7 What kinds of problems is a new producer of cake mixes likely to encounter when beginning operations?

8 What does the text mean with respect to marketing as a "system of action" and "systems of action"?

Marketing management and marketing strategy planning

Marketing has been defined as the performance of business activities which direct the flow of goods and services from producer to consumer or user, in order to satisfy customers and accomplish the company's objectives. From this definition, it should be clear that marketing is a total system of business action, not a hodgepodge of unrelated activities. This system has evolved because it does the job of directing the flow of goods and services more efficiently than any other.

Hitting the target customer

The marketing manager's job consists of trying to satisfy a particular group of customers, the target group, with a particular good or service, while still satisfying the objectives of the firm and operating within the resources and constraints imposed by the firm.

The selection of the target group for a given product is an important part of the marketing manager's job. But it is only the beginning. Out of the almost infinite number of products offered to potential customers, the marketing manager wants to be sure that *his product* will succeed. How can he do this?

First, the marketing manager is a *manager*. It might be well, therefore, to look closely at the nature of the management job per se, whether in marketing or otherwise.

The management job in marketing

Management generally has three basic tasks:

1. To set up a general plan or strategy.
2. To direct the execution of this plan.
3. To evaluate, analyze, and control the plan.

For simplicity, this might be condensed to planning, execution, and control. The three-cornered diagram in Figure 2–1 shows the interrelation of these three basic tasks. The interrelation of the control and planning jobs is extremely important, since the feedback of information often leads to changes in the general plan or even a totally new plan. Thus the management job is *continuous*.

Figure 2–1 The management job

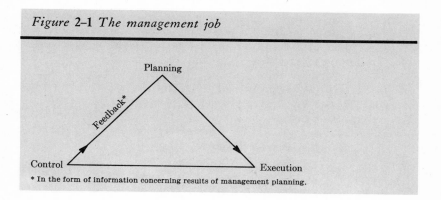

Planning

Feedback*

Control

Execution

* In the form of information concerning results of management planning.

The *marketing* manager's job consists of the same basic management tasks just listed. First, the marketing executive must evolve a plan—or as we will call it, a "marketing strategy"—aimed at a given group of customers. How this group is selected will be discussed later in this chapter. The development of a marketing strategy is of primary interest in this text. Without a well-defined master plan, there are no guidelines for execution, control, or evaluation.

Only after the basic strategy is developed can management concern itself with the implementation of that strategy (personnel selection, salary administration, dealer selection, commission rates, etc.). Implementation may, in fact, absorb a greater proportion of the manager's time, but it is not the major concern here. Detailed study of execution decisions must be left for your advanced work, after you have seen the "big picture," that is, when you have learned about planning marketing strategy.

We will emphasize control, too, since it provides the feedback that leads to the modification of marketing strategies The tools most frequently used by the marketing manager to exert this control are electronic data processing, marketing research, and accounting.

At first, it might appear that the planning and control jobs are only of concern to top management of large companies. This is not true. Even the smallest farmer, retailer, or wholesaler must plan his strategy. The salesman, however limited his territory, also must have a plan of attack. He may not have complete freedom because of the master strategy already outlined for him, but he usually has some latitude. He develops his own special strategy in the light of his own abilities and the problems of his particular territory.

The material we will discuss throughout this chapter and text will be helpful to all persons engaged in the marketing process, whether they are top-level managers or are primarily engaged in the execution of someone else's plan. You may need this information on your first, or even your present, job.

Importance of marketing strategy planning

We will place most of our emphasis on the planning phase of the marketing manager's job, for a very good reason. It appears that those "one-time" planning decisions—the critical decisions that determine what business the company is in and the general strategy it will follow—may be more important than has been realized. In fact, an extremely good plan might be badly implemented and still be profitable, while a poor but well-implemented plan might be unprofitable. The several case history examples that follow illustrate the prime importance of planning and show why we are going to be emphasizing strategy planning throughout this text.

General
Foods
study and
General
Foods
hypothesis

A recent study of the retail grocery industry was designed to explain why some retail grocery stores were more profitable than others. The General Foods study began with an extensive evaluation of traditional internal operating data such as turnover per square foot, etc. This was of little help, but when the study shifted its focus to the planning decisions, new insights *were* developed. It became clear that original strategy decisions about (1) where a grocery store was placed in relation to competition and (2) how large it was in relation to competition, seemed to explain varying profit rates of individual stores.[1]

Within this framework, an analysis of the effectiveness of the execution phase made sense. But it was clear that some well-managed stores were doomed to poor profitability because of the initial planning decision. Conversely, some well-placed stores were doing very well almost in spite of their operating management.

As a practical summary of this study, we will advance what we will call the *General Foods hypothesis:* Good strategy planning may be more important to the profitable operation of a business than good execution and control.

A practical application of the General Foods hypothesis can be seen in Gamble-Skogmo's effort to place relatively *large* discount stores in

---

[1] *McKinsey–General Foods Study* (New York: General Foods Corp., 1963).

18

small midwestern towns. Importantly, this strategy reverses a general tendency for discounters to stay close to larger cities and markets. When asked why he was moving into small towns, the president of Gamble-Skogmo answered: "If you're first, you're apt to be alone. Most of the towns we're in won't take two stores of that size."[2]

Gamble-Skogmo sought small-town markets

The General Foods hypothesis also helps to explain Sears, Roebuck's success since World War II. While other large retailers were concentrating downtown, Sears developed a new strategy—the development of stores with their own parking facilities in outlying and suburban areas where the population was growing fast. Some conventional retailers predicted dire results for Sears' new plan. But perhaps its success can be explained in the following terms: Sears put its new units away from competition, provided ample parking space, and then built stores so large and well stocked that the customer could do all her shopping under one roof.

Sears, Roebuck sought its own market

In short, instead of trying to meet competition head on, Sears developed a strategy for reaching some target markets that had not previously been completely satisfied. At the same time, the market itself was becoming centered in those outlying areas.

As another reflection of the growing acceptance of the marketing concept and the importance of strategic planning, U.S. Steel officials are setting long-run strategies. Rather than concentrating only on selling basic steel, U.S. Steel is looking for new opportunities to design steels that can be used in future products. A U.S. Steel vice president states: "The time to fight the market battle is in the design stage. We're confident that our salesmen will get our share of steel sold as a result."[3]

U.S. Steel seeks new opportunities

Henry Ford is often remembered for his development of the mass production techniques that *enabled* a car to be produced for the mass market. A closer look at his own recollection of his thinking, however, suggests that mass production developed *because of* his basic strategy decision to build a car the mass market could buy. That is, he decided to depart from the then-common practice of building cars for the wealthy, for the sports driver, and other specialty buyers, and to produce a car that would appeal to the majority of potential buyers. Ford felt that the low price which had to be set to appeal to so many buyers would force the new methods that would make the price possible.

Henry Ford's strategy worked

As Henry Ford saw it, the company set "a price so low as to force everybody in the place to the highest point of efficiency. The low price makes everybody dig for profits. We make more discoveries concerning manufacturing and selling under this forced method than by any method of leisurely investigation."[4]

Certainly additional production-oriented innovations were required

---

[2] "Small Town Greets the Discounters," *Business Week,* October 3, 1964, pp. 90–96.

[3] "How Steel Widens Its Targets," *Business Week,* March 27, 1965, pp. 119–23.

[4] Henry Ford, *My Life and Work* (New York: Doubleday, Page & Co., 1923), pp. 146–47; and Theodore Levitt, "Marketing Myopia," *Harvard Business Review,* July–August, 1960, p. 45.

to implement Ford's mass-market strategy. But analyzed in terms of current thinking about marketing, it appears that the really critical decision was the initial market-oriented decision that there was a market for millions of cars in the $500 price range. Much of what followed was merely implementation.

General Motors found a better strategy

A great deal has been written about the whys of the success of General Motors, but the focus has tended to be on its method of organization and financial arrangements. In his recently published memoirs, Alfred P. Sloan, Jr., the man who helped develop and guide General Motors Corp. to its position of dominance, adds new insights into General Motors' success. He claims that in the early stage of the reorganization of General Motors, he made only three really basic decisions. These concerned organization, financial controls, and product (product line). The balance of his tenure in the job was concerned with implementing those basic decisions. One of these three basic decisions was what we would call a marketing decision.

In the 1920's, Henry Ford, following a very successful strategy introduced many years earlier, was still offering a "mass-market" automobile in "any color you want as long as it's black." Ford had developed this strategy when he first decided to build his car for the masses.

Mr. Sloan and General Motors sensed that a new strategy was in order. They made a basic decision to add new colors and styling, even if this required raising prices. They also decided to see the market as several segments (based on price and model types), and then to offer a full line of cars with entries at the top of each of these price ranges. They planned to satisfy quality-conscious consumers, always offering good values.

Mr. Sloan acknowledges that the strategy was not immediately successful and that there were many who felt other strategies should be followed. But he persisted in his basic decision, and it is to this basic decision that Sloan gives credit, not the years of implementation.

As is now well known, General Motors persisted with this plan through the 1920's and slowly caught up with the unyielding Ford. Finally, in May, 1927, Ford closed down his assembly line and had to switch his strategy to meet the new competition. He stopped making the long-successful Model T and introduced the Model A. But General Motors already was well on its way to the commanding market position it now holds.[5]

General Motors and the replacement parts market

Thus far we have focused on success stories. But a failure may help us support the General Foods hypothesis even more effectively. We have shown that General Motors' automobile success was due, in great part, to a market-oriented decision. But it is important to note that while General Motors was successfully focusing on the automobile market, it was neglecting another very important market—the automobile replacement parts market. To be sure, parts were supplied— they had to be. But in the early days of auto manufacture, supplying

---

[5] Alfred P. Sloan, Jr., *My Years with General Motors* (New York: MacFadden Books, 1965), Introduction, chap. iv, and chap. ix.

20

parts was viewed by the auto makers more as a service than an important business. As a result, the market was left to many smaller suppliers who were quite willing to move into this increasingly profitable target market.

Even today, General Motors does not have the commanding position in the replacement parts market that it has in the original car market. In other words, Mr. Sloan's successful strategy was concerned with automobiles, not the whole concept of personal transportation and keeping the cars moving.

The essence of all these examples can be summed up in the position taken by one author who has been arguing for longer range thinking and innovation in marketing for some time. He says, "The real dough is in what economists call monopoly profits. I don't mean in a restrictive sense. I mean being first, the guy who skims the cream."[6]   **Good strategy planning pays off**

Further, these examples supporting the General Foods hypothesis show why we will emphasize marketing strategy planning in this text.

Now, without further justification, let us move on to this most important topic and see how to develop profitable marketing strategies.

Marketing strategy planning

Developing a marketing strategy consists of two distinct and yet interrelated steps.   **What is a marketing strategy?**

1. *Selection of the target market*—the selection of particular groups of customers to whom the company wishes to appeal.
2. *Development of a "marketing mix"*—the choice of the elements which the company intends to combine in order to satisfy this target group.

Most of the balance of this chapter is devoted to explaining these two steps.

Figure 2–2 illustrates the framework within which the marketing manager must operate. He can directly control the marketing mix which is shown around the customer (C). Surrounding these controllable factors are a considerable number of uncontrollable factors that he must consider even though he cannot control them. Included among these factors are the cultural and social environment, political and legal environment, economic environment, existing competitive business structure, and resources and objectives of the firm. All of these uncontrollable factors are considered in detail in Chapter 3, but we cannot afford to overlook them here. Just to illustrate their importance, let us look at possible company objectives.   **Decision framework —social, political, legal, etc.**

Objectives are extremely important to any manager and especially to the marketing manager. Since the objectives of the firm are both goals and guidelines for him, he cannot begin to develop a workable marketing strategy until these are defined. Although ideally the marketing manager should help set the objectives determined by top management,

---

[6] Theodore Levitt, in *Sales Management,* October 1, 1965, p. 32; and Theodore Levitt, *Innovation in Marketing* (New York: McGraw-Hill Book Co., 1962).

Figure 2–2 Marketing manager's framework

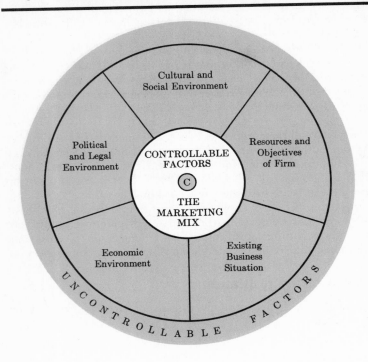

he does not always do so. And this fact may have an immediate bearing on marketing strategy planning.

Top management might decide, for example, that one of its objectives is to be the industry sales leader. This decision might exclude profitable but small target markets. In this situation, size might have to take precedence over profitability. Or the objective might be to dominate the low-price market, which might mean low prices combined with mass production and broad distribution.

But more about objectives in the next chapter. Here, we will focus on those variables the marketing manager *can* directly control.

Selecting target markets

Market grids help select target markets

Marketing management selects its target markets after analyzing (1) potential customers, (2) marketing mixes they might want, (3) its own ability to provide these, (4) company objectives, and (5) other, often uncontrollable, variables. When evaluating potential target markets, however, it is extremely important to realize that what is popularly considered as one market, actually may consist of many smaller, more homogeneous markets. It would be helpful to have an analytical procedure that isolates all or at least many of the possible variations. The market grid approach provides such a technique.

22

The market grid concept sees any market as a box that is cross-hatched, like a checkerboard or grid, on the basis of relevant *market* characteristics. Each of the squares in the large box represents a smaller, more homogeneous market. (See Figure 2–3.) Implicit in this approach is the understanding that only potential customers will be considered within the market grid that we draw.[7] On the market grid for men's clothing, for example, only the various characteristics of men would be considered. Children and women obviously are not potential customers in this market. They could be shown explicitly in a little area below the potential markets, perhaps surrounded by a dotted line as shown in **The bullseye is a box**

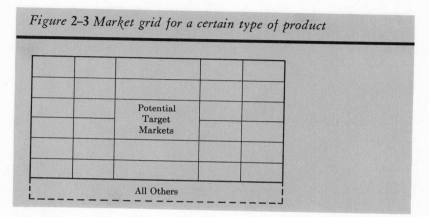

Figure 2–3 Market grid for a certain type of product

Potential
Target
Markets

All Others

Figure 2–3. But for practical purposes, such groups are not part of the potential market, and hereafter the dotted area will not be shown.

An example—the market grid for refrigeration. The refrigeration market is an excellent illustration. Remember that in the following analysis we are focusing on customers and their needs, not products that might satisfy them or that the company can produce. That is why we will consider "refrigera*tion*" rather than "refrigera*tors*."

Certainly there are many final consumers and businesses who need refrigeration. Refrigeration is used in homes, stores, institutions, and many other places, as shown in Figure 2–4. All these customers do not want the same product, nor are they equally accessible to the producer. Some of these market grid boxes might be satisfied by electric refrigeration, while others would prefer gas refrigeration. Some would require large walk-in coolers and others compact units. Picnickers would prefer a small ice chest. To show all of these possible variations on a market grid requires more breakdowns than those in Figure 2–4.

In Figure 2–5, the eastern food store market (shown with a large "X" in Figure 2–4) is analyzed. The food stores are listed by types: fruit and vegetable, dairy, fish, meat, and full-line grocery stores. These stores are of varying sizes, and this also may have a bearing on the type of refrigeration desired.

---

[7] The general term "market grid" should be credited to Professor J. R. Malone, College of Business Administration, University of Notre Dame.

23

Size of Market Grid Boxes Not Important Initially. The exact size of the markets represented by the boxes in Figure 2–4 and 2–5 need not concern us in this preliminary stage. Actually, it might take considerable market research to determine the potential sales volume in each of these boxes. But by developing a grid like this, the marketing manager

Figure 2–4 *Market grid for refrigeration*

East	Midwest	South	Mountain	Pacific	Region / Place of Use
					Home
					Food Stores
					Wholesalers
					Restaurants
					Hospitals
					Schools
					Military Reservations
					Business Offices
					Other Institutions
					Trailers
					Picnics
					Planes
					Trains
					Ships

is alerted to the possible existence of smaller, individualized markets. Perhaps many of these little markets can be satisfied by a single product. Before assuming this, however, it would be desirable to analyze them and perhaps do some formal marketing research to determine which if any of the many smaller markets can be merged and treated alike. This analysis is important, since *each unique target market implies the need for a separate marketing mix.*

When the marketing manager first constructs a market grid, each box can reflect what he feels to be the size of each market. In Figure 2–5, for example, the boxes for small stores are drawn larger than for the medium and large stores because there are many more small stores. This should be done with care, however, because the manager's intuitive notions about the market may reflect past, not present or future conditions.

Each Little Market Different. Each of the small markets within the larger refrigeration market shown in Figure 2–4 represents a homogeneous group of potential customers with special needs. But some of these groups may be quite similar to others, and one manufacturer may

---

Figure 2–5 *Market grid for refrigeration in eastern food store market*

Large Stores	Medium Stores	Small Stores	Size / Type
			Fruit and Vegetables
			Dairy
			Fish
			Meat
			Full-Line Groceries

---

cater to several boxes or perhaps to a whole row or column at the same time. In this particular case, it is unlikely that one manufacturer would cater to a whole column in Figure 2–4, since the products desired would be quite different. Yet it is entirely feasible for some of the large consumer refrigerator manufacturers to cater successfully to the "Home" row in Figure 2–4, as Westinghouse, General Electric, and others do.

The same market might be satisfied with different products, too. Gas and electric refrigerators of various types and sizes, and even old-fashioned ice boxes in some areas, would be suitable for the "Home" boxes shown in Figure 2–4. This acceptability of substitutes will affect the competitive situation.

Obviously these boxes could be divided in a more refined way to show the characteristics of *all* potential markets. Then, if there were no differences from box to box, they could be recombined.

If the variations in consumer demand from box to box are very great, or if some of the boxes are not very large, then it may be difficult or unprofitable for a particular firm to solicit the business represented by these boxes. In such cases, a market may go unsupplied. Or it may not be completely satisfied until some firm sees its need and caters specifically to it.

Flexible view of grids needed

The lack of profit potential in some target markets helps explain why some customers are poorly serviced or dissatisfied with the products available to them. Or sometimes, due to changing consumer preferences, a new target market has developed and has not yet been recognized. These boxes should not be seen as static markets, since they are in a constant state of flux.

Certain boxes may have so few "occupants" that mass production for them is not feasible. This presents an opportunity for smaller producers, wholesalers, or retailers to supply smaller volume and perhaps custom-fabricated products. A firm need not be small, though, to cater to the customers in small target markets. It merely needs to be flexible enough to recognize, and produce a product for, the needs of the customers in each particular box.

Any firm may find that its total market consists of the customers in many boxes, although they may not all be adjacent to each other on the grid drawing. This is especially true if a large market is broken down geographically and then further subdivided. Even these differences may be important, however. The customers in various geographical markets—say New York, Los Angeles, and Paris—may require different methods of distribution and, at the very least, will necessitate different wholesalers and retailers. Thus *each market grid box may require a unique marketing mix and should be thought of as a separate market.*

What dimensions to use in splitting the grid

The dimensions used to split up the market grid should be the characteristics and needs of *potential customers* for the type of product or service being considered—*not* the characteristics of present or possible products. For example, we would reject the traditional production-oriented approach used in the automobile industry, splitting up its markets into compacts, foreign cars, low-price, medium-price, and luxury cars.

We want to look at potential markets, first, in an effort to locate new opportunities, not just to find places where we can "get rid of" our existing products. There may even be some markets that cannot be satisfied with existing products, and this may represent a "breakthrough" opportunity for a firm.

Only after we have split up the market, using potential customer dimensions, do we become concerned with the size of the various boxes. Available data often is useful for estimating gross potentials. Alternately, some marketing research may be needed. (A great deal more about customer behavior, available data, and grid analysis will be found in later chapters.)

The selection of grid dimensions requires consideration of what characteristics may be relevant to the purchase of the potential prod-

26

Table 2-1 Potential dimensions for market grid analysis for which data is usually available*

Data for Households	Data for Household Heads
Geographic	Age
County size	Sex
Urban vs. rural	Education
Region	Occupation
Age of children	*Data for Housewives*
Family size	Age
Family income	Education
Home ownership	Employment
Dwelling characteristics	*Data for Business Customers*
Goods owned	Size of firm
Data for Individuals	Dollar sales
Age	Number of employees
Sex	Geographic location
Education	Centralized vs. decentralized
Marital status	purchasing
Occupation	Nature of target customers
Color	Nature of business (SIC codes)

* See William M. Wellbacher, "Standard Classification for Consumer Characteristics," *Journal of Marketing*, Vol. XXXI (January, 1967), pp. 27–31, for finer breakdowns on these dimensions.

ucts. This is where considerable management judgment and marketing research are needed. The number of potential dimensions is quite large. Table 2–1 suggests some of the possibilities for which there are often published data. Table 2–2 suggests some more qualitative ones which might develop out of marketing research or management "feel" for the situation.

Obviously, not all of these characteristics can be used at the same time, but often many sets of grids can be linked as we began to do in the refrigeration example. Sometimes several dimensions can be combined into a summary one. This will be illustrated in the two examples following.

Table 2-2 Potential dimensions for market grid analysis for which data must be gathered or estimated

Needs for:	Desire for:
Status	Hardiness
Affection	Durability
Privacy	Dependability
Convenience	Warmth
Distinctiveness	Softness
Economy	Speed
Variety	Activity
Newness	Movement
Security	Fun
	Excitement

The possibilities are almost unlimited for subdividing market grids. It should be noted that such subdividing often can be done, almost as an exercise, to stimulate marketing management's thinking. The very act of reviewing many of the possible variations is a significant step forward in the planning process. After many grids have been drawn, however, it may be necessary for management to make some arbitrary summary judgments and merge several dimensions together under headings that identify certain segments of the market. This will be

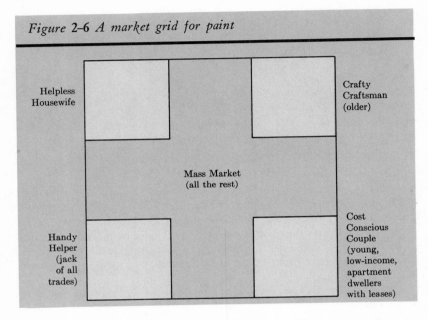

Figure 2–6 A market grid for paint

Helpless Housewife

Crafty Craftsman (older)

Mass Market (all the rest)

Handy Helper (jack of all trades)

Cost Conscious Couple (young, low-income, apartment dwellers with leases)

easier if the marketing analysts have done some interviewing of potential customers and have begun to get a "feel" for the market.

From helpless housewife to cost-conscious couple. A paint manufacturer in England did considerable interviewing and analyzing of the various needs for the kinds of products he could offer. Finally, by combining several dimensions, he came up with the view of the market shown in Figure 2–6.

There was a large mass market representing about 60 percent of the potential for all kinds of paint products. He did not give much consideration to this market because he was not a large manufacturer and he did not want to compete directly with the many companies already in the market. The other four markets, which he placed in the four corners of a market grid simply to show that they were different markets, were entitled Helpless Housewife, Handy Helper, Crafty Craftsman, and Cost-Conscious Couple.

The Helpless Housewife really did not know much about home decorating or specific products. She needed a helpful paint dealer who could supply not only paint and other supplies but also considerable

28

advice. And the dealer who sold her the paint would want it to be of fairly good quality so that she would be satisfied.

The Handy Helper was a jack-of-all-trades who knew a great deal about paint and painting. He wanted a good-quality product but was willing to buy from quite a different kind of retailer. The old-fashioned hardware store or lumberyard, which would be primarily a male hangout, was quite satisfactory.

Similarly, the Crafty Craftsman was willing to buy from a retailer who would *not* attract female customers. In fact, this older man didn't want to buy paint at all, but pigments, oils, and other ingredients to mix his own paint.

Finally, the Cost-Conscious Couple was young, had low income, and leased an apartment. In England, an apartment dweller with a lease must paint the apartment during the course of the lease, and it is this element that becomes critical to at least some tenants as they choose their paint. If you were a young apartment dweller with limited income, what sort of paint would you want? Some such couples in England do not want very good paint! And this manufacturer finally decided to cater to this market and offer them something that was not much better than whitewash.

His marketing strategy included selecting this group and then establishing a distribution system that concentrated primarily on lower income apartment neighborhoods in urban areas. This manufacturer has been extremely successful with his strategy, giving customers what they want even if it is a lower quality–lower cost product.

Seeing strategy in the needs of swingers. As part of the market grid analysis, it may be desirable to incorporate some of the needs expressed by potential customers. This edges into using product characteristics—because only specific products satisfy specific customer needs—but this temptation should be resisted as long as possible.[8]

The market grid for housing illustrates the possibility of combining customer characteristics (in summary form) with product-related housing needs. The customer characteristics shown in Figure 2–7, such as *swingers, sophisticates, newly married,* and so on, are summary descriptions of several simpler dimensions. For example, the swingers are young (in their 20's), unmarried, active, fun-loving and partygoing. The housing needs X'd in Figure 2–7 indicate what the swingers want. (It is interesting to note that they do *not* want "strong management." Most college students will probably understand why!)

A very successful appeal to the swingers in the Dallas, Texas, area includes a complex of apartments with a swimming pool, a putting green, a nightclub that offers jazz and other entertainment, poolside parties, receptions for new tenants, and so on. And to maintain their image, the management insists that tenants who get married move out shortly so that new swingers can be accommodated.

Descriptions of the other market segments are shown below Figure 2–7. Each of these market segments required and was offered a differ-

---

[8] We will use "products" to refer to both goods and services.

ent marketing mix, and as a result, apartment occupancy rates were extremely high in such buildings while, at the same time, other builders were experiencing severe difficulties in filling their apartments. These other builders, by way of contrast, were offering apartments that were "little boxes," intended to satisfy everybody but really satisfying nobody. It is interesting to note, also, that the idea of building apart-

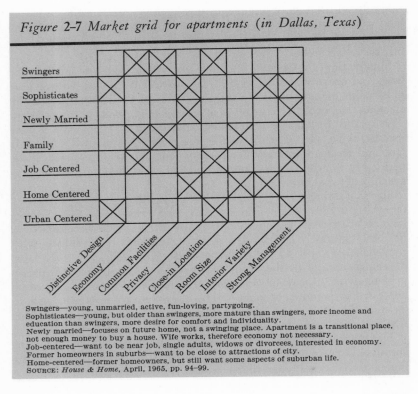

Figure 2-7 Market grid for apartments (in Dallas, Texas)

Swingers—young, unmarried, active, fun-loving, partygoing.
Sophisticates—young, but older than swingers, more mature than swingers, more income and education than swingers, more desire for comfort and individuality.
Newly married—focuses on future home, not a swinging place. Apartment is a transitional place, not enough money to buy a house. Wife works, therefore economy not necessary.
Job-centered—want to be near job, single adults, widows or divorcees, interested in economy.
Former homeowners in suburbs—want to be close to attractions of city.
Home-centered—former homeowners, but still want some aspects of suburban life.
SOURCE: *House & Home*, April, 1965, pp. 94–99.

ments to appeal to distinct target markets seems to be spreading. The swingers, especially, seem to be a group that appeals to apartment developers.[9]

Summary: the right box or boxes

Analyzing potential target markets using market grids requires considerable judgment and analysis of customers. But educated judgment and painstaking analysis are two of the major qualities expected of a marketing man. He must know his customers' needs, preferences, and desires. He should be expert in locating available data to add substance to the gridding process. He needs to be able to develop statistics as to the size and economic potential of possible target markets. As we said before, much more will be said on these topics in Chapters 6–9, which discuss potential customer behavior.

[9] "Singles Swing for Landlords," *Business Week*, March 5, 1966, pp. 38–40; "Catering to the Young for Fun and Profit," *Parade*, April 2, 1967, pp. 4–5; *Time*, August 26, 1966, p. 49; and "Segmented Demand," *House & Home*, April, 1965, pp. 94–99.

Hereafter, whenever we speak of target markets, we will mean customers in one or more boxes. Each box may require several dimensions, however, to fully describe the customers in it.

The market for a particular firm may consist of the customers in one or several of these boxes. At any one time and for a particular product, a particular customer probably would be in only one box. Markets are not static, however, so shifts must be anticipated, and marketing strategy planning must be adjusted to allow for them.

In our increasingly affluent society, some customers may have different demands that would place them in two or more boxes simultaneously. Consider, for example, the large family with teen-agers. They may see the need for more than one car and desire quite different things in each car because they have different uses in mind. It is possible that these demands can only be satisfied by quite different products, perhaps ones produced by different producers, say an Oldsmobile, Willys Jeepster, and a Rambler station wagon.

In general, each unique target market requires a unique marketing mix—which is why it is imperative to consider customer needs and dimensions in the selection of target markets rather than focus on product characteristics. The latter focus is a hangover from the production-oriented era.

Developing marketing mixes

Developing marketing mixes must be an integral part of the selection of the target market. That is, all the ingredients of a marketing strategy must be set simultaneously.

Many routes to the customer's satisfaction

There are a multitude of possible ways to satisfy target customers. A product can have many different tastes, colors, and appearances. The package can be of various sizes, colors, or material; the brand names and trademarks can be changed; services and returned-goods privileges can be adjusted; various advertising media (newspapers, magazines, radio, television, billboards) may be used; a company's own salesmen and perhaps various other sales specialists can be employed. Many different prices can be charged; cash discounts and markups can be changed; a higher caliber of salesman may be hired or a different type of distributor may be used; intensity of sales effort may be varied from one locality to another; credit policies may be adjusted; and so on.

Each of these many variations could have many shades of differences, making the number of possible marketing mixes extremely large. With so many variables available, the question becomes: Is there any way of simplifying a consideration of marketing mixes? And the answer is yes.

An analysis of the problems that face both large and small companies shows that it is possible to reduce the number of variables in the marketing mix to four basic ones:

> Product
> Place
> Promotion
> Price

It may help to think of the four major ingredients of a marketing mix as the "four P's." Figure 2–8 emphasizes their interrelationship and their focus on customers (*C*). This text includes a set of chapters on each of the four P's, but for the present each is discussed briefly in the following paragraphs.

Product—the right one for the target. In Chapters 10 to 14, we will consider all the problems of developing the product or service that the company has decided to offer to each target market. Most of this text will be concerned with tangible products, but the principles in most cases also apply to services. It is important to keep this in mind, since the service side of our economy is growing.[10]

Under *Product*, we will specifically cover the problems of (1) selecting a product or product lines, (2) adding or dropping items in a product line, (3) branding, (4) packaging, and (5) standardization

Figure 2–8

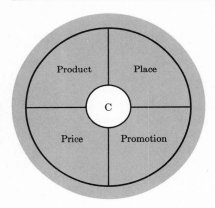

and grading. In short, the product area is concerned with *developing the right "product" for the target market.*[11]

Place—reaching the target. A product or service is not much good to a customer if it is not available when and where he wants it. We must consider where, when, and by whom the goods and services are to be offered for sale. Sometimes, for example, complicated channels of distribution are necessary, while at other times very simple methods are effective. Wholesaling, retailing, transportation, and storage play a part in the distribution of most goods and services.

In Chapters 15–20, then, we will consider under *Place* all the problems, functions, and institutions involved in *getting the right product to the target market.*

---

[10] See Donald D. Parker, *The Marketing of Consumer Services* (Seattle: Bureau of Business Research, University of Washington, 1960); John M. Rathmell, "What is Meant by Services?" *Journal of Marketing*, October, 1966, pp. 32–36.

[11] It is tempting to use the terms "product mix," "place mix," etc., refer to all the aspects of each variable. But we will just use Product, Place, etc., in a broad sense. Finally, all four variables must be blended into one marketing mix, and concern with several *mixes* might lead to confusion with *the marketing mix.*

Promotion—telling and selling the customer. The third P, *Promotion*, is discussed in Chapters 21–23. It is concerned with any method that *communicates to the target market* about the right product to be sold in the right place at the right price. Promotion encompasses sales promotion, advertising, and personal selling. All are complementary methods of communicating with customers.

Price—making it right and fair. While the marketing manager is developing the right product, place, and promotion, he also must decide on the right *price*, one that will round out his marketing mix and make it as attractive as possible. In setting the price, he must consider the nature of competition in his target market as well as the existing practices on markups, discounts, and terms of sale. He also must consider legal restrictions affecting prices.

In short, Chapters 24–28 on *Price* are concerned with *determining the "right" price* to move the right product to the right place with the right promotion for the target market.

All four P's, we have seen, are essential to the marketing mix. But is any one of them more important than the others? Generally speaking, the answer is no. When a marketing mix is selected, all decisions about the P's should be made at the same time. That is why, in the diagram, the four P's are arranged around the Customer (*C*) in a circle to indicate they are coequal. **Relative importance of four P's**

Some sequence is needed in our discussion, however, and the following one has logical advantages. We develop a *Product* that we feel will satisfy the target customers. Then we find a way (*Place*) to reach our target customers. *Promotion* tells the target customers about the availability of the product that has been designed for them. Then the *Price* is set in the light of expected customer reaction to the total offering.

Implementing marketing strategy

This text is concerned with developing and evaluating marketing strategies—primarily the analysis of target markets and the four P's. **Making choices is not easy**

The framework may appear simple enough, but the task of making choices within this framework is fairly complex. For one thing, each of the four P's has many potential variations, thereby making the number of possible marketing mixes very large. For example, if there were 10 variations in each of the variables (10 prices, 10 products, etc.) there would be 10,000 possible marketing mixes. Yet 10 is a very small number of variations for each of these variables, and as the number of variations increases, the number of possible mixes increases geometrically.

It is obvious that no human mind is capable of accurately evaluating all possible mixes, but progressive elimination of the least desirable can reduce the problem to manageable proportions. And, fortunately, there are many combinations, not just a single combination, that could succeed, as target markets are continually changing in our dynamic markets. **No human mind can do it**

One approach is to frame possible strategies in general terms, then trace the probable outcome and likelihood of success for each of them.

If the firm is profit-oriented, it can assess the relative desirability of each strategy by calculating the profit it is expected to produce. Then, assuming the decision maker is willing to accept expected profit as the criterion, the strategy that is likely to produce the highest expected profit can be chosen. For example, in Table 2–3, strategy 3 would be

Table 2–3 Evaluation of various alternatives

Alternatives	Payoff (In Dollars of Profit)	Probability of Occurrence	Expected Profit
1.	$ 100,000 or	.50	$ 50,000
	0	.50	
2.	25,000 or	.90	22,500
	0	.10	
3.	1,000,000 or	.20	200,000
	0	.80	
4.	500,000 or	.30	150,000
	0	.70	

chosen. An extremely conservative decision maker, however, might select strategy 2 because of its seeming certainty.

Frequently the possible outcomes of the various strategies cannot be specified quite as clearly as it is suggested in Table 2–3. Managerial judgment must then come into play. It may also be that maximum profits are not the main objective of the firm. In this case, the evaluation of strategies may have to be even more subjective.

Pointing the company toward its goal

The first and most important step in applying the marketing concept is wholehearted acceptance of a customer orientation. Without acceptance of this concept, at least by top management, any change in the organizational structure will be purely mechanical. Such acceptance has been likened to a magnet applied to the bottom of a piece of paper sprinkled with iron filings. "The force of the magnet orients all of the filings toward the common point."[12]

Marketing is everybody's job

The kind of change which may be needed is illustrated by the Worthington Corporation's experience. Long a conservative manufacturer of custom-made heavy machinery, Worthington revamped its organization when it shifted its viewpoint from the factory to the marketplace. Worthington feels that the marketing concept is just a "bunch of words until it comes out in performance."

To obtain performance, Worthington has followed a twofold approach: (1) a companywide reorganization along product lines, and

---

[12] Robert E. Ringle, "The Marketing Concept in the Defense Industry," *Marketing Digest* (Southern California Chapter of American Marketing Association, June, 1961), p. 28. See also, "Why Marketing Gets Bogged Down," *Printers' Ink*, February 9, 1962, pp. 53–56.

(2) an educational program designed to sell the idea of marketing, with all of its implications, to company personnel from the top down to the foremen in the shop.

Worthington is trying hard to keep marketing from being only the marketing manager's job. Instead, it would like every employee to feel that marketing is his job. To encourage this approach, the company has utilized task forces composed of men from various branches of the company to solve developing problems. These groups frequently make many changes beyond the solution of the original problem; most of these changes are designed to serve their customers better.

According to the president, "Marketing is more a way of thinking than it is of organizing."[13]

After top management has accepted the marketing concept, some formal reorganization usually is desirable. The product planning function often is under the production or engineering departments; pricing is under the finance or accounting departments; and both sales and advertising often are separate departments. Sales forecasting and budgeting frequently is done in a separate department, or by the finance or accounting departments.

Some organization structure helps

All of these activities are concerned with the customer and properly ought to be under the direction and control of the marketing manager. The marketing manager normally should report directly to top management along with the heads of production, engineering, finance, and accounting. The exact arrangement of the marketing management department depends somewhat on the needs of a particular company and the personalities involved. Organization charts showing the structure in one company before and after acceptance of the marketing concept are shown in Figure 2–9.[14]

Some companies have specific marketing activities delegated to specialized managers, such as product managers, pricing managers, distribution managers, promotion managers—in keeping with the four-P concept.

Many marketing managers probably will come from the ranks of sales management because they are more likely to be familiar with potential target customers. But this will not always be the case. Some sales managers would make poor marketing managers because of their almost blind allegiance to personal selling and their unwavering loyalty to the sales force. Similarly, an advertising manager may be so advertising-oriented that he believes almost any difficulty can be overcome by a larger advertising program. Production managers, research and development engineers, and accounting and finance experts as well may be plagued by this sort of myopia.

Who is suited to lead a marketing-oriented company?

---

[13] "Shifting the Stress to Marketing," *Business Week,* October 4, 1958, pp. 57–60; and "Worthington Corporation Adopts New Marketing Philosophy, Builds Capacity for Growth," *Printers' Ink,* October 3, 1958, pp. 41–44.

[14] Eugene B. Mapel, "What is the 'Marketing Concept'?" Barrington Associates, New York; reprinted from *Sales Management,* July 5, 1957; for other examples of specific marketing jobs, see Henry Bund and James W. Carroll, *The Changing Role of the Marketing Function* (Chicago: American Marketing Association, 1957), 59 pp.

The American Management Association official who predicted that every company president elected from 1965 on will be a marketing man was not speaking necessarily of promoted sales managers, or any other specialist for that matter. Rather, he was thinking of men who "think marketing."

Figure 2–9 *A company's organization chart before and after acceptance of the marketing concept**

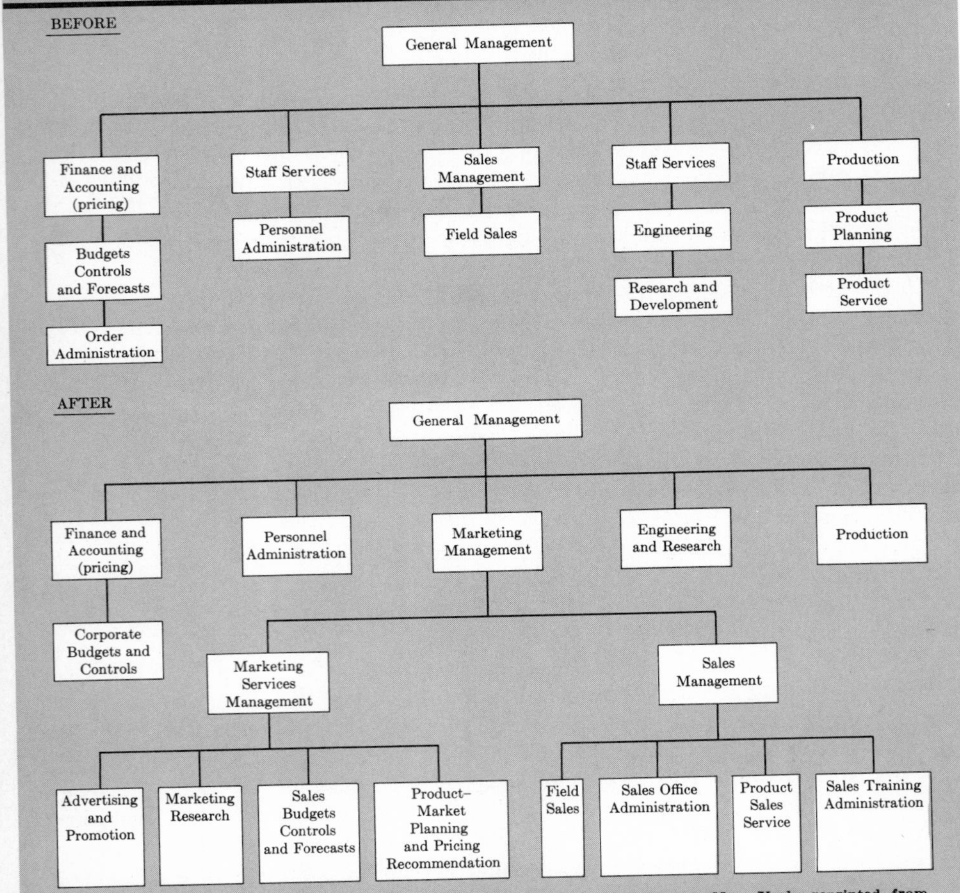

* Eugene B. Mapel, "What Is the 'Marketing Concept'?" Barrington Associates, New York; reprinted from *Sales Management*, July 5, 1957.

Theoretically, at least, the marketing manager and the prospective marketing-oriented president could come from any specialty. In one cosmetic company, as might be expected in this type of business, the advertising and sales promotion manager gradually assumed major planning and coordinating responsibilities in the company's marketing organization. In another firm, however, which produced highly technical custom-built products, the production manager was the leader in the move toward the application of the marketing concept.

The most important consideration is that the marketing manager and top management must accept the marketing concept—satisfying the customer, at a profit.

The marketing concept is less well understood in foreign markets, and consequently there are great opportunities for those who understand it and want to apply it abroad.

More profits in world enterprises

Some companies are expanding into worldwide operations. Sometimes they move from strictly domestic operations to some exporting and licensing of foreign producers. Such operations are often treated as separate little departments, with resultant neglect. Increasingly, though, such companies are aggressively pursuing foreign market potentials, often finding foreign operations much more profitable than domestic operations. As a result, they are paying more attention to worldwide markets. Domestic and foreign operations may even be integrated under one executive. Deere & Co., a farm machinery manufacturer, and Procter & Gamble, for example, have taken this step.

The involvement in international business may ultimately reach the point that the firm sees itself as a worldwide enterprise. The chief executive of Abbott Laboratories, a pharmaceutical company with plants in 22 countries, said: "We are no longer just a U.S. company with interests abroad. Abbott is a world enterprise, and many major, fundamental decisions must be made on a global basis."

A Texas Instruments executive had a similar view: "When we consider new opportunities and one is abroad and the other domestic, we can't afford to look upon the alternative here as an inherently superior business opportunity simply because it is in the U.S. We view an overseas market just as we do our market in, say, Arizona, as one more market in the world."

A General Motors executive sees this trend as: ". . . the emergence of the modern industrial corporation as an institution that is transcending national boundaries."[15]

Conclusion

The job of marketing management, it should be clear, is one of continuous direction. The marketing manager must select target customers and design a marketing mix or mixes to sell his product(s) to them. But that is only the beginning of his task. He also must see that this strategy works successfully. If it does not, he must adapt and modify this strategy during the execution stage.

Target customer groups can be divided and subdivided almost without end. Market grids can be used to segment potential markets. Then, potential marketing mixes can be considered for each of the boxes to evaluate their potential. Some boxes may be likely markets. Others may actually subdivide into several markets, each requiring different mixes.

---

[15] "Multi-National Companies," *Business Week*, April 20, 1963, pp. 62–86.

And still others may not be worth penetrating when expense is weighed against potential profit.

To limit the scope of the problem of choosing a marketing mix, without oversimplifying the problem, we settled on the four P's—Product, Place, Promotion, and Price—to identify the main decision areas of the marketing manager. The problem, in brief, is to satisfy our target customers with the *right* product, available in the *right* place, promoted in the *right* way, and available at the *right* price.

For practical purposes, there is no "best" marketing mix because market conditions are in continual flux. Marketing management may have to estimate the probabilities of success of the alternative strategies and act accordingly. All of this will be accomplished with greater ease if the company has adopted the marketing concept, which may entail the development of a new organization structure.

The four P's give the manager a framework within which he can operate logically. His eventual success will be determined by the wisdom of his choices, his ability to modify his mix in the face of uncertainly and change, and his follow-through. To give you some picture of all the details a marketing manager must consider and what is to come in the text, a checklist of marketing considerations is presented below. Do not try to memorize this list. It should be treated as a "list of considerations," to give you a feel for the many factors that the marketing manager must consider.

CHECKLIST OF MARKETING CONSIDERATIONS[16]

1. CUSTOMERS AND MARKETING CONSIDERATIONS
   A. *The Nature of the Market*
      Number of potential buyers—by region.
      Number of buyers—by region.
      Characteristics of buyers—age, income, occupation, education, sex, size of family, color, race—by region.
      Characteristics of users, if buyers and users are different—by region.
      Where buyers and users live—region, city size, urban and suburban.
      Where buyers buy—urban, suburban, rural; trading center, local; type of store.
      Size of purchase.
      When buyers buy—time of week, time of month, time of year, frequency of purchase.
      How buyers buy—brand specification or not; impulse or planned; personal inspection at counter; cash or credit.
      Why buyers buy—attitudes, motivation.
      Who influences buying decisions—type of product and brand.
      Uses for product.
      Unfavorable attitudes of buyers of brand.
      Indications of changes in buying habits.
   B. *The Structure of the Market*
      Number of competitors.
      Number of brands—national, regional, local.

---

[16] Adapted from: A. W. Frey, *The Effective Marketing Mix* (Hanover, N.H.: Amos Tuck School, Dartmouth College, 1956).

Share of market by brands, total, regional, city size, type of
store.

Characteristics of leading brands.

Differentiation of own brand from leaders.

Policies, the offer, methods and tools of principal competitors.

2. PRODUCT

A. *The Product*

Quality—materials, workmanship, design, method of manufacture.

Models and sizes.

Essential or luxury.

Convenience or shopping.

B. *The Package*

Attributes of protection, convenience, attractiveness, identification, adaptability to type of retail outlet, and economy,
through: material; size; shape; construction; label—design, color, copy; closure; competitive value.

C. *The Brand*

Adequacy with reference to memory value, suggestiveness,
pleasingness, family expansion, legal protection, goodwill
value.

D. *Service—Kind, Quality and Quantity*

Installation.

Education in use.

Repair.

Provision of accessory equipment.

Delivery.

Credit.

Returned goods.

3. PLACE

A. *Distribution Channels*

Total number of retailers, each type by region.

Total number of wholesalers, each type by region.

Percent retailers, each type, handling brand by region.

Degree of aggressive retailer cooperation, by region, store
type and city size.

Indications of shift in relative importance of channels.

4. PROMOTION

A. *Personal Selling*

Recruiting and selection methods.

Training procedures.

Supervision procedures.

Stimulation devices.

Compensation plan.

B. *Advertising*

Size of space and time units—effectiveness.

Appeals and themes—effectiveness.

Use of black-and-white and color—effectiveness.

Methods of merchandising advertising.

C. *Sales Promotion*

Types of activity—deal, premiums, bulletins, portfolios, and
so on.

Cooperative advertising arrangements.

D. *Publicity*

Volume and nature—releases, clippings, mentions.

5. PRICE
   At factory.
   To wholesalers, by type, size and regions.
   To retailers, by type, size and regions.
   Discounts—functional, quantity, cash, other.
   Allowances and deals.
   Service charges.
   Price maintenance.

---

1 Explain the General Foods hypothesis. What is its relevance to marketing?

2 Explain why it may be desirable to define target markets and market grids in terms of *people's* needs rather than in terms of products or people. Further, explain why considerable ingenuity may be needed to develop market grids which clearly define market opportunities.

3 Distinguish clearly between a marketing strategy and a marketing mix. Use an example.

4 Why is the customer placed in the center of the four P's in the text diagram? Explain, using a specific example from your own experience.

5 Develop a market grid for footwear in general, using as many customer needs and other characteristics as seem appropriate. Then discuss the many types and qualities of footwear which might appeal to the customers in your market grid boxes. Do not attempt to collect data.

6 Develop a market grid for the "automobile" market, using several customer-related dimensions—*not* product characteristics. Show where you are on the grid. Then, consider the products which are now available in the light of your breakdown and see if you can identify any unsatisfied target markets. Might they offer any substantial potential? Is your "ideal" available? Should it be?

7 Outline a marketing strategy for each of the following new products:
   a) A radically new design for a hair comb.
   b) A new fishing-reel.
   c) A new "wonder drug."
   d) A new industrial stapling machine.

Uncontrollable variables affect marketing management

The marketing manager does not work in a vacuum. He must consider much more than just the four P's and choosing target markets. As we noted in Chapter 2 (see Figure 2–2), the uncontrollable variables he must work with can be placed in the following categories:

1. Cultural and social environment.
2. Political and legal environment.
3. Economic environment.
4. Existing business structure.
5. Resources and objectives of the firm.

In the long run, the marketing manager's actions may affect some or all of these variables. This in turn would affect his future strategies. But in the short run we will take these variables as uncontrollable *by the marketing manager.* Some of them, however, may be controllable by other people, either inside or outside the firm.

The marketing manager cannot be concerned only with "marketing." He must understand how his firm, and other businesses, operate; he needs to have some knowledge of the social sciences, in order to anticipate future business and social trends.

The marketing manager should seek ways to relate and interrelate the findings and analytical approaches of many other disciplines. For example, he should try to integrate the newer work being done in the behavioral science areas of sociology, anthropology, psychology, and social psychology, in order to gain a better understanding of the

41

cultural and social environment. He should try to understand the traditional fields of political science, history, philosophy, law, and economics to understand the political and legal environment. The fields of economics and business administration, as well as the natural sciences and engineering are relevant to an understanding of the economic environment. And business administration and economics are necessary for an understanding of the existing business organizations and how they operate.

How important these variables are, and how they add to the complexity and challenge of marketing management, will be seen in this chapter.

Cultural and social environment

The cultural and social variable is completely beyond the control of the marketing manager—in the short run, at least. The traditions and values of various cultures and social classes are extremely relevant to marketing, and these tend to change very slowly. Obvious differences from country to country may come to mind quickly: Americans, for example, generally tend to accept and encourage change, while more tradition-bound societies are more resistant to innovators. But more subtle differences in customs, which can mean the difference between success and failure in marketing, are too often overlooked.

Friendliness and hushpuppies
Since customer behavior is given extensive treatment in Chapters 6–9, we will treat it only briefly. A few examples will suffice to emphasize the possible impact of customer behavior on marketing strategy planning.

Americans are often stereotyped as a friendly people, but actually this varies by regions. People on the West Coast, for example, tend to be more open and, at least superficially, more friendly. This is in part because many have moved west to find a new life and have left behind the more tradition-bound social structures of the smaller towns of the Midwest and the East. People on the West Coast also seem more willing to travel great distances. Some Californians, for example, think nothing of driving several hundred miles on a weekend, while this would be a major trip for a New Yorker. This has an effect on the location of retail facilities and loyalty to particular stores.

Eating habits vary to some extent among regions and within urban areas. For example, biscuits and hushpuppies are much more popular in the South, and Mexican food is gaining popularity in the Southwest. Within large metropolitan cities, we still find national and religious pockets that represent very distinct markets for some goods and services. Large midwestern and eastern metropolitan areas often have distinct neighborhoods of Irish, Italians, Poles, Jews, Puerto Ricans, and Negroes. These urban areas have newspapers, radio stations, restaurants, grocery stores, and record shops which cater specifically to these culturally defined target markets.

This great diversity within the American "melting pot" is ignored by the marketing manager only at his peril. Many foreign and American

42

businessmen have tried to use the New York City market as a test of how products will be received in the United States, thinking that because New York is in itself a melting pot, it will provide typical American consumer reactions. Such businessmen have been badly misled. The New York metropolitan market is probably the most unusual market in the world; while it includes many ethnic and national groups it is, by its diversity, typical of no one market. The New York area has about as many Jews as Israel, about 30 percent of the world Jewish population. There are more Puerto Ricans in New York City than in San Juan, the largest city in Puerto Rico. But New York does not have as many Scandinavians as Chicago or Minneapolis–St. Paul, or as many Japanese as Los Angeles. It is no wonder that businessmen who ignore these obvious statistics fail to understand some of the subtleties discussed in Chapters 6–9.

Besides consumption behavior differences, we also must consider cultural attitudes toward business institutions and the changes, sometimes due to marketing itself, taking place in these attitudes. Here, too, we should generalize with care. For example, the *mañana* attitude of South America is not typical of Venezuela, which is more eager than many of her neighboring countries to accept the improvements of modern technology. The explanation is probably a large influx of Germans who long ago came to develop mining enterprises and brought with them the spirit of the north European businessman.[1]

***Mañana* is today in Venezuela**

It is clear that a country's attitudes toward business and new enterprise has something to do with the rate of its growth and the direction of its development.[2] This is important to students and companies thinking of going into international business. Logical improvements in marketing methods may nevertheless be blocked by local distrust and prejudice against change and business. In some countries, the word "earn" has the connotation of "outwit," and new methods are suspect. Even the established businessman, no matter how wealthy and successful, is sometimes regarded as inferior. This was true in the time of Plato, it was true in Japan prior to the 19th century, and it is still true today in many countries. Where such attitudes exist, they are often reflected in the political and legal environment.

Political and legal environment

As the role of business grows in our society, the attitudes and reactions of the populace, social critics, and governments become increasingly important to the marketing manager. In our discussion, we will separate political and legal environments, although in practice this separation is hard to maintain. A change in political environment often leads to changes in the legal environment or the administration of existing legislation.

[1] Talk by Professor Edward Barnet, Tri-State Marketing Conference, Michigan State University, May, 1962.

[2] David C. McClelland, "Business Drive and National Achievement," *Harvard Business Review*, July–August, 1962, pp. 99–112.

Political environment

The political environment generally is, or should be, an expression of a peoples' attitudes toward the management of the whole economy. At one time, Americans expected the federal government to do relatively little for them. Today, more and more voters are expressing their preference for greater federal involvement in planning and controlling the economy. This has had a direct impact on many businessmen.

Less ad money for soap, fewer ads for Canada. In 1962, for example, the steel industry withdrew a price increase under direct pressure from President Kennedy. In the following years, other basic industries "backed down" on price increases under government pressure. Business executives have come to anticipate "guidance" from federal authorities. In the same way, British businessmen have been carefully watching investigations of their soap industry. Already, some price cuts have been forced on nonadvertised brands. If the pressure grows, drastic cuts in advertising budgets and prices may be required.[3]

The impact can cross national boundaries, too. Canadians have issued guidelines to "foreigners"—principally U.S. businessmen—on "good corporate behavior." Such guidelines can be extremely important in both domestic and international business because most businesses must obtain permission to operate. In some political environments, the routine is straightforward and clear-cut; in others, considerable red tape is involved and personal influence is sometimes important.[4]

If a company or industry fails to watch the political environment carefully, adverse legislation or administrative rulings may result. Governments frequently make swift and even arbitrary changes in tariffs, quotas, embargoes, and foreign exchange regulations, especially when competition hurts. Recently, legislation was passed to restrict the flow of American advertising specifically aimed at Canadian customers.[5] And foreign textiles moving to the United States have been regulated.

Nonparity in the Philippines, boycotts in Arabia. Political climates continually change. Often the results are predictable. It seems certain, for example, that the oil-rich countries will eventually obtain an even greater share of the oil profits.[6] Sometimes the shift in attitude is rather quick. For years, U.S. business was encouraged in the Philippines, while at the same time Chinese merchants were harassed by various regulations. In a recent court decision, however, a judge ruled for the first time that a U.S. company does not have parity rights with home-owned companies in the Philippines, although such rights supposedly were guaranteed by a 1954 agreement.[7] Similarly, Ford Motor Co. and Coca-Cola suddenly were added to an Arab boycott list, because they planned to establish plants in Israel.[8] Obviously this economic warfare reflects the political environment, and the probable impact on individual companies cannot be overlooked.

---

[3] *Time,* August 26, 1966, p. 75.

[4] "U.S. Companies Face Guidelines in Canada," *Business Week,* April 9, 1966, p. 34.

[5] "Ottawa Restricts U.S. Ads," *Business Week,* September 4, 1965, p. 36.

[6] *Business Week,* July 24, 1965, p. 90; and "Libya Acts to Bolster the Price of its Oil," *Business Week,* January 1, 1966, p. 16.

[7] *Business Week,* December 24, 1966, p. 72.

[8] "Arabs Bar Coke, Ford," *Business Week,* November 26, 1966, p. 52.

The political environment does not always have such negative implications. The worth of a politician is sometimes measured in the government contracts or subsidies he can bring to producers in a certain district or country. And many companies spend considerable money supporting lobbyists in an attempt to affect the political environment. Independent of such actions, governments may decide that encouraging business is a good idea.[9] Jamaica is currently offering tax holidays and other special treatment to companies that set up operations there,[10] and the U.S. government recently moved to clarify the tax structure on domestic and foreign subsidiaries in an effort to boost shipments overseas.[11] State and local governments also try to attract new businesses. Most legislatures are quite concerned with the effect the tax structure may have on their community as an attractive business site.

Whether the marketing manager is interested in domestic or international marketing, it is obvious that he must consider the political environment. And as already noted, the latter often has an impact on the legal environment.

U.S. legislative developments: encouraging competition

American economic and legislative thinking has been based on the assumption that competition among many small firms will guide the economy with an "invisible hand." This idea became popular after the publication of Adam Smith's *Wealth of Nations* in 1776. Great Britain accepted this idea during the 1800's, in principle at least, and it was enshrined in common law there and in the United States. According to this concept, attempts to restrain or limit trade were held to be against the public interest and unenforceable. Practices tending to fix prices, limit markets, or in any other way control trade, were considered undesirable.

This laissez-faire approach did not last long in Great Britain. England and the Commonwealth countries now permit (or at least tolerate) considerable restraint of trade, as do many other countries. But Americans have been especially reluctant to give up Adam Smith's free enterprise ideal. After the Civil War, however, industries began to grow larger, and some were consolidated by wealthy big-business tycoons of that day referred to as "robber barons." Their notion of free enterprise led to the formation of trusts, cartels, and monopolies, which restrained competition and tended to work hardships on smaller producers and consumers. As a result, there was a movement—especially among midwestern farmers—to curb monopolists. Beginning in 1890, we see the development of a series of laws that were basically anti-monopoly or pro-competition. The names and dates of these laws are shown in Table 3–1. The Sherman, Clayton, and Federal Trade Commission (FTC) Acts were early anti-monopoly laws. The FTC Act set up the Federal Trade Commission as a continuing body to serve as a watchdog for the public and to supplement the Justice Department's efforts to enforce the nation's laws affecting business.

---

[9] "Chile's Copper Beckons Once Again," *Business Week,* February 12, 1966, p. 76–81.
[10] "Industry's New Island In The Sun," *Business Week,* February 12, 1966, pp. 66 ff.
[11] *Business Week,* August 6, 1966, p. 38.

The losses of the depression of the 1930's, however, convinced many businessmen that too much competition had its disadvantages. The pendulum swung the other way, and some of the resulting legislation was basically anti-competition. Although the Robinson-Patman Act allegedly was concerned with avoiding "injury to competition," it was often interpreted by the courts to mean avoiding "injury to competitors," especially small retailers. The Miller-Tydings Act, passed in 1937 and strengthened in 1952 by the McGuire Act, provided exemptions to the basic antitrust legislation, thus permitting price fixing at the retail level.

Besides supplementing the Sherman Act, the Clayton Act was aimed at several specific practices: price discrimination, exclusive dealing arrangements that limit a buyer's choice of suppliers, and tying contracts (contracts requiring that some goods have to be purchased in combination with others that the company controls, even if the former

Table 3-1 Outline of federal legislation affecting competition in marketing

	Anti-Monopoly (Pro-Competition)	Anti-Competition	Anti-Specific Practices
1890	Sherman Act		
1914	Clayton Act		Clayton Act
	Federal Trade Commission Act		
1936	Robinson-Patman Act	Robinson-Patman Act	Robinson-Patman
1937		Miller-Tydings Act	Act
1938			Wheeler-Lea Amendment
1950			Antimerger Act
1952		McGuire Act	

can be obtained more cheaply elsewhere). These specific practices were singled out because the more general prohibitions of the Sherman Act did not seem to cover them. In a similar vein, the Robinson-Patman Act was aimed at price discrimination and price cutting, especially involving large price-competitive chains such as A&P, which were hurting small competitors. The existing legislation had been aimed at manufacturers, but the new threat to small middlemen now came from the large chain middlemen.

The Wheeler-Lea Amendment to the FTC Act was likewise aimed at specific practices. In this case, unscrupulous advertisers were singled out. These firms had escaped prosecution under the earlier laws because such laws were concerned with injury to competition rather than individual consumers.

The Antimerger Act of 1950 is an amendment to the Clayton Act. This was designed to make it easier for the Federal Trade Commission to regulate those mergers that might substantially lessen competition. The application of this law has led to tighter and tighter control over

46

mergers, extending even to the acquisition of noncompetitive firms by larger firms. The intention of both the Federal Trade Commission and Justice Department has generally been to maintain competition in the market. Yet it is difficult even for lawyers and justices of the Supreme Court to know where all this is leading. In a recent landmark case in which Procter & Gamble was ordered to dispose of Clorox, one of the justices agreed with the conclusion—but complained that the Court's opinion was so broad and generalized that it "leaves the Commission lawyers and businessmen at large guessing as to what is to be expected of them in future cases of this kind."[12]

Knowing what the government must prove to obtain a conviction in such matters will help one to understand the development of federal legislation. In the following list of legislative acts, a phrase is included after the name of each act to indicate what must be proved. It should be noted that the more recent laws are worded to make it easier to prosecute those whom consumers feel are not acting in their interest:

Sherman Antitrust Act (1890)—Monopoly or conspiracy in restraint of trade.
Clayton Act (1914)—Substantially lessen competition.
Federal Trade Commission Act (1914)—Unfair methods of competition.
Robinson-Patman Act (1936)—Tends to injure competition (but often applied as tend to injure competitors).
Wheeler-Lea Amendment (1938)—Unfair or deceptive practices in commerce.

Prosecution is a serious matter. It is important to note that we have both criminal and civil laws. Many business affairs are regulated under civil laws, and the penalties are limited to blocking or forcing certain actions, together with fines. Where criminal law applies, jail sentences can be imposed.

This is an important point to understand. Some business executives have gone to jail or received suspended jail sentences in recent years because they have violated the criminal law provisions of antitrust legislation. The imposition of jail sentences is a relatively recent development and has added a new note of seriousness to the consideration of the political and legal environment.

State and local regulations: Sunday laws, spreading disease. In addition to the U.S. legislation discussed above which affects interstate commerce, marketers must be aware of state and local laws which affect intrastate commerce. Here legal advice and/or extensive knowledge of community or state politics is even more important. Some laws, for example, impose such harsh penalties that the local prosecutors are

---

[12] *Marketing Insights,* April 17, 1967, pp. 3–4; for further discussion on this, see "Anti-Trust Turns Tougher," *Business Week,* September 12, 1964, pp. 98–112; "High Court Tightens the Anti-Trust Reins," *Business Week,* June 18, 1966, p. 40; "High Court Dissolves A Sudsy Conglomerate," *Business Week,* April 15, 1967, pp. 40–41; Peter Asch, "Conglomerate Mergers And Public Policy," *MSU Business Topics,* Winter, 1967, pp. 61–67; Betty Bock, *Mergers And Markets Studies In Business Economics No. 85* (New York: National Industrial Conference Board, 1964); and Betty Bock, *Mergers and Markets Studies In Business Economics No. 87* (New York: National Industrial Conference Board, 1965).

reluctant to enforce them. Thus, for practical purposes, the law is inoperative.

There are state and city laws regulating minimum prices and the setting of prices (to be discussed in Chapter 28); regulations about going into business (licenses, examinations, and even tax payments); and in some communities, regulations prohibiting certain activities, such as door-to-door selling or selling on Sundays or during evenings. This latter problem has been especially important in recent years, as old "blue laws" have been rolled out by established retailers as a defense against discounters. Sunday selling is often offensive to religious groups as well.

Some states have regulations about movement or importation of agricultural commodities, ostensibly to protect the quality of goods offered or to prevent the spread of animal or crop diseases. Some of these, of course, are justifiable, but others are simply a means of restricting the movement of goods to enable local producers to obtain higher prices. This has been especially true as regards milk, some citrus products, and wine. This is also true of the buy-local and buy-American provisions of some government contracts.

Legislative developments abroad: trade for the common good

The English preceded us in a policy of unrestrained competition, and then backed off when many of their businessmen decided that they did not actually want so much competition.[13]

The common law, based on statutes and court decisions, has generally been followed in English-speaking countries. But even within the English-speaking community, laws vary from country to country, and a specific knowledge of this legislation is necessary. Even more study is required in non-English countries, where there are often special courts dealing only with business matters and specific laws replace our common-law system.

As we move from marketing within one country to multi-national marketing, things become somewhat more complicated, especially within blocks of countries that are attempting to develop a common market.

The European Common Market—which consists of six countries in continental Europe (to be described in more detail in Chapter 7)—has approved some extremely tough antitrust legislation that is binding on all members and on all foreign businessmen who wish to sell their products within this Common Market. This legislation labels as illegal "any agreements which are likely to affect trade between member states which have as their object or result the prevention, restriction, or distortion of competition."

How this regulation will work out in practice has yet to be seen, but a recent decision by the highest court of the Common Market suggests that it may be quite effective, despite the cartelizing and restrictive practices that have been traditional with continental European businessmen.[14]

---

[13] For more recent developments, see Richard C. Osborn, "Postwar Control of Restrictive Trade Practices in Great Britain," *Journal of Business,* October, 1962, pp. 367–85.

[14] "Another Trade Wall Crumbles," *Business Week,* July 23, 1966, p. 32; and "Cartels Fence In European Steel," *Business Week,* September 3, 1966, pp. 94–98.

48

Because legislation must be interpreted by the courts, students should **Know the laws, follow the courts** continually follow not only legislative developments but also the tenor of thinking of the courts. Often laws are vaguely phrased by legislators to convey intent but not specific detail. It is then up to the courts and administrative bodies to spell out the details. And good legal assistance is needed to keep up with all these details.

If business students and businessmen better understand the intent of the makers and interpreters of the laws—the legislators and jurists— there might be less abrasion between business and government and fewer "embarrassing" mistakes. With such an understanding, business- men might come to accept the political-legal environment as simply another framework within which business must function and develop its marketing strategies. After all, it is the consumers, through their governmental representatives, who determine the kind of economic system they want. Businesses cater to customers' needs and have to operate within the framework specified by these customers. This does not preclude businessmen from studying how and why an economic system should work and lobbying for the development of a more effective system.[15]

Economic environment

An otherwise good marketing strategy may fail if a country is experiencing a depression or rapid business decline. For this reason, the marketing manager cannot ignore macroeconomics—the analysis of the behavior of whole economic systems. The plans of the business commu- nity to invest and the plans of the government sector to spend may have a major impact on the overall level of the economy. Consumers' willingness to buy, and the probable reaction to proposed tax increases or decreases, may have a bearing on future economic prospects. These matters are discussed more fully in Chapter 5 with respect to sales forecasting.

Tax changes, for example, provide a good illustration of why the **What will customers do?** marketing manager must study the economic environment. The fed- eral government makes a practice now of using monetary and fiscal policies to help smooth out economic fluctuations. A reduction in automobile excise taxes might be proposed to stimulate the automobile industry and, because of the latter's size, the economy as a whole. For the marketing manager, however, this would mean that he would have to anticipate when the announcement was to be made and the probable

[15] In this regard, see E. T. Grether and R. J. Holloway, "Impact of Government upon the Market System," *Journal of Marketing,* April, 1967, pp. 1–5; Seymour Banks, "Commen- tary on 'Impact of Government upon the Market System,'" *Journal of Marketing,* April, 1967, pp. 5–7; "A Changing Balance of Power," *Business Week,* July 17, 1965, pp. 85–106; J. G. Van Cise, "Regulation—By Business or Government?" *Harvard Business Review,* March–April, 1966, pp. 53–63; Ray O. Werner, "Marketing and the United States Supreme Court," *Journal of Marketing,* January, 1967, pp. 4–8; J. F. Barron, "'Normal' Business Behavior and the Justice Department," *Journal of Marketing,* January, 1963, pp. 46–49; Wayne G. Broehl, Jr., "Insights into Business and Society," *Harvard Business Review,* May–June, 1966, pp. 6–37; Stanley C. Hollander, "Social Pressures and Retail Competition," *MSU Business Topics,* Winter, 1965, pp. 7–14; and Daniel J. Murphy, "The Federal Trade Commission of the 1960's," *Journal of Marketing,* April, 1963, pp. 1–5.

customer reactions while the issue was being discussed. He might have to modify his marketing mix to tell target customers about the impact of the tax cut. And he might even have to cut prices immediately or promise rebates if the cut is voted, to keep the business going and avoid inventory pileups at both the retail and manufacturer levels.

Alternately, a tax change might force an entirely new marketing strategy and perhaps the development of new institutions. High purchase (sales) taxes in Great Britain have had this effect. A 45 percent purchase tax on radio and television sets has led to a large rental market—from 75 to 85 percent of the TV sets being rented, not bought.[16]

What will the government do? Inflation is a major factor in many economies, and it is of concern to the marketing manager, especially as regards pricing. In South America, inflation has become almost a way of life. Most people have come to assume that prices will always go up, and they buy and sell accordingly. This behavior usually encourages further inflation. From 1953 to 1960, the price level increased more than nine times in Chile; more than six times in Argentina; more than four times in Brazil; and more than three times in Uruguay. This can be contrasted with an 11 percent rise in the consumer price level in the United States. Even including our post–World War II inflation, our price index rose only 65 percent from 1945 through 1960.[17]

Sometimes the political and economic environments overlap, especially as government becomes an increasing force in modern economies. In 1962, President Kennedy's administration had a marked impact on the U.S. steel industry. Using the prestige of the Executive Office, and a veiled threat of antitrust legislation, the government forced the steel industry to rescind announced price increases. As a result, other firms held the line, and prices returned to the earlier level.[18] Canada's Finance Minister had a similar confrontation with the Steel Company of Canada in 1966, with similar results.[19] Corresponding examples can be found in other countries.

Obviously, the economic environment may be a special factor to the marketing manager. In contrast to legal and cultural environments, economic environments change continuously and may move rapidly up or down.

Existing business structure

The phrase, *existing business structure,* refers to the number and types of competitors facing the marketing manager in his various target markets, the degree of their competitiveness, and the nature of the

---

[16] *Business Week,* May 19, 1962, p. 100.

[17] *Economic Policies and Programs in South America* (Report of the Subcommittee on Inter-American Economic Relationships of the Joint Economic Committee of the Congress of the United States [Washington, D.C.: U.S. Government Printing Office, 1962]), p. 121; and *Statistical Abstract of the United States, 1962* (Washington, D.C.: U.S. Government Printing Office), p. 348.

[18] "Behind U.S. Steel's Price Blunder," *Fortune,* August, 1962, pp. 75 ff.

[19] "Canada Rolls Back Prices, Too," *Business Week,* September 24, 1966, p. 56.

marketing strategies being used in the various markets by the competitors (or being considered by them). This topic is a major concern of this text and of the marketing manager. A few examples will illustrate the importance of the marketing manager's concern with competition.

The marketing manager can expect a great deal more competition, and probably much more emphasis on price, if the industry is composed of many small producers and retailers. For example, there are at least 650 boat builders and 4,000 engine and accessory manufacturers attempting to sell their products through more than 17,000 marine dealers and 3,500 marinas.[20] Competitive strategies in this industry are very different from those in the aluminum or computer industries, for example, where there are relatively few competitors.

The competitiveness of the business structure also depends on the attitudes of the businessmen and varies from country to country. In France, the highly individualistic small retailer does everything in his power to avoid competition, particularly price competition. He will even join a "syndicate" which determines rules of doing business and fixes prices—a seeming contradiction to his desire for individualism. Such groups seek to discourage competitors and innovations. Their counterparts can be found among producers, wholesalers, and retailers throughout the world.[21]

In this book, competition is treated as an uncontrollable consideration. But what he or his competitors do may affect competition. Therefore, by intelligent consideration of what he might do in a particular situation—by putting himself in the competitors' shoes—he should be able to make intelligent plans in the light of the existing and potential business structure.

Resources and objectives of the firm

Two separate variables are involved here: resources and objectives. Top management, either past or present, may have set these variables, and the variables may impose real restrictions on short-run strategy planning. In the short run, the marketing manager must work within these constraints, but in the long run he will want to help shape the objectives and perhaps modify the resources.

One of the first things that a marketing manager must face is that his firm has some unique resources. As a result of its own history, experiences, and personnel, it has strengths and weaknesses that distinguish it from other firms. A good marketing strategy should make extensive use of the firm's strong points. Various resources to consider when developing a marketing strategy include those discussed below.[22]

Resources of the firm —the unique strength

Financial strength. There is no escaping the fact that industries such as steel, public utilities, oil refining, and chemicals require large

---

[20] "From Back Yard Boats to Yachts," *Business Week,* August 28, 1965, pp. 28–29.

[21] *Experiment in Union: Latin America Broadens Its Market* (New York: Vision, Inc., 1961), p. 21.

[22] Charles H. Kline, "The Strategy of Product Policy," *Harvard Business Review,* July–August, 1955, pp. 91–100.

amounts of capital to build efficient facilities. There is little reason for smaller companies to consider these businesses. This is especially true because larger facilities in such businesses may benefit from what are called "economies of scale." This means that the cost of production per unit decreases as the quantities produced increase. The smaller producer would be at great disadvantage if he tried to compete in these lines.

Some businesses, however, do not have economies of scale. In these lines, smaller, more flexible firms may be quite effective. That explains why large companies often have difficulties when they enter low-investment-type businesses. In one situation, a large chemical processor, because it was producing the basic plastic sheets, attempted to make and sell decorated shower curtains. The firm lost heavily on the experiment, however, because the smaller shower curtain manufacturers and distributors could change their styles and policies more rapidly, meeting retailer demands for many product variations and styles.

Industries that require large amounts of capital to introduce products or to withstand cyclical instability are usually dominated by larger concerns. The same is true of industries that require a great deal of basic, applied, or product research. Middlemen, on the other hand, typically require lower financial investment, and these businesses provide good opportunities for those with less financial strength.

Raw material reserves. Firms that own or have assured access to basic raw material resources can realistically consider businesses that require these resources. But companies, large or small, that are not in this position may find—especially in times of short supply—that they have difficulty even remaining in operation. Chemical and paper manufacturers usually attempt to control timber resources, and the large wallboard manufacturers usually control sources of gypsum rock. Historically, the metals and petroleum companies have controlled their own resources.

Independent owners of raw materials often have difficulty selling all their output during times of ample supply, and little difficulty during times of tight supply. This is because most of the large producers use their own resources for the bulk of their needs and buy on the outside only during especially busy times. A smaller firm that requires some of these basic raw materials or intends to sell to larger integrated producers must be aware of the behavior of its potential customers and competitors.

The availability of raw material reserves has less relevance to retailers, wholesalers, and certain types of manufacturers, which are far removed from the processing of such raw materials. They would consider this factor, however, when selecting sources of supply for the finished goods they need.

Physical plant. Some lines of business require large aggregations of productive facilities that may already be available. This is certainly true in the steel, chemical, and railroad industries.

In other industries, much less physical plant is necessary, and it is easier to sell or buy. Renting or leasing rather than buying may be a

52

possibility. A trucker can rent a truck, warehouse, and office facilities. His roadbed is provided by the city or state, and repair facilities are available at most garages or truck manufacturers' branch offices. A wholesaler can rent a warehouse and delivery trucks. A retailer can rent a store and delivery truck, and used store fixtures are available. Farms can be leased.

The existing physical plant may have considerable bearing on the development of a marketing strategy because one of the firm's objectives—even if it is not stated—may be to use its existing plant as fully as possible. Any logical strategy will attempt to make use of existing physical facilities, or include provision for their disposal, so that the capital can be used more efficiently elsewhere.

Location. High transportation costs, product perishability, and demand variations in local markets may force the marketing manager to adopt a marketing strategy that emphasizes production for local or regional markets. Perishable food products, such as bread, potato chips, and dairy products, are produced and distributed in relatively small markets and present great opportunities for smaller firms.

Sometimes the reverse is true. Being close to basic raw materials—hogs, in this case—a meat products producer, such as George A. Hormel Co., may produce certain kinds of meat products in one or several plants and then distribute over a wide area. But the marketing manager here is able to use an entirely different strategy with canned or smoked meat than with fresh meat, which must be sold much more rapidly.

Patents. Patents are of primary concern to manufacturers. To the patent owner, they grant a 17-year "monopoly" to develop and use his new product, process, or material as he sees fit. If a producer obtains a patent and is unwilling to license it, producers of any size may have difficulty competing. If the patent covers a basic process, other producers may be forced to use second-rate processes, and their efforts may be doomed to failure. Many large firms attempt, through basic research, to protect their interests in their operating fields by securing patents covering most or all of the basic formulas and devices in these fields. Small producers, not engaged in this type of research, would be well advised to avoid direct competition with manufacturers who emphasize and are successful at basic research.

Public acceptance. If a large or small competitor has developed a loyal following of customers—a "customer franchise"—for its product or service, then others may have difficulty invading this market. A strong customer franchise is a valuable asset that the marketing manager should use in the development of marketing strategy. Lack of such a franchise can be a real liability.

Sometimes a firm must test the strength of its own or a competitor's franchise before knowing how to adjust its marketing strategy. In one case, a large manufacturer attempted to do this against a bakery product that had a strong customer franchise and had encountered little competition for more than 10 years. The large manufacturer found that his competitor's market strength could be overcome, but

53

only at prohibitive cost. After this market test, the big firm decided to develop another marketing strategy.

Personnel. Some organizations pay higher wages for skilled labor because trained workers may enable the marketing manager to develop a unique marketing strategy, perhaps emphasizing quality consciousness and flexibility. A skilled sales force is also an asset, whereas lack of good salesmen may restrict strategy planning. Even if the skilled production employees mentioned above can produce a new product, the sales organization may not have the contacts or know-how to sell it. This is especially true when a firm moves from the consumer goods to industrial goods field or vice versa.

Management attitudes. The attitude of top management is an important factor in growth, especially as it affects the development and introduction of new products.

The president of one New England manufacturing company was enthusiastic about the prospects for a new product. But after reviewing his company personnel and especially those in management, he dropped plans for the product. Why? He found that among his employees there was no ambition or interest in growth.

In another company, this one in the Midwest, it is unlikely that a new product ever will be accepted. Again, the reason is simple and sad. As the firm's top management expresses it, "Fortunately, not enough sensible ideas come along to cause us any trouble."

Objectives of the firm —getting there at a profit

It might have been best to treat the objectives of the firm first, perhaps even before marketing strategy was discussed, since the company's objectives shape the direction and operation of the entire business. But we have saved our treatment of objectives until this point because it is easier now to see how they can affect the development of marketing strategies.

Should set firm's course. Any firm should know where it is going or it is likely to fall into the trap expressed so well by the quotation: "Having lost sight of our objective, we redoubled our efforts."[23] In spite of the importance of objectives, studies of both large and small corporations show that they are seldom stated explicitly. In small businesses, they appear to be stated *after the fact!* And in some large businesses, there may be *several* implicit—but conflicting—objectives held by different executives. The relative importance of any of these objectives seems to depend upon the point of view of the man being interviewed.[24]

It would be convenient if we could say that a company should set one overriding objective, such as making a profit, and let that serve as a

[23] Charles H. Granger, "The Hierarchy of Objectives," *Harvard Business Review,* May–June, 1964, p. 63.

[24] Robert F. Lanzillotti, "Pricing Objectives in Large Companies," *American Economic Review,* December, 1958, pp. 921–40. This was a continuation of the study by A. D. H. Kaplan, J. P. Dirlam, and R. F. Lanzillotti, *Pricing in Big Business* (Washington, D.C.: Brookings Institution, 1958); F. Parker Fowler, Jr., and E. W. Sandberg, *The Relation of Management Decision-Making to Small Business Growth* (Management Research Summary [Washington, D.C.: Small Business Administration, 1964]).

guide. Actually, however, setting objectives is much more complicated —which explains why it is done so poorly if at all.

Setting objectives that really guide the present and future development of the company is a soul-searching procedure that requires top management to take a systems view of the whole business, relate its present needs and resources to the external environment, and then plot the broad outlines of the company's future course.

Taken together, the following three objectives provide a useful starting point and guideline for a particular firm. These three objectives could be phrased and made more specific in many ways. But these three basic objectives should be sought together because, in the long run, a failure in even one of the three areas might lead to the total failure of the enterprise:

1. Engage in some specific business activity that will perform a socially and economically useful function.
2. Develop an organization to perpetuate the enterprise and implement its strategies.
3. Achieve sufficient profitability to survive.[25]

Should be socially useful. The first objective suggests that the company should do something useful. This is more than a platitude. Businesses exist at the discretion of consumers, and if the activities of a business appear to be at variance with the "consumer good," that business can be wiped out almost overnight by political or legal action.

Should view business broadly as customer-satisfying activity. The first objective also implies that the firm should view its mission as satisfying customer needs rather than some more production-oriented objective such as using the company's resources, exploiting a patent, etc. The firm should define its efforts broadly, as we did in Chapter 2, when we focused on the refrigera*tion* market rather than the refrigera*tor* market. This should lead the company down "need-satisfying" paths rather than product-oriented paths. It may mean that the company will develop products or processes that will compete with, or even make obsolete, its present activities. But if this new offering will better satisfy customers (and probably will be discovered by other companies anyway), then developing it would seem to be a sensible defensive course.

Procter & Gamble produces many soap brands that compete with each other. The company feels that if there are markets which are not completely satisfied, Procter & Gamble may as well create new products to satisfy them, even if this means cutting into the sales of some of its existing products.

By following the need-satisfying approach, whole new businesses may develop. Whirlpool Corp., a large manufacturer of refrigerators,

---

[25] These were adapted from Peter F. Drucker, "Business Objectives And Survival Needs: Notes On A Discipline of Business Enterprise," *Journal of Business,* April, 1958, pp. 81–90; and for a discussion of how objectives might develop, see Harper W. Boyd, Jr., and S. J. Levy, "What Kind of Corporate Objectives?" *Journal of Marketing,* October, 1966, pp. 53–58; see also, William D. Guth and Renato Tagiuri, "Personal Values and Corporate Strategies," *Harvard Business Review,* September–October, 1965, pp. 123–34.

views itself in the food preservation field, and this may lead them to obsolete refrigeration *and* refrigerators. The reason for this seeming contradiction is that Whirlpool recently developed a process for reducing the oxygen, and therefore oxidation, in food storage containers. The new process has kept apples crisp and fresh for two years *without* refrigeration.[26]

The importance of a broad view should be obvious if objectives are supposed to help a company plan for the future. Too narrow a view may lead the company into a product area in which the product itself, because of changing customer needs, will soon be obsolete.[27]

Should organize to innovate. Consumers have granted businesses the right to operate and to make a profit if they can. But they do not expect them simply to exploit the status quo. Businesses are supposed to be dynamic—agents of change, adjusting their offerings to customers' needs. Competition is supposed to encourage innovation and efficiency, which is why we have antitrust laws and other legislation. Our patent system plus the support of customers give rewards to innovators and to those who provide new and better services or perform old services more efficiently. Assuming that our society will continue this approach, a business firm should develop an organization that will insure that these consumer-assigned tasks are effectively carried out and that the firm itself continues.

Should achieve some profit. It is sometimes assumed that profit making is the only objective of business. The traditional economic model of a firm assumes that firms do attempt to maximize profits, and it is certainly true that in the long run a firm must make profits to survive.

Yet simply stating that profit making is a company objective does not constitute the whole of a modern business firm's objective-setting function. The time period involved in the profit making also should be specified because long-run profit maximization may require losing money during the first few years of the plan.

Further, setting an objective to maximize profit seems to imply that a firm will make good profits, but actually competition may be so fierce that poor results are almost inevitable. It might be more appropriate to set, as a target, some rate of profit return that would tend to guide the business into avenues having some possibility of such a return. Some firms probably should seek even higher rates of return than they are now achieving and more than is available by profit maximizing in their *present* activities.[28]

The objectives probably should specify the degree of risk that management is willing to assume for possible larger returns. Very large returns might be possible in the oil prospecting business, for example, but the probability of success in that field might be quite low. If the business is to take a long-run view and intends to survive and be a useful member of the business community, it probably should include

---

[26] "Fresher Fruits, Vegetables on Way," *Detroit Free Press,* April 24, 1966, p. 12B.

[27] This point of view is discussed at much greater length in: Theodore Levitt, "Marketing Myopia," *Harvard Business Review,* July–August, 1960, p. 45 ff; Theodore Levitt, *Innovation in Marketing* (New York: McGraw-Hill Book Co., 1962).

[28] Drucker, *op. cit.,* p. 87.

the costs of risk and potential losses in its calculations of long-run potential profit.

Whatever objectives are selected by top management, they should be compatible with each other, or frustrations and even failure may result. The three broad objectives suggested above would help a firm avoid the blunder of working at cross-purposes with its various programs. But as these three guidelines are made more specific, care must be exercised. For example, management might choose to specify a 10 percent return on investment each year as one objective, while at the same time specifying that the current plant and equipment be utilized as fully as possible. Competition might be such that it would be impossible to use the resources fully and achieve this return, but the company managers might try to follow the resource-use objective through the course of the year and discover the incompatibility only at the end of the year!

Both hands must work toward the same goal

We are assuming that it is the marketing manager's job to work within the framework—within objectives—provided by the top executives. But some of these objectives may restrict marketing strategies, perhaps to the detriment of the whole business. This is why it is desirable for the marketing manager to help shape the company's objectives.

Management myopia may straitjacket marketing

A few examples will be helpful to illustrate how the marketing manager might have to choose undesirable strategies.

A quick return on investment is sometimes sought by top management. This might lead the marketing manager to the selection of marketing strategies that would yield quick returns in the short run but kill the "customer franchise" in the long run.

Top management might decide on diversification. This might force the marketing manager to choose strategies that are poorly suited to the company's resources.

Perhaps for status or humanitarian reasons top management might decide to serve certain target markets, without regard to the company's resources or market profitability. Some companies in the "health foods" business seem to be following humanitarian objectives. In such situations, the marketing manager might still be expected to pursue profits, but less aggressively.

Some top managements want a large sales volume or larger market share for its own sake. This may lead to good profits—but this is not always the case, as we shall see later.

Another business objective is domination of a market for a particular commodity. Sometimes this objective is stated in terms of the rate of growth or share of a market; plans may call for doubling or tripling sales in five years, or increasing the share 10 percent each year. This course places a tremendous burden on the marketing manager and may require an extremely aggressive marketing strategy. It the objectives are stated even more specifically, such as the share of market within a particular geographical area or for particular products, the marketing manager's scope is even more limited. And the possibility of maximizing profits may be limited too.

The marketing manager may have no choice in determining the overall company objectives, but he may set subobjectives within the framework of these overall objectives. In subsequent chapters, we will discuss Product, Place, Promotion, and Pricing objectives that should be developed within the larger framework and the policies which, in turn, are developed to implement these narrower objectives.

Conclusion

This chapter has been concerned with the forces which, while beyond the marketing manager's control, profoundly affect the strategies he will develop.

As we have seen, he must develop marketing mixes appropriate to the customs of the people in his target markets. He must be aware, for example, that promotion which is appropriate in Gary, Indiana, may be offensive to citizens of New Orleans, Louisiana, or Yokohama, Japan.

The marketing manager also must be aware of the legal restrictions limiting his actions, and sensitive to changing political climates.

The economic environment—the chances of increased government spending, business cycle fluctuations, or spiraling inflation—also will affect his choice of strategies, and the marketing man must try to anticipate, understand, and deal with such changes.

Always mindful of these factors, he must also examine the market itself: How well entrenched are his competitors? What action may he expect them to take?

Finally, he must bear in mind the resources and objectives of his firm, for his strategies should be planned to gain those objectives within the constraints imposed by the firm's resources.

Developing good strategies is obviously a very complicated procedure. The marketing manager must be well informed. He may turn to the fields of sociology, anthropology, psychology, economics, political science, and history for additional information. Most important, he must know his own field thoroughly, for he will have to use the information he has drawn from all these sources in the formation of his strategies. Marketing management is clearly an integrating discipline. In the next chapter, on marketing research, we will begin to see how the marketing manager can find answers to the many problems facing him.

---

1 For a new design of hair comb, or one of the items mentioned in Question 7 of Chapter 2, discuss the uncontrollable factors that the marketing manager will have to consider.

2 Why is it necessary to have so many laws regulating business? Why has not Congress just passed one set of laws to take care of business problems?

3 If the Federal Trade Commission is an arm of the government, why has it had difficulty in obtaining compliance with many of its rulings?

58

4 Why is the Miller-Tydings Act called the Fair Trade Act—that is, what is fair about it and to whom is it fair?

5 What and whom is the government attempting to protect in its effort to preserve and regulate competition? Is there much possibility of the government succeeding in obtaining a purely competitive society?

6 For each of the laws discussed in the text, indicate whether in the long run this law will promote or restrict competition. As a consumer, without any financial interest in business, what is your reaction to each of the laws discussed in the text?

7 Specifically, how would various company objectives affect the development of a marketing mix for a new type of baby shoe? If this company were just being formed by a former shoemaker with limited financial resources, list the objectives he might have and then discuss how they will affect the development of his marketing strategy.

8 Discuss how a company's financial strength might have a bearing on the kinds of products it might produce. Will it have an impact on the other three P's as well? If so, how? Use an example in your answer.

Gathering marketing information

Planning marketing strategies obviously requires information—information about potential target markets and their possible reactions to various marketing mixes, about competition, and about the rest of the uncontrollable environment.

It is the job of marketing research to help the marketing manager gather the information he needs to make wise decisions. This is not an easy job, because people and competitors are so unpredictable. It must be done, nevertheless. Without sound marketing information, the manager would have to "fly by the seat of his pants," and in our dynamic and highly competitive economy, this almost insures failure. Competitors would probably know more about such a manager's market and how he was doing than he knew himself!

What is marketing research?

Marketing research is concerned with developing and analyzing the "facts" that will help marketing managers do a better job of planning, executing, and controlling. Marketing research is much more than a bundle of techniques or a group of specialists in survey design or statistical techniques. Good marketing researchers must be both marketing- *and* management-oriented to assure that their research focuses on real problems on which action can be taken.

Some of the techniques of marketing research are as old as human history. The Children of Israel sent interviewers to sample the market and produce of Canaan. In medieval Europe, merchant families sometimes prospered because their contacts throughout the world enabled them to get information before their competitors.

Marketing research as we know it today began around 1900 and grew as more companies became interested in regional and then national markets. The development of sampling techniques in the 1930's, the use of the psychological interview, and other accurate attitude and opinion measurement techniques have expanded the field markedly.[1]

Investing money and faith

These and other refinements have increased the dependability of the findings and prompted businessmen to put more money and faith in research. In some consumer goods companies, no major decisions are made without the support, and sometimes even the official approval, of the marketing research department. As a result, some marketing research directors rise to high levels in the organization. For example, at Pillsbury, this activity is headed by the Vice President of Growth and Technology.

Marketing research departments are often involved with long-range decisions that are the concern of top management. What products and services will the firm's target markets want 5 to 10 years from now? Are there other target markets developing? Should the company be in entirely different lines? How much will potential target markets be willing to spend for products in the company's area of operation? What kind of distribution facilities are developing or may develop? And so on.

Tool of top management

Some long-range research is concerned with forecasting the economic environment and is often handled by the marketing research department. But marketing research should be used for much more than merely projecting economic trends. Limiting research to such projections implies that the firm plans to do no more than react to change in the economic environment.

But progressive researchers should be helping top management look for new opportunities so that the firm can be on the offensive. When the marketing research department either gains or is given such a role, it—and its firm—can grow in importance.

The marketing manager, sales manager, brand manager, and others responsible for current promotion and sales have immediate problems. In a new-product introduction, they have to decide which geographical areas to serve first. Even before this, they may have to decide which of several new products to test-market or move into full-scale introduction. They may have to decide on a brand name or a price or choose any of various marketing mix ingredients. These more immediate and sometimes "crisis" decisions occupy a good deal of the time of most marketing research departments. Sometimes answers are needed so urgently that "quick and dirty" work must be done. A little informa-

Tool of operating management

---

[1] Lawrence C. Lockley, "Notes on the History of Marketing Research," *Journal of Marketing,* April, 1950, pp. 733–36.

tion may be better than none. Even though the most scientific approach is not feasible when time is short, the researchers attempt to follow the best procedures possible.

At the center of the business information system

Marketing research is sometimes seen only as an aid to planning, but it is much more than this. Marketing research is a vital part of management's control function as well. Recall that in Chapter 2 we viewed the management process as a circular procedure, going from planning to execution to control and back to planning with the aid of a "feedback" function. Marketing research helps provide this feedback function. Thus it is a continuing process. Some marketing researchers see themselves in the center of an information system which helps integrate all the activities of the business, that is, helps implement the "total system of action" we discussed earlier.

It is obvious that marketing research has wide application. Its scope is so wide, in fact, that it cannot be adequately covered in one chapter. We will therefore devote three chapters to this subject, this chapter serving as a basic introduction. Sales forecasting will be treated in Chapter 5. The more control-oriented aspects of sales and cost analysis will be examined in Chapter 30, when we will have gained a better appreciation of what we want to control.

The scientific method and marketing research

In seeking to relate the scientific method and marketing research, we are not trying to formulate absolute scientific laws about marketing. The businessman is simply trying to make the "best" decisions possible, and this cannot be done without a logical approach. The scientific method is such an approach. In marketing, this logical method forces the analyst to follow certain procedures that reduce the possibilities of slipshod work or reliance on intuition. This is especially important when the researchers have to work quickly to meet a crisis.

The scientific method consists, basically, of four stages:

1. Observation.
2. Formulation of hypotheses.
3. Prediction of the future.
4. Testing of the hypotheses.

In this approach, we seek to develop hypotheses (such as "There is no significant difference between Breads A and B"),[2] and then to test each hypothesis. The formulation of the hypothesis is extremely important. In fact, much exploratory research is aimed at getting information and suggesting testable hypotheses. But the research should always be decision-oriented, even if it is a question of whether to act or not.

The application of the scientific method helps the marketing manager develop and test the best hypotheses. It takes a commonsense but rigorous approach—formulation of hypotheses, testing, perhaps modifying and testing again. The feedback principle is applied throughout.

---

[2] To those familiar with statistics, null hypotheses are developed and tested whenever appropriate.

To illustrate these stages in a simple nonmarketing case, consider a college student who develops a painful swollen ankle after a skiing accident. The ankle could be bruised, sprained, or broken. What should he do? If he goes to a doctor, he will probably find the doctor following the scientific method:

1. Observation:	Pain seems to increase if foot is twisted, but pain is not unbearable.
2. Formulation of an hypothesis:	Since a sprain would be more painful than this, the ankle is broken.
3. Prediction of the future:	Pain and swelling will reduce, but bone may heal improperly if not set.
4. Testing the hypothesis:	X-ray the ankle; don't wait to see if hypothesis is correct in this case.

Let us now use the same framework to show how a businessman might use this method.

A man's shirt manufacturer had no major immediate problems, but he was alert to opportunities. The approach he took is shown below:

1. Observation:	Notices some competitors' sales increasing and many competitors shifting to a new plastic wrapping.
2. Formulation of hypotheses:	Assumes (*a*) that his products are similar and (*b*) that plastic wrapping is sole cause of competitors' sales increases.
3. Prediction of the future:	His sales ought to increase if he shifts to the new wrapping.
4. Testing the hypotheses:	Produce some shirts in new package and market-test them.

The market test showed that his prediction was correct—sales did increase. But what if they had not increased? In the answer to this lies one important merit of the scientific approach. Through careful control (making certain that the test was correctly designed and run) and evaluation of results, we should be able to isolate the reason why a given test failed and pinpoint where the hypotheses were in error.

In this case, either one of the hypotheses could have been wrong. Either increased sales by competitors were *not* caused by the new wrapping, or this manufacturer's products were *not* similar.

Assuming that the first hypothesis was wrong, further research might show that competitors' sales were rising simply because their promotion had been more successful. Or if the second hypothesis proved incorrect, it might be possible to identify ways the products differed and then to capitalize on these points.

Four-step approach to solving marketing problems

In marketing research, there is a four-step application of scientific method: (1) definition of problem, (2) situation analysis, (3) informal investigation, and (4) formal research project.

63

Observation, the first stage in the scientific method, is used during the first three marketing research steps. Once the problem is defined, *formulation of hypotheses* takes place, perhaps during the situation analysis or informal investigation. *Prediction of the future* takes place any time before a formal research project is planned. And *testing the hypotheses* is completed in the formal research project unless, as frequently happens, informal investigation solves the problem.

Actually, then, the scientific method is a vital part of marketing research. Table 4–1 may help us see the relationships. The precise meaning of these terms is explained in the following pages.

Table 4–1 *Relation of scientific method to marketing research*

Scientific Method Stages	Used during the Following Marketing Research Steps
Observation	Definition of problem
	Situation analysis
	Informal investigation
	Formal research
Formulation of hypotheses	Situation analysis
	Informal investigation
	Formal research (Planning)
Prediction of the future	Situation analysis
(Action implications)	Informal investigation
	Formal research (Planning)
Testing hypotheses	Formal research (Unless management is satisfied with an earlier but more intuitive solution.)

It should be emphasized again that this orderly procedure helps us keep clear what we are doing. Mastery of this approach will greatly improve your ability to plan and visualize the execution of marketing research projects.

Definition of the problem

Defining the problem is the most important and often the most difficult job of the marketing analyst. It is slow work, requiring careful observation and sometimes consuming well over half the time spent on a research project. But the time is well spent if the problem is precisely defined. The best research job on the wrong problem is wasted effort; it may even lead to more costly consequences, such as the introduction of a poor product or the use of an ineffective advertising approach.

Problem definition sounds simple, but unfortunately it is not. It is easy to mistake the isolation of symptoms for the definition of the problem. For example, say that the continuing sales analysis that is part of the control function (to be discussed more fully in Chapter 30) shows that the company's sales are decreasing significantly in certain territories while sales expenses are remaining constant, with a resulting decline in profits. Would it be helpful to try to define the problem by asking the simple question: How can we stop the sales decline? Probably not. This would be the equivalent of asking how to lower a patient's temperature instead of first trying to identify the cause of the fever.

We must discover *why* sales are declining—whether the cause is competitive activity, product deficiencies, inadequate support by company sales personnel, prices that are not competitive, inefficient advertising, or some other cause. If one or more of these factors can be isolated as the real problem, then the marketing executive is on the way to an effective solution.

The real problem may be very elusive. In the isolation of his own office, the marketing manager may conceive of several likely problems he can work on. But without further investigation and evidence, he should not assume too quickly that he has defined the actual problem. Instead, he should take his list of possible problems and then go on to the next step, trying to discover which of these is the fundamental cause of his trouble.

Situation analysis

When the marketing researcher feels that he has begun to focus on the problem, he can proceed to this next step. He need not (and probably should not) commit himself completely to any particular problem yet. Through this and the following steps, he should think of the problems he has isolated as subject to revision or restatement in the face of new facts. This rethinking is continuous. Even after he has developed and tested an hypothesis by formal research, it is possible that new factors will arise so that a new statement of the problem and a new hypothesis test may be necessary.

In the situation analysis, the analyst tries to "size up the situation"—but without talking to outsiders. He talks to informed executives within his own company, and studies and evaluates internal company records that are generated as part of the control function. He also searches libraries for all available published material. **No talks with outsiders**

This research is vital, since the analyst must be thoroughly familiar with the environment in which he must work. He analyzes information about his own company, its products, the industry, the specific markets in which they are operating, their dealers, their own promotion, and their competitors' activities. The libraries contain vast stories of information, but once the researcher has begun to narrow the scope of his problems, he can look for specific kinds of information.

Unless he knows what he is looking for, the researcher may be overwhelmed by the information available within his own company and in the libraries. Some of this is described below.

The data we are concerned with here is called *secondary data*. This is data which is already published by some government or private agency. **Data sources**

Primary data is gathered specifically to solve the current problem. Gathering primary data is discussed later, but it must be emphasized now that too often researchers rush out to gather primary data when there is already more secondary information than the researcher can use. And this data may be available immediately, at little or no cost!

One of the first places a researcher should look for secondary data is a good library. Familiarity with the references in the library's card catalog and bibliographies will enable the researcher to pursue other secondary sources more knowledgeably. Frequently, you need not go beyond your local library to find the answer to a question.

Government sources. The federal and state governments publish data on almost every conceivable subject. It is difficult for even large libraries to maintain a complete and readily accessible library of government documents. The federal government publishes a monthly guide to its current publications, but it is more practical to refer to federal government summary publications to obtain leads to more detailed documents.

Three useful summaries, available from the U.S. Department of Commerce for less than $5 a year and also found in most libraries, are the *Statistical Abstract of the United States,* the *County and City Data Book,* and the *Survey of Current Business.*

The most useful of these summaries, the *Statistical Abstract of the United States,* is similar to an almanac. It is issued each year and lists more than 1,000 summary tables from most of the work being published by the federal government as well as other groups. Included are detailed footnotes that a student can follow if he is interested in more specific detail on a topic. Each issue contains a "Bibliography of Sources and Statistics," about 40 pages in length, that lists all *Abstract* sources, classified by type of subject.

Every student should be familiar with the *Abstract* because it is probably the best starting point for locating statistical data. Marketing men must be experts on the sources of information, and the time to start developing this expertise is *now*.

The *County and City Data Book,* published about once every three years, gives more local, geographical detail than the *Abstract*. It presents a selection of statistics for all counties and for cities of more than 25,000.

For more current data on a wide variety of subjects, monthly and quarterly statistics are published, without geographical detail, in the *Survey of Current Business*. Each issue of this monthly periodical also features articles on economic trends and other business subjects.

The U.S. Department of Commerce serves as a distribution agency for statistics compiled by all other federal departments. Commerce Department branch and field offices, located in major cities throughout the United States, are fertile sources of data. Staff members can provide assistance and suggestions for locating specific data.

Some city and state governments have similar agencies that will provide leads to local data. University bureaus of business research may also prove helpful.

Private sources. Many private research organizations, advertising agencies, newspapers, and magazines regularly compile and publish data. Some of this data is available inexpensively as a customer service to clients of advertising agencies or buyers of advertising space or time. For example, J. Walter Thompson Co., an advertising agency, and the *Chicago Tribune* maintain continuing panels of housewives for consumer research purposes. These panels enable researchers to see trends, an extension of vision not easily obtained in one-time surveys.

Research by subscription. There are a number of research firms whose exclusive business is supplying, by subscription, research data that will aid the marketing manager in the situation analysis. Two of the better known organizations specializing in continuing research are the Market Research Corporation of America (MRCA) and A. C. Nielsen Co. MRCA makes available information on product movements through some grocery chains, using data from a consumer panel of about 5,000 families located throughout the United States. These families are expected to record, in diaries, all food and drug items, plus other selected items purchased each week. They list not only each item but its price and the store where it was purchased. This data is used by many large food and drug manufacturers to measure the rate of consumption of their products at the consumer level.

Similar reports are provided by A. C. Nielsen, which audits about 2,000 retail food stores and drugstores to measure movement at the retail level. These two services ought to provide roughly the same measure of movement of products at the consumer level. The Nielsen data, however, provides additional information about competitors' use of retail displays, 2 for 1 sales, and other activities. For this reason, some large companies subscribe to both services. They often find out more about the activity and sales of their smaller competitors than some of these competitors know about themselves.

Trade associations also may be a good source of information about a particular industry. They not only compile data from and for their members but also publish magazines that focus on the problems and important topics in the industry.

If the problem is clear-cut, it can sometimes be solved at this point without additional expense. Perhaps someone else already has conducted a study that answers almost exactly the same question. If not solved, the problem area may be drastically narrowed, making further research easier.[3]

Problem solving during the situation analysis

The fact that further research *may* be reduced or eliminated is important. Too often the procedure followed by researchers is to rush out a questionnaire to 100 or even several thousand persons or firms. This gives the impression that the analyst is "really doing something." An effective situation analysis, however, usually is much less impres-

---

[3] *Problem Definition* (Marketing Research Techniques Series No. 2 [Chicago: American Marketing Association, 1958]), pp. 9–10. Other examples of this approach can be found in "Finding Out What Consumers Will Buy," *Steel*, July 14, 1958, pp. 101–8; and "Consumer Questions Set the Key," *Business Week*, October 20, 1956, pp. 125–34.

sive. If a supervisor asks the analyst what he is doing, about all he can say is, "I'm sizing up the situation" or "I'm studying the problem."

What the situation analyst is doing is trying to determine the exact nature of the situation and the problem. Actually, the one who rushes out all the questionnaires may be doing this, too—although this may surprise him! The point is that when the results of his questionnaire come in, he may finally see the problem, but he still won't have the answer. He will still have to proceed to the next step in analysis, just the same as the more "scientific" researcher.[4]

Informal investigation

During the informal investigation, the analyst is still attempting to define his problem and formulate hypotheses. But he now gets outside the company and the library, and begins to talk to informed people, sometimes including customers. By informed people, we mean intelligent and efficient retailers, wholesalers, customers, and other knowledgeable people in the industry. No formal questionnaire is developed, as the analyst is not yet *testing* hypotheses, except intuitively.

When considering the development of machine tool products, for example, it might be desirable to talk to a few machine operators, plant superintendents in more efficient factories, design engineers at independent research organizations or universities, and perhaps a few good industrial distributors who have close contact with many potential customers.

Fast, informative, inexpensive

While these talks would be informal, they may help the analyst state his problem and hypotheses. By this time, he should have the problem area narrowed down. This is important, because asking informed people to discuss *general* problems will not be productive. Only specific questions will elicit specific answers.

The virtues of the informal investigation are that it takes little time and may be very informative. Moreover, it is inexpensive compared with a large-scale survey.

On the basis of the information gathered in a situation analysis and informal investigation, the analyst should now be formulating some specific hypotheses. Or he may be able to refine his hypotheses at this point, developing an answer to his problem without further research. This is especially likely in the industrial goods area, where the number of customers is limited and where they behave fairly rationally. Here the views of a few well-informed people may be representative of the industry.

If management must make a decision quickly—if it cannot wait for a formal test—then well-considered hypotheses may have to serve as the basis for an intuitive solution. Occasionally speed is more important than precision. In such cases, care in the preliminary steps is even more important.

---

[4] R. J. Holloway, "Marketing Research Is More Than Surveys," *Journal of Marketing,* January, 1953, pp. 297–300.

Planning the formal research project

If the analyst has failed to reach a solution to his problem by this time, then he may have to develop a formal research project to gather primary data. There are three basic methods that he can use: (1) the observation method, (2) the survey method, or (3) the experimental method.

Each method has its appropriate uses, and unless the problem is complex, only one would be used in a single project. It is the analyst's task to choose which method is best, according to problem characteristics as well as the time, funds, facilities, and personnel available to him.

The *observation method,* recognizing the possible pitfalls in direct questioning, avoids face-to-face interviews. Sometimes, however, asking questions cannot be sidestepped. Then a good *survey* can be very helpful. The *experimental method* may use either or both of the preceding methods. Its distinguishing characteristic is a more rigorous design, which usually includes establishing control groups and applying advanced statistical techniques.

Observation method: not asking but watching

In pinpointing the problem, we have been using observation—asking ourselves what is happening inside and outside the firm. It is logical to continue using observation in the research project. But this observation will be focused on a specific, well-defined problem.

Here, the researcher avoids talking to the subjects. If a retailer or a bread manufacturer were interested in bread-buying behavior in supermarkets, for example, he could station a man at the bread counter to observe what takes place. This person could, for example, note the length of deliberation in the choice of a brand, the amount of label reading that takes place, or the extent of multiple purchases.

In other situations, films are made of consumers under varying situations. Their behavior can then be analyzed carefully by running the films at very slow speeds or actually analyzing each frame. This might be useful, for example, in studying product selection in a supermarket or department store.

If a supermarket operator were interested in the distance customers traveled to his store, he could take down license numbers in the parking lot and trace addresses. Or, traffic flowing by a particular location can be counted to give some estimate of potential for a shopping center.

Information by instrument

The Audimeter permits adaptation of the observation method to radio and television audience research. This machine is attached to the radio or TV set in the homes of selected families. It records when the set is on and what station or channel is tuned in. This method is used by the A. C. Nielsen Co., and the results are widely used for popularity ratings. Nielsen claims that once families get used to the meter, their behavior is no longer influenced by its presence. This method, however, does not "observe" whether anyone is actually *listening* or *viewing,* and the sample sizes used may not be sufficient to yield the precise ratings

69

users would like. Yet this is basically a matter of economics. If users want more reliable ratings, a larger number of families will have to be audited, and this may make the information too costly.

Survey method: asking enough people the right questions

When researchers feel that to solve their problems they must talk directly to someone, they use the survey method. Sometimes surveys are conducted to test hypotheses, but they may merely be exploratory efforts to size up the situation before doing more research. Such an exploratory survey might provide the background data which, in another case, already would have been located during the situation analysis.

Usually some type of questionnaire is used in conducting a survey. In some unstructured surveys, however, the researchers may only provide the interviewer with a series of questions intended as a guide. Thereafter he "plays it by ear." The desirability of these various approaches will be discussed below.

By phone, mail or face-to-face. There are basically three types of surveys: telephone, mail, and personal interview. Each has its advantages and disadvantages.

Telephone Surveys. Telephone interviews are effective for obtaining quick answers to short, simple questions, especially when it is not important to identify the respondent or to know any of the characteristics of the person or family. Yet if consumer characteristics—such as age, income, condition of personal belongings, household furnishings or family composition—have a bearing on the analysis, then another survey method may be more appropriate.

Telephone interviewing is relatively low in cost and is satisfactory where the researcher is primarily interested in people who are likely to own telephones. In some areas, however, 10 to 20 percent of the families do not have telephones, and excluding them may bias the results.

Mail Surveys. The mail survey may be useful when the questionnaire is long. And it may be necessary economically if potential respondents are widely scattered. With the mail questionnaire, the person can take all the time he wishes to answer the questions and may be more willing to fill in personal or family characteristics. Unfortunately, the response rate on mail questionnaires is not very high unless there is extensive follow-up or unless the questionnaire is especially interesting. From 1 to 10 percent may be considered a "good" response, but the respondents may not be at all representative. Those who respond may be entirely different kinds of people from those who do not, and the results could be very misleading.

Mail surveys are inexpensive if a large number of persons respond. Conversely, they may be quite expensive if the response rate is poor, as it typically is, or if extensive follow-up is required. And with mail questionnaires, it is difficult to probe for additional answers to the questions or encourage respondents to elaborate on particular points.

Personal Interview Survey. The personal interview is used frequently because most people would rather talk than write. Each personal interview may be more expensive than each mail or telephone interview—but it offers the interviewer a chance to probe deeply on certain questions.

The personal interview also enables the interviewer to follow new lines of thought that might not have been anticipated earlier. New hypotheses or even new problems might be uncovered in the personal interview. Also, the interviewer has the opportunity to judge socioeconomic characteristics and to follow up on those people who are not at home the first time, perhaps reaching people who would not ordinarily answer mail questionnaires.

In this sense, the researcher using the personal interview has greater control over his sample, and the survey results may be better because they are more "representative" of the researcher's target population.

When considering whether to use a survey, and in particular, which type of survey, it is necessary to question critically both the validity and reliability of the proposed survey—the same critical approach that should apply when evaluating any kind of research. **Validity and reliability of surveys**

A survey is *valid* if it measures what it is supposed to measure. It is *reliable* if the results represent the whole population accurately.

Validity. The critical questions in testing for validity are, "What are we measuring? Does the research actually measure what we intend it to?" One sure way to get invalid findings is to ask consumers something they do not know. The main problem, however, is *not* that they don't know. Respondents usually want to help. They may not even know that they do not know, but they are obliging and will give answers.

Sometimes there is even the question of whether a survey measures anything at all. In one case, the researcher wanted to obtain some direction for his company's activities. After a great deal of effort, an 18-page questionnaire was constructed and sent to the company's *present list of customers*. They were, in effect, asked what other lines of business the company ought to go into. Many of them tried to answer, but the answers were not useful because the respondents were not familiar with the company's particular resources or alternate target markets.

In this case, the problem was poorly defined, and questions were aimed in every direction. The respondents to whom the questionnaire was sent were not even interested in the same problem or even informed about it, and could not give useful answers. If, by some chance, the answers had made any sense at all, it is frightening to think how the company might have used the answers. Finally, after several months of work, the research project was dropped.

In evaluating the validity of surveys—indeed, all research—the research user should continually question: (1) whether the data was obtained from an informed source, and (2) whether the problem has been answered with this data.

Reliability. The critical question in testing for reliability is, "Can we rely on these results as representative of the relevant population?"

For most commercial research, it is economically and physically impossible to include the total population in the research design. Even if you were interested in all retailers, only some of them could be interviewed. If the population were all college students, then only some of them would be chosen. These are *samples*. The representativeness of the sample has an important influence on the reliability of the research results.

If a sample is chosen in a random manner from a population, this sample will *tend to* have the same characteristics and be representative of the population. *Tend to* is important because it is only a tendency. The possible deviation of sample results can be predicted by sampling theory, *if* some random sampling technique has been used.

The simplest random sampling technique is called *simple random sampling*. Say, for example, that the total population to be sampled is all the students at a college. Using the *simple random sampling* technique, a list of all of the people in the college population is obtained; then the sample is drawn so that each of the members of the population has an equal chance of being included.

One of the many possible variations of simple random sampling is called *area sampling*. This approach may be used if it is not convenient or possible to develop a list of all the people in the population. Instead, the researchers might list all of the blocks in a city and then select at random some of the blocks to be sampled further. Within each of these selected blocks, every household or some smaller number selected at random could be interviewed.

Standing on the Corner Is Haphazard. In contrast, a *quota sample* or a more *haphazard sample* might be drawn. In such samples, not everyone has an equal chance of being selected. The researcher may specify that 10 percent of the survey population should consist of those with incomes over $10,000 a year, 20 percent in the next lower income bracket, and so on. Further, he may specify that a certain proportion of various age groups should be represented in each income bracket.

These specifications may insure that the sample is more or less representative of the population, *as far as those dimensions go*. But if some controls are not imposed so that everyone has a reasonable chance of entering the sample, the interviewers may further reduce the reliability by how they fill their quotas—for example, by talking to people who go through a railroad station or shop downtown on a particular day. The limitations of this approach are obvious, but the truth is that many samples are obtained in just this manner.

How To Decrease the Confidence Interval. If a random sampling technique has been used in designing the sample, then methods are available for measuring and stating the degree of reliability of the data obtained. These statements are in terms of "confidence intervals." For example, if a sample of 100 were taken (using a strictly random sample), and if it were found that 10 percent of the population preferred a new cake mix, the following statement could be made concerning your confidence in the 10 percent finding (with 95 percent certainty): The true percent preferring the new mix is between 4 and 16 percent of the population.

If this range of accuracy were not sufficient for management action, then a larger sample could be used to narrow the confidence interval. If a sample size of 1,000 were used and the same 10 percent preference were obtained, then the confidence interval would be approximately 8 to 12 percent instead of 4 to 16 percent.[5]

Statistical reliability and confidence intervals should be seriously considered when planning the formal research project. This is especially important if the final results are to be presented to managers who understand statistical theory! If they do, obviously the confidence they place in the results will be affected by the width of the confidence intervals.

Will management have confidence in research?

Further, it is important that both *validity* and *reliability* be considered in planning research. One study may be extremely valid but of questionable reliability, while another study, using precise statistical techniques, may have only pseudo accuracy because it lacks validity. Failure in either area may lead to incorrect decisions.

When a nonrandom sampling method is used, it is technically wrong to compute confidence intervals. Even so, some researchers who use such samples are inclined to imply a great deal. The majority of commercial research does use nonrandom sampling—because of the higher cost of selecting more reliable samples—and the results are somewhat suspect because of this.

Some researchers claim that with considerable judgment and caution in interpretation, such nonrandom samples may give good results at lower cost. This may be true in certain cases, especially in the industrial field where the total number of customers may be relatively small.

But the marketing researcher who relies heavily on nonrandom sampling should not be surprised if the marketing manager is reluctant to place much confidence in his results and relies on his own personal judgment instead.

Two extremes in approach can be used when developing a survey: the quantitative or the qualitative approach.

Selecting the general approach to a survey

Quantitative approach. Here the researcher asks, "How many persons do certain things, how many products are purchased in certain quantities," and so on. Straightforward yes or no or multiple-choice questions are often used. This approach is characterized by rather large and perhaps statistically reliable samples varying from several hundred

---

[5] Detailed treatment of confidence intervals is beyond the scope of this text and can be found in any introductory statistics book. Just to refresh memories for those who have had statistics, however, the formula used here for a 95 percent certainty confidence interval is:

$$p \pm \frac{2\sqrt{p \times q}}{n}.$$

In this formula p is the percent result; q is $100 - p$; and n is the sample size. For the 10 percent preference this yields:

$$10 \pm \frac{2\sqrt{10 \times 90}}{n}.$$

Obviously, increasing n will decrease the confidence interval, as stated.

to several thousand respondents. If the solution of a problem requires straightforward quantitative data, this approach can provide it. This kind of research sometimes helps management see what is happening in the market and, at the least, begin to understand why it is happening.

Qualitative approach. The strictly quantitative approach is more concerned with historical "facts"—with the *what, where,* and *when* rather than the *why*. But if a researcher is interested in what customers are going to do *in the future* or why they did something in the past, then some kind of qualitative *why* questions may be necessary.

Bible versus Burlesque Queen. Straightforward *why* questions, however, may be dangerous and reduce validity. Good judgment and careful design are vital in qualitative research, as the following case illustrates.

An analyst, attempting to predict newsstand sales of pocket-size books six months before they were marketed, asked a group of people what titles they preferred. He got the usual answers—the Bible, Shakespeare, and so on. Then, at the end of the interview, he handed respondents a list of book titles. He indicated that he would like to send them a free book for their cooperation in the survey. All they had to do was pick out the title they wished, by number. Included in the list were pocket-sized editions of the Bible, Shakespeare, and other classics as well as many of the titles that the company was considering. The favorite of the respondents was *Murder of a Burlesque Queen!*[6]

The research moral is that when you ask someone a question, he may react to you as a person or try to give you the answer he thinks you want. When given a choice of obtaining something free for himself, however, he acts in his own self-interest and shows his true preferences.

There has been enough evidence of this kind of consumer reaction in applied research to convince researchers that special techniques are necessary when trying to determine consumers' real opinions.

Motivation research—a qualitative tool. Motivation research applies the methods of the psychologist and sociologist, derived from clinical methods, to *why*-type problems. Rather than using large samples, the motivation researcher works with relatively small samples—perhaps only 25 to 50 persons. And instead of one-, two-, or five-minute interviews, he may use depth interviews taking one to two hours.

The interviewer using motivational techniques attempts to probe the respondent's subconscious thinking. The purpose is to determine the basic motives of the person and to see how these inner motives may be manifested in outward behavior when the person is faced with a specific choice.

Technically trained interviewers must conduct these interviews. It appears that the results obtained are, in part, a function of the experience, training, and judgment of the persons collecting and analyzing the data, as well as the attitudes and opinions of the individual respondents.

---

[6] "Don't Believe All You Hear," *Courier-Journal,* Louisville, Kentucky, May 26, 1957.

Explaining Prune Preferences. There is little or no possibility of quantifying the answers or developing an objective measure of the results of this approach. This is an important criticism, because the results seem to depend so heavily on the training of the research worker and his own point of view. This adds complications, since one study identified 39 different psychological schools of thought on human behavior.[7] *Yet only one group—Freudians—has* been prominent in the motivation research movement.

To illustrate these complications, two of the top motivation research agencies in the country were employed independently by two different groups interested in why consumers bought so few prunes.

One agency interviewed a sample cross section of Americans and presented a 62-page report explaining, with statements such as the following, why people disliked prunes: "They are dried-out, worn-out symbols of old age. . . . The prune fails to give security. . . . It is a plebeian food without prestige. . . . The prune is a witch."

Based on these findings, the agency conducting this survey suggested that the California Prune Advisory Board "rename them black diamonds; surround prunes with an aura of preciousness and desirability; and take prunes out of the fruit family and put them in the same context as nuts."

At the same time, the other research agency presented a 61-page report which concluded that Americans have no emotional block about the prune's "laxative connotation." On the basis of this finding, the researcher suggested that the prune promoters "exploit the core of the prune market by advertising the laxative features—and don't pussyfoot about this angle, either."

If only one of these studies had been made, then the prune producers would have had little difficulty in following the advice. But when two studies come up with such conflicting recommendations, there would seem to be reason to question the procedures.[8] Perhaps the results could be used in aiming at different target markets, but with the small samples used in this type of research it would be difficult to determine which specific markets had which views. It seems that the interest in motivation research is declining. As one researcher commented: "After all, Freud dealt with the abnormal personality, but the person we want to understand is the average consumer."[9]

Modified qualitative approach. Not all qualitative research is motivation research, although some motivation researchers have, in the

[7] Wroe Alderson, *Marketing Behavior and Executive Action* (Homewood, Ill.: Richard D. Irwin, Inc., 1957), p. 189.

[8] A good review of the arguments on both sides and the techniques involved can be found in Robert Ferber and Hugh G. Wales (eds.), *Motivation and Market Behavior* (Homewood, Ill.: Richard D. Irwin, Inc., 1958). Other sources are George H. Smith, *Motivation Research in Advertising and Marketing* (New York: McGraw-Hill Book Co., 1958); Robert J. Williams, "Is it True What They Say About Motivation Research?" *Journal of Marketing,* October, 1957, pp. 125–33; *Use of Motivation Research in Marketing* (Studies in Business Policy No. 97 [New York, National Industrial Conference Board, Inc.]); James U. McNeal, "The Disappearing Motivation," *Business Topics,* Autumn, 1964, pp. 30–36; and most basic marketing research texts.

[9] "New Way to Size Up How Consumers Behave," *Business Week,* July 22, 1961, p. 74.

interest of promoting their own techniques or agencies, tried to imply this. Any research that seeks subjective replies can be considered qualitative.

Some researchers have borrowed several of the more promising methods of the psychologist and sociologist, including some of the motivation research techniques, and remodeled them for use with traditional quantititiative questionnaires. In this modified approach, respondents are given a better chance to express their feelings and attitudes.

Instead of giving respondents the choice of yes or no on whether they plan to buy a product, for example, the analyst might list five alternatives: "Definitely yes"; "I am pretty sure"; "I think so"; "I do not think so," and "Definitely no." Or open-end questions seeking short, *free* answers may be used. Then the answers are categorized for quantitative tabulation.

To encourage responses to such questions, the interviewer may use cartoons with unfilled word balloons. The cartoon may depict a situation such as a woman buying coffee in a supermarket. The respondent is asked to fill in the balloon explaining what the woman is saying to her friend. Or the balloon may be removed and the respondent asked merely to comment on her feelings about a woman, say, buying instant coffee. Then these responses could be categorized and tabulated in a quantitative manner.

Surfacing approach. Some analysts make effective use of motivation research techniques as background or preparation for more extensive quantitative studies. Here, motivation research may provide hypotheses that can be tested and substantiated with quantitative research.

The name "surfacing approach" is given to this method of using several different techniques, each one in succession less and less subjective, until the final phase is a fairly objective test. As its name implies, it means beginning at the subconscious level (pure motivation research) and working closer and closer toward the surface of consciousness.[10]

Ideas plus "Harder" Measurements Lead to Action. Pure motivation research techniques, for example, might suggest that consumers would prefer real fruit flavor to artificial flavoring in a dessert being designed to compete with Jell-O gelatin dessert. Researchers using the surfacing approach might then put the identical product in each of two packages, indicating in some manner that one product was made with pure fruit flavor while the other was made with artificial flavoring. If consumers showed a strong preference for one or the other product after using it, there would be a quantitative measure of the importance of this claim—and the company and its advertising agency could act accordingly in the development of the product and its promotion.

The appeal of the surfacing approach is that the strictly qualitative techniques provide ideas, while the quantitative techniques produce "harder" measurements that afford a firmer base for action.

---

[10] C. Joseph Clawson, "The Coming Breakthroughs in Motivation Research," *Cost and Profit Outlook* (Philadelphia: Alderson Associates, Inc., May–June, 1958), p. 3.

Most marketing executives have now decided that both qualitative and quantitative research have their uses.

The observation method avoids approaching the customer, while the survey method relies upon direct interview. The experimental method utilizes either or both of these methods.

Experimental method: watching, asking, and trying

The major difference, as the name implies, is that experiments are set up. Statistical controls may be used in a market test so that random variations can be factored out by statistical analysis. Or mathematical models, perhaps utilizing computers, can be developed for simulating customer behavior or total marketing system behavior.

While detailed discussion of these techniques is beyond the scope of this book, experimental techniques are becoming increasingly important in applied research. Again, note the growing sophistication of marketing management and the challenge this field offers.[11]

The experimental method is often used in traditional sales and use tests. In a sales test, for example, a new product might be tried in one store, city, state, or region, while the marketing mix was held constant elsewhere. If a sales change takes place in all territories, only the net change in the trial territory will be attributed to the new factor. This method has been used by retailers to test packaging, displays, pricing, promotional plans, new products, and store equipment.[12]

It's what's up front that sells. By this method, a bread manufacturer or retailer could check the importance of display positions in different stores. Some bread deliverymen on commission have done this on their own initiative. They have found that a front position increases sales so much that they have been known to pay a store clerk—out of their own pockets—to walk over to the bread display occasionally and move their company's bread to the front.

In other situations, use tests may be developed. Potential customers are given the same or different products in different packages. Their response is analyzed, using various statistical techniques.[13]

A method that may hold promise is to have a representative group of consumers play experimental games in which various products, prices, or other alternatives are offered in turn. This is not fully realistic, but some interesting and encouraging results have been obtained.[14]

Little use now, but more later. There are four primary reasons why the experimental method is not used much at the present time:

[11] See Seymour Banks, *Experimentation in Marketing* (New York: McGraw-Hill Book Co., 1965); and Robert D. Buzzell, *A Basic Bibliography on Mathematical Methods in Marketing* (American Marketing Association Bibliography Series No. 7, 1962).

[12] William Applebaum and Richard F. Spears, "Controlled Experimentation in Marketing Research," *Journal of Marketing,* January, 1950, pp. 505–17; W. A. Lee, *Merchandising Potatoes in Retail Stores* (Pennsylvania State University, College of Agriculture, Agricultural Experiment Station Progress Report No. 142, February, 1957); Philip B. Dwoskin and Milton Jacobs, *Market Testing Potato Flakes—A New Form of Dehydrated Mashed Potatoes* (U.S. Department of Agriculture, Agricultural Marketing Service, 1956).

[13] Chi-square and analysis of variance tests, for example.

[14] Edgar A. Pessemier, *New-Product Decisions* (New York: McGraw-Hill Book Co., 1966); and L. K. Anderson, J. R. Taylor, and R. J. Holloway, "The Consumer and His Alternatives: An Experimental Approach," *Journal of Marketing Research,* February, 1966, pp. 62–67.

1. It is time-consuming, when most marketing decisions must be made quickly.
2. It is often more costly.
3. It may reveal plans prematurely to competitors.
4. Many market researchers do not have the statistical and mathematical training required to conduct such tests effectively.

This last factor is being overcome rapidly, and it is likely that this type of research will become more common as more trained researchers enter the field.

Execution and interpretation of the research project

How to organize and conduct research projects is beyond the scope of this text. These details include questionnaire and research design, training of field staff, tabulation, interpretation, and presentation of results, as well as the follow-through to be sure that these results are utilized effectively. Such matters provide the bulk of material in most *marketing research* texts and are specialized but highly important activities.[15] Without effective execution, presentation, and follow-up of results, careful planning of the preliminary steps may be of little value.

Marketing manager and researcher should work in concert

The interpretation step is especially important for marketing management. While managers may not be research specialists, they must evaluate the results of such research. The interpretation and presentation of the final results are a clue to the quality of the research and its planning.

If the report, for example, does not have action implications, it may have little value to management and may suggest—at least to management—poor planning by the researcher. If confidence intervals are not specified, then the manager has no basis for evaluating statistical reliability. The width of the confidence interval depends on the size of the sample, as we have seen already. If the research method and the reliability of the data are not presented, the marketing manager must use even greater judgment in evaluating the data. In fact, if the researcher does not explain his methods and then suggest action implications, he should not be surprised if the marketing manager chooses to ignore his work.

The desirability of close working relationships between the marketing manager and the marketing researcher should be obvious. Both of them should be focusing on making the best decisions.

Cost and organization of marketing research

Relatively little, perhaps too little, is spent on the typical marketing research department. Often the marketing research department's budget is about 0.2 percent of sales or $100,000 for a company with a $50 million sales volume.[16] This is in contrast to new-product research budgets that frequently run to 5 or 10 percent of sales. Unfortunately,

---

[15] H. W. Boyd and R. Westfall, *Marketing Research* (rev. ed.; Homewood, Ill.: Richard D. Irwin, Inc., 1964).

[16] "Scouting the Trail for Marketers," *Business Week,* April 18, 1964, pp. 90–116.

this situation sometimes leads to the development of products with little or no market potential.

Even on modest budgets, however, good work can be done.[17] When a problem is carefully defined, formal research projects may not be necessary. This is especially true in industrial marketing research because of the relatively small number of industrial customers. But taking shortcuts increases the risk.

More dependable research can become expensive. A large-scale survey could easily cost from $10,000 to $100,000, and the continuing research available from companies such as A. C. Nielsen or MRCA could cost the company from $25,000 to $100,000 or more a year. But as noted, companies who are willing or able to pay the cost of *marketing* research may learn so much that they know more about their competitors and their market than the competitors know themselves.

The potentially high cost of extremely valid and reliable research must be balanced against its probable value to management. You never have all the information you might like to have—it comes at a cost. Very sophisticated surveys or experiments may be "too good" and "too expensive" and "too late" if all that is needed is a rough sampling of dealer attitudes toward a new pricing plan by *tomorrow*.

Marketing managers must take risks because of lack of complete information. That is part of their job and it always will be. They might like more data, but they must weigh the cost of getting it against its likely value, in terms of validity, reliability, and timeliness. If the risk is not too great, then the cost of getting more or better information may be greater than the potential loss from a poor decision. Faced with a continuous flow of risky decisions, the marketing manager may seek help from research only on the problems where he feels the risk can be reduced substantially at reasonable cost.[18]

Most larger companies have a separate commercial or marketing research department to plan and conduct these projects. Even some of these larger departments, however, frequently use outside specialists, such as interviewing or tabulating concerns, to handle particular tasks that they face only occasionally. Few companies with sales of less than $2.5 million have separate market research departments, relying instead on sales personnel or top executives for what research they do conduct.

Some marketing research is done by most companies, even if it is not called by that name. The majority of marketing executives would agree with the manager of marketing research for Dow Chemical Co. who states:

I feel that it is impossible to run a company today without market research, whether it is done by the president, the sales manager, or a separate group set up specifically to perform the function. Few companies are small enough

Shortcuts and the value of information

Who does the work?

No firm can afford to do without marketing research

---

[17] Donald F. Mulvihill, "Marketing Research for the Small Company," *Journal of Marketing,* October, 1951, pp. 179–82.

[18] For more discussion, see P. E. Green and D. S. Tull, *Research for Marketing Decisions* (Englewood Cliffs, N.J.: Prentice-Hall, Inc., 1966), pp. 454–59.

to afford the luxury of having their market research done by the president. No company can afford not to do market research at all.[19]

Conclusion

In this chapter, we have shown that marketing research is not a mysterious cult practiced by statisticians. Rather, it is or should be a management tool. It should help the manager make better decisions. The manager should understand research procedures, and the researcher should understand management's problems of planning, executing, and controlling marketing strategies. Without such a close working relationship, the output of a marketing research department may be sterile, and the department may be relegated to a mere collector of data.

Marketing research tries to apply the scientific method to the solution of marketing problems. Some applications have been presented in this chapter, and many more will be presented in the later chapters on Product, Place, Promotion, and Price. Where such applications are presented, you should think through the process used by the researcher, to develop your own facility for stating problems and seeking their solution. You should concentrate on stating the problem—the real problem—since this is the most difficult aspect of any kind of research.

It should be stressed that there is more to marketing research than surveys. Surveys provide helpful information when they are needed, but there are many occasions when other methods would provide better information at the same or lower cost. While the survey method is certainly glamorous—with all its possibilities for applying Freudian psychology, mingling with consumers and delving into personal preferences—it should be remembered that whenever people must be interviewed, there are chances of error. These errors are caused by the respondent himself, by the interviewer's bias and by nonrepresentative sampling.

Other research techniques are the observation and experimental methods, as well as the less formal approaches used in the situation analysis and informal investigation. Search for (and study of) available literature, together with an analysis of company data, may provide interesting and unique ways to avoid the cost and pitfalls of a formal research project. Such a literature search and data analysis can help the marketing manager make better and faster decisions—always a prime goal of marketing managers.

Questions and problems

1 Marketing research entails expense, sometimes a considerable expense. Why does the text recommend the use of marketing research even though a highly experienced marketing executive is available?

[19] William A. Marsteller, "Can You Afford a Market Research Department?" *Industrial Marketing,* March, 1951, pp. 36–37 and 122–24; see also, *Marketing, Business and Commercial Research in Industry* (Studies in Business Policy No. 72 [New York: National Industrial Conference Board, 1964]).

2 Explain the steps in the general scientific method and then how the steps in marketing research are similar.

3 How is the situation analysis any different from the informal investigation? Could both these steps be done at the same time in order to obtain answers sooner? Is this wise?

4 Explain how you might use each of the research methods (observation, survey, and experimental) to forecast market reaction to a new kind of margarine which is to receive no promotion other than what the retailer will give it. Further, it should be assumed that the new margarine's name will not be associated with other known products. The product will be offered at competitive prices.

5 If a firm were interested in determining the distribution of income in the state of Ohio, how could it proceed? Be specific.

6 If a firm were interested in the sand and clay production in Georgia, how could it proceed? Be specific.

7 Explain the difference between validity and reliability of surveys. Would it be possible to have a survey with very high reliability and no validity? If not, why not? If so, suggest a situation.

8 Go to the library and find (in some government publication) three marketing-oriented "facts" which you did not know existed or were available. Record on one page and show sources.

Forecasting market
opportunities

Good sales forecasts are vital for effective marketing management. The marketing manager is badly handicapped in his planning without a realistic estimate of future sales. But he cannot develop a forecast until he has some tentative plans. In other words, forecasting and marketing strategy planning are interdependent. Sales are not just "out there for the taking." Market opportunities may be "out there," but they must be seen *and* taken.

Market opportunities—current and potential demands—may be available, but whether a particular firm converts these opportunities to sales depends upon the marketing plan developed. This plan, then, should be incorporated into the sales forecasting process.

Sales forecasts are needed by others besides the marketing manager. Accountants and financial officers base their planning and budgeting work on these forecasts. Production schedules, purchasing plans, and manpower forecasts hinge on sales forecasts. Good forecasts are needed for control, too, since it is practically impossible to evaluate performance without a measure of expected achievement. In fact, a business organization is a system, and actual and anticipated sales keep the system going.

The main job is turning opportunities into sales

The balance of this chapter is concerned with various techniques for forecasting market opportunities. The term "market opportunities" is used sometimes rather than "sales," to emphasize that sales come after opportunities. We must first estimate the opportunities before we can estimate what share of these opportunities the particular firm may be able to realize.

Our primary concern here will be with short-run forecasts—forecasts for a year or less. The same methods are useful for long-run forecasts, but since more things can change, more assumptions must be made about future conditions when forecasting for longer periods.[1] Further, long-run forecasting should become involved with shaping and interpreting the company's objectives, including what business fields the company should plan to enter or continue to serve in the future. These ideas were discussed briefly in Chapters 2 and 3, and we cannot go further here. By the end of the text you should have a better appreciation of the short-run problems of the marketing manager and why he should be deeply involved in his company's long-range planning *and* forecasting.

Various approaches may be used at the same time for forecasting market opportunities. Although this multiplicity may at first seem confusing, in practice the variety proves to be an advantage. Forecasts are so important that management often prefers to develop forecasts in two or three different ways and then reconcile the differences before preparing a final forecast.

Extending past behavior

The first step in extending past sales behavior is to determine *why* sales fluctuate. This is the most difficult and time-consuming aspect of sales forecasting. Usually we can gather considerable data about the product or market and about the economic environment. But unless the *why* of past sales fluctuations is known, it is difficult to predict in what direction and to what degree sales will move. Once we know why sales fluctuate, it usually is quite easy to develop a specific forecast—just as the execution function follows naturally from planning.

We assume here that we are forecasting sales for existing products or product lines, not wholly new products. Our basic approach is to try to project past behavior into the future while making, we hope, suitable adjustments for some or all of the many factors that have caused sales fluctuations in the past.

There is often considerable fluctuation not only in sales of individual product and product lines but in the company's sales as a whole. Ours is a dynamic economy, and future sales are affected by many factors, including fluctuations in the level of the whole economy, business investments, government expenditures, birth rates, housing starts, and competitive activity.

The basic factors affecting sales of a particular product are not all equally significant. Some affect the whole economy, some affect only the industry, and some, the specific company or product's sales. For this

---

[1] *Forecasting Sales* (Studies in Business Policy No. 106 [New York: National Industrial Conference Board, 1964]); Elmer C. Bratt, *Business Forecasting* (New York: McGraw-Hill Book Co., 1958); *Sales Forecasting, Uses, Techniques, and Trends* (New York: American Management Association, Inc., 1956); Delbert C. Hastings, *The Place of Forecasting in Basic Planning for Small Business* (Small Business Management Research Reports [Minneapolis: University of Minnesota, 1961]); and marketing research texts.

reason, a common approach to sales forecasting—and the approach we will follow—is to:

1. Develop an *economic forecast* for the whole economy and use this to . . .
2. Develop an *industry sales forecast,* which in turn is used to . . .
3. Develop a *specific company or product forecast.*

Developing national economy forecasts

Gross national product (GNP) is widely used as a measure of the economic health of an economy. GNP is an estimate of the market value of goods and services produced in a year and is roughly equal to the national income.[2] Sources for this and many other economic measures are discussed later in the chapter.

An estimate for GNP is a good starting point for developing industry and company sales forecasts, since sales curves usually rise when GNP goes up, and vice versa. In special situations—perhaps a firm has developed an especially attractive marketing strategy—sales by one firm may run counter to national trends. But in such cases, the firm is usually well aware of the situation and can make appropriate adjustments in the general forecasting procedures discussed below.

The naïve approach— oversimplified analysis

The simplest approach to estimating GNP is to assume that next year's level will be the same as this year's. Or a slight refinement might adjust for the general upward trend in the economy—approximately 3 percent a year in the United States. This oversimple approach is widely used because it is easy and works reasonably well when the economy is stable or growing slowly. But it may be unreliable when the economy has been changing rapidly.

Trend extension —several years are better than one

The trend-extension approach seeks to project GNP into the future on the basis of several years rather than on just one year's experience. Here, historical data—say data on GNP for the last 10 or 20 years—is plotted on a graph. What is obtained is called a scatter diagram. (See Figure 5–1.) By drawing a trend line through the scattered points on this diagram, the forecaster attempts to judge where the next point will fall.

Depending on the location of the many points, either a curved or a straight line may seem more appropriate for summarizing past experience. A freehand line may be drawn, as is done in Figure 5–2, with a dotted line projecting into the future to show, hopefully, future values of the variable. Or the "least squares" statistical technique can be used to draw a straight line.[3]

---

[2] Actually, national income is slightly less than GNP, but both are sometimes used as a measure of the aggregate activity of the economy. For a detailed discussion of these measures, see any beginning economics text.

[3] The goal here is to find a straight line such that the sum of the squared distances from each of the points to the straight line is a minimum. Readers unfamiliar with the least squares technique are referred to standard statistics texts. See, for example, Samuel B. Richmond, *Principles of Statistical Analysis* (New York: Ronald Press Co., 1957), chap. xviii; John Neter and William Wasserman, *Fundamental Statistics for Business and Economics* (2d ed.; Boston: Allyn & Bacon, Inc., 1961), chaps. xiii and xv.

84

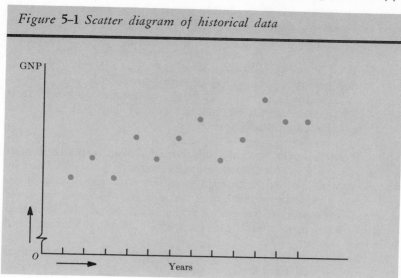

Figure **5–1** *Scatter diagram of historical data*

A major limitation of the trend-extension method is that it assumes that conditions in the past will continue unchanged into the future, with the extension of the line (or curve) indicating future values. To be sure, trend extension often *is* accurate, since aggregates such as GNP and industry sales often change slowly. Most businesses, in fact, have little difficulty making forecasts when the economy is rising or declining at a steady rate.

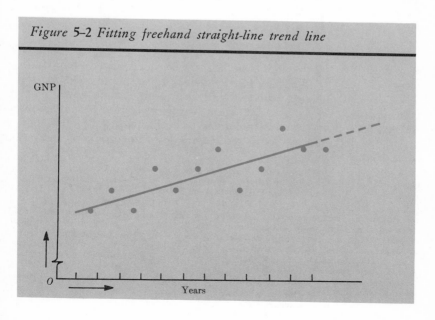

Figure **5–2** *Fitting freehand straight-line trend line*

But keep in mind that the future is not always like the past. The trend-extension approach usually will be wrong whenever there are important fluctuations.

Major business problems arise when economic conditions change quickly. If GNP rises rapidly, businesses may miss sales opportunities; but if it declines rapidly, they may be embarrassed with large inventories. For this reason, although they may use trend extension for one estimate, most forecasters seek another method that will help them anticipate sharp economic changes.

Time series and leading series: the ups, the downs, and staying ahead

Not all past behavior can be neatly extended with a straight line or even a simple curved line. Much economic activity is characterized by ups and downs. To cope with such variation, statisticians have developed time-series analysis techniques. A detailed discussion of these techniques is beyond the scope of this book, but it should be noted that there are techniques to handle daily, weekly, monthly, seasonal, and annual variations.[4]

The dream of all forecasters is to find accurate leading series. This is a time series which, for a logical reason or reasons, changes in the same direction *but ahead of* the magnitude to be forecast. Although we are interested here in forecasting national aggregates, leading series are sought also for industry sales and company sales.

No single series has yet been found that leads GNP, but the search continues. Lacking such a series, most forecasters watch indices—statistical compilations of several series—in an effort to find some index that will lead the magnitude they are attempting to forecast. Some indices of this type are published monthly by the Census Bureau of the U.S. Department of Commerce in a booklet, *Business Cycle Developments*.[5] And business magazines, such as *Business Week,* publish their own series.

Macroeconomic models— seeing the whole as a whole

Another method being used by many industry and government economists as a check on other approaches considers the economy as an integrated whole and develops a model to describe this whole economy. These models include factors for consumer, business, and government expenditures.[6] They utilize data from surveys of consumers' intentions to buy, surveys of business intentions to build plant and equipment, and the budgets of state, local, and federal governments. Some analysts

---

[4] See most basic statistics textbooks under time-series analysis; and U.S. Bureau of the Census, *Estimating Trading Day Variation in Monthly Economic Time Series* (Technical Paper No. 12 [Washington, D.C.: U.S. Government Printing Office, 1965]).

[5] *Business Cycle Developments* also includes about 70 other indicators and about 350 series of various economic magnitudes. One or a combination of several of these might be more useful in a particular case than the aggregate measures, such as GNP, that are being discussed. This may require considerable analysis, but the general approach discussed above would be used. Some forecasters are also experimenting with combinations of series, called diffusion indices, which they hope will better describe the fluctuations in the economy. See *Diffusion Indices* (Technical Paper No. 13 [New York: National Industrial Conference Board, Inc., 1963]). NICB's diffusion indices are published weekly and monthly in its own publications.

[6] Students who have had economics may recognize a familiar equation which is used in such models: National income $= C + I + G$.

merely add together the forecasts gathered from various sources. Others use these data in mathematical equations.

The mathematical model builders try to consider the interaction of the various sectors which make up the whole economy. In estimating GNP, for example, the intentions of business to expand plant and equipment might be discovered by a survey. But when companies find that consumers are reducing their purchases, they may decide there is less need for expansion. They may then cancel their plans, thus laying off workers whose reduced buying will further curtail consumer expenditures. The mathematical model builders attempt to include all these interactions in their models.

In the last few years, more sophisticated analysis, such as input-output models analysis have come into wider use. Input-output analysis uses tables which look like market grids filled with data and show the interaction of various segments of the economy. The data is manipulated to determine how various parts of the economy will affect other parts and to indicate the result on the economy as a whole. Such a model has been used to estimate the activity of the U.S. economy and its parts up through 1975.[7]

Developing industry sales forecasts

Once an aggregate forecast for the whole economy has been made, the next step is to make a forecast for industry sales. The two are often closely related. Automobile sales, for example, are related to the level of national income, since automobile sales normally rise as national income rises. But it would be most unusual for such relationships to be direct, i.e., a 1 percent increase in some national aggregate seldom leads to a 1 percent increase in industry sales. Instead, it is necessary to determine the relationship between the two (or more) variables.

Filling in a scatter diagram is a simple approach, but usually more advanced time-series analysis techniques are used, including multiple regression.[8] Then, once the relationship is determined, the forecast for the larger aggregate is used to determine the industry forecast.

Input-output analysis has shown that simple trend projection may be dangerous. A seemingly remote development in another part of the economy may have a direct impact on a particular industry. For example, a manufacturer of sulfuric acid, which is used in manufacturing paper pulp, might more accurately predict his future sales with the input-output approach which could consider the following interactions.

An additional $1 billion in federal aid to education would lead to a

More money, more books, more acid— with input -output analysis

[7] Clopper Almon, Jr., *The American Economy to 1975* (New York: Harper & Row, Publishers, 1966); for more details, see any elementary economics textbook, or E. F Beach, *Economic Models* (New York: John Wiley & Sons, Inc., 1957); J. Tinbergen, *Econometrics* (Philadelphia: Blakiston Co., 1951); "Computers Take to Prophecy," *Business Week,* June 1, 1963, pp. 47–48; and "Planners Put Big Picture on a Grid," *Business Week,* September 23, 1967, pp. 63–65.

[8] Although space does not permit a detailed explanation of this approach, generally the least squares approach is extended. These topics are discussed in most statistics texts, and when mastered, become a highly useful tool of the marketing analyst.

predictable increase in the number of textbooks used, which in turn would increase paper consumption and therefore paper pulp manufacturing, which uses his firm's sulfuric acid. But if this manufacturer, in developing his forecast for the product in question, focused only on past sales in the paper pulp business, his forecast might be seriously in error.

Input-output analysis is now more readily available for industry forecasting because companies such as IBM–Dun & Bradstreet and Fortune–CEIR have begun offering custom-tailored services at prices that even smaller companies can afford (often under $10,000).[9] These special services analyze data from the U.S. Bureau of the Census, current reports from credit reporters, and actual company sales.[10]

Someone else may forecast

Any company should consider the probable economic activity of the national economy and the industry when forecasting its own future; but it need not do all this aggregate forecasting itself. Some aggregate estimates are published regularly by government agencies, banks, trade associations, and business publications. And some private firms do forecasting for others at reasonable prices.

While a marketing manager need not do all this work himself, he should know what is being done. Then he will be able to use the forecasts properly at the next stop—forecasting his own company and product sales—where less outside help is available and his own and competitors' actions make forecasting more difficult.

What is your industry?

An industry forecast makes considerable sense in industries such as steel, cement, plywood, and housing. It suggests the opportunities available to members of the industry. But considering that our emphasis in this text is on developing unique marketing strategies, we will play down emphasis on the size of the industry's opportunities.

The more a firm tries to narrow its sights on some particular target market, the less attention it should pay to the aggregate opportunities of the industry. In the extreme, a firm might attempt to develop such a unique marketing strategy that it would, in effect, be creating its one-firm "industry." Then the firm would be more concerned with developing a forecast for the company and its specific products.

Company and product forecasts

Trend-extension and time-series analysis, including the search for leading series, may be useful in forecasting both company sales and specific product sales, especially if conditions are not changing too rapidly.

---

[9] "Input-Output Analysis: Its Use in Marketing," *Printers' Ink*, June 24, 1966, pp. 15–16.
[10] H. Russell Henderson, "Relating Company Markets to S.I.C.," *Journal of Marketing*, April, 1963, pp. 42–45; "Lifting the Haze from the Future," *Business Week*, December 17, 1966, pp. 100–102; "Industry's Slide Rule Is Updated by Eleven Years," *Business Week*, November 21, 1964, pp. 166–68; Celanese Puts Marketing Planning on the Grid," *Sales Management*, November 1, 1967, pp. 35–38; and "Planners Put Big Picture on a Grid," *Business Week*, September 23, 1967, pp. 63 f.

Analysis of past sales relationships may have shown, for example, that a particular bread manufacturer regularly achieved one half of 1 percent of the total retail food sales in his target markets. Estimates of retail sales for the coming period in these areas, then, could be used by this firm to forecast its bread sales (by multiplying 0.005 times the expected retail food sales in each market). **To estimate sales, calculate buying power**

The retail sales estimates might be based on past sales figures in sources such as *Sales Management* magazine. Figure 5–3 shows the kind of geographically detailed data available each year in one of the May or June issues of *Sales Management*.[11]

This data is carefully updated year after year and has correlated with surprising accuracy with the U.S. censuses upon which it is based. Evanston, Illinois, for example, accounts for 0.0432 of the U.S. population, but a much larger share, 0.0933, of effective buying income. The food sales dollar figure—$38,580,000—is an estimate of last year's food sales in this city. By extending any past trends, an estimate of future food sales could be obtained. Then by finding his firm's usual share—0.5 percent—he would have his estimate. Or if he planned an especially aggressive promotion campaign, he might up his estimates by multiplying forecasted food sales by 0.0055 rather than 0.005, to include an expected increase of 10 percent in his geographical sales estimate.

It is important to see that extending past and current data also could be used for estimating the potential of a new product if the new product is rather similar to the old or is going to substitute for it. *Sales Management* data, for example, could be used to establish the upper bounds of the potential for new entries into the market. For example, a new furniture manufacturer entering a market should not expect to sell more than the current total sales of his type of furniture in the market. When phrased this way this fact is obvious—but some firms have entered markets with high hopes for big sales unaware that the markets were not as large as they imagined. **Unbelievable but true**

All this may seem unbelievable to you, but production-oriented executives and firms have blundered badly for this reason. Clearly, one important tool the student can bring to the business world is a good knowledge of source materials and what can be done with them. More will be said about this in Chapters 6–9 on customer behavior.

Estimating future market sizes

When we are trying to estimate the future rather than just extending the past, we have to go beyond the trend-projection methods discussed in the preceding section. We must add a bit of judgment, perhaps some marketing research, and some of the techniques discussed below.

Judgment is increasingly important in our dynamic markets be-

---

[11] Look for the "Survey of Buying Power" issue. Similar current data are published by others. Standard Rate and Data Service, for example, provides less detailed monthly data of this type. *The Editor and Publisher Market Guide,* published annually by the Editor and Publisher Co., is another source. *Printers' Ink* and *Industrial Marketing* magazines also publish annual data supplements.

Figure 5-3 Sample page from Sales Management, "Annual Survey of Buying Power," Retail Sales Estimates

Illinois COUNTIES CITIES (continued)	Met. Area Code	POPULATION ESTIMATES SM 12/31/62			EFFECTIVE BUYING INCOME Estimates SM 1962		RETAIL SALES—SM ESTIMATES, 1962										SALES—ADVG. CONTROLS*		
		Total (thousands)	% of U.S.A.	Households (thousands)	Net Dollars (000)	% of U.S.A.	Total Retail Sales ($000)	% of U.S.A.	Food ($000)	General Mdse. ($000)	Apparel ($000)	Furn.-House-Appl. ($000)	Auto-motive ($000)	Gas Stations ($000)	Lumb. Bldg. Hdwre. ($000)	Drugs ($000)	Sales Activity Index	Buying Power Index	Quality Index
Evanston		81.0	.0432	26.4	354,408	.0933	167,623	.0712	38,580	40,406	17,590	9,588	27,887	7,762	5,021	4,949	165	.0767	178
Evergreen Park		27.8	.0148	7.2	76,082	.0200	53,495	.0228	10,125	22,719	7,727	875	3,897	1,652	834	184	154	.0198	134
Forest Park		14.3	.0076	4.9	38,558	.0101	26,688	.0113	4,515	257	109	1,278	3,234	2,538	1,724	642	149	.0100	132
Harvey		31.7	.0169	9.6	73,597	.0194	53,133	.0226	17,514	3,849	3,157	1,256	14,552	3,537	1,087	2,342	134	.0199	118
La Grange		16.3	.0087	4.7	68,813	.0181	55,347	.0235	12,011	8,926	3,989	2,143	12,148	4,122	5,270	1,231	270	.0178	205
Maywood		27.2	.0145	8.1	69,995	.0184	33,711	.0144	6,840	3,404	862	969	12,114	4,525	1,112	1,214	99	.0164	113
Melrose Park		25.0	.0133	7.2	61,801	.0163	50,599	.0215	13,360	8,165	2,666	1,485	1,219	2,940	9,288	3,056	162	.0173	130
Morton Grove		23.8	.0127	6.1	65,720	.0173	32,965	.0140	11,127	4,420	1,776	1,107	2,525	2,053	644	1,468	110	.0154	121
Niles		25.6	.0137	6.9	68,776	.0181	17,990	.0077	7,743	588	148	222	637	2,140	214	812	56	.0141	103
Oak Lawn		32.4	.0173	8.3	79,421	.0209	59,798	.0254	17,951	2,157	1,671	1,447	17,068	4,348	5,058	1,280	147	.0215	124
Oak Park		60.4	.0322	20.7	254,739	.0670	150,379	.0640	23,535	22,320	21,723	5,024	54,977	6,456	2,481	4,635	199	.0591	184
Park Forest		35.6	.0190	9.0	90,175	.0237	28,411	.0120	11,973	8,037	1,788	2,049	663	439	371	1,288	63	.0193	102
Park Ridge		36.4	.0194	10.3	152,197	.0401	62,301	.0265	13,882	10,959	3,233	1,784	20,940	3,213	2,587	3,040	137	.0319	164
River Forest		13.2	.0070	3.7	82,870	.0218	51,730	.0220	5,755	26,971	568	3,147	4,463	2,030	6,700	466	314	.0189	270
Skokie		66.0	.0352	18.4	228,412	.0601	180,617	.0767	26,383	54,599	11,014	6,153	30,823	7,471	6,913	6,272	218	.0601	171
Wilmette		31.4	.0168	8.6	169,782	.0447	51,375	.0218	14,941	11,268	1,876	1,647	10,407	3,117	1,691	1,967	130	.0323	192
Winnetka		13.7	.0073	3.9	114,231	.0301	30,838	.0131	6,711	1,219	6,476	1,979	4,960	2,029	1,527	1,247	179	.0204	279
Crawford		20.6	.0110	7.0	38,030	.0100	23,745	.0101	5,953	1,895	1,012	740	4,228	2,009	3,703	811	92	.0103	94
Cumberland		9.8	.0053	3.2	14,096	.0038	7,799	.0033	1,546	1,229	201	489	625	857	1,626	89	62	.0039	74
De Kalb		54.6	.0291	15.6	112,613	.0296	76,274	.0324	16,123	5,857	3,948	3,172	15,215	5,394	8,342	2,393	111	.0304	104
De Kalb		18.7	.0100	5.0	44,274	.0117	33,641	.0143	6,767	4,444	2,499	1,554	7,515	2,124	2,907	1,235	143	.0121	121
De Witt		17.4	.0093	5.7	30,346	.0080	23,382	.0099	5,243	1,631	899	747	6,074	2,048	3,256	410	106	.0088	95
Douglas		19.9	.0106	6.3	36,342	.0095	25,523	.0109	5,635	962	626	506	4,642	1,868	6,709	656	103	.0101	95
Du Page		357.3	.1908	95.9	1,012,922	.2666	406,126	.1726	123,475	26,776	18,360	10,229	66,273	39,016	37,748	17,560	90	.2233	117
Downers Grove		24.1	.0129	6.8	69,553	.0183	38,282	.0163	12,578	3,445	1,859	976	7,127	2,885	3,522	1,727	126	.0166	129

SOURCE: *Sales Management*, June 10, 1963, p. 246.

* Buying Power Index (BPI) is a weighted average of each market's strength. Each market's share of U.S. population is multiplied (weighted) by 2, its income by 5, and its retail sales share by 3. The resulting sum is divided by 10 (the total weighting) to give the BPI.

Quality Index shows whether a market's BPI is above or below average. The BPI is divided by the market's share of U.S. population to get the Quality Index. It is similar to the Quality Index except that the population share is divided into the retail sales share.

Sales Activity Index provides a measure of each market's sales traffic.

It is usually advisable to consider all three indices along with the household income breakdowns when evaluating an area's potential.

cause competitors' and the firm's own marketing mixes affect both potential and actual sales. There may be some potential "out there" in the various market grid boxes, but it becomes a part of forecasted sales only when management decides to try to reach those market grid boxes. What proportion of the potential in each of the grid boxes will be achieved depends on competitors' marketing strategies and the reactions of the target customers to the various strategies. This kind of forecasting requires much more than just extending past behavior.

Some of the methods discussed below are suitable for developing company or product-line estimates, but basically, from this point on, we will be interested in estimating sales potential for specific markets or products. Marketing strategies must focus on customers, and customers buy specific products.

Jury of executive opinion

One of the oldest and simplest methods of forecasting, the jury approach, is an attempt to combine the opinions of several executives, perhaps from marketing, production, finance, purchasing, and top management. The idea here is to utilize as much of the seasoned management judgment as possible, while at the same time relying on all the past data analysis that has been done.

The main advantage of the jury approach is that it can be done quickly and easily. On the other hand, the results may not be spectacular because they consist of the average of a number of views. Further, the jury method is most suitable for aggregate estimates, but ultimately what operating managers need is a more precise breakdown by products, time intervals, and specific geographic markets.[12]

Salesmen's estimates

This approach is similar to the jury approach, except that the opinions sought are those of sales personnel. This approach may be much more reliable where competition is dynamic.

The sales force is more likely than home office analysts to be familiar with customer reactions and to hear about what competitors are doing and is, therefore, more able to anticipate changes. Salesmen's estimates are especially useful in industrial goods markets which are composed of a limited number of customers who are well known to the salesmen. But this approach is useful in any type of market. A good retail clerk has a "feel" for his market, and his observations should not be ignored.

Two qualifications concerning the use of salesmen's estimates, however, should be kept in mind.

First, salesmen normally are not familiar with expected changes in the national economic climate, nor even with proposed changes in the company's marketing mix. As a result, their estimates must often be adjusted by the home office in light of national and industry forecasts and other factors.

[12] For more discussion on this and other approaches and examples of their application, see *Forecasting Sales* (Studies in Business Policy No. 106 [New York: National Industrial Conference Board, 1964]).

Second, sales force estimates must be used with care because of changes in sales personnel and because of the methods used in determining salesmen performance. If the turnover of salesmen is high, not much reliance can be placed on sales estimates. Some salesmen's forecasts, moreover, are related to a subsequent measure of their performance, to the firm's compensation system, or to the promotion budgeted to each territory. In these cases, it is only human for salesmen to tailor their forecasts to their own advantage.

Keeping these qualifications in mind, sales force estimates can provide another basis for comparison before final forecasts are developed.

Surveys, panels, and market tests

Instead of relying heavily upon salesmen to estimate customers' intentions, it may be desirable to use the marketing research techniques discussed in the last chapter. Special surveys of final buyers, retailers, and wholesalers may be illuminating. Some firms use panels of stores or final consumers to keep track of buying behavior and to determine when the use of simple trend extension has become inadequate.

Survey techniques are sometimes combined with market tests when the company wants to estimate the reaction of customers to possible changes in the marketing mix. In one such market test, a product gained 10 percent in its share of the market when its price was dropped 1 cent below competition. Yet this extra business was quickly lost when the price increased 1 cent above competition.

Such market experiments may enable the marketing manager to make realistic estimates of future sales when one or more of the four P's are changed.[13]

Fast sales analysis by computer

The availability of electronic data processing equipment is enabling more and more firms to analyze its own internal sales data for individual items or product categories very quickly, and use this data for current operating decisions. Food chains, discount houses, department stores, mail-order houses, and manufacturers are finding it both feasible and profitable to use computers to pick up and project sales trends.[14]

Fast analysis of sales data beyond a firm's boundaries may be helpful, too. Where there is a lag between the purchases of final consumers and the receipt of orders by manufacturers (because consumer purchases are reflected through retailers' and wholesalers' inventories), rapid

---

[13] R. J. Weber, "The Relationship of Advertising to Pricing Policy," *Pricing and Prosperity* (Marketing for Executives Series No. 1 [Chicago: American Marketing Association, 1956]), pp. 16–17.

[14] "Where the Computers Care Too," *Business Week*, March 12, 1966, pp. 140–146; "Now Retailers Put It All on Tape," *Business Week*, January 16, 1965, pp. 30–31: "EDP Tells Main Street," *Business Week*, August 8, 1964, p. 66; Irvin R. Whiteman, "Improved Forecasting Through Feedback," *Journal of Marketing*, April, 1966, pp. 45–61; *Time*, January 26, 1959, p. 84; Carl Vreeland, "The Jantzen Method of Short-Range Forecasting," *Journal of Marketing*, April, 1963, pp. 66–70 (which uses samples); and Robert L. McLaughlin, "The Breakthrough in Sales Forecasting," *Journal of Marketing*, April, 1963, pp. 46–54.

analysis of retail sales is an aid in forecasting sales at the wholesaler and manufacturer levels.

Some wholesalers handling major appliances, for example, send in weekly reports of sales, by model, to guide the manufacturer and enable him to forecast sales trends. Here, the wholesalers have agreed to accept shipments to replace units they have sold. This is an example of a "total system of action" which extends beyond a particular firm's boundaries. Rapid sales analysis is the feedback through the bigger "total" system. It seems likely that more such total systems will develop in the future.[15]

Forecasting for new products

Forecasting sales for new products is the most difficult task of all—and the most risky. If the product is really new, there is no relevant historical data that can be extended and no experience to indicate which leading series might be relevant. It is also unrealistic, as noted in Chapter 4, to expect potential customers or even salesmen to have valid opinions about things with which they are unacquainted.

The situation is not hopeless, however. The substitute method, marketing research on the potential market grid, and market tests can be useful. These techniques are discussed next.

Since few products are entirely new, careful analysis of the sales of products which the new one may displace may provide, at the least, an upper limit on potential sales. With imagination and research, it is possible to list most possible uses and to determine the potential in the various target markets. Once the potential upper limits of the markets have been ascertained, these figures can be scaled down by market realities, including actual customer preferences at various price levels.

Substitute method

This procedure can be illustrated by the forecasting done by DuPont for a plastic resin product.

The chemical company started by estimating the size of the various end-use markets—shown as the left series of boxes in Figure 5-4. These were markets where the resin product was technically suitable for use, including automotive, electrical, electronic, construction, personal, and toy products. The sum of the potential in all of these boxes indicated the upper limit on demand. Then a harder look at the suitability of the product in comparison with those currently being used indicated that one of the potential automotive and construction uses should be dropped.

The markets where the new product was technically preferable for use are shown in Figure 5-4, in the second bar from the left. These first two market-possibility bars, however, ignore potential selling prices which are realities in any market. So the potential demand at various selling prices was considered. The five right-hand bars in Figure 5-4

[15] Felix Kaufman, "Data Systems That Cross Company Boundaries," *Harvard Business Review*, January–February, 1966, pp. 141–55; and John Diebold, "What's Ahead in Information Technology," *Harvard Business Review*, September–October, 1965, pp. 76–82.

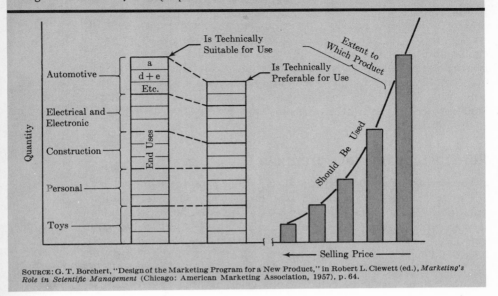

Figure 5–4 Size of market possibilities

SOURCE: G. T. Borchert, "Design of the Marketing Program for a New Product," in Robert L. Clewett (ed.), *Marketing's Role in Scientific Management* (Chicago: American Marketing Association, 1957), p. 64.

show the various quantities of the product that technically should be used at various price levels. The extreme right-hand bar indicates that if prices were low enough, all of the potential users on the extreme left-hand bar would use the product.

Many potentials but one forecast. The data in Figure 5–4 are shown in a different way and with more detail in Figure 5–5. Here the relation to the market grid concept becomes clearer. At a high selling price, interest would be shown by one of the potential automotive markets and by electrical and electronic users (markets *a, b,* and *c*). If the price were dropped slightly, additional automotive users (*d* and *e*) and a construction industry user (*f*) would add to the potential market. In other words, potential target markets are being specified as part of the sales forecasting procedure.

This approach, however, merely specifies market potentials. Determining a specific sales forecast requires a decision to go after particular target markets with the necessary marketing mixes. Many marketing strategy decisions—one for each potential target market—must be made. When all of these decisions are made and combined with judgments about the probability of achieving certain market shares, the sales forecast will come as a by-product.

Sales forecasting, it should be clear, is intimately linked with the determination of marketing strategy.

Filling market grid boxes

If the product is so new that no present product can be used as a guide, the forecaster can try to determine who will be interested in the product—and not just who the company executives *think* are likely to be interested.

94

Figure 5-5 Framework of market possibilities

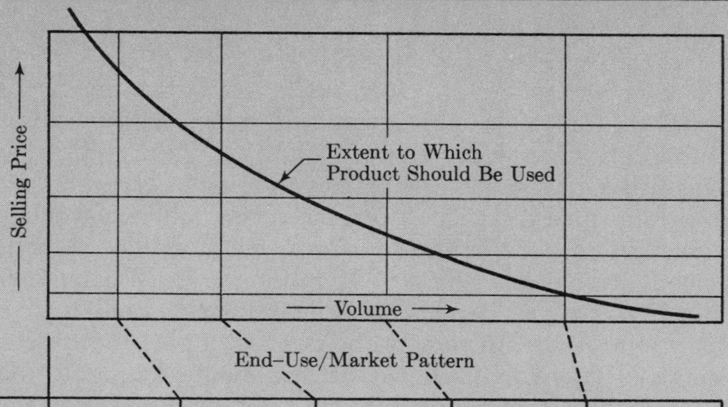

Market Areas		End–Use/Market Pattern			
Automotive	a	+ d, e	+ g, h, i	+ o	xxx
Electrical and Electronic	b, c	—	j, k, l, m	—	xx
Construction	—	f	*End Uses*	+ p, q	xx
Personal	—	—	n	+ r	xxxx
Toys	—	—	—	s	xxxx

SOURCE: G. T. Borchert, "Design of the Marketing Program for a New Product," in Robert L. Clewett (ed.), *Marketing's Role in Scientific Management* (Chicago: American Marketing Association, 1957), p. 66.

When potential target customers have been carefully described—when the boxes on the market grid are well defined—it is necessary to estimate the size of each of the potential markets. This may require the use of government and private statistics. Unfortunately, such statistics may not be readily available and a survey may be necessary.

This sort of forecasting may be crude in comparison with the techniques described previously, but it is no less important. Careful analysis of this type may show clear alternatives. It may show that the highest attainable sales volume for a product either is too small to warrant further research and development, or the outlook may prove to be so attractive that, despite the crude estimate, enthusiasm seems justified.

Calculations killed this slide rule. The following simple example illustrates this approach.

A firm developed a 5-inch plastic slide rule that could help the housewife determine which was the "best buy" among several products and packages at a supermarket. After discussion with a few friends, the executives were sure some housewives would be interested. But how many? And which ones? Men probably should have been considered, too, because men do some shopping, but the executives limited their initial investigation to housewives.

A small-scale survey of women was discouraging since only 5 percent of the housewives questioned showed any interest. The survey was not large enough to specify all characteristics on a housewife market grid, but it appeared that more highly educated, younger housewives were the only ones who might be interested—and only if the retail price of the slide rule were under 70 cents.

The company then talked to retailers to see how they would receive the product. Informal investigation with some retailers indicated a lack of enthusiasm, though some were willing to try the product.

It looked as if the achievable potential would be quite low. Specific figures confirmed this. The 5 percent of the housewives who *might* be interested, multiplied by the approximately 50 million American families, suggested an upper limit of 2.5 million units. When potential retail availability was considered, this potential upper limit was reduced to 100,000 units *or less*. In view of the fact that a premium price could not be obtained (the rule itself would cost about 25 cents to make), and that repeat sales were highly unlikely, the project was dropped.

Market tests— what will the S-curve look like?

Sometimes the only way to estimate the market potential of a new product is to actually try it in the market. Several test markets can be used, and assuming these are fairly representative, the results can be extended to a larger area.

Forecasting from market test results, however, can be misleading, since the very novelty of the product seems to attract some customers. This means that analysis of the sales pattern in the market test must consider what is called the "S-curve" effect. This refers to the phenomenon of sales increasing considerably just after the product is introduced and then declining quickly before leveling off—and then *perhaps* rising as a market of repeat customers develops.

Haste makes mistakes . . . or success. The major problem is estimating not the initial peak but where the market will level off. This may require continuing market research over several months or even a year or two, depending upon the product and the eventual repeat share rate.

Some companies have been misled by the initial peaking. Others have been misled by the early results *plus* their eagerness to market their product ahead of competition. Hurried testing may lead to mistakes—but more extensive market testing may prove a luxury in our highly competitive markets, especially if more venturesome competitors watch the initial reaction and beat the innovator to national distribution. This has happened often enough to discourage some firms from using tests for new products.

Accuracy of forecasts

The accuracy of sales forecasts may vary considerably, depending upon the number of components in the magnitude being forecast. The more aggregate the value being forecast, the more accurate the forecast is likely to be. This is because small errors in various components of the estimate tend to offset each other and make the aggregate estimate more accurate.

Annual forecasts of national aggregates, such as GNP, may be accurate within 5 percent. Industry sales forecasts, which tend to be more specific, are usually accurate within 10 percent, depending upon the inherent variability of the industry.

When estimates are made for individual products, there is even less chance of offsetting errors, except where errors from one salesman or territory offset those in another. Where style and innovation are important factors in an industry, forecast errors of 10 to 20 percent for *established products* are not uncommon. The accuracy of specific *new-product* forecasts is even lower. Many new products fail completely, while others are overwhelmingly successful.

Data on the accuracy of specific product forecasts is not easy to obtain because individual forecasting departments are reluctant to admit errors. They tend to magnify their successes and hide their failures.

Inaccuracy can happen easily

One forecaster of new consumer and industrial products claimed he had an excellent overall average for a particular year. He was off by only 2 percent on the average. His inaccuracy on specific product forecasts, however, was frightening. Many products did not sell at all—he missed by 100 percent—and others exceeded his expectations by 200 to 300 percent.[16]

Probably even less accuracy can be expected on sales forecasts in international markets. The data is poor, forecasters are less familiar with the markets, and the markets are less homogeneous due to inadequate transportation, natural barriers, illiteracy, and language differences. In Colombia alone, the four major population centers are almost isolated from each other by high mountains. Each major city has a different climate, population makeup, dialect, and mode of living.[17] The market grid boxes will be numerous and small, and as a result the forecast will be less accurate.

Conclusion

This chapter has discussed several approaches to forecasting market opportunities. The most common approach is to extend past behavior into the future. Where market conditions are fairly stable, reasonably good results may be obtained. Unfortunately, extending the past into the future is weak whenever sharp market changes are taking place—and it is precisely at those times that good forecasts are most needed.

To compensate for this weakness, the manager must use his own experience and judgment. There are also several analytical approaches to guide executive judgment or gather new information that can lead to better forecasts.

A forecast should represent a goal that the company expects to

[16] Checking the accuracy of forecasts is an intricate subject. For more detailed treatment, see Bratt, *op. cit.,* chap. xiii; *Sales Forecasting, Uses, Techniques, and Trends, op. cit.,* p. 148; and *Forecasting in Industry* (Studies in Business Policy No. 77 [New York: National Industrial Conference Board, 1956]).

[17] William Copulsky, "Forecasting Sales in Underdeveloped Countries," *Journal of Marketing,* July, 1959, pp. 37–38; and Henry Alderson, "Problems Peculiar to Export Sales Forecasting," *Journal of Marketing,* April, 1960, pp. 39–42.

achieve—with concentrated effort. A good forecast should consider the expected impact of the company's proposed marketing strategies as well as competitors' strategies. In other words, *the forecast should estimate the effectiveness of the whole business as a single integrated operating system in competition with other systems.*

Now that we have seen the importance of marketing strategy planning and have examined some research and forecasting tools, we will go on to chapters about customer behavior and the development of marketing mixes. At the end of the text, we will return to a discussion of tying together the whole business system so that it can regularly locate and capitalize on its opportunities.

In Chapter 30, we will consider the control function, returning to a discussion of forecasts and how they can be compared to actual results. We will see that these performance analyses can be fed back into the planning function to help the marketing manager develop new and better strategies. This further emphasizes the circular nature of the marketing management function. The manager must be continually planning, executing, and controlling.

Questions and problems

1 Suggest a plausible explanation for sales fluctuations for (*a*) bicycles, (*b*) baby food, (*c*) motor boats, (*d*) baseball gloves, (*e*) wheat, (*f*) woodworking tools, and (*g*) latex for rubber-based paint.

2 Explain the difference between a forecast of market opportunities and a sales forecast.

3 Discuss the relative accuracy of the various forecasting techniques. Explain why some are more accurate than others.

4 Given the following annual sales data for a company which is not planning any spectacular marketing strategy changes, forecast sales for the coming year (7) and explain your method and reasoning.

(*a*)		(*b*)	
Year	*Sales (in 000's)*	*Year*	*Sales (in 000's)*
1	200	1	160
2	230	2	155
3	210	3	165
4	220	4	160
5	200	5	170
6	220	6	165

5 Discuss the impact of the following events on industry sales forecasts for automobiles: (*a*) a large tax cut for consumers; (*b*) a large increase in government expenditures without accompanying tax increases.

6 Discuss the relative market potential of Wilmette and Winnetka, Illinois for: (*a*) prepared cereals, (*b*) automobiles, and (*c*) furniture.

7 Discuss how a General Motors market analyst might use the substitute method if the company were considering the potential for an electric car which might be suitable for salesmen, commuters, housewives, farmers, and perhaps other groups. The analyst is trying to consider the

potential in terms of possible price levels—$1,000, $1,500, $2,000, $3,000, and $4,000—and driving ranges—10 miles, 20 miles, 50 miles, 100 miles, and 200 miles—which would typically be desired or needed before recharging. He is assuming that gasoline-powered vehicles would become illegal for use within the major urban cities. Further, it is expected that while personal gasoline-driven cars still would be used in rural and suburban areas, they would not be permitted within some suburban areas, especially around the major metropolitan areas.

Consumers:
the American market

The CUSTOMER is the focal point of all business and marketing activities. Customers in the aggregate are markets, but the market grid concept leads us to thinking of markets as having many submarkets. Three important questions should be answered regarding any such "market":

1. How big is it?
2. Where is it?
3. What are its characteristics?

Answers to these questions will help locate attractive target markets and serve as a basis for planning marketing strategy. A considerable amount of data is available and is especially helpful if the marketing manager must make hurried decisions. The available data may not be as recent and precise as he would like, and he might prefer to apply some of the marketing research techniques discussed earlier—but considerations of time and money may force a quick decision.

Forget the Texas or New York stereotypes

Regardless of the approach the marketing manager uses, he will make some basic assumptions about the characteristics of potential markets which he hopes will reflect reality as faithfully as possible.

The marketing manager should not fall into the trap of accepting common stereotypes about the size or potential of various markets, such as those illustrated in one artist's version of a New Yorker's and a Texan's view of the United States (Figure 6–1), which may be humorous but of no real value to him.

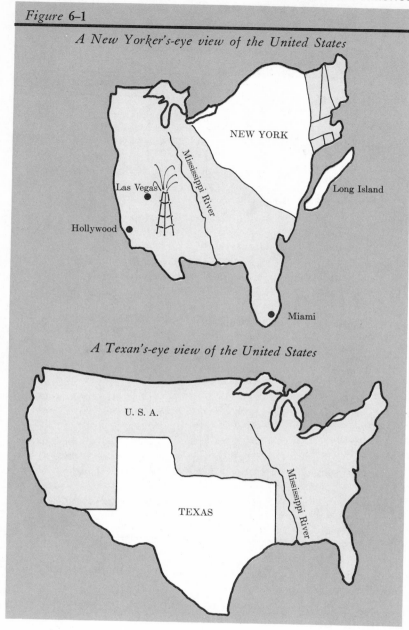

Figure 6–1

A New Yorker's-eye view of the United States

NEW YORK

Mississippi River

Las Vegas

Hollywood

Long Island

Miami

A Texan's-eye view of the United States

U. S. A.

TEXAS

Mississippi River

Since valid data is available, there is no excuse for decisions based on misconceptions or regional propaganda. Data on *final consumers* will be presented in this and the following two chapters. In Chapter 9, we will present data for other types of customers: businesses, farmers, and government buyers. The characteristics and behavior of wholesalers and retailers—important customers for manufacturers and retailers—

Table 6-1 Population by states and for Puerto Rico: 1910 to 1965*

State or Other Areas	Population (1,000)					
	1910	1920	1930	1940	1950	1965
United States	92,228	106,022	123,202	132,165	151,326	193,795
Regions:						
Northeast	25,869	29,662	34,427	35,977	39,478	47,617
North Central	29,889	34,020	38,594	40,143	44,461	54,089
South	29,389	33,126	37,858	41,666	47,197	60,017
West	7,082	9,214	12,324	14,379	20,191	31,983
New England	6,553	7,401	8,166	8,437	9,314	11,146
Maine	742	768	797	847	914	986
New Hampshire	431	443	465	492	533	673
Vermont	356	352	360	359	378	404
Massachusetts	3,366	2,852	4,250	4,317	4,691	5,361
Rhode Island	543	604	687	713	792	891
Connecticut	1,115	1,381	1,607	1,709	2,007	2,830
Middle Atlantic	19,316	22,261	26,261	27,539	30,164	36,471
New York	9,114	10,385	12,588	13,479	14,830	18,106
New Jersey	2,537	3,156	4,041	4,160	4,835	6,781
Pennsylvania	7,665	8,720	9,631	9,900	10,498	11,583
East North Central	18,251	21,476	25,297	26,626	30,399	38,231
Ohio	4,767	5,759	6,647	6,908	7,947	10,241
Indiana	2,701	2,930	3,239	3,428	3,934	4,893
Illinois	5,639	6,485	7,631	7,897	8,712	10,641
Michigan	2,810	3,668	4,842	5,256	6,372	8,317
Wisconsin	2,334	2,632	2,939	3,138	3,435	4,140
West North Central	11,638	12,544	13,297	13,517	14,061	15,858
Minnesota	2,076	2,387	2,564	2,792	2,982	3,562
Iowa	2,225	2,404	2,471	2,538	2,621	2,758
Missouri	3,293	3,404	3,629	3,785	3,955	4,492
North Dakota	577	647	681	642	620	652
South Dakota	584	637	693	643	653	686
Nebraska	1,192	1,296	1,378	1,316	1,326	1,450
Kansas	1,691	1,769	1,881	1,801	1,905	2,248
South Atlantic	12,195	13,990	15,794	17,823	21,182	28,748
Delaware	202	223	238	267	318	503
Maryland	1,295	1,450	1,632	1,821	2,343	3,534

will be discussed, together with these important marketing institutions, in Chapters 17 and 18.

Population

Present population and its distribution

Table 6-1 presents data on population by states for 1965. The first rank of California should sober the New Yorker and the Texan, and explain why some marketers are focusing on the West Coast market. On the other hand, the heavy concentration of population in New York and a few adjacent states—altogether twice as populous as the entire West Coast—does lend a certain validity to the New Yorker's

Table **6–1**—*Continued*

State or Other Area	Population (1,000)					
	1910	1920	1930	1940	1950	1965
Dist. of Columbia	331	438	487	663	802	802
Virginia	2,062	2,309	2,422	2,678	3,319	4,420
West Virginia	1,221	1,464	1,729	1,902	2,006	1,815
North Carolina	2,206	2,559	3,170	3,572	4,062	4,935
South Carolina	1,515	1,684	1,739	1,900	2,117	2,550
Georgia	2,609	2,896	2,909	3,124	3,445	4,391
Florida	753	968	1,468	1,897	2,771	5,796
East South Central	8,410	8,893	9,887	10,778	11,477	12,819
Kentucky	2,290	2,417	2,615	2,846	2,945	3,173
Tennessee	2,185	2,338	2,617	2,916	3,292	3,850
Alabama	2,138	2,348	2,646	2,833	3,062	3,486
Mississippi	1,797	1,791	2,010	2,184	2,179	2,309
West South Central	8,785	10,242	12,177	13,065	14,538	18,540
Arkansas	1,574	1,752	1,854	1,949	1,910	1,941
Louisiana	1,656	1,799	2,102	2,364	2,684	3,560
Oklahoma	1,657	2,028	2,396	2,336	2,233	2,448
Texas	3,897	4,663	5,825	6,415	7,711	10,591
Mountain	2,634	3,336	3,702	4,150	5,075	7,693
Montana	376	549	538	559	591	703
Idaho	326	432	445	525	589	693
Wyoming	146	194	226	251	291	330
Colorado	799	940	1,036	1,123	1,325	1,949
New Mexico	327	360	423	532	681	1,014
Arizona	204	334	436	499	750	1,575
Utah	373	449	508	550	689	904
Nevada	82	77	91	110	160	434
Pacific	4,449	5,878	8,622	10,229	15,115	24,290
Washington	1,142	1,357	1,563	1,736	2,379	2,973
Oregon	673	783	954	1,090	1,521	1,938
California	2,378	3,427	5,677	6,907	10,586	18,403
Alaska	64	55	59	73	129	267
Hawaii	192	256	368	423	500	710
Puerto Rico	1,118	1,300	1,544	1,859	2,211	2,633

* Insofar as possible, population shown is that of present area of state.
SOURCE: *Statistical Abstract of the United States*, 1967, p.12.

view of the U.S. market. The population of Texas is large, but its partisans' views are based on area, not population, and now that Alaska has been admitted to the union, Texas is no longer even the biggest state.

Obviously, if numbers of people are important in a company's marketing strategy, the marketing manager should rely on the latest census statistics for market grid analysis rather than guesswork or some parochial view of the importance of a particular area.

The map in Figure 6–2 is included to emphasize the concentration of population in various geographic regions. It shows the area of each state in proportion to its population. Notice the importance of the

103

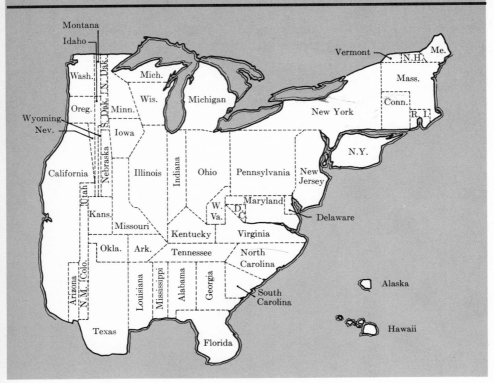

Figure 6–2 Map showing each state's area in proportion to its 1965 population

Midwestern states and the Southern states when viewed as a group. These regions, too, are often viewed as unique target markets by marketers anxious to avoid the extremely competitive East and West Coast markets. Note, too, the relative absence of population in the Plains and Mountain states, which explains why some mass marketers pay less attention to these areas. Yet they may provide an opportunity for an alert marketer who is looking for less competitive market situations.

Where are the people today and tomorrow?

Population figures for a single year fail to convey the dynamic aspects of markets. The U.S. population has been growing continuously since the founding of the country, doubling in the 50 years from 1910 to 1960. But—and this is important to marketers—the population did *not* double everywhere. Some states have seen great and rapid growth, while others have grown only a little and slowly.

These different rates of growth are especially important to marketing. For example, sudden growth in one area may make many new shopping centers necessary there, while old facilities may be more than adequate in other areas. In fact, the introduction of new marketing facilities in slow-growing areas may create severe competitive problems

104

for existing merchants, while in other areas demand may be growing so rapidly that even poorly planned and managed facilities may be profitable.

It seems certain that U.S. population will continue to grow.[1] The big question is, "How fast?" The birth rate is now dropping. As recently as 1958, the U.S. census projected that the U.S. population might grow to slightly over 300 million people by 1985. But by 1964 the estimate had been revised downward to slightly more than 275 million, and in 1966 it was again revised downward to 273 million.

It is obvious that new attitudes toward marriage, family size, and

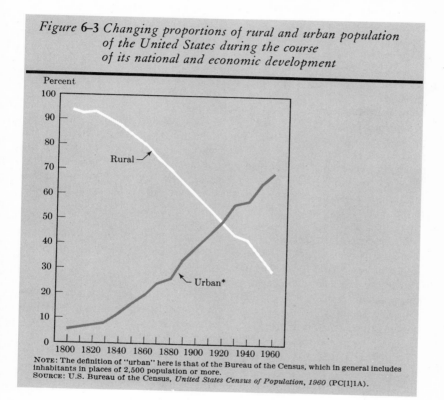

Figure 6–3 Changing proportions of rural and urban population of the United States during the course of its national and economic development

NOTE: The definition of "urban" here is that of the Bureau of the Census, which in general includes inhabitants in places of 2,500 population or more.
SOURCE: U.S. Bureau of the Census, *United States Census of Population, 1960* (PC[1]1A).

family planning should be carefully watched by marketers, because these factors obviously will have an impact on future market sizes.[2]

Migration from rural to urban areas has been continuous in the United States since 1800, as Figure 6–3 shows. In fact, in the last few decades the migration may have been even faster than suggested in Figure 6–3 because many people classified as rural residents by the U.S. census do not live on farms. The old rural-urban definitions may be

Shift to urban and suburban areas

[1] Detailed data on population growth and projections are available from the U.S. census. As a starting point, see the latest *Statistical Abstract*.

[2] "U.S. Population Stops Exploding," *Business Week*, July 2, 1966, p. 48; and "Have Stork's Wings Been Clipped a Bit?" *Business Week*, July 25, 1964, p. 28.

misleading about the size of the rural market because of the new factories and the suburban building in "rural" areas. About 7.5 percent of the U.S. population lived on farms in 1960 compared to about 15 percent in 1950. Clearly, we are becoming an industrialized society, and it seems possible that farming will eventually be dominated by corporate agricultural enterprises. This subject is explored further in Chapter 9.

From city to suburbs to city again

Since World War II, there has been a veritable race to the suburbs, which have grown about six times as fast as the central cities. As people have moved to the suburbs, retail and service businesses have followed. And as middle-income people have moved out of the cities, lower income consumers, often with different racial and national backgrounds, have moved in, thereby changing the nature of target markets in the center of the city.

A partial reversal of this trend seems possible, however. Some families have become disenchanted with the dream of suburbs, which they have found to be a nightmare of commuting, yard and housework, rising local taxes, and gossiping neighbors.

The movement back to the city is most evident among older and sometimes wealthier families. Their children are usually married or ready to leave home. They feel hemmed in by the rapid expansion of suburbia and especially by the large number of lower income families who are moving there. These older families are showing increased interest in high-rise apartments close to downtown shopping, recreational, and office facilities.

Developing a new concept of the urban area

These continuing shifts to and from urban and suburban areas mean that the usual practice of recording population by arbitrary city and county boundaries may lead to misleading descriptions of markets. Marketing men are more interested in the size of homogeneous marketing areas than in the number of people within political boundaries. To meet this need, the U.S. census has developed a separate population classification, the Standard Metropolitan Statistical Area, and much data is collected on the characteristics of people in these areas.

The Standard Metropolitan Statistical Area (SMSA) is an integrated economic and social unit having a fairly large population nucleus. Specifically, an SMSA must contain one city of 50,000 or more inhabitants, or "twin cities" which have a combined population of at least 50,000. The SMSA includes the county of such a central city or cities and adjacent counties that are found to be metropolitan in character and economically and socially integrated with the central city.

SMSA's are designated differently in New England because many of the cities in that compact, densely populated region are closer together, and counties must be split. Some SMSA's, especially those in the western part of the country, are exceptionally large geographically because of their huge county boundaries. Generally, however the SMSA's are basically urbanized, with a central city and surrounding suburbs.

Figure 6–4 shows the location of the nation's biggest urban areas, 212

Figure 6-4 Standard Metropolitan Statistical Areas

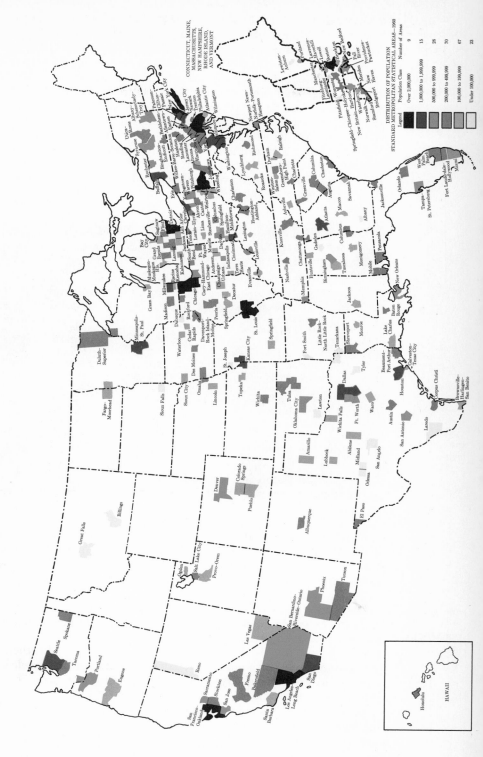

SMSA's that accounted for almost 65 percent of the country's population in 1965. Notice that this map further emphasizes the concentration of population in specific places—here, in SMSA's.

Big targets are easier Some national marketing organizations are concerned solely with these metropolitan areas and, in fact, with only certain ones among them because of the large concentrations of population within easy reach of their major distribution facilities. Table 6–2 shows the size of the top 15 SMSA's in 1965.

These larger target markets also offer greater sales potential in dollars and cents than population alone would indicate, in part because of generally higher wages in metropolitan areas and the concentration of higher paying occupations.

Table 6–2 Population and rank of top 15 Standard Metropolitan Statistical Areas in 1965

Rank	SMSA	Population
1	New York	11,366,000
2	Los Angeles—Long Beach	6,765,000
3	Chicago	6,689,000
4	Philadelphia (Pennsylvania—New Jersey)	4,664,000
5	Detroit	3,987,000
6	San Francisco—Oakland	2,918,000
7	Boston	2,589,000*
8	Washington, D.C. (Maryland—Virginia)	2,408,000
9	Pittsburgh	2,372,000
10	St. Louis (Missouri—Illinois)	2,249,000
11	Cleveland	2,000,000
12	Baltimore	1,854,000
13	Newark	1,851,000
14	Minneapolis—St. Paul	1,612,000
15	Buffalo	1,320,000

* 1960 Census Report.
SOURCE: *Statistical Abstract of the United States*, 1967, pp. 18–21.

The SMSA's should be considered as potential dimensions in market grid analysis. The farther customers are from major marketing centers, the more expensive they are to serve. Densely populated areas offer great opportunities—*if* the competition is not too great!

The age of the continuous city Despite the return of some families to the central cities, the trend to the suburbs seems likely to continue. An expanding population must go somewhere, and the suburbs combine pleasant neighborhoods with easy transportation to higher paying jobs in the city. Further, the continuing decentralization of industry may make the suburbs closer to the jobs than the central city itself. Not only people but industries have been fleeing the old cities.

These sometimes rapid shifts into new communities can create overnight opportunities for alert marketers. Here, however, less reliance can be placed on the usual census data; it's too old. Both intuition and careful study of local trends are necessary.

This growth in suburban population may create a new kind of urban-suburban strip called "interurbia" or "megalopolis." J. Walter Thompson Co.—a large advertising agency that has done much work in projecting population growth in various areas—sees a 600-mile-long "city" stretching along the East Coast and joining the citizens of Boston, New York, Baltimore, Philadelphia, and Washington and their suburbs into one giant community. This particular interurbia constitutes 6 percent of U.S. land and 20 percent of the population (see Figure 6–5). Other interurbia areas occur around the Great Lakes and

Figure 6–5 Projected growth of "interurbias"

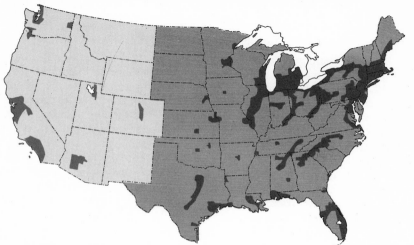

SOURCE: J. Walter Thompson Co.

adjoining areas in Pennsylvania, Ohio, and Missouri; in southern Florida; in the San Francisco Bay region; and in southern California. People who see the whole world becoming more urbanized look at these areas as laboratories of urban evolution.[3] The shaded parts in Figure 6–5 represent areas which are already fairly densely populated and can be expected to grow more.

It appears that the central cities in these interurbia areas gradually will be attractively rebuilt as the former slum areas are cleared with the aid of federal funds. Some may become higher income residential areas, drawing heavily from the suburbs.

The U.S. city of the past 70 or 80 years has been depicted as

[3] For a detailed study of the Northeast area, see Jean Gottmann, *Megalopolis* (New York: Twentieth Century Fund, 1961); Wolf Von Eckardt, *The Challenge of Megalopolis* (A Twentieth Century Fund Report based on the original study by Jean Gottmann [New York: Macmillan Co., 1964]).

consisting of a series of concentric rings or bands ranging from low-income slums at the city center outward through progressively higher income areas to the wealthy suburban areas at the outer fringe. The city of tomorrow may be more heterogeneous with many small neighborhoods—some wealthy, some middle income, and some poor—intermingled throughout the whole area from the central city to the suburbs.

This urban redevelopment already can be seen in the Los Angeles, Chicago, and Philadelphia areas; it will make the use of the market grid concept even more important. For example, retailers will have to find a way to cater to various kinds of customers, to carefully specify their target markets and then specifically develop marketing mixes for the selected target markets. Aiming at the "mass market" may be fatal.

Included in this analysis, of course, should be some estimation of how fast the population shifts will take place. Marketing decisions often must be lived with for quite a few years, and so the grid analysis should incorporate market potentials for the course of the planning period.

The mobile ones are an attractive market

It is important to remember that none of these population shifts is necessarily permanent. People move, stay awhile, and then move on again. In fact, approximately 20 percent of Americans move each year.[4] The 20–24 age group shows the greatest mobility, the rate dropping steadily as people grow older. It appears that mobile people are an important economic market, because their moves are often caused by promotions and job transfers, and they have money to spend. Moreover, it is clear that the movers must make many market-oriented decisions fairly quickly after their move. They must locate new sources of food, clothing, medical and dental services, and household goods.

Alert marketers would be well advised to try to pinpoint these people and inform them of their market offering. Research work is being done on mobile Americans, and we should know a great deal more in the near future about identifying and catering to this attractive market.[5]

Another dimension of mobile Americans should be noted, too—their willingness to travel about and try new things.

In a very tradition-bound society, people tend to get one job and stick with it, partly because jobs are in short supply and partly because they are not aware of opportunities elsewhere. But in the United States, the idea of mobility has been a tradition dating from the 17th-century beginnings of this nation. Pioneering, and homesteading and prospecting, more recently the cheap tin lizzie, the Great Depression and wars, all have contributed to a feeling of mobility and impermanence.

---

[4] *Sales Management,* April 16, 1962, p. 44.

[5] Alan R. Andreasen, "Geographic Mobility and Market Segmentation," *Journal of Marketing Research,* November, 1966, pp. 341–49; and James Bell, unpublished Ph.D. thesis, Michigan State University, 1967. Also, the extensive studies that are now being conducted in connection with the development of road systems may be extremely useful for marketing decisions. Both location and mobility have a bearing, and considerable data is becoming available. See Henry K. Evans, "A Vast New Storehouse of Transportation and Marketing Data," *Journal of Marketing,* January, 1966, pp. 33–40. Several interesting applications are offered.

110

The millions of military veterans who have traveled extensively during the wars of the past 25 years have expanded their horizons, and many have found new locations more attractive. The development of better highways since World War II has enabled workers to live at greater distances from their jobs. The increased popularity and availability of automobiles—brought about by the steadily rising prosperity of the 1950's and 1960's—has had a profound effect on the development of marketing institutions. Consider such developments as shopping centers in the metropolitan areas, and the retail facilities, marinas, and specialized services that cater to owners of second homes, vacation cabins, travel trailers, and boats.

Income

So far we have been concerned primarily with population characteristics. It is obvious, however, that unless a person has money or the assurance of acquiring it, he cannot be regarded as a potential customer. The amount of money he can spend also will affect the type of goods he is likely to buy. For this reason, most marketing men supplement population statistics with income data.

Growth at least until the year 2000

Income is derived from producing and selling goods or services in the market place. As already noted, a widely available measure of the output and the growth of the economy is the gross national product, which represents the total market value of goods and services produced in a year. The GNP has increased at the rate of approximately 3 percent a year since 1880. This means that GNP doubles, on the average, every 20 years.

If past trends continue, as is expected, the whole economy will probably continue to grow at about the same rate, that is, doubling every 20 years. Even though taxes have increased, and further increases are likely, we can nevertheless project continued growth of consumer spending power. Some researchers see continued growth, with no serious drain on resources, until the year 2000.[6]

The income pyramid capsizes!

These aggregate figures are meaningful when expressed in terms of family income and its distribution.

Family income has been moving up, but it is even more important for marketing men to note that the distribution of income has been changing drastically and will probably continue to change. Figure 6–6 shows that as recently as 1930 most of the families were bunched together in the lower income levels, and the distribution looked something like a pyramid. The data in Figure 6–6 is in terms of 1965 dollars, which means the effects of price inflation over the years have been removed.

By 1965, we see that the pyramid has turned over! Projections into

[6] Hans H. Lansberg, *Natural Resources for U.S. Growth—A Look Ahead to the Year 2000* (Baltimore: Johns Hopkins Press, 1964); "Plenty of Resources if We Use Them Right," *Business Week,* April 6, 1963, pp. 84–86. And the basic study: Hans H. Lansberg, Leonard L. Fischman, Joseph L. Fisher, *Resources in America's Future* (Baltimore: Johns Hopkins Press, 1963).

the future indicate that income will not only continue to grow but that more families will find themselves near or at the top of the income distribution.

Is
$10,000
bare
subsistence?

The income distribution data in Figure 6–6 cannot be stressed too much. Gross marketing strategy errors have been made by overestimating the amount of income available in various target markets. It is all too easy for businessmen to fall into such errors because of the natural tendency we all have of associating with others in similar circumstances and then assuming that almost everyone lives the same way. This was brought home most forcefully to the author when a group of students confronted him with what they felt was an error in a textbook. They

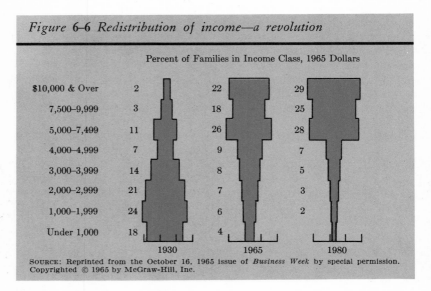

Figure 6–6 Redistribution of income—a revolution

Percent of Families in Income Class, 1965 Dollars

	1930	1965	1980
$10,000 & Over	2	22	29
7,500–9,999	3	18	25
5,000–7,499	11	26	28
4,000–4,999	7	9	7
3,000–3,999	14	8	5
2,000–2,999	21	7	3
1,000–1,999	24	6	2
Under 1,000	18	4	

SOURCE: Reprinted from the October 16, 1965 issue of *Business Week* by special permission. Copyrighted © 1965 by McGraw-Hill, Inc.

questioned the statement in the book that many people made less than $5,000 a year. No one, they felt, could possibly survive on such a low income. They felt that $10,000 or more a year was necessary for "bare subsistence." This was in 1955. Figure 6–6 shows that 10 years later—1965—only 22 percent of the country's families made more than $10,000. Furthermore, 34 percent of the families were making less than $5,000 a year.[7]

Only
disposable
income is
spent

Consumer budget studies suggest that the majority of consumers spend their income as a family or household unit. If the housewife or the children work, they usually pool their income with the husband or father when planning family expenditures. Thus most of our discussion on expenditures uses household or family income as a base.

[7] For a fuller discussion of the growth of the mass market and the implication for marketing strategy planning, see Walter Gross, "Income Flow Diffusion and Marketing Strategies," *MSU Business Topics,* Autumn, 1966, pp. 70–77; see also, "Cartier Opens Its Door Wider," *Business Week,* October 15, 1966, pp. 71–74; and Charles J. Collazzo, Jr., "Effects of Income upon Shopping Attitudes and Frustrations," *Journal of Retailing,* Spring, 1966, pp. 1–7.

Since governments, with their tax demands on income, are silent "spending" members of each family, most consumers are able to spend only a part of their income—the part called *disposable income*. Out of its disposable income—together with gifts, pensions, cash savings, or other assets—the family makes its expenditures. It is these expenditures that are our primary concern here.

The growing mass market with greater purchasing power is important to marketing men. It was once true here (and still is in some foreign countries) that the market consisted of a relatively few wealthy families. The masses of people could afford only the necessities. This is certainly no longer the case in the United States. Middle-income consumers today can afford almost anything except very expensive items such as yachts, helicopters, and limousines.

Discretionary income, luxuries, and necessities

Not all of the growing income is uncommitted, however. Most households have allocated a goodly portion of their income to "necessities"—such as food, rent or house payments, car and house furnishings payments, insurance, and so on—which are defined in various ways by various researchers and consumers. Their purchase of "luxuries" is made out of the remainder, or what has been called "discretionary" income. This is a rather elusive concept, because the definition of necessities varies from family to family and over time. Yet it also is an important concept, because if consumers do not feel they have *any* discretionary purchasing power, they may stop buying certain kinds of "luxuries" altogether.

In 1966, sales of durable goods dropped considerably, apparently because of a slow gain in consumers' discretionary purchasing power. The National Industrial Conference Board has developed a means of measuring discretionary purchasing power, and in 1966 it found that in sharp contrast to a rise of 5.8 percent in money income, discretionary income rose only 0.5 percent. This difference was due to increased federal and state taxes, as well as rising food and other costs.[8]

The U.S. Bureau of Labor Statistics has made numerous studies of city workers' budgets, and these have been used to develop measures of discretionary income. These studies are primarily concerned with the impact of income and family size on discretionary income, but in reality a particular family's discretionary income would depend not only on its income and size but also on its composition, social environment, life-cycle stage, and perhaps some other factors. Still, using only income and family size, some very interesting implications can be seen. One analysis, for example, showed that a proportionately small increase in income might significantly increase the discretionary income. A family with $8,000 gross income may have almost four times the discretionary income of a family with $6,500 gross income.[9]

The possible difference between money income, and especially discretionary income, and expenditures will lead us to emphasize expenditure data rather than income data in the following discussion. Our

[8] "Why There's Less Left to Spend," *Business Week*, November 26, 1966, p. 48.
[9] Thomas T. Semon, "Family Income and Spending Capacity," *Journal of Marketing*, April, 1962, pp. 26–30.

major reason for emphasizing expenditures rather than discretionary income, however, is that expenditure data is rather concrete and substantial data is available. Discretionary income measures, on the other hand, are not as widely available, apply only to some purchases, and probably need to be tailored to the needs of each individual situation. A color television set, for example, might be purchased out of discretionary income by a lower income family but considered a necessity by a higher income family.

Depending on a company's target markets, the data would be analyzed differently and different marketing mixes would be developed to deal with these different buying attitudes.

Consumer expenditure patterns by income

Engel's Laws. Some generalizations about consumer expenditure patterns are possible. These generalizations are commonly referred to as "Engel's Laws" because they grew out of the work of a German statistician by that name who published the first study of consumer spending patterns in 1857. Followers have rephrased these "laws," until now they are stated in three parts:

1. As a family's income increases, the percentage spent on food will decrease.
2. As a family's income increases, the percentage spent on housing and household operations will be roughly constant (with the exception of fuel, light, and refrigeration, which will decrease).
3. As a family's income increases, the percentage spent on all other categories and the amount saved will increase (with the exception of medical care and personal care items, which are fairly constant).

Engel was primarily concerned with working-class families who spent *all* their income. This fits in with our emphasis on analyzing consumer *expenditures*. Note that it is implied in Engel's Laws that as a family's income increases, *more will be spent absolutely in all categories*. The decreases or increases occur as a percentage of the total.

Engel's Laws are useful only for predicting the behavior of an individual family or groups of families moving from one income category to another. They should be used with care when it comes to predicting the expenditure pattern that will develop in the whole economy when the gross national product changes. Engel's Laws were not based upon such movements, but rather on a comparison of the budgets of individual families. They can still be useful to marketing men, however. An established retailer, for example, might use Engel's Laws to forecast how the expenditure patterns of his present customers would change if a new industrial plant coming into the community were likely to increase their incomes.

Recent expenditure data. Generalizations such as Engel's Law are valuable when precise data is not available, but fortunately we do have some detailed data available on consumer expenditure patterns. The National Industrial Conference Board (NICB) has developed an extremely comprehensive breakdown of data gathered by the Bureau of Labor Statistics as part of its project to revise its Consumer Price Index.

To make this revision, approximately 12,000 nonfarm families were

114

interviewed during 1961–62 concerning their purchases of approximately 700 individual products and services. All of this data has been analyzed and cross-classified with 11 different family characteristics, and presented in detailed tables.[10] Some of this data will be presented in this chapter to show the variety of information that is available in most libraries, and how this information may be used in market gridding.

Table 6–3 shows the average annual expenditures by household for major categories of expenditures, as developed in this study. These aggregate measures serve as bench marks, and as noted earlier, should keep you from making wild estimates based only on your own experience.

Why lower income consumers may be ignored

Table 6–3 *Average annual family expenditures by family income*

Item	Total	Family Income (Before Taxes)					
		Under $3,000	$3,000– $5,000	$5,000– $7,500	$7,500– $10,000	$10,000– $15,000	$15,000 and Over
Percent distribution of:							
All families	100%	22.4%	20.8%	26.2%	16.1%	10.7%	3.7%
Total expenditures	100	8.9	15.6	27.1	21.2	18.0	9.1
Average family size	3.2	2.1	3.0	3.5	3.7	3.9	3.8
Expenditures for current consumption:	$5,152	$2,043	$3,859	$5,315	$6,788	$8,679	$12,687
Food	1,259	600	1,015	1,318	1,624	1,970	2,550
Alcoholic beverages	81	21	55	81	117	152	242
Tobacco	93	42	84	105	123	126	134
Housing and household operations	1,236	620	968	1,263	1,552	1,889	3,002
Housefurnishings and equipment	269	83	185	284	376	476	690
Clothing and accessories	525	145	348	528	720	1,001	1,550
Transportation	781	176	560	848	1,093	1,450	1,891
Medical care	342	174	269	350	425	539	771
Personal care	148	61	118	156	194	241	312
Recreation and equipment	205	48	133	201	291	419	597
Reading and education	100	26	55	88	126	215	440
Other expenditures	113	47	69	93	147	201	508

SOURCE: Adapted from Fabian Linden (ed.), *Expenditure Patterns of the American Family* (New York: National Industrial Conference Board, 1965), p. 18.

As would be expected from Engel's Laws, the expenditure data shows that those with higher incomes spend more. The data in Table 6–3 shows that those in the upper income categories spend a large share of the total spent for goods and services. The families making over $7,500, for example, comprise only 30 percent of the population but account for almost half the expenditures. This may not be surprising information, but it does help to explain why some business organizations tend to ignore the lower income consumers.

[10] Fabian Linden (ed.), *Expenditure Patterns of the American Family* (New York: National Industrial Conference Board, 1965).

115

The data in Table 6–3 can help a marketing manager understand how his potential target markets are spending their current income. For example, if he is seriously considering consumers in the $15,-000-and-over income bracket, he can analyze how the families in the sample distributed their expenditures, and then he can consider how they would have to rearrange those expenditures to purchase his proposed offering.

Who is ready to take the plunge? A swimming pool manufacturer could calculate that such families spent about $600 a year on recreation and equipment. If his proposed pool would cost approximately $600 a year, including depreciation and maintenance, then it would follow that for the average family in this income category such a purchase would necessitate a realignment in its budget.

Clearly, the data will not give the pool maker the answers that he finally seeks, but they provide some of the raw material that he will need in making his decision. If he feels that he needs more data, he can develop some of his own, using marketing research techniques. For example, he might want to make some budget studies on consumers who already have swimming pools to see how they adjusted their expenditure patterns. As part of this analysis, he also would want to incorporate differences in expenditure patterns such as are available in the NICB study, based on age of household head, stage in the family life cycle, family size, earner composition of family, occupation of head, geographical region, color, market location, home ownership, and education of the household head. How some of these dimensions might be used are discussed in the following example.

A refrigerator gridding example. The NICB study provides data not only on aggregate categories but also on 700 products and services. Swimming pools are not such a category, but refrigerators are, and we will use them to illustrate the kind of detailed data which is available for the large number of items usually purchased by consumers. To make this more concrete, we will consider the problem of a soft-goods department store manager who is thinking about adding refrigerators and similar large appliances.

The store manager knows that he is now serving a lower income target market and wants to obtain some estimate of the relative magnitude of their current refrigerator purchases. His credit records give him a good measure of the number and income of his regular customers. He finds that about half are in the under-$3,000-a-year family income bracket, while the other half are in the $3,000-to-$5,000 bracket.

One of the tables in the NICB study shows that while the average expenditure for refrigerators was $14.56, the lowest income category spent only $6.17 for refrigerators, and the $3,000-to-$5,000 income group spent only $12.90.[11]

To sell the customer, know the customer

As would be expected, the higher income group spent more, probably reflecting both more frequent purchases and purchases of larger units. Data did show, nevertheless, that the lower income consumers were

[11] Fabian Linden (ed.), *Expenditure Patterns of the American Family* (New York: National Industrial Conference Board, 1965), pp. 70–75.

buying refrigerators. By multiplying the average purchase per family times the number of families in each of the income groups, the department store manager was able to develop an estimate of the total purchases of his target market. By making similar calculations for the other major appliances he was considering, he could estimate the total expenditures on such commodities.[12]

The more the department store manager knows about his present target market, the more he can make use of the available data. For example, if his customers are mainly older people, the NICB data will show that their expenditures on refrigerators are below average among refrigerator buyers. If most of his customers have no children or are unskilled workers or have lower educational achievement levels, they will spend less on refrigeration.

Some of these characteristics are interrelated and will have to be used with care. Unfortunately, the data in this study and in most such studies is not cross-classified according to income *and* education *and* occupation *and* age and so on. Still, expenditure data is available to guide and supplement judgment on the behavior of alternative target markets. Bear in mind that expenditure data analysis does not provide final answers.

After the department store manager has developed an estimate of the expenditures of his target customers, he then would have to estimate the likelihood of his obtaining some share of this business. He would also have to evaluate the possibility of attracting other people, including those like his present customers, if he added appliances to his line. And before the final decision was made, the manager would have to consider competition and the relative profitability of appliance lines. At the start, however, the expenditure data would add hard facts to the analysis.

It should be clear that a manufacturer, a chain retailer, or other marketer could use the basic approach of our department store manager. First, he would have to select target markets, and then he could carry out the analysis in many more geographic areas. Much more judgment and greater care would be needed in such an analysis, because competition and local preferences would have to be considered. The local retailer might have a far better "feel" for this than someone in a headquarters office. This helps explain why some small retailers can compete very successfully with chain outlets that attempt to apply one marketing mix in differing areas.

Expenditure pattern variations

Income has a direct bearing on expenditure patterns, but there are other factors that should not be neglected in any careful analysis of market grids. Several of these factors and general relationships are discussed below.

---

[12] The NICB study provides a variety of data, including information on the following appliances: refrigerators, home freezers, dishwashers, gas stoves, electric stoves, floor waxers, garbage disposal units, vacuum cleaners, washing machines, dryers, air conditioners, dehumidifiers, sewing machines, and ironers.

The location of a consumer's household, either inside or outside a metropolitan area, has a distinct bearing on expenditure patterns. On Table 6–4, note especially that total expenditures are much lower outside metropolitan areas. This fits with our earlier comment about the importance of Standard Metropolitan Statistical Areas. But the detailed variations also are important. Note how the shares spent on major expenditure categories shift in several places, always remembering that a 1 percent share represents a lot of money. Consumers in metropolitan central cities spend much less on transportation and much

Table 6–4 *Average annual family expenditures by market location*

| | | Market Location | | | | |
| | | In Metropolitan Areas | | | Outside Met. Area | |
Item	Total	Central Cities	Urban Fringe	Other Areas	Urban	Rural
Percent distribution of:						
All families	100%	34.9%	26.5%	6.0%	16.1%	16.5%
Total expenditures	100	34.8	32.4	6.6	14.0	12.2
Average family size	3.2	2.9	3.4	3.7	3.1	3.3
Expenditures for current consumption:	$5,152	$5,132	$6,303	$5,665	$4,482	$3,813
Food	24%	25%	24%	23%	25%	26%
Alcoholic beverages	2	2	2	1	1	1
Tobacco	2	2	2	2	2	2
Housing and household operations	24	25	24	24	24	21
Housefurnishings and equipment	5	5	5	6	5	6
Clothing and accessories	10	11	10	10	10	9
Transportation	15	13	16	16	15	18
Medical care	7	7	6	7	7	7
Personal care	3	3	3	3	3	3
Recreation and equipment	4	4	4	4	4	4
Reading and education	2	2	2	2	2	2
Other expenditures	2	2	2	2	2	2

SOURCE: Adapted from Fabian Linden (ed.), *Expenditure Patterns of the American Family* (New York: National Industrial Conference Board, 1965), p. 21.

more on housing than those in outlying areas. And rural families spend a larger share on food, perhaps because there is less competition in rural areas for the grocery dollar. But incomes tend to be lower in rural areas, and Engel's Laws may explain some of this. The more detailed NICB data that is available would have to be analyzed to answer specific questions.[13]

For the marketing man, geographical location is also relevant. Table 6–5 breaks the United States into four regions. As probably would be expected, total expenditures in the South are lower than in other regions because incomes are lower. The important share differences here, again, are in housing and transportation. Then, as noted before,

[13] See also, Donald F. Blankertz, "A Marketing Analysis of Suburban and Urban Expenditure Patterns," in Reavis Cox *et al., Theory in Marketing* (Homewood, Ill.: Richard D. Irwin, Inc., 1964), pp. 289–309, re. Engel's Laws.

higher or lower expenditures in some categories change the whole budget pattern. These differences must be considered when evaluating the potential in various geographical target markets.

Two other dimensions of population—age of persons and number of children—seem to have a direct bearing on consumption patterns and are therefore important to marketing men.

The young buy colored tissues

Age has a bearing on the acceptance of new items, for example. Younger people seem to be more receptive to new products. The

Table 6–5 Average annual family expenditures by geographical region

Item	Total	Geographical Region			
		North- east	North Central	South	West
Percent distribution of:					
All families	100%	26.9%	27.8%	28.9%	16.3%
Total expenditures	100	30.1	27.2	24.8	18.0
Average family size	3.2	3.2	3.2	3.2	3.2
Expenditures for current con- sumption:	$5,152	$5,761	$5,028	$4,410	$5,677
Food	24%	25%	24%	24%	24%
Alcoholic beverages	2	2	2	1	2
Tobacco	2	2	2	2	2
Housing and household operation	24	25	24	23	23
Housefurnishings and equip- ment	5	5	5	6	5
Clothing and accessories	10	10	10	10	10
Transportation	15	13	16	16	16
Medical care	7	6	7	7	7
Personal care	3	3	3	3	3
Recreation and equipment	4	4	4	4	5
Reading and education	2	2	2	2	2
Other expenditures	2	2	2	2	2

SOURCE: Adapted from Fabian Linden (ed.), *Expenditure Patterns of the American Family* (New York: National Industrial Conference Board, 1965), p. 20.

under-35 group was the first to use cellulose sponges, fitted bed sheets, liquid detergents, and colored two-ply paper tissues. Then, too, younger families—usually with no children—are still accumulating durable goods such as automobiles and housefurnishings. They have much less need for food. It is only as the children begin to arrive and grow that the emphasis shifts to soft goods and services such as education and medical and personal care. This tends to occur when the household head reached the 35-to-44 age bracket.

In the over-55 age bracket, there is more interest in drugs and medical care products—that is, those that will aid health, sleep, and digestion. These older families also have more interest in travel, recreation, and self-education.[14]

Table 6–6 presents the NICB findings concerning families in the various stages of the life cycle and their purchasing patterns. The relatively high expenditures by young families, especially those with some older children, should be noted. These families are numerous, and their expenditures are high, especially for food and clothing.

Table 6–6 *Average annual family expenditures by stage in life cycle*

| Item | Total | Families with Child under 6 | | 6 or Over Only | | No Children | |
		Some Under 6	All Under 6	All 6 to 11	Any 12 or Over	Husband-Wife	Other
Percent distribution of:							
All families	100%	14.5%	12.7%	4.6%	25.7%	24.1%	18.4%
Total expenditures	100	17.1	13.3	5.4	33.4	21.3	9.5
Average family size	3.2	5.5	3.6	3.7	4.1	2.1	1.2
Expenditures for current consumption:	$5,152	$6,070	$5,406	$6,045	$6,710	$4,549	$2,664
Food	24%	27%	22%	24%	25%	23%	24%
Alcoholic beverages	2	1	1	2	2	2	2
Tobacco	2	2	2	2	2	2	2
Housing and household operation	24	24	26	23	21	25	31
Housefurnishings and equipment	5	5	7	5	5	6	4
Clothing and accessories	10	11	9	11	12	8	8
Transportation	15	14	16	15	15	16	12
Medical care	7	6	7	6	6	8	7
Personal care	3	3	3	3	3	3	3
Recreation and equipment	4	4	4	5	4	3	3
Reading and education	2	2	1	2	3	1	2
Other expenditures	2	2	1	2	3	2	2

SOURCE: Adapted from Fabian Linden (ed), *Expenditure Patterns of the American Family* (New York: National Industrial Conference Board, 1965), p. 17.

Young families and families with young children are also good markets for homes and home improvements.

Reallocation for teen-agers

Much research on life cycles is being done because today's marketing man knows he must be familiar with the family characteristics of his market. It is fairly easy to obtain such data, since accurate information is available on births, marriages, and ages of children.

Considerable attention, for example, has been directed to the babies born in the period from 1940–50 and in general to those under 25 years

[14] S. G. Barton, "The Life Cycle and Buying Patterns," in Lincoln H. Clark (ed.), *Consumer Behavior* (New York: New York University Press, 1955), Vol. II, pp. 53–57. There are several other interesting articles in Vol. II on the relation of the life cycle to consumer behavior. See also, "Census-Eye View of Sales in '70's," *Business Week*, June 10, 1967, pp. 120–24.

of age. These persons will be key markets for decades. (See Figure 6–7.) Some are teen-agers who are eating more, beginning to wear more expensive clothes, and developing recreational and educational needs that are hard on the family budget. Their parents may be forced to reallocate their incomes to cover these expenses, spending less on durable goods such as appliances, automobiles, household goods, and houses. This, of course, would affect the producers of these goods.

As those teen-agers grow into young adults, we can expect a sharp increase in marriages, and perhaps a recurrence of the 1940–50 baby boom. These young adults, in turn, will buy durable goods until their

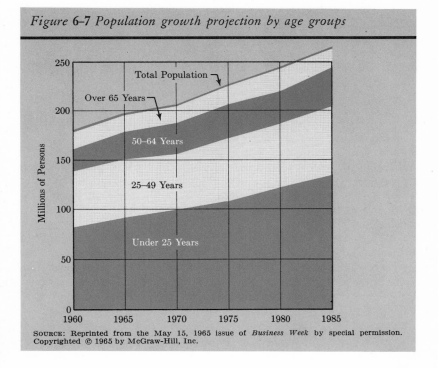

Figure 6–7 Population growth projection by age groups

children become older, and then they, too, will have to reallocate their budgets to provide for food, clothing, education and recreation.[15]

Selling to the empty nest

There is an important group in the 50–64 age category that has sometimes been called the "empty-nesters." Their children have been raised, and now they are able to reallocate their resources. It is an elusive group, however, because some people marry later and are still

---

[15] Paul Gilkison, "What Influences the Buying Decisions of Teen-Agers?" *Journal of Retailing*, Fall, 1965, p. 33; "Young, Single Spenders Pour It on the Market," *Business Week*, January 1, 1966, pp. 62–63; William D. Wells and George Gubar, "The Life Cycle Concept in Marketing Research," *Journal of Marketing Research*, November, 1966, pp. 355–364; William H. Reynolds and James H. Myers, "Marketing and the American Family," *MSU Business Topics*, Spring, 1966, pp. 57–66; "Catering to Kids," *Wall Street Journal*, September 17, 1962, p. 1; and "Why the Consumer Is Losing His Enthusiasm for Goods," *Business Week*, February 1, 1958, pp. 46–50.

raising a family as they move into this age group. It is empty-nesters who are moving back into the smaller, more luxurious apartments in central cities. They also may be more interested in travel, smaller sports cars, and other things that have not been realistic possibilities for them until now.[16]

Old folks are a new market

Finally, the "senior citizen" market is one that should not be neglected. The number of people over 65 is increasing rapidly because of modern medicine, improved sanitary conditions, and better nutrition. Between 1950 and 1960, the over-65 population increased about twice as fast as the total population. It is estimated that by the year 2000 this group will constitute 10 percent of the population.

Although these persons generally have reduced incomes, they represent a unique target market.[17] Many firms, in fact, are already catering to the senior citizen market. Special food products and diet supplements have been produced, and there are even housing developments designed especially to appeal to older persons.[18]

More education means less for food and clothing

Both education and occupation appear to have a bearing on consumption patterns, too. The NICB study provides data on both of these dimensions, but they are not presented here due to space limitations. Several observations are in order, however.

If the household head is a college graduate, we find that he spends proportionately less on food and clothing than others. He spends more on house and automobile expenses. This study does not attempt to discover why, but when drawing market grids, these facts should be considered.

Since educational levels are rising, differences due to education will probably become increasingly important. More students are completing high school and college. In 1950, barely a third of the adult population had completed high school. By 1970, more than half will have had a high school education, and many will have had some exposure to college.

Other factors affecting consumer expenditures

Are savers spenders?

One factor logically related to consumers' ability and willingness to spend income is their asset position. It is reasonable to assume that if a consumer has a substantial bank account or a nest egg of savings bonds, he will be more willing to spend his current income and even go into debt. This concept has interested the Federal Reserve System, which has some control over credit policies and the use of liquid assets, and it collects data on the matter.

Tables 6–7 and 6–8 indicate the kind of data available and shows that the majority of consumers have less than $1,000 in liquid assets. Compa-

---

16 "When Offspring Fly the Coop," *Business Week*, July 11, 1964, pp. 52–62.

17 John A. Reinecke, "The 'Older' Market—Fact or Fiction?" *Journal of Marketing*, January, 1964, pp. 60–64; and "The Family," *Time*, August 3, 1962, pp. 46–50.

18 "Retirement City—Haven or Ghetto?" *Business Week*, April 11, 1964, pp. 128–30; and "How the Old Age Market Looks," *Business Week*, February 13, 1960, pp. 72–78.

*Table 6-7 Family units—percent distribution
by liquid asset holdings, 1965*

Asset Size-Class	1965	Asset Size-Class	1965
All family units	100	Own assets—Continued	
		$2,000 to $4,999	14
Own no assets	20	$5,000 to $9,999	9
Own assets	80	$10,000 and over	8
$1 to $199	17		
$200 to $499	11	Median holdings	$575
$500 to $1,999	21		

SOURCE: The University of Michigan, Survey Research Center; *Survey of Consumer Finances.*

nies planning to sell products by persuading consumers to use their savings should bear this in mind. There will probably be more and valuable research along these lines.[19]

The data available now on asset position and credit availability is aggregative, but in any case it should probably be incorporated into market grid analysis whenever major expenditures are involved.

America may be called the "melting pot," but there are still relatively distinct racial and nationality groups that require special consideration when the marketing man is developing a market grid. This is obvious for some products, but there are other differences that may be ignored by the superficial observer.

Nationality and race and buying

Table 6-8 Average net worth of families by income, 1962

Item	Total Net Worth	Tangible Assets		Busi-ness Profes-sion	Insur-ance	Liquid Assets	Invest-ment Assets	Miscel-lane-ous Assets	Less Per-sonal Debt
		Own Home	Auto-mo-bile						
All families	22,588	5,975	637	3,912	1,376	2,579	7,063	1,528	483
1962 income:									
0 to $2,999	8,875	3,752	149	1,418	190	1,330	2,128	113	205
$3,000 to $4,999	10,914	3,544	412	1,902	635	1,738	2,925	137	378
$5,000 to $7,499	15,112	4,973	643	2,050	1,135	1,716	3,710	1,339	453
$7,500 to $9,999	21,243	7,499	868	2,577	1,879	2,722	4,779	1,632	712
$10,000 to $14,999	30,389	9,527	1,346	5,174	2,975	4,233	6,969	749	584
$15,000 to $24,999	74,329	15,188	1,816	9,088	5,196	9,241	30,638	3,664	502
$25,000 to $49,999	267,996	32,215	2,875	66,144	10,819	19,098	92,663	48,736	4,553
$50,000 to $99,999	789,582	45,961	2,803	251,977	19,559	41,845	345,728	86,313	4,604
$100,000 and over	1,554,152	85,634	4,011	288,915	32,309	54,426	1,004,246	96,879	12,268

SOURCE: Board of Governors of the Federal Reserve System; *Federal Reserve Bulletin*, March, 1964.

[19] See a basic study: Robert J. Lampman, *The Share of Top Wealth-Holders in National Wealth* (Princeton, N.J.: Princeton University Press, 1962).

In recent years, interest has been focused on differences in consumption between Negroes and whites, especially as the Negro consumer has become wealthier. Extensive analysis of available data has led one analyst to the following major conclusions:

1. Total consumption expenditures of Negroes are less than for comparable-income whites, that is, Negroes save more out of a given income than do whites with the same income.
2. Negro consumers spend more for clothing and nonautomobile transportation, and less for food, housing, medical care, and automobile transportation than do whites with comparable incomes.
3. Comparing Negroes and whites, there is no consistent difference in expenditures for either recreation and leisure or home furnishing and equipment at comparable income levels.

Differences associated with geography as well as race may have to be used together in a market grid, since the findings seem to depend somewhat on when and where the differences have been studied.[20] Several other observations are important here. The median age of U.S. Negroes is considerably lower than that of whites. This means that many more are in an earlier stage of the life cycle and therefore are a better market for certain goods, especially durable goods. Some Negroes seem to be striving for what they believe is the white middle-income standard in material goods; others have abandoned the attempt. Those who are striving seem to be more brand conscious, and this definitely has a bearing on the development of marketing strategy.[21]

When the wife earns, the family spends

A relatively new phenomenon that may require more consideration with respect to expenditure patterns is the growing number of married women who hold jobs. In 1965, about 15 million wives were on the nation's payrolls—more than double the number when employment of wives was at a high level because of World War II.

In families where the wife works, about 40 percent of all the family spending power is derived from her income. Half of all U.S. families in the $10,000-to-$15,000 income bracket have achieved this income because the wife is working.

A study by the U.S. Department of Agriculture showed that while a wife's employment outside the home seems to have little effect on the nutritive value of her family's food, working wives do *spend more* for food and do choose more expensive types of food.

Families with working wives also spend more on clothing, alcohol and tobacco, housefurnishings and equipment, and automobiles.

In short, when a wife works, it has a very distinct bearing on the expenditure pattern of the family. This fact must be considered when developing market grids for certain types of products.[22]

---

[20] Marcus Alexis, "Some Negro-White Differences in Consumption," *American Journal of Economics and Sociology,* January, 1962, pp. 11–28.

[21] Raymond A. Bauer, "Negro Consumer Behavior," in J. Newman (ed.), *On Knowing the Consumer* (New York: John Wiley & Sons, Inc., 1966), pp. 161–66 and pp. 13–14.

[22] "More Moms on Payroll," *Business Week,* December 31, 1966, p. 59; *U.S. Department of Agriculture Food and Home Notes,* July 13, 1960; and Margaret S. Carroll, "The Working Wife and Her Family's Economic Position," *Monthly Labor Review,* April, 1962, pp. 366–74.

The growth in income has been accompanied by a reduction in working hours, and this in turn has given the consumer much more time for leisure activities and play.

In the United States, television takes the largest share of leisure time, regardless of a person's occupation.[23] After television, there are a large number of active and spectator sports and hobbies that interest many people, as Table 6–9 shows.

The do-it-yourself hobby is growing in importance. Among many families, especially wage earners, it is a way of life.[24] Some people just like to putter, but for others it is a chance to work with their hands and save money as well. Some of this activity evidently has been encouraged by the shoddy work of servicemen and contractors.

Table 6–9 Leisure time use

Five Leading Participation Games and Sports	Number Engaged (In millions)
Cards	132
Fishing	35
Boating	25
Bicycling	22
Bowling	17

Five Leading Spectator Sports	Estimated Yearly Attendance (In millions)
Softball	125
Basketball	115
Football	70
Baseball	65
Horse racing	50

Five Leading Hobbies	Number Engaged (In millions)
Do-it-yourself	60
Photography	45
Gardening	40
Needlecraft	30
Playing musical instruments	28

SOURCE: Rene DeYoe, *The Leisure Market* (New York: J. Walter Thompson Co., 1957).

One recent development in do-it-yourself activities is an interest in sewing. Millions of women now rate sewing as their first, and sometimes only, hobby. There is more involved here than just a desire to save money. Apparently, sewing provides a way of expressing creative ability now that so many household activities have been simplified by machines and prepared or packaged food.[25]

More people seem to want to participate in sports rather than simply watching, as a growing interest in skin diving, skiing, boating, fishing,

---

[23] This, and other material not otherwise credited, was derived from Rene DeYoe, *The Leisure Market* (New York: J. Walter Thompson Co., 1957).

[24] "How the U.S. Plays," *Tide*, March 24, 1956, p. 23.

[25] "Sew and Reap," *Time*, November 10, 1958, pp. 78–81.

and badminton indicates.[26] Owning and riding horses appears to be a fast-growing recreation—especially among suburbanites.[27]

Consumers are also showing a growing interest in cultural activities. Art festivals, art museums, exhibits, operas, chamber music programs, and symphony concerts have had a marked increase in attendance since World War II. There has been growing interest in books and adult education programs.[28]

All in all, consumers have a great deal of leisure time and money to spend, and—most important to marketers—the desire to take part in leisure-time activities. This may create both opportunities and problems in the future.

Currently the consumer spends about 10 percent of his disposable income on leisure activities. As incomes and population continue to rise, growing pressures will be placed upon present leisure-time facilities. The federal government has studied this situation, and sees a pressing need for increasing outdoor recreation facilities in and *near* the major metropolitan areas.[29]

Present data is wanting

So far in this chapter, we have tried to show that there are underlying consumer expenditure patterns associated with various socioeconomic characteristics. Many specialized studies have shown such relationships. These analyses probably should be improved and made more precise, because it is obvious that consumers are multidimensional while the data we have been discussing is concerned primarily with one dimension at a time, for example, population *or* income *or* race.

Make the product hit the bullseye

Fortunately, as the idea of catering to smaller and smaller target markets becomes more widely accepted, we see specific data with cross-classifications becoming available. More attention is being directed to the female market, the teen-age market, and the senior citizen market, among others.

Even the 1960 census data is now available from a private source that supplements the official census data with additional cross-classification. For example, if a firm were interested in knowing how many households had incomes between $7,000 and $9,999 *and also* had five or more persons in the household, *and also* owned no car, one car, two cars, or three or more cars, such data is available.[30]

[26] "The Oddities of the Consumer," *Business Week*, September 6, 1952, pp. 123–26.

[27] "Everyone's Getting a Horse Now," *Business Week*, June 9, 1962, pp. 32–33; and *Wall Street Journal*, January 24, 1962, p. 1.

[28] "The Arts Become Good Business, Too," *Business Week*, January 19, 1963, pp. 68–69; "The New Consumer—Skilled, Choosey, Culture-Hungry," *Business Week*, May 4, 1957, pp. 62–77; and "Culture for Everybody," *Royal Bank of Canada Monthly Letter*, October, 1962, pp. 1–4.

[29] See *Outdoor Recreation Resources Review Commission's Report*, presented to President Kennedy in February, 1962. This report listed 60 specific recommendations designed to meet the needs of the nation's expanding population; also see Nels Anderson, *Work and Leisure* (New York: Free Press of Glencoe, 1961); and George Fisk, *Leisure Spending Behavior* (Philadelphia: University of Pennsylvania Press, 1963), p. 204.

[30] This basic study is entitled: *People and Homes in the American Market* (Detroit: S. J. Tesauro & Co., 1961).

It is likely that there will be more such cross-classification as firms become more interested in specific target markets rather than just "the market." As we have noted already, this movement is well under way. The apartment developers we discussed earlier are an example. And the Maytag Co. sought out and won a part of the high-priced washing machine business. Maxwell House developed a special coffee, called "West Blend," to satisfy the western taste for stronger coffee. And Johnson & Johnson introduced a disposable diaper for the specific use of families traveling during the summer season.

But now we must present the other side of the story.

There is often no pat answer to why specific goods or services sell while others do not. This is partly because of the rising consumer incomes and the increasing importance of discretionary spending. In fact, it could be argued that consumers have almost complete latitude in their choices and that almost all purchases are for nonnecessities. One economist showed, for example, that in 1950 a person could have had a nutritionally adequate diet for about $72 a year. To be sure, this was not a very attractive diet, consisting solely of wheat flour, evaporated milk, cabbage, spinach, and dried navy beans.[31]

Do we know why anybody buys anything?

But the point is that purchase of a variety of foods, strictly speaking, is primarily to satisfy emotional needs. On the basis of this reasoning, one could maintain that most food purchases are *not* for necessities. And once we get beyond necessities, it becomes more difficult to anticipate how much of any specific product or types of products a consumer will want. This applies to clothing, shelter, and other things, too. In fact, very few specific products are absolute necessities.

The absence of "captive demand" for necessities puts a considerable burden upon marketing managers and their firms. They usually are trying to sell specific products, in competition with many others, to consumers whose preferences are shifting continually. The factors discussed in this chapter may be extremely helpful in many market situations, but it seems that there are more (and sometimes hard to specify) dimensions affecting what an individual person or family will buy. Some of these dimensions are discussed in Chapter 8—and fortunately, can be incorporated into the market grid process.[32]

Conclusion

In our study of the American consumer, we have moved from the general to the particular. We first studied population data, leaving

---

[31] George J. Stigler, *The Theory of Price* (rev. ed.; New York: Macmillan Co., 1952), p. 2.

[32] For further discussion on the inadequacies of using socioeconomic characteristics only, see James A. Carman, *Studies in the Demand for Consumer Household Equipment* (Berkeley, Calif.: Institute of Business and Economic Research, University of California, 1965); Newman, *op. cit.*, pp. 15–16 and 173–86; Steven C. Brandt, "Dissecting the Segmentation Syndrome," *Journal of Marketing,* October, 1966, pp. 22–27; and M. Alexis, L. Simon, and K. Smith, "Some Determinants of Food Buying Behavior," in M. Alexis *et al., Empirical Foundations of Marketing: Research Findings in the Behavioral and Applied Sciences* (Chicago: Rand McNally & Co., forthcoming). On the positive side, see *How Consumer Characteristics Relate to Product Usage* (Technical report for *National Geographic* [New York: Market Math, Inc., May, 1966]).

behind various misconceptions about how our approximately 200 million people are spread over the United States. In so doing, it became apparent that the potential of a given market cannot be determined by numbers alone. Income, stage in life cycle, geographic location, occupation, education, and other factors are important, too.

We also noted the growth of interurbia, such as the megalopolis of the Atlantic Seaboard. These urban-surburban systems may suggest the shape of future growth in this country. It is also apparent that one of the outstanding characteristics of the American is his mobility. For this reason, even relatively new data is not foolproof. The wealth of available data can only aid judgment, not replace it.

Engel's so-called "Laws" are useful generalizations about consumption patterns. They help predict individual and family buying behavior. But the American consumer is different from Engel's workingman in a very important respect, namely, he is among the most affluent in the world, and this affluence affects his buying behavior. Beyond the necessities of life, he is able to buy a wide variety of products. In fact, it could be argued that little he buys is an absolute necessity.

This is extremely important to a marketing manager because it means that he must continually win target customers from the many choices open to them. It also means that consumers can delay their purchases for months or years, or shift them completely to more satisfying alternatives.

We saw that studying past consumer expenditure patterns can be very useful for estimating the market potential within market grids. We also saw that continual study of market behavior is necessary and that ultimately management judgment must be applied to interpret trends and evaluate data. Judgment is especially important because, in spite of all the population, income, and other data related to past expenditures which is available, we still are not always able to predict what consumers are going to do.

In fact, the kind of data we were studying in this chapter often does not fully explain actual customer behavior toward specific products. A fuller understanding of customer behavior may require more sophisticated and different kinds of analysis. More will be said on this in Chapter 8, where we discuss the decision-making behavior of individual consumers and of household groups. A knowledge of the American consumer's psychological and sociological makeup will help marketing men satisfy target customers more effectively and more often.

Questions and problems

1 Some socioeconomic characteristics are more important than others in determining market potential. For each of the following characteristics, identify two products for which this characteristic is *most* important: (*a*) size of geographic area, (*b*) population, (*c*) income, (*d*) stage of life cycle.

2 If a large new atomic research installation were being built in a formerly small and sleepy town, how could the local retailers use Engel's Laws in

planning for the influx of newcomers, first of construction crews and then scientists?

3 Name three specific examples (specific products or brands—not just product categories) illustrating how demand will differ by geographic location *and* market location, that is, with respect to size and location inside or outside a metropolitan market.

4 Explain how the continuing mobility of consumers as well as the development of "interurbia" areas should affect marketing strategy planning in the future. Be sure to consider the impact on the four P's.

5 Explain how the redistribution of income has affected marketing planning thus far and its likely impact in the future.

6 Explain why the concept of the Standard Metropolitan Statistical Area was developed. Would it be the most useful breakdown for retailers?

7 With the growing homogeneity of the consumer market, does this mean that the market grid idea is less useful? Do you feel that all consumers of about equal income will probably spend their incomes similarly and demand similar products?

8 Specify which kinds of consumers would be most likely to buy a new type comb selling for $1. Then estimate the number of potential customers. The factors which might be relevant in specifying the potential market are income, sex, stage in life cycle, and age. Use all of these factors which are relevant. State any assumptions you make and apply the data in the text.

9 If a recent college graduate is now earning between $10,000 and $15,000 a year before taxes, has some children under six, and is living in the western part of the United States in a surburban (urban fringe) area, how much would you expect him to be spending annually on (*a*) clothing and accessories, (*b*) transportation, (*c*) and housing and household operations? (Use the data in the text when developing your answer.)

Consumers:
international markets

$\mathbf{M}$ost Americans are proud of the United States' economic position in the world. This is understandable, for we are relatively rich and enjoy a high standard of living. But this viewpoint may have given us myopia regarding the economic state of the rest of the world.

We hear our politicians, for example, speak of exporting our "free enterprise system" to aid the "less developed countries" of the world, and we know that our government spends billions of dollars annually on foreign aid programs. It is only natural that many Americans think of foreign countries as poor, with little market potential. While this sometimes may be true, such thinking ignores the fact that there are many opportunities in international markets. Some foreign consumers already have high standards of living, and markets in many countries are growing, some very rapidly.

Importance of world markets to the United States

As a nation grows, its trade grows

All countries trade to some extent, since we live in an interdependent world. But it may surprise Americans to know that the United States is the largest exporter and importer of goods in the world. Even the United Kingdom, which has built its growth on trade, exports, and imports, has less than two thirds as much as the United States.

Figure 7–1 shows that all types of nations—whether large or small, wealthy or poor—engage in trade. This figure shows the percentage of total world trade accounted for by the major trading nations of the

130

Figure 7-1 Map of the world showing each country's proportion of total foreign trade

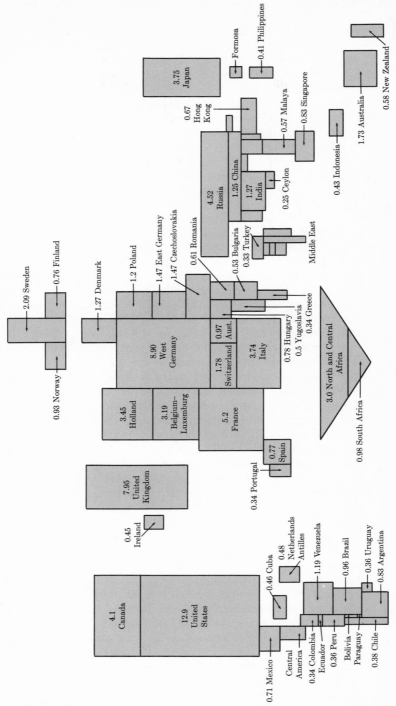

Source: *Clipper Cargo Horizons*, April, 1966. Drawn originally by Ing. G. Palacios Hardy.

world. It is easy to see that most of the largest traders are highly industrialized nations. Trade seems to expand, not contract, as a country grows and industrializes.

But while the United States is the biggest trading nation in the world, foreign trade does not dominate our economy. On a per capita basis, it is less important to us than it is to many other nations. This seeming paradox is explained by the larger size of our gross national product. Our foreign trade makes up a relatively smaller part of our GNP—less than 10 percent—but the smaller part is nevertheless greater in total dollars than in other major trading countries.

Favorable balance of trade supports government programs

This large volume of trade has been a distinct asset to America's foreign policy. U.S. exports since World War II have consistently been greater than imports, leading to a favorable balance of trade. The net gain from this surplus of exports over imports has been used primarily for foreign aid and the support of our troops in foreign countries.

"Balance of trade" should not be confused with "balance of payments," which includes capital movements, cash gifts, transportation, travel and military expenditures, among others. Our balance of payments has not always been as favorable as our balance of trade, in part because of the overseas commitments of our government. The balance-of-payments problem is a critical one for government planners because when the balance is negative, it must be settled in gold, and the U.S. gold supply has been dwindling rapidly.

In recent years, the government has attempted to control and restrict foreign trade and foreign investment for the purpose of compensating for its various commitments overseas which impair the balance of payments. These actions are just another one of the uncontrollable considerations that must be met by world enterprises.[1]

Many American manufacturers, seeing the growing opportunities, have developed a substantial stake in international markets. Companies such as Eastman Kodak, Pfizer, Caterpillar Tractor, International Harvester, Corn Products, 3M, Standard Oil, Mobil Oil, National Cash Register, Singer, Burroughs, Colgate-Palmolive, H. J. Heinz, Gillette, and others gain from 30 to 50 percent of their sales abroad. Some, as already noted, have come to think of themselves as worldwide operations and do not see foreign sales as a strange, separate entity.

Making exports where you sell them

At one time, foreign sales were handled by exporting domestic production—but increasingly, these worldwide companies are setting up factories and distribution facilities in other countries. Capital and technical know-how may be exported, but the actual production often is handled on the continent involved. Between 1960 and 1966, over 2,400 U.S. companies invested in about 7,000 separate global activities, primarily the construction of new plants or the expansion of existing operations.

In the long run, this investment in worldwide operations may cause some difficulties to U.S. government planners, because a smaller share

---

[1] "Stanching the Dollar Outflow," *Business Week,* July 3, 1965, pp. 38–41.

of GNP may be exported. In 1964, only one fifth of the worldwide sales by U.S. corporations were supplied by exporting domestic production. In the long run, the share may decline further, and there may be a narrowing of the favorable balance of trade. Nevertheless, the expansion continues, mostly in Canada and Western Europe.[2]

Some observers believe this continued growth, and merging of large companies, will create a relatively few supranational corporations that will dominate the world economy. It has been estimated, for example, that 300 corporations (not just U.S. companies) will control more than 75 percent of all industrial assets by 1975. **The Big Powers by 1975**

One of the reasons for the continued growth of world operations is the profit possibilities overseas. For example, the following companies have derived more than half of their *profit* from nondomestic sales: National Cash Register, Chesebrough-Ponds, Standard Oil of New Jersey, Mobil Oil, Singer, Burroughs, and Colgate-Palmolive.

U.S. companies are going worldwide, in part for profit but in part because they are almost compelled to do so. There are economic advantages to production specialization and then trade, and the only way to get along and improve your own and your country's welfare in our competitive world is to do business wherever you have some comparative advantage. We may not be "one world" politically as yet, but trading patterns are rapidly moving in that direction; the old cliché, "trade follows the flag," may have to be revised to "the flag follows trade." The recent dropping of world trade barriers following the "Kennedy Round" of negotiations (1967) is further evidence that the world political leaders are recognizing the economic interdependence of their economies. **Company planning must be global**

The complete blending of domestic and worldwide operations can be illustrated nicely with the Bell & Howell operation. This firm:

1. Imports and sells a full line of cameras from Japan.
2. Manufactures and sells a line of cameras in Japan.
3. Purchases low-cost components from Japan for assembly in the United States.
4. Exports low-cost U.S. cameras to any foreign market.[3]

Real growth opportunities exist for these global enterprises. One important reason is that the marketing concept has *not* spread as rapidly to the rest of the world. This gives American businessmen a head start. Catering to the world market puts an even greater burden on the marketing manager, but the opportunities are too great to ignore.

---

[2] "World Markets Are Still a Lure," *Business Week,* August 7, 1965, pp. 26–27; "U.S. Business in the New Europe," *Business Week,* May 7, 1966, pp. 94–120; "Big, Bigger, Biggest—American Business Goes Global," *New Republic,* April 30, 1966, pp. 14–18; "How to Profit in Foreign Markets," *Printers' Ink,* June 5, 1964, pp. 19 ff.; "Where the Cash Grows in Africa," *Business Week,* June 19, 1965, pp. 134–38; and "How Big Are Foreign Opportunities for Smaller U.S. Firms?" *Printers' Ink,* July 27, 1962, pp. 44–45.

[3] "How Big Are Foreign Opportunities for Smaller U.S. Firms?" *Printers' Ink,* July 27, 1962, pp. 44–45.

Phases of economic development

Not all markets are the same, whether domestic or foreign. Many foreign markets are much more advanced and/or growing more rapidly than others. Various countries are at different stages of economic development; this means their demands will vary and, in fact, even their marketing systems will vary. Let us look at these stages which, for convenience and clarity, we have divided into six phases.

Stage 1—Agricultural self-supporting phase

In this phase, most of the people exist as subsistence farmers. There may be a simple marketing system—perhaps occasional markets—but most of the people are not even in a money economy. Some parts of Africa and territories such as New Guinea are in this stage. In a practical marketing sense, these people do not represent a market, since they have no money income to purchase goods.

Stage 2—Preindustrial or commercial phase

Some of the countries in Sub-Sahara Africa and the Middle East are in this second stage. During this phase of economic development, we see more market-oriented activity. Raw materials such as oil, tin, and copper are extracted and exported. Agricultural and forest crops such as sugar, rubber, and timber are grown and harvested for the market and exported. Often this is done with the aid of foreign technical skill and capital. A commercial economy may develop along with, but unrelated to, the subsistence economy. These activities may require the beginnings of a transportation system to link the extracting or growing areas to shipping points. A money economy will be functioning at this stage.

There will be demands for imports of industrial machinery and equipment, and huge construction projects may require many specialized supplies. Buying for these needs may be handled by purchasing agents and engineers in industrial countries. There will be a need for imports, including luxury goods, to meet the needs and satisfy the tastes of the technical and supervisory personnel; these may be handled by company stores rather than local retailers.

The relatively few large landowners and those who benefit by this commercial activity may develop expensive tastes. The relatively few natives who are employed by these larger firms and the small businessmen who serve them may develop a small, middle-income class. But the majority of the population is still in the first phase, almost entirely outside the money economy and for practical purposes not in the market. This total market may be so small that local importers can easily handle the demand, with little incentive for local manufacturers to attempt to supply it.

Stage 3—Primary manufacturing phase

In the third stage, there is some processing of metal ores or the agricultural products that formerly were shipped out of the country in raw form. Sugar and rubber, for example, are both produced and processed in Indonesia, and the same is true for sisal in Tanganyika and oil on the Persian Gulf. More local labor becomes involved, and a domestic market develops. Even small businesses may be started to handle some of the processing or to service larger firms.

Even though the local market expands in this third stage, a large segment of the population is still at the subsistence level and almost entirely outside the money economy. There still may be a large foreign population of professionals and technicians essential to the developing agricultural-industrial complex. The demands of this group and of the growing number of wealthy natives are still quite different from the needs of the lower class and the growing middle class. A domestic market among the local citizenry begins to develop, but local manufacturers still may have difficulty finding enough demand to justify operation.

Stage 4—Nondurable and semi-durable consumer goods manufacturing phase

At this stage, small local manufacturing begins, especially in those lines requiring low capital investment relative to output. Often these industries are an outgrowth of small firms that developed to supply the primary manufacturers dominating the last phase. For example, plants making sulfuric acid and explosives for extracting mineral resources might expand into soap manufacturing.

Paint, drug, food and beverage, and textile industries develop in this phase. The textile industry is usually one of the first to develop. Clothing is a necessity, and the articles imported for the upper-income and foreign markets are too expensive for the majority of potential customers now entering the money economy. This early emphasis on the textile industry in developing nations is one reason the world textile market is so vigorously competitive.

Some of the small manufacturers become established members of the middle or even upper-income class, and help to expand the demand for imported goods. But as this market grows, local entrepreneurs begin to see sufficient volume to operate profitably. The heavy dependence on imports for nondurable and semidurable goods then declines, though consumer durables and capital goods are still imported.

Stage 5—Capital goods and consumer durable-goods manufacturing phase

In this phase, the production of capital goods and consumer durable goods begin. These classes of goods include automobiles, refrigerators, and machinery for local industries. Such manufacturing in turn creates other demands—raw materials for the local factories, and food and fibers for clothing for the rural population now coming into the industrial labor force.

Full-fledged industrialization has begun. But the economy is still heavily dependent upon exports of raw materials, either wholly unprocessed or slightly processed.

It still may be necessary to import specialized heavy machinery and equipment to build the capital facilities needed at this stage. There still may be imports of consumer durable goods in competition with the local products. The foreign community and the status-conscious wealthy still may prefer imports, and this demand can continue to provide an attractive market.

Stage 6—Exporting of manufactured products phase

Countries that have not progressed beyond the fifth phase are primarily engaged in exporting raw materials and in importing manufactured goods and equipment to build their industrial base. In the sixth stage, export of manufactured goods becomes dominant. The country may specialize in certain types of manufactured goods, such as iron and

135

steel, watches, cameras, electronic equipment, and processed food. Large countries (Germany or Japan are examples) may have many specialties.

The opportunities for importing and exporting are great, since these countries have grown more affluent and have needs (and the purchasing power) for a great variety of products. In fact, countries in this stage often carry on a great deal of trade with each other, each trading those goods in which they have production advantages. By this phase, almost all consumers are in the money economy, and there may be a large middle-income class. The United States and many Western European countries are at this last stage today.[4]

What these phases mean

A good starting point for evaluating the market potentials in a country is to estimate its present phase of economic development and whether and how fast it is moving to another stage. Actually, the speed of movement, if any, may be the most critical factor in whether market opportunities are there or are likely to open. But just identifying the country's present stage can be very useful in marketing strategy planning. Manufacturers of automobiles, expensive cameras, or other consumer durable goods, for example, should not plan to set up a mass distribution system in a country that is in the preindustrial (stage 2) or even primary manufacturing (stage 3) phase. The market would be too limited.

Among the foreign population and the wealthy landowners, nevertheless, there may be a small but very attractive market for luxury models. A simple distribution system with one or a few distributors may be quite adequate. The market for U.S. "necessities," however—items such as canned foods or drug products—may not yet be large. Large-scale selling of these consumer items depends on a large base of cash or credit customers, and as yet too few are part of the money economy.

On the other hand, a country in the nondurable-goods manufacturing phase becomes more attractive, especially for durable-goods producers. Incomes and the number of potential customers are growing, yet there is no domestic competition.

Opportunities still might be good for durable-goods imports in the next phase, while the domestic producers are attempting to get started. But more likely, the local governments would raise some restrictions to aid local industry. Then the foreign producer might have to move into licensing local producers or building a local plant.

Pursuing that attractive inverted pyramid

Countries in the final phase often will represent the biggest and most profitable markets. While there is admittedly greater competition, there are still many more customers with higher incomes. We have already

[4] This discussion is based on William Copulsky's, "Forecasting Sales in Underdeveloped Countries," *Journal of Marketing,* July, 1959, pp. 36–37; and *Aspects of Economic Development* (Freedom from Hunger Campaign Study No. 8 [United Nations, 1962]), pp. 4–7. Another set of stages is interesting although less marketing-oriented. See W. W. Rostow, *The Stages of Economic Growth—A Non-Communist Manifesto* (New York: Cambridge University Press, 1960).

136

seen how the income distribution shifted in the United States from a pyramid to a more equal distribution, with a large middle-income mass market. This kind of development, which can be expected during the latter phases, makes mass marketing increasingly attractive.

As incomes rise, we see expenditure patterns somewhat similar to our own. This can be seen developing in Western Europe, and it should not be surprising, since the original work on Engel's Laws was done in Europe. The mass market is growing fast in increasingly affluent Japan, too.[5]

Overview of world market dimensions

Markets, in the simplest of terms, are people with money and a willingness to spend. The market grid concept is even more applicable in world markets than in the American economy. This is because demands vary according to a country's stage of development and its potential for growth—as well as other economic, social, and cultural factors.

While an entire chapter has been devoted to the American consumer, it is clearly impossible to cover all the characteristics of all the world markets in this chapter. On the other hand, we cannot ignore either the potential or the problems in world markets, and we would be foolish to be content with the stereotypes and half-truths that circulate about "foreigners." Therefore, we will sketch some of the dimensions of world markets and suggest some of the problems of working in this larger business environment.

Data, yes, but not always the best

Unfortunately, data sources for some areas abroad are not as voluminous and the data is not as accurate as that available for the United States. The foreign data may be unsatisfactory in some cases because the countries where it is compiled do not have the resources or facilities for frequent compilation of information. Brazil, for instance, started to take a census in 1950 and ran out of funds before the work was completed.

The *Statistical Abstract* and the U.S. Department of Commerce Bureau of International Commerce would be a good place to start locating current data. In its publication, *International Commerce,* the Department of Commerce issues a semiannual checklist of material it feels will be helpful to businessmen interested in the world market. The *Statistical Year Book* of the Statistical Office of the United Nations is also a good source of basic data.

The number of people is staggering

Although you may be overwhelmed by the crowds of people you have to compete with in our urban areas, the 200 million population of the United States is less than 5 percent of the world's population of over 4 billion.

[5] "How the British React to Affluence," *Business Week,* January 19, 1963, p. 44; "Sweden Goes All Out for the Leisure Boom," *Business Week,* September 7, 1963, pp. 32–33; "Three Europes, One Boom," *Business Week,* September 10, 1966, pp. 116–38; "Young Italy Spends Big," *Business Week,* May 13, 1967, p. 184; "Vive Les Teen-Agers!" *Business Week,* November 23, 1963, p. 49; and "Consumer's Day Dawns in Land of Rising Sun," *Business Week,* May 21, 1964, pp. 129–36.

Sheer numbers are important. Rather than trying to show the specific population of various countries—and getting into tedious details—we will content ourselves with a map showing the area of each country in proportion to its population. Figure 7–2 reduces the United States to relative insignificance because of our relatively small population in relation to land area. The same is true of Latin America and Africa. In

Figure 7–2 Map of the world showing area in proportion to population

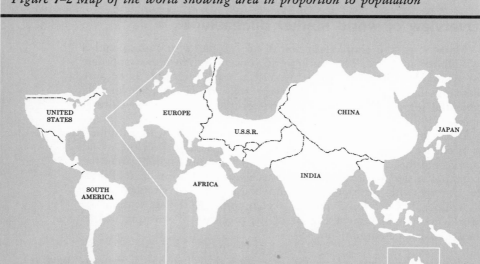

contrast, Western Europe is considerably larger than it is usually shown, and the Far Eastern countries are even bigger.

But people are not spread out evenly. As we saw in Chapter 6, there is a worldwide move off the farm and into industrialized and urbanized areas. These shifts, combined with an already dense population, have led to extreme crowding in some parts of the world.

Figure 7–3 shows a map of the world emphasizing density of population. The darkest shading indicates areas with more than 250 persons per square mile. Actually, density in these dark areas often far exceeds 250. For example, in 1956, New York State had a density of 303 persons per square mile; Massachusetts, a density of 638 persons per square mile; Belgium, 753; the United Kingdom, 541; and Germany, 528.[6]

The developing interurbias in the United States show up clearly as densely populated areas. Similar areas are found in Western Europe, along the Nile River valley in Egypt, and in many parts of Asia. In

---

[6] *The European Market* (New York: Publicus, 1958), pp. 17–20.

Figure 7-3 Map of the world emphasizing density of population

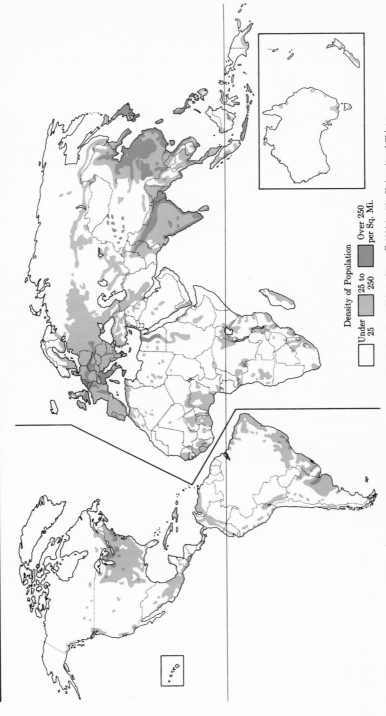

Density of Population

Under 25

25 to 250

Over 250 per Sq. Mi.

Adapted from *Atlas of Economic Development* by Norton Ginsburg by permission of The University of Chicago Press. © 1961 by The University of Chicago.

contrast, many parts of the world, like our western plains and mountain states, are sparsely populated.

Your own knowledge of the United States should help you avoid misreading a population density map. There are cities throughout the world, just as in the sparsely populated western United States, that are important markets even though they are surrounded by sparsely populated areas. Such cities may be extremely important as markets if they serve as trading centers for a large region. Still, for locating large numbers of people, population density maps are invaluable.

Population densities are likely to increase in the foreseeable future. Birth rates in most parts of the world are high (higher in Africa, Latin America, Asia, and Oceania than in the United States), and death rates are declining as modern medicine is more widely accepted. Generally, population growth is expected in most countries, but the big questions are, *How rapidly?*, and *Will output increase faster than population?* This has great relevance for marketing men because it has a bearing on how rapidly some economies evolve to higher stages of development and the kinds of goods that consumers will have the income to buy.

You must sell where the income is

Profitable markets require income as well as people. The best available measure of income in most countries is gross national product. Unfortunately, this may understate consumer well-being in many countries because the methods commonly used for calculating GNP may not be directly comparable for widely different cultures and economies. For instance, do-it-yourself activities, household services, and growing produce or meat by family members for their own consumption are not normally calculated as part of GNP. Since the activities of self-sufficient family units are not included, GNP can greatly underestimate economic well-being in less developed countries. The expenditures on fuel, heavier clothing, and more substantial housing needed in temperate climates add to GNP, yet no offsetting adjustment is made in tropical countries where such expenditures are not necessary and where the income available for other spending, therefore, is accordingly higher. Such expenditures may absorb 10 to 15 percent of consumer income in temperate climates.[7]

Gross national product, nevertheless, is a useful and sometimes the only available measure of market potential in many countries. Table 7–1 shows the population and total GNP of major regions of the world, except the Soviet bloc countries and mainland China. It is quite clear that the more developed industrial regions have the lion's share of the world's GNP. This is why so much trade takes place between these countries, and why they are viewed by many companies as the more important markets.

Income per capita may be more revealing

Since individuals and families rather than whole countries are buyers, it may be more revealing to consider GNP per capita. This is a commonly available figure—though it must be used with care. When

[7] Carl F. Shoup, *Principles of National Income Analysis* (New York: Houghton Mifflin Co., 1947), p. 13.

140

GNP per capita is used for comparison, we assume that the wealth of each country is distributed evenly among all consumers. However, this usually is not true, as we noted earlier. In relatively underdeveloped South Vietnam, for example, 75 percent of the population is supported by agriculture, but these people obtain only 24 percent of the income of the country. The annual income per capita in the late 1950's was somewhere between $50 and $70 (U.S.), but many city dwellers in Saigon had incomes of about $500 (U.S.) a year. This unequal division of income between rural and urban families is common in Asia, the Middle East, Africa, and Latin America as well.[8]

Still, care must be exercised in assuming that the urban market is the best market. In tropical Africa, it is estimated that the extremely large population in the rural villages spends more in *total* than the relatively few but more prosperous consumers in the urban centers. Equally

Purchasing power is where you find it

Table 7–1 Population and gross national product of major geographical regions of world* (in 1965 prices)

Region	Population (Millions)	Percent	GNP ($ millions)	Percent
North America	217.2	10	732,568	45
Latin America	235.6	11	90,926	6
Western Europe	354.4	16	508,437	32
Near East	88.5	4	23,304	1
South Asia	642.1	29	64,059	4
Far East	373.7	17	120,257	7
Oceania	17.5	1	28,722	2
Africa	264.3	12	40,637	3
	2,193.3	100	1,608,910	100

* Except Soviet bloc countries and mainland China.
SOURCE: Reprinted with permission from the June 26, 1967, issue of *Advertising Age*. Copyright 1967 by Advertising Publications Inc.

important, these two quite different markets have different demands.[9] The urban consumers, for instance, are more interested in imported "luxuries." Obviously the market grid concept is needed here.

Income is not distributed equally *within* cities, either. For instance, a 1954 survey in Beirut, Lebanon, showed that only 30 percent of the estimated 35,000 native families had incomes exceeding $1,500 (U.S.) a year, the amount considered necessary to maintain a minimum standard of living. Only 4 percent of these families had incomes exceeding $8,000 (U.S.).

[8] Richard W. Lindholm, "An Economic-Development-Oriented Land Reform Program for Viet Nam," in Walter Froehlich, *Land Tenure, Industrialization, and Social Stability* (Milwaukee, Wis.: Marquette University Press, 1961), pp. 181–82.
[9] Edward Marcus, "Selling the Tropical African Market," *Journal of Marketing*, July, 1961, p. 27.

Even further up the income scale in such cities, we usually find numerous foreigners. For example, there were an estimated 2,500 Americans living in Beirut.[10] We already noted that an entirely different way of life may exist in foreign communities. Sometimes these "compounds" are supplied through company stores or purchasing facilities, but in other cases local marketing units develop to serve these obviously different customers. The point is that their incomes help raise GNP estimates in a given nation and may give a false picture of the buying power of the masses in that nation.

To provide some bench marks, the GNP per capita of a variety of countries is presented in Table 7–2. The range is wide, from $41 U.S. per capita per year in Malawi to $3,501 in the United States.

The average world GNP per capita is $733, excluding consideration of Soviet bloc countries and mainland China, for which comparable data is even less reliable.

In the upper income levels are the United States and Canada, most of Western Europe, Australia, and New Zealand. Near the bottom are most of Asia and the Far East, the Near Eastern countries and a few Latin American countries, though most of Latin America lies at a considerably higher level than most of Asia and Africa. And Japan, while coming up rapidly, lies just above the world's mean.

A business opportunity and a human opportunity

These data indicate that a large share of the world's population lives in extreme poverty. Many of these countries are in the early phases of economic development, with large parts of their population engaged in agriculture and perhaps living only barely within the money economy. More than one half of the world's active population is engaged in agricultural occupations, and these occupations typically bring only a small monetary return.[11]

These people, however, have needs, and many exposed to Western ways are now anxious to better themselves. But they may not be able to raise their living standards without outside help. This presents a challenge and an opportunity to the industrialized nations and their business firms. There may be many opportunities for investments in basic industries, as well as the marketing and transportation facilities that are needed in a modern nation. As we noted in Chapter 1, marketing institutions can speed economic development by helping to expand markets and develop opportunities for local producers.

Reading, writing, and marketing problems

The ability of a country's people to read and write has a direct bearing on the development of the economy and on the marketing strategy planning of a firm planning to do business there. One research study showed the link between the literacy of a country's population and its economic development.[12] Certainly the degree of literacy affects

---

[10] Charles F. Stewart, "The Changing Middle East Market," *Journal of Marketing,* January, 1961, pp. 47–49.

[11] Norton Ginsberg, *Atlas of Economic Development* (Chicago: University of Chicago Press, 1961).

[12] The Indians in Latin America do not speak Spanish, for example, and as a result are more or less blocked from entering the money economy. See Douglas F. Lamont, "A Theory of Marketing Development: Mexico" (unpublished Ph. D. dissertation, University of Alabama, 1964).

Table 7–2 Gross national product per capita for major
regions of world* and selected countries
(in 1965 U.S. dollars)
and population (in millions in 1965)

	GNP/Capita for Countries	GNP/Capita for Regions	Population
North America		$3,372	217.2
United States	$3,501		194.6
Canada	2,451		19.6
Latin America		386	235.6
Argentina	718		22.4
Brazil	270		81.5
Haiti	70		4.7
Mexico	455		42.7
Western Europe		1,435	354.4
United Kingdom	1,817		54.6
France	1,910		48.9
Italy	1,100		51.6
Portugal	407		9.2
Sweden	2,498		7.7
Turkey	261		31.1
Near East		263	88.5
Israel	1,325		2.6
Egypt	160		29.3
South Asia		100	642.1
India	101		489.6
Far East		322	373.7
Indonesia	100		104.5
Japan	863		98.0
Philippines	161		32.3
Oceania		1,641	17.5
Australia	1,980		11.5
Africa (exc. Egypt)		154	264.3
Algeria	225		11.7
Ethiopia	58		20.2
Ghana	285		7.7
Kenya	90		9.4
Malawi	41		4.0
Nigeria	114		42.7
South Africa	532		20.1

* Except Soviet bloc countries and mainland China.
SOURCE: Reprinted with permission from the June 26, 1967, issue of *Advertising Age.*
Copyright 1967 by Advertising Publications Inc.

the communication of information—which in a marketing context means promotion.

An extensive analysis of literacy data in 136 countries showed that only 56 percent of the world's population is literate.[13] But this number must be interpreted with care. Most such data are based on census materials that were compiled by asking the question, "Can you read and write?" A simple yes, as a second-grader might answer, would not indicate a person's literacy level.

The low literacy rates in some countries indicate that a large-scale,

---

[13] Ginsberg, *op. cit.*

basic, and expensive educational task faces these nations. Generally, there is a band of countries with low literacy rates extending from Latin America through Africa and the Near East to eastern Asia. At the other extreme, higher rates of literacy are found in Australia, Canada, United States, Western Europe, the Soviet bloc of Europe and some Latin American countries.

Forty percent of the 136 countries for which data was available have literacy rates above the mean of 56 percent. These countries include almost the same percentage of the world's population. On the negative side, however, 43 percent of the countries have literacy rates of 25 percent or less—and they account for 31 percent of the world's population.

Beat the drums, draw a picture

To compound marketing difficulties, some of these countries are multilingual. For example, the low literacy in India—only 15 percent of the population is literate—makes national advertising as we know it practically impossible. Further, there are 51 dialects in India, and no single language is used by more than 50 million persons.[14]

Some imaginative Indian merchants hire "drummers" who walk through the streets beating a drum to get attention and stop periodically to give the merchant's message in the local dialect. Clothing merchants, for example, use a drummer when they receive a new shipment of goods or offer special price concessions.

Low literacy sometimes causes difficulties with product labels and with instructions for which we normally use words. In highly illiterate Africa, some manufacturers have found that placing a baby's picture on food packages is unwise, since illiterate natives believe that the product is just that—a ground-up baby! Singer Sewing Machine Co., met this lack of literacy with an instruction book which used no words.[15]

Even in Latin America, which has generally higher literacy rates than Africa or Asia, a substantial proportion of the population cannot read and write. Promotional programs have to use symbols, colors, and other nonverbal means of communication if they wish to reach the mass market.

Perhaps two promotional campaigns could be used—one for the literate and one for the illiterate. But even where the literacy rate supposedly is high, considerable care must be exercised. Literacy often means only that one can read and write *simple* ideas. So it may be nearly as effective to develop one campaign for the illiterate, assuming that the literate are really not *very* literate.

New economic and geographic configurations

Some countries have a long way to go to achieve the high living standards we enjoy. But it also is obvious that dynamic and energetic people frequently have overcome natural obstacles and achieved much higher living standards. The Japanese economic miracle certainly at-

[14] Ralph Westfall and Harper W. Boyd, Jr., "Marketing in India," *Journal of Marketing,* October, 1960, p. 15.
[15] Edward Marcus, "Selling the Tropical African Market," *Journal of Marketing,* July, 1961, p. 30.

tests to the possibility of rapid growth without benefit of generous supplies of fertile land or natural resources.[16]

We also see nations banding together in cooperative groups to speed their mutual development. They have dared to abandon old ideas and nationalistic prejudices in favor of cooperative efforts to reduce tariffs and other restrictive arrangements.

Tariffs—taxes on incoming goods—vary, depending on whether the country is attempting to raise revenue or restrict trade. Restrictive tariffs often block all movement, but even revenue-producing tariffs lead to red tape and discourage free movement of goods such as we have within the United States.

Let us look at some of these economic arrangements, because they should be considered in any market grid analysis of worldwide markets. Where older arrangements have been superseded by broader organizations, it is important to realize the depth and strength of this cooperative effort in appraising the present situation.

Benelux. *Be*lgium, The *N*etherlands, and *Lux*embourg created the Benelux Customs Union in 1944. The participating countries formed a common market among themselves, abolished internal tariffs, and faced the world with a common tariff system.

GATT. Until 1948, not only the Benelux group but also most of the countries in the world made bilateral arrangements on trade. Perhaps we can say that Benelux showed the way. In any case, most of the nations of the free world accepted the idea of multilateral negotiations. In 1948, they signed the *G*eneral *A*greement for *T*ariffs *T*rade (GATT). They agreed to meet every two years and negotiate for reductions in tariffs. This organization is still continuing, and through six major negotiation conferences has been very effective in lowering tariffs and encouraging greater trade. In 1967, the Kennedy Round of negotiations resulted in substantial reductions in tariffs.

This multilateral bargaining is especially important because most of the major trading nations use the "most-favored-nation" clause, which says that a significant tariff reduction offered to one nation immediately will be offered to all participating nations.

OEEC and OECD. Benelux specifically showed the way to breaking down trade barriers in Europe. In 1948, 17 European nations signed the Convention for European Economic Cooperation, forming the Organization for European Economic Cooperation (OEEC). This group of nations agreed to work toward a common solution of their economic problems while retaining full national sovereignty.

In 1960, OEEC evolved into OECD (Organization for Economic Cooperation and Development). This organization now includes not only 18 European countries as full members, but also Japan, Canada, and the United States. This is a consultant agency only, however, and has no binding power over its members.[17]

---

[16] "Can Japan Maintain the Pace?" *Business Week,* December 19, 1964, pp. 71–82; and "Exports Spur Japan's Economy," *Clipper Cargo Horizons,* August, 1966, pp. 2–6.

[17] W. A. Hoellige, "International Business and OECD," *National Trade Review,* February, 1965, pp. 9–12.

Coal and Steel Community. The first supranational economic institution developed in 1952 when Belgium, France, Germany, Italy, Luxembourg, and The Netherlands signed the Coal and Steel Community Pact. In this agreement, some national sovereignty was surrendered to the higher body for the purpose of establishing a free market for iron ore, steel scrap, coal, and steel.

The goal of the Coal and Steel Community was the development of a regional, rather than national, pattern for the production and distribution of these products. Since none of these countries was self-sufficient in the production of steel, the agreement made considerable sense. It showed that economic integration, even without political integration, was possible when it was logical and when it was sought by the countries involved.

The six nations in the Coal and Steel Community remained part of the OEEC, but were willing to go further than most of the members of that organization—to the extent of sacrificing some national sovereignty.

European Economic Community. As a result of the smooth functioning of the Coal and Steel Community, these same six nations met in Rome in 1957 to sign a treaty establishing a European Economic Community (EEC) and a European Atomic Energy Community. They were, in effect, applying the concept behind the Coal and Steel Community to their entire economic life. These six nations formed the nucleus of the European Common Market.

By the middle 1960's, it was obvious that this large free-trade market was breaking down old nationalistic and restrictionist attitudes, expanding employment and investment, reducing prices, and generally helping to raise the standard of living in these communities. So impressive are the advances made by the Common Market nations that a number of other nations are applying for or considering membership in the Common Market.

European Free Trade Association. Not all the original members of the OEEC, however, were willing to go this far toward political union. They were willing to cooperate and did not want to be left out completely, but still wished to retain control of their individual economies. Seven of these nations (Great Britain, Norway, Sweden, Denmark, Portugal, Switzerland, and Austria) organized a partially integrated economic organization in 1959. It was named the European Free Trade Association (EFTA). This group is working toward a reduction, and gradual elimination of tariffs and other restrictive measures among its members, but it does not have common external tariffs, as does the EEC. Prior arrangements not directly affecting all the member countries were permitted to continue. For example, the Imperial Preference System used in the British Commonwealth is still permissible within EFTA.

As of this writing, Britain is seeking to join the Common Market, perhaps modifying or even relinquishing its Commonwealth ties. If this occurs, it will be a significant economic change. Great Britain has long been an importer of raw materials from Commonwealth countries

146

and an exporter of finished manufactures. Modification or elimination of the Commonwealth system would have a profound influence on Commonwealth members, especially Canada, New Zealand, and Australia, who may be forced to seek new markets and sources of goods.[18]

Latin American Free Trade Association and Central American Common Market. Organizations akin to the European Common Market also have developed in Latin America, where two groups have been formed. The Latin American Free Trade Association (LAFTA) was formed in 1960 and included Argentina, Brazil, Chile, Mexico, Paraguay, Peru, Uruguay, and later, Colombia and Ecuador. The second group, also formed in 1960, is known as the Central American Common Market and consists of El Salvador, Guatemala, Honduras, Nicaragua, and later, Costa Rica.[19]

The success of the European Common Market bodes well for the future. Such a venture may not be a panacea for all economic ills, but it has proved itself in its early years, and it should continue to foster economic growth in the future. It probably will encourage other cooperative arrangements as well, and long-range marketing plans should include the possibility of such developments.

Market grid concept vital

The opportunities in international marketing are exciting ones, but the diversity presents a real challenge to marketing management. Obviously the market grid concept should find special application when a firm is planning to serve these markets.

The grid concept is especially important because often there are subtleties that we would not pick up unless we were aggressively seeking all the possibilities. Our nearby neighbor, Canada, affords an excellent example.

Some Americans think of Canada only as our northern neighbor which is very much similar to us. Actually, however, the province of Quebec, which includes 29 percent of Canada's population, is a unique market. Quebec is predominantly French in heritage and language. The French-Canadians of Quebec feel they have suffered at the hands of the English-speaking majority of Canada. There is even a movement for the secession of Quebec and its establishment as a separate nation. This attitude finds its expression in the marketplace, where French Canadians support local producers, buying their goods in preference to those of firms from other parts of Canada or from Great Britain, or the United States.

Canadians are different

---

[18] This discussion is based upon George Donat and Lawrence Dowd, "Formation of the European Economic Community," in Lawrence P. Dowd, *The European Economic Community* (Michigan Business Reports No. 36 [Ann Arbor: Bureau of Business Research, University of Michigan, 1961]), pp. 1–12. See also, "In Europe, Economic Unity Becomes a Fact," *Business Week,* December 31, 1966, pp. 52–54.

[19] "Why Central America Moves to a Faster Beat," *Business Week,* September 11, 1965, pp. 114–23; "Central America Closes Ranks," *Business Week,* March 16, 1963, pp. 47–52; and "Adios to Latin Tariff Barriers," *Business Week,* June 9, 1962, pp. 78–80.

The differences between the other Canadian provinces and the United States are less extreme. Even so, recent elections have shown there is considerable anti-U.S. feeling in Canada, caused by U.S. domination of the Canadian market in some industries. These differences in outlook, sometimes verging on hostility, must be given full consideration in market planning.[20]

If the French Canadians are individualistic, so are the French, and this national characteristic must be considered in marketing planning for sales in France. A sales slogan such as "Everybody's buying it" might cause sales of a product to drop in France, even though similar slogans might be successful in the United States.

What are you drinking?

Tastes differ across national boundaries. French Burgundy wine intended for Belgian export must have a higher sugar content than the Burgundy intended for consumption in France. Burgundy shipped to Sweden must have still another sugar concentration to be sold successfully there.

Even close neighbors in Europe have very different drinking habits. The average Frenchman in 1951, a fairly typical year, drank 137 quarts of wine and only 19 quarts of beer. In contrast, his Belgian neighbor drank 115 quarts of beer and only 9 quarts of wine. Coca-Cola has made such inroads in Spain that the Spanish wine producers have felt compelled to launch a rather defensive national campaign imploring Spaniards to "drink 10 percent more wine."[21]

Milk-drinking habits also differ substantially. Scandinavians consider milk a daily staple, while Latins feel that milk is only for children. A former French premier, Mendès-France, was able to get his picture on the front page of every Paris newspaper simply by drinking a glass of milk in public. Milk consumption figures are revealing. The Italians use 117 pounds per capita a year, while the French use 195.5 pounds, Americans 352 pounds, Swedes 487, and Norwegians 516 pounds per capita.[22]

Up with skirts, out of the cafe

The youth market seems to be of growing importance throughout Europe and the world. It is the young who have adopted the "Mod look" in London, but the impact of youth goes far wider and deeper than a current style in clothing. The youth of the world are no longer placidly accepting traditional values and behavior patterns.

The impact of television is also quite significant, because now more people can learn more quickly about how others are living. Many European consumers, especially the younger ones, are becoming much more interested in style and are willing to discard things much sooner than their parents and grandparents.[23] Even the classic French cafe seems to be losing out to the living room television and the kitchen

---

[20] "Canada: New Boom, New Outlook," *Printers' Ink,* June 26, 1964, pp. 25–39; and "Canada: Growth and Headaches for the U.S. Marketing Man," *Printers' Ink,* May 11, 1962, pp. 21–32.

[21] "Three Europes, One Boom," *Business Week,* September 10, 1966, pp. 116–38.

[22] *The European Common Market* (Paris: Publicis S.A., 1958), pp. 21–22.

[23] "Three Europes, One Boom," *Business Week,* September 10, 1966, pp. 116–38.

refrigerator, in which the Parisian can keep his wine, ice, and mixers so that he can serve his friends in newfound elegance.[24]

Such diversity demands marketing research to ascertain the habits and preferences of the many market grid boxes. Prejudices and stereotypes will not do. The African market, for example, is not interested only in beads, trinkets, and beer, as suggested in some movies. Africans may not buy as much as others per capita, but they are extremely sophisticated and fussy about what they do buy.

Who wears the makeup in France?

The purchase of a fez—only a brimless, red, conical cap to most Americans—justifies considerable shopping by an African. He will distinguish among the many shapes and color shadings, as well as the thickness and type of material and the extent and composition of the embroidery. He may have a strong loyalty to a brand that has proved satisfactory.[25]

The need for continuing marketing research perhaps can be dramatized even more by the following results from a large-scale survey of European Common Market adults:

The average Frenchman uses almost twice as many cosmetics and beauty aids as does his wife.

The Germans and the French eat more spaghetti than the Italians.

French and Italian housewives are not as interested in cooking as their counterparts in Luxembourg and Belgium.[26]

Conclusion

The international market is large and growing in population and income. New economic groupings such as the European Common Market are being developed in the hope of expanding output and incomes even more. Many American companies are becoming aware of the enormous opportunities open to alert and aggressive businessmen.

The great variations in phases of economic development, income, population, literacy, and other factors, however, mean that foreign markets must be treated as many separate little target markets—and each studied carefully. Lumping foreign nations together under the common and vague heading of "foreigners" or, at the other extreme, assuming that they are just like U.S. customers, is almost a guarantee of failure. So is treating them like common movie sterotypes. It is clear that marketing management, marketing research, and the market grid concept all can play a significant role in international marketing.

Much of what we will discover about American marketing in subsequent chapters will also apply in the world market. Actually, not too many adjustments are necessary to sell to the world market—*except* to realize that the all-important customers may behave differently from

---

[24] *Time,* March 31, 1967, p. 33.

[25] Edward Marcus, "Selling the Tropical African Market," *Journal of Marketing,* July, 1961, p. 27.

[26] Robert L. Brown, "The Common Market: What Its New Consumer Is Like," *Printers' Ink,* May 31, 1963, pp. 23–25.

what we would expect or hope. They may require different marketing mixes. And marketing research may be needed to avoid errors.

The major stumbling block to success in international markets is an unwillingness to learn about and adjust to different peoples and cultures. To those who are willing to make these adjustments, the returns can be great.

Questions and problems

1 Discuss the importance of the size of a country's population on its (*a*) phase of economic development and (*b*) the volume of its foreign trade.

2 Discuss the value of gross national product per capita as a measure of market potential. Refer to specific data in your answer.

3 Discuss the prospects for a Latin American entrepreneur who is considering building a factory to produce machines which would manufacture cans for the food industry. His country happens to be in stage 4—the nondurable and semidurable consumer goods manufacturing phase. The country's population is approximately 20 million and there is some possibility of establishing sales contacts in a few nearby countries.

4 Discuss the possibility of an international marketer using essentially the same promotion campaign in the United States and in many international markets.

5 Evaluate the growth of "common markets" in relation to the phases of economic development of the members. Is this basically a movement among the underdeveloped countries which are seeking to "catch up"?

6 Discuss the kinds of products which you feel may become popular in Europe in the near future. Does the material on U.S. consumption behavior discussed in the last chapter have any relevance here?

7 Discuss the probable importance of the market grid concept within the European Common Market.

Consumers:
a behavioral science
view

Basic data on population, income, and consumer expenditure patterns in U.S. and international markets was presented in the last two chapters. With such data, it is possible to predict aggregate trends in consumer expenditure patterns.

But how can marketing management predict which of a given group of products will be purchased by consumers? For what reasons? In what quantities?

Unfortunately, when many firms are selling similar products, the traditional socioeconomic analysis we discussed in the last two chapters is of relatively little value in predicting which *products* and *brands* will be purchased. Yet whether its products and brands will be chosen, and to what extent, are extremely important to a firm.

To find better answers, we must better understand people. Many marketing analysts have turned to psychology, sociology, and the other disciplines that study human behavior. The approaches and the thinking in these behavioral sciences are the topic of this chapter.

The behavioral science approach

Our primary emphasis will be on psychology, sociology, and social psychology. Psychology is the study of *individual behavior*. Sociology is primarily concerned with the *behavior of groups*.[1] and social psychology is concerned with the *behavior of individuals as affected by groups*. Anthropology is also concerned with man—usually in the primitive

---

[1] For more details, see Christen T. Jonassen, "Contributions of Sociology to Marketing," *Journal of Marketing*, October, 1959, pp. 29–35.

state—but it, too, has something to offer to our understanding of how to bring consumers the goods they want and need.[2]

At the outset, we should be realistic about the prospects for fully understanding people and why they like, choose, buy, and use the products they do. The behavioral sciences are still at a relatively primitive stage, and their areas of interest overlap only occasionally with that of marketing. No discipline can give us one theory to explain all human behavior, and in fact, prominent men in the same disciplines often disagree among themselves. Each discipline, nevertheless, can offer some insights and frameworks that may prove useful.[3] Our job in marketing is to combine the various approaches and apply them, when relevant, to marketing management.[4]

Why a person buys products

Needs lead to wants and perhaps · · · Purchase behavior

Psychologists generally agree that people have *needs* and *wants*. Some needs are physiological—that is, they have to do with the person's physical body. Other needs are psychological or sociological or cultural—they are concerned with the individual's view of himself and his relationships to others. Wants are less basic; these are learned during the course of the individual's life.

When a need or a want is not satisfied, it leads to a *drive*. The food need, for instance, leads to a hunger drive. The drive state is one of tension in which the individual tries to find ways of satisfying his drive. Drives are, in effect, the reasons or "motives" underlying certain behavior patterns. The drive tensions lead to behavior that will satisfy the need or want and thereby reduce the drive tension.

Needs— learned or innate?

Trying to separate learned from unlearned needs is not very fruitful, and we will not try to do so here. But brief consideration of the idea is desirable because some critics feel that marketing has created and warped needs.

It might be argued that all *basic* needs are innate in humans. A small child develops strong desires for "things," certainly before advertisers have had a chance to influence him. Similarly, it is hard to believe that a small girl has "learned" all the feminine wiles she displays at the age of one and two.

Even the need for status, which some marketing critics feel is related to the influence of advertising, is found among animals and in human societies where there is no such influence. Studies of birds show that there is a definite pecking order in flocks. In a study of jackdaws, for

---

[2] Charles Winnick, "Anthropology's Contribution to Marketing," *Journal of Marketing*, July, 1961, pp. 53–60.

[3] Louis C. Wagner, "What Responding Behavioral Scientists Feel Their Disciplines Could Contribute to Certain Specialized Areas of Advertising," in William M. Stevens, *The Social Responsibilities of Marketing, Proceedings of the American Marketing Association, 1962.*

[4] William Lazer and Eugene J. Kelley, "Interdisciplinary Horizons in Marketing," *Journal of Marketing*, October, 1960, pp. 24–30. For a summary of current knowledge, see G. Steiner and B. Berelson, *Human Behavior: An Inventory of Scientific Findings* (New York: Harcourt, Brace & World, Inc., 1964).

instance, it was found that the female, upon mating, acquires the status of her mate.[5] In the human realm, African villagers raise domesticated cattle and goats purely as signs of wealth and social status. For food, they hunt wild animals.[6]

When the human baby is born, his needs are simple. But as he grows, he learns various and complex behavior patterns to satisfy the drives stemming from these needs. As needs become more sophisticated and specific, they may be called wants. The need for food, for instance, may lead to many specific food wants, depending on the experience of the person. The resulting hunger drive may only be satisfied by the specific food desired. The people of Western nations find beef attractive, and children learn to like it. In India, however, Hindus regard the cow as sacred and will not eat beef. Hindu children learn to eat and like other foods. Many foods, in other words, can satisfy the hunger drive—but in a particular culture, an individual might *want* a hamburger, and the hunger drive might not be fully satisfied until he had eaten one.

Liking hamburger is learned behavior

Since wants and behavior patterns are learned, it is here that marketing may have an impact. Marketing can offer many items to satisfy the consumer; it is then up to the consumer to decide what is best for *him*.

Psychologists studying the learning process have isolated a number of steps in the process. They see a drive as a strong stimulus that motivates the individual to some *response,* in an effort to satisfy the drive. The specific response chosen depends on the *cues* existing in the environment, and *reinforcement* occurs when the response is followed by a reduction in the drive tension.

The hunger drive might be satisfied by a McDonald hamburger (response) if the person happened to be driving around and saw a McDonald's sign along the highway (cue). If the experience was satisfactory, this would be the *reinforcement,* and he might be quicker to satisfy this drive in the same way in the future.

Reinforcement strengthens the relationship between the cue and the response and may lead to a similar response the next time the drive occurs. Repeated reinforcement obviously would lead to the development of a habit. To the marketing manager, this underlines the importance of developing good products which *also* live up to the promises of the firm's advertising.[7]

Some schools of thought in psychology make distinctions between motives and drives.[8] Others dismiss motives as far too simple an

Who are you and what do you want?

[5] Robert Ardrey, *African Genesis* (New York: Atheneum Publishers, 1961), chap. iv.

[6] *U.S. News and World Report,* September 25, 1961, p. 78.

[7] Gerald Zaltman, *Marketing: Contributions from the Behavioral Sciences* (New York: Harcourt Brace & World, Inc., 1965), pp. 20–21.

[8] Clifford T. Morgan, *Introduction to Psychology* (2d ed.; New York: McGraw-Hill Book Co., 1961), chap. iii; Ernest R. Hilgart, *Introduction to Psychology* (New York: Harcourt, Brace & Co., 1953), chaps. v–vi; Norman L. Munn, *Psychology—The Fundamentals of Human Adjustment* (2d ed.; Boston: Houghton Mifflin Co., 1951), chaps. x–xii; and S. H. Britt, *Social Psychology of Modern Life* (rev. ed.; New York: Rinehart & Co., Inc., 1949), chaps. vi–vii.

explanation of consumer behavior. They feel that a person may have several motives for buying as he does, and they see him attempting to develop a balance between the forces driving him.[9]

Other psychologists attempt to arrange motives in a hierarchy according to their strength. This approach sees consumers attempting to satisfy certain needs before others, although they may be willing to satisfy the highest priority ones only partially before going on to others.[10] Food may have a high priority, but not all the expenditures will go for food. After some food has been assured, monies may be allocated to satisfy urgent needs for clothing, housing, and medical care.

Still other psychologists are concerned with the self-image concept. They see consumers as having several selves: the way you are, the way you see yourself, the way you would like to be, and the way you think others see you. In their view, consumers are continually trying to develop a better self-image, and it is obvious that any products or services, such as a new car or suit, or a new hair-do, that help achieve this goal might be attractive.[11]

The many motives for eating a hamburger

From a marketing standpoint, there are several problems here. Not all these psychological theories have been thoroughly tested, nor are they compatible with each other. Furthermore, as mentioned earlier, psychology tends to focus on the individual—while marketing often must be concerned with groups. Although a particular psychological theory might be more helpful than another in explaining a particular consumer's behavior, another theory might be needed for his neighbor.

Sorting all of this out might require more marketing research than the average firm would want to undertake. A more practical approach is to try to keep the various theories and approaches in mind when evaluating potential customer behavior, thus avoiding the dogmatism of only one approach.

In the following pages, we are going to discuss a list of motives that glosses over some of the distinctions between the psychological theories discussed above. In fact, we are going to lump together needs, wants, and drives, and call them all *motives—the reasons why people buy.* This is crude but practical.

Some advertising agencies use checklists of hundreds of motives. Our list of motives is a marketing man's approach to considering the reasons why consumers behave the way they do. It is not an all-inclusive list that explains all behavior, but rather a list to stimulate thinking about the various reasons why people behave the way they do.[12] Several motives may be operative at the same time, perhaps in a

---

[9] See the literature on cognitive dissonance: L. Festinger, *A Theory of Cognitive Dissonance* (Evanston, Ill.: Row, Peterson & Co., 1957); Bruce C. Straits, "The Pursuit of the Dissonant Consumer," *Journal of Marketing*, July, 1964, pp. 62–66; James F. Engel, "Further Pursuit of the Dissonant Consumer: A Comment," *Journal of Marketing*, April, 1965, pp. 33–34; and Robert J. Holloway, "An Experiment on Consumer Dissonance," *Journal of Marketing*, January, 1967, pp. 39–43.

[10] John Douglas, George A. Field, and Lawrence X. Tarpey, *Human Behavior in Marketing* (Columbus, O.: Charles E. Merrill Books, Inc., 1967), pp. 62–64.

[11] *Ibid.,* pp. 64–67.

[12] Francesco M. Nicosia, *Consumer Decision Processes* (Englewood Cliffs, N.J.: Prentice-Hall, Inc., 1966), p. 41.

hierarchy. In fact, a particular behavior system may be imbedded in a consumption system. That is, a consumer does not just eat a hamburger to satisfy a food need, but may also buy several other products at the same time and in a particular place to satisfy needs for sociability, affection, and perhaps other reasons.[13]

The motives we will discuss are not new but are the classical ones presented by Copeland in 1924.[14] More recent work has merely expanded the list or provided other organizational schemes.

These motives are arbitrarily classified as "emotional" and "economic." This is certainly an oversimplification, and you should remember that in any particular buying decision a consumer may have *several* motives for buying as he does. But this dichotomy, nevertheless, is useful to understanding consumer behavior.

We do make emotional decisions. Americans, perhaps because of heritage, are generally reluctant to admit this, preferring to rationalize their actions in terms of economic necessity. People in other countries, for example the Latin nations, are much less concerned about economic justification. Although some lists of motives present hundreds of emotional motives, we will discuss them under only eight headings. They are: **Emotional motives drive many consumers**

1. Satisfaction of senses
2. Preservation of species
3. Fear
4. Rest and recreation
5. Pride
6. Sociability
7. Striving
8. Curiosity or mystery

Satisfaction of senses. Satisfaction of the five senses—*touch, taste, sight, smell, and hearing*—seems to be one of the most important motives. An appeal to this motive would emphasize the *enjoyment* or *satisfaction,* rather than nutritional values one might get from food or drink. Since most Americans live beyond the subsistence level, this motive obviously is more complex than simple hunger and thirst.

Advertisements illustrating full meals or "a man's dinner" could appeal to this motive, but so could appeals concerning the *more subtle variations* sensed by the taste buds or the nostrils. An appeal to the sense of taste or smell might show a man inhaling cigarette smoke or a woman sampling a food delicacy.

This same motive would be concerned with eliminating unpleasant sights, smells, or noise and *avoiding discomfort or pain.* Particularly appealing here would be special kinds of mattresses, air conditioners, stomach aids, liniments, corn plasters, soft cashmere sweaters, creams which make your skin "nice to touch," and personal-care products to assure that you will be nice to be near—all day.

Preservation of species. The drives of *courtship and mating* are strong in most humans. The subsequent *care of children* is also strong in some societies, though there are variations here. In some cultures, the father and older children as well as the mother join in the details of

---

[13] Harper W. Boyd, Jr., and Sidney J. Levy, "New Dimensions in Consumer Analysis," *Harvard Business Review,* November-December, 1963, pp. 129–40.

[14] For more details, see Melvin T. Copeland, *Principles of Merchandising* (New York: A. W. Shaw Co., 1924), chap. vi.

caring for the children in the family. In other cultures, the care of children is primarily the mother's responsibility.

Marketing appeals made to women (and especially young girls) are relying on this motive when they mention the possibility of finding a mate through the purchase of pretty clothing, perfumes, and body-care products. Many products useful to newlyweds are presented in an aura of marriage and wedded bliss. Silverware, china, new furniture and appliances, honeymoon vacation trips, and even easy-to-follow cookbooks are in this category.

An appeal to this motive may be used to promote a variety of products for children—ranging from encyclopedias to cough syrup.

Fear. An appeal to *self-preservation,* or to *the protection of our family and friends,* may be emphasized here. For many people the uncertainties of the future, including the possibilities of accidents, sickness, and death, are of grave concern. Insurance, vitamins, and safety equipment in homes and automobiles appeal to this motive.

Rest and recreation. *Sleep* and *rest* are certainly basic needs, but flowing from these seem to be wants to *lighten or eliminate work* and to *obtain greater leisure time.* Then, once this time is obtained, there is the need to fill it or face boredom. Of appeal here would be sports, camping, travel, or indoor games, reading, television viewing, playing musical instruments, and spectator sports.

Pride. Pride in *personal appearance* or the *appearance of one's property* appears to be a strong drive. Many persons want to maintain their own "dignity" without regard for impressing others. Cleanliness, neatness, and personal appearance are related to this motive, and any product facilitating these ends would be attractive, such as soaps, cleaning compounds, toothbrushes, washing machines, cosmetics, polishing waxes, and dust cloths. These could be sold more effectively by appealing to the *pride* motive rather than selling the items as ends in themselves.

Expression of artistic taste is a further manifestation of pride. The consumer wants to have confidence in his own ability to choose esthetic articles for his own use or for others. The emphasis again is not on what others think about a person, but what he thinks about himself. Note that in making marketing plans, this *pride* motive should be distinguished from acts or motives concerned with impressing others.

Sociability. Sociability is concerned with the individual's drive *to be a part of his group.* Belonging to clubs and organizations, especially those offering special drinking or dining opportunities, might satisfy this motive. Coca-Cola is often shown as part of a happy social situation. Pepsi-Cola has used the advertising theme: "Be Sociable—Have a Pepsi."

Striving. The drive for *social achievement* can be very strong. Here the consumer may be concerned with achievement of success in social relationships by showing good sense in managing and participating in social affairs. Any products that help develop signs of good taste and manners might appeal to this motive.

Remember that striving can take various forms: Some people strive for their *own satisfaction,* just because they personally want to do a good job. Many strive for *distinctiveness*—that is, to do or have things which are not done or possessed by others. Others, by contrast, strive to *emulate*—to be the same as someone else. Different appeals would be needed for each group, and these appeals might have to change with time. What brings personal satisfaction now might have less appeal in 5 or 10 years. Today's distinctive product may be too popular tomorrow, and what is generally popular today may be a dead issue next year.

Finally, some people desire to emulate economically. Appeals to this motive might stress the offer of the very latest styles at budget prices.

Curiosity or mystery. Some people just like to try new things. Others have romance in their souls. Anything that appeals to their sense of curiosity or mystery may be attractive. This includes anything *new, different, or exotic*.

Ocean trips or travel in general appeal to this motive. So would a new hot-weather drink or a salad dressing or herb cookery. An example of curiosity at work is the success of an "Around the World Shoppers' Club," an organization that monthly sends knickknacks from foreign lands. The main appeal to buyers is not the knickknacks themselves but the novelty of getting something different from faraway places.

Economic motives

In contrast to the emotional motives, economic motives are primarily concerned with making the most effective use of the customer's scarce resources. A product that is easier to use or which will last longer, at lower cost, clearly accomplishes this purpose. These motives require less elaboration than the emotional motives. Eight categories are listed below.

1. Handiness.
2. Efficiency in operation or use.
3. Dependability in use.
4. Reliability of auxiliary service.
5. Durability.
6. Enhancement of earnings.
7. Enhancement of productivity of property.
8. Economy of purchase or use.

Here, more quantitative or specific appeals can be used—in contrast to the more subtle or descriptive appeals designed to reach emotional motives. Specific dollar savings, differences in weight, length of life, and other such measurable factors can be emphasized.

Why consumers buy a specific product

We have been discussing why consumers might buy various kinds of products. But we cannot say why they buy *specific products* and *specific brands*. Different target markets might buy for different reasons. The best general-purpose answer we can give is that consumers buy the set of goods and services that are most appealing to them, *as they see it*.

Budget experts or businessmen might feel they should buy differently, but in our economy the consumer does as he wishes. It is important to understand this and all its implications. It means that the marketing manager must design a marketing mix that will appeal to some consumers more than the many competing marketing mixes.

A successful mix may be based on his intuitive insight about how some target customers behave, while the "average" mix may just aim at "everyone"—or the manager's view of "everyone," which is really a projection of himself. Our motive-type analysis of why people might buy carries the investigation of buying decisions farther than many business firms go. Even this oversimple approach might lead to significant insights and the development of a successful marketing mix, because it aims at *some* unsatisfied customer needs.

So far we have been discussing insights which grow out of psychology. Yet consumer behavior actually may be determined not only by forces within a particular consumer but also by his relations with others. We will turn to this matter now. Then in Chapters 11–13 we will see that how people buy may be related to the kinds of products they are buying and the degree of brand preference which has developed.

Interaction of person with others

Social psychologists and sociologists see market behavior as a response to the attitudes and behavior of others. We will review this thinking in terms of the interaction of the individual with his family, social classes, and reference groups.

The individual is not completely a free agent. Society provides a framework for the individual's judgments, and applies pressure to keep his decisions within the realm of socially acceptable behavior. Often he must consult his family. He certainly considers his group's values. Some men, for example, would certainly prefer to wear comfortable sports clothes to formal dances, rather than a constricting tuxedo and starched shirt—but custom rules otherwise. In the same way, many women who find a new fashion unattractive, will still buy and wear it.

Family considerations may overwhelm personal ones

Most decisions are made within a framework developed by experience within the family. The individual may go through much of the thinking discussed above when developing his own preferences for various products and services. But this analysis may be only one of the influences in the final decision. Social processes—such as power, domination, and affection—may be involved, too. This decision-making process may be the subconscious result of much social learning.

A boat for father or a TV for mother. The interaction of various social forces can be illustrated using a choice between two products which could appeal to rest and recreation motives—say a television set and a boat with outboard motor.

The husband in a family might be particularly interested in the boat and motor for his camping and fishing trips. Weekend pleasure outings with the family would be only incidental. But in his arguments, he can present his preference in the desirable terms of *family wants and uses*. At the same time, his wife might prefer a new television set. It would enhance the beauty of her home and, secondarily, would be used as an entertainment medium for herself, her husband, and the children. She, too, could argue that this purchase is *for the family*.

The actual outcome in such a situation is unpredictable. It depends on the strength of the husband's and the wife's preferences; their individual degree of dominance of the family; who contributes the most money to the family's income; the need for affection; and the response of other family members.

Knowing how all these forces interact would be most helpful to the marketing manager. Unfortunately, each family may behave differently, and an overall marketing strategy may have to deal with tendencies or averages. Yet an individual retail salesman in direct contact with the family might sense how the family is operating and be able to adjust his marketing mix, especially his sales presentation, accordingly.

One person will often make the purchase, but when planning strategy, it is important to consider who is the "real" decider on the selection of a specific product or brand.

Who is the real customer?

Traditionally, the housewife has been considered the family purchasing agent. Presumably she has been the one who had the time to shop and run the errands. As a result, most product promotion and advertising have been aimed at women. But the situation may be changing. As more women work, and as night shopping and Sunday shopping becomes more popular,[15] the housewife may be playing a less dominant role as family buyer. One study found that 80 percent of the wives surveyed check with their husbands on any purchase of $50 or more, and nearly half check on smaller purchases.[16]

Men now have more time for and interest in shopping, and they may make the decisions involving large purchases or buy products of special interest to them, such as beer, liquor, automobiles, tires, life insurance, air conditioners, electric shavers, shaving creams, and outboard motors.[17]

Apparently the father is primarily concerned with buying decisions that involve functional items. Of the two parents, he tends to be more concerned with matters external to the family. The mother is more concerned with those buying decisions that have expressive values, and she is more concerned with internal matters. These distinctions may apply even if the user of a purchased product is the other parent. For example, the wife may buy the husband's clothing accessories, while the husband might buy household appliances.

The husband and wife may work together where internal-functional or external-expressive matters are involved, because the husband-wife roles may overlap. Husbands and wives may share in home improvements, for example, because they involve both functional and internal matters.[18]

[15] "The Sunday Driver Becomes Big Market," *Business Week,* June 8, 1957, pp. 62–68.

[16] "Queen of the Family Purse—Or Is She?" *Business Week,* August 10, 1963, pp. 26–27; and *Printers' Ink,* December 13, 1957, pp. 40 ff.

[17] *Males vs. Female Influence on Purchase of Selected Products, an Exploratory Depth Interview Study with Husbands and Wives* (New York: Fawcett Publications, Inc., 1958), p. 6; and "Liquor Store Survey Uncorks Potent Data: Two-Fifths of the Customers Are Women," *Business Week,* May 13, 1967, p. 187.

[18] W. H. Reynolds and James H. Myers, "Marketing and the American Family," *Business Topics,* Spring, 1966, pp. 58–59.

The trend among families, especially young adult families, to do things together has changed some shopping habits. The whole family often goes grocery shopping together, and usually spends more money than when the wife goes alone or only with the children.[19]

Yet, despite these *trends,* it appears that women still are responsible for about 60 percent of all personal consumption expenditures in the United States. (It is difficult to measure the exact figure, because if the housewife has carefully planted an idea in the husband's mind, she is not likely to admit it, and he may not even know it. Researchers are considerably handicapped, not knowing the exact relationships within families.)

It appears that the wife handles *all* the money and bills in about 38 percent of all U.S. families and shares the job with her husband in 31 percent of families. She also is responsible for nearly 100 percent of the personal-care expenditures.

The obvious conclusion is that the wife still has a big influence on total family purchases—but her influence may be waning.

The question of spending by the family, however, is not limited to mothers and fathers. As the life-cycle stages of the family change, the children begin to handle and spend more money. While children under age 13 may spend less than $2 weekly, as they grow older, the expenditures increase. A boy or girl aged 13 to 15 may spend about $4.50 and one aged 16 to 17 may spend about $15 a week. These expenditures are based on allowances and earnings and do not include expenditures made on behalf of the child or specific transactions for which the child merely carries cash.[20]

In many cases, however, the person actually doing the shopping is merely acting as an agent for persons who may have specified rather exactly which products should be bought. Small children may want specific kinds of cereals; the father may want a certain brand of cigarettes or golf balls.

Current research findings are helpful, but we still need greater understanding to see why different families come to widely different decisions when faced with a choice among many available products. For one thing, it would be valuable to know the family's present and past experience and future expectations in relation to society's values and the family social class position. Social class is extremely important here, and is discussed next.

Social class relationships Up to now, we have been concerned primarily with the individual and his relation to his family. Now we consider how society looks at an individual and perhaps his family—in terms of social class.

The mere mention of class distinctions in the United States provokes a defensive reaction. We like to think of America as a land of equality. We have been brought up to revere the statement in the Declaration of Independence, "All men are created equal." Our class system is far less pronounced than those in European and Asiatic nations where the system is tied to religion, blood kinship, or landed wealth. Nevertheless,

[19] *Business Week,* November 30, 1957, p. 58.

[20] *The Dynamics of the Youth Explosion—A Look Ahead* (Los Angeles Chamber of Commerce, 1967), pp. 33–35.

sociological research bears out the contention that a class structure *does* exist in this country.

In discussing class structure, we will use the traditional technical terms, "upper," "middle," and "lower." But a word of warning is needed. The choice of these terms, even though in general use, is unfortunate, because they have a connotation of superior and inferior. In sociological and marketing usage, however, no value judgment is implied. In fact, it is not possible to state that a particular class is "better" or "happier" than any other. Any such value judgment would be biased, as it could only be made from the vantage point of the individual making it, and his judgment would be colored by his own class values.

Some people strive to enter a "higher" class because they find the values of that class more admirable; others are comfortable with the standards of their own group and prefer to remain where they are.

The marketing man's concern should be with learning the characteristics and typical behavior patterns of each class so that he will be better able to develop unique marketing strategies involving class differences.

The American class system is an individual and a family system. While a child is a member of a family, his social status will probably depend on the status of his family. But grown children often "join" a different class than their parents. This is especially the case when they attain higher educational levels or take up different occupations from those of their parents.

Occupation, rather than just income, is an important factor in determining U.S. social class—which in turn has a bearing on buying behavior. To illustrate, in recent years blue-collar workers (factory and service workers, exclusive of office workers) have had a rapid rise in income. If social position had been based on income only, it might have been expected that these workers would automatically be accepted into the same class as the white-collar workers of equal income. We would expect them to follow similar buying patterns. This has not proven to be the case, however, as revealed in several studies discussed below.

Wage and salary town study. This study of people living in various communities showed that people could be divided into four groups based on occupation.[21] These groups were: High-town (professional and managerial class), Salary-town (white-collar workers), Wage-town (blue-collar workers), and Low-town (unskilled workers). The size and relative market importance of these groups are indicated below.

Social Group	Percent of Population	Market Significance
High-town	10	Small but important
Salary-town	14 ⎫	
	⎬ 68	Middle majority which buys the most goods
Wage-town	54 ⎭	
Low-town	22	Little market value

[21] Adapted from *The New America—Your Market Potential for 1957* (New York: MacFadden Publicatio s, Inc., 1957), p. 4.

This study found that, while the Wage-towners and Salary-towners may be earning roughly the same income, they are not at all alike. Wage-town people live in different neighborhoods and have different interests, habits, ways of life, associations, and ideas of home. They "speak a different language" and respond to different stimuli. In general, they read different magazines. Most of them have little interest in *Fortune, Holiday, Vogue,* or *Ladies Home Journal*—just as the average Salary-town wife has little desire to read *True Story.*

It is not the amount of income, but the source of income (how and where it is earned) and the neighborhoods in which they live that separate the people in Wage-town from those in the three other "towns" within the city. Bricklayers may earn more than office managers, electricians more than senior draftsmen, and truck drivers more than bank tellers. As these blue-collar workers' incomes increase, however, they do not buy the same things as white-collar workers making the same amount of money.[22] Some of the differences will be noted after a similar study is described.

Warner-Chicago Tribune studies. The occupational classification by "towns" is similar to one developed by Lloyd Warner, a social psychologist, but not nearly as comprehensive as his. He developed a class system for cities in the 10,000–25,000 population range. Rather than using only occupation, his class system is based on *income, occupation, house type, and residence area.* Warner's classifications, though widely used in sociology, had found little use in marketing until the *Chicago Tribune* undertook several studies with Warner's social class system to determine whether it had validity in larger metropolitan areas, especially concerning family buying patterns.[23]

After three years spent analyzing various marketing problems under the guidance of Warner, a population breakdown was derived for metropolitan Chicago, probably typical of a big industrial city. Many of the findings are interesting to marketing managers. Let us look at the *Chicago Tribune*'s five class breakdowns first and then consider some of the findings.

1. *Upper Class* (0.9 percent of population). This was defined as old families (upper-upper class) and the socially prominent new rich (lower-upper class). This group has been the traditional leader in the American community. Most large manufaccturers, bankers, and top marketing executives belong to it. It represents, however, less than 1 percent of the population. Being so small, the two upper classes were merged into one in this study. In some of the *Chicago Tribune* studies, these two classes are broken out separately, and a six-class breakdown is used.

2. *Upper-Middle Class* (7.2 percent of population). These are the successful businessmen and professionals and the best salesmen. These first two groups constitute the "quality market." The advertising professional speaks from this viewpoint, reflecting the tastes and codes

---

[22] *Ibid.,* pp. 14–15.

[23] Pierre Martineau, "The Pattern of Social Classes," in R. L. Clewett (ed.), *Marketing's Role in Scientific Management* (Chicago: American Marketing Association, 1957), pp. 233–49.

of these groups. Yet, combined, groups 1 and 2 represent only 8.1 percent of the population.

3. *Lower-Middle Class* (28.4 percent of population). These are the white-collar workers—small tradesmen, office workers, teachers, technicians, most salesmen. The American moral code and the emphasis on striving has come from this class. This is the most conforming, church-going, morally serious part of society. We speak of America as a middle-class society, but the middle-class value system stops here. Two thirds of our society is *not* middleclass.

4. *Upper-Lower Class* (44.0 percent of population). These are the factory production workers, the union labor groups, the skilled workers, the service workers, and the local politicians and union leaders who would lose their power if they moved out of this class.

5. *Lower-Lower Class* (19.5 percent of population). This group includes unskilled laborers, racial immigrants, and people in nonrespectable occupations.[24]

The *Chicago Tribune* class studies suggest that an old economic maxim, "A rich man is simply a poor man with more money," may not hold true. While Engel's Laws may still apply in general, it appears that a person belonging to the lower class, given the same income as a middle-class individual, handles himself and his money very differently. The various classes patronize different stores, buy different brands of products (even though their prices are approximately the same), and have different spending-saving attitudes.

The marketing implications of these studies are apparent, especially for advertising. Different classes may read quite different meanings into advertisements. One beer advertisement, for example, was built around a fox hunter in full costume, with scarlet coat, boots, and cap. The target customers, however, were members of the lower class—who, unhappily for the manufacturer, had no inclination to go fox hunting. In fact, the advertisement was repugnant to them because it seemed "snobbish." In this case, all the effort and expense had been wasted. **Wrong symbols, wrong customers**

Again, testimonials by Broadway stage stars have little meaning for social classes who have no acquaintance with the legitimate theater.[25] To illustrate further the difference in perception of symbols and ideas by classes, lower class women may eagerly read a crowded, dark, screaming sale advertisement which to them means urgency and potential bargains, while those in the middle or upper classes will ignore such advertisements because they interpret them to mean large crowds and poorer merchandise.[26]

In a study[27] on lamp, furniture, and home styles, the lower class half

---

[24] Adapted from Pierre Martineau, *Motivation on Advertising* (New York: McGraw-Hill Book Co., 1957), p. 164.

[25] Pierre Martineau, *Motivation in Advertising* (New York: McGraw-Hill Book Co., 1957), p. 165.

[26] Sidney J. Levy, "Symbols by Which We Buy," a paper delivered at 41st National Conference, American Marketing Association, December 30, 1958. For a popular version about the class system, see Vance Packard, *The Status Seekers* (New York: David McKay Co., Inc., 1959). See also, Richard P. Coleman, "The Significance of Social Stratification in Selling," in Martin L. Bell (ed.), *Marketing: A Maturing Discipline* (Chicago: American Marketing Association, 1961), pp. 171–84.

[27] Pierre Martineau, *Motivation in Advertising, op. cit.*, p. 168.

of the market selected completely different styles than did the top half. This lower group did not want the modern ranch homes and the two-story colonial homes, nor the severely plain, functional styling of furniture preferred by the higher classes. Instead, they preferred over-stuffed and ornate furnishings (sometimes called "borax" goods) and conventional, less conspicuous one- or two-story homes.

A similar study of women's fashions is equally interesting:

1. In the "old-money" families (the upper-upper class), the women maintain a certain independence of current shifting fashions. Their clothes may remain roughly the same for several years. The taste of these women is more British than French, running to tweeds and woolens, and avoiding the "daring" which is characteristic of French styling. Ads appealing to this group stress adjectives like "aristocratic," "well-bred," and "distinguished."
2. In the class just below (the lower-upper), the women of newer but often greater fortunes are the Paris-conscious style leaders, preferring high fashion. To them, clothes are symbols related to wealth and high living rather than to family background. These women seek to combine opulence with quiet elegance. They must spend a great deal on clothes but must appear not to have done so. Fashion advertising for them stresses clothes of inbred superiority and the adjectives revolve around "chic" and "sophistication"—although the word "glamor" is never used, because it sounds cheap.
3. In the middle and lower classes, fashion has a different meaning. High style is regarded with some suspicion. Paris styles are characterized as too extreme. Respectability is the standard, not breeding or effect. "Smart" is the right word, and "smart" means what everyone in the same social class is wearing. Hollywood stars are appropriate models (rather than socially prominent, sophisticated style leaders) because they exemplify "glamor," which in these classes means "femininely pretty."[28]

Middle and lower classes compared. Several studies have been cited to illustrate the varying behavior of different classes. These findings are not "facts" about consumers but are support for the idea of a social class system insofar as marketing is concerned. The summary in Table 8–1, comparing the attitudes and characteristics of the middle class to the lower class, accents general differences between classes as revealed in these and many other studies.

Once marketing men are aware of these general differences, they can adjust their mixes. Seeing that the lower classes are concerned with the present, for example, stores aiming at these classes frequently emphasize credit sales so that target consumers can satisfy their needs *now*. In such stores—such as credit jewelers and credit furniture stores—it is often difficult even to determine the total price. The salesmen talk about the small down payment and easy monthly payments with little mention of the number of such payments. Furthermore, the lower classes seem to be more concerned with financial security, and some stores catering to these groups offer insurance on the life of the bread-

[28] *Ibid.*, pp. 168–69.

winner so that the housewife will not be left with a debt should her husband die.

The lower classes seem to be confused by variety and apparently have difficulty in making choices. As a result, such buyers look on furniture salesmen, for example, as friends and advisors. The middle-class buyers are much more self-confident in contrast. They know what they want and prefer a furniture salesman to be an impersonal guide.[29]

The increasing affluence of the skilled worker (the upper-lower class) and his attitude that the "world revolves around his family" has led to a strong desire for home ownership in "respectable" city neighborhoods or suburban developments where other blue-collar people

Table 8–1 A comparison of attitudes and characteristics for two social classes

Middle Class	Lower Class
1. Pointed to the future.	1. Pointed to the present and past.
2. His viewpoint embraces a long expanse of time.	2. Lives and thinks in a short expanse of time.
3. More urban identification.	3. More rural identification.
4. Stresses rationality.	4. Nonrational essentially.
5. Has a well-structured sense of the universe.	5. Vague and unclear structuring.
6. Horizons vastly extended or not limited.	6. Horizons sharply defined and limited.
7. Greater sense of choice making.	7. Limited sense of choice making.
8. Self-confident, willing to take risks.	8. Very much concerned with security and insecurity.
9. Immaterial and abstract in his thinking (idea-minded).	9. Concrete and perceptive in his thinking (thing-minded).
10. Sees himself tied to national happenings.	10. World revolves around his family.

SOURCE: P. Martineau, "The Pattern of Social Classes," *op. cit.*, pp. 246–47.

live. These people don't seem to seek high-status neighborhoods, but simply want a good home for their families. They may want different retail facilities, too, such as discount stores.[30]

In contrast, the middle classes seem more concerned with selecting a house that has status value and might enable the family to rise in the social class structure. Housing location, and even social and political affiliations, may be chosen with a view to the family's social future.

From this review, it is obvious that social class cannot be ignored when analyzing market grids and developing marketing strategy.[31]

---

[29] *Advertising Age,* February 22, 1960, p. 63.

[30] David J. Rachman and Marvin Levine, "Blue Collar Workers Shape Suburban Markets," *Journal of Retailing,* Winter, 1966–67, pp. 5–13.

[31] For more discussion on this, see Richard P. Coleman, "The Significance of Social Stratification in Selling," in Martin L. Bell, *Marketing: A Maturing Discipline, Proceedings of the 1960 Winter Conference of the American Marketing Association* (Chicago: American Marketing Association, 1961).

And fortunately, it appears that some fairly objective and readily available data may be useful for estimating social class. In particular, U.S. census measures of occupation, education, and expenditures on housing may serve well.[32]

Reference groups

A reference group is a segment of people that the individual looks to when forming his opinions, attitudes, and beliefs. A person normally has several reference groups for various subjects.[33] Although he need not be associated directly with these references groups, he may take his values from "them" and make purchasing decisions based on what he feels they would accept. *Playboy* magazine, for instance, and the "in" people who presumably read it, might be a reference group for *Playboy* readers.

The reference-group concept has grown in importance in recent years as more people live and work together in today's larger corporations, schools, governments, communities, churches, and social action organizations. The larger company employee—the "organization man" —seems to be especially responsive to group pressures and puts "getting along" with the group above other values.

This group consciousness has been described by Riesman as a sign of the transition from the "inner-directed" man to the "other-directed" man. The inner-directed man has his own value system and directs his own activities, whereas the other-directed person is the one whose character is formed chiefly by those around him. Other-directed people—a large proportion of our society according to Riesman—are led by each other, and consequently there is a strong tendency to conform.[34]

Reaching the leaders who are buyers

A trend toward other-directedness could have a profound effect on marketing through its effect on the way individuals and groups change their values and desires. Advertising, and promotion in general, might have to be more concerned with affecting trend leaders and whole groups rather than individuals.[35]

In this drive for conformity, some people are more effective than others as "opinion leaders" or "communicators." It is important to note that these communicators are not restricted to the higher income people or the better educated. Rather, they are spread throughout all levels of society in varying proportions. Communicators on one subject are not necessarily communicators on another.

Housewives with larger families may be looked to for advice on cooking, while young girls may be the leaders in new clothing styles and cosmetics. And all of this may take place within the various social classes, i.e., different opinion leaders in the various classes.[36]

[32] James A. Carman, *The Application of Social Class in Market Segmentation* (Berkeley, Calif.: Institute of Business and Economic Research, University of California, 1965).

[33] Zaltman, *op. cit.*, pp. 77–78.

[34] David Riesman, N. Glaser, and R. Denney, *The Lonely Crowd* (Garden City, N.Y.: Doubleday & Co., Inc., 1950).

[35] Harold H. Kassarjian, "Social Character and Differential Preference for Mass Communication," *Journal of Marketing Research*, May, 1965, pp. 146–53.

[36] Carman, *op. cit.*, pp. 21 and 61; *Printers' Ink*, November 22, 1957, pp. 58 ff.; Elihu Katz and Paul E. Lazarsfeld, *Personal Influences* (Glencoe, Ill.: Free Press, 1955); and George Katona, *The Powerful Consumer* (New York: McGraw-Hill Book Co., 1960).

The influence of communicators and of the group pressures to conform has been credited with great increases of sales of such post–World
War II products as air conditioners, garbage and waste disposers, and
automatic dishwashers. Apparently an unusual set of forces works
within the group. The earlier adopters may be looked up to and copied
if their innovations prove successful. Then follows a period of imitation
by more members of the group, and finally the rest of the members may
be dragged along for fear of offending the others because refusal to
accept and buy the innovation may be interpreted as disapproval of the
group's values. We will say much more about this process when we
talk about Promotion planning in Chapter 21.

The effect of this group interaction (as well as class and stage in the **Who keeps**
life cycle) is illustrated in a study of buying behavior in two North **cool in**
Philadelphia areas. The study found that the older middle-income **Philadelphia?**
neighborhoods had a low saturation rate on air conditioners, as did the
older upper-income neighborhoods. In contrast, the largest concentrations of air conditioners were in the new row-house neighborhoods.
There was, however, a marked difference in concentration among individual row-house neighborhoods.

After more intensive research, it was found that there was a low
concentration in the row-house neighborhoods populated by factory
workers but a high concentration in those populated by the younger
white-collar workers. Figure 8–1 illustrates how the demand for this
appliance spread in one neighborhood, apparently indicative of a strong
desire to conform to group values, particularly among young white-
collar groups who are striving to get ahead.[37]

Integrating the behavioral science approaches

We have been discussing various approaches to explaining why
individuals and families buy as they do. The relationship of all of these
may not be immediately clear to you. It would be desirable to have an
integrating framework to relate the various influences on buying behavior and the theories about these influences.

Unfortunately, we do *not* have such a framework. The behavioral
scientists have developed many approaches, but those who are not
directly involved in "selling" a particular approach are frank to admit
that what we have now is not too useful as a precise guide to policy
making. Furthermore, it is not clear *how* such an integrating system
will be developed.[38] In other words, for the near future at least, even
after the marketing manager has reviewed all the behavioral data, he
may still have to rely on his own intuition and marketing research to
help him estimate the expected behavior of various target markets.

The behavioral sciences have not answered all of our questions. But
they do provide us with some insights. They force us to think beyond

---

[37] William H. Whyte, Jr., "The Web of Word of Mouth," in Lincoln H. Clark (ed.),
Consumer Behavior, Vol. II, *op. cit.,* pp. 113–22. Reprinted from *Fortune*, November,
1954. For additional examples of reference-group significance, see Zaltman, *op. cit.,* p. 93.
[38] Nicosia, *op. cit.,* pp. 141–42.

Figure 8–1 *The web of word of mouth*

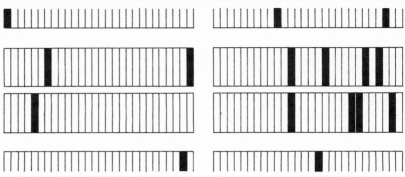

The four North Philadelphia areas above show some of the relationships between word of mouth, the age of the neighbor group, and purchases. From left to right, the blocks were built in 1922, 1953, 1951, and 1948. As the ratio of conditioned homes (black) in each block indicates, the age factor has a demonstrable effect on purchases. While other factors can change the ratio drastically, by and large there is a basic time progression.

To illustrate, let's assume a hypothetical couple called Dot and Ed. When we first meet them, they have been married a year, and are living with Dot's parents in an old row-house area like the one at the left. Ed is 25. At the moment conditioners mean nothing to them; they are thinking of little else except a house of their own. The parents don't think much about conditioners either. As papa remarks, he and mother lived very comfortably for 35 years without one, thank you.

At last the couple move into a house of their own in a brand-new block like the one second from the left. Everybody seems to be in the same boat, and the groups begin to form up around nuclei like those at the right end of the block. Two of the gang have conditioners but Ed and Dot, with one child already and a second on the way, are concentrating on babies' things and furniture.

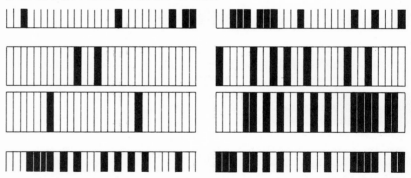

At the end of their third year on the block, the ratio of conditioned homes, like that of the area second from the right, has increased. Ed is making $5,500; they have already finished paying for their living-room and dining-room suites, and they have had an automatic washer for a year. Even with their payments on the car, they still have enough money left over for an $18-a-month installment loan; and, furthermore, almost all the other couples in their particular gang have a conditioner box sticking out their windows now, and on a hot night the whir of the motors in them has become psychologically deafening.

At the end of their seventh year on the block, by which time it resembles the one on the right, one phase of Ed's and Dot's cycle is drawing to a close. They are loaded with appliances (among other things, they have a second conditioner for the children's room), and they have begun thinking about a split-level home in the suburbs. Many of their friends have already moved away to the suburbs, and Dot feels a lower "element" is moving into the block. Just as one style of life is about set, they are now ready for another.

SOURCE: William H. Whyte, Jr., "The Web of Word of Mouth," courtesy of *Fortune*, November, 1954, pp. 142–43.

the typical stereotypes (or our own misconceptions) about consumer behavior. One behavioral scientist has developed a framework visualizing a family's character as having six basic parts that determine buying behavior. These six parts, shown in Figure 8–2, combine psychological and sociological needs and motives with socioeconomic characteristics and the family values resulting from life experience in today's environment. Figure 8–2 does not provide answers, but it does show the interaction of consumer characteristics and behavior. A few comments about this integrating framework are in order.

Block A (Social Placement) is concerned with data on education, occupation, and financial status (discussed in Chapter 6). But in Block A another dimension, social position, is added. Our discussion of social class is relevant here.

Block B (General Values) is concerned with society and its social, moral, and religious values. If a particular society views the family, for example, as an important institution, then homemaking and the purchase of homes and home furnishings may be viewed differently than in a society that does not consider the family so important.

Religious values may tend to discourage interest in certain kinds of entertainment, material goods, or even education. Some religious sects, for example, discourage dancing, card playing, drinking, and smoking. Some regard certain educational ideas as dangerous, and others even insist upon having their own school systems.

Block C (Family Goals, Policies, Life Styles), again, is concerned with social class values and their impact on various motives discussed earlier in this chapter. How a particular family has adapted to society's general values is also relevant here.

Block D (Family Organization) is primarily concerned with family size, stage in life cycle, and family interrelationships.

Block E (Potential for Family Action) is similar to the family organization block but is more concerned with the impact of the husband-wife relationship on decision making.

Block F (Career Patterns) deals with the family's history, for its past experience has a real bearing on current and future behavior. Some success has been achieved by market-oriented psychologists and sociologists who assume that past and present income and assets have a bearing on consumer behavior. In an effort to predict consumers' purchasing behavior, they relate these data to consumers' expectations and attitudes about the future.[39]

Block G (Effectiveness in Long-Range Planning) reflects past effectiveness in planning as a guide to the likelihood of future effectiveness. This factor may be especially important because experienced buyers behave differently from first-time buyers.[40]

Block H (Accumulation of Assets) involves the amount of money and goods available to carry out the family decisions.

---

[39] See George Katona, *Psychological Analysis of Economic Behavior* (New York: McGraw-Hill Book Co., 1951) and *The Powerful Consumer* (New York: McGraw-Hill Book Co., 1960) for additional discussion of this approach.

[40] Joseph W. Newman, *On Knowing the Consumer* (New York: John Wiley & Sons, Inc., 1966), p. 14.

Figure 8–2 Six parts of a family's character that determine how it buys

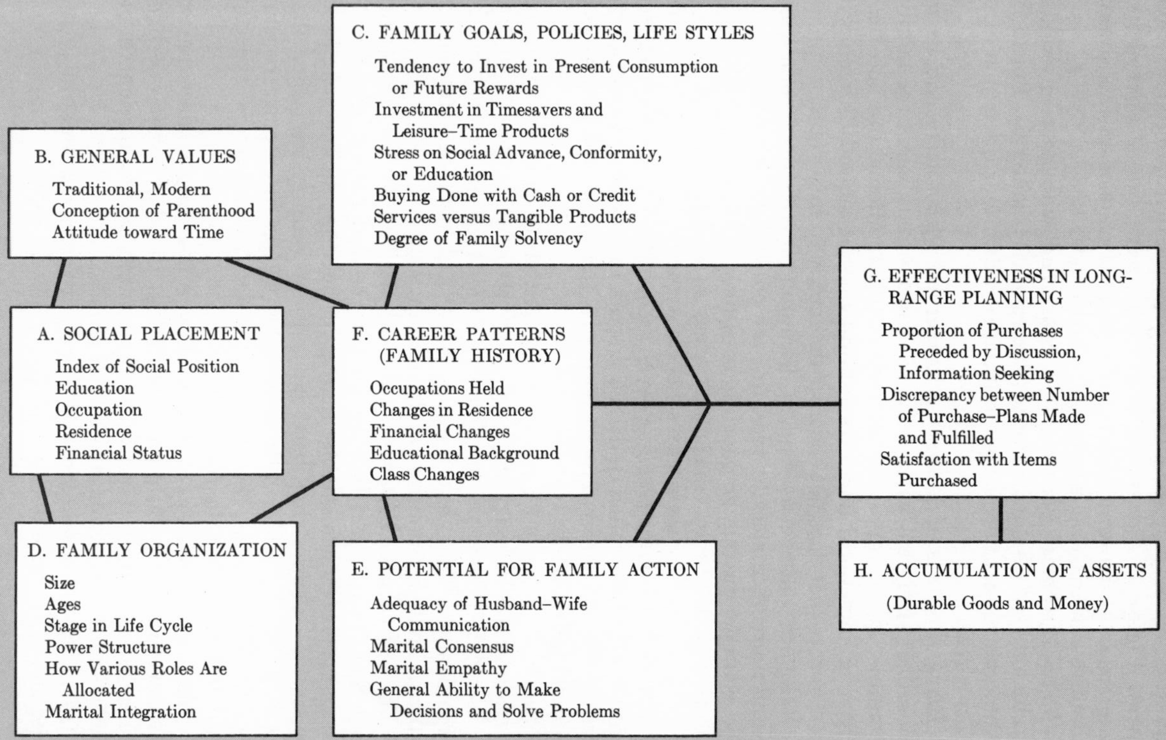

B. GENERAL VALUES

Traditional, Modern
Conception of Parenthood
Attitude toward Time

A. SOCIAL PLACEMENT

Index of Social Position
Education
Occupation
Residence
Financial Status

D. FAMILY ORGANIZATION

Size
Ages
Stage in Life Cycle
Power Structure
How Various Roles Are
    Allocated
Marital Integration

C. FAMILY GOALS, POLICIES, LIFE STYLES

Tendency to Invest in Present Consumption
    or Future Rewards
Investment in Timesavers and
    Leisure–Time Products
Stress on Social Advance, Conformity,
    or Education
Buying Done with Cash or Credit
Services versus Tangible Products
Degree of Family Solvency

F. CAREER PATTERNS
(FAMILY HISTORY)

Occupations Held
Changes in Residence
Financial Changes
Educational Background
Class Changes

E. POTENTIAL FOR FAMILY ACTION

Adequacy of Husband–Wife
    Communication
Marital Consensus
Marital Empathy
General Ability to Make
    Decisions and Solve Problems

G. EFFECTIVENESS IN LONG-
RANGE PLANNING

Proportion of Purchases
    Preceded by Discussion,
    Information Seeking
Discrepancy between Number
    of Purchase–Plans Made
    and Fulfilled
Satisfaction with Items
    Purchased

H. ACCUMULATION OF ASSETS

(Durable Goods and Money)

SOURCE: *Tide*, September 19, 1958, p. 29.

This framework shows the interaction of the influencing factors we have discussed. It should help the student remember that the consumer does not live in a vacuum, apart from all influences; he is considering not one but many competitive products.

How to build on the framework

Within this framework, some specialized research findings may prove more meaningful to the marketing man. Instead of just saying, "Well, that's very interesting" (and wondering how it all fits), he can categorize his thoughts within this framework.

Suppose a marketing manager was faced with evaluating research data that suggesed men were buying many articles long purchased exclusively by women. He might reason: "This has some bearing on family organization. I should study the male consumer to see which men are leading this trend."

He might ask himself some pertinent questions: "Is the trend related to income? What occupations are involved? Is society likely to discourage this trend? Are the family roles changing? Does this trend seem to represent a basic change in consumer behavior? Will we have to discover what men think of our product and other competing products?"

His next step should be to conduct research to get answers.

Why consumers select particular stores

We have discussed individual behavior, family behavior, group behavior, and social class behavior, all in terms of the process by which consumers or families make buying decisions about *products*. One more important area remains: *The choice of stores.*

The motives listed below are similar to the economic motives for products and help explain why consumers buy at one store rather than another.

Economic motives— What is rational and irrational?

1. Convenience.
2. Variety or selection.
3. Quality of goods—freshness, purity, craftsmanship, etc.
4. Courtesy of sales personnel.
5. Integrity—reputation for fairness in dealings.
6. Services offered—delivery, credit, returned-goods privileges.
7. Value offered.

Customers patronize stores that seem to offer the conveniences and services they want, at the lowest prices consistent with all the service they want. Some consumers want a great deal of service and are willing to pay for it. Others who do not want a lot of service (or at least don't want to pay for it) often think of those who patronize such stores as irrational, citing their apparent lack of concern about higher prices. But are the service-minded customers irrational? Perhaps they like these services and value their own time highly.

The conventional thinking in retailing tends to emphasize the economic motives, especially the value offered or, more narrowly, low

171

Emotional motives—Where do you find prestige or comfort?

prices. But it appears that there also may be important emotional reasons for patronizing particular stores. The product motives of sociability, distinctiveness, pride, or emulation may be relevant here.

Some people visit a store because they may meet their friends there. Others feel certain stores are distinctive and wear the labels of these institutions with pride. As a result, others may patronize these same

Figure 8–3 Customer profiles: store choices of people in different social classes (observed choices as percentage of expected choices)

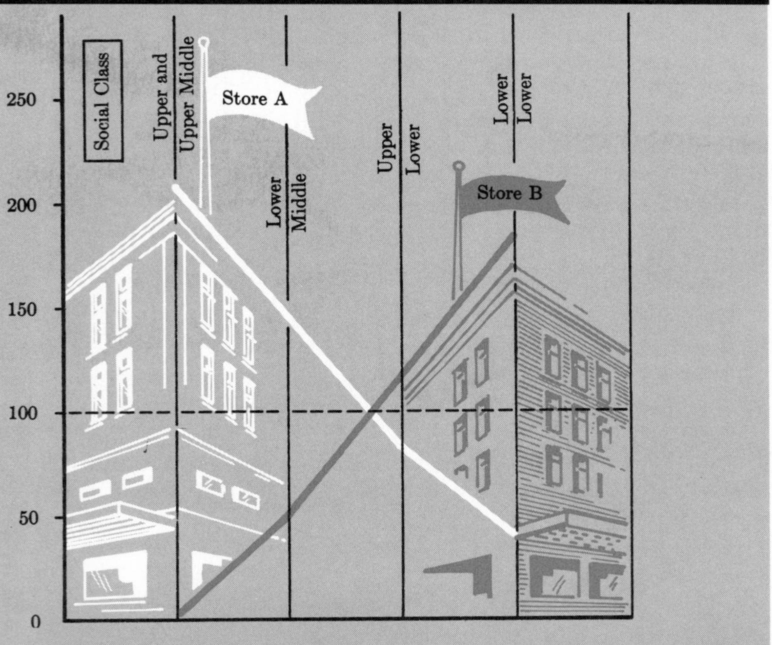

SOURCE: Pierre Martineau, "The Personality of the Retail Store," *Harvard Business Review*, January–February, 1958, p. 49.

stores to emulate the leaders. By contrast, they might not patronize another store because they would be embarrassed to carry home packages bearing the insignia of an obviously "inferior" store.

Social class seems to be especially important in consumers' selection of stores. In one study, it was found that the lower class woman thinks that if she goes into a higher class store, the clerks and the other customers in the store may "punish her in various subtle ways." "The clerks treat you like a crumb," one woman said.[41]

In Figure 8–3, the social class profiles of two large Chicago stores selling furniture are presented. Each had a broad range of prices and

[41] Martineau, "The Pattern of Social Classes," *op. cit.*, p. 234.

felt it was catering to "everybody." Yet the profiles reveal that each is patronized by different classes.[42]

Not all stores have so distinct an image. Often they try to avoid creating a class image because they want to appeal to a wide audience. Macy's in New York, for example, tries to create a fairly universal appeal. John Wanamaker, in Philadelphia, thinks of itself as a family store with a friendly atmosphere; as a result, it (like Macy's) has departments that carry some very expensive merchandise and others that handle goods for the mass market. Carson, Pirie, Scott & Co., in Chicago, caters to the large middle majority. Its objective is to have a friendly family store that will satisfy the broad market, some of which might feel uncomfortable in a high-fashion outlet.

By contrast, Robert Hall Clothes, Inc., a national clothing chain, aims at the lower class market. It tries to attract the average family who wants good clothing, not *high* fashion, and it emphasizes lower price. At the other extreme, Lord & Taylor in New York and I. Magnin in San Francisco—as well as some of the shops in Marshall Field & Co. in Chicago—emphasize high-fashion merchandise and aim at the upper classes. The prestige of these stores enables them to hire sales personnel with the "company" attitudes. The personnel reinforce the image the management wishes to convey. Lord & Taylor says, "We try to have a well-bred store, run by well-bred people, for well-bred customers." But the store is quick to point out that this does not necessarily mean high prices: "There is no price tag on taste."[43]

If consumers expect different things from stores, then perhaps different kinds of stores are needed. One sociologist classified shoppers into four categories: *economic shoppers, apathetic shoppers, personalizing shoppers,* and *ethical shoppers.* Each type might need a different type of store. **Various kinds of stores may be needed**

The largest group discovered in the study were the *economic shoppers,* the economists' "economic men;" middle-class shoppers tended to be in this group. They were primarily interested in price, quality, and variety, and looked with disfavor on practices (or salespeople) that inhibit or slow down their shopping.

The *apathetic shoppers,* a much smaller group, have practically no interest in shopping and are willing to patronize the most convenient store.

Personalizing shoppers seek stores in which they feel socially com-

---

[42] These profiles were obtained when people in various classes answered the following question:
"If you were going to buy new living room furniture for your home, at which store would you be most likely to find what you want?"
If each store were equally attractive to each class we would expect, on the basis of chance, that about half the members of each class would pick each store. The profiles show observed choices as a percentage of expected choices.
If there were only chance differences, we would expect each store to have a rating of 100. Instead, we see that Store A appealed strongly to the upper-middle and upper classes, and Store B appealed strongly to the lower-lower class. Pierre Martineau, "The Personality of the Retail Store," *Harvard Business Review,* Vol. 36, No. 1 (January-February, 1958), p. 49.
[43] "What Makes a 'Favorite' Store?" *Business Week,* June 14, 1958, pp. 57–60.

fortable. They are inclined to rate stores in terms of the closeness of their relationship to the sales personnel. Sometimes such a shopper refers to the store she patronizes as "my store." These shoppers tend to be from the lower classes.

Ethical shoppers seem to feel that they ought to support particular stores, especially neighborhood stores or small shops, because they sometimes appreciate their availability.[44]

It is obvious that if there were enough of each of these types of shoppers in a neighborhood, different kinds of stores could exist.

Clearly, the market grid concept has relevance in the consumer's selection of stores, and this should be noted by retailers because it means that consumers might attach themselves to stores rather than products. It should also be noted by manufacturers and wholesalers because it points up the importance that particular retailers could play in reaching certain target markets. Some consumers may be more store-loyal than brand-loyal.

Conclusion

In this chapter we have analyzed the individual consumer, the consumer operating in a group, and the way individuals and groups view products and stores. We have stressed that individual consumers behave very differently, sometimes motivated by economic and sometimes by emotional considerations, and often by a combination of the two. To assume that everyone behaves the way we do—or even the way our friends or families do—may lead to grave marketing errors.

Consumer buying behavior is the expression of the consumer's efforts to satisfy his needs and wants. We discussed some motives that may be helpful in suggesting why consumers buy, but saw that consumer behavior cannot be explained by a list of motives. On the other hand, motives may be useful until a tested theory of consumer behavior is developed.

We also saw that our society is characterized by social classes, which does help explain some consumer behavior. And fortunately, it is possible to develop some estimates of the size of social classes, using readily available data on education, occupation, and housing expenditures.

A framework was presented in this chapter to help the student interpret and integrate the various approaches and data he might obtain from marketing research. As of now, the behavioral sciences can only offer insights and theories which the marketing manager must blend with his own intuition and judgment in developing his marketing strategies.

Marketing research may have to be used to answer specific questions. But if neither the money nor the time is available for research, then management will have to rely on the available description of present behavior and "guesstimates" about future behavior. You should study carefully the popular magazines and the nation's leading newspapers,

---

[44] Gregory P. Stone, "City Shoppers and Urban Identification: Observations on the Social Psychology of City Life," *American Journal of Sociology*, July, 1954, pp. 36–45.

for these publications often mirror the public's shifting preferences. You also should be familiar with the many studies concerning the changing consumer that are published regularly in the business and trade press. This material, added and related to the information in these last several chapters, will aid your decision making.

Remember that the consumer, with all his likes and preferences, may be elusive—but not invisible. We do have data and some understanding of consumer behavior—much more than is used by many businessmen.

Questions and problems

1   What buying motives are being appealed to in the following statements?

   a) "Don't hide your copper!" (Copper-bottomed cooking utensils.)
   b) "Choose (our appliance) and welcome a tradition into your home . . . a tradition of quality. Because of it (our appliances) will serve you faithfully, year after year. And their classic beauty never dims. In fact, many are still in daily use today, after 20 or more years of service."
   c) "Sign of good taste. Be really refreshed . . . have a (soft drink)!"
   d) "America's best-selling honey. This honey is pure, clear, and golden as the sunshine. With a wonderfully mild, wholesome flavor created by Mother Nature—honey pure and delicious. Try it."

2   Cut out two recent advertisements: one full-page colored ad from a magazine and one large display from a newspaper. Indicate which of the buying motives are being appealed to in each case.

3   What is the basic difference between emotional and economic motives? Is any use served by classifying motives into these two categories?

4   How is the "pleasing the sense of taste" motive different from "satisfaction of the appetite"?

5   Illustrate the interaction of the individual and the family from your own personal experiences. Do you feel that other families behave in exactly the same way? Can some principle be developed out of this experience?

6   List three products for which the preferences of the actual user have no bearing on the purchasing decision.

7   How do society's values have an impact on purchasing behavior? Give two specific examples.

8   How should the social class structure affect the planning of a new restaurant in a large city? How might the four P's be adjusted?

9   What social class would you associate with each of the following phrases or items?

   a) Sport cars.
   b) *True Story, True Romances,* etc.
   c) *New Yorker.*
   d) *Life.*
   e) Women listening to "soap operas."
   f) TV bowling shows.
   g) Families that serve Martinis, especially before dinner.
   h) Families who dress formally for dinner regularly.
   i) Families which are distrustful of banks (keep money in socks or mattress).
   j) Owners of French poodles.

175

In each case, choose one class, if you can. If you are not able to choose one class, but rather feel that several classes are equally likely, then so indicate. In those cases where you feel that all classes would be equally interested or characterized by a particular item, choose all five classes.

10 What is "web of word of mouth" and how could it be used by the marketing man?

11 What new status symbols are replacing the piano and automobile? Do these products have any characteristics in common? If they do, what are some possible status symbols of the future?

12 On the basis of the data and analysis presented in Chapters 6 and 8, what kind of buying behavior would you expect to find for the following products: (1) canned peas, (2) toothpaste, (3) ball-point pens, (4) baseball gloves, (5) sport coats, (6) dishwashers, (7) encyclopedias, (8) automobiles, and (9) motorboats? Set up a grid for your answer with products along the left-hand margin as the row headings and the following factors as headings for the columns: (1) how do you think consumers would shop for these products, (2) how far would they go, (3) would they buy by brand, (4) would they wish to compare with other products, and (5) any other factors which they should consider. Insert short answers—words or phrases are satisfactory—in the various grid boxes. Be prepared to discuss how the answers you put in the grid boxes would affect each product's marketing mix.

Intermediate customers and their buying behavior

T he term "customer" is interpreted by most of us to mean the individual final consumer (or family). Yet most final consumers probably would be startled to find that the bulk of purchases are made, not by final consumers, but by intermediate customers.

This chapter will be devoted to these intermediate customers—who and where they are, and something about their buying habits. We want to dispel misconceptions about the nature and size of these "other" markets. In fact, there are great marketing opportunities in catering to intermediate customers, and it is very probable that a college-level student will eventually work in this area. We also want to show that the market grid concept may have even greater application here because of the great diversity of demand and types of intermediate customers. While we will limit our discussion to the United States to keep it specific, many of the ideas are applicable to the world market.

Who are intermediate customers?

There are many kinds of intermediate customers. The various kinds and their numerical importance are shown in Table 9–1. Although there are about 200 million final consumers, there are only about 11 million intermediate customers. These customers may: (1) buy goods for resale to others; (2) buy items that they incorporate into their

177

Table 9-1 Kind and number of intermediate customers in 1963

Agriculture, forestry, and fisheries	3,491,000
Service industries	2,521,000
Retailers	1,940,000
Contract construction	848,000
Wholesalers	505,000
Manufacturers	408,000
Governmental units (1962)	91,000
Others	1,558,000
Total	11,362,000

SOURCE: *Statistical Abstract of the United States, 1966*, pp. 416 and 486.

own product for eventual resale to others; and (3) buy plant and equipment that enable them to operate their businesses.

Farms, service, retailing

The most numerous intermediate customers are those engaged in *agriculture, forestry, and fishing.* While many of these are small farmers, each represents an individual decision-making unit and a potential customer. Farms are given separate treatment in this chapter.

The service industries are the second largest group of intermediate customers. These include establishments such as restaurants, hotels, motels, barbershops, beauty shops, hospitals, medical clinics, and laundries and dry cleaners. Their great diversity and, frequently, small size make it difficult to generalize about their buying behavior. In addition, labor is a big element in their operation, as opposed to materials, but the subject of labor relations is beyond our scope. Further, the owner's own labor may be the major cost.

We will not treat the service industries separately, but how industrial customers (manufacturers) buy probably will be applicable to the buying of goods and services by service industries also. This will be especially the case where the service industries are linked together into a chain or are part of a franchise operation.

Retailers are the next most numerous group of intermediate customers. Their buying behavior with respect to plant and equipment will be similar to that of industrial customers. Their buying of goods for resale, however, is so intimately linked to their selling activity that we will delay discussion of this until retailing is discussed in Chapter 17.

Contract construction is the business of manufacturing homes, roads, buildings and other structures, and in this respect is similar to manufacturing in general. The two will be considered as similar in our discussion of manufacturers in this chapter.

Wholesalers, a somewhat smaller group, also would behave like manufacturers in the purchase of plant and equipment. In buying for resale, however, they, like retailers, find their buying and selling policies closely related. We will delay this discussion until we treat wholesaling in Chapter 18.

Manufacturers, while even less numerous, are discussed extensively in this chapter because their total volume of purchases is large and it is possible to generalize about their buying behavior.

A seemingly small group—*governmental units*—includes states, counties, cities, school districts, sanitary districts, and the federal government. But governments are of growing importance, especially for certain types of products. Our federal government is especially important, for it is the largest single buyer in the world. Governmental buyers will receive special treatment in this chapter.

A large number of firms fall into the "other" category—mining and quarrying, communications, and public utilities (all of which are basically manufacturing enterprises), *plus* transportation, finance, and real estate (all of which combine some aspects of manufacturing and the service industries). While the general principles we will discuss apply to these various enterprises, their specific needs, buying behavior, etc., are too specialized to be treated in this text.

The importance of intermediate customers

Intermediate customers are essential in the marketing process. Although few final consumers are aware of what is going on behind the scenes, *more goods and services are sold in total to farmers, manufacturers, wholesalers, retailers, and other intermediate customers than are sold to final consumers.*

At first glance, this may be difficult to understand. How can more goods and services be sold than are consumed by final consumers? The answer is that in our complex, interrelated society, a good deal of buying and selling goes on while the goods and services are being produced and on their way to final consumers. In fact, the same good may be sold *several times* before it is in "final" form and sold to retail customers.

Several intermediate customers may handle same product

Many farmers or manufacturers do not themselves produce the finished products desired by final consumers. Rather, many producers in our economy specialize in that aspect of production in which they are most efficient and then sell their goods for further processing or sale. Eventually someone assembles the specialized products of many producers and either physically combines them (manufacturers), or presents them in an attractive assortment (wholesalers or retailers) for the next customer, be he an intermediate or a final consumer. And each time these goods change hands, a sale is recorded.

An example may clarify this process. The small manufacturer of electric fans obviously does not produce iron ore, steel, copper, paint, raw materials, or other such products which are basic ingredients of electric fans. He buys the components from firms specializing in motors, metal castings, stampings, and so on. When this manufacturer has finished fabricating and assembling the fan, it is doubtful that he would sell it direct to the final consumer. Rather, wholesalers might buy the fans, sell them to plants or offices for their use and to retailers for resale to their customers.

179

As you can see, a great deal of marketing activity is involved before a product reaches the final consumer. The complexity and magnitude of this flow of goods and services in the United States has been diagrammed in Figure 9–1. The sizes of the various streams represent roughly the value of the goods and services flowing to the next customers. Notice the small amount of activity between the retail level and the final consumers compared to the activity between other levels. Retailing is important, certainly, but a great deal of marketing is going on behind the scenes—wholesalers to other wholesalers and manufacturers, for example, as well as manufacturers to other manufacturers.

**Where does
the value of
products
come from?**

Notice in Figure 9–1 that the streams going into the blocks representing agriculture, manufacturing, wholesaling, and retailing are smaller than the streams coming out. The higher selling price of the goods coming out represents the "value added" by that particular sector. This is sometimes called "value added by manufacture," "value added by wholesaling," and so on. It represents the value of all goods and services, labor payments, and entrepreneurial profit added by the firms in that activity. Notice that the values added by agriculture and manufacturing were relatively large, indicating a considerable amount of processing and labor. Retailing adds relatively less cost and value, and wholesaling least of all.

This concept of value added must be interpreted carefully. It is based primarily on the *cost and profit added,* rather than on the *amount of satisfaction or usefulness contributed*. The relatively small value added by wholesaling does not necessarily mean that wholesaling is unproductive. The wholesaler may be extremely efficient, operating at low cost and therefore adding little "value" according to this approach to measuring productivity. Unfortunately, there still is no accurate measure of added value in terms of customer satisfaction.

The main point to be derived from Figure 9–1 is that a large volume of goods and services flow between all the various levels of intermediate customers. All these flows are important to the efficient operation of our interdependent, free economy.

The size of these flows also suggest important opportunities for alert marketing managers. Firms selling to intermediate customers seem to be more production-oriented than those selling directly to final consumers, and therefore the marketing-oriented firm may be even more successful here.

Industrial customers

While we will emphasize the size and behavior of manufacturers, many other intermediate buyers behave like manufacturers, both in buying their plant and equipment and the goods and services they incorporate into their products. Thus many of the comments will be applicable to other intermediate customers.

**How big are
the targets?**

Probably the most striking fact about the industrial market is its small number of customers compared to the final consumer market,

Figure 9–1 The flow of goods and services in the United States (the size of each channel indicates the sales volume in that flow)

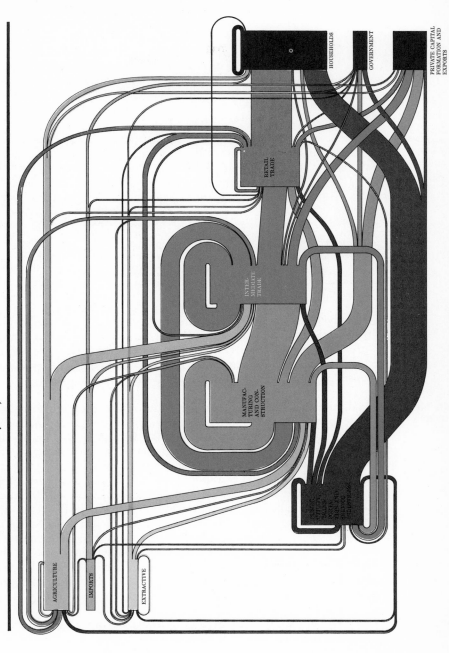

AGRICULTURE

IMPORTS

EXTRACTIVE

MANUFAC-
TURING
AND CON-
STRUCTION

INTER-
MEDIATE
TRADE

RETAIL
TRADE

PUBLIC
UTILITY
GAS
WATER
COMMUNI-
CATION
SERVICE
MISCELLANEOUS

HOUSEHOLDS

GOVERNMENT

PRIVATE CAPITAL
FORMATION AND
EXPORTS

SOURCE: Reavis Cox, *Distribution in a High Level Economy*, © 1965. Reprinted by permission of Prentice–Hall, Inc., Englewood Cliffs, N.J.

where we find about 200 million people in more than 57 million households. In the industrial market, there are about 410,000 manufacturing plants, and the majority of these plants are quite small, as indicated by the data in Table 9–2.

Table 9–2 Size distribution of manufacturing establishments, 1963

Number of Employees	Number of Establishments	Value Added by Manufacturing	Total Number of Employees	Percentage of Firms	Percentage of Value Added	Percentage of Employees
1–4	112,036	2,109,939	203,647	36.5	1.1	1.3
5–9	48,461	3,045,060	326,093	15.8	1.6	2.0
10–19	46,778	6,155,413	645,606	15.3	3.2	4.0
20–49	47,376	14,241,093	1,480,682	15.4	7.4	9.1
50–99	22,886	15,832,033	1,590,601	7.5	8.2	9.8
100–249	17,614	28,826,390	2,726,693	5.7	15.0	16.8
250–499	6,639	25,662,713	2,297,394	2.2	13.3	14.1
500–999	2,942	25,390,653	2,014,698	1.0	13.2	12.4
1,000–2,499	1,375	29,237,192	2,052,759	0.4	15.2	14.3
2,500 or over	544	41,819,313	2,898,617	0.2	21.7	23.0

SOURCE: *1963 Census of Manufactures,* Vol. III, *Area Statistics,* pp. 2–8, 2–9.

A relatively few large manufacturing plants employ the majority of workers and produce a substantial share of the value added by manufacture. For example, in 1963, 29,114 plants—about 9.5 percent of the total—employed 80.6 percent of the production employees and were responsible for 78.4 percent of the value added by manufacture.

Where the customers cluster

In addition to concentration by size, industrial markets are characterized by concentration in particular areas. Figure 9–2 is an industrial map of the U.S. showing the area of each state in proportion to the value of manufactured products in that state. The dominance of the Middle West and Middle Atlantic states is noteworthy.

As we found with final consumers, political boundaries leave something to be desired when describing industrial concentration. Big metropolitan areas are big industrial markets too. The 212 SMSA's account for approximately 63 percent of the value added by manufacturing in the United States. Marketing managers can focus their attention on a relatively few clearly defined markets and be within reach of the majority of the business. This has a definite bearing on the number and type of wholesalers that manufacturers use and the kinds of wholesalers who develop, as we will see in subsequent chapters.

Concentration by industry

Not only do we see concentration by size of firm and geographical location but also by industry. Manufacturers of advanced electronics systems and instrumentation are concentrated in the Boston and New York areas and on the West Coast, for example. The steel industry is heavily concentrated in the Pittsburgh and Chicago areas. Other indus-

182

tries have similar concentrations based on the availability of natural or human resources.

The salesman's job of selling to some industries is made even easier because some large companies with multiple plants may do all of their buying from a central office and that central office is usually located in

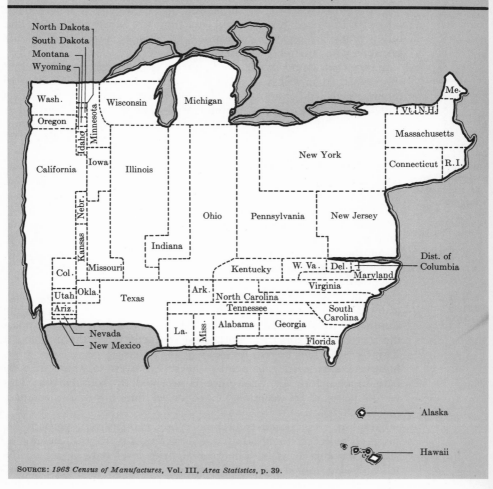

Figure 9–2 *An industrial map of the United States showing area of each state in ratio to other states based on value of manufactured products (based on the 1963 Census of Manufactures)*

SOURCE: *1963 Census of Manufactures*, Vol. III, *Area Statistics*, p. 39.

one of the large metropolitan areas. One of the large building material manufacturers, for example, does the bulk of its buying for more than 50 plants from its Chicago office. In such a case, the salesman may be able to "sell" his products all over the country without leaving his home city.

This makes it easier for him, but also for his competitors, and he may have to compete in an extremely competitive market. The selling job may be easier, but the marketing job may be much harder, because all the customers are close together.

The size of some industrial operations has made the buying function extremely important. Many have developed buying specialists, known as purchasing agents. Some of them have banded together, forming the National Association of Purchasing Agents in an effort to improve the effectiveness and status of professional buyers. This is the kind of buyer that faces those who wish to sell to the industrial market.

The industrial buyer, or purchasing agent, usually is the man all salesmen must see first before contacting any other employee. The buyer holds an important position and may be prejudiced against salesmen who attempt to bypass him.

Rather than being "sold," these buyers expect precise and accurate information that will help them buy wisely. They appreciate help in buying as efficiently as possible. They like information on new products and services and tips on potential price changes, strikes, and other changes in business conditions. Most industrial buyers are serious, well-educated men, and salesmen should treat them accordingly.

In various circumstances, industrial buyers (really, buyers of all types, including final consumers) use four basic approaches to evaluating and buying products: (1) inspection, (2) sampling, (3) description, and (4) negotiated contracts.

Inspection. The inspection method is used for products that are not standardized, and require examination. Here, each product is different, as in the case of some fruits and vegetables, and livestock. One-of-a-kind products, such as used buildings and cars, also must be inspected.

Products that require inspection are often bought at auction, especially if there are several possible buyers. Auctions, for instance, are commonly found at the wholesale level. The potential buyers inspect the merchandise and then bid against competitors for the product. If there are too few buyers to make a good market at any one time, however, a price may be set by the seller. Even so, there may be bargaining before the final price is accepted by both parties. This would be true, for example, in the used building and machinery market.

Sampling. As products become more standardized, perhaps because of more careful grading and better quality control, buying by sample becomes feasible. The general price level may be set by the seller or determined by an auction-type market for standard grades. The price then may be adjusted from this level according to the quality of the specific sample.

In the grain market, for example, the general price level for standard grades is set by demand-and-supply factors. Then the price for a specific carload is the market price for the appropriate grade plus or minus an adjustment for quality variation based on a sample taken from the carload.

184

Description. Today, most manufactured items and many agricultural commodities can be subjected to more rigid quality control or grading. When quality almost can be guaranteed, buying by description—grade, brand, or specification—may be satisfactory, at least when there is mutual trust between buyers and sellers. In recent years, more wholesale and retail buyers have come to accept government grading standards for some fruits and vegetables. Now, much of this merchandise is packed in the fields and sold without any further inspection or sampling. This, of course, reduces the cost of buying and is used by buyers whenever practicable.

In modern economies, most products are purchased by description. Grocery, hardware, and dry goods items are examples. By contrast, in primitive economies, most buying is done by inspection or sampling, regardless of the products. The reason is skepticism and uncertainty about quality, or lack of faith in the seller.

Various pricing practices are used for products that can be bought by description. Some firms set fixed prices, and the buyer has little choice, especially if the seller has succeeded in developing a unique marketing mix. But if there is competition among several suppliers, then buyers may ask for bids and choose the seller with the lowest bid. This practice is formalized and made mandatory in much government buying. As an alternative, the buyers may bargain for lower prices.

Negotiated contracts. The three methods discussed above are concerned with tangible products or products and services which can be described sufficiently well so that suppliers know what is wanted and can submit definite prices or bids. Usually a price is set for each shipment or order, or perhaps for a series of shipments against the same order. But a price is set for some fairly definite, agreed upon, product and marketing mix.

Sometimes, however, the buyer knows roughly what he wants but cannot describe it exactly. Perhaps he plans to change the specifications or total requirements as the job progresses, or maybe some of the details cannot be anticipated. This is found, for example, in research and development work and in the building of special-purpose machinery and large buildings. In such cases, the general project is described, and a basic price may be agreed upon, with provision for adjustments both upward and downward. Or a supplier may be willing to work under a contract that provides some type of incentive over coverage of costs, such as full coverage of costs plus a fixed fee, or full costs plus some percentage profit based on costs. The whole contract may even be subject to renegotiation as the work proceeds.

Industrial buyers are usually less emotional in their buying habits than final consumers. The basic objectives or motives of their purchasing can be stated as follows:

Basic purchasing motives of industrial buyers

1. To maintain continuity of supply to support the manufacturing schedule.
2. To do so with a minimum investment in materials and inventory consistent with safety and economic advantage.
3. To avoid duplication, waste, and obsolescence of materials.

4. To maintain standards of quality and materials, based on suitability for use.
5. To procure materials at the lowest cost consistent with the quality and service required.
6. To maintain the company's competitive position in its industry and to conserve its profit position, where material costs are concerned.[1]

Specifically, buyers tend to look for certain product characteristics, including economy, both in original cost and in use; productivity; uniformity; purity; and ability to make the buyer's final product more suitable.[2]

In addition to the product characteristics, buyers consider the reliability of the seller; his general cooperativeness; his ability to provide quick repair service; past and present relationships (including previous favors); continuous supply under all conditions; and certain, fast delivery.

Emotional motives. Industrial purchasing does have some emotional overtones, too. At one time, it might have been fair to characterize buyers by the following quotation:

The typical buyer is a man past middle life, spare, wrinkled, intelligent, cold, passive, noncommital, with eyes like a codfish, polite in contacts, but at the same time unresponsive, cool, calm, and damnably composed as a concrete post or a plaster-of-paris cat; a human petrification with a heart of feldspar and without charms; or the friendly germ, minus passions or a sense of humor. Happily they never reproduce, and all of them finally go to hell.[3]

Such a view does not apply to a modern purchasing agent, who places less emphasis on price and more on value. He has a broader view of the purchasing function, usually has a sense of humor, and often can be approached in a lighter vein. International Minerals and Chemicals Co., a manufacturer of standardized chemicals, once even used a dramatic consumer-type promotion (including jets, rockets, and pretty models) for a trade-show presentation.[4]

Modern buyers, being human, want to have friendly relationships with suppliers.[5] Some buyers seem eager to emulate progressive competitors, even to be the first to try new products. In other words, the emotional product motives discussed in the last chapter may have some relevance here.

The purchasing agent may have another important motive, namely, to protect his own position in the company. Most buyers, like people everywhere, seek to increase their chances for promotion without taking too many risks. And they, perhaps more than many executives,

---

[1] Stuart F. Heinritz, *Purchasing: Principles and Application* (3d ed.; Englewood Cliffs, N.J.: Prentice-Hill, Inc., 1959).

[2] "Component Buyers Seek Tangible Savings," *Electronic Procurement,* May, 1962, pp. 26–29.

[3] Adapted slightly from Charles A. Koepke, *Plant Production Control* (2d ed.; New York: John Wiley & Sons, Inc., 1949), p. 104.

[4] "Putting a Sales Idea into Orbit," *Business Week,* June 28, 1958, pp. 70–74.

[5] "How to Use Emotional Factors That Trigger Industrial Sales," *Steel,* April 6, 1959, for a motivational survey conducted in the metalworking industry by F. R. Shoaf of New York University.

have to make decisions involving many uncontrollable factors. A new product may not work out, and the buyer may be blamed. Poor service, interrupted or late delivery, or low quality can reflect upon his ability. Any product or service, therefore, that assures the buyer that he will "look good" has a definite appeal. In fact, it might make the difference between a successful and an unsuccessful marketing mix.

Multiple buying influence

Much of the work of the typical purchasing agent consists of placing orders to fill routine requisitions flowing from various production, warehouse, and office departments. Similar orders may have been placed many times before, and to obtain the goods, the purchasing agent may merely refer to his "source file" where he has recorded notes on his past relations with various sources of supply, their prices, and their dependability. For such routine items, he may place the order without further consultation with anyone.

In other cases, the buyer is not the only company executive participating in the purchasing decision. In fact, sometimes five or more executives may be involved. The bigger and more important the purchase, the higher the level at which the decision will be considered, if not made. The more technical the decision, the more likely that technical employees will be involved, perhaps to the extent of writing specifications so that only one supplier can meet them.[6]

The nature of the multiple buying influence must be studied in each particular case. It can even be another dimension in the market grid for a particular product. Knowledgeable salesmen could probably help describe the nature of the multiple buying influence, though marketing research may be necessary in some cases. Table 9–3 shows how the Amercoat Corp. outlined its corrosion-control sales job. Although representing a specific case, the table should be studied carefully, since it shows the difference in outlook of the various levels of executives. A salesman might talk to every one of those possible "influencers," but he would take up different topics and stress different factors for each of them.

Sharing of buying decisions among a number of executives leads to a relatively long selling period. Paper work must pass many desks. Approval of a routine order may take anywhere from a week to several months. On very important purchases—say the purchase of a new computer system, a new plant, or major equipment—the selling period may stretch out to a year or more.

Supply sources must be dependable

Many industrial products are produced and sold as branded items or to meet certain specifications. As long as suppliers at least meet these minimum specifications, buyers can concentrate safely on other factors, such as price, dependable service, delivery, and credit terms. But it is important that quality be kept up. The cost of a small item may have little to do with its importance. If it causes malfunctioning of a larger unit in which it is incorporated, it may cause a large loss regardless of its own value. Buyers are understandably concerned about consistent

[6] For more detail, see John H. Platten, Jr., "How Industry Buys," *Scientific American,* September, 1950.

Table 9-3 *Analysis of customer buying behavior*

This table shows how Amercoat Corp. isolated the group of men who may exert buying influence on the corrosion-control plan they sell. Correlated paragraphs summarize each man's job influence, his knowledge and interest in corrosion control, his knowledge and interest in control methods, and his buying habits. The same technique can be used by any company that sells to the industrial market, working, of course, with its own key men.

Key Men	Contributor Factor Rating	Job Influence	Knowledge and Interest in Corrosion Control	Knowledge and Interest in Control Methods	Buying Habits
General manager	"A"	Primarily interested in results. Likely to leave details to others.	Limited knowledge. May have active interest in obtaining better results.	Little knowledge. Interest likely to be in anticipated results only.	May make final decision. Likely to leave details to others.
Manufacturing director	"A" or "B"	Primarily interested in results. Likely to be important factor in obtaining action.	Knowledge likely to depend on size and nature of the company. Should have active interest if aware of own hazards.	Knowledge probably limited. Should have active interest in best methods.	May have authority to place or initiate order. Important factor in any case.
Plant manager or superintendent	"A" "B" or "C"	Degree of importance depends on size of company and operating practice.	If operating in place of manufacturing director, likely to have above average degree of knowledge and interest in both subjects. Otherwise, may be figurehead. His goodwill, however, is important.		Unlikely to have authority to buy. Recommendation or requisition may be important.
Maintenance or corrosion engineer	"B"	Important factor in companies where charged with responsibility for maintenance costs.	Likely to have both interest and knowledge particularly if operating as corrosion engineer.	Should have active interest and some knowledge. May be prejudiced regarding some methods of control.	Unlikely to have authority to place or initiate order, but recommendation important.
Purchasing agent	"C"	Negative rather than positive, but in many companies must be seen first.	Limited, if any.	Limited, if any.	Close buyers, but largely influenced by other department heads and by top management.

Table 9–3—Continued

Key Men	Contrib- utor Factor Rating	Job Influence	Knowledge and Interest in Corrosion Control	Knowledge and Interest in Control Methods	Buying Habits
Research department	"B"	Negative as regards operating costs. Positive as applied to products and testing.	Knowledge and interest may be purely "scientific," rather than from dollars and cents viewpoint.	Knowledge and interest likely to be "scientific" and possibly prejudiced.	Usually have no authority to place or initiate orders. Tests likely to be important.
Plant engineer	"B" or "C"	Degree of importance depends on size of company and operating practice	If operating in place of maintenance or corrosion engineer, likely to have most of his knowledge and interest in both subjects. Otherwise, important only from standpoint of goodwill.		May have authority to "requisition"; otherwise recommendation may carry some weight.
Paint foreman	"C"	Usually follows "line of least resistance." Interest and pride need to be stimulated, especially if new method involves extra effort.	Neither knowledge, nor interest except in rare cases.	Except in rare cases, no knowledge beyond methods now using and no active interest except in easier ways to do the job.	Usually have no authority to place or initiate orders. Goodwill and willingness to handle products properly are important.

Key to Contributor Factor Rating:
"A"—The men who must make the final buying decision and who have the authority to authorize the expenditure.
"B"—The advisory, intermediate or subordinate men who must also be sold; otherwise the "A" men are likely to withhold approval.
"C"—Other men who may influence the buying decision. As a rule, these men have no authority but can block the sale by direct opposition or a negative attitude.
SOURCE: A. E. Turner, "Finding the Men Who Can Influence the Sale," *Sales Management*, September 15, 1953, p. 41.

quality, and some even set up statistical quality control procedures to inspect all incoming lots.

Because of the importance of dependable product quality to industrial buyers, some producers deliberately seek to make products that are slightly above required specifications, thereby giving a greater assurance of dependable quality to the buyer. This is *the* important selling point for some firms. In effect, this "makes" their marketing mix.

The availability of this "higher-than-needed" quality helps explain the behavior of some buyers who appear to favor certain suppliers. While several products may meet the minimum requirements, the buyer may choose suppliers of extra-quality products because his own future is involved in the buying decision.

To be assured of dependable quality, a buyer may also develop loyalty to certain suppliers. This is especially important when buying nonstandardized products. When a friendly relationship is developed over the years, the supplier practically becomes a part of the buyer's organization—without the buyer assuming the additional cost of plant and working capital or the problems of management. This friendly, loyal relationship may be good business for all concerned. In an emergency, one can sometimes help the other.

Most buyers have a sense of fair play, and when a salesman proposes a new idea that saves the buyer's company money, he usually attempts to reward that salesman with orders. This encourages future suggestions.[7] In contrast, buyers who use a bid system exclusively—either by choice or necessity, as in some government and institutional purchasing—may not be offered much beyond the basic products or services. They are interested primarily in price. Marketing managers who have developed "better" products and technical or other assistance programs may not solicit such business, at least with their "better" mix.

Even if a firm has developed the most ideal marketing mix possible, it probably will not get all of the business of its industrial target customers. Purchasing agents usually seek several dependable sources of supply, to protect themselves from unpredictable events, such as strikes, fires, or floods in one of their suppliers' plants. But still, a good marketing mix is likely to win a larger share of the total business.

Buy EOQ quantities, especially if use EDP

Some buyers in larger companies which have well-developed electronic data processing systems (EDP) have been able to delegate a considerable part of their routine order placing to computers. They develop decision rules that tell the computer how to order economic order quantities (EOQ) and then leave the details of following through to the computer. This is possible because there generally is a lowest cost order quantity toward which the purchasing agent would aim, anyway.

The delivered cost of goods can be visualized as shown in Figure 9–3. This figure shows that cost per unit is high for very small quantity buying, declines as the quantity ordered increases, and then begins to rise again as greater quantities are ordered. Ideally, buyers will seek to purchase that quantity for which the unit cost is lowest.

---

[7] "Rival's Purchasing Philosophy," *Pet Food Industry,* June, 1962, pp. 8–9.

Figure 9–3 Relation of total cost (including storage) per unit to quantity ordered

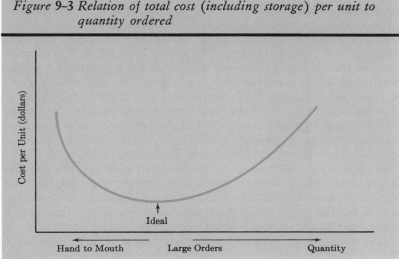

Some factors that cause the curve in Figure 9–3 to decline as the quantity purchased increases are as follows:

1. Price discounts are sometimes given as quantity purchased increases.
2. Transportation costs are usually lower as the quantity shipped increases.
3. Purchasing costs may be relatively fixed per order, not per unit ordered. As quantity increases, therefore, the per unit ordering costs decrease. An average purchase order may cost $5 to $10 regardless of the number of items ordered.[8]

The following factors cause the curve to rise and suggest the purchase of smaller quantities:

1. Interest, insurance, and taxes will be higher on larger quantities held in inventory.
2. Space costs will be higher, especially if additional warehouse space must be rented.
3. The risks of deterioration and obsolescence of inventory are increased as the quantity held in inventory is increased.

The costs of carrying inventory often are underestimated because some are intangible. Careful estimates, however, show that the total cost of carrying inventory range from 15 to 30 percent of the cost value of the average inventory.[9]

Some formulas have been developed to objectively relate all of the various factors in a particular buying situation and determine the EOQ's. These formulas are beyond the scope of this book, but the very fact that formulas and computers are used shows that buying is becom-

---

[8] Actually, the curve would look more like a series of steps, depending on the relation of costs to quantity, but a curve is a fair approximation in most cases. A curve is assumed in the manipulation of mathematical formulas which are frequently used in determining the quantity to buy.

[9] T. M. Whitin, *The Theory of Inventory Management* (Princeton, N.J.: Princeton University Press, 1953).

ing increasingly analytical and that every effort is being made to reduce guesswork and intuition.[10]

Ideally, the buyer would appraise all of these factors on a continuing basis and adjust his economic order quantities accordingly. Actually, however, most buyers are faced with such a large number of items to purchase that they could not fully analyze all these factors all the time. When they have a computer system available, they tend to "delegate" as much as they can. Then they watch the general movement of economic conditions, and when conditions require, these buyers modify the basic formulas they have given to the computer. When nothing unusual happens, however, the computer system may continue to "grindout" new purchase orders to the established suppliers.

It is extremely important, then, for a supplier to be one of those that the computer will consider. In such a situation, the critical thing is not whether a particular salesman will get a particular order, but whether he will be considered one of the major suppliers. Obviously this is a much bigger "sale." It also is obvious that such a buyer might be more favorably impressed by an attractive marketing mix, perhaps for a whole line of products, rather than just a lower price on a particular order. It might be too costly and too much trouble to change his whole buying system just because somebody is offering a low price on a particular day.

Inventory policy may determine sales

Industrial firms generally try to maintain an adequate inventory—at least enough to insure that the production lines keep moving. Nothing is viewed as a greater calamity in a factory than to have a production line close down.

Adequate inventory often is expressed in terms of number of days' supply—for example, 60- or 90-days' supply. But what constitutes 60- or 90-days' supply depends upon the level of demand facing the company. If the demand rises sharply, say by 10 percent, then total purchases will expand by more than 10 percent to maintain customary inventory levels *and* meet the new needs. On the other hand, if sales decrease by 10 percent, actual needs *and* inventory requirements decrease, and total purchases may decrease drastically while the inventory is being "worked off." During such a contraction, a seller would probably have little success with efforts to stimulate sales by reducing price or offering more favorable credit terms. The buyer is just not in the market at this time.

The buyer's first concern when sales are shifting rapidly is to bring inventory into line with sales, perhaps preparing for either further declines or rises in sales. The severity in changes in buyer's demands in the market will depend in part on how rapidly the buyer insists upon adjusting his inventory. And this in turn may depend on the firm's economic situation and the policies of its financial officers. Another factor is computer systems. We may even see mechanical and rapid adjustments upward or downward if a firm has moved its inventory

[10] S. F. Heinritz, *Purchasing* (2d ed.; Englewood Cliffs, N.J.: Prentice-Hall, Inc., 1951), pp. 177–95; Whitin, *op. cit.;* and Winston C. Dalleck and Robert B. Fetter, *Decision Models for Inventory Management* (Homewood, Ill.: Richard D. Irwin, Inc., 1961).

control procedures to a computer. This may lead to extremely rapid swings both upward and downward in the flow of orders.

In recent years, some alert purchasing agents have expanded their view of their job to include consideration of whether the product requisitioned should be purchased at all or if it is the most suitable one for the job. This broader approach is called *value analysis,* or sometimes *value engineering.* It requires that the purchasing agent become involved with areas outside his own department.

Value analysis

With this approach, perhaps 75 percent of the purchasing agents' effort will be required in *selling* new ideas and methods to engineering, manufacturing, and top management.[11]

A purchasing agent with such a broad view of his job would obviously be increasingly appreciative of suggestions and new ideas. Price, of course, is never ignored, but purchasing agents are coming to realize that the lowest price may not provide the best value.

Reciprocity implies that if "you buy from me, I'll buy from you." If a company's better customers also can supply products which the firm purchases, then the sales departments of both buyer and seller may seek to "trade" sales for sales. Purchasing agents generally prefer to buy the required quality at the lowest prices consistent with dependable quality, delivery, and so on. This leads them to resist reciprocity, but often it is forced upon them by their sales departments.

Reciprocity

Reciprocal buying and selling is commonplace in some industries, particularly in paints, chemicals, and petroleum. Usually both prices and product qualities are competitive, and it becomes difficult to ignore the pressures of the sales departments involved. One chemical company brought purchasing under marketing to handle this problem.[12]

When prices and quality are competitive, an outside supplier seldom can break such a reciprocal relationship. He can only hope to become an alternate source of supply and wait for his competitors to let quality slip or prices rise. In this case, alert sellers provide a service to buyers who are not sympathetic with these reciprocal arrangements.

The U.S. Justice Department also frowns upon reciprocity. It has now launched a program to block reciprocal buying on the grounds that it is an attempt to monopolize, restricting the normal operation of the free market. This may force those firms that place heavy reliance on reciprocal dealing to reevaluate their marketing strategies.[13]

These general buying habits and practices apply in the purchase of many industrial products. Specific habits and practices, however, vary according to the type of product, a subject which is covered in Chapter 13. These specifics, however, apply within the framework of our discus-

Buying practices vary by product

[11] Burke B. Cochran, "Human Factors Important in Value Analysis," *Electronic Procurement,* July, 1962, pp. 24–27; see also, Lawrence P. Miles, *Techniques of Value Analysis and Engineering* (New York: McGraw-Hill Book Co., 1961); and "How Valuable Is Value Analysis?" *Business Week,* May 15, 1965, pp. 78–82.

[12] "The Chemical Boom: Will New Stress on Marketing Make It Even Bigger?" *Printers' Ink,* November 17, 1961, pp. 22–28.

[13] "Suit Hits Two-way Buying," *Business Week,* March 11, 1967, pp. 162–64.

sion of the geographical location and concentration of industrial customers, their basic purchasing motives and methods, the importance of the multiple buying influence, and other general considerations.

The farm market

Agriculture is fundamental to almost all economies. As we saw in Chapter 7, agriculture absorbs almost all of the work force in some countries. In the United States, however, the percentage of the population engaged in agriculture has been declining steadily, and even further decline is predicted. (See Table 9–4.)

				1975
1850	*1900*	*1930*	*1960*	*(estimated)*
64%	38%	22%	9%	6%

Table **9–4** *Percent of U.S. labor force working on farms*

SOURCE: "Big Farms, Little Farms, in 1970," *Looking Ahead*, National Planning Association, May, 1962, p. 1.

American farmers have been progressive in the adoption of new equipment and farming techniques. From 1950 to 1960, output per man-hour in agriculture went up 5.1 percent per year, while manufacturing gained only 2.7 percent.[14] This high rate of productivity has caused some embarrassment in the farm market when surpluses (sometimes related to price supports) have continually depressed prices.

The following discussion will emphasize the U.S. farm market, but it has wider application to international agricultural marketing.

Where are the farms and farmers going?
As already noted, farmers are the most numerous intermediate customers. Yet just as the percentage of the population engaged in agriculture is declining, so is the number of farms. In the 20-year period from 1940 to 1959, more than 2 million farm units disappeared, the total dropping from more than 6 million to less than 4 million farms. The remaining farms have absorbed some of this acreage, and from 1940 to 1959, the average farm increased in size from fewer than 200 acres to more than 300 acres.

The degree of concentration is seen more clearly if it is realized that about a million and a half farmers produce about 87 percent of the total farm output. One tenth of all farms in the United States exceed 500 acres, and it is the farmers of these larger, more productive tracts who have known how to work with and around agricultural subsidy programs. The idea of subsidy programs, justified politically and economically as supporting the small farmer's "way of life," is dying hard. But it is clear that many small farmers continue to leave the land and that more and more farming is being done by larger corporate farms.

The rapid decline in the number of farms is extremely important to a

---

[14] *Looking Ahead*, May, 1962, p. 2.

marketing manager. He has fewer but larger potential customers. Further, however, competition has changed. There has been a decline in the number of manufacturers catering to this market, a decline from a high of about 1,600 manufacturers in 1950 to something more than 700 in 1964.[15]

There also has been a similar decline among middlemen. The National Farm & Power Equipment Dealers' Association indicates that their membership declined from about 34,000 to 17,000 between 1940 and 1960.

Many middlemen who were in once rural areas have switched to lawn tools for the new suburbanites or to equipment for the new industrial plants which have moved out of the central cities. Other dealers have simply gone out of business.[16]

Tailoring products to customers' specialization

Another important factor is that farmers are tending to specialize in one or a few products—such as wheat alone, or wheat plus oats and corn, or fruit and nuts, or poultry. These farmers are interested in only specific kinds of products.

A cotton farmer, for example, may have little interest in hen houses or antibiotics. Or a wheat farmer in the northern plains where hard wheat is grown would have different needs from those of a farmer further south where soft wheat is preferred.

Market grids for such different customers should be developed in great detail; fortunately, much data is available from the U.S. Department of Agriculture.

Studying this market carefully makes it obvious that marketing mixes may have to be tailored for each individual farmer—and in some cases this is happening. Fertilizer producers have now moved far beyond selling an all-purpose bag of fertilizer. Now they are able to blend the exact type needed for each farm and load it directly onto fertilizer spreaders which do the job more economically than manual methods. Some producers, in fact, are working directly with farmers, providing a complete service—including fertilizing, weeding, and debugging—all tailored to each individual farmer's needs.[17]

Every farm dollar counts

Sheer numbers of farms, like sheer numbers of people, do not make markets. Customers must have buying power to be of interest to sellers. This part of the farm picture is not nearly so bright.

In 1959, more than half the farms in the United States sold less than $5,000 worth of merchandise each, and less than a quarter of the farms sold more than $25,000 worth.[18] The number of larger farms has been increasing and small ones decreasing. But still there are many potential customers who are poor attractions from the market point of view.

In 1959, the average farm took in $8,218 in cash receipts from product sales.[18] There are, however, many farms with sales far above this

[15] "The Farm Sees a New Revolution," *Business Week*, October 24, 1964, pp. 116–72.

[16] "Farm Tool Retailers Diversify to Lift Profit as Old Clients Dwindle," *Wall Street Journal*, November 30, 1962, p. 1.

[17] "Monsanto Moves into Farmers' Backyard," *Business Week*, February 6, 1965, pp. 60–62.

[18] Computed from data in *Statistical Abstract of the United States*, 1962, p. 612 and pp. 616–17.

average; they make for an attractive market for farm equipment, new buildings, and consumer goods.[19] But from this average income exceeding $8,000, various expenses must be subtracted for running the farm—and hopefully, supporting the house and family. It is easy to see that the average farmer does not have any great surplus to spend.

Groceries and feed in the station wagon

The income figures mentioned above make it easier to understand why farmers are often seen as conservative and slow to buy. Quite simply, many farmers do not have the money to buy much.

But the owner of the larger farm is another matter. He is just as questioning, but he is more knowledgeable and more receptive to change. He tends to run his farm as a business rather than a way of life, and consequently is susceptible to presentations stressing savings and increases in productivity. And he may have the assets to act on his decisions.

Some studies of farmer purchasing behavior, however, indicate that for some products, buying motivations are not much different from those for consumer goods.

Many farmers seem unwilling to shop around for the lowest price, preferring the convenience of patronizing the nearest farm implement or feed dealer. Some emulation was found, especially in the purchase of farm machinery. This is understandable when you consider that a farmer's home and place of business are the same. Some manufacturers take pride in office facilities and factories, and the same sort of motive may affect farmer purchasing behavior. Among owners of smaller farms, a new tractor may offer just as much status as a new car would to an urban cousin. Moreover, the farmer's roles as a businessman and a final consumer sometimes overlap. For example, a station wagon might be used for carrying feed and the family's groceries. Then the motives that drive both final consumers and businessmen may become intertwined.

Agriculture is becoming a business

Another factor that may have growing importance is the tendency for farmers to engage in contract farming. Here, the farmer obtains his supplies and perhaps working capital from local dealers or manufacturers who agree to purchase his output, sometimes at guaranteed prices. This limits his buying freedom, since he becomes, in effect, an employee. Such arrangements are becoming more frequent, especially in raising chickens and turkeys and in growing fresh vegetables for commercial canning. These arrangements give stability to the agricultural structure but also limit the markets for sellers. It is all part of the move toward bigger and more businesslike agricultural enterprises.

In some parts of the country, we already see the development of corporate farms and closely integrated operations. Some large feed millers, for example, have moved into the poultry industry in order to assure an outlet for their feed. Some have integrated their operations all the way down to processing the broilers and eggs and then moving them toward retailers.

---

[19] "Farmer: A Market with New Status," *Printers' Ink*, March 15, 1963, pp. 21–26.

Where such contractual arrangements (or actual ownership) are common, marketing managers will have to adjust their marketing mixes. Perhaps they will have to sell directly to the large manufacturers or dealers who are handling the arrangements rather than to the farmer himself.[20]

In summary, the modern farmer is becoming more knowledgeable and more businesslike and seems willing to accept help and new ideas—but only when he feels sure they will help him improve production.

The government market

Government is the largest customer in the United States. Approximately 30 percent of the gross national product is spent by various governmental units. These units buy almost every kind of commodity. They run not only schools, police departments, and military organizations but supermarkets, public utilities, research laboratories, offices, hospitals, and liquor stores. And government expenditures for all these operations are growing continually.

Size and diversity

Spending by all government units totals slightly more than $200 billion, and the federal government, the largest of all the governmental buyers, accounts for approximately 58 percent of the total. The states' share of this total is only 15 percent; local governments spend about 27 percent.[21] Expenditures of this magnitude cannot be ignored by an aggressive marketing manager.

Bidding is common. Many government customers buy by description, using a mandatory bidding procedure which is open to public review. Often the government buyer is forced to accept the lowest bid. His biggest job, after deciding generally what he wants, is to correctly describe his need so that the description is unambiguous and complete. Otherwise, he may find sellers bidding on a product he does not want. By law, he might have to accept the low bid for the unwanted product.

General buying methods

Drawing specifications carefully is not an easy task, and buyers usually appreciate the help of knowledgeable salesmen. Legally, the buyer probably cannot draw the specifications so that only one supplier will be able to meet them (although this has been done!), but if all the relevant specifications are included, then the bidding must be on the items desired. The customer can then obtain the product he wants. And the knowledgeable salesman may get the business, even though his bid is not the lowest, because the lower bids do not meet the minimum specifications.

Not all of the items that governments buy, however, create specification difficulties. Many branded items or items for which there are widely accepted standards are routinely purchased through the conven-

---

[20] L. R. Kohls, "The Farm Today," *Journal of Marketing*, October, 1959, pp. 59–62; "New Farm Market—Down in Customers, But Up in Money," *Printers' Ink*, March 16, 1962, pp. 23–28; *Wall Street Journal*, November 30, 1962, p. 1; and *Time*, November 9, 1962, p. 20.

[21] *Statistical Abstract of the United States, 1966*, p. 418.

tional bidding procedures. School supplies, construction materials, gasoline, and so on, would fall into this category.

Negotiated contracts. For items that are not branded or easily described, or for products requiring research and development, or in cases in which there would be no effective competition, contracts may be negotiated directly. Depending on the government involved, the contract may be subject to audit and renegotiation, especially if the contractor makes a larger profit than was expected.

Negotiation often is necessary when there are many qualitative and intangible factors. Unfortunately, this is exactly where favoritism and "influence" can slip in. Such influence is not unknown, especially in city and state governments. Nevertheless, negotiation is an important buying method in government sales, and there is a definite need for a marketing mix that emphasizes more than just price.

Approximately 85 percent of the items purchased by the U.S. Defense Supply Agency are acquired through negotiation.[22]

Life-cycle buying. It appears that the current buying procedures of government may be unsuitable for some of the many specialized products that are now needed in an increasingly scientific and technical age. The Pentagon has found, for example, that it may spend 10 times the original purchase price of a piece of military hardware just to own and operate it during its lifetime, even though Defense Department buyers themselves have traditionally focused only on the initial price of the equipment. Now they are experimenting with a new approach to buying that may replace the traditional low-bid practice, and bring a new dimension into negotiated buying.

This new approach, called life-cycle buying, focuses on the total cost of owning an item throughout its life, rather than just the original cost. This certainly fits nicely with the marketing concept that emphasizes satisfying customer needs rather than just selling them products, and it probably will be viewed most favorably by progressive businessmen.

This approach to buying is illustrated in Table 9–5 which shows how a low bidder may actually lose the order under this new system, because the total cost of buying and operating his equipment is higher than his competitor's offerings. Life-cycle buying will require a complete rethinking on the part of engineering, design, and production people—really a switch to the "total system" approach—so that the company's whole marketing mix will be better than others in satisfying the customer's *long-run* needs.[23]

Learning what government wants

Since most government contracts are advertised, the prospective supplier focuses on who he wants to cater to and learns the bidding procedures of that particular government. The marketing man can make a big contribution at this point, because there are so many different bidding procedures and possibilities.

The marketing man should be an expert on the potential govern-

---

[22] "DSA Is the Shopper for GI's Everywhere," *Business Week,* August 20, 1966, pp. 150–56.

[23] "Picking the Winners with a New System," *Business Week,* May 13, 1967, pp. 62–67.

Table 9–5 Where the low bidder loses

Under Pentagon's life-cycle costing this theoretical
contract would go to Z Corp.; in conventional
bidding, X Corp. would have won

	X Corp.	Y Corp.	Z Corp.
Bid price	$ 42,000	$ 60,000	$ 47,000
Five-year Maintenance	129,000	116,000	84,000
New inventory items	10,000	20,000	10,000
Five-year inventory management	45,000	30,000	42,000
New documentation	12,000	18,000	12,000
Operational training	8,000	8,000	8,000
Total	$246,000	$252,000	$203,000

SOURCE: Reprinted from the May 13, 1967 issue of *Business Week* by special permission. Copyrighted © 1967 by McGraw-Hill, Inc.

ment target markets, using the assistance available from government directories. For example, the U.S. government offers a purchasing and sales directory that explains its procedures;[24] and various state and local governments also offer assistance. There are trade magazines and trade associations providing information on how to reach schools, hospitals, highway departments, park departments, and so on. These are unique target markets and must be treated as such when developing marketing strategy and approaching them.

Selling to government sometimes involves costly red tape and even renegotiation of contracts. And it also requires learning the idiosyncrasies of many new, and sometimes very competitive, markets. One might ask why firms go through all of this. The answer is that many of the government target markets are large, offering good profits. **Why sell to government?**

On some types of contracts, too, firms hope to gain valuable experience that will have later commercial application. In such cases, prospective suppliers actually may bid below their cost in order to get the opportunity of working on the project.

At one time, Bendix Corp. estimated that a research and development contract to develop a new radio device would cost approximately $500,000. They bid $300,000 in an effort to obtain the job. But a competing firm was so anxious to obtain the experience that it bid $1 and won the contract.[25]

Competitive pressures may "force" firms to do business with government, at least on research and development work. And it is clear that marketing has a role to play in government markets, even in the defense market which has traditionally been production-oriented.[26]

---

[24] *U.S. Government Purchasing and Sales Directory.*

[25] Malcolm P. Ferguson, "The Corporation as Supplier to the Government," *Business Topics*, Summer, 1961, pp. 37–50.

[26] Walter B. Wentz, "Aerospace Discovers Marketing," *Journal of Marketing*, April, 1967, pp. 27–30; William H. Reynolds, "The Marketing Concept and the Aerospace Business,"

Conclusion

In this chapter we have considered the number, size, and buying habits and practices of various intermediate customers. We saw that intermediate customers—farmers, retailers, wholesalers, manufacturers, and others—do considerable buying and selling among themselves before products reach the final consumer. We saw that this buying is generally less emotional than that of final consumers. Intermediate customers may buy by inspection, sampling, description, and negotiated contracts, with the latter two methods becoming more popular.

We have concentrated our attention on manufacturers, farmers, and governmental units, postponing until later chapters the detailed discussion of wholesalers and retailers.

The first concern of modern industrial buyers is dependability of the supplier—dependability of quality, service, and delivery. Price is considered, but usually in relation to dependability and quality. In large companies, buying may be quite complex, with various people handling different products or exerting influence on final decisions. Reciprocity may be an important factor, too, especially in certain industries. Finally, there remains the human element—the personality of the purchasing agent, his need to protect his reputation, and his desire for good relationships with his suppliers. The successful salesman will not overlook these emotional needs.

In considering the farm market, we have emphasized the rapid changes taking place there. The trend is toward fewer, larger, more productive farms. This trend will have a great impact on those who sell to the farm market and must adjust as the market changes.

Today's large commercial farmer is not only better off financially but is better informed and more progressive. He is willing to listen to new ideas, and to invest in machinery, fertilizers, and other products that he feels will increase his production. More and more, he tends to specialize. But the farm picture is not all bright. There are still many small, low-income farmers who offer little market potential.

Finally, we have seen that the government is a fast-growing market and an extremely complex one. Much government purchasing is done through prescribed bidding procedures. On nonstandardized goods and services, however, various types of negotiated contracts are used. Much federal government defense spending goes into research and development, and as we have noted, some companies are willing to bid below their cost in order to obtain a research contract and the valuable experience it will provide.

This review of intermediate customer buying habits and practices has tried to stress basic similarities. Actually, however, the practices among various buyers vary a great deal. Personal preferences and organizational setups cause differences. Furthermore, the nature of the specific products being purchased requires modification of the general princi-

Journal of Marketing, April, 1966, pp. 9–11; John J. Kennedy, "Defense-Aerospace Marketing: A Model For Effective Action," *Business Horizons,* Winter, 1965, pp. 67–74; and Leonard Marks, Jr., "The Aerospace Management Challenge," *Business Horizons,* Spring, 1966, pp. 19–24.

ples. The nature of specific industrial products is discussed in Chapter 13; at that time, variations in buying behavior will be discussed by product category.

The need for specialized research on the buying habits and preferences of specific target customers should be obvious. The market grid concept clearly is needed when developing marketing strategies for intermediate customers.

Questions and problems

1   Discuss the importance of applying the market-grid concept when analyzing intermediate customer markets. Be sure to consider how easy it is to isolate homogeneous market segments.
2   Discuss the advantages and disadvantages of reciprocity from the industrial buyer's point of view. Are the advantages and disadvantages merely reversed from the seller's point of view?
3   Is it always advisable to buy the highest quality product?
4   How does the kind of industrial good affect manufacturers' buying habits and practices? Consider lumber for furniture, a lathe, nails for a box factory, and a sweeping compound.
5   Discuss the geographic concentration of industrial buyers and estimate the share of the total value added by manufacture in the area east of the Mississippi River, and north of the Ohio River and the southern edges of Pennsylvania and New Jersey.
6   How much latitude does an industrial buyer have in selecting the specific product and the specific source of supply for that product, once the product has been requisitioned by some production department? Consider this question with specific reference to pencils, paint for the offices, plastic materials for the production line, a new factory, and a large printing press. How should the buyer's attitude affect the seller's marketing mix? Can you develop any principles out of your discussion?
7   Discuss the impact of value analysis on promotion.
8   Discuss the impact of the decline in number of commercial farmers on the marketing mixes of manufacturers and middlemen supplying this market. Also consider the impact on rural trading communities which have been meeting the needs of farmers.
9   The government market is obviously an extremely large one, yet it is often slighted or even ignored by many firms. "Red tape" is certainly one reason, but there are others. Discuss the situation and be sure to include the market-grid concept in your analysis.
10   Based on your understanding of buying by (1) manufacturers, (2) farmers, and (3) governments, outline the basic ingredients of promotion to each type of customer. Use two products as examples for each type. Is the promotion job the same for each pair?
11   Distinguish among the four methods of buying and indicate which would probably be most suitable for furniture, baseball gloves, coal, and pencils, assuming that some intermediate customer is the buyer.

Product—introduction

Beginning in this chapter and continuing through the next several chapters, we will look at the job of developing products and product lines to satisfy the ever changing desires of customers. This involves developing the right Product, which then can be distributed to the right Place, with the right Promotion and Price.

Developing the right product is not an easy task. Not only are customer needs and preferences changing but competition also continually makes current products obsolete. In some lines of business, the development of new products is so rapid that 50 percent or more of the products made by a given firm were not even in planning 5 to 10 years earlier.

Not only American firms, but also businessmen of other nations are realizing the importance of continually developing and improving products.

At a 1960 trade fair in Vienna, Russian and American tools were displayed side by side. Both functioned equally well, but although the Russian tools were priced lower, the U.S. tools were more readily sold. Manufacturers attributed this to better industrial design, expressed in both function and appearance. Apparently the Russians did, too, since they sent delegates for the first time to the International Council of Societies of Industrial Design when it met the following year. It would seem that buyers throughout the world, even in developing nations, are interested, not just in any products, but in *better* products.[1]

---

[1] "Reds Seek Better Product Design," *South Bend Tribune,* October 6, 1961, p. 24.

In Chapters 10–14, we will consider the role of products in marketing strategy planning. This may have first-job relevance to you, because many companies have organized their production and marketing activities along product lines. Some multiple-product producers, for example, maintain separate sales forces for each of the company's product lines, and wholesalers and retailers frequently have salesmen and buyers who specialize along product lines.[2]

What is a product?

First, we must decide what we mean by a "product."

If we are selling a washing machine, are we selling a certain number of nuts and bolts, some sheet metal, an electric motor, and a plastic agitator?

If we are selling the detergent to be used in this washing machine, are we selling several chemical raw materials?

If we are selling a delivery service, are we selling so much wear and tear on a delivery truck and so much operator fatigue?

The answer to all of these questions is *no*. Instead, we are *selling the capacity to give the satisfaction, use, or perhaps the profit desired by the customer.*

All the housewife asks is that her washing machine do a good job of washing and continues to run. She does not care how it was made. Further, she wants to clean with her detergent, not analyze it. And when she orders something, she doesn't really care how much out of the way the driver had to go or where he has been. She merely wants *her* package.

When producers and middlemen buy products, they are interested in the profit to be obtained from their purchase, through use and resale, not how they were made.

The concept of product—as potential customer satisfactions or benefits—cannot be overstressed. Many business executives, trained in the production side of business, are concerned about the number of nuts and bolts, the tightness of the nuts, the fertilizer application per acre, and other technical problems. Middlemen, too, are often concerned with their technical details. But while these are important to *them,* they have little bearing on most customers' conception of the product.

Customers buy satisfaction, not parts or ingredients

The *total product* is more than just the physical product with its related functional and aesthetic features. It includes any accessories needed, installation, instruction on use, the package, perhaps a brand name which fulfills some psychological needs, and the assurance that service facilities will be available to meet the customer's needs after the purchase.

Total product is physical product— plus

Customers want their needs satisfied. They want dependable products that will work, and prompt service if they do not. If a product breaks down easily and is difficult to repair or have serviced, it is of little use.

Guarantees that satisfaction will continue

[2] Stanley C. Hollander, "Merchandise Classification and the Commodity Approach," *Journal of Marketing,* Vol. XX, No. 3, p. 275.

Dependable quality and prompt service may be even more critical in the industrial sector. More than just customer inconvenience is involved here, since a whole production line may be shut down when the total product is not satisfactory. Such malfunctioning is now formally considered in some industrial and government purchasing. That is, the cost of the product over its life rather than just the initial cost is considered in the buying decision.

To overcome customer objections, some market-oriented firms are designing more quality into their products and then extending longer and stronger guarantees or warranties, such as the automobile warrantees for 50,000 miles or five years. But even such guarantees or warrantees may not satisfy the customer if they are limited to repairing or replacing the products. What is a customer supposed to do if an electric iron or electric shaver breaks down and cannot be repaired for two or three weeks? Must he have a second item in reserve for such contingencies? If the objective of the firm is to satisfy customer needs, these questions must be answered.

Some companies, such as Proctor Silex Corp. and Sears, Roebuck & Co., have met this problem by extending a one-year *replacement*—not just repair—guarantee on their appliances.

Although our approach to developing a total product that satisfies customer needs may seem very logical, some production-oriented companies feel that service is not their business.[3] Some, such as the automobile manufacturers and some appliance manufacturers, have passed on to the wholesalers and retailers the job of assuring that the physical product does work. *Sometimes* this job gets done, but production-oriented manufacturers appear not to care. Outside the United States, most retailers do not feel that service is their responsibility, and few maintain any repair facilities.[4]

By contrast, other businessmen are seeing very clearly that the customer wants more than just the physical product. General Electric and Maytag, for example, have developed manufacturer-owned or -franchised appliance service facilities to be sure that the total product *is* satisfactory. They see that this is part of the product and must be provided as part of the marketing mix if they are to develop more attractive marketing strategies than their competitors.

The best product is the total product

We have been emphasizing a single physical product and the related services that make up a single total product. But customer needs cannot always be satisfied by a single product. Several foods, for example, are eaten at the same meal, and most sports require several kinds of equipment. Marketing managers may have to think in terms of an assortment of goods and services that will satisfy customers' needs. The marketing manager may not have to supply them all, but at least he should include these needs in his strategy planning.

Manufacturers and wholesalers may have to offer a complex total product to their intermediate customers. Likewise, retailers may have

---

[3] "Guaranteeing More, Enjoying It Less," *Business Week,* January 26, 1963, pp. 46–48.

[4] Charles F. Stewart, "The Changing Middle East Market," *Journal of Marketing,* January, 1961, p. 49.

to offer a wide assortment in their "total product." This may include the total assortment of goods they offer as well as related services. Good parking facilities, gift wrapping, elevators and escalators, charge accounts, and delivery services probably should be considered as part of the retailer's product—yet some retailers provide most of these related services only grudgingly.

In our discussion, we will tend to focus on a single product for convenience of exposition. But it should not be forgotten that several products *and* services might have to be combined to develop the most effective "product" as part of the most effective marketing strategy.

Total product affects other three P's

We stress a good total product—one of our four P's—because a poor product will put an undue burden on the other three P's. Frequently, and especially when repeat purchases are sought, the right Price, Place, and Promotion will not compensate for a poor Product. Remember that in the Russian tool example, lower prices were not able to offset poor product design.

Products as seen by customers

Following the marketing concept, we start our planning with the customer and work back. This is relatively easy to do with respect to products, because it actually is the product that customers buy. True, they *are* influenced by the total marketing mix, but usually it is the more or less tangible product part that directly satisfies their need.

The economists have provided us with some very useful analytical tools to describe how customers view the total product. We will review their thinking in the next several pages.

Individual customers choose among alternatives

Economics is sometimes called the "dismal" science because it shows that customers simply cannot buy everything they want. Since most customers have a limited income over any time period, they must balance their needs and the costs of various products.

Economists usually assume that a customer has a fairly definite set of preferences. When he is given a set of alternatives, it is assumed that he evaluates these alternatives in terms of whether they will make him feel better (or worse) or in some way improve (or change) his situation.

But what exactly is the nature of the customer's desire for a particular product?

Usually the argument is presented in terms of the extra utility he can obtain by buying more of a particular product or how much utility would be lost were he to have less of the product. (Students who wish further discussion of this approach should refer to *indifference curve analysis* in any standard economics text.)

Utility is a conceptual framework. It may be easier to grasp this idea if we consider what happens if the price of one of the customer's usual purchases changes.

Suppose that a consumer were buying potatoes in 10-pound bags at the same time he bought some other foods, such as meat and vegetables. If the consumer is primarily interested in purchasing a certain number of calories, and the price of potatoes drops, it seems reasonable to expect that he will switch some of his food money to potatoes and away from some other foods. But if the price of potatoes rose, it seems reasonable to expect that our consumer would probably buy fewer potatoes and more of other foods.

The general interaction of price and quantity illustrated by this potato example has been called "the law of diminishing demand." This law states that *if the price of a commodity is raised, a smaller quantity will be demanded; conversely, if the price of a commodity is lowered, a greater quantity will be demanded.*

When our hypothetical consumers are considered as a group, we have what is called a "market." It seems reasonable to assume that many consumers in a market will behave in the same way—that is, if price declines, the total quantity demanded will increase, and if the price rises, quantity demanded will decrease. And empirical data supports this reasoning.

The relationship between price and quantity demanded in a market is illustrated in Table 10–1. It is an example of what economists call a

Table **10–1** *Demand schedule for potatoes*

	Price of Potatoes per Bag P (1)	Quantity Demanded (Bags per Month) Q (2)	Total Revenue per Month P × Q = TR (1) × (2) = (3)
A	$0.80	8,000,000	$6,400,000
B	0.65	9,000,000	
C	0.50	11,000,000	5,500,000
D	0.35	14,000,000	
E	0.20	19,000,000	

"demand schedule." It should be noted that, as the price decreases, the quantity demanded increases. In the third column, total dollar sales or total revenue of the potato market is shown. Notice, however, that as prices go lower, the total *unit volume increases,* yet the *total revenue decreases.* It is suggested that you fill in the missing blanks and observe the behavior of total revenue—an important figure for the marketing manager.

If your sole interest is seeing at which price customers would be willing to pay the greatest total revenue, the demand schedule may be adequate. But in our subsequent analysis, it will be helpful to think in terms of a "picture" of the relationship between price and quantity. When the demand schedule is graphed, the resulting curve is called a *demand curve*. Figure 10–1 shows the demand curve for potatoes, which is actually a plotting of the demand schedule. It shows how many potatoes would be demanded by potential customers at various possible prices. This is known as a *downsloping demand curve*.

Most demand curves have this downsloping appearance. A downsloping demand curve merely indicates that if price were decreased, the quantity that customers would demand would increase.

Note that the demand curve only shows how customers would react to various prices. Usually, in a market, we see only one price at a time, not all these prices. The curve, however, shows what quantities will be

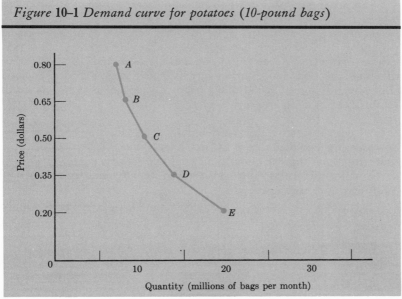

Figure **10–1** *Demand curve for potatoes (10-pound bags)*

sold, depending upon what price is set. It would seem that most businessmen would like to see the price set at a point where the resulting revenue was large.

Before discussing this, however, we should consider the demand schedule and curve for another commodity to get a more complete picture of what is involved in demand-curve analysis.

A different demand schedule is the one for refrigerators shown in Table 10–2. Column 3 shows the total revenue that would be obtained at various possible prices and quantities. Again, as the price of refrigerators goes down, the quantity demanded goes up. But here, contrary to the potato example, total revenue increases—at least until the price drops to $150.

Refrigerator demand curve looks different

Table 10–2 Demand schedule for refrigerators

	Price per Refrigerator P (1)	Quantity De- manded per Year Q (2)	Total Revenue per Year $P \times Q = TR$ $(1) \times (2) = (3)$
A	$300	20,000	$ 6,000,000
B	250	70,000	17,500,000
C	200	130,000	26,000,000
D	150	210,000	31,500,000
E	100	310,000	31,000,000

These general demand relationships are characteristic of all products, but each product has its own demand schedule and curve *in each potential market,* no matter how small the market. In other words, a particular demand curve has meaning only with reference to a particular market. We can think of product demand curves for individuals, regions, and even countries. And the time period covered really should be specified, although this is often neglected as we think implicitly of monthly or yearly periods.

The difference between elastic and inelastic demand

The demand curve for refrigerators (see Figure 10–2) is also downsloping, but note that it is flatter than the curve for potatoes. It is quite important that we understand what this flatness means.

We will consider the flatness in terms of total revenue, since this is of most interest to businessmen.[5]

When you filled in the total revenue column for potatoes, you should

Figure 10–2 Demand curve for refrigerators

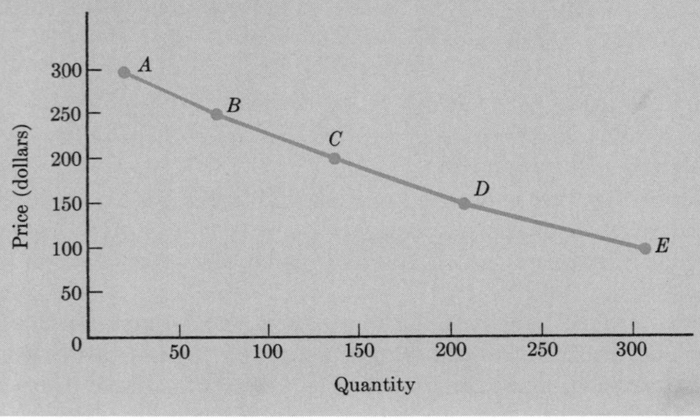

[5] Strictly speaking, two curves should not be compared for flatness if the graph scales are different, but for current purposes we will do so to illustrate the idea of "elasticity of demand." Actually, it would be more correct to compare two curves for one commodity—on the same graph. Then, both the shape of the demand curve and its position on the graph would be important.

have noticed that total revenue decreased continually as the price was reduced. This is undesirable from a businessman's point of view, and illustrates what is known as *inelastic demand*. This means that although the quantity demanded increases as price decreases, the quantity demanded does not "stretch" enough—that is, it is not elastic enough to increase total revenue.

In contrast, the quantity of refrigerators demanded did stretch enough—at least for a while—to increase total revenue as price was dropped. *This portion* of the refrigerator demand curve is an example of *elastic demand*.

Note that as the refrigerator price dropped from $150 to $100, total revenue *decreased*. It can be said, therefore, that when the price is less than $150, demand is inelastic—that is, total revenue is decreasing.

Thus, elasticity can be defined in terms of changes in total revenue. *If total revenue increases as price is lowered, then demand is said to be elastic. If total revenue decreases when price is lowered, then demand is said to be inelastic.*

A point that often is missed is that in an elastic demand situation, total revenue would *decrease* if prices were *raised,* but in an inelastic demand situation total revenue would *increase* if prices were *raised.* If total revenue remains the same when price is changed, then we have a very special case known as *unitary elasticity of demand.*

These ideas are illustrated graphically in Figure 10–3. Here, total revenue is conceived of as the rectangular area formed by a price and its related quantity.

P_1 is the original price here, and the total potential revenue associated with this original price is shown by the area with the diagonal lines slanted down from the left. The total revenue area associated with the new price, P_2, is shaded, with lines running diagonally upward from the left. In both cases, there is some overlap, and so the important areas are those with only a single shading. Note that in the left-hand figure, where demand is elastic, the revenue added when price is increased is less than the revenue lost (compare only the single-shaded areas). When demand is inelastic, however, only a small single-shaded revenue area is given up for a much larger one when price is raised.[6]

It is important to note that it is *improper to refer to a whole demand curve as elastic or inelastic*. Rather, elasticity for a particular curve refers to the change in total revenue between two points on a curve and not along the entire curve. The change from elasticity to inelasticity can be seen in the refrigerator example. Generally, however, adjacent points are either elastic or inelastic, so it is common to refer to a whole curve by the degree of elasticity of the curve in the price range that normally is of interest—the *relevant range*.

At first, it may be difficult to visualize why one product should have an elastic and another an inelastic demand. Many factors, such as the availability of substitutes, the importance of the item in the customer's

Availability of substitutes helps explain elasticity of demand

---

[6] It is possible to compute coefficients of elasticity of demand that will represent a numerical value for the degree of elasticity. We will not go into this here. Interested students should refer to any basic economics text under the topic "coefficient of elasticity of demand."

budget, and the urgency of the need and its relation to other needs, influence demand for a particular product. By examining one of these factors, the availability of substitutes, we should better understand why demand elasticities vary.

Substitutes are goods or services that offer a choice or an alternative to the buyer. The greater the number of good substitutes available, the greater will be the elasticity of demand, the term "good" here referring to the degree of similarity or homogeneity that customers see in a group of products. If they see the products as extremely different or heterogeneous, then a particular need cannot be satisfied by easily interchanging them, and the demand for the most satisfactory product may be quite inelastic.

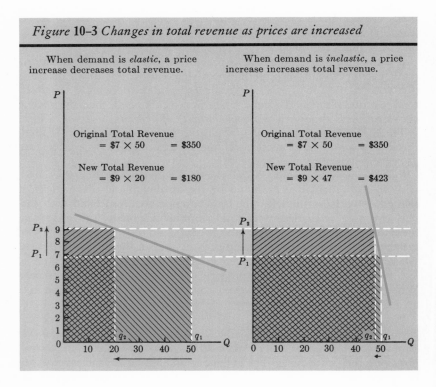

Figure **10–3** *Changes in total revenue as prices are increased*

When demand is *elastic*, a price increase decreases total revenue.

When demand is *inelastic*, a price increase increases total revenue.

Original Total Revenue
= $7 × 50 = $350

New Total Revenue
= $9 × 20 = $180

Original Total Revenue
= $7 × 50 = $350

New Total Revenue
= $9 × 47 = $423

As an example, if the price of hamburger is lowered (and other prices stand constant), the quantity demanded will increase considerably as will total revenue. The reason is that not only regular hamburger users will buy more hamburger, but those consumers who formerly bought hot dogs, steaks, or bacon probably will buy hamburger too. But if the price of hamburger rose, the quantity demanded would decrease, perhaps sharply. Consumers would still purchase some hamburger, depending on how much the price had risen, their individual tastes, and what their guests expect (see Figure 10–4).

In contrast to a product which has many "substitutes," such as

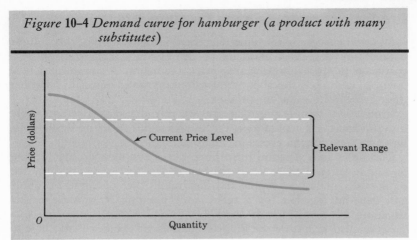

Figure **10–4** *Demand curve for hamburger (a product with many substitutes)*

hamburger, consider a commodity with few or no substitutes. Its demand curve will tend to be inelastic. Salt is a good example. Salt is needed to flavor food. Yet no one person or family uses great quantities of salt. And even with price changes *within a reasonable range,* it is not likely that the quantity of salt purchased would change much. Of course, if the price dropped to an extremely low level, people might buy more, say for yard fill (Figure 10–5). Or, if the price rose to a

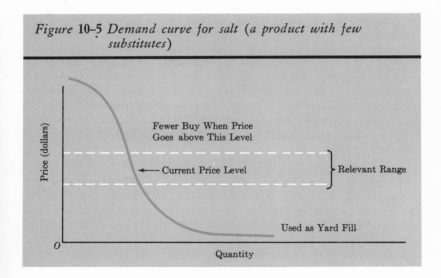

Figure **10–5** *Demand curve for salt (a product with few substitutes)*

staggering figure, many people would have to do without. But these extremes are outside the relevant range.

Remember that the terms elasticity or inelasticity are applied only along a range of the demand curve somewhat above and below the normal price level—that is, within the relevant range.

211

Product markets as seen by suppliers

Demand curves are introduced in the Product section of this volume because the degree of elasticity of demand is a characteristic of a particular product in a particular market situation. It summarizes how potential customers feel about the total product, and especially, whether there are substitutes for the product.

Economists' thinking on demand was introduced to give an insight into product-market situations. But to obtain this fuller understanding, we must continue this economic analysis.

Customers may demand something, but if suppliers are not willing to supply it, then there is no market. So we are going to study the economist's analysis of supply and then finally bring analysis of supply and demand together for a fuller understanding of product-market situations.

Economists often use the kind of analysis we are discussing here to explain pricing in the marketplace. This is *not* our intention. Here we are interested in product markets and the interaction of customers and potential suppliers. The discussion in this chapter does *not* explain how individual firms set prices or should set prices. That will come in the Price chapters.

Supply curves reflect supplier thinking

Generally speaking, suppliers' costs have a bearing on the quantity of products they are willing to offer on the market during any period. In other words, their costs affect their supply schedules and supply curves. While a demand curve shows the quantity of goods customers would be willing to buy at various prices, a supply curve shows the quantity of goods that will be supplied at various possible prices by all of the suppliers together (if we are thinking of a total market) or one supplier (if we are thinking of a single firm's situation). Eventually only one quantity of goods will be offered and purchased, and so a supply curve is really a hypothetical description of what would be offered at various prices. It is, however, a very important curve. Together with a demand curve, it summarizes the attitudes and probable behavior of buyers and sellers with respect to a particular product in a particular market.

Curving potatoes, vertical strawberries

We usually assume that supply curves are somewhat upsloping, that is, suppliers will be willing to offer greater quantities at higher prices. If a product's market price is very high, it seems only reasonable to assume that producers will be willing to produce more of the product and even put workers on overtime or perhaps hire additional workers in order to increase the quantity they can offer. To go further, it seems likely that producers of other products will switch their productive facilities (farms or factories) to the production of the commodity that is in great demand.

Contrariwise, if a very low price is being offered for a particular commodity, it seems reasonable that producers will switch to other products, reducing supply. A supply schedule (Table 10–3) and a supply curve (Figure 10–6) for potatoes illustrates these ideas. This

212

Table **10–3** *Supply schedule for potatoes*

	Possible Market Price per 10-Lb. Bag	No. of Bags Sellers Will Supply per Month at Each Possible Market Price
A	$0.80	17,000,000
B	0.65	14,000,000
C	0.50	11,000,000
D	0.35	8,000,000
E	0.20	3,000,000

supply curve shows how many potatoes would be produced and offered for sale at each possible market price for a particular month.[7]

In the very short run (say over a few hours, a day, or a week), a supplier may not be able to increase the supply at all. In this situation, we should see a vertical supply curve. This situation is frequently of practical significance in the market for fresh produce. Fresh strawberries, for example, continue to deteriorate, and a supplier must sell them quickly—preferably at a higher price—but in any event he must sell them. For less perishable commodities, he may set a minimum price floor and, if necessary, store his goods until market conditions are more favorable.

Elasticity of supply

The term "elasticity" also is used to describe supply curves. An extremely steep or almost vertical supply curve, often found in the very short run, is called *inelastic* because the quantity supplied does not

Figure **10–6** *Supply curve for potatoes (10-lb. bags)*

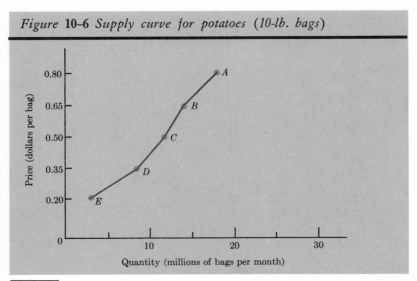

---

[7] This supply curve is for a month to emphasize that farmers might have some control over when they delivered their potatoes. There would be a different curve for each month.

stretch much (if at all) if the price is raised. A flatter curve is called *elastic* because it does stretch more. A slightly upsloping supply curve is characteristic of longer run market situations. Given more time, suppliers have a chance to adjust their offerings and plan their production.

Demand and supply interaction

Now, market supply and demand forces must be brought together to show their impact on market price. The demand curve for potatoes introduced earlier is now graphed against the supply curve presented in Figure 10–6. See Figure 10–7. Demand and supply curves intersect at the market price. At this price the market is said to be in *equilibrium*.

In this potato market, the demand is inelastic; the total revenue of all the potato producers would be greater at higher prices. But the market price is at the equilibrium point, where the quantity and the price that sellers are willing to offer are equal to the quantity and price that buyers are willing to accept. The 50-cent equilibrium price for potatoes yields a smaller *total revenue* to potato producers than would a higher price. This lower equilibrium price comes about because the many producers are willing to supply enough potatoes at the lower price. *Demand is not the sole determiner of price level. Cost also must be considered, via the supply curve.*

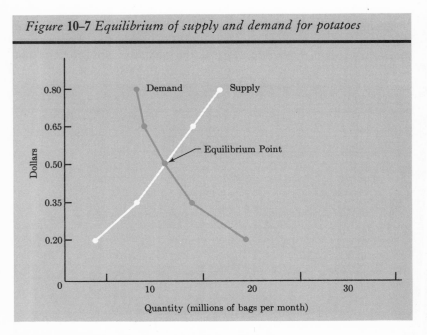

Figure 10–7 Equilibrium of supply and demand for potatoes

Nature of product market situations

The elasticity of demand and supply, and the interaction of demand and supply curves, helps explain the nature of product-market sit-

214

uations. We will emphasize two basically different kinds of market situations: pure competition and monopolistic competition. A third type, called monopoly, is encountered so infrequently that it will not be treated separately. Usually monopolies are controlled by local, state, or federal authorities. Where they are not, they can be treated as monopolistic competition, since monopolies are simply an extreme case of monopolistic competition.

A clear understanding of these product-market situations is quite important because some situations considerably reduce the freedom of a marketing manager. For example, if the demand for a particular product of a firm is completely elastic—the demand curve is completely flat—the marketing manager would have no control whatsoever over price. And it also would mean that his job with the other three P's would not be easy, since target customers apparently do not believe that his product is different from others.

If his demand curve is inelastic, however, he may have much more freedom in varying the other three P's.

In pure competition, we find something approaching a perfectly flat demand curve for a particular firm. Each of our individual potato producers was in such a situation.

Pure competition

Pure competition develops in markets characterized by many buyers and many sellers offering extremely similar or homogeneous products. It is assumed here that all buyers and sellers have perfect knowledge of the market forces and that there is ease of entry for all of these buyers and sellers—that is, new firms have little difficulty starting in business and new customers can easily come into the market. This is more or less true in the potato industry, which is why we would call it a pure-competition situation.

Although the potato industry as a whole has a downsloping demand curve, each individual potato producer has a demand curve that is perfectly flat at the going market price—the equilibrium price.

To explain this in more concrete terms, let us consider the demand curve for the individual potato producer. Say that the equilibrium price for the industry is 50 cents. This means he can sell as many potatoes as he chooses at 50 cents. The quantity he and all of his fellow producers choose makes up the supply curve; but acting alone, he can do almost anything he wants to do.

If this individual farmer raises $1/10,000$th of the quantity offered in the market, for example, it is obvious that there will be little impact on the market whether he goes out of business or doubles his production.

The reason the demand curve is thought of as flat in this example is that the farmer probably could not sell any potatoes above the market price, and there is no point in selling below 50 cents. (The subject of deciding the best quantity to offer is discussed in Chapter 26, where we cover pricing and output decisions.)

The relation between the industry demand-curve situation and the demand curve facing the individual farmer in pure competition is shown in Figure 10–8.

Not many markets can be characterized as purely competitive, where the competitors are facing a perfectly elastic demand curve. But there

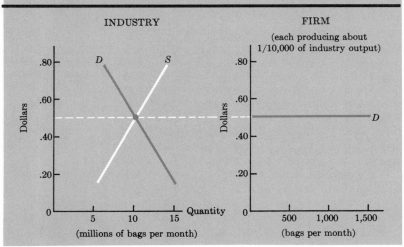

Figure **10–8** *Interaction of demand and supply in the potato industry and resulting demand curve facing individual potato producers*

are enough markets with some of these characteristics to allow us to talk about extremely competitive situations in which the marketing manager may have to accept the going price.

Squeeze on the orange growers

Florida orange growers, for example, have essentially homogeneous products, and they have little control over price. When there is an extremely large supply, prices drop rapidly and are beyond the producers' control. The 1967 crop was 50 percent larger than the 1966 crop, and most operators sold their oranges below their costs. Oranges "on the tree" cost 75 cents a box to grow and sold for $1.25 in 1966. In 1967, they were selling for 35 cents a box.[8]

Similar situations are found in many agricultural commodities, and farmers often seek government help to "save" them from pure competition. Agricultural parity programs are designed in part for this purpose, usually working to increase price by reducing supply. In 1961, the cling peach growers in California voted to destroy part of their crop in an effort to raise the market price.[9] And the Brazilian government, faced with a wholesale price drop for coffee from 95 cents a pound in 1954 to less than 35 cents in 1962, burned coffee trees to reduce supplies.[10]

Nor are such highly competitive situations restricted to agriculture. In any field where many competitors sell essentially homogeneous products—such as chemicals, plastics, lumber, coal, printing, and laundry services—the demand curve seen by *each producer* tends to be flat.

[8] *Business Week,* May 13, 1967, p. 187; and "Orange Crush," *Time,* January 27, 1967, p. 67.

[9] *Wall Street Journal,* July 9, 1962, p. 2.

[10] *Wall Street Journal,* July 10, 1962, p. 1.

Assuming no collusion among the firms, there is a tendency for each firm to expand production—and the action of all the producers forces the market price lower.

The impact of an extremely competitive situation can hit even a large firm such as E. I. du Pont de Nemours & Co. Competitive activity among the producers of synthetic fibers has been extremely active in recent years. Major U.S. and world producers had been working for years to expand production capacity, and finally supply more than caught up with demand. Almost overnight the many large competitors were cutting prices drastically; Du Pont's profits declined, and their declining stock price even dragged down the Dow-Jones industrial stock average.[11]

As industries become more competitive—on the way to pure competition—more competitors generally enter, the supply is increased, and the current equilibrium price is pushed downward. This tends to force profits down until they are eliminated. Economists describe the final equilibrium position as that point at which there are no entrepreneurial profits, only sufficient return to keep the present competitors in the business.

On the way to this final equilibrium position, it is possible that competition will become so vigorous that the equilibrium point will be passed, and industry profits actually may be negative as the industry price goes below the equilibrium level and some firms are driven out of business. This may take some time, though finally the industry price may move up to the equilibrium level so the remaining companies can survive. At the economist's final equilibrium point, however, none of the firms make a profit!

When competition is monopolistic

From the above discussion it is easy to see why firms would want to avoid pure competition situations. They prefer a market that is more truly *their own*.

To avoid a purely competitive market, marketing managers seek to develop a differentiated or heterogeneous product, one perhaps of special interest to certain segments of a market grid. If these efforts are successful, the firm becomes, in effect, the "industry" for this product. Since target customers recognize the product as "different," the firm does not have to share *this* industry demand with all competitors. Such a market situation is called *monopolistic competition*.[12]

The term "monopolistic" indicates that the firm is attempting to attain its own little monopoly, but the term "competition" indicates that there is still competition. The extremely vigorous—even cut-throat—competition of the purely competitive market is reduced, although there usually remain somewhat similar products (substitutes) providing competition to the monopolistic competitor.

[11] "Sagging Du Pont Casts Shadow over Dow," *Business Week*, April 8, 1967, pp. 118–20; and "Du Pont Says Net in First Period Fell by 24 Per Cent from 1966," *Wall Street Journal*, April 11, 1967, p. 32.

[12] Sometimes it is called heterogeneous competition to emphasize that nonhomogeneous products are involved—to provide more contrast with pure competition where homogeneous products are characteristic.

In monopolistic competition, the firm has its own downsloping demand curve, but the shape of the curve depends somewhat on competitors' actions. Each monopolistic competitor has freedom, but not complete freedom, in his own little "industry."

Judging elasticity, if not shape Since the firm in monopolistic competition has its own downsloping demand curve, it must make a conscious price decision as part of its marketing mix. Here, the elasticity of the firm's own demand curve becomes extremely relevant. If it is highly inelastic, the firm may decide to raise prices to increase total revenue. But if demand is highly elastic, this may indicate many competitors with acceptable substitutes, and the company may have to focus attention on product improvements, place, and promotion.

The terms "elastic and "inelastic," used in relation to demand, give us a helpful shorthand for describing the nature of competition and demand facing a firm. The degree of elasticity is something the marketing manager can judge, even though he may not be able to specify the exact shape of the demand curve. This judgment can be very helpful in describing the nature of the market and can affect his overall strategy. (More is said on demand estimation in Chapter 26. For now, rough judgments will meet our need.)

Why are some products offered in pure competition?

Why would anyone compete in essentially profitless pure competition? The usual explanation is either that the firm was already in the industry, or enters without knowing what is happening or is going to happen, and then must stick it out until its resources are depleted. Production-oriented people seem more likely to make such a mistake than the market-oriented businessman. Avoiding pure competition seems advisable, and certainly fits with our emphasis on trying to develop unique marketing strategies, catering to unsatisfied target markets that will see the company's product as heterogeneous rather than homogeneous.

Despite their desire to avoid pure-competition conditions, however, some firms find that (at least for part of their operation) they cannot do so. In some cases, production processes make this inevitable. For instance, in the chemical industry, caustic soda is produced as a by-product in the production of more profitable chlorine. At one time, the supply of caustic soda was so great that it was being dumped as waste into the Gulf of Mexico. Obviously this had a depressing influence on the market and the nature of competition!

Some industries appear almost purely competitive, yet new firms keep entering or replacing the casualties, possibly because they may not have more attractive alternatives and can at least earn a living in the industry. Examples of such industries include small retailing and wholesaling, especially in less developed economies. Modern farmers are continually attempting to shift their production to more profitable crops, but since there are many thousands of other farmers making similar choices, almost pure competition is inevitable.

Pure competition leads to standardization efforts

A marketing manager caught in nearly pure competition may, and often does, want to encourage or participate in an industry standardization program to reduce the variety of products he has to offer and thereby reduce his costs.

Standardization is the determination of specifications or grades to which manufactured goods must conform or into which the products of agriculture and extractive industries may be sorted. Standardization usually involves a reduction in the number of grades offered and agreement on which ones will be offered. Standards may be set by the government or by industry members.

Government standards usually are set up or suggested by an agency, such as the U.S. Department of Agriculture or the U.S. Bureau of Standards, a unit of the Department of Commerce. The standards are not established specifically for the products of any one firm but are applied generally to the grading and standardization of such commodities and products as wheat, corn, and apples; mechanical equipment; and nuts, bolts, and screws.

Industry standards are similar to government standards except that they are set by a trade association or group of firms. Examples are can and bottle sizes, and shoe and clothing sizes.

Standards may be based upon quantitative factors, such as weight per volume, or ingredients or performance. Standards also may be based on a variety of qualitative factors such as ripeness, color, flavor, taste, and texture.

Generally, quantitative standards are preferred because of ease of measurement. But for many products, strictly quantitative measures are not enough. Raw materials for paint manufacturing, for example, defy complete description, so paint buyers often specify "the same as the last satisfactory shipment" on purchase orders.

Standardization has been called a "facilitating" function, since it frequently simplifies trade. Uniform quality and a reduction in the number of grades make buying and selling easier, more economical, and frequently save time. Comparison between the selling prices of competitors is facilitated, and sales by sample or description becomes feasible.

For agricultural commodities, the use of standard grades facilitates sorting. Commodities then can be traded like quality-controlled manufactured products. Standardized grades permit the use of published market statistics and facilitate the development of a more competitive market.

If there are grades for which demand can be predicted, the producer has some assurance of product acceptance and a stable market, and he may be willing to lower prices. Standardization may also reduce the amount of promotion necessary on commonly accepted standard items.

For the consumer, standardization may lower prices and reduce buying risk for all of the reasons just enumerated.

Approaches for developing separate product markets

Standardization efforts may make sense if it is obvious that the firm must remain close to, or in, pure competition. But monopolistic competition is more attractive to a marketing manager than pure competition. The key to achieving monopolistic competition is to have a markedly different marketing mix. By differentiating its product, the firm may be able to "carve out" a special target market for itself.

Making a market

There are two basic ways to achieve some control of your market: market segmentation and product differentiation.

Market segmentation is the process of isolating previously unsatisfied target markets and designing a unique product for that part of the market grid. Here, the intent is to develop a uniquely different and more satisfying product.

When there are direct competitors for the customers in a particular market grid box, however, then it becomes necessary to stress product differences. This latter approach is called *product differentiation*. Sometimes a firm may be following both approaches at the same time. Its successful market segmentation efforts may attract competition and force it to rely on product differentiation too. These ideas are explained more fully below.

Product differentiation, not customer exclusion

Product differentiation seeks to direct customer demand toward one manufacturer's or middleman's product even though it may be quite similar to the competitors' products.

In other words, the firm tries to shift its own demand curve to the right.

This approach, which often stresses promotion, also may involve physical changes, including new packages or brands, new features, new flavors, or new novelties slipped into the box.

Even if physical changes are made, the intention is not to focus on the demand of small target markets but to improve the company's position in many target markets, perhaps all the way across the market grid. The aim is to differentiate but not to become so unique that general appeal is lost. The theory here is that a firm should offer a "better" homogeneous product rather than a unique heterogeneous product desired only by a few.

Some firms use promotion heavily in their product differentiation efforts because the actual differences among various competitive physical products may be minor—but these minor differences nevertheless may be very important to some target customers.

Some differences may exist mainly in the eye of the beholder. If a woman truly believes that one cosmetic is more suited to her personality, she will use it. But different customers have different needs. Some women may be concerned with cleanliness, others with beauty, and others with glamour. A single cosmetic advertisement might appeal to all of them, but for different reasons.

Product differentiation is employed for most widely advertised products appealing to mass audiences—products such as cigarettes, soaps,

220

cosmetics, foods, and automobiles. It also is seen in the industrial goods area, where firms try to meet generally accepted specifications but with improved products.

Control Data Corp., a small computer manufacturer competing with IBM, for example, tries to make better and cheaper computer equipment, but all of it meshes with IBM's systems.[13] With product differentiation you want to be different—but not so different that you narrow your markets, excluding some customers. You may not uniquely satisfy anyone better than competitors can, but you hope your general appeal will be satisfying enough to a sufficient number of people to prove profitable.

In this approach, we attempt to develop a special total product to satisfy target customers in different market grid boxes. Here, more drastic changes, perhaps even in the physical product, may be made in the total product to appeal to smaller target markets. The result may be the achievement of more inelastic demand curves in several different markets. **Market segmentation to satisfy "very well"**

A market segmentation approach recognizes that there may be different demand curves in different parts of the market grid. This focus on smaller markets would tend to provide greater satisfaction to customers and would therefore provide greater security for the marketing manager and his firm.

Although a product differentiation policy would attempt to satisfy a lot of people "pretty well," market segmentation would attempt to satisfy a smaller number of people "very well."[14]

Market segmentation may lead to considerable product diversification and expansion of a manufactuer's line. There might be a special product for each market grid box, or even for each individual customer! Actually, this policy is seldom carried to its logical conclusion. Few customers' desires for different products are so strong that they will pay the higher costs that completely individualized products probably would entail. A market segmentation policy, nevertheless, can expand product lines markedly.

Thom McAn Shoe Co. has found it necessary to have 150 different styles, exclusive of different widths and lengths. Instead of trying to explain that one basic shoe model will fit every customer's personality, the company produces many different shoes to satisfy the varied demands. **If the shoe fits, buy it**

Market segmentation may enable a small producer to move itself away from pure competition into monopolistic competition. For example, the Wolverine World Wide Co. came out with "Hush-Puppies," a casual, split-pigskin shoe, that enabled it to move into the extremely competitive U.S. shoe market with spectacular success while

---

[13] "Poor Man's IBM," *Time,* August 14, 1964, pp. 62–63.

[14] For the original and classic discussion on product differentiation and market segmentation, see Wendell R. Smith, "Product Differentiation and Market Segmentation as Alternative Marketing Strategies," *Journal of Marketing,* July, 1956, pp. 3–8.

conventional small shoe manufacturers were existing in almost pure competition.[15]

The highly profitable operations of Magnavox and Zenith in the extremely competitive television industry further illustrates the profit possibilities of a market segmentation policy. Magnavox, which aims at the top of the market, earned approximately a 30 percent return on its invested capital in 1966.[16] Zenith, appealing to the quality- and reliability-conscious, at several price levels, also has done well.[17]

Market segmentation combined with product differentiation

Even if a firm attempts a market segmentation policy, it probably will find that one or more competitors will quickly follow. Then it will have to shift emphasis to product differentiation.

The automobile industry has developed many different kinds of cars to appeal to different target markets. But the various companies and divisions within companies have quickly copied each other. Sometimes the car builders frankly admit that one car was designed to compete directly with another—for example, Chevrolet's Camaro with Ford's Mustang. Then the competitive focus tends to shift from the whole product to minor differences in features, trim, and accessories, together with psychological perceptions of the different products, styles, and brand names.

Even if a marketing manager preferred to follow a market segmentation policy, the extreme competition that most firms find in the marketplace might force him to use product differentiation along with market segmentation.

It's the intent that counts

It often is difficult for an outsider to tell which policy a firm is pursuing. As we have already seen, there is no simple, "correct" way to analyze market grids and precisely define the needs of different target markets. What one firm would see as a unique market, another might see as many markets and systematically design products and marketing mixes to satisfy some of them. It might see itself following a market segmentation policy, while the first firm might see its own and all the competitive efforts as product differentiation, aimed at the same larger market. Which firm would win would depend on how the market(s) respond(s) to the competing products and mixes. If there really are need differences which are correctly seen and satisfied, then the (perhaps more costly) market segmentation effort may be more profitable. But if the whole market really is more or less homogeneous, then the product differentiation effort may be just as successful, perhaps at lower cost.

As always, the customer decides which policy satisfies him best. A market segmentation policy tries harder, but it requires more careful analysis of the market and more risk. Product differentiation, on the other hand, tries to satisfy broader markets "pretty well." Given our

[15] "This Little Pigskin Went to Market," *Business Week,* December 7, 1963, pp. 48–50.

[16] "Only the Best," *Time,* January 20, 1967, pp. 76–78.

[17] Talk by Nelson Foote, General Electric Company, at Market Segmentation Conference sponsored by the American Marketing Association, Chicago, in February, 1967; and "Zenith Aims at the Top in Color TV," *Business Week,* September 11, 1965, pp. 128–34.

present knowledge of customer behavior analysis, this may be the safe path. But it will lead one into fairly direct competition from others following the same course. Safety may be purchased at the price of the attractive profits which usually accompany marketing breakthroughs.

Conclusion

This chapter has visualized a "product" very broadly. It is not only the physical product or service, but the package, brand, installation, repair service, and so on, that satisfy customer needs.

The economist's traditional demand and supply analysis provides us with useful tools for analyzing the nature of demand and product-market situations. It is important that you master the concepts of a demand curve and demand elasticity and their relationship to pure and monopolistic competition. Businessmen usually try to avoid pure competition in favor of monopolistic competition. In pure competition, the individual firm faces a highly elastic demand curve and has little control over price, or the other three P's for that matter, since essentially homogeneous products are being offered by all competitors.

In an effort to achieve a monopolistic competition situation, a marketing manager may use either a product differentiation or market segmentation policy. A product differentiation policy seeks to adapt the firm's product to broad audiences by focusing on minor but still important differences. Promotion may be quite important when a product differentiation policy is followed.

Market segmentation, on the other hand, tries to satisfy fewer markets in depth; it often requires the development of quite different products and services. The two policies are not incompatible, however, because competitors usually quickly follow a firm's successful market segmentation, and the marketing manager of that firm will have to resort to product differentiation.

Following either a product differentiation or a market segmentation policy, a marketing manager may be able to achieve relatively inelastic demand curves in one or many market grid boxes. He may operate more profitably than the many product-oriented firms that typically focus on lowering costs rather than satisfying customer needs and as a result find themselves in profitless pure competition.

---

1 Explain how the addition of guarantees, service, and credit can improve a "total product." Cite a specific case where this has been done and explain how customers viewed this new "total product."
2 What "products" are being offered by an exclusive men's shop? By a night club? By a soda fountain? By a supermarket?
3 Distinguish between product differentiation and market segmentation. Which policy is being followed if cold cream is offered in a new, more distinctively shaped jar? Which if only the label is changed to gold foil for distinctiveness?

Questions and problems

4 If the general market demand for men's shoes is fairly elastic, how does the demand for men's dress shoes compare to it? How does the demand curve for women's shoes compare to the demand curve for men's shoes?

5 If the demand for fountain pens were inelastic above and below the present price, should the price be raised? Why, or why not?

6 If the demand for steak is highly elastic below the present price, should the price be lowered?

7 If a manufacturer's well-known product is sold at the same price by many retailers in the same community, is this an example of pure competition? When a community has many small grocery stores, are they in pure competition? Specify very carefully the characteristics of a purely competitive market.

8 List three products which are sold in purely competitive markets and three in monopolistically competitive markets. Now list three products for which the sellers seem to be using product differentiation and three more where they appear to be using market segmentation. Do any of these products have anything in common? Can any generalizations be made about the relation between these approaches and market situations? Would it be expected that the marketing mix for any of these products would be similar? If so, which ones and how?

Packaging and branding

A total product is much more than the basic physical product. The physical product probably will need some packaging. And physical products and services probably should be branded to assure that they will be clearly identifiable.

In the same sense, there is much more to packaging and branding than just buying a cardboard box and applying the company's name.

These important matters are discussed in this chapter. In some cases, the packaging and branding decisions may be more important than the physical product decisions. They may enable a firm to differentiate its homogeneous physical products and escape from pure competition.

What is packaging?

Sometimes a distinction is made between packing and packaging—the former being more concerned with protection and the latter with promotion. We will *not* make this distinction. The difference is seldom clear-cut. Modern packaging tries to do both jobs. It is important to note, however, that management conflicts may develop over the relative importance of these two packaging functions.

The production, shipping, and transportation departments of a manufacturer and the physical handling departments of middlemen and customers may be more interested in protection. The sales department may be more interested in the promotion aspects. And final consumers may be more interested in the use characteristics of the package. All these interests must be balanced in developing a marketing strategy. The need for this balancing emphasizes the importance of having top management involved in this aspect of marketing strategy planning.

Growing importance of packaging

Packaging is costly but plastic cuts costs

The importance of packaging is partially illustrated by its cost. About $14 billion was spent on packaging *materials* alone in 1965, and it is expected that this may rise to $24 billion by 1970.[1] The actual cost of packaging may be twice as high, however, when all the costs of handling, storing, and moving containers are included.

Packaging expenses as a percentage of the manufacturer's selling price vary widely, ranging from 1 percent to 70 percent. Low packaging expenses are found in such fields as office machines (1.4 percent), hardware (4.0 percent), cutlery (5.0 percent), and automotive parts (5.0 percent), where the primary job is protection and the value of products is relatively high. On the other hand, expense percentages are higher for candy (21), foods (21), drugs (26), and cosmetics and toiletries (36).[2] The really high percentages apply to soaps (50) and toothpaste (70).

Packaging costs per unit, however, seem to be going down. A recent study of consumer goods manufacturers showed that their total packaging costs had declined nearly one third between 1954 and 1967, dropping from an average 27.9 cents per gross sales dollar to 18.6 cents. These lower costs were attributed to increased packaging-line mechanization and newer, less costly materials.[3] Putting food in a plastic bag, for example, may promote sales and cut costs at the same time.

Higher corporate status for packaging

The purchasing agent was in charge of packaging in many companies when protection was the major function of the package. But now, as some companies are establishing corporate packaging staffs, the product manager, or perhaps a specialist in packaging, has taken over this job.

General Foods Corp. appointed a Manager of Packaging Development and Procurement Services, when it reached the conclusion that packaging is an important tool of management. This manager coordinates packaging activities with the various product managers. The National Biscuit Co. has a vice president of packaging acting as chairman of the packaging committee.[4]

This newfound status for packaging occurred in part because of the growing competitiveness in many markets. This status also reflects the costliness of packaging errors and the difficulty of correcting them. An advertising campaign, for instance, might prove ineffective and could be dropped. Its ineffectiveness might lead to a loss of money but have no impact on potential customers. In contrast, a poor package could

---

[1] *Modern Packaging,* Encyclopedia Issue, 1967, December, 1966, pp. 39–41.

[2] *Modern Packaging,* March, 1954, p. 127 and April, 1959, p. 146.

[3] "What Does Packaging Really Cost?" *Modern Packaging,* May, 1967, pp. 90–93.

[4] "The New Power of Packaging: Management Takes Control," *Printers' Ink,* June 11, 1965, pp. 13–18.

have long-term effects, killing the product for customers who try it and creating ill-will among middlemen.

Strategic importance of packaging

Marketing strategy planning tries to match target market needs and preferences to the marketing mix offered—and packaging is part of the mix. Packaging materials, sizes, and designs should be examined with the final target market(s) in mind. But in so doing, intermediate customers wants and preferences cannot be neglected either. A new package may make a new strategy, but it should be designed with consideration of the needs of all those who will buy or handle it.

When the package makes the product

A new package can become the major factor in a new marketing strategy by significantly improving the total product. A better box, wrapper, can, or bottle may even enable a relatively small, unknown firm to compete successfully with the established competitors. Carter Products Co., not previously in the men's toiletries field, introduced its first men's product, Rise shaving cream, in aerosol cans and was able to compete effectively. The normal tube and carton might not have been so successful.[5]

A package change often creates a "new" product by giving either the regular customers or new target markets the existing product in a new form or quantity that is more satisfactory. Packaging frozen vegetables in 1-pound packages instead of 10-ounce packages served larger families better. The small package held too little for them, while two packages held too much. Some producers are carving large turkeys into quarters to stimulate year-round sales. One such experiment expanded sales 200 percent.[6]

Multiple packs may be the basis of a new marketing strategy, too. Consumer surveys showed that some customers were buying several units at a time of products such as soft drinks, beer, and frozen orange juice. This suggested an unsatisfied market grid segment. Manufacturers tried multiple packaging of units in 4-, 6-, and 8-packs, and this has gained wide acceptance. Such multiple packaging has advantages for both retailers and customers, for handling ease and lower cost. Multiple packs demonstrate why it is difficult (and may be a mistake) to try to distinguish the protective and handling aspects from the promotional aspects of packaging.

Satisfy the wholesaler, help the retailer

Better protective packaging is especially important to intermediate customers, such as manufacturers and wholesalers, who may have to absorb the cost of goods damaged in transit. Sometimes the cost of such damage can be charged to the transportation agencies, but still there are costs for settling such claims—and getting them settled is a nuisance. Moreover, goods damaged in shipment may delay production and cause lost sales.

---

[5] "New Packaging Concepts Sell, Resell, and Satisfy Customers," *Printers' Ink,* November 21, 1958, pp. 21–27; see also, "Packaging Brings a Sleeper to Life," *Printers' Ink,* March 22, 1963, pp. 48–49.
[6] *Ibid.*

Packaging is important to retailers. They are interested in both the protective and promotional aspects of packaging. Estimates are that better packaging could reduce supermarket handling costs by as much as 4.5 percent of total sales and increase sales 7.4 percent. The sales increase could total more than $3 billion a year, of which some $1 billion might be passed on to consumers as reduced prices.[7]

Packaging which gives better protection, supermarket operators claim, can reduce store costs by lessening breakage, shrinkage, and spoilage; preventing discoloration; and stopping pilferage. Packages that are easier to handle can cut costs by speeding price marking, improving handling and display, and saving space. And packaging can increase sales by such promotionally oriented moves as offering smaller or larger sizes, more multi-packs, better pictures of the product itself and pictures of the product in use, and more effective use of color.

Food retailers attach such importance to packaging that they have formed supermarket industry committees to criticize manufacturers' packages and to encourage improved packaging. And retailers also make their feelings known individually. In South Bend, Indiana, for example, some supermarket retailers refused to carry one manufacturer's gelatin products because he would not supply the products in larger cartons. The storekeepers maintained that the firm's small cartons, designed to serve small retailers, were a nuisance and cost too much to handle.

What makes a good package design?

There are no easy rules-of-thumb for the marketer making packaging decisions. The right package depends upon such factors as:

1. Susceptibility of the product to damage.
2. The hazards to which the product *normally* will be exposed—in commercial packaging, it is too costly to protect against every possible hazard.
3. The length of time the product must remain in the package and still be in satisfactory condition.
4. The promotional role of the package.

The right packaging, enough packaging

Experience shows that *a specific package must be developed for each specific product*. The package must safely transport its contents, serve in a specific climate (especially if the product is to be exported), and last for a specific time. To provide such packaging, the manufacturer must know his product, his customers, and how the product will be brought to them. *Under*packaging costs money for damage claims or poor sales, but *over*packaging also costs money because dollars are spent but no gains are realized. Glassware, for example, needs to be protected from even relatively light blows that might smash it. Heavy-duty machinery seldom needs protection from blows but may need protection from corrosion caused by moisture.

Some of the factors a package designer must consider, perhaps with the help of marketing research, are detailed in Figure 11–1. To view

[7] *Modern Packaging*, October, 1957, pp. 121 ff.; and "The Case of the Crumbled Cookie," *Printers' Ink*, January 13, 1967, p. 3.

Figure 11–1 *Packaging considerations*

A. *Package in the Home or Place of Use:*
 1. Package immediately destroyed?
 2. Package used to store contents until used up? How long is this period?
 3. Should package have a dispensing device?
 4. What is average amount of contents used each time?
 5. Is package designed for reuse?
 6. Is package returnable?
 7. Where is package stored? Before use? During use?
 8. Where is the package used?
 9. Is the package used later to store other material?
 10. What effect does the foregoing have on size, color, material?

B. *Package in the Store:*
 1. What types of store will sell the package?
 2. What class of customers do they serve?
 3. Must the package do most of the selling?
 4. Does the package form part of the display?
 5. At what distance must package be identified?
 6. How is identification of contents achieved?
 7. What is the rate of turnover?
 8. In what is package kept in the selling space?
 9. How is package handled in the storeroom?
 10. What can be done to simplify handling of packages?

C. *Package in Transit:*
 1. How is package shipped? What types of carriers?
 2. Are standard cartons or crates used?
 3. How do these factors affect dimensions?
 4. What protective measures are required against temperature, moisture, shock, pilferage, vermin?
 5. Have the carriers any recommendations or standards to be considered?

D. *Package in the Warehouse:*
 1. How is package stored?
 2. How is it handled?
 3. What are usual units of shipments?
 4. How are inventories taken?
 5. How long is package warehoused?
 6. What protective measures are required?

E. *Package at Plant:*
 1. In what form is package received? Quantities?
 2. Where are empties stored?
 3. What are filling and labeling methods?
 4. What types of machines are used?
 5. What grades of employees are involved?

F. *Package and Other Design in Promotion Consideration:*
 1. Are there trademarks? color? type face? or art work problems?
 2. Are there established customs in the industry that affect packages?

G. *The Package and the Law:*
 1. What government requirements exist as to size, description of contents, grades?
 2. What trade customs exist within the industry?
 3. What patent information is required?

SOURCE: Adapted from Benjamin L. Webster, "First Steps in Package Design," *Distribution Age*, June, 1957.

packaging through the eyes of the designer or manufacturer, study this list in relation to a specific product, such as frozen peaches, table salt, women's sweaters, or television sets. When it is obvious that you do not (and the package designers probably would not) know the answer to a packaging problem, marketing research would be indicated before making major packaging decisions.

The impact on costs

May lower total distribution costs

It is apparent that packaging costs money—but in many cases this money may reduce total distribution costs (1) by providing more protection and ease in physical handling, thereby reducing damage and loss, and (2) by so increasing sales and turnover that costs decline, that is, by achieving some of the economies of mass distribution.

The value of protective packaging is clear. Some airlines have developed aluminum containers that can be loaded at the shipper's own plant, *sealed,* and delivered still sealed to the customer. This reduces costly packing and is reputed to be lossproof, weatherproof, and tamperproof. Similar containers have been developed for water shipments. The Volkswagen factory in West Germany, for instance, uses lightweight containers in shipments to its U.S. distributors. Each distributor's container holds several dealers' orders of prepackaged parts, which are ready to go on the shelf with minimum handling.[8]

Promotionally oriented packaging also may reduce the total distribution costs. An attractive package may so speed turnover that total costs will decline as a percentage of sales. While more will be said on this in subsequent chapters, rapid turnover is one of the important ingredients in the success of self-service retailing. Without packages that "sell themselves," self-service retailing would not be possible.

Or . . . may raise total distribution costs

In other cases, total distribution costs may rise because of packaging—and yet *everyone may be satisfied* because the packaging improves the total product.

Consider sugar as an example. In 100-pound bags, the cost of packaging sugar is only 1 percent of the selling price; in 2- to 5-pound cartons, 25–30 percent; and for individual serving envelopes, 50 percent. Yet most housewives do not care to haul a 100-pound bag home, and are quite willing to pay the added costs for more convenient packages. Restaurants use one-serving envelopes of sugar, finding that they reduce the cost of filling and washing sugar bowls and that customers prefer the more sanitary little packages. In both cases, packaging adds value to the total product—or more accurately, it creates new products and new marketing strategies.

Housewives versus packaging

Despite all the time and money now spent on packaging, there is still much room for improvement. In one survey, 85 percent of the house-

---

[8] "Hauling Freight by the Package," *Business Week,* September 16, 1961, pp. 84–86.

230

wives interviewed told of having been hurt when opening a package. Women were especially vocal about having to use knives to open containers of frozen strawberries. Complaints were general about bottles that break, metal containers with sharp edges, reclosable baby-food jars that are practically unopenable, sardine tins and coffee cans without windup keys, sugar bags that are almost impossible to open, and flour-bags that invariably spill.[9] The result is unsatisfied target markets.

Some consumers complain about partially filled packages. Others are confused by the many and varied sizes. Critics of business allege that some package designs are misleading, perhaps deliberately. They feel the great variety of package designs makes it difficult for consumers to make value comparisons readily.

The concern of some consumers finally led to the passage of the Federal Fair Packaging and Labeling Act of 1966. This act provided that, initially, the federal authorities would encourage industry to draw up its own simplified package standards which will give the customer more information and perhaps reduce the number of package sizes. If this is not done, it is possible that Congress will pass legislation that is much more definitive.[10]

Packaging must fit into the strategy

Considerable research and ingenuity may be necessary to do a good job of packaging and to avoid such "goofs" as the recent packaging of a soft drink in an attractive new aluminum can that was fine for supermarket shelves but too tall for vending machines.[11]

In planning packaging, however, packaging is only part of a total marketing strategy. The marketing manager must be alert to make the packaging fit into the total strategy—and not vice versa.

Branding the product

Brands are so numerous and commonplace that we are inclined to take their significance for granted. In the grocery products area alone, there are approximately 38,000 brands, even though the average supermarket can stock only about 6,500.[12] The following section discusses the importance of branding for individual firms and for the economy as a whole.

From our review of Western economic history, it will be recalled that production for the marketplace began early in recorded history, lapsed after the fall of Rome and during the Middle Ages, and expanded again as the feudal villages began to trade with each other. During this revival, craft guilds (similar to labor unions) and merchant guilds formed to control the quantity and quality of production. One require-

Use of brands evolved to meet economic needs

---

[9] "The Perfect Package: It's Not Here Yet," *Business Week*, August 12, 1961, pp. 106–8; and "Cut Fingers in the Kitchen," *Time*, October 20, 1961, p. 56.

[10] "What Effect Will the 'Fair Packaging & Labeling Act' Have on Marketing Practices?" *Journal of Marketing*, April, 1967, pp. 58–59.

[11] "RC Cola's Package 'Too Tall to Vend,'" *Printers' Ink*, May 12, 1967, pp. 56–57.

[12] *The Nielsen Researcher*, No. 1, 1967, p. 11.

ment was that each producer mark his goods so that output could be restricted when necessary. This meant that inferior quality, which might reflect unfavorably on other guild products and discourage future trade, could be traced back to the offending producer. Early trademarks also were a protection to the buyer, who could now determine the source of the product.

Not restriction but identification

More recently, brands have been used primarily for identification rather than restriction of output.

The earliest and most aggressive brand promoters in America were the patent medicine manufacturers. They were joined by the food manufacturers, who grew in size after the Civil War. Some of the brands started in the 1860's and 1870's, and still going strong, are Dr. Lyon's Tooth Powder, Borden's Condensed Milk, Quaker Oats, Vaseline, Pillsbury's Best Flour, and Ivory Soap.[13]

Indians prefer sugar to chalk dust

Today, a good brand usually assures high or at least constant quality and encourages repeat purchasing. This works where there is some trust of sellers by buyers and where the sellers can protect their brand. This is generally true in the United States, but much less so elsewhere. For example, in Formosa there are about a dozen red-and-white striped toothpaste packages of varying quality with brand names remarkably similar to Colgate—Coalgate, Goalgate, Goldkey, Goldcat, and Goldrat.[14]

Customers are willing to buy by brand rather than by inspection when there is some assurance of quality. In many countries, however, the consumer doesn't feel he has any such assurance. In India, inspection is common because there is a complete lack of confidence in packaged goods and brands. This distrust has a solid foundation. In 1957, it was estimated that in Delhi, 25 percent of all food was adulterated. Sawdust, husks, colored earth, and ground seeds accounted for 10–50 percent of the weight of many products. As a result, Indian customers avoid buying packaged or prepared foods. They prefer to buy sugar in extremely coarse crystals, and grain rather than flour, because both fine-granulated sugar and flour can be adulterated easily with chalk-dust.[15]

Soviets prefer brands

The importance of brands in a nation's economy can be seen clearly in the Soviet experience. The U.S.S.R. evolved toward an enthusiastic use of branding—after instances of economic disaster forced it upon them.

Several Russian factories were manufacturing supposedly identical 17-inch TV sets, but actually one of the plants regularly was shipping "lemons." When customers became aware of this, they stopped buying all 17-inch sets, because they could not identify the bad ones. This

---

[13] Frank Presbrey, *The History and Development of Advertising* (New York: Doubleday & Co., Inc., 1929).

[14] *Time*, June 15, 1962, p. 83.

[15] Ralph Westfall and Harper W. Boyd, Jr., "Marketing in India," *Journal of Marketing*, October, 1960, p. 17.

obviously caused considerable inventory problems for the central planners. It also caused some public discontent with the Soviet system. Shortly thereafter, factory marks on products were required to help the planners identify the production source. Subsequently, plants that were producing poorer quality products began to have difficulties meeting their economic plans. Soviet consumers rather than planners forced the plants to pay more attention to quality. Interestingly, before long there were more than 25 state-sponsored advertising agencies to tell people about the "quality" of various factories. Now, advertising courses are even offered in Russian universities![16]

The important thing to note here is that the brands were created by the customers rather than the planners. The factory identification numbers had been added originally to help the planners—but the consumers quickly adapted them to their own use.

Why branding is used and valued

Well-recognized brands make shopping feasible in a modern economy. Think of the consumer's dilemma in a grocery store, for example, if she had to consider seriously the advantages and disadvantages of each of 6,500 items every time she went shopping.

Advantages for the customer

Many customers are willing to buy new things, but having gambled and won, they like to buy a "sure thing" thereafter. The customer may even be willing to pay a premium for brands with which she has had favorable experience. And noneconomic considerations may enter here, too. A housewife considering a well-known brand versus a lower priced and unknown brand of frozen peas, for instance, may evaluate the possible savings. She will also think hard about her embarrassment if her entire dinner is ruined because of hard or unappetizing peas.

There is considerable evidence that if the housewife used well-known brands rather than high prices as an indication of good quality, she might be further ahead. One study of grocery products found that the known brands usually had fairly consistent quality, but there was little assurance that a high price meant high quality.[17]

Furthermore, lower class housewives may buy well-recognized manufacturers' brands, not for status, but for assurance of quality within their more narrowly perceived range of choices.[18]

Brands give status. Customer satisfaction depends on more than the physical product. It involves the *assurance* included in the total product when a dependable brand name is attached to it. Some customers derive psychic satisfaction from the use of well-known branded articles because they feel some of the status or prestige of the product may become associated with them.

---

[16] T. Levitt, "Branding on Trial," *Harvard Business Review,* March–April, 1966, pp. 28–32.

[17] Robert H. Cole, "The Battle of Brands in Canned Goods," in S. H. Rewoldt (ed.), *Frontiers in Marketing Thought* (Bloomington, Ind.: Bureau of Business Research, Indiana University, 1955), pp. 153–59.

[18] James A. Carman, *The Application of Social Class in Market Segmentation* (Berkeley: Institute of Business and Economic Research, University of California, 1965), p. 28.

Advantages to branders

Brands obviously would not be used so aggressively by branders if target customers did not respond to them. Many of the advantages of brand promotion to the branders are a function of the advantages to customers. A good brand speeds shopping for the customer, and so it reduces the marketer's selling time and effort. When a customer finds it convenient to repeat purchases by brand, promotion costs are reduced and sales volume is increased. A marketing manager who consistently attempts to provide a good "buy" and maintain quality can be assured of his reward by using brands.

Another important advantage of successful branding is that the brander may be able to carve out a market for himself among loyal customers.[19] Whether the brander is a manufacturer, wholesaler, or retailer, this brand loyalty protects him from competition, because the brander, in effect, is given a customer franchise by the customers he is reaching. In other words, he achieves a monopolistic competition situation or even a little monopoly, and this gives him greater control in planning his marketing mix.

A brander also can use various brands to segment markets and meet the needs of various intermediate customers. Instead of merely selling "motor oil," for example, the marketing manager could offer three grades (and brands) to cater to final consumers' varying demands for oil quality. But if he were selling this oil to various competing wholesalers and retailers who did not want to compete directly with each other, he might offer them identical or almost identical products under different brand names. Such practices help explain why there are so many brands on the market.

The bigger the better the brand

There is evidence that the bigger or more successful that customers think a company is, the better impression they have of it and its products. The U.S. Steel Corp., with its many large subsidiaries, found that industrial customers who were aware of the relationship of U.S. Steel to its subsidiaries viewed the subsidiaries more favorably. This was important in their choice of supplier, especially when competing products were basically similar. For this reason, in 1958, U.S. Steel redesigned its trademark and began to identify all the subsidiaries with it.[20]

Growing acceptance that a good customer image is important has led some companies to change their corporate name so that the name either is more descriptive of the firm's activity or more inclusive so that it can cover a variety of activities. Cities Service, for instance, took the name Citgo, and spent considerable money popularizing the new name and the new symbol because the old name seemed inappropriate.[21] And U.S. Rubber, with its various foreign subsidiaries, adopted the Uniroyal name and trademark because the new name was a more accurate designation.[22]

---

19 Ross M. Cunningham, "Brand Loyalty—What, Where, How Much?" *Harvard Business Review*, January–February, 1956, pp. 116–28.
20 "What's Behind the New Look That U.S. Steel Is Sporting," *Business Week*, March 29, 1958, pp. 88–93.
21 "Cities Service Hangs New Shingle," *Business Week*, May 8, 1965, pp. 72–77.
22 "One Name to Girdle the Globe," *Business Week*, August 1, 1964, pp. 74–75.

Achieving brand insistence is not an easy thing

Recognition and respect for a brand must be earned, by producing a good product and persistently promoting it. There are many brands which, for practical purposes, are valueless because they have no meaning to target customers.

Three degrees of brand familiarity are significant: (1) recognition, (2) preference, and (3) insistence.

Brand recognition means that customers remember having seen or heard of the brand. This is perhaps a significant achievement if there are many nondescript brands on the market. **Brand recognition**

Rather than just gaining brand *recognition,* some branders would prefer to reach the stage called "brand preference" in which target customers will choose this brand out of habit or past experience. At this stage, the firm may have achieved a favorable position in a monopolistic competition situation. **Brand preference**

"Brand insistence," a logical extension of brand preference, is the stage at which customers insist upon a product and may even search extensively to find it. This stage is the goal of most product differentiation and market segmentation activities. Here, the firm has developed a strong "customer franchise" and may enjoy a very inelastic demand curve. **Brand insistence**

While the degree of brand familiarity achieved will have an important bearing on the development of a marketing mix, it may be necessary to conduct marketing research to determine exactly what the firm has achieved and in what target markets. Research on specific target markets may be needed because, in many situations, company executives feel their products have achieved a higher degree of brand familiarity than they actually have achieved, and the firms develop their marketing mixes accordingly. This self-delusion can only lead to burdening the other ingredients in the marketing mixes. Studies show that some brands do not reach even the brand recognition stage. One study, for example, showed that two out of every five housewives could not even name the brand of furniture they owned.[23] **Knowing how well you're known**

By offering customers what amounts to a "guarantee" of quality, branders may be able to obtain a price that is higher than the cost of giving this guarantee. This is important because maintaining quality and providing a guarantee does, in fact, cost something. One study **Branding may return more than it costs**

---

[23] *Business Week,* February 20, 1960, p. 71; see also, Dik W. Twedt, "How Does Brand Awareness-Attitude Affect Marketing Strategy?" *Journal of Marketing,* October, 1967, pp. 64–66; "Women Flunk Identity Test," *Business Week,* April 6, 1965, pp. 50–52; Henry L. Munn, "Brand Perception as Related to Age, Income, and Education," *Journal of Marketing,* January, 1960, pp. 29–34; Seymour Banks, "The Relationship Between Preference and Purchase of Brand," *Journal of Marketing,* October, 1950, pp. 145–57; and Kenneth P. Uhl, "Shareowner Brand Preference," *Journal of Business of the University of Chicago,* January, 1962, pp. 57–69.

showed that customers were willing to spend approximately 13 percent more for food to pay the extra cost of well-known brands. The customers preferred the well-advertised brands about 3 to 1, and were willing to pay approximately $1 billion a year extra to get them.[24]

Brands must be seen to be appreciated

Spending money on branding makes sense only if the customer who is going to make the buying decision will see the brand and be impressed by it.

Those who make items that are incorporated into others, say into a car, have a particularly difficult branding problem. Producers of automobile tires, spark plugs, and batteries have been successful branders, but makers of wheel bearings, door handles, radiators, and other such parts have not. Producers in the latter kinds of industries tend to face almost pure competition.

Choosing a brand name

In choosing a brand name, a firm may, (*a*) coin a name (Kodak), or (*b*) adapt and adopt words (Keen Kutter, or Perfection), or (*c*) use a name under license or agreement (Batman).

It is difficult to pinpoint what constitutes a good brand name. The names of some products defy even the obvious rules, and yet the products are successful. Many of these items, however, got started when there was relatively little market competition. Where possible, a good brand name should be:

Short, simple, and easy to spell and read.
Easy to recognize and remember.
Pleasing when read and easy to pronounce.
Not disagreeable sounding.
Pronounceable in only one way.
Always timely (does not get out of date).
Adaptable to packaging or labeling requirements.
Available for use (not in use by another firm).
Pronounceable in all languages (for goods to be exported).
Not offensive, obscene, or negative.
A selling suggestion.
Adaptable to any advertising medium (especially billboards and TV).

Deciding what's in a name

Examples of good brand names are *Caterpillar, Pestroy, Rinso, Duz, Sunkist, Band Aid, Zerone,* and *Frigidaire.*

Most suppliers of industrial goods use their own name or something closely associated with their name—although some manufacturers believe that the names of industrial products should indicate such qualities as strength, dependability, or durability.

There are no easy rules for choosing a good brand name; marketing research probably should be used in the selection. For example, after preliminary screening, a large soap manufacturer selects brand names for new products by testing them on consumer audiences, as follows:

---

[24] J. O. Peckham, *Planning Your Marketing Operations for 1959 . . . and the Years Ahead* (Chicago: A. C. Nielsen Co., 1958), p. 15; and "How A Small Packer Does Better than the Giants," *Business Week,* November 22, 1958, pp. 140–52.

Association Test. Names are read or shown on cards. The audience makes notations of things that immediately come to mind.

Learning Test. This measures the ease of learning, reading, pronouncing, writing, and spelling of the names.

Memory Test. A list of names is read off, and the audience tries to recall the names.

Uniqueness Test. After the names are read or shown on cards, the audience writes down all similar brand names. This identifies which names might be confused with established brand names.

Preference Test. The audience states its preferences for the few names left in the running.[25]

What is a brand?

We have used the terms branding, brand names, and trademarks interchangeably so far, but it is important to distinguish among them because of the legal implications each term has.

Branding refers to the use of a name, a term, a symbol, or design (or a combination of these), to identify goods or services of one seller or a group of sellers and to distinguish them from those of competitors.[26] This is a broad term that includes the use of brand names, trademarks, and practically all other means of product identification.

Brand name has a narrower meaning. It is a word, letter, or a group of words or letters that can be spoken.

Trademark, however, is essentially a legal term and includes only those words, symbols, or marks that the law designates as trademarks.

The word "Buick" can be used to illustrate these distinctions. The Buick car is *branded* under the *brand name* "Buick," whether it is used orally or printed in any manner. When "Buick" is printed in a certain kind of script, however, it becomes a *trademark.* A trademark need not be attached to the product. It need not even be a word. A symbol can be used.

These distinctions may seem technical, but they are very important to business firms that spend much money to protect their brands.

Protecting brand names and trademarks

Common law assures the rights of the true originators and users of trademarks and brand names, stating that the ownership of brand names and trademarks is established by continued usage without abandonment. Clearly, by now Morton Salt, Coca-Cola, and Bon Ami are unmistakably identified with particular products.

The exact procedure for protecting trademarks and what could be protected were not clear, however, until the passage of the federal Lanham Act in 1946. This act specifies what types of marks (including brand names) can be protected by law, and it makes provision for

---

[25] Gustav E. Larson, *Developing and Selling New Products—A Guidebook for Manufacturers* (2d ed.; Washington, D.C.: U.S. Government Printing Office, 1955), pp. 40–41.
[26] "Report of the Definitions Committee," *Journal of Marketing,* October, 1948, p. 205.

registration records to facilitate their protection. It applies to goods shipped in interstate or foreign commerce.[27]

No federal tests or policing

The Lanham Act does not make registration compulsory. Even getting onto the registration records does not establish ownership of a mark. It is still necessary to show that the firm was the first to use the particular trademark and that the trademarked product actually has been offered for sale on a continuing basis.

Registration under the Lanham Act merely gives public notice of a company's intention to use a particular trademark. Then, after a certain period of years, some marks—such as Morton Salt's little girl spilling salt—do become incontestably the property of the firm that has registered them.

Registration does not imply that the federal government endorses the product or that the product has passed any federal tests of quality. Neither does registration under the act with the U.S. Patent Office mean that the Patent Office will police the owner's rights to a mark. He himself still must bring suit against any infringers.

A principal reason for registering under the Lanham Act is to protect a trademark to be used in foreign commerce. Some countries require that a trademark be registered in its home country before it can be protected in that country. For this reason, the Lanham Act provides for two registers, the Principal Register, with rigorous requirements, and the Supplemental Register, more inclusive and basically a register for goods in foreign commerce.

Will Orlon go the way of shredded wheat?

A legally valid trademark can be a real asset to a company. Every effort should be made to develop a trademark that will not become a common descriptive term for that kind of product. A unique product group may come to be known by its leading brand name rather than its common descriptive name. When this occurs, the brand name or trademark becomes public property, and the owner loses all his rights to it. This happened with the names *cellophane, aspirin, shredded wheat,* and *kerosene,* and there was concern that *Scotch Tape* and *Frigidaire* might become public property.

Companies with meaningful brands are careful in their promotion to indicate which of their product names are brand names and which are purely descriptive. Orlon is a brand name for acrylic fiber manufactured by Du Pont, which is very careful to require that all reference to Orlon indicate that it is a brand name and *not* a generic name for that type of acrylic fiber.

Conditions favorable to branding

Most marketing managers accept branding as desirable and are primarily concerned with assuring the success of the brand name of the product(s) they are marketing.

The following conditions would be favorable to successful branding:

---

[27] A detailed treatment of the requirements for trademark registration appears in *Printers' Ink,* December 19, 1947; see also, *Trademark Rules of Practice,* U.S. Department of Commerce, January, 1959.

1. The demand for the general product class should be large but with various market segments so that the brander will have something to offer each.
2. The demand should be sufficiently strong so that the market price will offer a large enough margin over additional promotion cost to make the effort worthwhile.
3. It is best when there are economies of mass production. If the branding were really successful, the cost of production would decline with additional volume, thereby increasing profits.
4. The product quality being offered should be the best for the price in the market being served, and the quality should be easily maintained.
5. The product should be easily identifiable by a brand or trademark. This is easier said than done. Many products do not lend themselves easily to conspicuous marking. Few consumers would like to have a furniture manufacturer's label sewn conspicuously on their sofa or lounge chair. But if the label or mark is inconspicuous, then much of the brand prestige value is lost.

    Some producers are ingenious in placing labels. Walnut and orange growers stamp their brand names directly on their products; some coal producers color their coal; and large meat packers place metal foil brand labels inside self-service meat packages.
6. Consistent and widespread availability is necessary. When a customer starts using a brand, she should be able to continue finding it in her stores.
7. Brand promotion will be more successful if the brander can be assured of favorable positioning of his products in the stores. For some manufacturers, this is just a hope or a goal for their salesmen. But when wholesalers and retailers brand their own products, this is something they can control.

What kind of brand to use?

Branders who manufacture or handle more than one item must decide whether they are going to use the same brand name for all their items—called a family brand—or individual brands for each item.

The old established family name

The use of the same brand for many products is sensible if all are essentially the same in nature and quality. The goodwill attached to one or two products may reflect on the others. This reduces the promotional overhead, tends to build a customer franchise for the family brand, and paves the way for the introduction of new products.

Examples of family brands are the Heinz "57" food products, A&P brands (Ann Page, Sultana, and Iona, each in different price classes), Sears, Roebuck's Kenmore appliances, and the Pittsburgh Plate Glass line of paints and other home products.

Use the family brand with care. But just because the company has an established name is no absolute assurance that products bearing this name will find customers with open arms. Much depends on the strength of the customer franchise and the nature of competition. Sunkist is a good example.

The owners of the Sunkist brand were late in entering the frozen citrus concentrate market. When they did enter, they assumed that the brand name Sunkist would have the same appeal printed on frozen

239

juice cans that it does stamped on fresh fruit. They were wrong. Sales were poor, and Sunkist had to fight for its share of the frozen concentrate market just like any other newcomer.

It is obvious that when a family brand name is used, it should be applied to approximately the same type and quality of product. Pillsbury, for example, uses its family name on baking mixes, refrigerator products, and farm feeds, all of which share some common point of origin as milled grain products. Pillsbury's president says: "The Pillsbury name should not mean everything to everybody. . . . If Pillsbury were to enter the appliance business, it shouldn't use the Pillsbury name for the same reason that a housewife probably wouldn't respond to a General Electric cake mix."[28]

Individual brands: outside and inside competition

Individual brands frequently are used by a manufacturer when his products are of varying quality or type. If the products are distinctly different, such as meat products and glue, individual brands probably are preferable. Or the quality and higher price of one of the company's well-known names may be protected while another brand (perhaps identifying a lower priced line) is used as a "fighting" brand to meet competition. Use of individual brands is preferred, too, if there is any risk of the failure of one product damaging the reputation of others.

The market grid concept and market segmentation—trying to aim straight for the right customer with exactly the right product—help explain why some large grocery products manufacturers, such as General Foods, Procter & Gamble, and Lever Brothers, follow a policy of individual branding for many of their lines.

Procter & Gamble has found that its brands appeal to different customers, who feel that they have very individualistic and definite needs. But sometimes these customers decide that a particular product does not satisfy their needs and switch to another product with a different brand name. Frequently this will be one of P&G's other products. If a family P&G brand name were used, however, and the customer specifically identified the product as a P&G item, it is possible that the disgruntled customer might switch to a product of Lever Bros. or some other competitor.

Sometimes firms use individual brands to stimulate competition *within* the organization. This is true, again, with P&G brands. Each brand is the responsibility of a different group; management feels that internal competition keeps everyone alert. The theory is that if anyone is going to take business away from a P&G brand, it ought to be another P&G brand. The same kind of competition is found among General Motors' brands, where Chevrolet, Pontiac, Oldsmobile, Buick, and even Cadillac compete with each other.

Who should do the branding?

Manufacturer brands versus dealer brands

Frequently wholesalers and retailers decide to use their own brands in preference to manufacturers' brands, commonly called "national brands" because of their promotion across the nation or in large re-

[28] *Advertising Age,* September 15, 1958, pp. 2 ff.

gions. Such manufacturers' or national brands include Kellogg's, Stokely, RCA-Whirlpool, International Harvester, Sheetrock, and IBM.

The term "national" is not always an accurate designation, however, since many wholesalers' and retailers' brands have achieved national distribution and are advertised nationally, while some manufacturers' products have only regional distribution. Kroger, A&P, Sears, Roebuck, and Montgomery Ward brands, for example, are all advertised and distributed more widely than many so-called "national brands."

For this reason, instead of the term "national brands," we will use *manufacturers' brands* to refer to this type—as contrasted to wholesalers' and retailers' brands. These latter brands frequently are called "private brands." But to reduce confusion, we will call the wholesalers' and retailers' brands *dealer brands*.

Should a manufacturer make dealer brands?

Our major thrust in this book is on developing unique and profitable strategies which the firm controls. Making products for others—for example, dealer brands made to dealers' specifications at relatively low prices set in almost purely competitive markets—does not fit with our main emphasis. Nevertheless, we must note that some manufacturers choose this strategy and others are forced into it by lack of resources (human and financial) to do the marketing job. Such firms have basically given up marketing and are dependent on the fortunes of their middlemen customers. They may receive enough profit to keep them in business, at least when economic conditions are good, but they are not likely to achieve the profits earned by those who locate and satisfy new target markets.

Some manufacturers emphasize their own brands but produce dealer brands too. The main reason is to utilize capacity more fully. They realize that dealer branders will probably find someone to produce for them, so there is no point in worrying about increasing competition. This was a major concern of producers some years ago, but now most manufacturers will produce dealer brands if they feel it is profitable to them. They see the battle for sales in the market and plan to win their share there rather than by trying to restrict output. General Electric recently decided to make appliances for J. C. Penney. And RCA-Whirlpool does the same for Sears. These products usually are made to the dealers' specifications and become parts of different—and perhaps competing—marketing strategies. We will say more about pricing later, but here we should note that dealers usually are able to buy from manufacturers at relatively low prices because they take over the whole marketing job.

Before launching a dealer brand

For a dealer brand to be successful, a number of conditions should exist:

1. If there are several manufacturers' brands, none should be strongly entrenched in the market.
2. A dependable quality and quantity of ingredients or raw materials for the dealer brand should be available at a reasonable price to insure a good margin in case the brand meets with acceptance.
3. It helps if manufacturers' brands are overpriced, so the dealer brand

can be priced under them, yet with a larger-than-normal gross margin, to cover higher promotional costs.

4. Although the dealer's brand must be promoted, the promotion should not be so expensive as to use up the extra gross margin.
5. There should be an adequate, well-established market; dealers may find it difficult and expensive to pioneer the introduction of new products.
6. Product quality should be easily and economically determined by inspection or use; customers will be more willing to experiment if a dealer's brand does not present too much of a risk.
7. If the dealer brand is lower priced, depressed business conditions may help its sale—customers are more price conscious.

Dealer brands in the food and drug lines usually are offered at slightly lower prices than manufacturers' brands. Dealer brands, however, are not always priced lower. Sometimes dealers, having analyzed their target market, choose to offer a prestige-laden, higher quality product and then price it even higher than major manufacturers' brands. Some such decisions have been successful.

Advantages and disadvantages of branding for dealers

Our discussion of branding so far has applied to manufacturers as well as dealers, but branding has some special advantages and disadvantages for dealers.

Advantages of manufacturers' brands —more prestige, less inventory

The major advantage of selling a popular manufacturer's brand is that the product already is presold to some target customers. Furthermore, it may bring in new customers. It may encourage higher turnover with a reduced selling cost, and some of the prestige of the manufacturer's brand may rub off on the dealers. But in case the manufacturer doesn't maintain his quality, *he* receives the blame, not the dealer, and the customer can be shifted to another manufacturer's brand or a dealer brand. The dealer does not lose *his* customer.

Since manufacturers' brands usually are readily available at the wholesalers' or manufacturers' warehouses, the dealer needs to carry less inventory. Another major advantage for some retailers is that the retailer can advertise special prices on items which are carried in other stores and thereby call attention to his store as a source of bargains.

Disadvantages of manufacturers' brands —lost products, lost customers

The major disadvantage of manufacturers' brands is that manufacturers normally offer a lower gross margin than the dealer might be able to earn with his own brands. This, however, may be offset by higher turnover.

Another disadvantage is that the manufacturer still maintains control of his brand and may withdraw it from the dealer at any time. Wholesalers are especially vulnerable in this respect. If customers become loyal to a manufacturer's brand and the dealer does not or cannot carry the product, then the customers may go elsewhere. Here, loyalty may be tied to the brand rather than to the dealer.

In some respects, the advantages of dealer brands are the converse of the disadvantages of manufacturers' brands. The dealer may be able to buy products at lower prices and so be able to obtain higher gross margins even with lower retail prices. He may have greater price flexibility for his own brands because price comparisons are not as easy as with manufacturer's brands, and also because there is no manufacturer to dictate pricing policy.

Advantages of dealer brands—loyal salesmen, the best shelves

Another advantage of dealer brands is that dealers easily can change from one supplier to another if any one firm can't offer the quality and price needed. By using their own brands, dealers may be able to protect themselves from the arbitrary action of manufacturers.

Wholesaler brands protect wholesalers from the defection of their salesmen—and the salesmen's customer following—to other wholesaling firms. Why? Wholesaler brands give the wholesaler, rather than his salesmen, a claim to customer loyalty.

Since the dealer's own brand ties customers to him, he may be able to estimate demand and buy more effectively. His salesmen can also control the point of sale and may be able to give their products special shelf position or displays.

The dealer must stimulate his own demand, and this may be costly, especially if turnover is typically slow in his lines. He must take the blame for inferior quality. He may have difficulty getting consistently good quality at low prices, especially during times of short supply such as wartime inflationary periods. And the dealer must purchase in fairly large quantities from suppliers, assuming the risk and cost of carrying inventory.

Disadvantages of dealer brands—taking the blame, buying big quantities

The battle of the brands—who's winning?

Manufacturers and dealers have been vying with each other in what has been called the "battle of the brands." No criticism of branding is implied in the term "battle." It is simply a question of whose brands are to be more popular and who is to be in control.

Some motivation research findings suggest, in food products at least, that manufacturers' brands may be losing ground. In 1951, manufacturers' brands seemed to be preferred by a ratio of 2 or 3 to 1. Even higher prices were accepted. By 1956, however, similar research indicated that some customers had shifted in favor of some of the major dealer brands. This trend seems to be continuing. Referring to "Ann Page," one research respondent said: "You get a feeling that the whole personality of the store is behind each of its products, and when you buy you have a tendency to follow through on this pattern."

One of the reasons for this shift is that some of the manufacturers' brands have come to symbolize elegance and are regarded as a luxury, while the dealer-branded chain store products are seen as necessities.[29] The chains' dealer-branded products also seem to be more widely recognized and *are* more likely to be in stock. One consumer's quote

[29] E. Dichter, "Brand Loyalty and Motivation Research," *Food Business,* January and February, 1956; see also, *Printers' Ink,* March 1, 1963, p. 5.

may be revealing in this connection: "When something is highly advertised, I find it short in the supermarkets."[30]

The growth of dealer branding has been pushed by the established chain stores, who often use their brands as a competitive weapon against discount houses. But this in turn sometimes leads manufacturers to bring out lower priced lines of their own. Goodyear, for example, brought out a third-line nylon tire to compete with dealer-branded tires being sold at lower prices.[31] Department stores, supermarkets, service stations, clothiers, appliance dealers, and drugstores are all going more deeply into dealer branding.

Perhaps the end of dominance

The "battle of the brands" certainly is far from over, but the former dominance of manufacturers' brands may be ended. Some retailers are becoming so large that dealer brands frequently sell in large volume and are nationally advertised. Some wholesalers have developed extremely strong brands and have ties to regional chains with literally hundreds of stores. As long ago as 1957, one such wholesaler had a strong dealer-branding program, covering 600 food and related items. He was serving a group of 27 regional food chains that operated 650 stores.[32]

Manufacturers may become only manufacturers

In the future, retailer-controlled brands may seek broader distribution among other retailers and perhaps wholesalers too. It seems logical that as retailers begin to advertise nationally but have only a limited number of sales outlets, they may find it profitable to permit others to carry their brands. This might be a serious challenge to manufacturers' brands.

If this trend continues, manufacturers could become just that—only the producers. Retailers and wholesalers might come to dominate marketing. Certainly the latter are closer to final consumers and may have greater control of the final sale situation.[33]

Conclusion

Packaging and branding can create a new total product. Variations in packaging can make a product salable in various target markets. Branding can be used by the marketer in creating and building a customer franchise for a given product.

A specific package must be developed for each product. Both underpackaging and overpackaging can be expensive. Although the final

---

[30] "Private Brands Score Well," *Printers' Ink,* May 12, 1967, p. 3.

[31] "A Wider Track for Tire Sales," *Business Week,* March 20, 1965, pp. 55–58; and *Business Week,* February 13, 1960, p. 80.

[32] John V. Ziemba, "Private Labels Climb into Key Marketing Positions," *Food Engineering,* July, 1958, pp. 52–54.

[33] H. W. Boyd, Jr., and R. E. Frank, "The Importance of Private Labels in Food Retailing," *Business Horizons,* Summer, 1966, pp. 81–90; "Manufacturers' Brands vs. Distributors' Brands," *Grey Matter,* March, 1963; "Private Labels Peril Concept of Brand, GMA Told," *Advertising Age,* June 24, 1963, pp. 3 ff.; "Private Label: A New Round in the Retail Revolution," *Drug & Cosmetic Industry,* March, 1963, pp. 285–86 ff.; and E. B. Weiss, "Will Retailer-Controlled Brands Seek Broader Distribution?" *Advertising Age,* September 23, 1957, pp. 106 ff.

customer remains the ultimate factor, the packager also must remember the needs of wholesalers and retailers. A small retailer might prefer the smaller package units that a supermarket operator would resist.

To customers, the main significance of brands is an assurance of quality. This confidence leads to repeat purchasing. For marketers, such "automatic" buying means reduced promotion costs and increased sales.

Should brands be stressed? The decision depends on whether the costs of brand promotion and honoring the brand guarantee can be covered and made profitable by a higher price or more rapid turnover, or both. The cost of branding may reduce other costs by relieving pressure on the other three P's.

In recent years, the strength of manufacturers' brands has declined and dealer brands have become more important. The dealer-labeled products may win in the "battle of the brands," perhaps because dealers are closer to customers and may choose to promote their own brands more aggressively.

Branding gives a marketing manager considerable latitude. He can add brands and use individual or family brands. Ultimately, however, customers express their approval or disapproval of the total product (including the brand). The degree of brand familiarity obtained is a test of management's ability to carve out a separate market, and has considerable impact on Place, Price, and Promotion decisions.

Questions and problems

1 Justify the increasing interest in packaging, not only for consumer goods but industrial goods. Is this likely to continue?

2 Suggest an example where packaging costs probably: (*a*) lower total distribution costs, and (*b*) raise total distribution costs.

3 Compare the kind of packages typically used for frozen peas and for phonograph records with respect to the considerations in Figure 11–1. Do these packages have anything in common? How are they dissimilar? Compare these packages to shoe packages. Why are they different?

4 Is there any difference between a brand name and a trademark? If so, why is this difference important?

5 Is a well-known brand valuable only to the owner of the brand?

6 Would it be profitable for a firm to expend large sums of money to establish a brand for any type product in any market situation? Why, or why not? If the answer is no, suggest examples.

7 Evaluate the suitability of the following brand names: (*a*) Star (sausage), (*b*) Pleasing (books), (*c*) Rugged (shoes), (*d*) Shiny (shoe polish), (*e*) Lord Jim (ties).

8 Explain family brands. Sears, Roebuck and A&P use family brands but they have several different family brands. If the idea is a good one, why don't they have just one brand?

9 What is the "battle of the brands"? Who do you think will win and why?

10 What does the degree of brand preference imply about previous promo-

tion efforts and the future promotional task? Also, how does the degree of brand preference affect the Place and Price variables?

11 One of the larger furniture manufacturers in England recently embarked upon an aggressive promotional campaign stressing his brand name with the objective of obtaining between 40 and 50 percent of the English market. He started with about 3 to 4 percent of the market. What are his prospects?

12 If you have been operating a small supermarket with emphasis on manufacturers' brands and have barely been breaking even, how should you evaluate the proposal of a large wholesaler who offers a full line of dealer-branded groceries at substantially lower prices? Specify any assumptions necessary to obtain a definite answer.

Consumer goods

There are two major problems in discussing consumer goods. One is that it is impossible to discuss the marketing process for the thousands of goods. The other is that some products usually considered consumer goods also may be industrial goods, since they are destined for use by intermediate customers.

Consumer goods are those goods or services destined for the ultimate consumer in such a form that they may be used without additional processing. These contrast with *industrial goods,* which are those goods and services destined for use in producing other goods or services.[1] All goods fit into one or the other of these two categories.

The type of customer who will finally use the good determines whether it should be classified as consumer or industrial. Although the same physical product may be involved, the two types of customers may need entirely different marketing mixes.

Many products and services can be either consumer or industrial goods, depending upon the final customer. Examples include typewriters, typing paper, rugs, decorators' services, lighting fixtures, brooms, and plumbing services.

A further breakdown for the consumer goods category is included in this chapter and for the industrial goods category, in Chapter 13.

---

[1] *Marketing Definitions* (Chicago: American Marketing Association, 1960), pp. 11 and 14.

Need for a classification system

Fresh meat, canned salmon, and lettuce are all foods, yet all are marketed differently. Hosiery and women's party dresses are clothing items, but the marketing mixes for each are quite dissimilar. Hosiery is available in many different types of outlets and has a much simpler fitting problem. Hosiery has been successfully branded, but relatively few women's dress brands are widely known.

There are many other examples of apparently similar products with dissimilar marketing problems. The nature of the product has considerable bearing on how the four P's are combined in a marketing mix. To avoid treating every product as unique, we must try to develop sensible, if tentative, generalizations about how products are related to marketing mixes. If we can so classify products, this can be highly useful as a starting point for developing marketing mixes for new products and evaluating present mixes.

A number of classification systems are conceivable. One type might be based on the kind of outlet through which the products are marketed. Another could be based on a division of all products into either necessities or luxuries. A third could be classification by the degree of demand elasticity. Each has its deficiencies.

A useful classification system

Let the buyer be satisfied

A particularly workable and useful product classification system would be one based on *the way people buy products*. Since the purpose of the marketing process is to satisfy customer needs, basing product classification on customer behavior makes the most sense.

In a classification system based on customer behavior, goods can be separated into four categories: (1) convenience goods, (2) shopping goods, (3) specialty goods, and (4) unsought goods.

Convenience goods are those that customers want to buy immediately, with minimum shopping effort, i.e., where the busy customer feels she stands to gain little from making price and quality comparisons.

Shopping goods are those goods for which customers do shop, comparing the price and quality of various brands by shopping in several stores, studying performance evaluations, and reading advertisements.

Specialty goods are those that customers insist upon finding, and search for until they find.

Unsought goods are those items that potential customers don't want yet, or don't know they can buy, or aren't looking for.

How much do people want what they buy?

Convenience and shopping goods are characterized by specific kinds of *shopping* behavior. In this sense, these goods are at the extremes of a customer shopping effort continuum. The amount of customer search and comparison mounts higher going from shoestrings (a convenience good) to suits and dining room furniture (shopping goods).

Specialty and unsought goods are not on the same continuum of shopping effort. They are special cases. Unsought goods are not

248

shopped for at all. Customers will travel extensively to find a particular specialty good they already know they want—but they are not shopping in the comparing sense. This doesn't mean, though, that the customer looking for a specialty good will have to look very far. Many retailers may carry such specialty goods, knowing that if they don't have these items, they will lose the business of the customers who want them.

In marketing, we have traditionally focused on physical goods almost to the exclusion of services. This reflects the production orientation of most manufacturers and the physical handling emphasis of most middlemen.

Services are goods, too

Some writers, likewise, have been inclined to ignore services, while others treat them as vastly different from physical goods. We will do neither. Services now account for about 40 percent of personal consumption expenditures; they cannot be ignored and they should not be treated as unique.

In this text, we stress that the purpose of marketing is to satisfy customers, not just to get rid of physical products. Customer needs are satisfied not only by tangible products but also by services, or some combination of them. Indeed, one author has suggested that there are very few pure products or pure services. Most goods are a combination of both.[2]

An automobile without repair services, for example, is not a very useful product. The customer wants not just the physical automobile but the maintenance and repair service to keep it running. To a consumer, the physical product and the service to keep it operative should not be separated—although this separation seems to exist in the minds of production-oriented businessmen.

In terms of their potential for satisfying customer needs, some services are even superior to physical goods. A rented car, for example, may be far more practical temporary transportation than an owned car.

We will not make a distinction between goods and services but will call them all goods or products. Where the intangibility of a service as contrasted to the physical nature of a product is of special significance, we *may* take some notice of the distinction. For the most part, however, we will focus on the similarities—based on customer buying habits and preferences—of various physical products and services. This will be a sound method and of great help in planning effective marketing strategies.

Product classifications help set strategy

The attitudes of a group of target customers who see a product in the same way pretty much determine what *their* "ideal" marketing mix would look like. And this means that if we accept as practicable the

---

[2] John M. Rathmell, "What Is Meant by Services?" *Journal of Marketing,* October, 1966, pp. 32–36; Robert C. Judd, "The Case for Redefining Services," *Journal of Marketing,* January, 1964, pp. 58–59; William J. Regan, "The Service Revolution," *Journal of Marketing,* July, 1963, pp. 57–62; and Dik W. Twedt, "What Is a 'Convenient Food'?" *Journal of Marketing,* January, 1967, pp. 67–68.

development of marketing mixes to satisfy target customers, then we are predetermining the general outline of the marketing mix when we select a goods classification to summarize how some target group views the product.

Research does support this approach, having found that customer-behavior-related goods classifications are related to marketing mix development. Further validation is the clustering of retail stores according to goods classifications, especially as found in shopping centers.[3] More will be said on this in Chapter 17 on Retailing.

Product classifications not automatic or unique

There is no simple, automatic classification for a particular good. While this may be bothersome, it means that there is no need to memorize a long list of products according to classifications. Yet the corollary of eliminating the list is that the manager must develop a theory about how different groups of target customers will regard his product—and proceed accordingly.

Different target markets sometimes take different views of the same service or physical product. For a particular product, two or more product classifications combined with two or more marketing strategies might be needed to satisfy all potential customers.

A tale of three motels

Motels are a good example of a service that is viewed as three different kinds of goods. Some motorists—tired ones—are satisfied with the first motel they come to (a convenience good); other travelers shop for the best facilities at the best price (a shopping good); still others study their road guides and drive or phone ahead until they find a vacancy in a recommended motel (a specialty good).

Perhaps the same motel could satisfy all potential customers, but it would take some doing to produce a marketing mix attractive to everyone. Those looking for convenience would want easy access; the shopping tourists would want attractive appearance and comfort relative to price; specialty-goods travelers would require a listing in their touring guides.

The market grid for motels in one geographical area might appear as shown in Figure 12-1, with a very large convenience-goods market. This might suggest that motel owners should try harder to get convenient locations even if it meant skimping on facilities that would appeal to the shopping-goods travelers.

In other areas, the market grid might look more like Figure 12-2,

---

[3] Arno K. Kleinenhagen, "Shopping, Specialty, or Convenience Goods?" *Journal of Retailing*, Winter, 1966–67, pp. 32–39 ff; Louis P. Bucklin, "Testing Propensities to Shop," *Journal of Marketing*, January, 1966, pp. 22–27; William P. Dommermuth, "The Shopping Matrix and Marketing Strategy," *Journal of Marketing Research*, May, 1965, pp. 128–32; Gordon E. Miracle, "Product Characteristics and Marketing Strategy," *Journal of Marketing*, January, 1965, pp. 18–24; Richard H. Holton, "The Distinction Between Convenience Goods, Shopping Goods, and Specialty Goods," *Journal of Marketing*, July, 1958, pp. 53–56; and Leo V. Aspinwall, "The Characteristics of Goods Theory," in William Lazer and Eugene J. Kelley (eds.), *Managerial Marketing: Perspectives and Viewpoints* (rev. ed.; Homewood, Ill.: Richard D. Irwin, 1962), pp. 633–43; Perry Bliss, "Supply Considerations and Shopper Convenience," *Journal of Marketing*, July, 1966, pp. 43–45; S. Kaish, "Cognitive Dissonance and the Classification of Consumer Goods," and W. P. Dommermuth and E. W. Cundiff, "Shopping Goods, Shopping Centers, and Selling Strategies," *Journal of Marketing*, October, 1967, pp. 28–36.

Figure 12–1 *How the motel market looks to some motel owners*

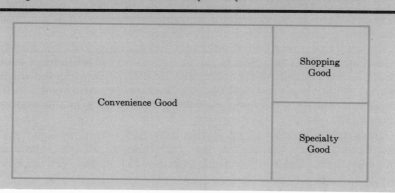

Figure 12–2 *Another view of the motel market*

which shows large shopping-goods and specialty-goods markets—which may be the best view of the motel market today. The newer motels not only are conveniently located but also have rather sumptuous layouts and offer charge card and free reservation services to your next stop.

These motel examples show that if each marketing manager analyzed his own potential target markets in terms of these goods classifications, it would force him to clarify his thinking about consumers' behavior and marketing mixes. To better understand these classifications, let's look at them more carefully.

Convenience goods

Convenience goods—those goods the customer wants but isn't willing to spend much of his valuable time shopping for—include such items as cigarettes, soap, drugs, newspapers, magazines, chewing gum, candy, and most grocery products.

These products are bought frequently and readily, require little

251

service or selling, are not very expensive, and may even be bought by habit. The classic cigarette slogan, "I'd walk a mile for a Camel," tried to imply that Camels were not a convenience good, but it is doubtful that many consumers think of their own cigarette brand in this light.

At the same time, you should also be careful about too readily classifying goods as convenience goods. Remember the attitudes of your target customers as they are influenced by income, wealth, and other factors. A 10-cent novelty might be a convenience good for most adults, but it is definitely a shopping good for a child with a 20-cent weekly allowance.

Convenience goods can be further classified into three sub-types, again primarily on the basis of how customers think about products and buy them. These sub-classifications are (1) staples, (2) impulse goods, and (3) emergency goods.

Staples— as inevitable as death and taxes

The staple food and drug items used regularly in every household are usually bought frequently, without much thought beyond the initial decision to buy. Branding becomes important because brand recognition helps the customer reduce shopping effort.

Staple items are offered for sale in many convenient places such as food stores, drugstores, and hardware stores, as well as vending machines, because customers don't want to search far for them. Some customers, in fact, value convenience so highly that they prefer to have such goods as milk, bread, newspapers, and orange juice delivered directly to their homes. This may cost slightly more, but customers are willing to pay for the convenience.

Shopping for staples may not even be planned. Since many housewives do their meal planning while passing shelves in the supermarket, modern supermarkets have been laid out to facilitate this. Complementary goods such as strawberries and shortcake mix (biscuit mix) or sponge cake are sometimes placed next to each other. This encourages even more unplanned buying.

Such spontaneous purchasing of convenience goods does not mean that this buying is completely haphazard. One study did show that the buying of about 50 percent of all grocery items might be classed as unplanned, but nearly 86 percent of these purchases were products and brands that had been purchased before.[4]

Unplanned purchasing of this kind is sometimes called "impulse buying," but this may be a misuse of the term. Rather, it would seem that some customers—especially experienced shoppers and those buying large quantities—are shifting their meal planning from the home to the store; this may be a very sensible way for them to buy.[5]

Impulse goods— buy it now or never

Impulse goods are bought as unplanned purchases, but not in the same sense as are unplanned purchases of staples. Customers typically are not out shopping for impulse goods. Yet true impulse goods are

---

[4] David T. Kollat and Ronald P. Willett, "Customer Impulse Purchasing Behavior," *Journal of Marketing Research*, February, 1967, pp. 21–31.

[5] *Ibid.*, p. 27.

items that the customer decides to purchase on sight, probably has bought the same way many times before, and wants immediately.

If a housewife were to pass a street corner vendor, for example, decide eating ice cream would be a good idea, and purchase an ice-cream bar, this bar would be considered an impulse good. The important distinction is that if the same housewife were to buy a box of ice-cream bars in the supermarket with the intention of using them for a family dessert, then the bars would be regarded as staples because she was looking for desserts.

There is an important distinction between buying something for *immediate gratification* and buying for *subsequent use*. If the customer does not purchase an impulse good immediately, the need may disappear and no purchase will be made. But if the customer needs some desserts, she will eventually buy them.

This distinction is important because it affects Place and the whole marketing mix. Place is extremely important for impulse goods, because if they don't cross paths with the buyer, the potential sales may be lost forever. As a result, special methods have developed for selling impulse goods. Impulse-good specialists, such as ice cream vendors, specialize in putting these goods where they'll be bought. Department stores often place impulse goods on the first floor near main doors; supermarkets and drugstores put them near the checkout counter. Impulse goods sometimes achieve a strong brand preference—as in the case of Coca-Cola and some brands of candy bars.

Emergency goods are purchased only when the need is urgent. The customer wants these products immediately; price and perhaps even quality are of small concern. The demand for such goods may be extremely inelastic.

Emergency goods— the price you're willing to pay

Examples are ambulance services, umbrellas or raincoats during a rainstorm, and tire chains during a driving snowstorm.

Some retailers deliberately handle emergency goods to meet such needs. Small gasoline stations in rural areas and the big service stations on turnpikes carry tires to meet emergency needs. The buyer probably could get a tire at a lower price back home, but with a damaged tire on his car, he will pay what he has to.

Some small, neighborhood grocery stores meet the "fill-in" needs of customers who make only one major buying excursion to the supermarket each week and need something else between trips. Usually these small stores charge higher prices for this service, but customers find it worthwhile because they take a different view of the products they buy there. One study found that almost 80 percent of the housewives who were surveyed used such a "fill-in" store.[6]

Place is an important part of the marketing mix for emergency goods. Clearly, the marketing mix for emergency goods will be different from the one for staples, at least regarding where goods are placed.

---

[6] M. Alexis, L. Simon, and K. Smith, "Some Determinants of Food Buying Behavior," in M. Alexis, R. Hancock, and R. J. Holloway, *Empirical Foundations of Marketing: Research Findings in the Behavioral and Applied Sciences* (Skokie, Ill.: Rand McNally & Co., forthcoming).

Everything is becoming a convenience

Convenience goods traditionally have been regarded as small, frequently purchased items. We accept this view, except that emergency goods are not purchased as often. But as consumers grow increasingly affluent, they seem to prefer the luxury of treating more goods as convenience goods, and even as impulse goods.

One marketing executive has taken the extreme position that "almost anything that costs less than a new car is impulse-purchased. Packaged goods, particularly, are bought on the fly today. There is far less thoughtful, considered buying than there used to be."[7]

In addition to foods, some consumers seem to be buying toys, jewelry, cosmetics, some women's clothing, books, and phonograph records on impulse. The author has seen a $300 freezer bought without any searching or comparison—an isolated example, perhaps, but one that may become more common in the future.

You should watch the growing tendency to buy goods quickly, with little shopping, because this kind of buying may drastically alter marketing distribution patterns in the future. There seems to be a trend among neighborhood drugstores, variety stores, and grocery stores to carry increasingly high-priced goods that apparently are bought as convenience goods.

Shopping goods

Shopping goods are those products that a customer feels are worth the time and effort to examine carefully and compare with competing products.[8]

Shopping goods can be divided into two classifications, depending on what customers are seeking: (1) homogeneous and (2) heterogeneous shopping goods.

Homogeneous shopping goods— the price must be right

Our earlier discussion of homogeneous products—those that consumers view as essentially similar—begins to bear fruit here. You will recall that when consumers view the various brands of a product as essentially the same, each competitor has an almost perfectly elastic demand curve. Since a slight price cut on such products could substantially increase sales volume, we might expect vigorous price competition.

This, in fact, is the condition in many markets. Some consumers feel that certain sizes and types of refrigerators, television sets, washing machines, and even automobiles are essentially similar, and are primarily concerned about shopping for the best price.

Each manufacturer seeks to emphasize his differences, and every retailer tries to promote his "better service." But if the customers do not believe these differences are real, they will base their shopping decisions on the one variable they feel is or can be different—price.

---

[7] E. J. Kelley, "The Importance of Convenience in Consumer Purchasing," *Journal of Marketing*, July, 1958, p. 33; see also, Hawkins Stern, "The Significance of Impulse Buying Today," *Journal of Marketing*, April, 1962, pp. 59–62.

[8] For a graphical approach to analyzing shopping behavior and its implications, see William P. Dommermuth, "The Shopping Matrix and Marketing Strategy," *Journal of Marketing Research*, May, 1965, pp. 128–32.

This is particularly true in large urban areas where there are many firms selling the same physical product and similar services. In this situation, target customers decide on the model they want, after perhaps seeing it advertised or talking to their neighbors, and then seek the "best buy."

In a recent study of automobile purchasing behavior, about 56 percent of those interviewed wanted the "best price or deal," and about half of those interviewed did shop at more than one dealership.[9]

Some consumers, interested only in price, try to simplify their search by attempting to obtain comparative prices by telephone. But some retailers refuse to give prices by telephone, feeling that they are selling more than the physical product—and want to be able to tell the customer face-to-face about their services.

It is this buyer emphasis on price, then, that helps explain the development of certain types of discount houses.

Even some inexpensive items like butter, coffee, and other food items may be treated as homogeneous shopping goods by some people. Some customers carefully read food store advertising for the lowest prices on these items, and then go from store to store getting the items—doing what is known as "cherry picking" in the grocery trade. Still, these customers may fill other needs while on their rounds, and this could enable the store to make profitable sales to offset the bargains they offer.

In some international markets where consumer incomes are low, we see more homogeneous shopping goods. With limited buyer power, the consumers in these areas seem unwilling to treat goods as convenience goods and prefer instead to shop extensively. One author reported, for example, that "virtually all goods are shopping goods" in Nigeria.[10]

Even if some manufacturers' branded products have achieved the brand preference stage, they still may be treated by some price-conscious consumers as homogeneous shopping goods when offered by several competing retailers who add nothing to the total product. At the retail level, price may be all-important if everything else in the marketing mix seems equal to target customers.

Heterogeneous shopping goods—the product must be right

These are products that the customer sees as nonstandardized and wants to inspect for quality and suitability. Examples are furniture, draperies, dishes, and clothing. Style is important, and price is secondary.

Even if an item costs only $5 or $10, consumers sometimes will seek it in three or four stores to be sure they have done a good job of shopping.

Price is not totally ignored in this kind of buying. But for nonstandardized merchandise, there are fewer bases for price comparison. Once the customer has found the right product, he may not be too concerned about price, provided it is reasonable. That is, the demand for the product may be quite inelastic. The more close substitutes there are, the more elastic becomes the demand. But it does not approach the extreme elasticity found with homogeneous shopping goods.

[9] L. P. Feldman, "Prediction of the Spatial Pattern of Shopping Behavior," *Journal of Retailing,* Spring, 1967, pp. 25–30 ff.

[10] Henry L. Munn, "Retailing in Nigeria," *Journal of Retailing,* Fall, 1966, p. 30.

Branding may be less important for heterogeneous goods. The more a consumer wants to make his own comparisons of price and quality, the less reliance he places on trade names and labels. These goods usually are branded, but often little effort is made to publicize them. While women's dresses have labels, they don't show. Style and quality usually are more important.

When status sells. The fact, however, that branding has not been common with heterogeneous shopping goods does not mean that they can't be branded effectively. Achieving the brand recognition stage might noticeably affect heterogeneous product choices. As with other types of products, if the customer is unsure about several apparently similar items, he may choose the brand he recognizes and which he thinks carries status. This status aspect may grow increasingly important if more consumers become other-directed. At the very least, a well-recognized brand may be useful for some parts of the market grid.

Service, please! Often the buyer of heterogeneous shopping goods not only wants but expects some kind of help in buying, the kind and degree often depending on the socioeconomic class of the purchaser.

If the purchase is costly, the buyer may want expensive service, such as alterations of clothing or installation of appliances. For most customers, a sport shirt picked up on the run, as a convenience good, need not fit so precisely as a good suit—a heterogeneous shopping good.[11]

Specialty goods

Specialty goods are those consumer goods that a significant group of buyers want and will make a special effort to buy. The buyer knows he wants the product. Shopping for the specialty good consists not of comparing the product but merely finding it.

Specialty goods usually are not product categories but specific branded products that have passed the brand preference stage and achieved brand insistence. Product differentiation and market segmentation efforts aim at creating specialty goods.

There are some instances in which a unique new product, even though not branded, also might be a specialty good. This could be true of a new drug or fertilizer, available only by generic name. Generally, however, a specific brand is involved.

Accept no substitutes! Contrary to a common view, specialty goods need not be relatively expensive, durable items that are purchased infrequently. Any branded item that develops a strong customer franchise may achieve specialty-goods status. Consumers have been observed asking for a drug product by its brand name and, when offered a substitute (even though chemically identical), actually leaving the store in anger.

As might be expected, the demand for specialty goods will be relatively inelastic, at least within reasonable price ranges, since target customers are willing to insist upon the product.

Ready availability of a product does not eliminate it as a specialty

---

[11] For a basic study on shopping behavior in department stores, see Stuart U. Rich, *Shopping Behavior of Department Store Customers* (Boston: Harvard Graduate School of Business Administration, 1963).

good. Although some customers might be willing to look hard to locate it, the following conditions in the competitive market structure might make extensive searching unnecessary:

1. If many retailers want to obtain a share of this specialty goods market.
2. If the manufacturer, uncertain of his success in creating a specialty good, tries to obtain distribution in more outlets than really are needed to satisfy the specialty-goods market.
3. If the product is basically a staple convenience good and the major effort is directed at that target market.

As we noted earlier, the same physical product might be classified in two or three ways, depending on how potential customers regard it. If consumers view the product as both a staple and a specialty good, the same Place facilities could serve both target markets. Yet the marketing manager would want to recognize the two distinct markets so that he could intelligently interpret research findings and comments from the field. He might, for example, be very pleased to find that some retailers are impressed with the apparent brand loyalty of those customers who continue to treat the product as a specialty good—but he should remember that the bulk of the market considers his product a staple.

Unsought goods

Unsought goods are those that potential customers do not yet want or know they can buy and, therefore, do not search for at all. In fact they probably would not buy these goods even if they came upon them unless additional promotion were used to show the value of these goods or services.

There seem to be two types of unsought goods, and they can be called *new* unsought and *regularly* unsought.

The *new* unsought goods are products offering *really new* concepts with which potential customers are not yet familiar. The concepts are such, however, that informative promotion can help convince consumers to accept or even seek the product.

Regularly unsought goods are such products as life insurance, encyclopedias, and gravestones that may remain unsought but definitely not unbought forever. These products may represent some of the biggest expenditures a family ever makes, but few people would even drive around the block to find them.

Not all "new" products are unsought goods. Just any new brand of shoe polish, for instance, would not be an unsought good. Most customers probably would consider it a staple—as just another entry in the shoe polish market. The marketing manager's job would be to get distribution and hopefully some brand preference. Dow-Corning's Shoe-Saver, a silicone waterproofing product for shoes, was another matter.

Making dry shoes a convenience

Dow-Corning fought an uphill battle to gain acceptance for Shoe-Saver. It was not a polish, and cost more than polishes. The marketing manager's job, here, was to end its unsought status by informing potential target markets that a new kind of product was available for shoe protection. Subsequently, Shoe-Saver was accepted by retailers and consumers as another convenience good.

Regularly unsought goods are a different problem. Goods such as encyclopedias and life insurance must be promoted continually to achieve any sales, but there probably is little hope that they will move out of the unsought category for most consumers. Greater stress is needed on Promotion, and it is likely that aggressive marketing will have to continue.

By imaginatively searching for unsatisfied customer needs, however, it may be possible to locate some target market that would find the unsought good so attractive that they might seek it, or at least buy with enthusiasm. This would make demand fairly inelastic.

A producer of grave markers, for example, recently abandoned the not very productive approach of relying on a location close to cemeteries in the hope that customers would simply come in. Instead, he began using aggressive sales techniques.

He had considerable success with a TV advertising appeal, finding a good market particularly among guilt-ridden sons and daughters who long ago had buried their parents without a gravestone. Now, after years of uneasiness about the poorly marked grave(s) and with a newfound affluence, the heirs were willing to seek the gravestone seller and discuss price and quality.

One product may be seen as several goods

We have been focusing on one good at a time, but it is critical to understand that the *same product* might be viewed as *different goods* by *different target markets* at the *same time*.

The marketing manager might find that his general market consists of several clusters of people who have similar attitudes toward his product, as shown in Figure 12–3. This figure clusters people in terms of their willingness to shop, and brand familiarity or preference—and is a simple way of summarizing our goods discussion.

Each of these clusters might require a different marketing strategy. Or closer analysis of each cluster might suggest the possibility for several profitable strategies, depending on how homogeneous the clusters are. Generally, we are looking for homogeneous target markets so we can design marketing mixes to satisfy each market grid box more exactly.

Clustering by goods classifications and then subdividing these clusters where necessary can be very revealing. Further, it is a common-sense approach which enables anyone with some market judgment to organize his thinking without extensive preliminary marketing research.

Need for consumer research to properly classify goods

Although the marketing manager can use his market judgment to classify a good, he probably could do a more reliable job by using

258

marketing research. This is especially important if the marketing manager wants to cater to various-sized target markets and develop really good marketing mixes.

Marketing research may show many dimensions of consumer attitudes about products. One exploratory study of gasoline purchasing behavior found 19 factors that may influence the choice of particular brands;[12] another study might develop still other factors. While not all factors would have equal weight in a particular situation, each would have some influence.

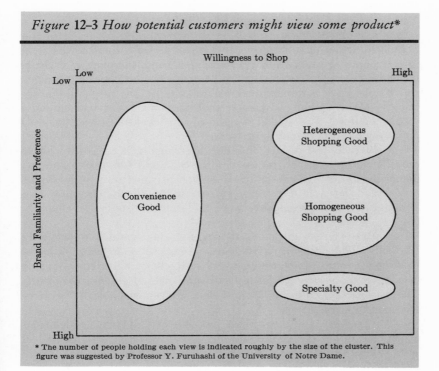

Figure 12–3 How potential customers might view some product*

* The number of people holding each view is indicated roughly by the size of the cluster. This figure was suggested by Professor Y. Furuhashi of the University of Notre Dame.

This multiplicity of factors influencing brand choice points up the importance of using marketing research. For a particular product, the relative value of the various factors might be isolated, or it might be possible to isolate two important classes of factors—qualifying and determining factors.

Qualifying and determining factors may make the difference

The *qualifying factors* affecting a product are those that are necessary for the consumer even to consider buying it. The *determining factors* carry the consumer a step farther, actually deciding him on a particular product. If the qualifying factors are about equal for a number of products, the determining factors, although they may seem minor, can become all-important in the final buying decision.

[12] William F. Brown, "The Determination of Factors Influencing Brand Choice," *Journal of Marketing*, April, 1950, pp. 699–706.

**Fast
service,
clean rest
rooms, and
five shares
at 46⅜**

The behavior of a female schoolteacher buying gasoline illustrates this process. The teacher always bought major brands of gasoline because she was afraid that "cheap" brands would ruin her car's engine. She bought several major brands at various times because she felt that all of them were quite similar. She never drove into a gasoline station unless it looked clean, and normally she patronized the stations nearest her home so that they would recognize her and be ready to give advice when she had mechanical problems. To her, therefore, the major brands were basically staple convenience goods.

From this description, it would appear that the qualifying factors here were experience, price, convenience, dealer's service, and prestige. Yet these factors did *not* determine her choice.

Her requirements were met by three major-brand service stations— Standard, Shell, and Mobil—located on different corners of the same intersection, one block from her house. Although the margin of choice seemed narrow, she stated that until recently she had been patronizing the Mobil station. After considerable questioning, she admitted that she felt the Mobil station was larger than the others and had extensive repair facilities. The added weight of the dealer's service facilities appeared to be the determining factor.

But this was still not an absolute determinant, it turned out. Two months earlier, she had acquired some Standard Oil stock—and this ownership factor had caused her to switch her purchases to the Standard dealer. So a minor factor proved to be the determining one, although the qualifying factors were vital to the narrowing of choice.

In general, the gasoline study showed that most gasoline buyers were favorably influenced by a standard group of *qualifying factors*— including prestige, advertising, and satisfactory experience—but in most cases the *preference for a particular brand of gasoline was weak*. The various *determining factors* were convenience, dealer services, salesmanship, and chance.

It would seem, from this, that gasoline fits into the convenience-goods category. Once most consumers have evaluated the factors (at least subjectively), their judgment leads to rather consistent brand selection—what might appear to be specialty-good behavior. But it is more accurate to say that this is a case of brand preference rather than insistence, and that gasoline producers would be better advised to consider their product a staple convenience good rather than a specialty good.

Even rough judgments will suggest strategy implications

The product classifications we have introduced may seem somewhat arbitrary, but they are workable. In developing marketing strategies, even rough judgments about how significant groups of customers view products are helpful. Since we will use these goods classifications throughout the rest of this book, you should have a real understanding of them.

For greatest efficiency in an actual marketing program, we would use marketing research to determine the proper goods classifications and the size of the market for each. In the following examples, however, to clearly demonstrate what these goods classifications mean, we will use the intuitive approach to classifying products. And in each example, the potential impact on strategy planning will be suggested.

How should the drugs listed on a doctor's prescription be classified? The patient is seeking a specific product and will probably pay whatever price is charged. This has all the earmarks of a specialty good, yet the consumer has little or no choice of product brand or price.

Prescription drugs . . . specialties and bargains

In some areas, pharmacists would fill the prescription with similar products but at different prices. While it might be worthwhile for the patient to shop around, comparing prices is somewhat impractical and could be embarrassing to some customers because at each store they would have to ask the pharmacist to decipher the prescription and then quote his price. Besides, the customer buying a prescription usually wants his order filled as quickly and as conveniently as possible. Most consumers, therefore, probably think of prescriptions as convenience goods, either staples or emergency goods.

For an alert pharmacist, there is an opportunity in this situation. He could promote his establishment so effectively that consumers would have greater confidence in his products and his ability to fill prescriptions. If successful, he might turn his service into a specialty good. In the past, other pharmacies have conceived of their products as homogeneous shopping goods, emphasizing lower prices in their efforts to attract customers.

How are saltine crackers classified? Major commercial baking firms produce a number of well-advertised saltine cracker brands. Does this mean that these individual brands of soda crackers are specialty goods or close to it?

Saltine crackers —that's how the cracker crumbles . . . crisply!

Researchers found that most consumers thought of a saltine as "just" a saltine—they saw little difference among brands and were not interested in investigating other crackers. This implied a staple convenience good, and attempts by the bakers to distinguish their crackers through promotion met with considerable indifference.

Additional research on saltines found, however, that consumers *did want* their crackers fresh and crisp. This led one firm to develop a new inner-seal package, enabling consumers to open only part of the package at a time, preserving the freshness and crispness of the other unopened crackers. This package modification creating a "new" product, allowed the baker using it to differentiate his product for a time.

This differentiation did not attract flocks of consumers. But the differentiation was strong enough to obtain some brand recognition and even brand preference for the product, even though it remained a convenience good.

Ski resorts probably fit into the heterogeneous shopping-goods category. Skiers watch the snow reports carefully and go to the lodges where the snow is good. Their preference for a ski instructor and chalet

Ski resorts make good snow

accommodations may be qualifying factors but seldom overcome the one determining factor—snow.

In an effort to eliminate snow as a variable, some ski resorts have been installing snow-making machines. This puts an end to shopping for snow and has made it possible for some resorts to differentiate their service and to become specialty goods in the minds of some customers.

Railroad service— cheaper sleeping and fashion shows

What kind of a good is railroad passenger service? It might be a convenience good, because it would seem to be economically priced. Yet many consumers compare all the costs and advantages of various forms of transportation before climbing aboard anything. Indeed, the trend toward driving and flying in preference to train travel indicates that travelers base their choices on a number of factors, of which price is only one.

Thinking of their service as an heterogeneous shopping good, a few of the railroads have been experimenting with new and improved services. When the Baltimore & Ohio Railroad introduced its "slumber coach" service—more reasonably priced berths—it attracted many customers who otherwise would have gone by air.[13]

One of the extras offered on the Great Northern's Empire Builder, dinner by reservation, is intended to end a traditional bugaboo of train travel—queuing up in the diner.[14] The Atlantic Coast Line's Florida Special offers fashion shows, coloring books and crayons for the children, free champagne for the parents, and group singing in the lounge car (shades of the airlines!).[15]

Butter and other agricultural products

Butter is probably a homogeneous shopping good for many people. Why some consumers have focused so much attention on this product is not clear, but their practice of shopping for the lowest butter prices has made the retail butter market extremely competitive.

To escape from this extreme competition, Land-O'-Lakes Creameries, Inc., a producers' cooperative, branded its butter as "quality butter" and sought to promote Land-O'-Lakes butter to a specialty-goods status. Land-O'-Lakes has had some success in its efforts, as have the Idaho potato growers and the Sunkist orange growers in similar programs.

The brand preference and even insistence is so strong for the products in some markets that producers can command a slightly higher price, in addition to a substantial share of the market. Among some customers, these cooperatives may have achieved the specialty-goods status. Yet they continue to distribute these products as convenience goods because most customers probably see them this way.

Conclusion

A consumer product classification system based on consumers' buying habits and behavior has been introduced in this chapter. These

[13] "Do Experiments Attract Customers?" *Railway Age,* December 15, 1958, p. 21.

[14] *Business Week,* May 19, 1962, p. 123.

[15] *Wall Street Journal,* October 11, 1962, p. 1.

classifications will simplify our study of marketing and the development of marketing mixes because the attitudes of target customers almost determine the marketing mix which should be designed to satisfy them.

The four major categories of goods—convenience, shopping, specialty, and unsought—are arbitrary but workable. They provide a framework for subsequent analysis. They also relate to the concept of elasticity of demand. If customers do not give much thought to price when purchasing a product, as in the case of convenience goods, or if consumers have extremely strong brand insistence, as for specialty goods, then the demand for these products will be relatively inelastic. On the other hand, if consumers have a strong interest in comparing the products, as they do with shopping goods, then demand may be more elastic.

You should become familiar with these classifications and their subclassifications and begin to observe how marketing institutions handle specific products. Your firsthand observations applied to this analytical framework will speed the development of your "marketing sense."

The way customers in various market grid boxes view the same physical product may help explain how seemingly poor or irrational marketing mixes may become successful. Much of the diversity and complexity of the marketplace can be explained in terms of different product classifications in different market grid boxes.

Questions and problems

1 What kinds of goods are the following: (a) fountain pens, (b) men's shirts, (c) cosmetics? Explain your reasoning and draw a market grid in each case to help illustrate your thinking.
2 Some goods seem to be treated perpetually as "unsought goods" by their producers. Give an example and explain why.
3 Illustrate what is meant by the statement: "Convenience goods and shopping goods are at either ends of a continuum of customer searching effort."
4 How would the marketing mix for a staple convenience good differ from the one for a homogeneous shopping good? How would the mix for a specialty good differ from the mix for a heterogeneous shopping good? Use examples.
5 Which of the P's would receive greatest emphasis in the marketing mix for an unsought good? Explain why, using an example.
6 Would the marketing mix for all convenience goods be essentially the same? Discuss, using an example for each type of convenience good.
7 In what types of stores would you expect to find: (a) convenience goods, (b) shopping goods, (c) specialty goods, and (d) unsought goods?
8 Draw market-grid boxes showing your view of the relative sizes of the markets for the products discussed in the last few pages of the chapter, i.e., specifically (a) prescription drugs, (b) saltine crackers, (c) ski resort services, (d) railroad service, and (e) butter.

Industrial goods

Wwhile a consumer goods classification system is useful for developing effective marketing mixes, an industrial goods classification is even more valuable. Over the years, industrial firms have developed a rational system of buying that is related to the goods classification system we will discuss in this chapter. Before considering the various product *differences,* however, we will note some important product *similarities* that have a direct impact on marketing strategy planning for industrial goods.

General characteristics of industrial goods[1]

One demand derived from another

The outstanding characteristic of the industrial goods market is derived demand—the demand for industrial goods is derived from the demand for final consumer goods. There would be little need for fertilizer if there were no demand for food products. There wouldn't be much demand for cans or canmaking machinery if consumers didn't want their food products packed in cans.

Derived demand is clearly illustrated in the steel industry. Almost all forms of steel, such as beams, plate, and rods, are sold to manufacturers for the production of other products. About one fifth of all steel products goes to the automotive industry, which is highly dependent on

[1] Many of the ideas presented in this chapter are based on R. S. Alexander, "Goods for the Market: Industrial Goods," in C. F. Phillips (ed.), *Marketing by Manufacturers* (Homewood, Ill.: Richard D. Irwin, Inc., 1950), pp. 34–60.

final consumer demand. If a car manufacturer hopes to sell 50,000 cars of a particular model each month, then it will order enough steel to produce those automobiles. No amount of price cutting or other adjustments in the marketing mixes by the steelmakers will increase the total amount of steel demanded by this auto producer. Each steel producer may try to get a larger share of this total available business by developing a more attractive marketing mix, but the total amount demanded is limited by the expected final consumer sales.

The relationship between steel and automobiles is direct and fairly obvious. But the suppliers of bolts, screws, castings, textiles, and other industrial products find it is easy to forget that the need for their products is derived from the demand for final consumer products. As long as business is good and markets are growing, the derived nature of this demand does not seem very important. But it assumes great importance when final consumer preferences are shifting rapidly or in times of recession, when even the most efficient and aggressive companies lose sales because their customers cannot get business.

At such times, even a seemingly good marketing mix aimed at intermediate customers may not be very effective unless it has some impact on final consumer demand; industrial goods producers sometimes advertise directly to consumers, in an effort to stimulate demands.[2]

The very fact that demand for most industrial goods is derived means that industry demand will be fairly inelastic. To satisfy consumer needs, producers need a certain quantity of each of the components of their products, almost regardless of price. Since each of the components costs only a fraction of the total final cost of their product, the price behavior of any one item may have relatively little to do with the quantity of that item purchased. The cost of the spice in a box of cake mix, for example, might represent only one half of 1 percent of the manufacturer's total cost. Even if the price of this spice were doubled and passed directly along to consumers, it would have relatively little impact on the cake producer's price or the quantity demanded by final consumers. Therefore the price increase might not reduce the quantity of spice purchased either.

Pay the going price, even if industry demand is inelastic

Although the industry demand may be inelastic, the demand facing individual firms may be extremely elastic. This will be true if competitive products are essentially homogeneous and there are many sellers—that is, if the market approaches pure competition.

In the case of the spice ingredients, if the spices available from all suppliers are essentially similar and one spice supplier increases his price while his competitors do not, buyers probably will shift their purchases to the competition. Thus *there may be nearly pure competition among the suppliers of a product even though there is an inelastic industry demand.*

If the marketing manager faces an inelastic demand and has a unique product, perhaps protected by a patent, he may be in a very

[2] "Fundamental Differences Between Industrial and Consumer Marketing," *Journal of Marketing,* October, 1954, p. 153.

favorable position. Likewise, if there are only a few competitors and they have tacitly agreed not to emphasize price in their marketing mixes, then prices may tend to be higher than they would be in very competitive markets. (More is said on this in the Pricing chapters.)

An outstanding example of such a condition is the sale of labor services when a union has effectively organized the labor market. In effect, there is one seller, and wage rates may continue to rise in markets—such as the construction industry—where the workers are facing essentially inelastic demand *at any one time.*

Interest in price may vary

As we saw in Chapter 9, industrial buying is generally less emotional than consumer buying. An industrial goods buyer usually knows fairly precisely what and how much he needs. If there are many sources for such a product—if competing products are homogeneous—then primary emphasis may be placed on price, as well as dependable quality and delivery, and other services. Price competition may be vigorous as the market moves close to pure competition.

When competing products are heterogeneous, however, more negotiation may be necessary. The multiple buying influences may become important, and emotional motives may figure more importantly in the buying decision. There may be much less interest in price, which will be reflected in the kind of marketing mixes developed for such products.

Backward chain reactions can cause booms

Demand at the industrial good level may fluctuate much more than demand at the final consumer level. This is true because demand for industrial goods, which may be several steps removed from the final consumer demand, reflects in part the expectations and buying practices of various middlemen and other producers. Intermediate customers follow more erratic buying policies than final consumers because they attempt to: (1) anticipate price changes, (2) reduce costs by quantity buying, (3) anticipate demand, which may not materialize, and (4) place rush orders when their sales forecasts prove inadequate.

If intermediate customers believe prices are going to drop further, they may postpone all purchases. If they feel that prices are at their lowest point, they may buy in substantial quantities, anticipating future needs. Or firms may buy in large quantities to obtain quantity discounts and then work off the inventory as needed. On slow-moving items, this may mean that a firm will buy three to six months' inventory at one time to obtain a lower price.

Sales swings may be even more extreme when intermediate customers try to anticipate growing demand. Home air conditioners are sold primarily when hot weather arrives. Orders for air-conditioner compressors may be heavy before the summer selling season. If really hot weather never comes, though, the retailers, wholesalers, and air-conditioner manufacturers may become overstocked, and the orders for compressors will stop completely. Yet if there is a prolonged heat wave, it can deplete retailers' air-conditioner stocks—and a chain reaction will start backward to component manufacturers.

In this situation, retailers and wholesalers may attempt to build inventories in advance of the season. This will drain the producers' inventory and cause them to expand production, perhaps even going into overtime. The producers then place rush orders for compressors and the other components they need. This pattern can occur both in advance of and during the selling season.

If this sort of chain develops in an industry that is less seasonal than air conditioners, there may be pressures to expand the producer's plant capacity. Rush orders may develop for new plant and machinery, causing sudden "boom" conditions for these manufacturers.

These extreme but typical fluctuations have an impact on the nature of competition and the development of marketing mixes. Drastic changes in both price and promotion may be needed to handle these shifting conditions.

Paying taxes affects spending for equipment

The handling of the cost of a particular purchase on a firm's profit and loss statement may have a significant bearing on the buyer. If, in computing profits, the cost of a large machine could be charged to the current year's expenses, the company executives might be more willing to buy it. Even though the cost of the equipment reduced current profits, it also would reduce tax liability and increase the company's assets.

These are two general methods of charging costs: as capital and as expense items. Both are determined primarily by U.S. Internal Revenue Service regulations.

Capital items. Most large machinery and other durable, relatively long-lived items are treated as capital items. They are often called "capital goods." Internal Revenue regulations and accepted accounting procedure require that only a portion of the original cost be charged off or depreciated each year for a total depreciation period of 2 to 50 years, depending on the item. The depreciation rate usually is specified by the Internal Revenue Service.

In 1962, the federal government liberalized depreciation rules, because it decided that excessively long depreciation periods had discouraged purchase of capital items. And in 1964 a 7 percent investment tax credit was added to encourage capital expenditures.

It is clear that these rules have expanded spending on capital goods. It also appears likely that the temporary suspension of the 7 percent tax credit in 1966, designed to cool an inflationary boom, was effective, too.[3] Some businessmen were quite concerned about the federal government's use of investment incentives and depreciation rules to help regulate the economy.[4] It is clear, nevertheless, that businessmen do look at capital investments differently from the way they view expense items.

An opening for emotions. Businessmen generally are slower to buy capital items. The purchase of a capital item is, in effect, a long-term

---

[3] "Orders for Rail Equipment Sag Sharply; Producers Blame Tax-Credit Suspension," *Wall Street Journal*, February 27, 1967, p. 26; "When Business Is Almost Too Good," *Business Week*, September 24, 1966, pp. 198–200; and "Tax Credit Has Fans and Foes," *Business Week*, March 26, 1966, pp. 49–50.

[4] "More Realism in Fiscal Policy," *Business Week*, March 18, 1967, p. 196.

claim against future revenues. Yet management cannot predict exactly what the future holds. Since an error in judgment can have an influence for many years, company executives understandably are hesitant to make quick decisions. There seems to be little agreement on the best approach to capital expenditure decisions,[5] however, and this may offer opportunities for the marketer to introduce emotional considerations.

Expense items. In contrast to capital items, expense items are charged off as they are used—usually in the year of purchase. The potential value is more easily forecast and can be compared with the cost. Since the company is not putting a lien against its future when it buys expense items, it tends to be less concerned about these costs, especially if business is good. If sales decline, however, some expense purchases may be cut back sharply or eliminated temporarily.

Industrial goods classifications

The nonshopper and the wily buyer

Industrial goods buyers do relatively little shopping, compared to consumer goods buyers. The accepted practice is for the seller to come to the buyer. This means that a product classification system based primarily on shopping behavior is not appropriate.

The industrial goods classification we will use is determined by how buyers regard products and how the products are to be used. The categories of industrial goods are: (1) installations, (2) accessory equipment, (3) raw materials, (4) component parts and materials, (5) supplies, and (6) services.

While the consumer goods classification is tentative and perhaps arbitrary, the industrial goods classification is keyed directly to the way industrial purchasing departments and accounting control systems operate day to day. As an example, steel mills use categories similar to our industrial goods classifications for buying, maintenance, costing of orders, and control purposes.

The authority of certain plant executives to buy is limited frequently to one or more categories, either directly or by a dollar limit. Accessory expenditures, for example, might be limited to $10,000 an item to allow the department foreman some latitude in his requisitioning and, at the same time, to control expenditures. Yet by ingenuity an enterprising foreman can get around these controls. He might buy a large crane in pieces, including the bridge, $8,000; trolley, $4,500; two drums, $950 each; 800 feet of woven-wire cable, $3 a foot, etc. Under other control systems, perhaps the only items a plant foreman could buy without higher approval would be supplies, but it is remarkable what kinds of small machines and other accessories can be called supplies in this situation.

But these corruptions of organizational control procedures aside, our industrial goods classification system generally does make sense and is used extensively in the industrial goods market.

Installations, major capital items

Installations are large and expensive items that do not become a part of the final product but are expended, depleted, or worn out during

[5] Donald F. Istvan, *Capital-Expenditure Decisions: How They Are Made in Large Corporations* (Indiana Business Report No. 33 [Bloomington: Indiana University, 1961]), p. 97.

268

years of use. All installations are *capital items*. They represent major expenditures for the company and are depreciated over a period ranging from 2 to 50 years.

There are two major classifications of installations: *buildings and land rights,* and *major equipment.*

Buildings and land rights include assets such as factories, farms, stores, office buildings, mining deposits, and timber rights. Major equipment includes large items of machinery and production facilities such as diesel engines, tractors, papermaking machines, printing presses, and kilns.

Major equipment can be subdivided into two types: (1) custom-made and (2) standard.

Custom-made equipment is built to specification for a particular company. *Standard* installations are regular production items such as tractors, general-purpose diesel engines, lathes, and printing presses.

For our purposes in this text, *buildings* and *custom-made equipment* are treated alike, since both require special negotiations for each individual product. *Standard major equipment,* being more homogeneous, can be treated more routinely. All installations, however, are important enough to require high-level and even top-management consideration.

Size of market. These are long-lived goods, and the number of potential buyers at any particular time usually is small. For some custom-made machines, there may be only a half-dozen potential customers at any one time, compared to a thousand or more potential buyers for standard machines of similar type and capacity.

Potential customers generally are in the same or a related industry, permitting industry specialization by sales executives. The plants are likely to be geographically concentrated. The automobile industry, for example, is heavily concentrated in and around Michigan, the tire industry in Ohio, copper mining in the western states, and the aircraft industry—from a global view—in the United States.

Multiple buying influence. The importance of these items leads to considerable multiple buying influences. Negotiations can stretch over months or even years and often involve the top executives of the company, especially for buildings or custom-made products. This may complicate promotion, since these executives may be concerned with quite different problems than purchasing agents and may not use the same evaluation procedures. The top executive may be less concerned, for example, with the product's suitability for current needs than with its flexibility and possible·usefulness in a new venture he is considering. The seller may need different sales approaches to cope with each of the possible influences.

Buying motives. Buying motives are essentially economic. They are concerned with the projected performance of the installation over its expected life. After comparing this performance factor to present costs and calculating interest, the expected return on capital can be calculated. Yet emotional motives, such as a desire for industry leadership and status, also may be involved. Emotion, for example, seems to have dictated some decisions to purchase computers.

Elasticity of demand. The demand for a particular installation may be completely inelastic up to a certain price, especially if the firm badly needs expanded capacity. The potential return on the new investment may be so attractive that any reasonable price might be acceptable.

While the demand may be very inelastic, however, the situation for sellers may be different. There may be many suppliers, such as building contractors, and so buyers of installations may be able to request bids and buy in a highly competitive market.

Installation industry, a "boom-or-bust" business. The installation industry has been described as a "boom-or-bust" business. During the upswing of a business cycle, businessmen want to expand production capacity rapidly and are willing to pay almost any reasonable price to do it. Competition is less vigorous, and profits are higher for the installation sellers. But during a downswing, buyers will have little or no need for new installations, and sales can fall off precipitously.

Installation manufacturers can even suffer a "bust" because consumer demand, although high, is no longer rising. At such times, the producers who previously needed additional installations to meet *rising* consumer demand are no longer in the market—except for replacements.

Installations may have to be leased or rented. Since installations are relatively expensive, the producer often will lease or rent the product rather than sell it outright. Examples are buildings and land rights and some specialized equipment, including electronic data processing machines. Such lease or rental arrangements are attractive to some target markets because they shift the expenditure from a capital item to an expense item.

Specialized services needed as part of the product. Since the expected return on an installation investment is based on efficient operation, the supplier may have to make service provisions to assure this efficiency. The sales contract may stipulate regular visits by servicemen; a serviceman may even be permanently attached to the company. Computer manufacturers may station service personnel with the machines, and shopping center owners sometimes provide maintenance and even promotion services to their tenants. The cost is included in the price or rent.

The more homogeneous the installation, the more likely it is that the seller will try to differentiate his product by offering specialized services, such as aid in installing his machine in the buyer's plant; training employees in its use; supplying repair service; and taking trade-ins on long-lived installations that a potential buyer already may have on hand.

Accessory equipment —important but short-lived

Accessory equipment, like installations, does not become a part of the final product. These products usually are less expensive and shorter-lived than installations and generally can be depreciated more quickly than installations, but are still *capital items*.

Accessory equipment is very similar to the smaller standard installations and includes tools and equipment that facilitate production or office activities. Examples include portable drills, sanding machines, electric lift trucks, typewriters, filing cases, accounting machines, wheelbarrows, hand trucks, and small lathes.

Size of market. Accessories are even more standardized than installations and are usually needed by more target markets. A large, special-purpose belt sanding machine, for example, might be produced as a custom-made installation for woodworking firms, but small sanding machines would be considered accessory equipment for general use in a variety of shops and factories. Since there is a larger number of target markets and less geographical concentration, different marketing mixes would be required for accessory equipment than for installations.

Multiple buying influences. Since these products cost less and last a shorter time than installation equipment, the multiple buying influence is less important. Operating personnel and purchasing agents rather than top-level executives may do the buying. Purchasing agents are more dominant in buying accessories, as these become more standardized and are bought by brand or at least by widely recognized standards.

The nearer that accessory items come to being expense items, charged off in one year, the less the consideration given to this purchase by higher level management. Some small accessories are treated as expense items, even if the Internal Revenue Service might prefer otherwise.

Leasing or renting accessories is attractive to some target markets because the costs can be treated as expenses. A manufacturer of electric lift trucks, for instance, was able to expand its sales by selling the basic truck outright but charging for the expensive battery system by the amount it was used. And these charges could be treated as operating expenses in some plants. This expanded sales because, as one of the company executives said: "Nobody worries about costs which are buried as an operating expense."[6]

Buying motives and elasticity of demand. Essentially the same economic buying motives that would apply to standard installations apply here. But since accessories are purchased more frequently than installations and have less bearing on the quality and cost of the final product, reciprocity requests are more likely.

As accessory items become smaller and more standardized, the more likely it is that there will be competitive substitutes. Then, although buyers may have inelastic demands, they still may be able to purchase in fairly competitive markets. And competition will be accentuated because when purchasing agents are buying less important items, they will be more willing to experiment with alternate suppliers.

Special services needed. Ordinarily, engineering services or special advice is less important for accessory equipment because of its simpler operation. Yet some companies have managed to add attractive services to their accessories, as in the case of the office equipment firms that offer advice on office layouts and office systems.

Raw materials are products that have been processed only as much as needed for safe, convenient, economical transport and handling.[7] Unlike installations and accessories, raw materials become part of the physical product.

Raw materials are *expense items* and may be purchased routinely by purchasing agents. But top executives may take part in buying when

Raw materials —a good price for eggs, an assured price for rubber

[6] "Switching the Charge on Batteries," *Business Week,* March 13, 1965, pp. 132–34.
[7] "Report of the Definitions Committee," *Journal of Marketing,* October, 1948, p. 213.

certain raw materials represent a large part of the firm's costs, as with wheat in the flour milling business. Moreover, to assure sources of supply, top executives may help negotiate the annual contracts for some important raw materials.

It is useful to break raw materials into two broad categories: (1) farm products and (2) natural products. *Farm products* include crops, livestock, and other commodities such as cotton, wheat, strawberries, sugar cane, cattle, hogs, poultry, eggs, and milk. *Natural products* include animal, vegetable, and mineral products as they occur naturally, including, for example, fish and game, lumber and maple syrup, and copper, zinc, iron ore, oil and coal.

Some raw materials, such as fruits and vegetables, poultry, eggs, and milk, can be used directly by final consumers. In this text, we will treat raw materials sold directly to consumers or through middlemen for sale to consumers as consumer goods, not industrial goods.

The buying attitudes and practices of the various middlemen handling raw materials will be quite different. As we will see later, different middlemen may develop to handle raw materials when they are destined for consumer rather than industrial target markets.

Farm products. The need for grading is one of the important factors distinguishing these products from other industrial goods. Nature produces what it will, and then someone must sort and grade the wheat, corn, tobacco, cotton, and other similar products to satisfy target customers. Some of the top grades of fruits and vegetables may find their way into the premium-quality consumer goods market, while the lower grades will be treated as industrial goods and be used in juices, sauces, and frozen pies.

Most farm products are produced seasonally, yet the demand for them is fairly constant throughout the year. As a result, storage and transportation are major activities in their marketing process.

As noted, buyers of industrial goods normally do not seek out suppliers. This is a complicating factor in marketing farm products, particularly because the many small farm producers usually are widely scattered, sometimes far from potential buyers. Often they need collective representation. Place and Promotion consequently are important factors in marketing mixes for these products.

Most buyers of farm products have specific uses in mind and generally prefer that products be sorted and graded. But since large buyers may have difficulty getting the quantities of the grades and types they want, contract production has developed. Here, the buyer deliberately seeks out potential sources of supply and makes contracts that assure the supplier a market for his goods. This has several effects. It tends to make the supplier a part of the buyer's operation and removes one more producer from the competitive market. This may be desirable from the suppliers' point of view, because it isolates him from a purely competitive market.

Elasticity of demand and prices. Most farm products have an inelastic market demand, even though the many small producers are in nearly pure competition. The market demand becomes more elastic

272

when there are many substitutes (such as beef for pork or corn for wheat). But within the usual price ranges, the demand for agricultural products is generally inelastic, and so it helps agricultural producers to control output and prices, perhaps through U.S. Department of Agriculture programs.

Most attempts to control prices in the farm products market are frustrated by slow adjustment of supply and the difficulty of organizing the many producers. Once a crop is planted, the potential supply is

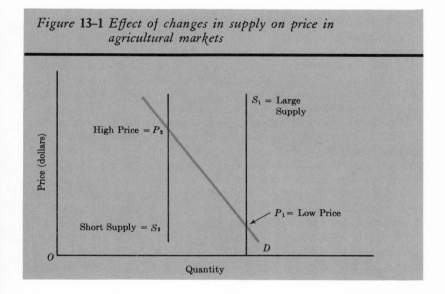

Figure **13–1** *Effect of changes in supply on price in agricultural markets*

more or less fixed (subject to weather, pests, etc.), and it is too late to change crop size that year. For some animal products, the planning cycle may be two or three years, and this further accentuates the problem of adjustment in supply.

At the end of a growing season, the quantity of available farm products is fixed. If this supply is large, the market price may be extremely low; if it is small, the price may be high. This can be seen in Figure 13–1 where vertical lines are used to show that in the short run, farmers would supply the same quantity regardless of the price.

This relatively long planning period has led to some peculiar cycles in production and prices. The poultry farmers in the Delaware, Maryland, and Virginia area traditionally went through boom-and-bust periods on an annual basis. High poultry prices one year attracted many growers the following year, who then overproduced, driving prices down below cost. This caused many small producers to leave the market, creating an inadequate supply and again raising price to a high level. Recently, however, the entry of a few large producers with better control over supply has reduced this seesawing of supply and prices.

Natural products. In contrast to the farm products market, with its

273

many producers, natural products are produced by fewer and larger companies. There are some exceptions, of course, such as the coal and lumber industries.

In general, the total supply of natural products is limited and cannot be expanded readily. But the supply harvested or mined in any one year *is* adjustable.

Most of the products are bulky and pose transportation problems. But storage is less important, since fewer are perishable and some can be produced year-round. Major exceptions are fish and game, which have runs or seasons and resemble farm animal products more than forest or mineral products in their marketing patterns.

Buying motives. As with farm products, buyers of natural products usually need specific grades and dependable supply sources to assure continued production in their own plants. Large buyers, therefore, often seek to buy, or at least control, their sources of supply. This is easier than with farm products because fewer and larger production facilities are involved.

One way to control supply sources is *vertical integration*—ownership of the natural product producer by the user. Examples are synthetic fiber and paper manufacturers who control timber resources, oil refiners who control crude oil sources, and tire manufacturers who control rubber plantations. Probably the best known are the steel producers who control not only iron ore and coal deposits but also the ships and trains to carry ore and coal.

When a great deal of integration has taken place in a given industry, there may be an erratic or spotty open market. This is because buyers and sellers will come into the market only when their own captive sources are producing too much or too little or the wrong quality.

Sellers in these markets who do not formally integrate with users normally find that their customers buy in large quantities and are interested in assuring themselves dependable sources of supply. This usually is done through contracts or "understandings," perhaps negotiated by top-level executives and referring to standard grades or specifications for products.

Elasticity of demand. The industry demand is derived and basically inelastic. The large producers of natural products are quite responsive to market demands and are inclined to limit supply to maintain stable prices. In the coal and lumber industries, however, where there are many producers, there is close to pure competition.

Component parts and materials —the sum is no better than. . . .

Like raw materials, component parts and materials become a part of the finished product. Both are treated as *expense items*. Component parts, however, undergo more processing than is required for raw materials and may require different marketing mixes.

Component parts include those items that are (*a*) finished and ready for assembly or (*b*) nearly finished, requiring only minor additional processing (such as grinding or polishing) before being assembled into the final product.

In the parts category are automobile batteries, small motors, tires, and forgings or castings, all of which are incorporated directly into a

274

finished product. It also includes other items, such as automobile jacks, that are sold with the product but not physically attached to it or incorporated into it.

Component materials are items such as wire, paper, textiles, or cement. They have already been processed but must be further processed before becoming part of the final product.

Multiple buying influences. Some component parts are custom-made. Much negotiation may be necessary between the engineering staffs of both buyer and seller to arrive at the proper specifications. If the price of the item is very high or if it is an extremely important component of the final product, top-level executives may become involved, as with raw materials.

Other component parts and materials are more likely to be processed to commonly accepted standards or specifications and produced in quantity. For such items, engineering or production people in the buying firm may specify quality. The purchasing agent will do the actual buying.

Buying motives. As with other types of industrial goods, the motives involved in buying components are basically economic and concern price, availability, quality, and suitability. Assurances of availability and prompt delivery are most important. A purchasing agent must do everything in his power to avoid a plant shutdown caused by unavailability of materials. Moreover, an assured source of supply will enable the buyer to reduce his inventory, reducing both his inventory investment and the risk of damage to, and obsolescence of, goods in stock.

Since components are incorporated in the firm's own product, quality is extremely important, too. The company's own name and whole marketing mix are at stake. Quality may be less important for component parts, however, if they are well branded—such as a tire or spark plug—and the blame for a defective product can fall upon the component supplier. Generally, however, a progressive buyer would attempt to buy from component sources that would help assure a satisfactory product to the final customers.

Elasticity of demand. Although the industry and individual firms' demand may be fairly inelastic for components, there usually are many possible suppliers, enabling buyers to purchase in a fairly competitive market. In fact, the market for many component parts and materials is extremely competitive. There are several reasons for this competition.

1. Most component buyers want to have several sources of supply, and encourage new suppliers.
2. There usually are many small producers—small tool-and-die shops, machine shops, and foundries—with general-purpose machinery that can produce a great variety of component parts.
3. There often are many suppliers of component materials willing to produce to widely accepted specifications or standards.

Design services may be important for some components, and this may enable an alert seller to achieve an inelastic demand curve. Or if the seller has obtained some design patents or in some way developed a particularly unique (heterogeneous) product, he may achieve an extremely inelastic demand curve.

Replacement markets may develop. Since component parts are incorporated in a finished product, a replacement market often develops. This market can be both large and very profitable, as in the case of automotive tires and batteries.

This replacement market may involve new target markets. The part originally may have been considered a component part when it was sold in the OEM (original equipment market), but as a replacement the same product may become a consumer good. The target markets are different, and probably different marketing mixes will be necessary.

Some component parts suppliers may be eager to have their parts used in the OEM market because the "after" market composed of final consumers is attractive.

The Mallory Battery Co. worked hard to get its small batteries installed as original components in cameras, watches, hearing aids, and dictating equipment because marketing research had told them that half of all final consumer battery buyers don't know what kind of battery powers their equipment. They simply walk into a store and say, "Gimme one just like this."

Mallory coordinated its efforts in both markets—the components and final consumer markets—and achieved a 50 percent increase in profits.[8]

**Supplies—
everybody
wants them
but
how much?**

Firms consume supplies, just as they do raw materials and component parts and materials. They are, therefore, *expense items*. But unlike raw materials and components, *supplies do not become a part of the physical product*. Although they are necessary, most supplies are not as vital as the products in the first four classifications—and when a firm economizes, supplies may be the first to go.

Supplies can be divided into three categories: (1) maintenance, (2) repair, and (3) operating supplies, giving them their common designation, *MRO* items.

Maintenance items include such things as paint, nails, light bulbs, sweeping compounds, brooms, and window-cleaning equipment. *Repair items* are nuts and bolts or parts needed to repair existing installations. *Operating supplies* include lubricating oils and greases, grinding compounds, coal, typing paper, ink, pencils, and paper clips.

Most supply items are used by industry in general and are similar to the kinds of items purchased by final consumers in hardware stores. Some supplies are more important than others, as noted below.

Important operating supplies. Some operating supplies needed regularly and in large amounts receive special treatment from buyers. Some companies buy coal and fuel oil in carload or tank-car quantities. Usually there are several sources for such homogeneous products, and large volumes may be purchased in highly competitive markets. Or contracts may be negotiated, perhaps by high-level executives. Such contracts have several advantages. Subsequent purchase requisitions may be drawn routinely against them. They sometimes assure lower

---

[8] "Will Tiny Cells Power Big Sales," *Business Week,* January 14, 1967, pp. 60–64.

prices, and they eliminate the buyer's concern about a dependable source of supply for these important operating supplies.

When several dependable sources are available and orders are large, reciprocity may become important. If quality and price are roughly the same, it becomes more difficult to refuse the sales department's request for reciprocity relationships. Purchasing departments usually resist such overtures, but this is one place where the sales department's arguments are strong.

Maintenance and small operating supplies. These items are similar to consumer's convenience goods and are so numerous that a purchasing agent cannot possibly be an expert in buying all of them. There usually is little multiple buying influence.

Each requisition for maintenance and small operating supplies may be for a relatively few items. The purchase requisitions may amount to only $1 to $2. Although the cost of handling a purchase order may be from $5 to $10, the item will be ordered because it is needed.

Branding may become important for such products. It makes product identification and buying of such "nuisance" items easier.

Industry demand for supplies may be fairly inelastic, and sellers may see fairly inelastic demand curves, too. Since only small amounts of money are involved and shopping around for bargains would hardly be worth the time, a purchasing agent may find several dependable sources of supply and patronize them for the bulk of such items.

A new company offering only one supply item might have trouble entering such a market. The job of buying these many small items is difficult enough, and buyers usually don't have time to review the small advantages of some new product or supplier. The purchasing agent wouldn't be as interested in price for such items—the breadth of assortment and dependability of the source are of utmost important in buying supply items. Yet a characteristic of a "dependable" source of supply is that it offers good values, and a skilled purchasing agent continually shops for good value. The threat of losing a substantial amount of business from one buyer tends to keep the various suppliers' prices in line.

Repair items. The original supplier of the installation or accessory equipment may be the only source of supply for repairs and parts. The cost of repairs relative to the cost of disrupted production may be so small that buyers are willing to pay the price charged.

Demand for repair items is quite inelastic. But if the demand for such items is large and steady—say for truck mufflers or power transmission belts—there may be many suppliers. The market then may become quite competitive even though each buyer's demand is relatively inelastic.

Services —you pay for what you get

Services supplied by specialists frequently are valuable in supporting the operations of a firm. Engineering or management consulting services might improve the plant layout or the organization of the company. Design services can supply designs for the physical plant, products, and graphic materials. Outside maintenance services can handle window cleaning, painting, or general housekeeping services. Other organizations can supply in-plant lunches and piped-in music to improve employee morale and production.[9]

All these services are considered *expense items*. The cost of buying them outside the firm would be compared with the cost of having company personnel provide them. For special skills needed only irregularly, an outsider may be the best source. Specialists are proliferating in our increasingly complex economy.

The demand for special services may be fairly inelastic if the supplier has a unique product. And the supply may be fairly inelastic, too, if the suppliers consider themselves professionals and charge accordingly. For example, engineers, architects, and medical doctors have commonly accepted fee schedules, and the competition among them is not based on price but on quality of service.[10]

Conclusion

The industrial goods classification system developed in this chapter is considerably easier to use than the one for consumers' goods because it starts with products and the way they are used. Buying behavior and market structure are related to the product classifications.

It is important that you have a thorough understanding of the various kinds of products and their distinguishing characteristics, since this has a significant bearing on where and how these products are distributed, promoted, and priced.

It also is important to distinguish between consumer and industrial goods. The same physical product may belong in both categories but require quite different marketing mixes.

An important characteristic of industrial goods is that demand is derived from demand for consumer goods. Further, *industry demand for industrial goods tends to be inelastic, but because of competition among suppliers, the demand facing any one industrial goods seller may be quite elastic.* Derived demand and industrial buying practices also may lead to violent and hard-to-forecast fluctuations in sales. Capital-goods producers, in particular, experience boom-and-bust cycles, because of changes in final consumer buying patterns.

In contrast to consumer buying, which may be emotionally motivated, industrial purchasing of all categories of goods is more concerned with economic factors. Some industrial goods even warrant top-level decisions.

While consumer goods classifications are somewhat arbitrary, those for industrial goods are not. Industrial purchasing and accounting systems use similar classifications, and areas of purchasing responsibility are frequently assigned according to these product classifications.

The following chapters will begin to use these product classifications to bring order out of a complex marketing structure. Before reading these chapters, you will profit by a serious consideration of what kinds

---

[9] For a discussion of the marketing problems associated with technical services, see James G. Hauk, *Technical Service in the American Economy: A Problem in Marketing Management* (Michigan Business Studies, Vol. XXI, No. 1 [Ann Arbor: University of Michigan, 1962]).

[10] Warren J. Wittreich, "How To Buy/Sell Professional Services," *Harvard Business Review,* March–April, 1966, pp. 127–38.

of marketing institutions might develop to distribute specific products and the functions which they would provide. This will enable you to better appreciate why certain marketing specialists have developed and why they use certain marketing practices.

Questions and problems

1 Present two examples of industrial goods which require a substantial amount of service in order to make them useful "products."
2 Would you expect to find any wholesalers selling the various types of industrial goods? Are retail stores required (or something like retail stores)?
3 What kinds of goods are the following?
   a) Nails and screws.
   b) Paint.
   c) Dust-collecting and ventilating systems.
   d) An electric lift truck.
   Explain your reasoning.
4 What impact does the fact that demand for industrial goods is derived and fairly inelastic have upon the development of industrial goods marketing mixes? Use examples.
5 How do farm product raw materials differ from other raw materials or other industrial goods? Do the differences have any impact on their marketing mixes? If so, what, specifically?
6 How would an Internal Revenue Bureau relaxation of depreciation regulations affect the marketing mixes of industrial goods? Would it affect all of them equally?
7 Discuss the kinds of wholesalers and retailers you might expect to find in the sale of farm-produced raw materials. Specifically what activities would you expect each to provide and why?
8 For the kinds of goods described in this chapter, complete the following table (use one or a few *well-chosen* words).

Goods	Kind of Distribution Facility(ies) Needed and Functions They Will Provide	Caliber of Salesmen Required	Kind of Advertising Required
Installations			
Building and land rights			
Major equipment			
Standard			
Custom made			
Accessory equipment			
Raw materials			
Farm products			
Natural products			
Components			
Parts			
Materials			
Supplies			
Operating supplies			
Maintenance and small operating supplies			
Services			

Product planning

So far in our discussion of Product, we have been concerned primarily with describing and classifying the various types of products and suggesting implications for marketing mix planning. At various places, we have noted that product markets are dynamic. To satisfy customers and meet competition, marketing managers must be concerned with the development of new products. We will now discuss the specific topic of product planning and new-product development.

Need for product planning

Products are not commodities
  Some production-oriented businessmen think of their company's product as the natural result of the production process. They see no need for product planning. Yet this view is at the root of many new product failures and weak marketing strategies.[1]

Long ago when economies were much simpler, most products were commodities—more or less homogeneous products that were in general demand. They were the natural result of the simple production processes available then. The idea of planning products to satisfy specific customers' demands was not prevalent.

Today, more aggressive competitors, even including agricultural producers, strive to satisfy specific markets. Production processes permit a growing number of choices. Farmers are offered not just one type of

[1] "NICB Discusses New-Product Failures," *Printers' Ink,* April 14, 1967, p. 57.

seed, but many types of carefully bred hybrid seeds. In the same way, a variety of foods, fibers, raw materials, and manufactured products compete with each other for the customer's favor.

The customer seldom has to be satisfied with a basic commodity. Usually there are many competitive products vying to satisfy the need which used to be met by a commodity. Product planning is necessary if the firm is to avoid selling its products as homogeneous commodities in very competitive markets.

Another factor forcing product planning is the extreme competitiveness and innovativeness of most product markets. New ideas can be copied quickly and made obsolete by better ones. Some progressive companies are planning 5 and 10 years ahead, and some even further. Westinghouse Electric Corp., for example, has planners working ahead to the year 2000 on developments in 21 different technological fields.[2] **Product markets are dynamic and innovative**

Products have life cycles

Since products, like consumers, have life cycles, it is essential that a company concentrate on the product-planning activity. We will discuss the product life-cycle concept. It is extremely important, and underlies material to be found later in the text.

The life of a product can be divided into four major stages: product introduction, market growth, market maturity, and sales decline. A product's marketing mix must change during these stages, because (1) customers' attitudes may change through the course of the product's life cycle, (2) entirely different target markets may be appealed to at different stages in the life cycle, and (3) the nature of competition moves toward pure competition.

Further, the sales history of the product varies in each of these four stages, and more importantly, the profit picture changes. It is significant that the two do not necessarily move together. Profits may decline while sales rise. Their general relationships can be seen in Figure 14–1.

In the introduction stage, promotion is needed to "pioneer" the acceptance of the product, since it is not sought by customers. Potential target customers must be told about the existence, advantages, and uses of the new product. **Introduction —investing in the future**

Even though a firm has successfully carved out a new market for itself, the product may not be an immediate success. This introductory stage usually is characterized by losses, with much money spent for promotion and product and place development. Funds, in effect, are being invested with the expectation of future profits.

In this second stage, the innovator usually begins to make substantial profits. Competitors start coming into the market, and each tries to develop the best product design. There is much product variety. Some competitors copy the most successful products. Monopolistic competition with downsloping demand curves is characteristic of both the **Market growth— many competing products and better profits**

---

[2] "Setting a Time Table," *Business Week*, May 27, 1967, pp. 52–61.

281

period of product introduction as well as that of market growth.

During this stage, the sales of the total industry are rising fairly rapidly as more and more customers enter the market. This second stage may last from several days to several years, depending on whether the product is hula hoops or color television sets. This is the time of peak profitability—*and* also the beginning of the decline of profits for all the competitors selling this product.

Market maturity— competition up, profits down

By the third stage, many competitors have entered the market. (In some cases, entry is not as easy, and the market behaves differently. If there are only a few large competitors and products are homogeneous, the situation is called oligopoly. This is discussed in detail in Chapter 27.)

In this stage, there is a more competitive situation, with declining

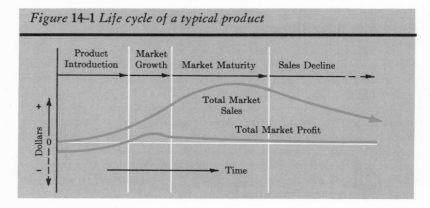

Figure **14-1** *Life cycle of a typical product*

profits. Promotion emphasizes the advantages of particular brands, but products actually differ only slightly because most of the companies have settled on the same way to appeal to the mass market, and there is a tendency to copy competing features. Mass production methods also discourage product variety.

This market, still characterized by monopolistic competition, is becoming much more competitive on product, price, and promotion. Basic product similarities and the need for lower cost mass production cause firms to resort to product differentiation. At this time, emotional appeals become more common—they are the only remaining way to add value to the product.

Industry profits decline throughout the market maturity stage because promotion costs climb, and some competitors begin to cut prices to attract business. Although each firm may still have its own demand curve, the curves are becoming increasingly elastic as the various products become almost homogeneous. Prices may be cut even as total industry volume is rising. This was the case recently in plastics and transistors, for example.[3]

[3] "Plastics Industry Paradox," *Business Week,* August 3, 1963, p. 24; and "Growth—at a Price—for Transistors," *Business Week,* April 6, 1963, pp. 102–6.

In the United States, the markets for most automobiles,[4] boats,[5] many household appliances, most groceries, black-and-white television sets, and tobacco products are in the market maturity stage.

The market maturity period may continue many years until a basically new product idea comes along to completely change the market. Gasoline-powered automobiles, for example, replaced horsedrawn carriages, and eventually may be replaced by some other method of transportation, such as electric autos and high-speed mass transit.

Sales decline

In the fourth and final stage of the life cycle, new products replace the old. Price competition from dying firms may become more vigorous, but companies with strong customer franchises may make profits almost till the end. These firms will have downsloping demand curves because they have successfully differentiated their products.

As the new products go through the introductory stage, the old ones may retain some sales by appealing to the most loyal target customers, perhaps older people or those who were uniquely satisfied.

Our earlier discussion of consumer behavior showed that some customers accept new ideas more readily than others. The former would shift first into the new product; more conservative buyers might switch later, smoothing the sales decline.

The early bird makes the profit

The total length of the cycle may vary from 90 days, as in the case of hula hoops, to possibly 90 years for automobiles. But technical progress, the passage of time, and changing customer preferences seem to make a sales decline inevitable for any product. Few products that originated 100 years ago have escaped substantial change—if indeed, they are still sold at all.

Product life cycles also seem to be shortening in the face of growing competition. One research study found the cycle for grocery products declining from about 36 months for those starting in 1962 to 18 months for starters in 1964.[6]

Du Pont's top executive says: "Lead time is gone. . . . There's no company so outstanding technically today that it can expect a long lead time in a new discovery."[7] Du Pont had nylon to itself for 15 years, but in just two years a major competitor, Celanese Corp., came out with something very competitive to Delrin, another synthetic fiber discovery that Du Pont considered potentially as important as nylon.

Six months after U.S. Steel came out with a new economical "thin tin" plate, competitors were out with even better products. Electric skillets, electric can openers, and electric toothbrushes also saw the fast

---

[4] R. J. Holloway, "Which Automobiles Will Be Here Tomorrow?", *Journal of Marketing,* January, 1961, pp. 35–36.

[5] *Wall Street Journal,* July 19, 1962, p. 1.

[6] Reported in a special presentation to an American Marketing Association Conference on Market Segmentation by A. C. Nielsen, Jr., president, A. C. Nielsen Co., February 24, 1967.

[7] "The Short Happy Life," *Time,* March 29, 1963, p. 83.

rise of competition. And color TV seems to have moved into the market maturity stage already.[8]

Even copying of products is not unknown, thus speeding the cycle more. Westinghouse found a company copying its new hair dryer *and* instruction book almost exactly.[9] Even patent protection may not be

Figure 14–2 *A. Significantly improved product starts a new cycle, but maybe with short introductory stage.*
B. Profit-oriented firm dropping out of market during market maturity stage.

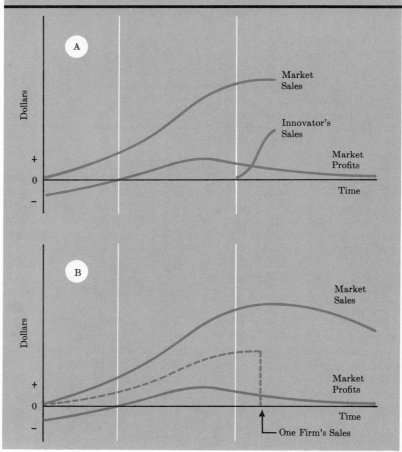

enough, since the product's life may be over before a case would get through the courts. What this means is that the modern firm must be

[8] William E. Bell, "The Maturing TV Industry," *Journal of Marketing*, April, 1966, pp. 12–15; "A Case of TV Nerves," *Business Week*, November 19, 1966, p. 48; and "Curtis Mathes Reports 3rd Period Loss; Firm Had Year-Earlier Profit," *Wall Street Journal*, April 10, 1967, p. 8.

[9] *Time*, March 29, 1963, p. 83.

developing new products continually and must seek to have a marketing mix (and not just a product) that will make the most of the early stages of the life cycle when profits are highest.

It is clear that a succession of new products is needed to offset the impact of competition and the product life cycle. Yet new or improved products do not just happen. Ideas for new products must be translated into tangible form, and existing products may have to be improved. More is said on this later in the chapter. **How to meet or beat competitive forces**

A company does not have to sit by in frustration and watch its product go through the complete product life cycle. It can either significantly improve the product and let it start off on a new cycle, or

Figure **14–3** *Sales patterns of products in company which regularly introduces new products*

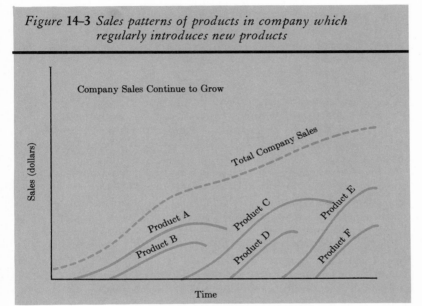

withdraw it before it completes the cycle (Figure 14–2). A company that continually offered new products could offset the effect of its declining products and actually see a growth in company sales (Figure 14–3). But this takes a continual flow of new products and only underlines the importance of this development process.

Style and fashion cycles

The concept of the product life cycle applies generally to most products, but another kind of cycle—a fashion cycle—can be seen clearly for products whose style or fashion are important to consumers. A whole category of consumer goods—the heterogeneous shopping good—exists, in part, because of the importance of style or fashion. Usually these goods must be examined to determine their suitability.

285

For instance, women must try on, feel, and look at hats, shoes, and dresses to appraise their subtle variations in style or fashion.

The short happy life of Batman

The words "style" or "fashion" commonly are used synonymously by consumers. Technically, however, they ought to be differentiated.

Style is a "characteristic or distinctive mode or method of expression, presentation, or conception in the field of art."[10] Various residential architectural styles such as colonial, Cape Cod, ranch, and modern, have come to popularity during certain periods of history.

Fashion, however, refers to the *currently* accepted or popular style in a given field. A particular style of house such as a ranch house or A-frame may be in style for a time and then lose its popularity. Or a certain color and style of women's dresses, such as empire style, may be in fashion one year, then outdated the next. It is still a style but no longer a fashion.

A fad is a particular fashion that seems fashionable only to certain groups—who are enthusiastic about it but so fickle that it is short-lived as a fashion. Such children's products as Batman capes and some teen-agers' records can be called fads.

Fashion cycles have stages, too

Consumer acceptance of fashions usually goes through a cycle which is closely related to consumer buying motives. A fashion cycle is commonly composed of three stages: the *distinctiveness, emulation,* and *economic emulation* stages, which roughly parallel the product life-cycle stages.

In the *distinctiveness* stage, some consumers, seeking new styles, are especially interested and willing to pay for products that are different from those possessed by the majority. Many have products custom-made or patronize manufacturers or distributors who make or handle goods in small quantities.

If a particular style "catches on" with a number of style leaders, then other consumers, because of their desire to emulate, may copy them. *Emulation* may come easier as manufacturers begin to make larger quantities of the products that seem to be "catching on." This stage can be likened to the early market growth stage of the product life cycle.

Then, if it seems assured that a fashion is going to be popular with a mass segment of the population, the product moves into a third stage, *economic emulation.* Manufacturers mass-produce large quantities of the product at low cost, and we move quickly through the market growth stage and maybe through the market maturity stage into sales decline.

Perhaps in the second stage, and certainly in the third stage, the style that began as the private possession of the few becomes less attractive to these original style leaders. But they already are seeking other styles—which eventually may become fashions and run through another cycle.[11]

---

[10] P. H. Nystrom, *Economics of Fashion* (New York: Ronald Press Co., 1958), p. 3.
[11] M. T. Copeland, *Principles of Merchandising* (New York: A. W. Shaw Co., 1924), p. 167.

How a particular fashion gets started is not well understood. Most present fashions are adaptations or resurrections of previously popular styles. Designers and entrepreneurs are continually seeking styles that will suit those consumers who want distinctiveness. The results may be exaggerations of earlier styles or perhaps new adaptations of styles from Japan, India, or Egypt.

Predicting what will sell is not easy. Fortunes can be lost in the fashion business by guessing wrong about consumer behavior. Ambrose Bierce once wrote, "Fashion is a despot whom the wise ridicule —and obey." And Thoreau commented, "Every generation laughs at the old fashions but follows religiously the new."[12]

Despite the chancy nature of any fashion-oriented enterprise, businessmen keep trying to find new fashions.[13] And there are a few generalizations that do seem to apply to consumer fashions:

1. Fashions cannot be forced, but many styles can be presented, and when one becomes fashionable, its cycle may be accelerated by aggressive promotion.
2. A higher standard of living and greater mobility encourage a greater interest in fashions.
3. The speed of communication affects the rate of change or acceptance of fashions.
4. Speed in change of fashions increases the cost of producing and marketing goods. There are losses due to the trial and error in finding acceptable styles, then producing them on a limited production basis because of retailers' uncertainty about the length of the cycle. These increased costs are not always charged directly to the consumer, since some manufacturers lose their investment and go out of business. But in the aggregate, fashion changes cost consumers money. This added cost resulting from consumer desire and preference for change should not be considered as the "fault" of marketing or business.

Need for product objectives

Guidelines are needed for the whole product-planning process. This is the function of product objectives, which are extensions and elaborations of company objectives. If company objectives are specific with respect to products, then there may be no need for product objectives. But if company objectives are very general and are concerned with such matters as sales growth and the possible future direction of the firm, then the marketing manager may have more latitude in his product planning.

To guide his planning, the manager should set down his product objectives. These objectives should apply to his whole program and not just to new products, since he is probably responsible for some established (and perhaps even declining) products, too. But product objectives cannot be conceived in a vacuum. They must flow from overall company objectives and be compatible with the Place, Promotion, and Pricing objectives.

[12] Alfred H. Daniels, "Fashion Merchandising," *Harvard Business Review*, May, 1951, pp. 51–60.
[13] "Marketing: Latest Thing in Fashions," *Printers' Ink*, April 26, 1963, pp. 25–30.

Ideally, product objectives are customer-oriented. But in practical terms, the marketing manager is limited by company resources. The company's productive and executive resources must be considered in developing product objectives, and in fact, wise use of resources might become a company objective. What happens when this kind of objective is taken is illustrated by the experience of the paper industry in the early 1960's. The industry was searching aggressively for new *paper products* to keep the mills going. Yet the emphasis was not on what paper products customers wanted but on what products they wanted that could be made out of paper.[14]

Take more shelves, ship by boxcar

While no one list of product objectives will suit all businesses, here are a few which suggest the range of possibilities.

1. One marketing manager might want to develop a line of products to satisfy not only several consumer markets but also to satisfy the wholesalers and retailers he supplies. He might want to offer a brand at the "top" of his line that would add prestige to the whole line even if the brand itself did not sell well. He might want to offer a "fighting" brand to give his retailers a low-priced brand to meet discount house competition.

2. Another marketing manager might want to offer a full line so that he could achieve more shelf space and reinforce his in-store image by increasing the "faces" before the consumer. And the full line might attract enough volume to warrant truckload or rail-carload-size orders, thereby reducing his delivery costs.

3. Another marketing manager might want to specify clearly that he wanted to practice as much market segmentation as possible. This would have a direct impact on both the new-product planning function and the production department. Such an objective probably would have to be cleared with the production department to avoid later conflicts over the size of production runs. This illustrates, again, why a business system should be considered as a total system.

Need for product policies

Product objectives serve as guides for writing explicit product policies. These policies give quick answers to routine questions. Consider the marketing manager who is continually faced with salesmen's requests to add new products to the line.

If he has specific policies about adding new products, the answer can be fast and simple. If he doesn't, every request may force him to reevaluate objectives or to give quick answers that he may regret later.

Product policies may actually be determined by specific product objectives or company objectives. For instance, if the top management were only interested in selling current products, then one product policy would be definite. All requests to add new products would be refused.

---

[14] "Mills Step Up Research on New Products, Hope to Utilize Idle Capacity," *Wall Street Journal*, December 1, 1961, p. 1.

As with product objectives, there is no set list of product policies. Generally, however, the policies are more specific statements than the objectives and usually they cover recurring problem areas. The product policies of one large manufacturer illustrates some possibilities. This firm developed nine statements of product policy on the following topics:[15]

Policies for telling "very good" from "very poor"

1. Sales volume.
2. Type and number of competitors.
3. Technical opportunity.
4. Patent protection.
5. Raw materials required.
6. Production load.
7. Value added.
8. Similarity to major business.
9. Effect on other products.

To illustrate what might be written on each topic, three statements are paraphrased from the policy definition of the manufacturer:

1. *Sales Volume.* Each product line should have a large potential volume of sales. It should be useful in a number of different applications and salable to a large number of customers.

4. *Patent Protection.* Each line should be well protected by patents arising from the company's own discoveries or acquired by purchase or other means.

9. *Effect on Other Products.* Each line should improve the company's overall sales and profit position, helping to promote the sales of the company's other products. If, however, any new line would hinder the sales of other company products, it should have a greater potential long-range profit than the products in conflict with it.[16]

Such product policies can be used in evaluating present products or selecting new ones. These topics could be used as a checklist. Each present or prospective product could be rated, for example, from "very poor" through "very good."

Table 14–1 shows the evaluation of two proposed products by this same manufacturer. In neither case were all the ratings "very good." But while the product in Case A was different from the present products, it looked very favorable—and it actually developed into a major new business for the company. Case B, however, showed a generally unfavorable pattern, with too many low ratings, and it was not considered further by the company.

When product policies are developed, they should be applied to the old products as well as the new. A regular procedure should be developed for reviewing established products. Conditions in and out of the company change, and what was wise years ago may prove less desirable now.

Apply product policies to established products, too

Some product lines may have become obsolete, or considerable effort

---

[15] Charles H. Kline, "The Strategy of Product Policy," *Harvard Business Review,* July–August, 1955, pp. 91–100.
[16] *Ibid.*

may be devoted to low-volume, relatively unprofitable products. If the company has only one major line, review may be easy.

When sales of White sewing machines were seriously challenged by competition from low-priced Japanese machines, the need for the White Sewing Machine Co. to adjust its product policy became clear. Upon evaluating the resources, White realized it had no special production strong points—but it did have strength in its marketing organization.

Table 14-1 Examples of summary product appraisals by a large materials processor

CASE A: A Generally Favorable Pattern	Rating				
	Very Good	Good	Fair	Poor	Very Poor
Sales volume	x				
Type and number of competitors	x				
Technical opportunity	x				
Patent protection		x			
Raw materials		x			
Production load		x			
Value added		x			
Similarity to major business				x	
Effect on present products			x		

CASE B: A Generally Unfavorable Pattern	Rating				
	Very Good	Good	Fair	Poor	Very Poor
Sales volume	x				
Type and number of competitors					x
Technical opportunity				x	
Patent protection					x
Raw materials		x			
Production load			x		
Value added		x			
Similarity to major business	x				
Effect on present products	x				

SOURCE: Charles H. Kline, "The Strategy of Product Policy," *Harvard Business Review*, July–August, 1955, pp. 91–100.

White adjusted its product policy accordingly, buying machines from Japan and distributing them under the White name in the United States. The company successfully capitalized on its resources of financial strength, public acceptance of the brand name, and sales and management experience.

For the company with many products and product lines, review of products and policies may be more difficult. A clear understanding of the company's whole strategy is important. Over the years, the sales department usually presses for expanding the product line, paying less attention to balancing or reducing the line. But the whole line may be the company's "product." Some seemingly unprofitable items may be very important to some target customers, and dropping them might lead to the loss of very profitable volume in other parts of the line. Understanding the company's overall strategy, therefore, is essential. If the marketing manager knows whom he is aiming at and what they want, then he can correctly define and evaluate the whole "product."[17]

Pruning products for better profits

A careful appraisal of the company's product policies plus detailed sales and cost analysis (to be discussed in Chapter 30) may show points at which substantial savings can be made and profits increased. One company with an annual sales volume of $40 million increased the sales volume 50 percent and its profits 20 times during a three-year period by eliminating from its line 16 products with a total volume of $3.3 million. This product pruning not only eliminated unprofitable products but enabled the company to spend more time on the profitable ones.[18]

Need for product managers

Product managers[19] have evolved to do the job of product planning as well as the ongoing management of established products. Product managers are especially common in large companies producing many kinds of products. Sometimes they are responsible for the profitable operation of the whole marketing effort for a particular product. In this capacity, they usually have to coordinate their efforts with those of other executives, including the sales manager, advertising manager, and production and research people.

Whether there is a product manager or not, however, it is obvious that someone must manage Product. The balance of this chapter will cover the special problems of designing and developing new products.

Designing new products

What is a new product— lemons!?

Since there is no common agreement on what constitutes a new product, a company should define what *it* means by the term. A simple technical change made by the engineering department might turn out to have an impact on the whole marketing mix or even the marketing strategy if new target markets were attracted by the change.

In this text, we will consider a product as new if it is *new in any way* for the company concerned. To be considered new, there need not even

---

[17] For a good selection of readings on product strategy, see Thomas L. Berg and Abe Shuchman, *Product Strategy and Management* (New York: Holt, Rinehart & Winston, Inc., 1963).

[18] Kline, *op. cit.* For further case histories on savings achieved by line simplification or product elimination, see Charles H. Sevin, *How Manufacturers Reduce Their Distribution Costs* (Economic Series No. 72, U.S. Department of Commerce [Washington, D.C.: U.S. Government Printing Office, 1951]). See also, R. S. Alexander, "The Death and Burial of 'Sick' Products," *Journal of Marketing*, April, 1964, pp. 1–7; and L. J. Houfek, "How to Decide Which Products to Junk," *Printers' Ink*, August 1, 1952, pp. 21–23.

[19] Sometimes they are called brand managers or merchandise managers.

be a physical change in the product, package, or brand—if different target markets are sought. Lemons illustrate the point.

In the marketing of lemons by one organization, no physical changes were made, but extensive promotion and consumer education created many "new" products. The same old lemons were promoted successfully for lemonade, mixed drinks, diet supplements, cold remedies, lemon cream pies, a salad condiment, dressing for fish, and many other culinary uses. For each of these markets, the product had to go through the early stages of the product life cycle.[20]

A product can be called "new" for only a limited time. Six months is the maximum time that a product should be called "new," according to the Federal Trade Commission. To be called "new," says the FTC, a product must be entirely new or changed in "a functionally significant or substantial respect."[21] While six months may seem a very short time for production-oriented businessmen, it may be reasonable in the light of our earlier discussion of the length of product life cycles.

Give the customer the right color

Following the marketing concept, customers' needs or wants should dominate product development. The final choice and design of the product should be compatible with a company's overall objectives and use its resources effectively. But it may be a costly mistake if production-oriented considerations are given precedence over customer wishes.

Customer-oriented decisions must be more than good intentions, however. Marketing research may be needed. A survey by Rubbermaid, Inc., of Wooster, Ohio showed that the firm's present customers preferred gray or neutral shades for its rubber drainer trays, dish racks, and sink basins. Rubbermaid, however, had been using color to "brighten the home," turning out products in bright blues, reds, yellows, greens. Rubbermaid's president noted, "We get all wrapped up with ourselves out at the plant, sometimes, and when I bring home a new product, my wife will often say, 'Who dreamed that up?' "[22]

Color generally is becoming more important, however, not only for final consumer products but industrial goods too. Black typewriters in perfect condition were retired by some businesses when the colored machines arrived. And more color is being used in industrial machinery and plant design.[23]

The product design must fit customer needs

The importance of marketing research in aiding product development is seen even more clearly in the context of world markets. Variations from one nation to another in taste and expectations emphasize the need for finding out what the target customer wants and needs.

The Japanese are designing their own "Western style" furniture because Japanese customers consider copies of Western designs uncom-

---

[20] See Chester R. Wasson, "What Is 'New' about New Products?" *Journal of Marketing,* July, 1960, pp. 52–56.

[21] *Business Week,* April 22, 1967, p. 120.

[22] *Business Week,* March 21, 1959, p. 92.

[23] "Trends in Consumers' Taste in Color Offer New Opportunities for Sales," *Printers' Ink,* December 5, 1958, pp. 71–72; and Ernest Dichter, "Color Can Stimulate Sales" (Small Marketers Aids No. 85, Small Business Administration, November, 1962).

fortable.[24] Picks, shovels, and even tractor seats designed for sale in Africa must be made smaller than those sold in Western countries, because the potential users are themselves smaller in size.[25]

To help assure good product design, the internationally minded management of one firm checks the factors listed in Table 14–2. These factors are general, and the answers might vary from target market to target market—but if any is found relevant, the implications for marketing mix planning are obvious.

Table **14–2** Considerations and their implications in designing for world markets

Considerations	Implications
Level of technical skills	Product simplification
Level of labor cost	Automation or manualization of product
Level of literacy	Remarking and simplification of product
Level of income	Quality and price change
Level of interest rates	Quality and price change (investment in high quality might not be financially desirable)
Level of maintenance	Change in tolerances
Climatic differences	Product adaptation
Isolation (heavy repair difficult and expensive)	Product simplification and reliability improvement
Differences in standards	Recalibration of product and resizing
Availability of other products	Greater or lesser product integration
Availability of materials	Change in product structure and fuel
Power availability	Resizing of product
Special conditions	Product redesign or invention

Reprinted from the *Journal of Marketing*, national quarterly publication of the American Marketing Association. Richard D. Robinson, "The Challenge of the Underdeveloped Market," *Journal of Marketing*, October, 1961, Vol. XXV, p. 22.

An example involving one of these factors, *level of maintenance,* shows why it is essential to know each market.

An African government purchased hand-operated dusters for applying pesticides to cotton fields. The product supplied by the American manufacturer was a finely machined device that turned more easily than competing equipment but required regular oiling for good care. Used in the African cotton fields, however, the duster seldom was oiled properly, and it quickly broke down. The government went back to an older French duster which didn't work as well but also didn't need regular oiling and so lasted longer. In this market, the French product was superior because it met the target customers' needs.[26]

---

[24] "Japan's Newest Quest for Quality," *Business Week,* July 28, 1962, pp. 98–100.

[25] Edward Marcus, "Selling the Tropical African Market," *Journal of Marketing,* July, 1961, p. 27.

[26] Richard D. Robinson, "The Challenge of the Underdeveloped Market," *Journal of Marketing,* October, 1961, p. 21.

Market research alone, however, cannot assure good product design. Some management judgment must be used. Consumers have been notoriously unreliable in predicting what they are going to like.

Since some judgment and risk probably always will be involved, the checklist in Figure 14–4 may help management to narrow the areas in which judgment is necessary.[27] This checklist is useful because it usually is safer to make 12 separate small judgments than one large judgment of "yes" or "no."

On this checklist, a score of "yes" on 11 or 12 questions would indicate a good design; 9 or 10 points, a fair design (with "no" answers indicating weak spots to be corrected); and below 9 points, a poor

---

Figure 14–4

Good Design: Does Your Product Have It?	Yes	No
1. Does the product's present design reflect quality?		
2. Is the present design economical to manufacture?		
3. Is the design well accepted by wholesalers, retailers, salesmen and customers?		
4. Is the design in tune with current design trends?		
5. Does the design have a comparatively long life?		
6. Are the details of the product well designed?		
7. Does the design contribute to the product's usefulness and convenience?		
8. Are the materials used practical for product's end use?		
9. Is the color right for use and environment?		
10. Is the size right for best use?		
11. Is the weight right for best use?		
12. Does the design stand up well with competition?		

---

design, probably indicating that profits will be reduced through lost sales and possibly through high manufacturing costs. This list is suitable for all products except high-fashion women's apparel—which is a world of its own.

To see how this list could be helpful, try it on some product you bought recently.

The product design selected by a firm may depend on whether it is following a policy of market segmentation or product differentiation. Market segmentation would suggest designing a product precisely to meet the needs of some unique target market.

Product differentiation might mean building several features into a product to make it more appealing to more people. For example, extra features might be added to a camera *without* making it too complicated for amateurs. This would enable the camera manufacturer to appeal to more buyers with the same product. This approach might appeal to production-oriented people in the firm because it might allow

[27] Victor Petertil, "Is Your Product Designed to Sell?" *Management Methods,* July, 1958, p. 48.

longer production runs, offsetting the added cost of adding extra features. Decisions about a step like this, however, should be made only after a careful analysis of the potential target markets. Adding more features to a camera might make it look more complicated and scare off more customers than it attracted.

All people who handle, sell, or use a product must be considered when developing the product. Manufacturers' marketing managers must look at their products through the eyes of intermediate customers as well as final consumers. For example, retailers or wholesalers might need a wider product line than the company is providing currently. Coca-Cola added several new products to its line—Fanta, Sprite, Tab, Fresca, and even orange juice—to satisfy bottler and consumer demands. Yet the company moved too slowly for some of its bottler customers, and they had begun promoting their own lemon-lime soda, "Veep."[28]

For the intermediate customer, new pop, better sales help

The trend of self-service in some retail outlets has forced product designers to make many product changes. Multi-packs may help the retailer as well as the consumer. And good product instructions and sizing aids may have to be built into the product to compensate for the lack of personal selling effort. One firm that sells its sleeper-suit pajamas through self-service outlets prints a size formula on the package. The customer can estimate the correct size without the help of a clerk. In fact, the information on the package may be an even better guide to selecting these clothes than the clerks.

New product development: a total company effort

A new-product development department or committee helps assure that new ideas for products are carefully evaluated and good ones profitably marketed. Delays may lead to late test marketing or market introduction and give competition a head start in the product life cycle. A delay of even six months may make the difference between a product's success or failure in one of the more competitive markets.

A well-organized development procedure might even enable a firm to copy others' attractive innovations quickly and profitably. This possibility should not be overlooked. No one company can hope to be first always, with the best.[29]

New-product development must have the enthusiastic support of top management and the whole organization. New products tend to disrupt the old routines that managers of established products may try in subtle but effective ways to maintain.[30]

A story of failure and rejection

[28] "Coke Tries New Ways to Refresh," *Business Week*, August 24, 1963, pp. 100–110; and *Printers' Ink*, February 10, 1961, p. 5.

[29] See T. Levitt, "Innovative Imitation," *Harvard Business Review*, September–October, 1966, pp. 63–70.

[30] William A. Bours, III, "Imagination Wears Many Hats," *Journal of Marketing*, October, 1966, pp. 59–61; John H. Murphy, "New Products Need Special Management," *Journal of Marketing*, October, 1962, pp. 46–49; S. C. Johnson and Conrad Jones, "How to Organize for New Products," *Harvard Business Review*, May–June, 1957; E. J.

Marketing new products is a total company effort, as Figure 14–5 shows. Here, we see that the whole process is a sequential activity involving personnel in management, research, production, promotion, packaging, and branding. The process moves from an early exploration of ideas and concepts (see Figure 14–5) to a development of the product and product-related concepts. Technical development of the product itself is not the first step in new-product development. Concept appraisal comes first. Many items can be produced—even a Rube Goldberg device can be developed, but who wants it?

After the product and related concepts have been developed, the total concept—really, the total marketing mix—is developed and matched against the company's resources to see whether the product looks profitable.

If the answer is yes, then management must make another decision: Does it want to test-market, before a full-scale market introduction? This is not a trivial decision because, as noted in Chapter 4, although test marketing may test out ideas, it also may tip the company's hand to competition. After seeing the speed of product life cycles, we can better understand why some managements are reluctant to test-market.

The role of marketing management and top management in product development is shown in Figure 14–5. Management has the power to push or veto development, but to keep it going it must commit more funds. These sequential decisions become more difficult as the process proceeds because the costs are increasing.

Some of the many marketing research techniques applicable in new product development are indicated in Figure 14–5. Yet even with these careful plans and studies many new products *do* fail—about 50 percent of all those marketed by larger companies. And the rate is even higher for smaller companies.[31]

The rejection rate for new ideas during this new-product development process is even higher. One study of 80 companies found that only 1 out of 40 new ideas survived the kind of organized development process we have just discussed. The rate of rejection, however, varies; an especially conservative organization, for example, might have even more rejects. A well-known investment firm found that of 2,100 new-product propositions studied, only 17 were considered meritorious.[32]

Putting it to a test may help sell   Some firms that are not strongly market-oriented may be nudged by outside testing organizations into a more careful consideration of the customer during the product development process. The work of these testing organizations affects the market in two ways:

Provides customer-accepted research reports.   Private testing laboratories may do testing for firms that do not have their own laboratories. But even more important, they can give their "seal of approval" to

McCarthy, "Organization for New Product Development?" *Journal of Business of the University of Chicago,* April, 1959, pp. 128–32; and James H. Wolter, "An Analysis of the Process of New Product Idea Evaluation for Consumer Goods" (unpublished Ph. D. dissertation, Indiana University, 1960).

[31] *Management of New Products* (Chicago: Booz-Allen & Hamilton, 1960), p. 14.

[32] Paul Stillson and E. Leonard Arnoff, "Product Search and Evaluation," *Journal of Marketing,* July, 1957, p. 33.

Figure 14-5 New-product market development sequence

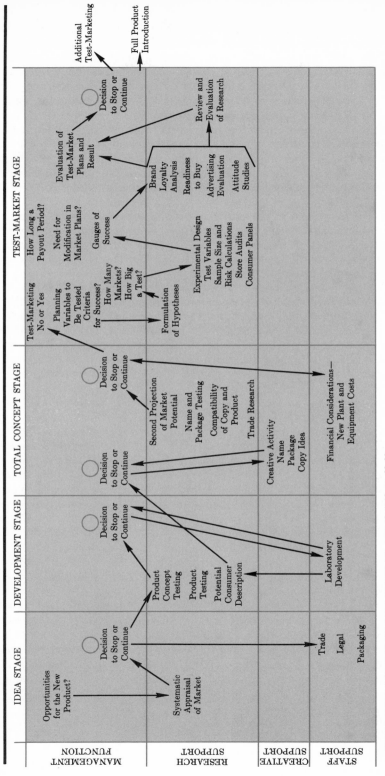

SOURCE: Benton & Bowles Research and *Printers' Ink*, April 13, 1962, pp. 22–23.

products, and this in itself may improve a product's chance for success.

Some of the organizations that evaluate products and allow use of their own brands, seals, or trademarks as an additional guarantee of the quality of the product are: the Underwriters Laboratories, the American Gas Association, the American Institute of Laundering, *Good Housekeeping, Parent's* magazine, *McCall's,* U.S. Testing Co., and the York Research Corp. (associated with *Reader's Digest*).[33]

Many customers have come to respect these product evaluations. For example, Glamorene, a home rug cleaning product, nearly put professional carpet cleaning firms out of business in 1951 after receiving the York Research Seal of Approval and a subsequent glowing endorsement from *Reader's Digest*. Glamorene sales shot from $500,000 a year to $1 million in just 60 days.[34]

Forces customer orientation. Two consumer-sponsored rating organizations in the United States report on and evaluate a wide variety of products in their own monthly magazines. High ratings in *Consumers Report* and *Consumers Research* have been known to increase sales, while low ratings have prompted product changes.[35]

Similar testing abroad by members of the International Association of Consumer Unions has been similarly effective.

An unfavorable report about an automatic washer in a German consumer publication caused the washer maker's market share to drop from 38 to 20 percent. Another manufacturer of spin driers lost his contract with a large mail-order company because of unfavorable ratings.

Evaluation of product planning

"Planned obsolescence" can't be all bad

Deliberately developing new products, sometimes only slightly updated, in the hopes of replacing older but still serviceable models has roused the ire of some critics of marketing. Such "planned obsolescence," as it is called by its critics, is especially common in the automobile, appliance, and clothing industries, where new styles or fashions are introduced at least once each year. The critics are concerned, among other reasons, because products that are not yet worn out may be discarded by some consumers.

"Planned obsolescence" certainly has some advantages for producers and middlemen, since new models may help them out of the market maturity stage of the product life cycle and back into the more profitable market growth stage.

But much of the continued innovation that is manifested in new-model introductions seems to have been forced upon producers by customer demands and competitor pressures. Continued novelty seems to satisfy some consumer needs. Marketing research sometimes shows that customers truly prefer a face-lifted model to the old model simply because it is new, perhaps for prestige reasons. Recall our discussion of

[33] For a description of testing techniques, see "Testing The Product," *Industrial Design,* November, 1960, pp. 41–51.

[34] "Product Testing Spurs Industry," *News Front,* June, 1958, pp. 30 ff.

[35] *Wall Street Journal,* March 15, 1962, p. 1.

the early stage of the fashion cycle. Catering to such needs can even be seen as a policy of market segmentation. Without this continued newness, these innovation-minded segments of the market would not be truly satisfied.

It can be argued further that "planned obsolescence" not only satisfies many customers but also encourages research and investment, helping to maintain high levels of employment.[36]

"Old" products, moreover, are not always wasted. There is a large secondhand market waiting in those markets where innovation and product changes are more rapid. In fact, a strong secondhand market seems to encourage change, making it less costly and economically more feasible for more customers. In the automobile market, for example, there is a ready secondhand market. A car may be sold several times before it is finally junked. The furniture market, on the other hand, has no organized secondhand market, and furniture is not replaced nearly as rapidly, to the sorrow of many housewives.

Further support for aggressive and continuing product differentiation and market segmentation comes from an unexpected source.

"Obsolescence" or "planning," it keeps customers supplied

The earlier Soviet practice of producing only homogeneous products was not successful. And so, responding to consumer wishes, Soviet production agencies have been expanding product variety. The Soviet radio-TV industry expected to offer 30 to 40 different brands of radios and phonographs and about 20 types of television sets in 1965.

In fact, Soviet interest in new products has even spread to laundry soap and detergents, important areas of product differentiation in the United States.[37] Viewing this development, one American specialist on Soviet economic affairs feels that many American critics of marketing may have underestimated the advantages of our present economic system and ought to reevaluate their thinking.

Clearly, what the critics call "planned obsolescence" and the marketing practitioners call "product planning," may have a number of desirable characteristics. In any case, these practices seem to be responses to customer demands in a competitive marketplace.

Conclusion

Product planning is an increasingly vital activity in a modern economy because it is no longer very profitable to sell just "commodities." And the product planning must be continuous to meet the dynamic and innovating competition which is causing product life cycles to shorten.

The product life-cycle concept is especially important to marketing strategy planning because it shows that different marketing mixes, and even strategies, are needed as a product moves through its cycle. This is especially important to understand because profits change during the

[36] See, for example, H. M. Case, "Designed Decay," *Harvard Business Review*, January–February, 1966, pp. 126–31.

[37] Marshall I. Goldman, "A New Perspective on Product Differentiation and Advertising: The Soviet View," *Business Review*, Boston University, Spring, 1962, pp. 3–12.

cycle, with most of the profits going to the innovators or fast copiers.

It is clear that effective management of Product is important, and this led us to a consideration of product objectives and policies, and of new-product development.

Once a company has decided on its overall objectives, it is wise to specify product objectives. These are simply more specific statements of the implications of the overall objectives with respect to products. Specifically, there might be statements about the type of products to be offered, the width of product line, and how much newness should be sought in new products.

Within the limits of company and product objectives, it is desirable to set down written product policies. These may be rewordings of the product objectives, but they should offer definite answers to recurring problems. If one objective is to cater to the mass market, then a product policy might state that all new products should satisfy this market (and by implication all products not aimed at this market would be rejected).

Possible product objectives and policies were suggested, although there is no single list applying to all situations.

We pointed out that a "new" product is not limited to physical newness. We will call a product "new" if it is new in any way—to any target market.

New products are so important to the survival of firms in our competitive economy that some organized method for developing them is needed. A general approach was discussed, but it is clear that it must be a total company effort to be successful. And the effort should be customer-oriented rather than production-oriented.

The failure rate of new products is high, but it is considerably lower for larger and better managed firms that have recognized product planning as a vital function in the business process. Some firms even have appointed product managers to manage individual product lines and new-product committees to assure that the process is carried out successfully.

Questions and problems

1 Discuss the life cycle of a product in terms of its probable impact on a manufacturer's marketing mix. Illustrate, using battery-operated toothbrushes.

2 If product differentiation or market segmentation efforts are especially successful, some people feel that this will accelerate the trend toward similar products. They point to the refrigerator market as an example. Comment on the idea of "success breeding its own downfall."

3 Distinguish among a fad, style, and fashion. How should a retailer adapt to them? Some people maintain that fads or fashions can be created by businessmen. Can you give an example of any business firm that has *consistently* created successful fads or fashions? *Consistently* is important, because anyone can be lucky a few times; the successes are publicized but the failures are not.

4 What overall objectives and product objectives might a recent business college graduate set for himself if he has a desire to go into business for himself. He has already had some electronics sales experience and has $30,000 to invest. After setting the objectives, what product policies logically flow from it? In answering this question, "product" must be considered broadly to include the services he may contribute to this enterprise.

5 A farmer has discovered a large deposit of sand just below his topsoil and is considering going into the sand and gravel business. After all, he feels, "I already have my product readymade." Evaluate his thinking. Should he go into this business? Specify any assumptions necessary to obtain a definite answer.

6 Explain why product policies should be written.

7 Should there be different product policies for new and for established products?

8 Discuss what is a new product and why it is important to make this distinction.

9 Discuss the thinking which should go into the design of washing machines for the Italian market, using the check-list in Table 14-2.

10 Discuss how the check-list "Good Design: Does Your Product Have It?" could be used to evaluate: (*a*) a can opener, (*b*) a baby stroller, (*c*) men's hats (fedoras), (*d*) a coffeemaker.

11 Explain the importance of an organized new product development process and illustrate how it might be used for: (*a*) an improved phonograph, (*b*) new frozen food items, (*c*) a new children's toy.

12 Some persons criticize planned obsolescence as it encourages the disposal of goods which are not yet completely worn out. What assumptions are they making about consumer preferences and behavior? Are these assumptions valid?

13 Discuss the social value of planned obsolescence policies, especially when they encourage people to discard products which are not "all worn out." Is this an economic waste? How worn out is "all worn out"? Must a shirt have holes in it? How big?

Place—introduction

Regardless of how good the product may be, it is of little use to the customer if it is not *where* he wants it *when* he wants it. The next six chapters consider all of the activities and institutions needed to provide "Place." For simplicity, we will use the term "Place" to refer to all of the things that go into providing the time, and place, and possession utilities that are needed to satisfy target customers, just as we use "Product" to mean the "total product" offered.

Place decisions may be concerned with the location of marketing facilities and the selection and use of marketing specialists, including transportation and storage agencies, wholesalers, and retailers. Some of the material we will discuss may seem theoretical and descriptive, but it is extremely important that the marketing manager understand the *why* and *what* of present distribution methods so that he can effectively plan for the future.

In our dynamic economy, marketing facilities are in such a constant state of flux that the marketing manager must continually evaluate his own (and his competitor's) current and possible place offerings. He should be constantly alert to market shifts that may provide new opportunities or cause new problems. Established place facilities may grow inefficient and need to be changed, or unfilled needs may offer an opportunity for a marketing "breakthrough."

Place doesn't just happen, contrary to the feelings of some production-oriented businessmen. To be sure, there are lots of wholesalers and retailers around. And there are many wholesale and retail facilities for rent to prospective middlemen. But are they the right place facilities?

The marketing manager's decisions on Place may be the most important ones he makes because they have long-range implications and are harder to change than Product, Price, and Promotion decisions. It is difficult to move retail and wholesale facilities once leases have been signed and customer movement patterns have been established. Cordial working arrangements with middlemen can take several years and a good deal of money to develop. Place decisions are likely to be the one-time strategic decisions whose importance we discussed in Chapter 2.

Place is so important and yet so poorly understood that we will examine the subject carefully, beginning with a theoretical discussion and then building our understanding on this solid foundation.

Decisions that are hard to move

Place provides time, place, and possession utility

Economists usually define four kinds of utility: form, time, place, and possession. So far we have considered only the creation of form utility—the development of a product. But the other three utilities are equally important. A customer can use a product only if it is in his *possession* at the right *time*. And to possess a product it must be in a *place* convenient to him.

We sometimes overlook why we can have a cup of coffee or a rubber tire or a woolen suit, apart from the fact that we have the money to buy it. One of the functions of marketing is to provide a product possessing form utility with time and place utility.[1] Only when this is done can the customer plunk down his 10 cents and enjoy possession utility of a cup of coffee.

There's an awful lot of coffee in Brazil—and Chicago

What is the importance of time and place utility? How much satisfaction would a Chicago consumer derive from owning a pound of coffee in Brazil? How happy would a coed be if her date brought her a certificate showing that she owned one orchid in Hawaii? Or consider the value of tire chains at the factory during a snowstorm or electric fans in the warehouse during a heat wave.

Look at Place in terms of supply and demand. Producers are willing to supply products and consumers may be demanding them, yet no transactions take place unless the buyers and sellers get together. Here, the job of marketing is to match supply capabilities to the demands of the many target markets, moving goods wherever they are needed.

Markets develop to facilitate exchange

The historical development of organizations specializing in providing time and place utility, which we call simply *Place*, was sketched in Chapter 1. You will recall that marketing was not necessary when

---

[1] Wroe Alderson, *Marketing Behavior and Executive Action* (Homewood, Ill.: Richard D. Irwin, Inc., 1957), p. 199. See also, Wroe Alderson, "The Analytical Framework for Marketing," in Perry Bliss, *Marketing and the Behavioral Sciences* (Boston: Allyn & Bacon, Inc., 1963), pp. 25–43.

families existed as self-sufficient units. As these family units developed surpluses and became interested in bartering for other products, Place became relevant. The products had to be brought together before they could be exchanged.

We assumed in our earlier discussion that this trade would be mutually beneficial. Now we must see why and how, for the marketing manager who understands the advantage of such exchange can find new and better ways to accomplish it.

Begin by asking why central markets have developed? Suppose a group of five families found that each has some special skill for producing some item. After meeting basic subsistence needs, each family might decide to specialize. This decision would be very practical. It is easier for one family to make two pots and another to make

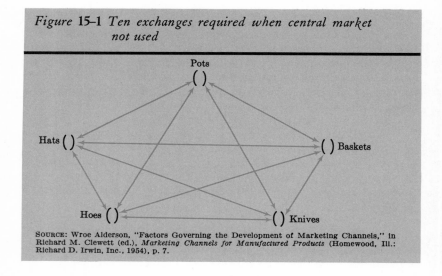

Figure 15–1 Ten exchanges required when central market not used

SOURCE: Wroe Alderson, "Factors Governing the Development of Marketing Channels," in Richard M. Clewett (ed.), *Marketing Channels for Manufactured Products* (Homewood, Ill.: Richard D. Irwin, Inc., 1954), p. 7.

two baskets than it is for either to make one pot and one basket. Specialization makes labor more efficient and more productive.

If these five families specialize in one product apiece, they will have to trade with each other. As Figure 15–1 shows, it would take the five families 10 separate trips and exchanges to obtain some of each of the products. If the families live near each other, the exchange process would be relatively simple. But if they are far apart, travel back and forth will be time-consuming. And who would do the traveling and when?

Faced with this problem, the families may agree to come to a central market and trade on a certain day. Then, each family would need to make only one trip into the market to trade with all the others, reducing the total number of trips to five. The reason for the development of central markets is clear. They facilitated exchange, left more time for production, and also served as social gatherings.

Modern economies are well beyond this simple example, but the principle still holds. The fundamental purpose of markets is to facilitate exchange and allow greater time for production.

Money system speeds trading

But while a central meeting place would simplify exchange, all of the individual bartering transactions would still take much time. Bartering takes a partner who wants what you have and vice versa. Each trader must find others who have products of approximately equal value. After trading with one group, a family might find itself with a collection of hats, knives, and pots, and then it would have to find others who were willing to trade for these products.

A money system would change all of this. A seller would merely find a buyer who can either use or sell his product, negotiate the price, and be free to spend his money to buy whatever he wants.

Specialists facilitate trade even more

Even though a money system simplifies the trading, considerable time and effort are needed to complete all transactions among the families. And once they were using money, each family head might have to open (and pay for) a stall at the market, while other family members shopped at other parts of the market.

The exchange process may be facilitated by the appearance of a dealer who is willing to trade with the families for *all* of their surpluses in exchange for what they need. See Figure 15–2. **Enter the middleman**

In our simple example, using the services of a dealer at a central market, the 10 exchanges needed are now reduced to 5. Such a dealer

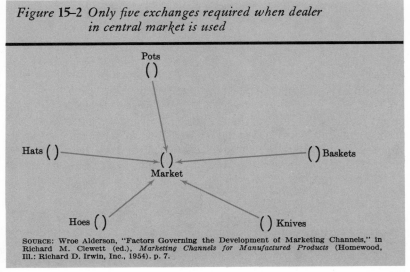

Figure 15–2 Only five exchanges required when dealer in central market is used

Pots
( )

Hats ( )

( )
Market

( ) Baskets

Hoes ( )

( ) Knives

SOURCE: Wroe Alderson, "Factors Governing the Development of Marketing Channels," in Richard M. Clewett (ed.), *Marketing Channels for Manufactured Products* (Homewood, Ill.: Richard D. Irwin, Inc., 1954). p. 7.

would make a charge for this service, but if the time saved were considerable, each family might have more time for production at home and visiting at the market. Each family could specialize in production and let the dealer specialize in trading.

Such dealers, offering permanent trading facilities, are known today as wholesalers and retailers. As the number of customers increases, the advantages of working with a dealer becomes substantial. That is why there are so many wholesalers and retailers in more complex economies.[2]

Discrepancies of quantity and assortment must be adjusted

Marketing managers must continually adjust supply to demand. The process is somewhat more complicated than the simple supply-and-demand analysis we discussed earlier, however, because there are (1) so many different demands on the market grid for a general type of product and (2) many different kinds of middlemen and producers with different costs and objectives. To simplify our introductory discussion, we will consider the discrepanices between producers and final users or consumers.

Bake a cake as fast . . . if you can

Rather than wanting large quantities of one item, customers usually are more interested in an assortment of products to serve some specific purpose. The value of an assortment has been called "the potency of the assortment."[3] A housewife baking her son's birthday cake illustrates the point. She needs a variety of ingredients, including sugar, shortening, eggs, milk, flour, and salt. As she begins mixing, she discovers she has no flour. At this point, she needs the flour quickly and may be willing to pay a premium for it, perhaps at an expensive but nearby "fill-in" store rather than the more distant supermarket. We would call this flour an emergency good. The "potency" of flour alone would not be strong if none of the other ingredients were available. But since only the flour is missing, and the need for it is urgent, the housewife's demand becomes extremely inelastic for this emergency good.

The assortment and quantity of goods wanted by a customer has little direct relation to the assortment and quantity of goods normally produced by a manufacturer. Probably no two products the housewife needed for the cake were made or produced by the same firm or farm, except perhaps the milk and eggs, though they could have been supplied by separate dairy and poultry firms. That missing flour would be produced by millers specializing in flour production who had purchased the wheat from farmers who specialized in wheat (or from middlemen who specialized in handling larger quantities of wheat).

---

[2] One author has developed a ratio of advantage that demonstrates clearly how the advantages offered by middlemen grow fast as the size of the market grows. See Wroe Alderson, "Factors Governing the Development of Marketing Channels," Richard M. Clewett (ed.), *Marketing Channels for Manufactured Products* (Homewood, Ill.: Richard D. Irwin, Inc., 1954), pp. 7–9 for further elaboration.

[3] *Ibid.,* pp. 10–11.

It is clear that there are discrepancies both of *quantity* and *assortment* between what producers normally make and what consumers normally want. It is important to distinguish between the two, especially if we want to understand why marketing specialists develop.

Earlier we saw that specialization by a firm often makes economic sense. A company offers those products (or services) that it can produce most efficiently, given its resources and objectives. Rather than offering small quantites of many items, most producers now specialize in producing larger quantites of a few items.

Discrepancy of quantity —don't put all your golf balls in one place

The large quantities that specialized production makes possible are the cause of discrepancy of quantity and a major factor in the development of specialists. Few customers have such large demands for specific items that they can consume a big part of the producer's output. If a customer did need a large quantity of an item, it might be more economical for him to make it himself.

Consider the movement of golf balls from manufacturers to golfers as shown in Figure 15–3. Most manufacturers of golf balls produce in large quantities such as 200,000, 500,000, or 400,000, in a given time period. The average golfer, however, is interested only in a few balls at a time—say 1 to 12 balls for this same time period.

For a golf ball manufacturer to deal directly with thousands of golfers—perhaps more than 100,000 in all—would be a Herculean task. For one thing, it would be necessary to use cash to avoid a costly investigation of each potential customer's credit rating, even though requiring cash would annoy many customers. And each individual order would have to be mailed to the customer's home, unless the manufacturer opened thousands of his own retail stores handling only golf balls.

A local specialist—a retailer—might develop to fill the obvious need of all these individual consumers for a product. If the demands from golfers in the locality totaled, say, 600 balls for some time period, the retailer could arrange to provide that quantity. Then each golfer could come in and inspect the balls before purchase and take them home immediately. This retailer also might extend credit.

But there still might remain a great discrepancy between the quantity the manufacturer produced and the quantity each retailer wanted. The manufacturer might still find this selling to retailers both difficult and uneconomical.

The solution of this problem would be wholesale outlets. They could develop to serve the market, selling to perhaps 100 retailers each. Now the manufacturer could deal only with a few wholesalers, establishing closer relationships that would facilitate credit checking and quantity shipments on credit.

If we limit our hypothetical discussion to golf balls alone, however, we only partially explain the development of specialists.

For instance, why can some independent wholesalers and retailers do this job more effectively than the manufacturer? Why doesn't the producer simply open his own outlets? This requires consideration of discrepancy of assortments.

Discrepancy of assortments—giving the customer a choice

The typical golfer needs more than golf balls. He needs golf gloves, hats, jackets, clubs, bags, carts, and tees. He wants a full line of golf supplies, and he probably would prefer *not* to shop around for each item. This would be especially true if he had to deal directly with many distant manufacturers. He wants only *one or a few* of each of many items, whereas producers specialize in making one or a few items in

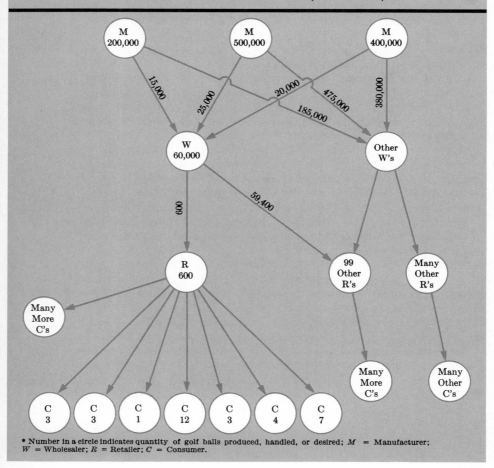

Figure **15–3** *Movement of golf balls from manufacturers to consumers** (*showing discrepancy of quantity produced, handled by wholesalers and retailers, and desired by consumers*)

* Number in a circle indicates quantity of golf balls produced, handled, or desired; *M* = Manufacturer; *W* = Wholesaler; *R* = Retailer; *C* = Consumer.

quantity. It is the job of specialists—wholesalers and retailers—to assemble assortments for their target customers.

The total value of all the golf supplies carried by one retailer may be substantial, yet the inventory of any *particular* item may be small. Such a small quantity seldom would be attractive to a manufacturer, but the

308

retailer's demand for *many* different items might be attractive to wholesalers who have assembled wide assortments from many manufacturers to supply their target market—retailers.

When a wholesaler assembles many orders from his retailers, the quantities he buys from each of his supplier-manufacturers becomes substantial and can represent an economical transaction.

Assembling, by wholesalers and retailers, of an assortment of golf supplies from many manufacturers is shown in Figure 15–4. Manufac-

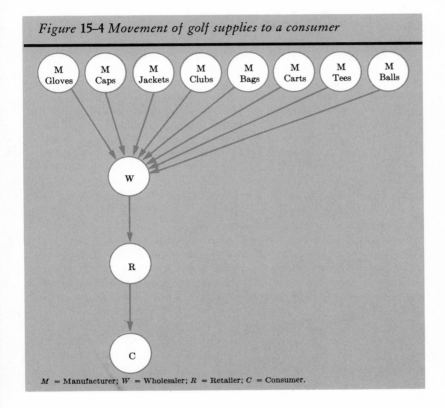

Figure 15–4 *Movement of golf supplies to a consumer*

M = Manufacturer; W = Wholesaler; R = Retailer; C = Consumer.

turers produce large quantities of individual items and then depend upon the wholesale and retail specialists to bring the proper assortments to their own retailer and final consumer customers.

In actual practice, bringing goods to customers is not quite so simple as in this golf example.

A retailer may buy golf supplies from many wholesalers, not just one, especially if they carry different brands. It is likely that both the wholesaler and retailer would carry more than golf supplies. The retailer might be a general sporting goods dealer, carrying golfing items only as a minor part of his line. In addition, there are wholesalers who supply other wholesalers, not retailers. These complications will be discussed later.

The point to remember is that discrepancies in quantity or assortment or both may cause specialists to develop.

Creating and adjusting discrepancies

Quantity discrepancies —cutting costs if possible

Collecting substantial supplies of homogeneous products—the *accumulation process*—creates the first discrepancy of quantity. In a factory, the products that pass inspection are accumulated over a day or a week for shipment in economic lots. In agricultural commodities, specialists (wholesalers) typically accumulate the production of a number of farmers, then ship these products in larger quantities to locations nearer the market.

The accumulation process is commonly practiced to obtain the lowest possible transportation rate by accumulating and shipping goods in truckload or carload lots. Transportation will be discussed in a subsequent chapter, but it should be noted here that the possibility of lowering transportation charges on larger shipments is one important reason for the existence of many marketing specialists.

Small farmers, for instance, seldom produce enough of particular grades or qualities of products to ship at the lowest rate.

Collecting, however, must be done with an eye to the needs of the potential target market because the qualities collected affect subsequent levels. Here, the expanded "total system" mentioned earlier becomes relevant because once collected, the goods may move through several specialists before reaching final consumers.

The Burmese government found it necessary to intervene in the collecting process for rice because farmers and even wholesalers in Burma were mixing different strains of rice to amass quantities large enough for economical handling. The mixing did cut transportation costs, but it caused milling problems—and lowered the quality of the final product.[4]

Once economical quantities have been accumulated and moved closer to potential customers, then *breaking bulk*—the *allocation process*—begins. The homogeneous supply is broken into smaller quantities, since the next level or group of customers have less need for such large quantities. Depending upon the product, wholesalers may sell smaller quantities to other wholesalers or directly to retailers. The retailers continue the allocation process, as they in turn break bulk for their customers. In a sense, the housewife even participates in the allocation process, buying food and serving it in individual portions.

Assortment discrepancies —get the customer what he wants

Discrepancy of assortment can be caused by the necessary process of using established standards to grade the heterogeneous production of farms, mines, forests, and factories into more homogeneous lots. This is called *sorting-out*. The quality control operations of manufacturers are an example of the sorting-out process. So is grading of agricultural products, such as apples, oranges, or wheat, by a grower or wholesaler.

Sorting-out may create assortments that are undesirable but exist

[4] J. C. Abbott, *Marketing Problems and Improvement Programs* (Rome: Food and Agriculture Organization of the United Nations, 1958), p. 188.

310

because of the inherent variability of the production process. These assortments may create additional opportunities or headaches for marketing managers.

There may be headaches if some of the output does not fit into a product line and must be distributed to entirely different target markets than originally aimed for. Minor defects in clothing, tires, appliances, sporting goods, and musical instruments may require the marketing manager to offer them, perhaps at little profit, as "seconds" in regular or even special outlets.

Or assortments may be created deliberately—to create a product line. This approach, called the *assorting process,* is one of putting together a line of heterogeneous products to give a target market what it wants. This usually is done by those closer to the final consumer or user, that is, retailers or wholesalers who are attempting to supply a wide assortment of products for the convenience of their customers.

An electrical goods wholesaler may take on a line of lawnmowers or even garden products for the convenience of his hardware retailer-customers. Even manufacturers participate in the assorting process when they attempt to develop a new product line to satisfy their customers.

The last member of the assorting chain is the final consumer or user, who assembles products from many different sellers—retailers, wholesalers, or manufacturers. Seldom does a single retail or wholesale marketing specialist satisfy all of the needs of final consumers.

Marketing opportunities come from spotting badly handled discrepancies

We have seen that marketing specialists may develop to facilitate exchange and to make adjustments for discrepancies in both quantity and assortment. These discrepancies may result from both the nature of the production process and customer demands. To overcome discrepancies of quantity and assortment, it may be necessary to use "regrouping" activities: accumulation (collecting), allocating (breaking bulk), sorting-out, and assorting (developing assortments). When one or more of these activities is needed, a marketing specialist may develop and fill this need.

Sometimes discrepancies are adjusted badly, especially when there have been rapid shifts in buying habits and preferences. Here, new firms are given a chance to fill these needs. In other cases, "breakthrough" opportunities may occur when some marketing specialist takes a "big picture" view of what he or some other specialists are doing.

A metal wholesaler, for instance, regularly had been supplying aluminum ingots in rather large quantities to aluminum fabricators. His major activity seemed to be adjusting the discrepancy in quantity between the aluminum ingot manufacturer from whom he bought the ingots and his aluminum fabricator customers to whom he sold them. On more careful analysis, he found that some customers were regularly melting down the ingots almost as quickly as he delivered them, while the ingot manufacturer-supplier was having to cool the aluminum to supply it in ingot form.

Since there was no substantial discrepancy of quantity in this case, the wholesaler bought a specially designed truck to haul molten aluminum directly from the ingot manufacturer to the fabricators. This wholesaler saw the "big picture" and developed a unique marketing mix to serve his customers better.

Specialists should develop to adjust discrepancies, if they must be adjusted, but there is no point in having intermediaries just because "that's the way it has always been done." The specialist must provide a real service, as most of them do. But in a dynamic economy, we see the development of new needs and the evaporation of old ones, while some producers and marketing specialists continue offering the same marketing mixes. Clearly, there always is an opportunity for the marketing manager who has an understanding of his customers' needs and how they can best be served.

Developing the channels of distribution

Goods and services do not flow from producers to consumers automatically. They move through channels of distribution where a great deal of marketing work is done. Any sequence of marketing institutions, from producer to final user or consumer, including any number of (or perhaps no) middlemen, is called a *channel of distribution*. A channel of distribution is an example of a larger total system mentioned earlier.

Sometimes a channel system is quite simple (or short), perhaps running directly from a producer to the final user or consumer. Often it is much more complex (or long). In Figure 15–5, four basic channels are presented: (1) direct from manufacturer or producer to consumer or user, (2) to a retailer, (3) through a wholesaler and then a retailer, and (4) through two levels of wholesalers (who provide a different set of marketing functions) to a retailer and then to a final consumer or user. These basic channels are not limited to the United States.

These four channels only suggest the possibilities. Actually, there may be many different kinds of retailers, and they expand the number of possible channels. There are many different kinds of wholesalers, too. Some provide only a few functions, such as promotion or transfer of title, while others actually handle the goods and provide varied services. The many variations of middlemen are discussed in later chapters. Other variations in channels of distribution are possible when manufacturers or producers use their own salesmen, branch warehouses, or retail stores.

Alternate channels may serve different target markets

The many possible variations should not be seen as competitive channels. Each should be considered a separate "possible" channel. A marketing manager may have many different target markets in mind, and this may require him to use several channels at *the same time* to reach the different parts of his market grid. It is important to think of these different channel systems as different entities. Each potentially is part of, and may require, a different marketing mix.

While one channel may be "best" for reaching a particular target market, it also may cater to other markets for which other channels are stronger. If the various channels consist of independent businessmen, it is only logical to expect these men to seek opportunities wherever they can. Yet this can lead to considerable interchannel rivalry. And if it leads to open price warfare, especially on well-known and branded merchandise, considerable ill will can result. The management of competing channels of distribution is a continuing and difficult problem for marketing managers.[5]

The marketing manager and competing channels

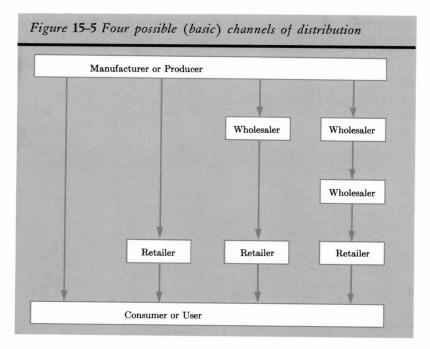

Figure 15–5 Four possible (basic) channels of distribution

The complexity that can develop in actual markets is illustrated in Figures 15–6 through 15–10, involving both consumer and industrial goods. Although these figures may appear somewhat complex, they actually are simplified pictures of what is happening in the real world.

Different channel, different package, same product

Note that each set of lines represents a channel consisting of many individual firms, each with its own peculiarities. Note further, that each of these channels may require a separate marketing mix. Sometimes a manufacturer not only will use a separate sales force for each channel, but supply his product to it, differently packaged, priced, and promoted.

Figure 15–6 shows the 10 separate channels used by one manufacturer of a wide line of wire and cable to reach its various target markets. But note that several channels are aimed at the same target markets. This, as noted, can lead to competitive problems.

---

[5] For more discussion on this point, see Martin R. Warshaw, "Pricing to Gain Wholesalers' Selling Support," *Journal of Marketing,* July, 1962, pp. 50–54.

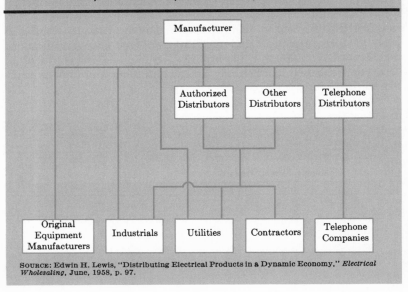

Figure **15–6** *Ten channels and various markets for a manufacturer of a wide line of wire and cable*

SOURCE: Edwin H. Lewis, "Distributing Electrical Products in a Dynamic Economy," *Electrical Wholesaling*, June, 1958, p. 97.

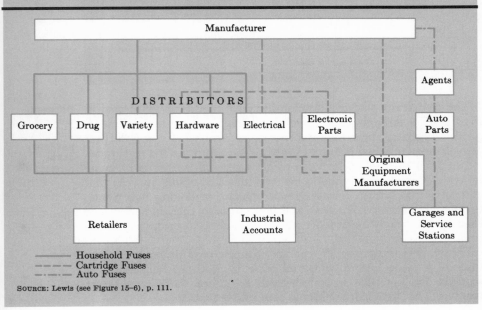

Figure **15–7** *Sales of fuses are made through many kinds of wholesalers*

SOURCE: Lewis (see Figure 15–6), p. 111.

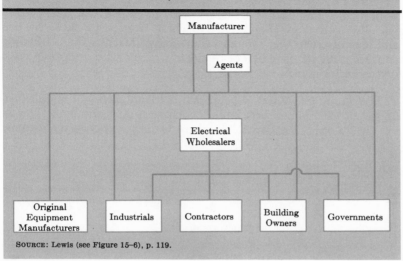

Figure **15–8** *Typical channels of distribution for commercial and industrial fixtures*

SOURCE: Lewis (see Figure 15–6), p. 119.

Figure **15–9** *Typical channels of distribution for residential fixtures*

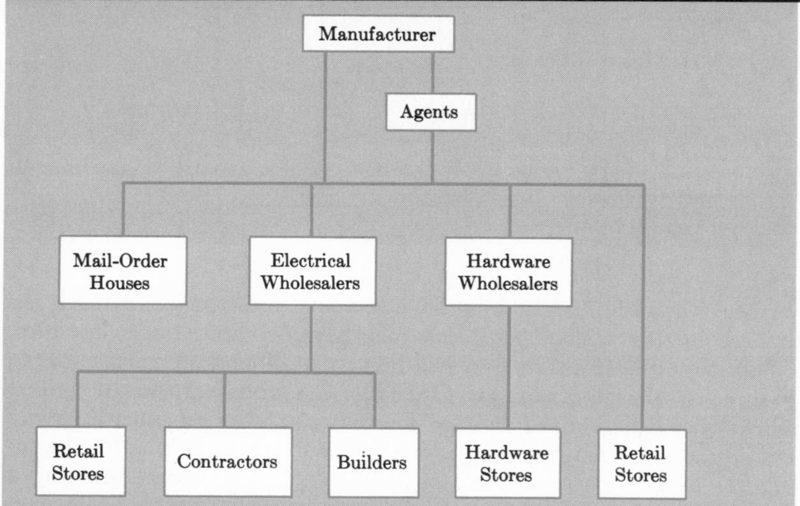

SOURCE: Lewis (see Figure 15–6), p. 119.

Figure 15–7 shows the many channels used by manufacturers of household, cartridge, and auto fuses. It should be noted that household fuses go through grocery, drug, variety, and hardware wholesalers, all of which supply goods to retailers who are accustomed to different

315

gross margins. Among such channels there is a great deal of opportunity for competition, including price competition.

Figure 15–8 and 15–9 show typical channels for the distribution of commercial and industrial lighting fixtures (Figure 15–8), and residential lighting fixtures (Figure 15–9). These fixtures are made by the same manufacturer, yet for the various target markets the marketing manager must set up different channels, perhaps with a separate sales force in each channel.

Sometimes there are no middlemen

These examples seem to suggest that there are plenty of middlemen around to form almost any kind of a channel of distribution. This is not always the case. Sometimes there is only one key middleman

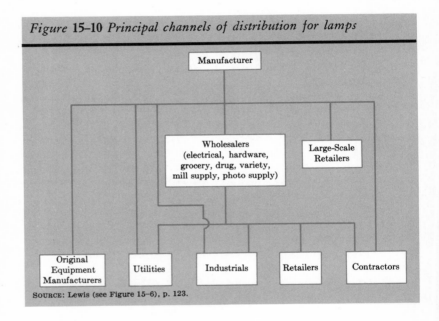

Figure **15–10** *Principal channels of distribution for lamps*

SOURCE: Lewis (see Figure 15–6), p. 123.

serving a market, and he may have a virtual monopoly. To reach the markets he serves, small producers may have no choice but to use him.

Sometimes there are just no middlemen at all, and a producer has to go directly to target customers. One large U.S. apparel maker described this kind of situation as follows: "There is a production super-highway and a retailing super-highway, but a cowpath in between." This manufacturer found it necessary to set up his own retail chain, building a channel directly from producer to the retail level.[6]

This U.S. apparel maker's problem is typical outside the United States, especially when aggressive, marketing-minded middlemen are needed. Such middlemen are scarce in Europe, for example.

Following the Treaty of Rome, which led to the European Common

[6] "Apparel Maker Sets Up Own Discount Chain," *Business Week*, September 16, 1961, pp. 70–75.

Market, many European manufacturers rapidly expanded manufacturing capacity without paying any attention to distribution facilities. Now, many are forced to establish their own controlled retail and wholesale outlets. This may be their only solution for years to come.[7]

Channel system may shift and share functions

Ultimately the channel system must deliver the goods and services desired by the target customers. Regardless of whether the marketing manager uses long or short channels, the channels he does use must provide all the functions of marketing. Some buying and selling are required. Transporting, storing, grading or sorting, financing, and risk taking are necessary in all channels. These functions can be shifted and shared, but not eliminated.

Figure 15–11 shows how the marketing functions were shifted and shared differently in two channels for auto parts. Note in Channel 1 that the manufacturer spent more time and money on marketing and so charged a higher price. But because of the manufacturer's activities the distributor had less to do, and so the price to retailers was the same in Channel 1 as in Channel 2, where the manufacturer's price was lower but the distributor had more to do.

If a manufacturer has been extremely successful in differentiating his product in the minds of customers, there may not be much for other channel members to contribute, and the manufacturer may not have to offer channel members very attractive returns for their efforts. Ford Motor Co., for instance, offered dealers a lower margin on its fast-selling Mustang in 1967 than on other, less popular, models.

Even if a producer takes goods directly to the user, the channel functions are not eliminated. The direct-to-user route may reduce the number of times the functions are performed—but it does not eliminate them, and it may *or may not* reduce the cost.

Passing on distributor's risks to customers

The Carborundum Co. has offered lower prices to its users of large volumes of a single abrasive grinding wheel *if* the customers are willing to assume some of the distributor functions, including carrying inventory. Further, the customer must agree to order a certain annual volume and take deliveries in economical order quantities, thereby reducing production costs. Lower volume business is still serviced through the regular distributors who are geared to perform the marketing functions needed for this kind of business.

Cities are different places

We already have seen the valuable functions performed by central markets and dealers when producers and the potential transactions among them are multiplying. It is only logical that marketing specialists would tend to congregate where they can conveniently serve more customers—in cities. Cities are not all the same, however, and do not

[7] Stewart C. Dalrymple, "Major Pitfalls in Sales and Distribution Methods in the Common Market," *International Trade Review*, January, 1963, pp. 12–13.

Figure 15–11 Shifts in marketing functions—manufacturer vs. distributor

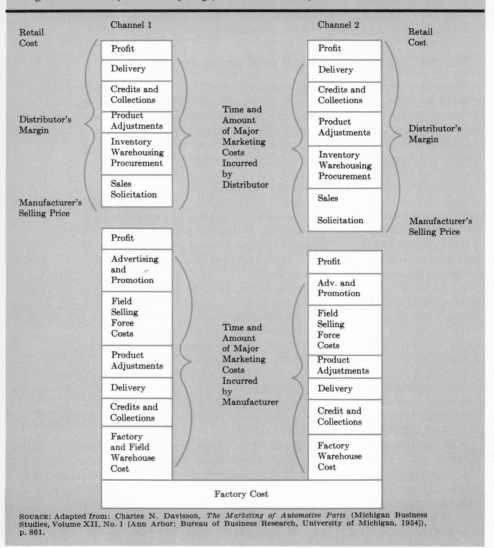

SOURCE: Adapted from: Charles N. Davisson, *The Marketing of Automotive Parts* (Michigan Business Studies, Volume XII, No. 1 [Ann Arbor: Bureau of Business Research, University of Michigan, 1954]), p. 861.

play the same kind of role in marketing. And we do *not* find marketing specialists evenly distributed purely on the basis of population. This fact is of importance to any marketing manager who must work with and through specialists.

An understanding of the role of cities is extremely important to the marketing manager because these roles may be changing in the future. For example, what will happen when computers can talk to computers and handle the buying and selling functions automatically? And what will happen when salesmen can call on customers with Phone-vision?

Will we need the kinds of cities we have now with their towers of offices and square blocks of warehouses? After seeing what cities do, perhaps you can decide what the future city will look like.

Retailing and service operations are important functions of many cities. But none of the world's major cities has grown large purely as a retail or personal service center. Most retail business is a service to the people who live and work in the community.[8]

What do the cities do—and where?

Basic employment is fundamental to the growth of cities. It is employment in activities that serve people outside the local community, and therefore is a kind of "export." Through basic employment, the city earns the revenue to pay for its "imports" from other areas. Detroit builds automobiles for customers throughout the world. Some are produced for Detroit residents, but only the cars sold outside of Detroit contribute to *basic* employment.

The remainder of the work done in the city is *service employment*—that is, "taking in each other's washing." But this service employment is not trivial. In most American cities, about three persons are employed in service industries for every two persons engaged in basic employment.

The major contributors to city growth are commerce and manufacturing. The term *commerce* refers to all the activities of trade between regions, including transportation, warehousing, wholesaling, and financing. The term *manufacturing* means factory production.

Commerce not only causes the major growth of cities but also attracts manufacturing. As a country's economy becomes more interdependent and trade becomes more important, greater volumes of goods must be traded in and through these cities. A commercial city might even grow rapidly without the added stimulus of manufacturing growth.

San Francisco is a good example of a U.S. city that is largely based on commerce. It services the far western part of the United States. As the volume of goods handled has increased, the San Francisco metropolitan area has grown at a much faster rate than the total population in the region it serves. Other examples of such cities include New Orleans, Chicago, Philadelphia, New York, London, Hamburg, Rotterdam, Amsterdam, Tokyo-Yokohama, and Manila.

By contrast, cities that are chiefly noncommercial—including smaller manufacturing towns and rural trading centers—generally have reached a certain size, then stopped growing. Their size depends on the growth and health of the particular manufacturers who happen to locate there, or the number and prosperity of farmers in the immediate trading area.

As the larger cities become more efficient at commerce, the growing

---

[8] The following discussion is based on Richard L. Nelson, *The Selection of Retail Locations* (New York: F. W. Dodge Corp., 1958), pp. 5–18; see also, Percy Johnson-Marshall, *Rebuilding Cities* (Chicago: Aldine Publishing Co., 1966), pp. 374; Morris L. Sweet, "History of Municipal Markets," *Journal of Housing,* June, 1961; Morris L. Sweet and Finn B. Jensen, "The Planned Community," *National Civic Review,* May, 1962, pp. 251–56; Raymond Vernon, *The Changing Economic Function of the Central City,* January, 1959; and Robert C. Wood, *Metropolis Against Itself* (New York: Committee for Economic Development, March, 1959).

interdependence of the economy actually may decrease the regrouping activities provided by the noncommercial areas. Remember that the advantage of dealers in central markets grows as the size of the market increases.

Kinds of cities

The marketing manager should recognize the qualitative differences among cities because marketing facilities and institutions differ from city to city. The following breakdown of U.S. cities into four basic types explains some of these differences more specifically:

1. The big commercial city, called "Commerce City."
2. The industrial city, called "Centertown."
3. The rural trading center, called "Countyville."
4. The dormitory suburb, called "Forest Lake."[9]

Most cities fit into one of these categories or are making a transition from one to another. The marketing manager should look for such transitions, for it is during this stage that present institutions may become inadequate to meet marketing needs. Note these city types carefully because they will be referred to later in our discussion of specific retailing and wholesaling institutions.

Commerce City

Most Commerce Cities have a population exceeding a half million and are located at transportation centers and on waterways. In Commerce Cities, wholesaling, warehousing, finance, and transportation usually are more important activities than manufacturing as the source of basic employment.

Often the downtown district has grown up along a river, lake, or ocean because the early development of the city depended upon the use of the waterfront. Expansion since that time has fanned out from the downtown area. Today the city, surrounded by suburbs, has difficulty expanding geographically.

The population of the city itself may have ceased to grow because of lack of room, but the dormitory suburbs in the city's metropolitan area are expanding rapidly. The suburban areas that first developed by stringing out along the railroads, now are beginning to fill between the rail lines as population grows and as automobiles and superhighways make commuting more acceptable to more people.

Nearly all highways and railroads radiate from the city center, a downtown area with multistoried department stores, tall office buildings, and well-defined sub-areas, such as financial, retailing, and entertainment sections.

On the major streets leading out from the downtown area are a number of large shopping districts, perhaps centered about one or two large department stores that are branches of the big stores downtown. Throughout the city, along major streets, there are strips of stores selling convenience-type goods in the grocery, drug, hardware, and liquor categories. A series of these stores may be repeated every three or

[9] Nelson, *op. cit.,* pp. 5–18.

four blocks, or in densely populated areas they may line solidly along the major business streets. Out in the suburbs, there are large shopping centers.

Commerce Cities usually have large warehouses and extensive shipping facilities, both rail and truck, and sometimes barge or ship. They are also the headquarters for large corporations with their buying offices. As noted already, this makes it convenient for sellers to reach many important buyers. There are large advertising agencies, banks, management consultants, and others providing services in these cities. Commerce Cities often are the homes of large distribution centers for the major mail-order companies. They may also be the homes of important dealer branders, who maintain their central offices and warehouses there.

Large manufacturers may find it desirable to maintain substantial warehouses in Commerce Cities rather than in the more numerous Centertowns because this enables them to reduce their total inventory. More is said on this later, but for now, note that centralization of marketing facilities often provides economies similar to those provided by centralized, mass production factories. This centralization of marketing activities takes place in Commerce Cities.

Centertown is likely to be a manufacturing-oriented community. It is called Centertown because most of the activities are in the center of the town. The downtown area is a concentration of stores and service facilities. In a larger Centertown, the downtown stores may emphasize shopping goods, while the downtowns of smaller Centertowns will consist of stores selling both convenience and shopping goods. **Centertown**

Sometimes the retail facilities are concentrated together in one or two blocks, but frequently they are wedged in among other service and political facilities. And even industrial suppliers for local industry may be found downtown.

In one study of Centertowns, more than 20 percent of the cities studied had a downtown street called "Main Street." It was or still is the main street through town, although there is a tendency for state and federal highways to avoid Main Street in favor of a faster, safer bypass. The retail stores usually originated at the intersection of Main Street and the railroad, or at the intersection of an important crossroad. But as newer buildings have been built, the center of downtown has often moved a little farther out along the main street, generally toward the area of largest population growth.

The outward growth most often takes the form of subdivisions similar to the suburbs of Commerce Cities. But these areas have few, if any, shopping facilities of their own, except perhaps stores carrying convenience goods. The major retail shopping facilities are downtown, including the majority of stores carrying shopping goods and specialty goods. But in some of the larger Centertowns, outlying discount stores and shopping centers are developing.

Depending on the proximity of Commerce Cities, there may be some wholesale and commercial facilities in Centertown. But the emphasis is on manufacturing (or education, medical facilities, or some other

321

noncommercial activity), and goods may be shipped directly to Commerce Cities for regrouping activities.

Countyville Countyville is a small, rural trading center. It frequently is built around a courthouse square or along a railroad. There usually is no suburban shopping center of any kind, and usually the majority of the commercial buildings are old and obsolete by modern retailing standards. There may be some limited shopping-goods facilities, depending upon the proximity to a Centertown or Commerce City.

The major function of a Countyville is to serve the agricultural market. Its role as an agricultural market may include the accumulation of enough volume of farm products from the region to achieve the most economical transportation rate and permit the commodities to be handled as a standard unit in subsequent markets. For example, the common unit in the wheat market is a rail carload.

If the Countyville middlemen who sell to farmers do a good job, they need not fear competition from Centertown businesses, which are oriented more toward manufacturing. The same may be true for those who buy the farmers' output.

But with the decline in the number of small farmers, many Countyvilles are having difficulties. The larger farmers who are becoming more important in U.S. agriculture may be able to deal directly with buyers in Commerce Cities or may make contracts with manufacturers either in Countyvilles or Centertowns. They also may search farther for their supplies. And as more farm families have money and can take superhighways into distant cities, the limited shopping-goods retail facilities in these towns are having troubles.

Forest Lake Forest Lake is a dormitory suburb. Most people who live in this suburb work in Commerce City. Many commute by train or car, via high-speed highways. The majority of retail stores sell convenience goods, and there is little or no wholesaling or other commercial activity.

Many suburban towns are overgrown rural trading centers which happened to be within convenient commuting distance of large cities. The majority of residents do their buying of shopping goods and specialty goods in Commerce City or in the large outlying shopping centers that are developing to serve several Forest Lakes.[10]

Conclusion

This chapter has discussed the role of Place in an economic system. The development of a satisfactory product provides *form* utility, but this is of little value unless it is combined with *time* and *place* utility to permit *possession* utility.

Possession utility can be achieved only when products are exchanged—usually in markets. We found that markets and marketing

---

[10] For a discussion of wholly new cities, both suburban cities and "total cities," see "Where City Planners Come Down to Earth, and Master Builder with a New Concept," *Business Week,* August 20, 1966, pp. 101–10.

specialists facilitate exchange and help adjust discrepancies of quantity and assortment.

Discrepancies of quantity occur when there is a difference between the quantity produced by individual producers and the quality demanded by individual customers. They also occur when the output of many small producers, especially farmers, must be accumulated to obtain the most economical transportation rate.

Discrepancies of assortment occur because producers tend to specialize in a few products although individual customers want variety. One of the roles of marketing is to help match these differences between supply and demand.

The combination of a number of marketing specialists to move goods from producers to final users or consumers is called a channel of distribution. Many different channels are possible—in fact, each target market may require a slightly different one. All channels must provide the same basic functions, though channels may shift and share the functions differently.

Finally, we discussed the kinds of cities where marketing specialists develop and work. The roles of these city types are important in marketing mix planning. Some marketing specialists are more likely to congregate in certain types of cities, while in others, adequate marketing specialists may not be available. This may provide an opportunity for a marketing manager to offer a unique marketing mix to his target markets.

---

1 Explain the differences among time, place, and possession utility. For the following products describe the kinds of business effort required to provide these utilities and the nature of business firms which could provide them (describe these firms in general—do not try to name specific types): **Questions and problems**
   a) Beefsteaks.
   b) Men's shoes.
   c) A drill press (for industry).
   d) A diamond ring.
2 Describe what the economic organization of your college town or city would be like if there were no organizations specializing in providing place utility (that is, explain the kind of economic activities in which each of the members of the community would participate).
3 Explain "discrepancies of quantity and assortment" using the clothing business as an example. How does the application of the concept of discrepancies change when coal for sale to the steel industry is considered rather than clothing? What impact does this have on the number and kinds of marketing specialists required?
4 Explain the four steps in the regrouping process with an example drawn from the building supply industry (nails, paint, flooring, plumbing fixtures, etc.). Would you expect many specialists to develop in this industry or would the manufacturers handle the job themselves? What

kind of marketing channels would you expect to find in this industry and what functions would be provided by various channel members?

5 Distinguish between channels of distribution and middlemen.

6 Why are there so many channels of distribution for electrical goods? Would you expect so many different channels in the sale of a perishable agricultural product like oranges? Why, or why not?

7 If a manufacturer has five different markets to reach, how many channels is he likely to use? If only one, why? If more than one, what sort of problems will this raise?

8 Why have Commerce Cities tended to grow more rapidly than the country as a whole? Is this trend likely to continue? Why, or why not?

9 Many Countyvilles and Forest Lakes are of approximately the same size. Which of these two would be a better market? For what kinds of goods?

Place objectives and policies

The critical Place questions are: How much market exposure is needed? And how should it be provided?

The marketing manager must develop Place policies to answer these questions. It is his job to see that the "right" Product reaches the "right" Place. As a guide in setting these policies, he must consider his Place objectives—the kind of distribution he would consider ideal. Place objectives should be based on customer preferences. They are closely related to the goods classifications discussed in Chapters 12 and 13.

In this chapter, we will discuss Place objectives and the basic Place policies that marketers must determine to accomplish these objectives. Here, we will be concerned primarily with the "ideal" channel or channels to reach the selected target markets—*the Place combination that will completely satisfy target customers.*

In concept, such an ideal channel is strictly customer-oriented. But the realities of costs and market conditions may cause the marketing manager to settle for something other than the ideal. Ultimately, he will select the "best" channel available to him—the one that comes closest to the "ideal", fits the entire marketing mix, and still satisfies the company's overall objectives. We will defer discussion of the development and management of channel systems until Chapter 20, when we will know more about the marketing specialists who might be part of a channel system.

Figure 16–1 Place objectives

CONSUMER GOODS

1. *Convenience Goods*
   a) *Staples*—need maximum exposure—need widespread distribution at low cost.
   b) *Impulse goods*—need maximum exposure—need widespread distribution but with assurance of preferred display or counter position.
   c) *Emergency goods*—need widespread distribution near probable point of use.

2. *Shopping Goods*
   a) *Homogeneous*—need enough exposure to facilitate price comparison.
   b) *Heterogeneous*—need adequate representation in major shopping districts or large shopping centers near other, similar shopping goods.

3. *Specialty Goods*—can have limited availability, but in general should be treated as a convenience or shopping good (in whichever category product would normally be included), to reach persons not yet sold on its specialty-goods status.

4. *Unsought Goods*—need attention directed to product and aggressive promotion in outlets—or must be available in places where similar products would be sought.

INDUSTRIAL GOODS

1. *Installations*
   a) *Buildings (used) and land rights*—need widespread and/or knowledgeable contacts, depending upon specialized nature of product.

Developing place objectives

All detailed objectives, including Place objectives, should be compatible with the company's overall objectives. And, of course, all four P's of the marketing mix must work together. This need for compatibility of the components in a marketing system is really an aid rather than an obstacle, however, especially when developing Place.

When we have selected some potential target markets, it is likely that these customers have similar attitudes toward our product or products. The goods classifications summarize our judgment on the nature of the product, including what the target customers think of it, their willingness to shop for it, and the amount of service desired.

These factors all have a bearing on the ideal Place objectives. The Place facilities we ideally should supply are related to customers' needs and preferences. For example, if some target customers think of several different grocery products as staples, it follows that Place should be handled similarly for all of them.

Figure 16–1 suggests ideal Place objectives for our consumer and industrial goods classifications. These ideal objectives are based on the

326

Figure 16-1—Continued

---

b) Buildings (new)—need technical and experienced personal contact, probably at top-management level (multiple buying influence).

c) Major equipment

1. *Custom-made*—need technical (design) contacts by man able to visualize and design applications, and present to high-level and technical management.
2. *Standard*—need experienced (not necessarily highly technical) contacts by man able to visualize applications and present to high-level and technical management.

2. *Accessory Equipment*—needs fairly widespread and numerous contacts by experienced and sometimes technically trained personnel.

3. *Raw Materials*

   a) Farm products—need contacts with many small farmer producers and fairly widespread contact with users.

   b) Natural products—need fairly widespread contacts with users.

4. *Component Parts and Materials*—need technical contacts to determine specifications required—widespread contacts usually not necessary.

5. *Supplies*

   a) Maintenance—need very widespread distribution for prompt delivery.

   b) Repairs—need widespread distribution for some, and prompt service from factory for others (depends on customers' preferences).

   c) Operating supplies—need fair to widespread distribution for prompt delivery.

6. *Services*—most need very widespread availability.

---

interaction of customer behavior and the nature of the products. Before studying this figure—and it should be studied carefully—it will be fruitful to consider what constitutes ideal Place facilities for each type of product.

Place objectives should be studied carefully, since they set the framework for developing the whole Place setup. But remember that different target markets' differing views of the same physical product can influence the development of Place. If some target customers think of a particular appliance as an heterogeneous shopping good, there is no need for the marketing manager to distribute in every store in the country. It would be enough to distribute where other shopping goods are displayed, because the target customers buying these are willing to shop around. Yet if the same appliance was an impulse good to other target markets, more outlets should be sought, particularly ones that would give preferred display positions.

Several place objectives may be ideal for appliances

Just as there are no automatic classifications of products, we cannot automatically determine the best Place arrangement. Place selection

327

depends on what customers like best and what various channel members can provide profitably.

Channel captain needed to guide place policy setting

Until now, we have considered the individual marketing manager as the integrating force in marketing planning. But now we see that there may be several firms and managers in a single distribution channel. If we follow the systems concept, we see that each *channel* should act as a unit, directed by someone we can call a "channel captain." The question is, which marketing manager should be the captain?

The concept of a single channel captain is useful, but we must recognize that some channels may not have an acknowledged captain, since the various firms are not acting as a system. The reason may be lack of leadership or lack of understanding that members of the system are interrelated. Many businessmen, more concerned with those firms immediately above and below them, seem almost unaware that they are part of a channel.[1]

But, like it or not, firms are interrelated, even if poorly, by their policies, and it would seem to make a lot more economic sense to make a whole channel work efficiently.

It should be remembered, however, that the role of channel captain is earned by leadership and market power, not by the fiat of an ambitious businessman.

In the middle and on top

In the United States, manufacturers frequently take the initiative in setting Place policies that affect channel relations. Middlemen (specialists) wait to see what the manufacturer intends to do and what he wants done. After the manufacturer sets his pricing, promotion, and place policies, the middlemen decide whether their roles will be profitable and whether they want to participate in the manufacturer's plans. Middlemen may not play an active role in the channel building, but they must be considered by manufacturers in their planning, if only because they (middlemen) have the power to say no. The marketing mix offered to them must be appealing if they are to become active members of the channel team.

There are large or strategically located middlemen who do take the initiative, especially in foreign markets where there are fewer large manufacturers. Such middlemen may determine the types of products their customers want and then seek out manufacturers—perhaps small ones—who can provide products at reasonable prices.

Such middlemen may develop their own dealer brands. Or they may handle manufacturers' brands, but on their own terms. These strong middlemen can even become, in effect, manufacturers. They specify the whole marketing mix for a product and merely delegate production to a factory.

---

[1] Phillip McVey, "Are Channels of Distribution What the Textbooks Say?" *Journal of Marketing,* January, 1960, pp. 61–65.

Large middlemen are closer to the final user or consumer and are in an ideal position to assume the channel captain role. Some students of marketing have even suggested that middlemen, especially retailers, may dominate the marketing structure of the future.[2]

We cannot overemphasize the importance of a whole channel system viewing itself in competition with other systems. Without this self-conception by members of the channel, one firm might adopt policies that clearly would be unfavorable to another member of his own system. In the short run, a stronger firm might succeed in forcing its policies by sheer weight of market power. Yet in the long run this might lead to the failure, not only of a weaker channel member but of the whole team.

Our captain, the producer

A good example of how *not* to act as channel captain is the manufacturer who loads his retailers with excessive inventory. He may make money in the short run, but he will not be welcomed back by the overloaded firms.

Clearly, the person or firm that helps direct an integrated system of action is the leader. We will consider him our channel captain. His identity may change from time to time—depending on the success of product development or promotional programs, financial reserves, and management personalities—but this does not change the concept or its impact on marketing.

For convenience, we will assume in the following discussion that the channel captain is a producer. Remember, though, that a middleman may play this role too.[3]

Need for place policies

The "ideal" Place system does not happen automatically. Place objectives are suggestive of what the system should be. But then someone must make specific decisions about how many middlemen, if any, should be in a geographic area and how the various marketing facilities should be linked together. These basic, almost strategic, decisions are the subject of the balance of this chapter. Manufacturers, wholesalers, and retailers must be concerned with Place policies, even if they are made by someone else in their channel system. Inevitably they are part of a channel system that must compete with other channel systems.

---

[2] David R. Craig and Werner K. Gabler, "The Competitive Struggle for Market Control," reprinted from *Annals of the American Academy of Political and Social Science,* May, 1940, pp. 84 ff., in J. H. Westing, *Readings in Marketing* (New York: Prentice-Hall, Inc., 1953), pp. 46–57; and Donald F. Dixon, "The Emergence of Marketing Systems," in G. Fisk and D. F. Dixon, *Theories for Marketing System Analysis* (New York: Harper & Row, Publishers, 1967), pp. 61–65.

[3] For further discussion on the idea of channel control, see Louis W. Stern, "The Concept of Channel Control," *Journal of Retailing,* Summer, 1967, pp. 14–20 f.; Bruce Mallen, "Conflict and Cooperation in Marketing Channels," in L. G. Smith (ed.), *Reflections on Progress in Marketing* (Chicago: American Marketing Association, 1965), pp. 65–85; and Valentine P. Ridgeway, "Administration of Manufacturer-Dealer Systems," in S. C. Hollander (ed.), *Explorations in Retailing* (East Lansing: Michigan State University Bureau of Business and Economic Research, 1959), pp. 250 ff.

Determining degree of market exposure

Although it might seem that all marketing managers would want their products to have maximum exposure to potential customers, we have seen in our earlier discussion of place objectives that while some products need widespread distribution, others need only limited distribution. What degree of market exposure should be sought?

Generally, the ideal market exposure should meet target customers' needs and preferences but not exceed them. Excessive exposure would merely increase the number and kinds of outlets, the work involved, and probably the total marketing cost.

We will discuss three degrees of market exposure: *intensive distribution, selective distribution,* and *exclusive distribution.* As we move from intensive to exclusive distribution, we give up exposure in return for some other advantage—including, but not limited to, cost reduction.

Intensive distribution is the sale of a product through any responsible and suitable wholesaler or retailer who will stock and/or sell the product. *Selective distribution,* as the name implies, refers to the choice or selection of only those middlemen who will do a good job with the product. *Exclusive distribution* is the choice of only one middleman in a particular geographical area.

In practice, this means that cigarettes are handled, through *intensive distribution,* by at least a million U.S. outlets, while Rolls Royces or expensive chinaware products are handled through *exclusive distribution,* by only a limited number of middlemen across the country.

A more detailed explanation of each of the three degrees of market exposure will clarify the differences.

Intensive distribution —sell it where they buy it

Intensive distribution is commonly needed for convenience goods and for industrial supplies—such as pencils, paper clips, and typing paper—used by all plants or offices.

Manufacturers of "new" unsought goods that must compete with convenience goods would like to achieve intensive distribution. They may not be able to get this degree of exposure because customers aren't demanding their products, and the channel consequently isn't willing to carry them; nevertheless, these manufacturers have an intensive distribution policy.

The manufacturer's intent is important here. Intensive distribution refers to the *desire* to sell through *all* responsible and suitable outlets. What this means depends on customer habits and preferences. If target customers normally buy a certain product at a certain type of outlet, then ideally we would specify this type of outlet in one of our Place policies. If customers prefer to buy hardware items only at hardware stores, we would solicit all hardware stores to achieve intensive distribution. But if, as it seems today, many customers will buy certain hardware items at any convenient outlet, including drugstores and food stores, an intensive distribution policy logically requires use of these outlets—using more than one channel to reach one target market.

Selective distribution covers the broad band of market exposure

330

between intensive and exclusive distribution. It may be suitable for all categories of products. Only the better middlemen, chosen on some predetermined basis, are used here. The usual purpose in going to selective distribution is to gain some of the advantages of exclusive distribution while still achieving adequate market coverage. **Selective distribution —sell it where it sells best**

A selective policy might be used to avoid selling to wholesalers or retailers who (1) have a poor credit rating, (2) have a reputation for making too many returns or requesting too much service, (3) place orders that are too small to justify making calls or providing service, or (4) are not in position, for any other reason, to do a satisfactory marketing job.

Selective distribution is growing in popularity over intensive distribution as firms decide it no longer is true that a company must obtain 100 percent coverage of the market in order to justify or "support" national advertising. A study by one company, for instance, showed that 41 percent of its wholesaler customers accounted for only 7 percent of its sales. These clearly were unprofitable customers to serve. Most of them gradually were dropped, and after four years of aggressively cultivating the remaining customers, sales increased 76 percent. Marketing expenses were reduced from 22.8 to 11.5 percent of this larger sales volume, and a net loss of 2.9 percent on sales was converted into a net profit of 15 percent.[4]

Selective distribution may produce greater profits for all channel members because of the closer cooperation among them. Here, the systems concept is relevant. Transactions become more routine, requiring less negotiation in the buying and selling process. Wholesalers and retailers may be more willing to give aggressive promotion to products if they know they are going to obtain the majority of sales produced through their own efforts. They may carry deeper stocks, wider lines, do more promotion, and provide more service, all of which contribute to increased sales.

Selective distribution may be appropriate for shopping and specialty goods, and for those industrial goods that require special effort from channel members. If the channel captain selects only "good" members for his team, this reduces interchannel competition and gives each of the members a greater opportunity to profit if they do a good job.

When selective distribution is used by manufacturers, fewer sales contacts have to be made, and fewer wholesalers may be needed. In fact, as in the garment industry, a manufacturer may be able to contact retailers directly if he uses selective distribution.

In the early part of the life cycle of a new unsought good, the marketing manager may have to use selective distribution to encourage enough distributors to handle his product. He wants to get his product out of the unsought category as soon as possible, but he can't as long as it lacks distribution. Well-known middlemen may have the prestige to get the product introduced—but perhaps on their own terms, which often includes limiting the number of competing outlets.

---

[4] Charles H. Sevin, *How Manufacturers Reduce Their Distribution Costs* (Economic Series No. 72 [Washington, D.C.: U.S. Government Printing Office, 1948]), p. 13. This text presents a large number of case studies showing similar results.

Exclusive distribution arrangements usually entail a verbal or written agreement stating that the channel members will buy all or most of a given kind of product or product line from a particular firm. In return, these middlemen are granted the exclusive rights to that product in their territory. Many dealers are so anxious to get a manufacturer's exclusive franchise that they will do practically anything to satisfy the manufacturer's demands. In effect, the dealer becomes a part of the manufacturer's organization. The dealer supplies the capital and local management, but the major policy decisions are made by the manufacturer.[5]

Exclusive distribution may be satisfactory for some shopping goods and the more expensive specialty goods. It also may be practical for many industrial products—including installations, larger accessory equipment, some raw materials, and component materials—that have limited markets and require special selling effort. When a middleman has a monopoly in an area, he is more likely to sell aggressively when he knows all the fruits of his efforts will come to him.

Exclusive distribution is especially useful when it is necessary for middlemen to carry large inventories to provide adequate service, as in sales of industrial machines, major household appliances, and some lines of men's suits. It also may be useful when extensive installation or repair services are needed, as in sales of automobiles and heating equipment.

Unsought-goods manufacturers may have to adopt an exclusive distribution policy if they cannot get distribution without granting exclusive rights to some middlemen. This must be done with care, however, especially if the product should have wider distribution. All the channel members should thoroughly understand the arrangement, and how long it will last. An exclusive middleman may agree to help move his product through the introductory stage only if attractive terms are offered, knowing that when the product has achieved greater customer acceptance, the producer will change to a selective or intensive distribution policy.

Exclusive distribution sometimes is used as a device to help control prices in a channel. For years, Magnavox Corp. maintained its list prices and high standards by selling only through 3,000 exclusive franchise dealers, but according to its own president, lost "tens of millions of dollars" by making it too difficult for potential customers to buy its product. To stop this loss, Magnavox relaxed its exclusive distribution policy and offered its products through Singer Sewing Machine centers as well.[6]

Exclusive distribution also may help to build a channel team. A producer is assured of reliable contact with target customers; this protects the goodwill developed by his advertising and product quality control. Since the producer using exclusive distributors doesn't have to

[5] For a good discussion of exclusive dealing, see K. J. Curran, "Exclusive Dealing and Public Policy," *Journal of Marketing,* October, 1950, pp. 133–44; and Leonard J. Konopa, "Exclusive Dealing Arrangements in Marketing," Michigan State University *Business Topics,* Summer, 1964, pp. 63–72.

[6] *Advertising Age,* May 6, 1963, p. 26.

do as much aggressive selling in the channels, his selling expenses are cut, and this permits more emphasis on assisting the exclusive middlemen. Furthermore, the producer using exclusive distribution can expect better feedback to aid his planning and control. And these assured outlets also protect the producer against the activities of competitors, at least in "his" outlets, because the exclusive arrangement bars those outlets to his competition.

Marketing managers must operate within the law, and any consideration of Place must raise the question of the legality of limiting market exposure. **But is it legal?**

Exclusive distribution, per se, is not illegal. But current interpretation of the various anti-monopoly laws gives the impression that almost any exclusive-dealing arrangement could be interpreted as an injury to some competitor somewhere. In 1967, for example, the U.S. Supreme Court decided that a franchise system used by Sealy Mattress was illegal because it tended to restrict competition.

It is also possible that the auto manufacturers' dealer structures may break down. Agreements among automobile dealers in larger metropolitan areas have already been declared illegal by a Supreme Court decision in 1966.[7]

As of 1966, the chief of the Antitrust Division of the U.S. Department of Justice saw only two justifications for giving dealers exclusive territories—the introduction of a new product or a new company's entry into a market. He added that these arrangements should be limited to, perhaps, less than three years.[8] Until the situation is clarified, it would appear that companies should be cautious about entering into exclusive dealing arrangements. The same would apply to selective distribution, only here less formal and binding arrangements are typical and the possible impact on competition more remote.

We have related the ideal market exposure to our goods classifications, but the exposure needed is also related to the degree of brand preference achieved by product and promotion efforts. If a product has attained only the brand recognition stage, it probably should be distributed as widely as consistent with its goods classification. Potential customers obviously won't search for it. **When to cater to the lowest common denominator**

When a product reaches the brand preference stage, more thought can be given to selective distribution, although this degree of buyer interest still cannot override the goods classification. But if selective distribution were indicated before, perhaps an even more selective policy would be possible now.

Finally, when the brand insistence stage is reached, selective distribution and perhaps even exclusive distribution become feasible.

Even though a product seems to have achieved the brand insistence

[7] "Are Supermarkets for Autos Next?" *Business Week,* May 7, 1966, p. 33; "Is the Franchise System Legal?" *Business Week,* April 3, 1965, pp. 66–68; "High Court Hits Sealy-Schwinn Franchise Plans," *Advertising Age,* June 19, 1967, pp. 1 ff.

[8] *Business Week,* July 2, 1966, p. 30.

stage with present target customers, the marketing manager still may not go all the way to exclusive distribution because new potential customers may be coming into the market all the time. In terms of the market grid concept, we can say that some target customers may insist on the brand, while others have not yet reached the brand recognition stage. In such situations, marketing managers probably would prefer to cater to the lowest common denominator—those who have not yet learned to recognize the brand.

An exclusive distribution policy (or an extremely selective one) usually is chosen for other reasons besides the level of brand preference. The aim may be to control price or to achieve a greater selling effort, but the degree of brand preference achieved cannot be neglected.

Determining type of channel system

Besides deciding how much market exposure he would like, a marketing manager also must decide which type of distribution system he will use to reach the various target markets. Two basic decisions are involved: (1) Should the firm go directly to the final user or consumer, or indirectly through specialists? (2) If the indirect method is used, should the members of the channel system be entirely independent or should some effort be made to integrate the system's efforts?

Direct channel systems

Many producers would prefer to handle the whole distribution job themselves. Perhaps they are yielding to a desire to control large organizations or perhaps it is simply a case of, "If you want a job done right, do it yourself." In any event, there are genuine advantages in selling directly to the final user or consumer.

When the producer is close to his target customers, marketing research is easier. He is more sensitive to changes in customer attitudes and preferences and is in a better position to promptly adjust his marketing mix. If aggressive selling effort or special technical service are needed, he can be sure that his sales force receives the necessary training and motivation.

Naturally short channels. Some products typically have short channels of distribution, and a direct-to-user channel is not surprising. For example, many industrial products are sold to a relatively few target customers, making a direct channel system logical. Or if the product is "used up" by the first customers, as in the case of machinery, or if it otherwise loses its identity so that no marketing effort is needed farther along in the channel, then a direct channel system may be sensible.

The typical channels used for various kinds of products are discussed and explained in Chapter 20; we will not elaborate on them here. The important point here is that a direct manufacturer-to-final-user channel is typical for some products in certain situations. It is not always necessary to use middlemen.

Corporate integration of typically longer channel systems. Some channels typically contain several firms, but we also find integrated firms developing full-channel systems. With corporate ownership

334

ranged all along the channel, we can say that the firm is going direct, but actually it may be handling manufacturing, wholesaling, *and* retailing. This is more activity than usually is implied when we refer to direct distribution.

We will treat integration extensively here because of its impact, not only on the type of channel systems used but also on the degree of market exposure. Vertical integration, in particular, may make it possible to avoid the legal problems entailed in exclusive distribution arrangements.

Integration usually refers to purchasing other firms, though a company can reach the same goal through internal expansion. Internal expansion is less likely to bring about government intervention because it is controlled only by anti-monopoly laws, while integration by acquisition is subject to specific anti-merger legislation. There has been considerable government restrictive and punitive activity in this area in recent years.

At first, it might seem that horizontal integration—the acquisition of firms at the same level of activity—would have little to do with channels of distribution, usually depicted as vertical. But discrepancies of quantity and assortment must be considered, too, and it is for these reasons that horizontal integration might make sense.

To integrate vertically, a firm might have to integrate horizontally or expand its horizontal operations by internal expansion. Woolworth's, Kresge's, A&P, National Tea Co., Safeway Stores, Kroger, Florsheim Shoes, Genesco, and J. C. Penney have expanded or integrated horizontally at the retail level. General Motors Corp. and U.S. Steel Corp. are integrated horizontally at the producer level.[9]

In vertical integration, control is expanded to two or more successive stages of production or distribution. A retailer might go into wholesaling and perhaps even manufacturing. Some companies are integrated both horizontally and vertically. A&P, Kroger, Genesco, Florsheim Shoes, and J. C. Penney are wholesalers or manufacturers as well as retailers. A&P, for example, has fish-canning plants. Genesco and Florsheim make their own shoes, and J. C. Penney controls textile plants. Firestone Tire and Rubber Co. has rubber plantations in Liberia, tire plants in Akron, Ohio, and Firestone label wholesale and retail outlets all over the United States.

There are many advantages to vertical integration, such as stability of operations, assurance of materials and supplies, better control of distribution, better quality control of products, an opportunity for larger research facilities, greater buying power, and reduction in executive overhead expense.

The economies of vertical integration may benefit the consumer, too, through lower prices and better products. Vertical integration brings smooth, routine operation of the traditional marketing functions and can cut costs. The business transactions that once required negotiations

---

[9] "How Far Can a Producer Retail?" *Business Week,* January 21, 1961, pp. 77–84; and *Time,* November 23, 1962, p. 76.

between separate firms now are routine requisitions, acknowledgements, and internal accounting transactions.

In conclusion, we can see that vertical integration is a method for assuring formal exclusive arrangements. Provided that the discrepancy of quantity and assortment is not too great at each level in a channel—that is, the firms fit together well—vertical integration may be extremely efficient and profitable.[10]

Indirect channel systems

Indirect channel systems seem to be most effective for certain kinds of products. There are various types of indirect channel systems, and the survival of a firm may depend on what type it joins or develops.

Traditional channel systems. We have noted already that there are operating advantages in corporately integrated channel systems, but there is a great deal less freedom of decision making too. On the other hand, in a traditional channel system, the separate firms (often with highly individualistic managers) have their independence, but the channel may be inefficient because of it.

In some highly independent channels, buyers may even prefer to wait until sellers desperately need to sell, hoping to force the price down. This leads to erratic production, inventory, and employment patterns that can only increase total costs.[11] More will be said about such businessmen in later chapters, but here it can be noted that such channels are declining in importance, and with good reason. They are still typical in some industries, however.

Administered channel systems. The inherent advantages of an integrated system have been understood by some progressive businessmen. But instead of integrating corporately, they have tried to develop formal and informal relationships with others in the channel system. Some have achieved the advantages of corporate integration while retaining some of the flexibility of the traditional system.

Norge Division of Borg-Warner Corp., for example, has an arrangement with its independent distributors to provide them automatically and continually with a six weeks' inventory of appliances, based on current inventory and sales, plus projected sales. Every week, Norge makes a thorough item-by-item analysis of 125,000–130,000 major appliance units valued at around $18 million. These units are located in many warehouses operated by 87 distributors throughout the country. Each week, all of this data is analyzed by the president and his managers of distribution, sales, and marketing research (as well as his manufacturing heads), and plans for production and sales activities for the following week and weeks are established.

Similar systems have been developed and coordinated by middlemen in the grocery, hardware, and drug industries. In fact, a retailer in these lines almost has to be a member of such a system to survive.

[10] This discussion is based on the advantages and disadvantages discussed in Nugent Wedding (ed.), *Vertical Integration in Marketing* (Bulletin 74 [Urbana: Bureau of Economic and Business Research, University of Illinois, 1952]), pp. 11–12, 30.

[11] For more discussion on this interaction, see Jay Forrester, "Industrial Dynamics—A Major Break-Through for Decision-Makers," *Harvard Business Review,* July-August, 1958, pp. 37–66.

In addition to their other virtues, smoothly operating channel systems also appear to be competitively superior.

In the consumer goods field, corporate chains that are at least partially vertically integrated account for about 26 percent of total retail sales; firms aligned with various administered systems account for an additional 37½ percent. This gives vertical systems in the consumer goods area a healthy majority of retail sales. Importantly, it appears that such systems will continue to increase their share in the future.[12] The inevitable conclusion is that vertical marketing systems are becoming the principal competitive units in the U.S. distribution system.[13]

This trend toward the development of vertical marketing systems suggests that both new and established firms should give serious consideration to becoming a part of such a channel system.

One reason for the movement toward integrated systems is that once channel captains see what must be done to spur sales and growth, they may have difficulty accomplishing it with their traditionally independent channel members. General Electric and Westinghouse may be moving in the direction of direct distribution of major appliances for this reason. The small retailers may not be completely eliminated, but some of their functions may be assumed, including stocking, delivery, installation, and service.[14]

Today, every independent firm should decide what kind of a channel system it wishes to be a part of. In the next several chapters, we will discuss the components of channel systems. Then, in Chapter 20, we will discuss how these components can be combined into effective systems.

Pushing or pulling through the channel system

A producer has yet another place decision: How to win channel cooperation to assure that his product reaches the end of the channel. (Middlemen, especially retailers, do not have this problem. They already control that end of the channel.)

The two basic methods of achieving channel cooperation are pushing and pulling.

"Pushing a product through the channels" means using normal promotional effort—personal salesmen and advertising—to help sell the whole marketing mix to possible channel members. This method is common, since these sales transactions are between rational, presumably profit-oriented businessmen. The approach emphasizes the impor-

[12] Bert C. McCammon, Jr., "Vertical Marketing Systems: An Exploratory Analysis," a paper presented at the 9th Annual Paul D. Converse Awards Symposium, University of Illinois, April 13, 1967.

[13] Bert C. McCammon, Jr., "The Emergence and Growth of Contractually Integrated Channels in the American Economy," a paper presented at the Fall Conference of the American Marketing Association, Washington, D.C., September 2, 1965.

[14] "Building a Faster Track from Factory to Home," *Business Week,* February 16, 1963, pp. 45–46; "Westinghouse Retail Outlet Will Double as Microscope to Scan the Consumer," *Business Week,* February 16, 1963, p. 50; E. B. Weiss, "Will Manufacturers Go into Retailing?" *Advertising Age,* December 31, 1962, p. 35; and "Has G.E. Taken Another Step Toward Retailing?" *Advertising Age,* September 3, 1962, p. 52.

tance of building a channel and securing the wholehearted cooperation of prospective channel members in a total system of action. The channel captain, in effect, is trying to develop a team that will work well together to get the product to the user.

Pulling policy— make them reach for it out there

By contrast, a manufacturer pulls a product through the channels when he tries to get channel support by making consumers want his product. This entails highly aggressive promotion to final consumers or users—perhaps using coupons or samples—temporarily bypassing the middlemen. If the promotion works, the middlemen are forced to carry the product to satisfy their customers.

This method, familiar in the soap industry, may be necessary if many products are competing already in all of the desired outlets, and the channel members are reluctant to handle a new product. They may be told about the promotion beforehand so that they can anticipate demands if the promotion is successful.

Regardless of how channel cooperation is won, the potential channel members must be convinced that the channel captain knows what he is trying to accomplish and why. The marketing manager's salesmen must be able to tell prospective channel members what is expected of them and how much competition they may have from other channels. And it may be a good idea to spell out how the firm and channel will react to probable competitive marketing mixes. In other words, Place policies must be integrated with the rest of the marketing mix if implementation is to be effective.

Conclusion

The development of Place objectives and policies has been discussed in this chapter. "Ideal" place objectives were outlined, based on the nature of customer demand as reflected in the goods classifications. Achieving the appropriate objective requires two basic place policy decisions: (1) How much market exposure is desired—*intensive, selective* or *exclusive distribution?* and (2) What type of channel is needed —direct or indirect?

We have seen that a decision to use a direct-to-final-consumer or-user channel might encourage vertical or horizontal integration, or both. Decisions to integrate, however, must be made carefully, because mergers may be subject to review and reversal in the federal courts, especially if they seem to threaten smaller competitors.

Administered channel systems made up of cooperating independent businessmen may achieve some of the same economies characteristic of corporate vertical systems. It appears that such vertical marketing systems must have some inherent advantages because they are coming to dominate the marketing scene.

Finally, we discussed two ways for producers to achieve channel cooperation—pushing and pulling the product through the channel.

In the next three chapters, we will consider the various kinds of specialists that have developed and can be used in a marketing mix and in a channel system. Then we can turn, in Chapter 20, to the development and management of distribution channel systems.

1 What do place objectives have to do with place policies? Be sure to illustrate.

2 In view of the place objectives suggested for convenience goods, what kinds of specialized marketing institutions would the manufacturer hope to find when he went into the market to implement the objectives? What kinds for shopping goods? For unsought goods? For industrial goods? (In your answer, don't be concerned with whether there are any such institutions, just indicate ideally what you would like to find.)

3 Relate the nature of the product to the degree of market exposure desired.

4 Relate the degree of brand preference achieved through branding and previous promotion to the nature of products, the nature of the market situation (pure or monopolistic competition), and the degree of market exposure which seems desirable. Illustrate with actual branded products.

5 Discuss the place objectives and place policies which might be used for the following products (indicate any special assumptions required to obtain a definite answer):
  a) A postal scale for products weighing up to two pounds.
  b) Children's toys: (1) electric train sets costing $20 or more, (2) balloons.
  c) Pneumatic nut tighteners for factory production lines.
  d) Caustic soda used in making paper.

6 Why would middlemen seek to be exclusive distributors for a product? Why would producers seek exclusive distributors? Would middlemen be equally anxious to obtain exclusive distribution for any type of product? Why or why not? Explain with reference to the following products: cornflakes, razor blades, golf clubs, golf balls, steak knives, hi-fi equipment, and industrial woodworking machinery.

7 Explain the present legal status of exclusive distribution. Describe a situation where exclusive distribution is almost assured to be legal. Describe the nature and size of competitors and the industry, as well as the nature of the exclusive dealing arrangement. Would the exclusive dealing arrangement so described be of any value to the producer or distributor?

8 Find an example of horizontal integration within the confines of your city. Do there appear to be any particular advantages from this horizontal integration? If so, what are they? If there are no such advantages, how do you explain the integration?

9 Explain how a "channel captain" could help independent firms compete with integrated ones.

10 Discuss the possibility of retailer-organized integrated channels (either formally integrated or administered) dominating consumer goods marketing.

11 Discuss the advantages and disadvantages of either a pushing or pulling policy for a very small manufacturer who is just getting into the candy business with a line of inexpensive candy bars. Which policy would probably be most appropriate for him? State any assumptions you need in order to obtain a definite answer.

339

Retailing

Retailing involves the sale of goods to the *ultimate* consumer. It is not concerned with industrial goods nor the sale of consumer goods to retailers or wholesalers.

Retailing consists primarily of buying a satisfying assortment of goods for some target customers, making these goods available at a reasonable price, and often convincing the target customers that the goods will satisfy them. Retailers often use the term "merchandising" to cover all these activities. For established retailers, this means developing a marketing strategy, adjusting all four P's—perhaps excepting the store location, which usually is fixed. This view of retailing makes it clear once again that everyone, regardless of his level in a channel system, should have a marketing strategy.

Marketing managers of consumer goods at all levels must understand retailing, since retailers eventually handle most consumer goods. If the retailing job is not effective, the goods may not be sold and *all* members of the channel will suffer. The kinds of retailers in a channel may make the difference between a product's success or failure.

Understanding retailing today is not simple because, in recent years, many different types of retailers have developed. Most retailers used to display goods, give credit, and deliver. Now, some announce proudly that they do none of these! Why? Will this continue?

In this chapter, we will consider the nature and development of retail facilities and will discuss retailers' methods of operation and trends that are now modifying these operations. We will *not* cover, in this chapter, the promotional and pricing aspects of retail merchandising. These problems are part of all marketing mixes and are discussed elsewhere in this text.

The customer's-eye view of retail facilities

Different target markets may have different images of the same store, as noted in Chapter 8. Individual retailers should be aware of these attitudes and so should the other channel members who may sell through their stores. If the target customers do not think a store is going to satisfy their needs, they won't shop there, and clearly, target customers will have no exposure to a product there.

Building on our earlier discussion of consumer behavior and the goods classifications, we can classify three types of stores: *convenience stores, shopping stores,* and *specialty stores*. There is no point in discussing *unsought stores*. They have no image at all. They cannot last long unless they do acquire an image in the eyes of some target customers.

These labels do not limit any store to one type of merchandise. A convenience store might stock specialty goods. Rather, the classification refers to the customers' image of the store.

A centrally located or neighborhood *convenience store,* for example, might draw many customers simply because it is convenient. They would go first to this store even for shopping goods.

Certain other stores seem to be favored by consumers shopping for such items as clothes, furniture, and household appliances. These stores carry all types of merchandise, but their attraction is the width and depth of their assortments. Such stores are classified as *shopping stores*.

Finally, a customer may develop an extremely strong allegiance to a particular store. Whatever his reasons—service, selection, or store reputation—the customer consistently will buy convenience, shopping, and specialty goods at this store. It would be classified as a *specialty store*.

Store type affects retailer and channel strategies

A retailer's planning must allow for customers' attitudes toward both the products and the store—that is, the planners must view product and patronage motives together. Classifying stores by type of goods, as shown in Figure 17-1, is a good way to see this complete view.

A retailer could try to better understand his potential market and competition by estimating the relative size of each of the market grid boxes, shown in Figure 17-1, and then identifying which retailers are satisfying which boxes. He may find that he and his competitors are all charging "head on" for certain kinds of customers, and completely missing a substantial number of others.

When the retailer sees more clearly what he is doing, he may continue his present marketing strategy more vigorously or he may alter it. The manager of a shopping store, for instance, would be wise to add something to the physical products he carries. And if he succeeds in making his store a specialty store, he may even be able to become the channel captain in his geographical area.

Consideration of store type should be part of a retailer's overall strategy; it affects a retailer's whole marketing mix. Type-of-store classification also is important to the strategies of manufacturers and wholesalers. If, for example, the majority of a manufacturer's target customers patronize convenience stores, intensive distribution may be necessary.

Store type could be used as another dimension on a multidimensional market grid to provide greater understanding of the needs, preferences, and behavior of customers. A dealer-branded product might be no

Figure 17–1 How customers view store-product combinations*

Product Type \ Store Type	Convenience	Shopping	Specialty
Convenience	Will buy any brand at most accessible store.	Shop around to find better service and/or lower prices.	Prefer store. Brand may be important.
Shopping	Want some selection, but will settle for assortment at most accessible store.	Want to compare both products and store mixes.	Prefer store but insist on adequate assortment.
Specialty	Prefer particular product but like place convenience, too.	Prefer particular product but still seeking best total product and mix.	Prefer both store and product.

* For more discussion of these ideas, see Louis Bucklin, "Retail Strategy and the Classification of Consumer Goods," *Journal of Marketing*, January, 1963, pp. 50–55.

better than a manufacturer's brand, but if the dealer's store is a specialty store for such products for some target customers, then the product may sell well despite its lack of superiority. An example involves Sears, Roebuck's washing machines, which are similar to competing manufacturers' brands. Some target customers seem to view Sears as a specialty store, and Sears' share of the home-laundry business is a healthy 28 percent.[1]

To determine store type takes detailed evaluations of individual retailers. Since implementation efforts are beyond our scope, we will de-emphasize store types in this chapter and stress the goods classifications. Students especially interested in retailing, however, can think of a store's entire offering of goods and services as its Product. Then many of the concepts discussed below will be applicable to stores.

---

[1] "Inside Sears, Roebuck," *Printers' Ink,* October 22, 1963, pp. 15–30.

Number and size of actual facilities available

Since retailers sell to final consumers, they usually are nearer to people than to production facilities. Retailers also are much more numerous than manufacturers because customers are widely dispersed and have greatly varied wants. In 1963, there were approximately 1.7 million retailers compared to about 290,000 wholesalers and 310,000 manufacturers.[2]

The extremely large number of retailers might suggest that retailing is a field of small businesses. To an extent, this is true. In 1963, for instance, 23 percent of the nation's retailers accounted for only 1.5 percent of total retail sales, grossing less than $20,000 each annually.

Retailing: many small businesses

Table 17–1 Retail trade, 1963—United States, sales by size of establishment

	Establishments			Sales Volume		
Sales Size of Establishments	Number (000)	Percent	Cumulative Percent	Sales (000,-000)	Percent	Cumulative Percent
Total, all establishments	1,708			244,202		
Establishments operated entire year, total	1,532.3	100.0		232,043	100.0	
With annual sales of:						
$1,000,000 or more	36.1	2.4	2.4	89,096	38.4	38.4
$500,000 to $999,999	43.4	2.8	5.2	30,062	13.0	51.4
$300,000 to $499,999	57.6	3.8	9.0	21,035	9.5	60.9
$100,000 to $299,999	306.1	20.0	29.0	50,683	21.8	82.7
$20,000 to $99,999	736.0	48.0	77.0	36,709	15.8	98.5
$19,999 or less	353.1	23.0	100.0	3,558	1.5	100.0

SOURCE: *U.S. Census of Business, 1963, Retail Trade.*

Yet in the aggregate, retailing is big business. Retail sales in 1963 totaled $244 billion, making retailing a key element in the U.S. economy. The larger retail stores—those selling more than $1 million in goods or services annually, such as supermarkets—do most of this business. Only 2.4 percent of the retail stores fell in this bracket, yet they accounted for more than 38 percent of all retail sales. Table 17–1 gives details on the number of retailers and the sales volume by various sales classes.

The many small retailers, however, cannot be ignored, especially because they frequently cause the marketing manager difficult problems. Their large number and relatively small sales volume make it expensive to work with them, and they often require additional mar-

[2] *Statistical Abstract of the United States, 1966.*

keting mixes. Yet these stores reach many consumers and often are invaluable channel members for some products and target markets.

Evolution of present retailing facilities

In the following section tracing the development of retailing institutions, we will try to get a better understanding of why there are so many stores—and especially so many small stores.

House-to-house retailers

House-to-house selling today is a relatively insignificant form of retailing, but it was an important step in the development of retailing. Its greatest advantage is that it offers marketing managers an opportunity to control their whole channel of distribution. It may be especially useful during the introductory stage of the life cycle of a product, for sales of unsought goods, or during a recession when goods need a special push. It is an old but still effective method inherited from the Yankee peddler.

The total number of house-to-house salesmen has increased over the years, but their share of total retail sales has declined to less than 1 percent. In 1963, about 66,000 house-to-house organizations were enumerated by the census. Most of these were one-man organizations. Only about 9,000 were large enough to employ salesmen, and many of these larger organizations were milk or bread distributors. The average annual sales volume of all of these, including the larger firms, was just under $36,000 compared to $141,000 for all retail establishments.

This is an expensive method of selling. True, overhead costs are lower because the house-to-house retailer has no store, but travel is costly and the number of personal contacts possible in a day is limited. Markups range from 30 to 50 percent, and often are higher.

Despite these disadvantages, though, this retailing method has its marked successes. Electrolux, which has been sold door-to-door since its introduction from Sweden decades ago, still claims the top position in the vacuum cleaner business and is able to sell all of its cleaners at list price!

Trading posts— general stores

Historically, these stores sold anything the local consumers might buy in sufficient volume to justify carrying it. Before the Civil War, they were the main kind of retail outlet in this country.

The main advantage of the general store is its convenient location for some target customers. It sometimes serves, too, as a social center and a collecting point for agricultural produce.

Such stores are still found at rural crossroads and sometimes in small Countyvilles, carrying mainly food and other convenience goods, but there are so few now that no longer is there a separate census category for them.

Single-line, limited-line stores

These types of stores became common after the Civil War, when the continuing expansion in the volume and variety of consumer goods began to make it impossible for the general store to offer depth and

344

breadth in all its traditional lines. Some stores began specializing in certain lines, such as dry goods, apparel, furniture, or groceries.

Most retail stores are still single- and limited-line stores—specializing in groceries, or hardware, or gasoline, or clothing, or sporting goods, for example—and this probably will continue to be true as long as customer demands are numerous and varied. The main advantage of a limited-line store is that it can satisfy some target markets better, perhaps achieving a specialty-store status, by adjusting its marketing mix—including store hours, credit, and product assortment—to suit some customers. Several such stores, catering to various parts of the market grid, can satisfy the whole market.

Such stores face a major disadvantage in having to stock some items in depth that are slow-moving but must be carried to satisfy the store's target market. Further, many of these stores have the disadvantage of being small, with high expenses relative to sales.

There are some extremely large single- and limited-line stores, especially in larger Centertowns and Commerce Cities. But the marketing manager must remember there are many more small limited-line stores in *both* large cities and small towns and adjust his mixes accordingly, even if this takes complicated channels with several middlemen.

Specialty shops

The specialty shop is a type of limited-line store found in downtown areas, fashionable shopping districts, and large shopping centers. It usually is small, has a distinct personality, and aims at a carefully defined market segment by offering a unique product assortment, knowledgeable salesmen, and better service.

Usually the specialty-shop designation is reserved for stores dealing in special types of shopping goods, such as high-quality sporting goods, men's exclusive ties, high-fashion dresses, clothes in special sizes, and women's shoes. The new "boutiques" opening around the country are specialty shops.[3]

Using the term "specialty" should not cause us to confuse specialty *shops,* specialty *stores,* and specialty *goods.* A successful specialty shop might achieve the specialty-store status, discussed earlier in the chapter, among a small group of target customers, but it probably would be more satisfied to be well known among a larger group for the distinctiveness of its line and the special services offered. Similarly, a specialty shop might carry specialty goods, but only if they fit into its narrow line and will benefit by the additional service and display the specialty shop offers.

The specialty shop's major advantage is that it caters to certain types of customers whom the management and salespeople come to know well. This familiarity simplifies buying, and the resulting quicker turnover cuts the costs due to obsolescence and style changes.

---

[3] See, for instance, a description of the operation of a sporting goods retailer of this type (Abercrombie & Fitch), "Caterer to the Outdoor Man," *Business Week,* December 16, 1961, pp. 84–89; see also, "Big-City Store Takes Fashion into a Barn," *Business Week,* May 27, 1967, pp. 32–33.

Specialty shops probably will continue to be a part of the retailing scene as long as customers continue to have such varied tastes and the money to satisfy them.

Department stores

Department stores handle a *wide* variety of goods such as women's ready-to-wear and accessories, men's and boys' wear, piece goods, housewares, and housefurnishings.

The distinguishing characteristic of department stores is that they are organized into separate departments like limited-line stores and specialty shops—for purposes of promotion, service, and control. They normally are large stores.

Some specialty shops, grown large and departmentalized, appear to be department stores, and we will treat them as such. As a rule, however, specialty shops do not carry complete lines. They frequently omit housewares, housefurnishings, and furniture, and prefer instead to emphasize depth of line and distinctiveness in the lines they do choose to carry. Neiman-Marcus in Dallas, for example, is departmentalized, but insists it is a specialty shop.

Department stores generally try to cater to customers seeking shopping goods. Originally they were located in downtown districts close to other department stores and convenient to many potential customers. Historically, this close grouping developed to facilitate shopping at the junctions of major railroad and streetcar routes, the principal forms of urban public transportation in the 19th century, when the major U.S. department stores began.

Since World War II, many downtown department stores have opened suburban branches in shopping centers to serve the middle and higher income groups who have moved to the suburbs, especially around the large Commerce Cities. The big J. L. Hudson store in Detroit was a leader in the movement toward building shopping centers around a large branch department store.

Some downtown department stores now are making renewed efforts to remain attractive in their traditional downtown locations by (1) carrying wide lines in the major shopping-goods items for which they have long been famous; (2) attracting the trade of conventioneers and tourists; and (3) appealing to the low-income groups remaining in the residential neighborhoods near the downtown area. New urban trends, including downtown apartment units and urban redevelopment, may provide new markets for the big downtown stores.

Department stores are often looked to as the retailing leaders in a community. Leaders, first, because they seem to be so generous in giving the customer services he can't get elsewhere—credit, merchandise return, delivery, fashion shows, and Christmas displays. And leaders also because they are big. In 1963 the annual sales volume of U.S. department stores averaged almost $5 million, compared to about $141,000 for the average retail store. The biggest—Macy's, Field's, and Hudson's—each top $100 million in sales annually. Although department stores account for less than ¼ of 1 percent (4,251) of the total number of retail stores, they accounted for 8.4 percent of total retail sales in 1963.

346

Some department stores are an important force to be reckoned with in their own strongholds. Some target markets may be reached *only* through particular department stores because of the strong specialty-store status they have achieved for *their* store. And some department store buyers make this situation very clear in their dealings with suppliers!

Catalog retailing—usually done by mail—should not be ignored by marketing managers. It may be useful for reaching widely scattered markets with products that otherwise might be considered unsought. A mail-order house in Los Angeles is successfully selling things "people really don't need but can't live without," such as electric back-scratchers and invisible thread for mending multicolored materials.[4] Some mail-order houses aim at narrow target markets, selling only electronic components, or phonograph records, or health foods. Others, such as the big mail-order houses, offer both convenience and shopping goods. **Catalog retailers**

Some of the early mail-order houses, including Sears, Roebuck and Montgomery Ward, were started shortly after the Civil War, as railroads and postal service expanded. They were so successful with their low prices and wide variety that some conventional retailers sought legislation to restrict their operations.

Yet catalog selling today isn't like catalog selling a century ago. The kitchen hardware and coveralls are still there, but there is an increasing emphasis on high-fashion women's and girls' wear, sporting goods, and luxury items.

The emphasis is no longer solely on low-price selling by mail. Product assortments and quality have grown. And some companies offer catalog stores, telephone service, convenient pickup depots, and delivery, to make catalog buying easier. The big mail-order houses started this, but now department stores and limited-line stores are seeing the profit possibilities and are becoming catalog retailers too.

To appeal even more strongly to customers, most catalog sellers have strong merchandise guarantees and liberal return policies. Because they can locate this part of their business in warehouse-type buildings and need limited sales help, they can offer wider selections at lower prices than conventional retailers. Sears' mail-order and catalog operation typically undersells its own retail stores by about 10 percent, and Europe's largest mail-order firm, Die Quelle, keeps its prices 15–20 percent below those of other retailers.[5]

Mail-order houses have continued to grow with the U.S. economy, numbering more than 4,000 establishments in 1963. Yet they have never achieved more than 1.3 percent of total U.S. retail sales, and in 1963 they were down to about 1 percent.

Mail-order houses seem to be making greater headway in Europe, where conventional retailers may be less effective and customers may want the convenience of ordering by mail as well as the lower prices. Mail-order sales accounted for 4.5 percent of all retail sales volume in

---

[4] "When the Needless Is Essential," *Business Week,* December 15, 1962, pp. 50–52.

[5] *Time,* April 19, 1963, p. 110.

Britain in 1966.[6] This may be a hint of things to come in the U.S. if our cities continue to grow and visiting stores in person becomes even less convenient. More is said on this under "Trends In Retailing," near the end of the chapter.

Vending machines

Although vending machines are the newest revolution in marketing methods, and their growth has been spectacular, automatic vending still represents less than 2 percent of total U.S. retail sales. But in certain lines, the vending machine is an important factor—16 percent of all cigarettes sold in the United States, 20 percent of the candy bars, and 25 percent of the bottled soft drinks are sold through machines.[7]

The largest part of the vending-machine business (about 40 percent) is in cigarettes and the next largest share is from hot and cold beverages (36 percent). For some target markets, clearly, the marketing manager cannot ignore this retailing method.

The major stumbling block in vending is high cost of operation. The machines are relatively expensive for the volume they sell, and they require much stocking time and repair labor. Mass marketers of similar, nonvended products can operate profitably on a margin of about 20 percent; the vending industry seems to require about 41 percent, and so usually must charge higher prices.[8] If costs come down and consumers' income and desire for convenience rises, perhaps we will see an even greater growth in this method of retailing.

Planned shopping centers

The planned shopping centers that have grown rapidly in the last 10 to 15 years can be viewed as both a new development and a variation of old marketing institutions. Their forerunners were the early villages and country fairs, and the department stores composed of many individual shops leased to merchants who operated them as limited-line and specialty shops within one large building.[9] The new shopping centers also are similar to the old shopping districts in larger cities, except shopping centers are planned as a unit. Shopping centers, often planned by a real estate developer to facilitate one-stop shopping, usually have substantial parking facilities, and some are pleasantly landscaped. Although the centers are composed of independent merchants, they sometimes act together for promotional purposes.

Shopping centers have been classified into three basic categories: (1) the neighborhood center, (2) the community center, and (3) the regional center.

Neighborhood shopping centers. These centers, similar to the many "strips" of convenience stores found in most Commerce Cities and Centertowns, usually include a supermarket, drugstore, hardware store, beauty shop and barbershop, laundry, dry cleaners, gas stations, and others, such as a bakery or appliance shop. They normally serve

[6] "Europeans Take Fancy to Buying by Book," *Business Week,* June 3, 1967, pp. 87–92.

[7] "Vending in 1964, and Vending in 1961," National Automatic Merchandising Association, Chicago, Ill.

[8] Douglas J. Dalrymple, "Will Automatic Vending Topple Retail Precedence?" *Journal of Retailing,* Spring, 1963, pp. 27–31.

[9] Paul E. Smith, "Prescription for a Successful Shopping Center," *Business Topics,* Autumn, 1966, p. 17.

348

7,500 to 20,000 people living within 6 to 10 minutes' driving distance. There were more than 6,000 such shopping centers in 1966.

Community shopping centers. These somewhat larger operations usually include a variety store or a small department store in addition to the stores found in the neighborhood center. There is more emphasis here on shopping goods (apparel and home furnishings), but the bulk of sales are of convenience goods. These centers must serve 20,000 to 100,000 people within a radius of 3 to 4 miles. They are quite common around Forest Lakes and are found around larger Centertowns. There were more than 500 such community centers in 1966.

Regional centers. These are much larger units. They include one or two large department stores and as many as 100 smaller stores. Most of these emphasize shopping goods; in fact, the stores that emphasize convenience goods often are at the edge of the center, where they will not interfere with customers primarily interested in shopping.

Regional centers must serve 100,000 to 200,000 persons within a radius of 5 or 6 miles. They closely resemble downtown shopping districts of Centertowns or even some small Commerce Cities, and usually are close to the Forest Lakes near large Commerce Cities. In 1966, there were about 250 regional centers in the United States out of a total of about 7,000 shopping centers.[10]

One aspect of shopping center development, important to manufacturer and wholesaler marketing managers, is that the financial requirements of shopping center developers often have barred small independent stores from the centers in favor of national chain stores. This sometimes has blocked manufacturers' brands from these important centers, since some chains tend to emphasize dealer brands.[11]

Mass marketing methods

So far we have been describing retail institutions primarily in terms of the width of lines carried and their physical facilities. But there are some important retail institutions that cannot be adequately described this way. Supermarkets and discount houses, for instance. could have been shoved into our previous classifications. But by so doing, we would have missed the essence of these mass marketers just as some conventional retailers did when these stores first developed.

Mass marketing institutions typically were started by nonretailers who were sure they could win substantial sales volumes by emphasizing lower price and faster turnover. They rejected the conventional retailer's notion of a fixed demand in his territory and were willing to depart from conventional behavior. Their success is history now. Some conventional retailers have adopted some of their methods and prospered. Other retailers have not and are out of business today. More

[10] *Ibid.*, pp. 17–26; "Shopping Centers and New York State's Retail Economy," *New York State Commerce Review*, September, 1958, p. 2; and "Specialty Fashion Center in Santa Ana Will Make 'Shopping Around' Easier," *Business Week*, March 8, 1958, p. 51. For a detailed list of available shopping centers, see *Directory of Shopping Centers in the United States and Canada* (Chicago: National Research Bureau, Inc., annual).

[11] "Small Concerns Are Frozen Out of Shopping Centers, Panel Is Told," *Wall Street Journal*, December 19, 1961, p. 28; and E. B. Weiss, "Retailing by Treaty," *Advertising Age*, March 11, 1963, p. 94.

probably will fail unless they begin offering something unique to some target customers.

**Super-
markets
started
move to
mass
marketing**

A supermarket is essentially a large store specializing in groceries. As late as 1930, most food stores were relatively small limited-line operations. In the early depression years, some innovators felt that price appeals could move merchandise in volume. Their early experiments in vacant warehouses proved an immediate success. Conventional retailers, both independents and chains, quickly copied the innovators— emphasizing lower prices and self-service.

Generally, $1 million is considered the minimum annual sales volume for a store to be classified as a supermarket. In 1966, there were 19,155 supermarkets meeting this definition, and they handled almost 57 percent of total grocery sales. Today, with supermarkets continuing to multiply, it appears they are beginning to reach the saturation level, yet new ones still do well when they are wisely located.[12] Supermarkets are growing in popularity all over the world, with several thousand in Europe alone.[13]

Supermarkets sell convenience goods, but in quantity. Their target customers don't want to shop for groceries every day as was common in pre-supermarket times. To facilitate quantity buying, supermarkets generally offer free parking facilities.

Present-day supermarkets are planned for maximum efficiency; some carefully analyze the sales and profit of each item, and allocate space accordingly. This approach helps sell more merchandise in less time, reduces the investment in inventory, makes stocking easier, and reduces the cost of handling goods.[14] Such efficiency is essential. Grocery competition is keen, and net profits after taxes in grocery supermarkets usually run a thin 1 percent of sales.

**Discount
selling
preceded
mass
merchan-
disers**

Discount selling has become quite popular since World War II, but price cutting or discounting dates from the beginning of marketing. Bargaining has always been the way to get a better price. And clergymen, teachers, members of labor unions, and members of various social groups have long received discounts in certain stores.[15]

Some discounting has been done through brokers and in "open showrooms" where furniture and similar bulky items ostensibly are shown only to wholesalers or retailers but actually are shown to anyone. The details of these arrangements vary. Sometimes retailers act as brokers between the consumer and the wholesaler. Usually these showroom operations are not well publicized, account for only a small portion of retail sales, and might better be termed discount selling.

[12] *Progressive Grocer,* April 1967, p. 63; Ben L. Schapker, "Behavior Patterns of Supermarket Shoppers," *Journal of Marketing,* October, 1966, pp. 46–49.

[13] *Business Week,* September 10, 1966, p. 132; "Europe Goes Shopping," *Business Week,* May 18, 1963, pp. 58–72; "Supermarts on the Seine," *Time,* April 12, 1963, pp. 95–96; and "Supermarkets in Siberia," *Chain Store Age,* November 1960, pp. 144 ff.

[14] For further discussion on this, see "How Super Valu Study Was Used to Lay Out Motts' New Super," *Progressive Grocer,* an undated reprint.

[15] Discount selling and discount houses have been discussed extensively in the literature. See a special-interest bibliography compiled by S. C. Hollander, *Discount Selling, Retail Price-cutting, and Resale Price Controls* (Chicago: American Marketing Association, 1956).

Discount houses are price-cutting operations that have expanded beyond discount selling. The early post–World War II discount houses formally adopted a policy of low-margin selling and were much more open about their operations. To obtain the lower prices, the customer would have to go to their low-rent facilities, pay cash, and take care of service and repair problems himself, because the lower prices didn't cover such extras (although manufacturers' guarantees were available on some items). **Discount houses upset some conventional retailers**

Word-of-mouth advertising made them well known, and eventually some discount houses advertised through local media. Such steps were taken very cautiously, however. Sales and profits were growing, and the discounters did not wish to antagonize their manufacturer-brand suppliers or conventional competitors because of fear that they might—as in fact they eventually did—put pressure on their sources to cut off the discounter's supplies.

In the early 1950's, with war shortages finally ended, goods became more plentiful, and a buyers' market developed. Discount houses became more attractive to suppliers, and the discounters themselves became more aggressive. Earlier they had emphasized products that had been bought cheaply but often with little regard to assortments. Now they were able to offer full assortments.

At this stage, many discounters sought "respectability," moving to better locations and offering more services and guarantees. They began to act more like regular retailers, but kept their prices lower than conventional outlets to keep turnover high.[16]

Discount houses are a new approach to retailing. In the face of discount house competition, some regular retailers have resorted to price cutting on highly competitive items. But these purely defensive tactics are just that—price cutting—while discounters make a standard practice of selling all of their goods with small markups.

More than just price cutting is involved, however. Careful buying with the firm's target markets in mind is essential, to assure high turnover. A major discounter's first venture into apparel sales flopped, for instance, because its buyers were appliance experts and knew little about fashions. The discount approach worked only after they hired experienced buyers from department stores.[17]

Unlike the early discount houses—which emphasized manufacturer-branded hard goods, such as appliances and TV sets, where it was easier to show that discounts were being given—the mass merchandisers tend to emphasize soft goods and, more recently, groceries. These "discount" stores are a force to reckon with. They are selling more food (among other things) per store than the chain supermarkets![18] **Mass merchandisers are more than discounters**

The mass merchandisers are simply large, departmentalized stores

[16] For a description of a discount house that has gone through these stages—Polk Brothers in Chicago—see "Chicago's Red Hot Merchandiser," *Fortune*, September, 1955, pp. 130–54; and Edward M. Barnet, "A Showdown in the Marketplace," *Harvard Business Review*, July–August, 1956, p. 89.

[17] *Time*, September 15, 1961, p. 100.

[18] "Discounters Sell More Food than Chain Markets," *Detroit Free Press*, February 26, 1967, p. 15C; see also, R. J. Minichiello, "The Real Challenge of Food Discounters," *Journal of Marketing*, April, 1967, pp. 37–42.

that are more *super* than the supermarkets. They have a wider range of goods, stress low price and self-service even more, and are bigger.

In 1966, there were more than 2,000 such outlets. By definition, their minimum floor space is 10,000 square feet, but the average mass merchandiser has about 60,000 square feet, which is three to four times the size of the average supermarket.[19]

Some of these units are run by relative newcomers to retailing, but two of the important competitors are Kresge with its K-Marts and F. W. Woolworth with its Woolco Stores. The K-Marts are 100,-000-square-foot full-line department stores that sell top-quality national brands at modest prices. In 1966, there were 122 of them, and plans call for building about 40 more each year. Kresge is now going into a slightly lower priced operation, Jupiter Stores, and Woolworth is going into this field too.[20]

Are today's innovators tomorrow's retailers?

Mass marketing, and especially food discounting, can be seen as a new marketing strategy in which primary emphasis is on price, with secondary emphasis given to in-store promotion, services, trading stamps, and giveaways—things the conventional retailers, including supermarkets, have been stressing more.[21] The apparent success of this strategy suggests that at least some target customers were not fully satisfied with the conventional strategies.

Mass merchandisers already have made some dent in the market, having about 3 percent of total grocery sales, 11 percent of health and beauty aids sales, and a larger but more difficult to estimate share of some general merchandise lines. Clearly there is a demand for this kind of store, and it is likely that the mass merchandisers will continue to grow using their present methods, because they see these methods as "conventional" for their type of operation.

Scrambled merchandising

Who's selling what to whom?

Current retailing might be called "scrambled merchandising." Variety stores (the old 5-and-10-cent stores) are almost indistinguishable nowadays from department stores and some discount houses. Department stores are selling houses, and mass merchandisers are selling groceries. Some discount houses are becoming department stores and want to be called "promotional department stores." Supermarkets are selling anything they can move in volume, including appliances, drugs, general merchandise, and clothing. Catalog houses are selling through supermarkets. Drugstores, seeing the loss of many health and beauty aid sales to supermarkets and mass merchandisers, are moving into movie cameras, costume jewelry, electric shavers, clocks, and watches. Camera and jewelry stores, in turn, are affected by these moves.

What is behind this scrambled merchandising? According to the "Wheel of Retailing" hypothesis, new types of retailers enter the mar-

---

[19] *The Nielsen Researcher*, No. 3, 1966, pp. 3–11.
[20] "Kresge's Triple-threat Retailing," *Business Week*, January 29, 1966, pp. 126–34.
[21] Minichiello, *op. cit.*, p. 42.

ket as low-status, low-margin, low-price operators. If successful, they go into more elaborate establishments and offer more services, with resulting higher operating costs and higher prices. They are then vulnerable to new low-status, low-margin, low-price outlets—and the wheel turns again.

The wheel of retailing, the ladder of success

Early department stores began this way, then became higher priced and built basement departments to serve the more price-conscious customers. The 5-and-10-cent store and the mail-order house were developed on a price basis, as were the food chains, economy apparel chains, drug chains, and the automotive accessory chains which developed during the 1920's. The supermarket, in turn, was started with low prices and little service.[22]

Today, conventional retailers are concerned about the competition offered by discount houses and the growing mass merchandisers. But some of these mass marketers are already offering more services and raising their prices. Perhaps they in turn will open the door to a new type of retailer.

But why should various types of retailers repeatedly go through this cycle from low cost and prices to higher costs and prices?

There are several possibilities. The original innovators may relax their vigilance and control as they acquire age and wealth. Or their successors may be less competent or aggressive than they were. Or they may simply want to trade up as some of their original customers grow affluent with age, leaving to others the younger, lower income customers. Or these firms simply may feel they have to add the additional services to remain competitive as the product (the retailers' whole offering) life cycle moves along.[23]

The wheel theory, however, does not explain all major retailing developments. Vending machines entered retailing as high-cost, high-margin operations. The branch trend of the department stores and the development of shopping centers have not been low-price oriented. On the contrary, they sometimes have even been high-price operations. Nor have all innovations been immediate successes. Some of the first department stores failed, while vending-machine history is filled with failures.

It's all in hearing the knock, perhaps

The probable cause of these cross currents has been summarized very well by Hollander:

. . . retailers are constantly probing the empty sectors of competitive strategy with many failures until someone uses exactly the right technique at the right time. In at least some cases, the merchant prince's skill may have been in judging opportunities rather than in originating techniques.[24]

---

[22] William R. Davidson and Alton F. Doody, "The Future of Discounting," *Journal of Marketing,* January, 1963, pp. 36–37.

[23] Alton F. Doody, Jr., "Historical Pattern of Marketing Innovations," in William F. Decker, *Emerging Concepts in Marketing, Proceedings of the Winter Conference of the American Marketing Association, December, 1962* (Chicago, American Marketing Association), pp. 245–56.

[24] Stanley C. Hollander, "Retailing: Cause or Effect?" in Decker, *op. cit.,* pp. 220–30.

This diagnosis is consistent with our emphasis on strategy and locating new opportunities. The product life-cycle concept helps here, too. The merchant prince may exploit new opportunity for a while, but if his judgment is correct, he can count on fairly prompt imitation and a squeezing out of the innovator's profits. Conventional retailers are far along in their cycle—some have already declined—while the current innovators are still in the market growth stage.

Will retailers keep scrambling for profits?

Scrambled merchandising may continue into the future. There are still many inflexibilities and rigidities in our marketing system, including the inflexibility of the traditional retailers' pricing policies. Pricing will be discussed in detail later, but it should be noted here that many

Table 17–2 Gross margins in selected retail trades for recent years

Gross Margin Ranges	Retail Trades
50 percent or more	Custom tailors, monuments, florists and nurseries, bakery shops, furs.
40 to 50 percent	Garages, jewelry, restaurants, eating places, furniture, and undertaking.
35 to 40 percent	Musical instruments, housefurnishings, dairy and poultry products, gifts, novelties, souvenirs, books, furniture, drinking places, taverns, bars, office equipment and supplies, floor coverings, shoes (family stores), electric and gas household appliances.
30 to 35 percent	Paint, wallpaper, glass, confectionery, drugs, women's accessory and specialty stores, men's clothing, stationery, men's furnishings, women's ready-to-wear, limited-price variety, automobile accessories and parts, family clothing, coal and other fuel.
20 to 30 percent	Hardware, sporting goods, dry goods, general merchandise, lumber, cigar stores and stands, filling stations, meats, hardware and farm implements.
Below 20 percent	Alcoholic beverage package stores, farm implements, motor vehicles, groceries and meats, groceries.

SOURCE: Dun & Bradstreet.

retailers have traditionally used fixed percentage markups for *all* items, regardless of the rate of turnover. The fast-moving items contributed nicely to profit, while the slow-moving items tended to reduce profits. If a firm were looking for opportunities, it would sell these fast-moving, high-profit items. And it is exactly these items that are crossing traditional lines and appearing in unexpected places.

Table 17–2 shows the ranges of gross margins conventional retailers have found necessary, to assure staying in business and making *some* profit. *Some* is emphasized because typically the net profit—the difference between a seemingly big gross margin and apparently necessary expenses—is only 1 or a few percent.

Mass merchandisers and discounters try to operate on gross margins and markups of 15 to 25 percent, but, as shown in this table, conventional retailers usually require much higher percentages. This table should give you a better idea of the "why" of scrambled merchandising and suggest possible directions it will take. This table shows, for example, why supermarkets, discount houses, and other scramblers want to sell bakery goods, jewelry, appliances, refreshments, and gifts. Try to analyze why some of the conventional retailers have such high gross margins and why other types of retailers can operate more economically.

Size and channel system thinking

As already noted, mass production is not the only source of the economies related to larger size. A few specific comments on how the advantages and disadvantages of larger size apply to retailing are pertinent.

The large and small advantages

The small independent retailer may satisfy his own psychic needs by being his own boss, and he can be extremely helpful to some target customers because of his flexibility. But he may be so small that he *seems* profitable only because some of the costs of doing business are ignored. He may not be allowing for depreciation or for family members clerking or keeping books without pay. Sometimes he can keep the doors open only because he is running the store and has a full-time job elsewhere. As we noted already, about 350,000 small retailers gross less than $20,000 of sales annually, which, after expenses, leaves hardly enough to support one person.

Even the average retail store is too small to gain economies of size. Annual sales for the average store of only $141,000 is not very impressive, especially considering that net profits as a percentage of sales range from 1 to 5 percent. We gain some perspective on size when we realize that grocery supermarkets sell more than $1 million worth of goods per year!

Retailing is easy to enter, and the mortality rate is predictably high. The new small storekeeper must be expert in almost all phases of the business immediately. In a larger organization, on the other hand, specialists take care of buying, accounting and taxes, and building maintenance.

But although larger organizations can buy in quantity at lower prices, take advantage of mass advertising, and hire specialists, larger size alone does not guarantee more efficient operation. It merely gives management an extra opportunity for efficiency.

The growth of large-scale retailing indicates that larger size can have economic advantages. Department stores, for example, achieve some of the advantages of horizontal integration, whether the store was formed by merging several limited-line stores or by internal expansion. As a single larger unit, the department store may be able to attract more customers by store-wide advertising. Once customers are in a store, they can cross departmental lines and buy on impulse.

355

But size does not automatically confer advantages. A large department store may be made up of many small-scale specialty shops and limited-line stores that require special management skills. Leasing of some departments—optical goods, hats, restaurants—may be necessary if specialized skill is required to operate them. Moreover, the departments in a department store may not be any larger than independent limited-line stores, and so there may be little or no possibility for volume buying.

There's strength in number of outlets

The disadvantages of small size, even among large department stores, has led to chain or association operations to achieve the advantage of larger operations.

Chains grew slowly until after World War I, then spurted ahead during the 1920's. The first Census of Distribution in 1929, designed in part to determine the importance of chains, found that more than 7,000 chain organizations controlled about 21 percent of all retail sales and a much larger share in certain lines. This discovery caused a number of states to pass antichain store legislation. The Robinson-Patman Act of 1936 was intended, in part, to stop some chain store practices, especially demanding and getting lower prices because of their size.

This legislative reaction may have inhibited some managements. Chains did continue to grow, but at a less dramatic rate. In 1948, 23 percent, and in 1963 about 30 percent, of the country's retail sales were made by chain stores.

Chains have done even better in certain lines. Variety store chains have 81 percent of sales in that field. Department store chains are an important factor across the nation in selling general merchandise. Such chains as Sears, Montgomery Ward, and J. C. Penney are in this category.

In the general merchandise field, chains of four or more establishments in 1963 handled 86 percent of sales, compared to only 60 percent of the volume in 1954. Grocery chains of four or more outlets have expanded from 39 percent to 49 percent of the market during the 1954–63 period.

You can lead the customer to the channel, but . . .

One of the reasons chain store sales have been climbing recently is that chain managements are paying more attention to achieving the economies of scale in distribution through horizontal integration and the development of vertical relations, either corporately or through administered systems. We already have mentioned corporate chains, but here we must note the development of cooperative chains, sponsored by retailers.

Cooperative chains are formed by independent retailers in their efforts to compete with chains. They band together to set up their own wholesaling organization, and cooperation in such groups has enabled many "independents" to meet chain competition effectively. Sales of cooperative chains have been rising.

Voluntary chains, operating similarly to cooperative chains except that they are sponsored by wholesalers, also have been most helpful to the "independent" retailers. Some are linked together by contracts specifying common operating procedures and the use of common storefront design, store name, and joint promotional efforts.[25]

Franchise operations—such as McDonald's Carry-Out Restaurants and Colonel Sander's fried chicken shops—are similar to voluntary chains. Someone has developed a good marketing strategy and the members of the group carry it out. The voluntary chains have tended to work with existing retailers whereas the franchisors have tended to work witth newcomers whom they train and get started. Sometimes they will locate the site, get it built, and run the initial promotion and opening.[26]

Cooperative and voluntary chains should not be confused with *consumer cooperatives,* which are groups of *consumers* who have banded together into voluntary buying associations and normally operate on a nonprofit basis with voluntary or poorly paid management. These consumer cooperatives have never been sizable in the United States, their high point being 1 percent of retail sales in 1954.[27]

Such cooperatives have been more successful in Europe where most retailers apparently have been high priced and inefficient. Most U.S. markets, on the other hand, have been so competitive that the cooperative patronage dividends, basic to co-op customer loyalty, have not been attractive enough to keep the customers coming to the typically out-of-the-way store for the (sometimes) unknown or co-op dealer brands.

The fate of consumer cooperatives is further evidence that size or goodwill alone do not make an efficient channel system. Economies of scale may be possible, but it takes some hardheaded business decisions to link the members of a channel system efficiently. As always, the final test is customer approval. Some of the large horizontally and vertically linked systems seem to be getting this approval.

How retailers operate

Retailing includes so many different kinds of operations that it is difficult to find generalizations that cover the behavior of both the smallest independent store operator and the highly specialized buyer in large integrated systems. Still, retailers do share many common characteristics, and so we will consider *what* goods retailers choose; *how* they choose and handle the goods; *when* they buy; and *who* does this buying.

Most retail buyers see themselves as purchasing agents for their target customers, remembering the old retailing maxim: "Goods well bought are half sold." Typically, they do *not* see themselves as sales

Retailer must buy for his customers and himself

[25] "Cooperatives Give Independent Retailers More Marketing Muscle," *Marketing Insights,* November 7, 1966, p. 20. "Prescribing for the Drug Stores," *Business Week,* September 10, 1966, pp. 149–52; "A Supermarket Chain That Isn't a Chain," *Business Week,* August 22, 1964, pp. 81–84, has a description of Super Valu, a Midwest food wholesaler running a voluntary group; and Russell L. Childress, "Trends in Affiliated Wholesale-Retail Food Operations," *Management Research Summary,* Small Business Administration, 1963.

[26] E. H. Lewis and R. Hancock, *The Franchise System of Distribution* (Minneapolis: The University of Minnesota Press, 1963).

[27] H. G. Canoyer and E. F. Cheit, Consumer Cooperatives in Minnesota," *Business News Notes,* School of Business Administration, University of Minnesota, November, 1952.

agents for manufacturers. Retailers have a selfish interest in serving customers well—their own survival and profit—and this comes before helping manufacturers sell their products.

Some retailers emphasize manufacturers' brands, then attempt to evaluate various manufacturers' promotional programs to anticipate future customer demands. They may even try to anticipate the success of a pulling policy. Other retailers, in contrast, have a deliberate and successful policy of promoting their own dealer brands.

There is no sure way to determine what items a retailer should stock. He should try to develop a marketing mix that includes an attractive product assortment for his target customers. This assortment will vary according to his customers and the kind of store (convenience, shopping, or specialty) he is operating. Even in a large chain operation such as Sears, the particular location determines what a particular store carries. The assortment offered in each of the 25 Sears retail stores in the Chicago area depends on the neighborhood in which the store is located. And as many as half of the items carried by a grocery chain may be specifically ordered for particular neighborhoods with the rest standard for all stores.[28]

The price policies of the channel also may affect the choice of products. Some retailers, especially druggists, have encouraged resale price maintenance and refused to carry merchandise not protected under the Fair Trade laws. Here, because they feel retail prices will not be favorable to them, the retailers are refusing to carry products that might be favorably priced for their customers, a slight twisting of the concept that the retailer is the purchasing agent for the consumer.

How retailers buy and why

Although most retailers carry a large number of items—drugstores carry up to 12,000 items, hardware stores from 3,000 to 8,000, and grocery stores up to 8,000 items—they do not often carry a large inventory of any single item. Instead, modern retailers seek to stock their shelves, perhaps keep some reserve stock, and depend on a continual flow through the channel. The size of their inventory depends on how efficiently and dependably the channel operates. To help simplify buying, most retailers, especially if they are affiliated with voluntary or cooperative chains, limit their buying to only a few wholesalers.

Often retail buyers are annoyed by the number of wholesalers' and manufacturers' representatives who call on them. These retailers feel that their sales of each item are so small that they cannot afford to spend much time choosing each product. The manufacturer's marketing manager should understand this attitude in developing his promotion. His marketing mix may be more successful if his salesmen emphasize display and shelf arrangement more—things that help the retailer directly—and product merits less.

As the retailer's sales volume expands, he can justify spending more time buying individual items. Buyers may begin to specialize in certain goods; some large chains buy such large lots that they can assign buyers

---

[28] "Coming: Customized Assortments," *Chain Store Age*, November, 1966, p. 69.

to find additional and lower cost sources of supply, especially important when they go into dealer branding.

Retail buyers constantly must decide how much of which products to stock and restock. One aid to the buyer is a form, the want slip, that salespersons, perhaps working directly for the buyer, make out to show customers' unfilled requests. Many retailers, however, can't afford to wait until wants materialize. They must anticipate them. To do this, they review trade papers, listen to ideas and plans of salesmen, and watch the sales of their competitors, especially the leaders in retailing. Often they look to New York City or nearby Commerce Cities for the latest trends. **Buyers must read the signs—and computer, too**

Buyers are not completely in the dark when they make their selections. Fads and fashions may come and go, but consumers always need suits, dresses, sugar, nails, and safety pins. Their sizes, appetites, and other needs don't change appreciably from year to year, and routine sales analysis and sales forecasting can be very helpful in anticipating future needs.

Retail buyers may be in charge of inventory control. To keep a close tab on stock on hand, most retailers—and especially the modern mass merchandisers—maintain detailed inventory controls. Some firms even use electronic computers to monitor the turnover of individual items. Inventory records are maintained on a dollar basis, unit basis, or both.

Dollar inventory control aggregates records for many products. Departments keep records in dollar terms on sales, gross margins, inventories, markups, markdowns, returns to sellers, and returns by customers. This kind of analysis shows general tendencies.

Unit control uses records of actual units—by types, sizes, styles, prices, colors, etc. These more detailed records help reveal best sellers, slow sellers, and any imbalance of stocks. Such close control makes it easier to buy intelligently and tends to make buying more routine.

Mass merchandisers are using unit control increasingly to quickly pinpoint sales of every product on their shelves. As one discounter put it, "We are not satisfied to know what we are selling in a thousand-foot area—we want to know quickly what we are selling on each table."

Over a given time period, such detailed data from the various stores in a chain can be used to identify trends and direct buying.[29]

In conventional retailing operations, however, much still depends on the buyer's judgment. Each buyer usually has a budget he stays within. This is a miniature profit-and-loss statement for each department or merchandise line. In an effort to make a profit, the buyer attempts to forecast sales, merchandise costs, and expenses. The figure for "cost of merchandise" is the amount the buyer has to spend over the period of the budget. If he has not yet spent it all, he is "open to buy." *The buyer, therefore, does have considerable latitude to exercise his judgment.* **Remember his ego, his invoice, his business**

[29] "What's the Sales Potential of Those Products Taking Up Space on a Store's Valuable Shelves," *Systems Management*, January, 1962, pp. 35 ff.

The buyer can be an important figure in a channel system.[30] He must be sold before the final consumer even has a chance to inspect the merchandise. His ego needs boosting just like an industrial buyer's. He is concerned about his future and buys accordingly. Nor are these trivial considerations. In most retailing operations, each buyer runs his own department and his decision is final. Special efforts may be needed to satisfy each one, even if this means invoicing in a certain way, packaging different assortments, and so on. In the extreme, each buyer may require a separate marketing mix.

When they buy—on Monday or in April

Proximity to sources of supply and speed of turnover help determine how often, and how far in advance, retailers place orders. Many retailers don't buy more than a week ahead because their wholesalers are nearby. Grocery supermarket buyers count on a continual flow from wholesalers and manufacturers and may place their orders every week. In grocery retailing, rapid turnover dictates frequent ordering.

Women's ready-to-wear retailers, on the other hand, may have to order well in advance of actual sale to assure delivery because some manufacturers may not make up the goods until they are sure of orders. Lead time, however, also depends on how far the retailer is from the central market. Dress buyers in New York City, for example, may buy several times a week; buyers in Pocatello, Idaho, may place their large orders only four times a year.

When a channel system has been developed, the retailers may be expected to place orders on a more regular and predictable schedule to smooth the flow of goods from manufacturer to wholesaler to retailer. This may change the retailer's ordering patterns somewhat, and perhaps increase or decrease inventory levels. But it all would be done to improve the efficiency of the whole channel.

Buyers are people who like to satisfy

The buyers in small stores usually are the owners or managers, since there is a very close relationship between buying and selling. In larger stores, buyers tend to specialize in certain lines. But usually those buyers sell as well as supervise the sales clerks who will sell the new merchandise. These buyers, therefore, are in close contact with their customers, *and* with their salespeople who are sensitive to the effectiveness of the buyer's efforts—especially when they are on commission. A buyer may even buy some items to satisfy the preferences of his salespeople.

As sales volumes rise, the buyer may specialize in buying only and have no responsibility for sales. Sears, for example, has a buying department of more than 3,000, supported by a staff department exceeding 1,400. There are 44 buying departments located in Sears' headquarters city, Chicago, with 6 in New York and smaller buying offices in Los Angeles, Dallas, Kansas City, Minneapolis, Atlanta, London, Brussels, Paris, Milan, Frankfurt, and Tokyo.

---

[30] For discussions of the importance of buyers, see E. J. Gross, "Bureaucracy, the 'Gatekeeper' Concept, and Consumer Innovation," *Journal of Retailing,* Spring, 1967, pp. 9–16, 64; "Prestige Store Grows Without Losing Gloss," *Business Week,* April 9, 1966, pp. 58–62.

Departments in Chicago and New York concentrate on a narrow assortment of items. Each is set up as an independent unit under a supervisor with a controller, a mail-order sales manager, a retail sales manager, and the buyers and assistant buyers.[31]

Resident buyers. Many department stores and ready-to-wear clothing chains handling fashion merchandise work with independent buying agents, called *resident buyers,* in the central markets of New York, Chicago, Los Angeles, and San Francisco. They cover new styles and fashions on the spot, and buy fill-in items as the retailers run out of stock during the year. Some resident buying organizations may buy everything except furniture, shoes, and food for their stores. Some resident buyers have hundreds of employees and buy more than $1-billion worth of goods a year.

Resident buying organizations fill a channel need to reach the many small manufacturers who cannot afford large selling organizations. Resident buyers' usually are paid an annual fee based on their purchases. The store's regular buyers often use the resident buyer's offices as headquarters on their regular buying trips to the central markets for fashion merchandise.

Committee buying and multiple buying influences. In some large chain store organizations, especially in grocery and variety lines, the major decisions—to add or drop lines or change buying policies—may be delegated to a committee. The seller still will contact the buyer, but the buyer does not have the final responsibility. In some organizations, the buyer prepares forms summarizing proposals for new products. The seller completes these forms but may not get to present his story in person to the buying committee.

This rational, almost cold-blooded approach reduces the impact of the persuasive salesmen, but it has become necessary because of the flood of new products. In an average week, 150 to 250 new items are presented for consideration to the buying offices of the larger food chains. If all were accepted, 10,000 new items would be added during a single year, more than their present stock! Obviously, buyers must be hardheaded and impersonal. About 90 percent of the new items presented to food stores are rejected.

Marketing managers must develop good marketing mixes when buying becomes so sophisticated and competitive. This approach is likely to become more common as computers facilitate sales and inventory analysis.[32]

What does the future look like?

The changes in retailing in the last 30 years have been extremely rapid. No end seems in sight. Scrambled merchandising may become more scrambled. Some analysts are forecasting larger stores while others are predicting smaller ones.

---

[31] "The Buying Story," reprinted from 1956 *Report to Stockholders,* Sears, Roebuck & Co., pp. 4, 5; "Inside Sears, Roebuck," *Printers' Ink,* October 22, 1965, pp. 15–30.
[32] E. B. Weiss, *The Decline of the Store Buyer* (New York: Doyle-Dane, Bernbach, Inc., 1961).

Perhaps the coming of servoselling

Any effort to forecast trends in such a situation is extremely risky, but the market grid approach may be helpful. Those who suggest bigger and bigger supermarkets and discount houses may be primarily concerned with the mass market. Those who look for more smaller stores and specialty shops may be expecting more small but increasingly affluent target markets, able to afford higher prices for different total products.

To serve these smaller but affluent markets, smaller, convenience-type grocery stores may continue to spread, and sales by vending machines—even with their higher operating costs and prices—may grow steadily. Certainly some customers are tiring of the large supermarkets that take so much of their time. Logically, convenience goods should be offered at the customer's convenience, not the retailer's as has been the case—some retailers still fight night and weekend hours, for example, when it is most convenient for many families to shop.

Telephone shopping is another possibility. The catalog houses and department stores already find phone business attractive. Telephone supermarkets, now a reality, sell only by phone and deliver all orders. Linking the phone to closed-circuit TV would enable the customer to see the goods at home while hearing well-prepared sales presentations. Then the customer could place an order through a small computer system or through a telephone system and have the billing and delivery arranged automatically. Some prophets are even talking about delivery systems directly into the home, just as gas and oil are delivered now.[33]

With present electronic and servomechanism capabilities, there seems to be no reason why the customer couldn't shop from his home instead of traipsing up and down the aisles of larger and larger shopping facilities.

Such an advanced form of automated retailing—perhaps the equipment involved would warrant the name "servoselling"—might take over a large share of the convenience-good and homogeneous shopping-good business.

If shopping centers are too conventional

Shopping centers may continue to grow but may feel increasing competition from mass merchandisers who were not able to or not interested in obtaining space in the planned shopping centers. If these shopping centers turn out to be strongholds of conventional retailers but don't meet the needs of today's target customers, then shopping centers may be forced to change their methods—or take the consequences. The branches of some department stores, for example, entered shopping centers with relatively high prices but are dropping them now.

Retailers becoming manufacturers and vice versa

We also may see more horizontally and vertically administered channel systems. One prophet foresees perhaps 50 giant corporate chains, together with perhaps 100 giant chains of independents, controlling most of the nation's retail sales.[34] These chains probably would

[33] E. B. Weiss, "What Will Retailing Be Like in 1975?" *Marketing Insights*, November 7, 1966, pp. 14–16; and A. F. Doody and W. R. Davidson, "Next Revolution in Retailing," *Harvard Business Review*, June, 1967, pp. 4–21.

[34] "Independent Retailing: New Outlook," *Printers' Ink*, April 5, 1963, pp. 53–54.

integrate vertically as well, or at the very least would work closely with their suppliers and perhaps become the channel captains.

All this would have a major impact on present manufacturers who already can see retailers developing their own brands and using manufacturers primarily as production arms. The large manufacturers themselves may go into retailing in the future for self-protection.

General Electric and Westinghouse, as noted earlier, are experimenting along this line. But they would not be the first, since Rexall Corp., Sherwin Williams, B. F. Goodrich, Van Heusen, and others already control or own retail outlets.[35]

One thing is certain—change in retailing is inevitable. For years, traditional retailers' profits have declined. And from 1958 to 1963, there was a 5 percent drop in their number. Even some of the newer discount houses and shopping centers have been posting disappointing records. Department stores and food and drug chains have experienced profit declines. The old variety stores have fared even worse. Some of these are shifting into mass merchandising operations, but this may only make that picture less attractive.

A selection of opportunities and problems

A few firms, among them Sears and J. C. Penney, have avoided this general profit squeeze. But generally, declining profits have helped cause the sometimes desperate moves into scrambled merchandising. Where it will all end is not yet clear, but it is safe to say that the imaginative marketing manager will find opportunities as well as problems in this unsettled situation.

Conclusion

There are many crosscurrents in today's retailing. Many new developments are resulting from changing customer preferences, rising incomes, aggressive action by competitors, and technical innovations.

But retailing is not completely chaotic. Some generalizations about the development of retailing institutions are possible. These can be summarized as follows:

1. Certain types of retailing facilities are extremely stable. It is likely that in every city in the country there are stores with ancient Roman counterparts, such as limited-line food and clothing stores.
2. Although the development of new retailers has frequently been viewed with alarm by conventional retailers, these newcomers have tended (*a*) to become a stable part of the retailing system, and (*b*) now account for only a relatively small percentage of retail sales. Sometimes the newcomers have encouraged changes—the traditional retailers have been forced into modifications—but they have not eliminated all the former leaders. This has been true for the department store chains, mail-order houses, and most recently, discount houses.
3. Changes in retail institutions appear to be evolutionary, not revolutionary, and usually reflect changes at the consumer level. Even changes caused by uncontrollable variables—the laws passed in the political

---

[35] E. B. Weiss, "Will Manufacturers Go into Retailing?" *Advertising Age,* December 31, 1962, pp. 35–36; "Has G. E. Taken Another Step Toward Retailing?" *Advertising Age,* September 3, 1962, p. 52; and "The Coming Crisis in Mass Retailing," *Advertising Age,* January 28, 1963, pp. 78–80.

environment, for instance—may be traced to the consumer. When very rapid changes do occur, it is usually because orthodox retailers have not recognized, or made adjustment to, changes in consumer behavior. Unmet demands open the door to innovators, and then conventional retailers may have to make swift and dramatic modifications to catch up. Such a situation very well may be in the making now.

Emphasizing the evolutionary nature of retailing does not mean that all competitors evolve at equal speed or with comparable success. Many do not see the portents of change until it is too late, or worse, attempt to ignore and resist them. Others simply do not have the resources to change their marketing strategy substantially.

It is vital that the marketing manager foresee these coming changes and estimate their impact on the existing retail structure and his own channels. The successful marketing manager will be the one who correctly anticipates—or at least meets—these changing customer demands by adjusting his place policies and marketing mixes accordingly.

Questions and problems

1 Identify a specialty store selling convenience goods in your city. Explain why you feel it is that kind of a store and why an awareness of this status would be important to a manufacturer. Does it give the retailer any particular advantage? If so, with whom?

2 Try to estimate the return to the owner and the profitability of a retail grocery store grossing about $150,000 in sales a year. First, compute the average daily sales volume needed to achieve this annual sales figure (assuming a six-day week). Then estimate the cost of help, rent, utilities, etc., that would be needed to handle this sales volume. Assume that competition would force him to operate at about a 20 percent gross margin. Briefly contrast the economics of this situation with that of the average supermarket.

3 What sort of a "product" are specialty shops offering? What are the prospects for organizing a chain of specialty shops?

4 A department store consists of many departments. Is this horizontal integration? Are all of the advantages of horizontal integration achieved in a department store operation?

5 Many department stores have a bargain basement. Does the basement represent just another department, like the hat department or the luggage department for example, or is some whole new concept involved?

6 Distinguish between voluntary and cooperative chains. Which is likely to be most effective in competing with corporate chains? Why?

7 Distinguish among discount houses, discount selling, and mass-merchandising. Forecast the future of low-price selling in food, clothing, and appliances.

8 In view of the wide range of gross margins (and expenses) in various lines of trade, suggest what the supermarket or scrambled merchandising outlet of the future may be like. Use care here. Are products with high gross margins necessarily highly profitable?

9 List five products which seem suitable for automatic vending and yet

are not normally sold in this manner. Generally, what characteristics are required?

10 Considering the nature of retail buying, outline the basic ingredients of promotion to retail buyers. Does it make any difference what kinds of products are involved? Are any other factors relevant?

11 How is the increasing professionalism of grocery chainstore buyers going to affect food processors' marketing mixes in the future?

12 Apply the "Wheel of Retailing" hypothesis to your local community. What changes seem likely? Does it seem likely that established retailers will see the need for change or will entirely new firms have to develop?

13 Discuss the kinds of markets served by the three types of shopping centers. Are they directly competitive? Do they contain the same kinds of stores? Is the long-run outlook for all of them similar?

14 Apply the product life-cycle concept to the growth and decline of various types of retailers, treating the retailer's total offering as a "product."

Wholesaling and
wholesalers

Wholesaling is extremely important in the marketing process. Wholesalers appear in many channel systems. To understand their role better, you should consider wholesalers primarily as members of channels rather than separate entities. You should ask how wholesalers fit into various channels, why they are used, and what effect they have on the marketing mixes of both manufacturers and retailers.

How to tell a wholesaler from a retailer

Precisely what is a "wholesaler?" What does he do?

These questions are hard to answer precisely, but one way to get at these definitions is to find out why a given firm wants to be considered a wholesaler rather than a retailer. There are several reasons why he might seek this classification.

First, in some channels, manufacturers permit only wholesalers to buy directly from them. The wholesalers, in turn, are expected to sell only to retailers. Exactly which firms will be permitted to buy from the manufacturer depends on how the manufacturer defines "wholesaler."

Second, and related to the first point, is the amount of discount granted. If retailers in a certain line normally expect a 30 percent discount off the suggested retail list price, then the wholesalers supplying them may be allowed a 45–50 percent discount off retail list price. They, in turn, are expected to pass on a 30 percent discount to their retailers. In practice, this can be much more complicated.

Some manufacturers set up a scale of wholesale discounts depending on the size of the wholesaler and the services he offers. Called "trade discounts," these are discussed further in the Pricing chapters. Correctly determining which firms are entitled to what trade discounts is especially important to manufacturers because of the provisions of the Robinson-Patman Act, prohibiting price discrimination and discriminatory discounts.

Third, some cities and states have retail sales taxes or taxes on inventories or gross receipts that apply only to retailers. These levies require record keeping and occasionally out-of-pocket costs when the retailer fails to collect the tax from the consumer. It is natural, therefore, that some firms should try to avoid classification as a retailer.

Fourth, fair-trade laws usually are binding only on retailer sales to consumers. Some discount houses have sold below the fair-trade price to consumers who were buying as "wholesalers." Being a member of a buying group—such as a labor union, church group, or local business concern—was sufficient rationalization for the purpose. Interestingly, some discount houses, although operating as wholesalers to avoid the manufacturer's ire, have not wished to risk prosecution by state taxing units and have charged a retail sales tax on these "wholesale" sales.

Any of these four points explains why a firm might wish to be labeled a wholesaler rather than a retailer. The *fifth* point operates in reverse. Retailers, but not wholesalers, are generally exempt from federal minimum-wage legislation, including the requirement that overtime be paid for more than 40 hours' labor a week.[1]

Despite the apparent difficulty in writing a single, hard definition of wholesaling, the *main* source of confusion is not simply semantic, but rather the wide variation in how wholesale firms operate—the functions performed, the cost of operations, and the operating policies followed.

Somebody has to do the wholesaling job

Many wholesalers perform more functions than we traditionally associate with the term. Some wholesalers engage in all four of the regrouping steps, and some of their sorting out and accumulation activities may even seem like manufacturing. As a result, we find some firms calling themselves manufacturer and jobber, or manufacturer and dealer. In addition, some use general terms such as merchant, dealer, distributor, or jobber because their actual operations are flexible, and they do not wish to be narrowly classified.

To avoid a prolonged technical and semantic discussion, we will use the U.S. Bureau of Census definition, the essence of which is:

Wholesaling is concerned with the activities of those persons or establishments which sell to retailers and other merchants, and/or to industrial, institutional, and commercial users, but who do not sell in significant amounts to ultimate consumers.[2]

It should be noted that producers who take over wholesaling functions are not considered wholesalers. However, if separate establish-

---

[1] For a detailed discussion of the definition of wholesaling and the operation and management of a wholesale business, see T. N. Beckman, N. H. Engle, and R. D. Buzzell, *Wholesaling* (3d ed.; New York: Ronald Press Co., 1959).

[2] Similar to definition in "Report of the Definitions Committee," *Journal of Marketing,* October, 1948, p. 217.

ments, such as branch warehouses, are set up, those facilities are counted as wholesalers by the U.S. census.

Wholesaling is a middleman activity. When a manufacturer goes direct, he still must assume the marketing functions that an independent wholesaler might provide. This is important from a channel standpoint. Wholesaling functions usually must be performed by some channel member, whether a wholesaler or the manufacturer himself.

Possible wholesaling functions

Wholesalers may provide functions for both their own customers and their suppliers—in short, for those above and below them in a channel. These wholesaling functions really are elaborations of the basic marketing functions—buying, selling, grading, storing, transporting, financing, risk-taking, and gathering market information. These wholesaling functions are basic to the subsequent discussion and should be studied carefully now. But *keep in mind that these functions may be provided by some but not all wholesalers.*

What a wholesaler may do for his customers

1. *Anticipates needs.* As a purchasing agent for his customers, the wholesaler forecasts his customers' demands and buys accordingly.

2. *Regroups goods.* The wholesaler provides at least one and sometimes all four of the regrouping steps in an effort to provide the assortment wanted by his customers at the lowest possible cost.

3. *Carries stocks.* The wholesaler carries inventory, relieving his customers of the necessity to carry a full inventory.

4. *Delivers goods.* The wholesaler frequently has transportation facilities and can provide prompt delivery service at low cost. Speed may be essential to keep factory production lines rolling or to satisfy a retailer's customers.

5. *Grants credit.* The wholesaler has traditionally extended credit to many of his customers, sometimes for several months. This financing function may be especially important to small customers and is sometimes the reason why they buy through wholesalers rather than directly from the manufacturer. Generally, the smaller the customer, the more financially dependent he is on wholesalers.

6. *Provides information and advisory service.* The wholesaler and his salesmen may be specialists in the products in which they deal. They are in a position to provide price and technical information as well as suggestions on how to install and sell products.

7. *Provides part of buying function.* Many customers appreciate the wholesaler having salesmen call on them. This relieves customers of the responsibility of looking for supply sources—that is, it simplifies *their* buying function. They have only to evaluate the worth of the various products offered.

8. *Owns and transfers title to goods.* Ownership of inventory permits a wholesaler and his customer to complete a sale without benefit of other intermediaries (such as a manufacturer or broker), thus facilitating the whole transaction.

368

1. *Provides part of producer's selling function.* The wholesaler sometimes seeks out supply sources, decreasing the number of salesmen the producer needs. The wholesaler also may participate in the producer's advertising and sales promotion programs.

2. *Stores inventory.* The classic wholesaling function of storing reduces a manufacturer's need for carrying large stocks, reducing his warehousing expenses.

3. *Helps finance by owning stocks.* Some producers, especially small ones, need financial assistance. When the wholesaler carries inventory, this reduces the producer's need for working capital.

4. *Reduces credit risk.* A producer's customers—retailers and other producers—are numerous, and some may be poor credit risks. It is expensive for a small producer, especially one far distant, to evaluate all of these potential credit risks when selling only one or a few products. The wholesaler who sells these customers many products is in a better position to evaluate their credit status. And if the wholesaler is a source of supply of many products, the customer may be more likely to pay him than to pay a manufacturer from whom he may not reorder.

5. *Provides market information.* The wholesaler is closer to the consumer and is in a better position to evaluate customer reactions. As an informed buyer and seller, he may reduce the producer's need for market research.

What a wholesaler may do for his producer-suppliers

Kinds and costs of available wholesale facilities

Table 18–1 lists the types, number, sales volume, and operating expenses of wholesalers operating in 1963. The differences in operating expenses suggest that each of these types is performing or not performing certain wholesaling functions. But which ones and "why?"

Why, for example, do manufacturers use merchant wholesalers costing 13.5 percent of sales when manufacturers' branches with stock cost only 10.6 percent?

Why use either when brokers representing sellers cost only 2.8 percent?

Is the use of wholesalers with higher operating expenses the reason why marketing costs are high—if, in fact, they are?

Historical background will help answer these questions.

In this text, we are emphasizing the evolutionary character of change in our economy. This concept applies fully to wholesaling. The American nation has transformed itself from colonial territory, dependent on the mother country for its finished goods in exchange for its raw materials, into a prime industrial nation. As output grew, so did the need for middlemen to handle it.

Each wholesaler found his niche

To serve the retail general stores of earlier times, early wholesalers carried a wide line of merchandise. They were called "general merchandise" wholesalers because their merchandise was so varied. We already have seen that the general store developed into a limited-line store as towns grew and more goods became available. To serve these stores, "single-line" wholesalers evolved; those specializing in very narrow lines were called "specialty" wholesalers. Single-line wholesalers were well established in the eastern grocery and dry-goods fields by the early 1800's. This same evolution took place a little later in the markets farther west.

Since wholesaling developed to distribute the greater production of

Table **18-1** *Wholesale trade, 1963, United States, by type of operation*

Type of Operation	Establish-ments (Number)	Sales (000,000)	Operating Expenses (Including Payroll) Percent of Sales
United States, total	308,177	$358,386	
Merchant wholesalers' total	208,997	157,392	13.5%
Service wholesalers:			
Wholesale merchants' distributors	194,121	135,857	14.6
Importers	5,724	9,243	8.9
Exporters	2,664	8,282	4.4
Terminal grain elevators	633	3,000	5.6
Limited function wholesalers:			
Wagon, truck distributors	5,825	1,010	13.0
Manufacturer's sales offices, sales branches, total:	28,884	116,443	7.2
Manufacturers' sales branches (with stock)	16,408	54,857	10.6
Manufacturers' sales offices (without stock)	12,476	61,586	4.2
Petroleum bulk plants, terminals, LP gas facilities, total	30,873	21,485	N. A.
Merchandise agents, brokers, total	25,313	53,245	3.6
Auction companies	1,894	5,141	2.6
Merchandise brokers	5,083	13,855	2.8
Commission merchants	3,416	9,524	2.7
Import agents	393	2,112	2.2
Export agents	544	2,179	2.8
Manufacturers' agents	11,189	10,941	6.0
Selling agents	2,574	8,292	3.9
Purchasing agents and resident buyers	220	1,201	2.6
Assemblers of farm products, total	14,110	9,820	9.0

SOURCE: *1963 Census of Business.*
(N.A.) Item not applicable.

the factories to an expanding population, wholesalers served not only retailers and final consumers but also manufacturers. Many manufacturers were so small that it was hard for them to contact the growing number of wholesalers or other manufacturer customers, and special wholesalers—called agents and brokers—developed to make these contacts. In general, specialized needs arose and specialized wholesaling institutions developed to meet them.

To get a clear understanding of wholesaling, we will identify and analyze as pure types, several specific kinds of wholesalers. Actually, however, it is difficult to find examples of pure types in wholesaling. No two wholesalers operate exactly alike. Rather, they are a blend of the basic types presented here. And it becomes even more difficult to identify the type by the name commonly used in a particular trade. Some so-called "brokers" actually behave as limited-function wholesalers, and some so-called "manufacturers' agents" operate as full-service wholesalers.

This casual use of terminology in the business world makes it important that you be thoroughly familiar with the pure types before trying to understand the hybrids. A manufacturer's or retailer's marketing manager should understand these differences *and* clearly specify his place objectives and policies before trying to select suitable wholesalers.

Learn the pure to understand the real

Merchant wholesalers

Merchant wholesalers are the most numerous. In 1963, they constituted about 68 percent of the wholesaling establishments—but handled only 44 percent of wholesale sales.

Their major distinguishing characteristic is that they take title; they assume the ownership of the goods they handle. They also provide some or all of the wholesaling functions. The two basic types of merchant wholesalers are: (1) service, sometimes called full-service, wholesalers, and (2) limited-function or limited-service wholesalers. Their labels are suggestive of their difference.

In international marketing, we find the same kinds of wholesalers in each country as we have in the United States. Also, there are merchant wholesalers who specialize in exporting and importing. They are sometimes called export merchants, distributors, import merchants, and importing wholesalers or jobbers. But again, names do not always identify function, and each firm must be evaluated individually.

Service wholesalers normally provide all of the functions discussed previously. Within this basic group are three main sub-types: (1) *general merchandise,* (2) *single line,* and (3) *specialty.*

Service wholesalers

General merchandise service wholesalers. General merchandise service wholesalers handle a broad variety of nonperishable staple items such as hardware, electrical supplies, plumbing supplies, furniture, drugs, cosmetics, and automobile equipment. With this broad line of convenience and shopping goods, they serve general stores, hardware stores, drugstores, electric appliance shops, and small department stores. In the industrial goods field, the mill supply house (or distributor) operates in a similar way. Somewhat like a hardware store, the industrial supply house carries a broad variety of accessories and supplies.

Single-line or general-line wholesaler. This type of wholesaler differs from general merchandise wholesalers or mill supply distributors in restricting himself to a narrower line—and sometimes to a specific line—such as dry goods, groceries, wearing apparel, paint, hardware, or certain types of industrial tools or supplies. In consumer goods, he

371

services the limited-line stores. In industrial goods, he covers a wider geographical area and offers more specialized service.

Specialty wholesalers. This type of wholesaler stocks only a narrow range of products. A *consumer goods* specialty wholesaler might carry only health foods or Oriental foods, rather than a full line of groceries. Or, the specialty house might carry only automotive items, selling exclusively to mass merchandisers. One such wholesaler, for example, is willing to arrange and stock his mass merchandisers' shelves, an important service to these retailers because their customers' behavior seems to vary according to geography. Final consumers in northern Indiana, for instance, respond to different shelf arrangements and products from those in southern Indiana.

The specialty wholesaler's task is to learn these differences, and adjust the stocks and displays accordingly. In this, he is going further than most merchant wholesalers. He is providing some of his customers' selling functions, since displays do most of the selling in mass merchandising outlets.

For industrial goods, a specialty wholesaler might limit himself to fields requiring technical knowledge or service, perhaps electronics or plastics.

The Cadillac Plastic and Chemical Co., in Detroit, became a specialty wholesaler serving the needs of plastics makers and users alike because neither the large plastics manufacturers nor the merchant wholesalers with wide lines were in a position to give individual advice to the many users (who often have little knowledge of which product would be best for them). Cadillac now carries 10,000 items and sells to 25,000 customers, ranging in size from the very small firms to General Motors.

Limited-function or limited-service wholesalers

The limited-function wholesaler, as the name implies, usually provides only some of the wholesaling functions. The full-service wholesaler frequently operates at higher cost because he does provide all of these services. Still, some customers do not want all these services, and some of the service wholesaler's policies do not exactly fit some customers' needs.

Rather than change or adjust policies for each customer, some wholesalers have set up separate departments or subsidiaries to give each customer the special assortment of services he wants. This usually means dropping one or more of the wholesaling functions discussed previously. Some full-service wholesalers have been slow to give the customer what he wants, however, and perceptive innovators have entered the market to supply the customer what he wants at the price he wants to pay.

Table 18–2 outlines the services typically provided by the various limited-function merchant wholesalers. It shows what services are, and are not, provided by each general type.

In the following paragraphs, the main distinguishing characteristics of each of the limited-function wholesalers will be discussed. These limited-function wholesalers are not numerous; in fact, they are not itemized separately in the 1963 census. They are, nevertheless, important in some trades. You should be able to identify the various pure

372

types of wholesalers so that you will be able to more fully understand the roles (and thus the operating costs) of the middlemen actually at work in the marketplace today.

Cash-and-carry wholesaler. Many small retailers, especially small grocers and garages, are too small to be served profitably by a service wholesaler. Discovering this, wholesalers establish a minimum charge or, in some cases, merely refuse to handle certain customers' business. Or they may establish cash-and-carry subsidiaries to give the small

Table **18–2** *Functions provided by limited-function merchant wholesalers*

	Limited-Function or Limited-Service					
	Cash-and-Carry	Drop Shipper (Desk Jobber)	Wagon or Truck	Mail Order	Coopera-tives	Rack Jobbers
Functions for customer:						
Anticipates needs	X		X	X	X	X
"Regroups" goods (one or more of 4 steps)	X		X	X	X	X
Carries stocks	X		X	X	X	X
Delivers goods			X		X	X
Grants credit		X	Maybe	May-be	Maybe	Consign-ment (in some cases)
Provides information and advisory services		X	Some	Some	X	
Provides buying function		X	X	X	Some	X
Owns and transfers title to goods	X	X	X	X	X	X
Functions for producers:						
Provides producer's selling function	X	X	X	X	X	X
Stores inventory	X		X	X	X	X
Helps finance by owning stocks	X		X	X	X	X
Reduces credit risk	X	X	X	X	X	X
Provides market informa-tion	X	X	Some	X	X	Some

retailer the products he needs in exchange for cash on the counter. This is like a retail store, but for small retailers; it can operate at lower cost because the retailer provides many of the wholesaling functions himself. And using cash-and-carry outlets may enable the small retailer to stay in business.

Drop-shipper (or desk jobber). A drop-shipper obtains orders from wholesalers, retailers, or industrial users, then passes these orders on to producers, telling them to ship directly to these customers. He takes title and technically owns the goods, but he does not physically handle, stock, or deliver them. This lowers his operating costs.

Drop-shippers most commonly deal in products that are so bulky that additional handling would be expensive and possibly damaging. Or the quantities may be so large that there is little need for "regrouping," as with rail carload shipments of coal, lumber, oil, or chemical products.

The drop-shipper's major function is selling, but he does have to locate supplies, arrange for transportation, finance customer purchases, and assume some of the risks that go with taking title to goods.

Wagon or truck wholesaler. This wholesaler is on the go, selling his stock from a wagon or truck. Handling perishable commodities in general demand, such as tobacco, candy, potato chips, and salad dressings, the truck jobber may provide almost the same functions as a full-service wholesaler. His major contribution is delivery of perishable lines that regular wholesalers prefer not to carry because of the special problems involved.

Truck wholesalers sometimes supply small service stations and back-alley garages with local delivery of the many small items they often forget to pick up from the service wholesaler. Truck wholesaler operating cost ratios are relatively high because they do a lot for the little they sell.

Mail-order wholesaler. We discussed catalog selling in the chapter on retailing. Wholesale mail-order houses operate in much the same way. In fact, many wholesale mail-order houses also will sell to *final* consumers who may, in some way, have access to their wholesale catalogs. To bona fide retailers, however, wholesalers give special discounts for ordering larger quantities. Otherwise, all the advantages and disadvantages of mail-order selling apply here. These houses operate in the hardware, jewelry, sporting goods, and general merchandise lines, often catering to small outlying stores.

Producers' cooperative. Producers' cooperatives are also limited-function wholesalers, although they frequently attempt to give the same service as service wholesalers. Here, the "profits" go to the cooperative's customer-members—in the form of patronage dividends.

The successful producers' cooperatives have emphasized the "sorting-out" process—to improve the quality of farm products offered to the market. They have also branded these improved products and then promoted the brands. These farmers' cooperatives sometimes have had success in restricting output and increasing price by taking advantage of the normally inelastic demand for agricultural commodities.

Examples of such organizations are the California Fruit Growers Exchange (citrus fruits), Sunmaid Raisin Growers Association, The California Almond Exchange, and Land O'Lakes Creameries, Inc.

Aside from demand stimulation and supply restriction activities, the cooperatives operate basically as service wholesalers.

Rack jobber—sells nonfoods in food stores. The rack jobber is a relatively new type of wholesaler, catering mainly to food stores and especially to supermarkets. He specializes in products, such as housewares, hardware items, and health and beauty aids, that frequently are displayed on wire racks he provides.

Many grocers do not wish to bother with reordering and maintaining displays of nonfood items, since it involves small quantities of so

374

many different kinds of goods. The regular wholesalers who were handling such items were not too interested in this business either, because opening up this new channel might jeopardize relations with their present customers. While many wholesalers specialize by product line, the rack jobber must handle a "scrambled" assortment because this is what consumers want.

The rack jobber is practically a service wholesaler, except that usually he is paid cash for the amount of stock sold or delivered. This is a relatively expensive operation, with operating costs calculated at 18.3 percent of sales in 1958, but sales have grown impressively because this way of selling offers convenience to some target customers. In 1960, nonfood sales through grocery stores almost equaled the total sales volume of hardware stores.[3] Although the large volume of nonfood sales from these racks has prompted some large chains to experiment with handling such items themselves, it appears now that rack jobbers can provide this service as effectively as (or more effectively than) the supermarket chains.

One of a merchant wholesaler's principal assets is his customer list. He attempts to offer a unique service to some customers. He may be the only one who does this particular job, and the manufacturer who wishes to reach the target customers served by this wholesaler may have to use him.

Wholesalers specialize by product and customer

Most wholesalers specialize by product or product line—an important fact for channel planners, and especially manufacturers who usually are product-oriented. The U.S. Census Bureau uses 140 categories to enumerate the kinds of businesses engaged in by merchant wholesalers. Most of these categories are by product classifications rather than by methods of operation.

Detailed data is available from the U.S. census on these various types of wholesalers. This data is not presented here, but for channel planning purposes it is important to know that such detailed information is available, usually by product categories.

The detailed census data also is categorized geographically. This enables the marketing manager to determine if there are potential channel members in his target areas.

Finally, the marketing manager must become intimately acquainted with specific firms that might be valuable in his channel system. Each of them might place different emphasis on the various marketing functions. Some might be classified as full-service wholesalers but also have flourishing separate departments providing limited functions.

The marketing manager must know what he wants done and then seek those who can do it most effectively.

Manufacturers' sales branches

The drive toward economic integration that began in the late 1880's had its effect in wholesaling, too. Many manufacturers set up their own

[3] James J. Sheeran, "The Role of the Rack Jobber," *Journal of Marketing,* July, 1961, pp. 15–21; and John D. Horn, "Merchandising Non-Food Items through Supermarkets," *Journal of Marketing,* April, 1954, p. 380.

sales branches whenever the sales volume or the nature of their products warranted it. By 1963, less than 9 percent of the wholesale establishments were manufacturers' sales branches, but they handled almost 32 percent of the total wholesale sales.

One reason for this disproportion is that these branches are usually placed in the most fertile market territories. This helps explain why their operating costs often are lower. But cost comparisons between alternate channels can be misleading, since cost allocation methods may differ. Sometimes the cost of selling is not charged to the branch but to the manufacturer's sales expenses. If all expenses were allocated similarly, it is likely that manufacturer's sales branches would prove more costly than they appear to be.

The U.S. Census Bureau collects extensive data showing the number, kind, location, and operating expenses of manufacturer's sales branches. Such data can help manufacturers determine competitors' distribution systems and probable costs. If many competitors are going direct, it may mean that there are no good specialists available—or at least none who can provide the functions desired.

Petroleum bulk plants, terminals and LP gas facilities

Another Census Bureau wholesale classification (see Table 18–1) covers wholesale petroleum product distribution. These specialized wholesalers work closely with the major oil companies. We will not treat them in detail here, since their major contribution to the marketing process is providing storage and handling facilities that are not generally applicable to other marketing management problems.

Merchandise agents and brokers

All merchant wholesalers at least take title to the goods, even when they do not actually handle them. These are the middlemen that most people picture when thinking of wholesalers. Yet there is another important group of middlemen—the merchandise agents and brokers —who do *not* take title. Their main service is to facilitate the producer's selling function. They normally provide even fewer functions than the limited-function merchant wholesalers. In certain trades, however, their contribution is extremely valuable, and they may operate at relatively low cost, say 1 to 5 percent of selling price.

Agents and brokers, like merchant wholesalers, generally specialize by customer type and by product or product lines, and so it is extremely important to determine exactly what each agent or broker does.

In the following paragraphs, only the most important points about each type of agent or broker will be stressed. For details on the functions provided by each, see Table 18–3, which continues the scheme used for merchant wholesalers, based on functions performed. It is obvious from the large number of vacant spaces in Table 18–3 that agents and brokers provide fewer functions than merchant wholesalers.

Auction companies are not numerous (see Table 18–1), but in certain lines they are extremely important. They are especially common in the

376

fruit, livestock, fur, tobacco, and used-car markets. For these products, demand and supply conditions change rapidly, and the product must be seen to be evaluated. Buyers and sellers, therefore, are brought together by the auction company, and demand and supply interact to determine price while the goods are being inspected.

Auction companies —just a shed down by the tracks

Facilities can be plain, keeping overhead costs low. Frequently, auction sheds are close to transportation facilities so that the commodities

Table **18-3** *Functions of agents and brokers*

Functions	Auction Companies	Brokers	Commission Merchants	Manufacturers' Agents	Selling Agents
Functions for customers:					
Anticipates needs		Some		Sometimes	
"Regroups" goods (one or more of four stages)	X		X	Some	
Carries stocks	Sometimes		X	Sometimes	
Delivers goods			X	Sometimes	
Grants credit	Some		Sometimes		X
Provides information and advisory services		X	X	X	X
Provides buying function	X	Some	X	X	X
Owns and transfers title to goods	Transfers Only		Transfers Only		
For producer:					
Provides selling function	X	Some	X	X	X
Stores inventory	X		X	Sometimes	
Helps finance by owning stocks					
Reduces credit risk	Some				X
Provides market information		X	X	X	X

can be reshipped quickly. The auction company charges a set fee or commission for the use of its facilities and services.

The broker's principal function is to bring buyers and sellers together. His "product" is information—about what buyers need and what supplies are available. He aids in buyer-seller negotiation and if the transaction is completed, earns a commission from whichever party engaged him.

Brokers— helpful guide in a strange land

Usually, some kind of broker will develop whenever and wherever market information is inadequate. Brokers are especially useful for selling seasonally produced products. For example, they could represent a small food canner during the canning season, then go on to other activities. Some have expanded their operations, still calling themselves "food brokers," but operating more like manufacturers' agents. They are discussed below.

Brokers also are active in used machinery, real estate, and even ships.[4]

[4] "Dealers in Ships, New and Old," *Business Week,* January 13, 1962, pp. 114–16.

These products are dissimilar, but the marketing functions needed are not. In each case, buyers come into the market infrequently, and someone with extensive knowledge of available products is needed to help both buyers and sellers complete the transaction quickly and inexpensively.

Commission merchants —to sell in absentia

Commission merchants are common in agricultural markets. When a producer does not use a local auction to sell his output, he may ship it to a big-city central market. There he needs someone to handle the selling function for him, since it is obviously not practical to accompany every shipment.

Commission merchants have grown up to meet this need. They are especially common in markets for livestock and grain, both commodities that buyers want to inspect and if they so choose, buy immediately. Commission merchants, although they do not take title, are generally permitted to sell goods at the market price or the best price obtainable above some stipulated minimum. They usually are numerous in central markets, each competing with the others and trying to get the highest price for his producer-sellers. Since prices in these markets usually are a matter of public record, the producer-seller has a check on the performance of his commission merchant. Usually costs are low because commission merchants handle large volumes of goods and buyers usually come to their central market location.

A commission merchant is similar to a broker, except that he actually handles goods, completes transactions, and remits the selling price (less his commission) to the seller.

Commission merchants sometimes are used in other trades, too, such as textiles, where many small producers wish to reach buyers in a central market without having to maintain their own sales forces.

Manufacturers' agents— free- wheeling, dealing, and selling

A manufacturers' agent works for several manufacturers almost as if he were each company's own salesman. He may cover one city or several states. If the sales potential of an area is low, he may be used in lieu of a company's own salesman. Or a small firm may have to use agents everywhere because sales volume is inadequate to support a sales force.

Manufacturers' agents can be useful in any field where many small manufacturers need representation. They are used frequently in the sale of machinery and equipment, dry goods, electrical goods, automotive products, clothing and apparel accessories, furniture, and some food products.

Manufacturers' agents usually know their own territory quite well and handle the noncompeting lines of several manufacturers. They work on commission and often can operate profitably in situations where a producer's sales force cannot. This is mainly because they have well-established contacts, detailed knowledge of an industry, and a wide line of goods obtained by representing several companies. This wide product line enables them to spread fixed selling costs over many products.

Like a manufacturer's salesman, the agent's main job is to call on

378

wholesalers or industrial customers or both. Orders picked up are sent to the producer, or the customer sends them directly to the producer, but in either case the agent is credited with the sale. Agents seldom have any voice in setting prices or determining the producer's policies.

As a service to customers, manufacturers' agents sometimes stock goods and make deliveries, but the majority concentrate on sales calls. The producer delivers the merchandise and bills the customers.

The distinguishing characteristic of manufacturers' agents is a rather freewheeling, independent, and aggressive approach to selling—especially in the sale of new products. They become specialists in certain lines and can be more effective than the producer's own sales force because of their wider experience and their good contacts with key customers.

In practicing their specialty of developing markets for new products, manufacturers' agents charge a healthy 10 to 15 percent commission. By contrast, their commission for large-volume established goods may be quite low—perhaps only 2 percent. The higher rates often come to be the agent's major disadvantage, from the manufacturer's point of view. The original commission rate may have seemed small when the product was new and sales volume was low, but once the product is selling well and large commissions are going to the agent, the agreed rate may seem high. At about this time, the firm often begins using its own salesmen, and the manufacturers' agent must look for another new product to develop.[5]

Food brokers—successful filling of a gap

Food brokers, operating like manufacturers' agents, have become extremely important in grocery distribution. More than half the processed goods sold by grocery stores is sold to them by these brokers.

Food brokers call on grocery wholesalers for their manufacturer clients. Some aggressive food brokers have become more involved with their client's marketing strategy than the typical manufacturers' agent. They may even work closely with the producer's advertising agency and marketing manager in planning overall strategy.[6]

For the usual commission of 5 percent of sales, these firms handle the whole selling function for manufacturers. For small manufacturers, they may perform a vital service; for large ones with many small divisions, they may be equally helpful.

Each food broker organization specializes in a given territory. Most manufacturers can achieve national distribution with between 70 and 100 food brokers.

The food broker fills a gap in the sales efforts of many manufacturers. The brokers generally have an effective sales force because they pay their salesmen well and keep them in the field. In contrast, manufacturers often use their sales territories as training grounds, and promote

---

[5] For a description of this situation in the electronic components industry, see "Easing the Squeeze on the Sales Rep," *Business Week,* July 13, 1963, pp. 130–31.

[6] "Food Brokers: New Force in Grocery Marketing," *Printers' Ink,* December 1, 1961, pp. 20–27; "Food Brokers Thrive on Local Sales Push," *Business Week,* June 17, 1961, pp. 55–62; and Frank Johnson, "Census Distortions of Food Broker Sales," *Journal of Marketing,* July, 1963, pp. 67–69.

their good salesmen to larger territories or home offices as soon as (or before) they have really become effective in their sales areas.

Selling agents— in effect, marketing managers

The selling agent functions somewhat like the manufacturers' agent, only he may handle competing lines. He usually takes over the whole *marketing* job nationally—not just the *sales* contacts in one area. He handles the entire output of one or more producers and has almost complete control of pricing, selling, and advertising. In effect, he becomes each producer's marketing manager.

Financial trouble is one of the main reasons a producer calls in a selling agent. The selling agent may provide working capital, but in turn he may take over the affairs of the business.

These agents have been especially common in highly competitive fields such as textiles and coal, and they also have been used for marketing lumber, certain food products, clothing items, and some metal products. In all these industries, marketing is much more important than production for the survival of firms. The selling agent provides the necessary financial assistance and marketing know-how.

International marketing is not so different

We find agents in international trade, too. Most operate much like those just described. Export agents, import agents, sales agents, indent agents, resident sales agents, and resident agents are all basically manufacturers' agents. Export commission houses and import brokers or factors are really brokers. Import commission houses may operate like commission merchants. Indent houses operate like the resident buyers described in the last chapter. A combination export manager serves as a blend of a manufacturers' agent and a selling agent, handling the entire export function for a number of manufacturers of allied but non-competitive lines.[7]

As with domestic agents, it is necessary to determine exactly what functions each institution provides before deciding to use it in a channel system. Agents are more common in international trade because of the critical problem of financing in that field. Many markets include only a few well-financed merchant wholesalers. The best many manufacturers can do is obtain local representation through agents and then handle the financing directly, often through banks with specialized services and facilities in international trade.

Assemblers of farm products

Assemblers are specialists in agricultural products. As already indicated, there are many small producers in the agricultural market. Output must be accumulated and sorted to ship it to market in the most economical quantities. Once accumulation and sorting are completed, the wholesalers already described may handle these commodities.

The specialists who do the sorting and accumulation are assemblers.

---

[7] To see the role some play, see "Japan's Giant Web of World Traders," *Business Week,* January 8, 1966, pp. 76–78; and "Decking the Halls with Imports," *Business Week,* December 17, 1966, pp. 134–38.

They also usually handle transportation, storage, grading, and financing, taking the risks these functions involve. The assembler's costs may be relatively modest, but for perishable items such as fresh fruits and vegetables, operating expenses may exceed 25 percent of sales. Such high handling costs help explain why farmers sometimes receive only 10 to 25 per cent of the retail price for some agricultural commodities.

Other specialized middlemen

Factors are specialists in financing. In effect, they are wholesalers of credit. They buy their clients' accounts receivables. Usually they specialize in certain lines of trade and are willing to extend credit for longer periods than commercial banks. Sometimes factors provide management advice or assistance and become almost selling agents. In fact, some are former selling agents who have concentrated on financing rather than selling. Like selling agents, factors are especially common in the highly competitive textile industry.

Factors— hiring a credit department

In buying accounts receivables, factors provide their clients with working capital. The factor's lending charge varies from 6 to 18 percent, depending on whether he has any recourse to the seller for collection in case of nonpayment. He may charge extra for his advice in customer selection and collection, and these additional charges may be 1 to 3 percent of the invoice face value. In effect, the factor may assume the function of a credit department, relieving his client of this expense.

Usually factors have many clients in a given line, such as textiles, and so are able to spread their risks over many customers. By specializing in a certain line, they get to know most of the buyers in the trade and are better able to evaluate the credit risks. One result is that while a buyer, for example, might be willing to delay payment to a single seller, he might not run a similar risk when he owes money to a factor. The factor might seriously hurt his credit rating or even cut off future credit.

Another specialist in financing is the field warehousing organization. If a firm has accounts receivable, it can use a factor or even borrow at a bank. But if it has financial problems and its goods are not yet sold, then borrowing may be more difficult. One solution to this problem is to move the goods to a public warehouse and obtain a warehouse receipt, which can then be used as collateral for borrowing at a bank. But moving goods can be expensive.

Field warehousemen— goods on hand are money from the bank

In field warehousing, the selling company's own warehouse is used, but a portion is formally segregated by the field warehouseman. The seller retains title to his goods, but control of them passes to the field warehouseman. He in turn issues a warehouse receipt, as collateral in borrowing. These field warehousing organizations usually know capital sources and may be able to arrange loans at lower cost than obtainable locally.

Using this method, large stocks may be maintained at various distribution points in anticipation of future needs. Or economical production runs can be made and then stored at the factory against future needs.

Sales finance companies normally deal only in consumer credit, but a number have become interested in financing inventories for middlemen, especially auto and appliance dealers. This type of financing is called "floor planning." Many auto dealers, for example, do not own outright any of the cars on their display floors. They may have only a 10 percent interest in each of them, the other 90 percent belonging to a sales finance company. The auto dealer has physical possession, but the finance company owns the cars, and the proceeds from sales may go directly to it.

In effect, these companies are providing part of the dealer's financing function. But because the goods are usually well branded, and therefore easily resold, there is relatively little risk. The charge to the dealer for these services may be as low as 6 percent a year, depending on the finance company's cost of borrowing money in the capital markets.

Geographical distribution of wholesalers

Wholesalers, like retailers, must consider both the location and preferences of their target customers when deciding on their own locations. And where they are affects the jobs of other channel members, too. Some wholesalers, such as petroleum distributors whose customers are widely dispersed geographically, are widely dispersed. Likewise, assemblers of farm products do most of their work close to the farm, often in Countyvilles.

Despite this dispersion, however, 42.3 percent of all wholesale sales in 1963 were made in the 10 largest standard metropolitan statistical areas, those with populations exceeding 2 million. And these 10 areas plus the next 14 largest SMSA's, with populations of 1 to 2 million, accounted for 59.1 percent of all wholesale sales.

This heavy concentration of wholesale sales in large cities is caused, in part, by the concentration of manufacturers' sales offices and branches plus agents and brokers in Commerce Cities, where there are more wholesalers and industrial buyers. Some large manufacturers buy for many plants through one purchasing department located in the general offices in those cities. And large general merchandise wholesalers often are located in these transportation and commerce hubs.

The prominent role played by the New York City area should be especially noted—16.1 percent of all wholesale sales. This results partly from the concentration of much of the U.S. wholesale clothing and jewelry industries in this one market. But it also points up the important role played by all large Commerce Cities in the nation's trade.

Methods of operation

Now that we know what the various kinds of wholesalers are like, let's see how they operate. This is especially important to manufacturers' marketing managers because they must know how wholesalers operate in order to deal with them.

This section will be concerned with *what* and *for whom* wholesalers buy, *how* they buy, *when* they buy, and *who* in the organization is responsible for buying. For the sake of clarity, we will limit our discussion to merchant wholesalers, since they are the most numerous and provide so many wholesaling functions.[8] The foregoing descriptions of the other wholesaler types are suggestive of their methods of operation.

That popular retailing philosophy, "Goods well bought are half sold," is equally appropriate for merchant wholesalers. Their main function is obtaining the products of many manufacturers and distributing them in smaller quantities to customers—that is, adjusting discrepancies of quantity and assortment.

Give the customer what he wants—period

The merchant wholesaler is not expected to judge the desirability of products but simply to get his target customers the products they want.

He is not in a position to educate consumers either, although some wholesalers have conducted limited consumer research in an effort to help their customers operate their businesses more profitably.[9] Few merchant wholesalers make such efforts but rely instead on their own judgment, their salesmen, and manufacturers' research.

Most wholesalers handle so many items that they cannot give continual individual attention to all of them. A grocery wholesaler may stock up to 20,000 items; a drug wholesaler, up to 125,000; and a dry-goods wholesaler, up to 250,000 items.

How they buy—the perpetual, automatic, contractual shopping list

Understandably, most wholesalers buy the bulk of their products on a routine, automatic reorder basis, once the initial decision to stock these products has been made. Most wholesalers try to maintain two months' inventory on most items, except faster moving items. They carry two weeks' to a month's inventory of these items and watch them more closely, so that there is time to reorder before supplies are too low.

Most dry-goods firms order standard items, such as sheets, pillowcases, and towels, on this basis. Drug wholesalers, hardware wholesalers, electrical wholesalers, and industrial distributors follow the same procedure for their standard items.

Careful maintenance of inventory records makes routine buying practical. Only a minority of wholesalers keep perpetual inventory records on all of their items, but most do keep records on the fast-moving or high-unit-value items. One drug wholesaler, for example, maintains a perpetual inventory record on 800 items that are extremely important to his operation.

Modern record-keeping systems—including Robot Kardex equipment, punched card accounting machines, and computers—enable progressive wholesalers to maintain perpetual inventory on all of their items, often at little or no increase in cost. One New York drug wholesaler modernized his inventory record system and expanded

---

[8] Much of this material is based upon R. S. Alexander and James Snitzler, "Wholesale Buying and Merchandising," *Journal of Marketing,* September, 1949, pp. 178–91. The *average* wholesaler has not changed too much since then.

[9] See, for example, "Streamlining the Middleman," *Business Week,* July 21, 1962, pp. 64–67.

sales volume 6.9 percent while lowering administrative costs.[10] A plumbing-heating wholesaler adopted Robot Kardex equipment and now maintains a perpetual inventory on 13,000 items. This system so speeds pricing and other activities, thereby cutting his other costs, that this inventory control system operates "for free."[11] This helps explain why more wholesalers are adopting such systems.

Companies lacking this timesaving equipment usually control inventory by taking a monthly count of all items and a biweekly count of fast-moving items. Assuming a normal two months' inventory, this procedure may be satisfactory. For the small firm, more accurate control might be too expensive compared to the cost of carrying "a little extra" inventory.[12]

Some wholesalers rely on the order pickers in the warehouse to assure maintenance of at least minimum stocks. But this procedure obviously depends on the reliability of the warehouse help.

Whatever the method of inventory control, some procedure must be developed for deciding how much to carry and when to reorder. Mathematicians and statisticians have been working with the problem of optimum inventory, and wholesalers are beginning to use their statistical techniques.

The previously mentioned wholesaler who adopted the Robot Kardex system uses a probability system for setting stock levels. He found it unprofitable to have every single item in stock at all times. Inventory levels, therefore, are set so that supplies of some items probably will be exhausted occasionally. Being willing to be out of stock on any item once in five years enabled this wholesaler to reduce the investment required to carry inventory. This wholesaler not only is willing to be out once in five years—he *plans* to be out that often. Using monthly sales and purchase records accumulated over several years, it is not difficult to adjust stock levels when items do not run out as planned.[13]

In addition to the routine buying, some wholesalers buy products on seasonal or annual contracts. Among products that may be bought in this way are antifreeze, blankets, rubber footwear, suntan lotion, cough syrups, lawnmowers, fans, heaters, garden hose. Seasonal or annual contracts assure the wholesaler of an adequate supply and also enable the manufacturer to plan his production, thereby reducing manufacturing costs. Channel system thinking can be seen in action here.

Seasonal items are sometimes bought 6 to 10 months before they are sold; such advance stocking adds to the cost of wholesaling. Some wholesalers attempt to reduce or avoid it when possible. They may insist that the material merely be consigned to them—they receive but do not own or pay for it—or they ask manufacturers to "forward-date"

[10] "Saving Money Is Fine; Making More Is Even Better," *Systems Management*, January, 1962, pp. 30 ff.

[11] "Aaron Company's Total Inventory Control of 13,000 Items," *Supply House Times*, February, 1959, pp. 48–70.

[12] Donald F. Mulvihill, "Inventory Control for Small Wholesalers," *Management Research Summary*, Small Business Administration, 1963; and "Controlling Inventory in Small Wholesale Firms," *Small Marketer's Aids*, No. 122, Small Business Administration, September, 1966.

[13] "Aaron Company's Total Inventory Control of 13,000 Items," *op. cit.*, p. 53.

their invoices so that payment is not due until a later date, perhaps during the actual selling season. In addition, a wholesaler may require that manufacturers guarantee the price of the goods they take in stock and even permit the return of merchandise if new or better products are brought out before the selling season.

It is obvious, then, that most wholesalers order rather routinely once the original decision to stock an item has been made. The next questions are, who makes the initial buying decision and how is this decision reached?

Who buys —and how can they do it for less?

Clerks handle much of the routine wholesale buying by simply reordering the items that the inventory control procedure shows to be out of stock. Unless the company has modern data processing equipment, the sheer bulk of paper work on so many items precludes extensive analysis of what products are selling best, which ought to be dropped, or what new items ought to be added.

Most wholesalers are reluctant to drop items, because they feel obligated to provide "service" to their customers. Under these circumstances, the manufacturer's major hurdle is to get his product onto the wholesaler's buying list in the first place. Since wholesale buyers seldom seek new supply sources, it is easy to understand why manufacturers must employ salesmen or agents to reach wholesalers.

In a small firm, the owners, partners, or general manager will make the decision to add or eliminate items. In larger firms, the buying decisions may be made by a committee including the president, general manager, or a vice president in charge of buying. Some firms include the sales manager in buying talks because of the interdependence of purchasing and sales in wholesaling businesses. In fact, some businessmen feel that the two activities should not be separated at all, and they use "merchandise managers" to direct and control both buying and selling in specific lines.

In larger companies, merchandise managers handle certain lines of goods. Reporting to them are buyers who are even more specialized in the items they buy but often have no control over the selling function. All of this is similar to the specialization we saw in retail buying.

The degree of buyer specialization depends on the size of the company and the variety of goods handled. A large grocery house in the Middle West employs nine buyers, some of whom buy as many as 50 types of articles. A medium-sized hardware house employs four buyers, specializing in garden tools and supplies, electrical appliances, general tools, and miscellaneous items. A large firm in the hardware field divides its buying work among 13 buyers, each specializing in one of the following lines of goods.

Mechanical and industrial supplies
Plumbing and heating
Farm and garden supplies
Sporting goods
Builders' hardware
Painters' supplies and drapery fixtures
Industrial supplies

Heavy hardware
Housewares and gifts
Major appliances
Electrical supplies
Guns and ammunition
Cutlery, toys, and wheel goods

At the other end of the scale is the small house which has two buyers, one purchasing builders' hardware and the other buying all other items.[14] Yet regardless of the buyer's title or scope, the wholesale buyer is basically economic in his choices—yet he, like industrial and retail buyers, is susceptible to ego boosting and other appeals.

Some wholesale firms, dispersed geographically, delegate some buying to independent purchasing agents or resident buyers who are located in central markets, such as New York or Chicago. Such agents maintain continuous contact with manufacturers on behalf of many wholesalers. These organizations are especially helpful to the smaller wholesaler, allowing him, in effect, to shift some of his buying responsibility to a specialist who can buy efficiently at minimum cost. Some wholesalers use these outside buyers for standard and routine items, handling the nonstandard and fashion items themselves.

Such outside buying groups are working for the buyer (the wholesaler, in this case) and not the seller. These buyers usually make a commission charge to the buyer; since the passage of the Robinson-Patman Act, their connections with the buyer preclude their obtaining additional discounts from the seller that are not justified by cost savings. Their existence depends upon providing additional information and better buying for less money than it would cost the wholesaler to do the job himself.

Comeback and future of the wholesaler

In the 1800's, the wholesaler held a dominant position in marketing. The many small producers and small retailers needed his services. As producers became larger, some bypassed the wholesaler by setting up their own sales organizations or by selling directly to industrial customers. When retailers also began to grow larger—and especially during the 1920's, when chain stores began to spread rapidly—many predicted a dire future for the wholesaler. Chain stores normally assume the wholesaling functions, and it was thought that the days of the independent wholesaler were numbered.

Not fat and lazy but enduring Some analysts and critics felt that the decline of the wholesaler might be desirable from the social point of view, for many wholesalers had apparently grown "fat and lazy," contributing little more than breaking bulk. Their salesmen often were only order takers; the selling function was neglected; high-caliber management was not attracted to the wholesaling industry, and it became a domain of vested interests which many persons felt should be eliminated.

Our review here, however, has shown that wholesaling functions *are*

[14] Alexander and Snitzler, *op. cit.,* p. 179.

386

necessary, and wholesalers have not been eliminated. True, their sales volume declined from 1929 to 1939, but wholesalers have since made a comeback. By 1954, they had regained the same relative importance they had in 1929,[15] and they have continued to hold their own since then.

Wholesalers have held their own, in part, because of new management and new techniques. To be sure, there are still many operating in the old ways, and wholesaling has had nothing comparable to the rapid changes in retailing. Yet progressive wholesale firms have become more concerned with their customers and with channel systems. Some are offering more services to their independent customers, and others are developing voluntary chains, as noted in Chapter 17, that bind them more closely to their customers.

Producing profits, not chasing orders

Today's *progressive* wholesaler no longer is a passive order taker. As part of the "new look" in wholesaling, not only have many of the salesmen been eliminated, but in place of the old order takers wholesalers are now using order slips similar to those used between a chain warehouse and chain retail stores.

Some modern wholesalers no longer require all customers to pay for services simply because some customers use them. This traditional practice had the effect of encouraging limited-function wholesalers and direct channels. Now, some wholesalers are making a basic service available at a minimum cost, then charging additional fees for any special services required. In the grocery field, for instance, the basic servicing of a store might cost the store 3 to 4 percent of wholesale sales. Then promotional assistance and other extra aids are offered at extra cost.

Modern wholesalers also are becoming more selective in picking customers as cost analysis shows them that many of their smaller customers are clearly unprofitable. With these less desirable customers gone, the wholesaler can give even more attention to the preferred customers. In this way, he is helping to promote healthy retailers who are able to compete in any market. The larger, more profitable customers receive the best service the wholesaler can give. As one executive said: "We try to train our people to evaluate profits beforehand, not just to chase after orders."[16]

Some wholesalers have renamed their salesmen "store advisers" or "supervisors" to reflect their new roles. These representatives provide many management advisory services, including location analysis; store design and modernization; legal assistance on new leases or adjustments in old leases; store-opening services; and sales training and merchandising assistance, and advertising help. Such salesmen, really acting as management consultants, must be more competent that the mere order takers of other days.

---

[15] Paul D. Converse, "Twenty-Five Years in Wholesaling: A Revolution in Food Wholesaling," *Journal of Marketing,* July, 1957, pp. 40–41.

[16] "The Changing Anatomy of Industrial Sales Distribution," *Dun's Review & Modern Industry,* January, 1963, pp. 37 ff.

Training a modern wholesaler's salesmen is not an easy task, and it is sometimes beyond the capacity of management in small wholesale firms. In some fields, such as the plumbing industry, wholesaler trade associations have taken the problem in hand. They organize training schools designed to show wholesaler-salesmen how they, in turn, can help retailers manage their businesses and promote sales. These schools may give instruction in bookkeeping, figuring a markup, collecting accounts receivable, advertising, and sales planning—all in an effort to train salesmen to improve retailers' effectiveness as channel members.[17]

We have noted that some wholesalers are now using electronic data processing systems, and in the next chapter, we will see what some wholesalers are doing to modernize their warehouses and physical handling facilities.

Some wholesalers are offering central bookkeeping facilities for their customers, realizing that their survival is linked to their customers' survival. In this sense, some wholesalers are becoming more channel systems minded, no longer trying to overload retailers' shelves but now trying to clear the merchandise *off* the retailers' shelves.[18] They follow the adage, "Nothing is really sold until it is sold at retail."

Despite these changes, though, not all wholesalers today are progressive. Many still follow outmoded practices; some of the smaller, less efficient ones may have difficulty in the future. While the average operating expense ratio is 13.5 percent for merchant wholesalers, some small wholesalers have expense ratios of 20 to 30 percent.

Low cost, however, is not the only criterion for success. The higher operating expenses for some smaller wholesalers may be a reflection of the special services they offer. Truck distributors are usually small and have high operating costs, yet some customers are willing to pay the higher cost of this service. Some of the apparently expensive, older, full-service wholesalers probably will continue operating because they offer the services and contacts needed by some small manufacturers. And, of course, some goods and some markets traditionally have slow turnover; wholesalers may be the best choice here even though they have high operating expenses.

Even making these allowances, though, it is clear that the smaller wholesalers and the larger, less progressive ones face future difficulty unless each has carved out a specific market for itself. Profit margins are not large in wholesaling, typically ranging from less than 1 percent to 2 percent. And they have been declining in recent years as the competitive squeeze has become tighter.

In short, the institution of wholesaling certainly will survive, but weaker, less aggressive wholesale firms may not. Retailers and industrial customers are motivated basically by economics. They will patron-

---

[17] *Dealer Development Institute Progress Report* (Chicago: Central Supply Association, August 27, 1958).

[18] For further discussion of these ideas, see E. H. Lewis, "Comeback of the Wholesaler," *Harvard Business Review*, November–December, 1955, pp. 115–25; E. B. Weiss, "The Independent Druggist Gets More Tranquilizer Pills," *Advertising Age*, June 3, 1963, pp. 88–90; and Robert L. Bull, "Counseling Affiliated Food Retailers," *Management Research Summary*, Small Business Administration, 1963.

ize those middlemen who help them most. They are concerned with their own success and with the efficiency of their channel, not with the success or failure of a particular wholesaling firm.

Conclusion

Wholesalers can provide functions for those both above and below them in a channel of distribution. These services are closely related to the basic marketing functions. There are many types of wholesalers. Some provide all the wholesaling functions while others specialize in only a few. Eliminating wholesalers would not eliminate the need for the functions they provide, and we cannot assume that direct channels will be more efficient.

Merchant wholesalers are the most numerous and account for a sizable share, although not the majority, of wholesale sales. Their distinguishing characteristic is that they take title and often physical possession of goods. Agents and brokers, on the other hand, act more like salesmen for sellers or representatives for buyers, and usually they do not take title or possession.

Despite various predictions of the demise of wholesalers, they continue to exist, and the more progressive have adapted to a changing economic environment. No such revolutions as we saw in retailing have yet taken place in the wholesaling area and none seems likely. But it is probable that some smaller and less progressive wholesalers will fail.

We have seen that some modern wholesalers are acting more like channel captains or at least close advisers to their associated retailers, especially when they are a part of voluntary or cooperative chains. Others are adopting modern data processing and materials handling methods, and trying to improve their position in the channel.

Independent wholesalers are still vital to some smaller manufacturers, retailers, and industrial customers, but some producers and retailers are big enough to handle the wholesaling functions themselves and do so when it is economically desirable. Some wholesalers also find competition from other wholesalers as well as from producers and retailers. As a result, profit margins are not large in wholesaling—and we find progressive wholesalers providing useful functions very economically in many channels of distribution.

---

1 Discuss the evolution of wholesaling in relation to the evolution of retailing.

2 What risks do merchant wholesalers assume by taking title to goods? Is the size of this risk about constant for all merchant wholesalers?

3 Why would a manufacturer set up his own sales branches if established wholesalers were already available?

4 What is an agent middleman's marketing mix? Why don't manufacturers use their own salesmen instead of agent middlemen?

Questions and problems

5 Explain the concentration of merchant wholesalers in Commerce Cities. Is this true of all wholesalers? Is this concentration likely to become more pronounced in the future? What impact will the continued development of Interurbia have on the location of wholesalers?

6 Discuss the future growth and nature of wholesaling if low-margin retailing and scrambled merchandising become more important. How will wholesalers have to adjust their mixes if retail establishments become larger and the retail managers more professional? Might the wholesalers be eliminated? If not, what wholesaling functions would be most important? Are there any particular lines of trade where wholesalers may have increasing difficulty?

7 Which types of wholesalers would be most appropriate for the following products? If more than one type of wholesaler could be used, provide the specifications for the situation in each case. For example, if size or financial strength of a company has a bearing, then so indicate. If several wholesalers could be used in this same channel, explain this also.

   a) Fresh tomatoes   e) Men's shoes
   b) Paper stapling machines f) An industrial accessory machine
   c) Auto mechanics' tools   g) Ball-point pens
   d) Canned tomatoes   h) Shoelaces

8 If you were operating a small grocery store (say $50,000 annual sales volume) in a Forest Lake where several large grocery chains were operating, would it be desirable to affiliate with a voluntary or cooperative chain? (Make any necessary assumptions about your product policy, etc., to obtain a specific answer.)

9 In view of the large size of many manufacturers and retailers, how can the existence of wholesalers be explained? It would seem that these large firms could buy and sell in quantity directly from each other.

10 Would a drop shipper be most suitable for the following products: coal, lumber, iron ore, sand and gravel, steel, furniture, or tractors? Why, or why not? What channels might be used for each of these products if drop shippers were not used?

11 Explain how factors differ from commercial banks and why factors developed.

12 Discuss the impact of field warehousing on place policies. How can this help the marketing manager?

13 Which types of wholesalers are likely to become more important in the next 25 years? Why?

Physical distribution

Physical distribution is the actual handling and moving of goods within individual firms and along channel systems. It is one of the most important and basic steps in bringing goods to customers. Nearly half the cost of marketing is spent for it.

Goods in the factory are somewhat like the "sound" of the fallen tree in the deserted forest. They really have no "use" at all. Possession utility is not possible until Time and Place utility have been provided. This usually requires the transporting and storing functions that are part of physical distribution.

As the marketing manager develops Place policies, he must consider how the transporting and storing functions can and should be divided within the channel. Who will store and transport the goods, and who will pay for these services? Merely deciding to use certain types of wholesalers and retailers does not automatically or completely answer these questions. A wholesaler may use his own trucks to haul goods from a producer to his warehouse and from there to retailers, but the manufacturer may give him a transportation allowance. Another wholesaler may want the goods delivered to him.

Knowing who will haul and store is essential

When developing a marketing mix, the marketing manager must consider precisely how these functions are to be shared. For this will affect the other three P's, especially Pricing.

The truth is, however, that there is no "ideal" sharing arrangement. Physical distribution can be varied endlessly in a marketing mix and in

391

a channel system. To appreciate the possibilities, we need to know more about the transporting and storing functions and the specialists who handle these functions.

In this chapter, we will discuss these subjects and also some important new developments in physical distribution, including the distribution center, the total cost approach, and the physical distribution manager.

Remember that physical distribution is an important, though often neglected, activity. It even has been called the "other half" of marketing.

Today, marketing-oriented firms are not neglecting physical distribution. This chapter deserves careful study.

The transporting function

From backpack to cargo planes

Transportation, so vital to an interdependent society, now accounts for nearly 10 percent of the U.S. gross national product.[1] Without transportation there could be no mass distribution with its regrouping activities, or any urban life as we know it today. We see this most clearly during a major rail or truck strike.

Before powered vehicles, when the movement of goods was limited to what a man could carry on his back or haul in a wagon, transportation was so difficult, expensive, and time-consuming that most people didn't try to transport much. They lived where the goods were, on self-sufficient farms. They traded their surpluses in nearby markets. Such poor transporting facilities still exist in many underdeveloped countries and inhibit economic development.

Early societies developed along seacoasts or rivers partly because transportation of goods by water was easier than by land. Yet even most commercial river transportation was one-way—downstream—until the development of steamboats in the early 1800's. Then the major river valleys, such as the Ohio and Mississippi, prospered. Cincinnati, for example, became a great wholesale and meat-packing center after the steamboats began plying the Ohio in both directions.

The introduction of the first practical steam locomotive in 1829 opened up a whole new era for inland transportation. In the United States, rail transport made it possible to ship midwestern farm produce to the eastern industrial area, lowering food prices there considerably. Later, motor trucks and highways brought even small towns and remote farms closer to the markets.

Air transport has not had as spectacular an impact on marketing as other modes; the reason is its higher cost. For higher value items, though, shipping by air is of growing importance.

The availability of air transport, ironically, may have an unfortunate side effect in less developed countries. It may discourage the development of more basic transportation facilities in areas such as Central and South America, and some parts of Africa, where air transportation is developing rapidly—but at the expense of other methods. Ultimately,

[1] J. L. Heskett, R. M. Ivie, and N. A. Glaskowsky, Jr., *Business Logistics* (New York: Ronald Press Co., 1964), pp. 10–17.

dependence on air transportation could severely limit trade in and among these countries.

The cost of shipping an average product by rail is about 5 percent of wholesale cost.[2] For many bulky or low-value products, however, the percentage of cost is much higher. Transporting sand and gravel, for example, costs about 56 percent of its value; bituminous coal, 41 percent; cabbage, 37 percent; watermelons, 28 percent; and iron ore, 18 percent. At the other extreme are lighter or more valuable commodities, such as copper ore and copper concentrates and business and office machines, at less than 1 percent of wholesale cost; cigarettes, cotton cloth, and butter, less than 2 percent.[3]

Can you afford to get to the target?

Transportation costs may limit the target markets that the marketing manager can consider. Shipping costs increase delivered cost, and this is what most interests the customer. High costs for goods in outlying areas, caused by higher transportation costs, encourage local production. The high costs of shipping sand and gravel dictate that these materials be sold in the limited geographical areas near the pits where they are extracted.

If a product is unique in some way, however, customers who really want it will have to bear the transportation costs. A unique clay product selling for only $12.50 a ton in Georgia costs an additional $12 a ton to ship to an Ohio paint factory. A unique paint ingredient, pyrophyllite, costs only $20 a ton in the Carolinas but another $21 a ton to transport to a California paint plant.

The transportation rates we have been referring to are those charged by *common carriers,* such as the railroads and major truck lines. These carriers, given a franchise by a government regulatory body, must accept merchandise from any shipper and maintain regular service. They usually must obtain permission to discontinue service or change their rates.

How transportation costs are decided

In contrast to common carriers are *contract carriers,* who are less strictly regulated and do not maintain regular schedules. They make up a more freewheeling group. They can work for anyone for an agreed sum and for any length of time. Like agents and brokers, they will appear wherever needed.

In the following discussion of transportation rates, we will concentrate on *rail common carrier rates,* since they set a competitive standard. Most other transportation rate structures have similar characteristics.

The railroad rate structure was developed by governmental regulatory commissions. The underlying rationale of the rate structure was that the railways could carry the heavy and bulky items—such as sand and gravel—at a relatively low charge per ton; carry the more valuable, less bulky items at higher rates per ton; and then balance the low

[2] D. Philip Locklin, *Economics of Transportation* (4th ed.; Homewood, Ill.: Richard D. Irwin, Inc., 1954), p. 35.
[3] D. Philip Locklin, *Economics of Transportation* (5th ed.; Homewood, Ill.: Richard D. Irwin, Inc., 1960), p. 33.

charges against the high charges to show a profit. As we will see, however, this has not worked out as planned. The railroads have been carrying the heavy bulky items at low rates, but trucks and airlines have been taking the high-rate business.

There are three basic types of rates: (1) class, (2) commodity, and (3) exception. These three kinds of rates are quoted for carloads (CL, 60,000–100,000 lbs.), truckloads (TL, 15,000 lbs. or more), less than carloads (LCL), and less than truckloads (LTL).

Rates on these smaller shipments vary but are often twice as high as those on larger shipments. These rate differentials are one reason for the development of wholesalers, who buy in larger quantities than most users need to get the advantage of large-shipment rates and then sell in the smaller quantities the users *do* need.

Bear in mind that there need be nothing absolutely final about the present rate structure; since it is man-made, it could be changed. If it were changed, it might lead to a vastly different, and perhaps more efficient or more equitable, transportation system. In some other countries, for instance, these rate differentials are much smaller or nonexistent. As a consequence, goods are shipped in much smaller quantities, freight cars are smaller, and wholesalers and retailers handle smaller quantities.

Class rates—higher rates for smaller volume. The railroads handle so many different products that they have had to develop a freight classification system covering more than 10,000 different articles or groups of articles. Each class is assigned rates based on the cost and value of the service, the size of the shipment, and the distance shipped.

Most of the goods shipped under class rates are general manufactured products that are shipped in volumes too small to justify much negotiation by shippers. Between 2 and 4 percent of the volume shipped by rail comes under these rates, and these are the rates which were supposed to offset the low rates on bulky, low-value items.

Commodity rates—lower rates for big bulk. In many instances, there is no provision among the 10,000 class-rate classifications for the specific characteristics of certain commodities, especially bulky or low-value items. Commodity rates are set for transporting specific commodities, usually between specific points or over specific routes. These rates frequently develop out of negotiation between shippers and railroads.

There are special commodity rates for most bulky items, such as wheat, iron ore, coal, lumber, or any products shipped regularly in substantial volume. Some of the negotiated commodity rates are called "blanket rates," because the same rate applies over a large geographical area regardless of the distance between specific points within that area. Fresh fruits and vegetables, for example, can be shipped from the West Coast to almost any place on the East Coast for the same rate. Approximately 90 percent of the rail carload traffic moves under commodity rates.

Exception rates—special rates for special conditions. If a certain producer needs lower rates so that he can compete in other markets, or if competition from other methods of transportation is especially

394

strong, the carriers sometimes are forced to "reconsider their costs" and set special rates.

Railways have been forced to grant "exception rates" on many items to meet truck competition in certain territories. But less than 10 percent of carload traffic moves under these rates.[4]

Correct rate not easy to determine

The large number of rate classes, and the many exceptions, makes traffic management a difficult job. A freight agent frequently charges a higher rate when a lower rate should apply. Some companies find it profitable to audit all freight bills before payment. There are even private firms specializing in this kind of work.

It is not that carriers are deliberately overcharging, but that the agents who determine the appropriate rates must choose from a vast number of possible rates and rate combinations. Determining the lowest correct rate gets more complex each year, since more than 150,000 rate changes are made annually.[5] And the basic rate books do not show cross-references to all of these new rates. For this reason, some channel members prefer to have prices quoted on a delivered basis.

Marketing manager may affect rates

The previous discussion has been concerned primarily with how to operate within the existing rate structure. Yet, as noted previously, these rates are *regulated,* not *permanently fixed.* Changes can be made in them relatively quickly (1 to 30 days) and easily, as indicated by those 150,000 changes made each year.

Most rates are based originally on supply considerations, that is, the cost of providing necessary services—loading, product liability, regular scheduled service even though it is not used, special equipment such as refrigerated cars, and so on.[6] But supply factors are not the final determinants of transport rates. Rather, they determine the rate the carrier *would like to charge.* The rates actually charged are determined by competition among the various carriers and alternate methods of transportation. It is by capitalizing on these factors that an aggressive marketing manager can influence the cost of the transporting function.

Be aggressive, buy for less

Carriers usually are interested in stimulating business in their areas. If the marketing manager can show that he could expand his business if lower rates were granted into certain territories, the carriers may be willing to grant these lower rates.

On shipments to western points, New England railroads for many years have charged the same rates from New England as from New

---

[4] F. M. Cushman, *Transportation for Management* (New York: Prentice-Hall, Inc., 1953), pp. 173–74; Locklin, *op. cit.* (5th ed.), p. 163; and Heskett, *op. cit.,* pp. 91–103.

[5] C. A. Taff, *Traffic Management* (rev. ed.; Homewood, Ill.: Richard D. Irwin, Inc., 1959), p. 292.

[6] Locklin, *op. cit.* (4th ed.), pp. 436–43, 464–77.

York, enabling New England industries to compete on equal terms with those in New York. When the textile industry developed in the South, the carriers serving the southern mills reduced their rates on finished cotton goods so that these mills could sell in northern territories in competition with New England mills.[7] Note the behavior of competing channel systems, again, with the railroads as part of the channel.

The creative marketing manager and channel captain can capitalize on the opportunity to bargain for rate changes. Whoever can provide the transporting function most economically and effectively is most likely to develop an effective channel team. And this is the kind of team that individual companies will be eager to be part of.

When buying goods from other channel members, for example, a channel captain might provide a valuable service to them by helping with the transporting function. He could specify the best routes, determine the rates, negotiate with the transportation agencies, if necessary, and check their invoices. When selling to others in the channel, he could sell on a delivered basis and assume the same functions.

Some manufacturers and middlemen maintain traffic departments staffed by 10 or more employees to provide just these services. This is another area of specialization in distribution activities that may be well worth the cost.

By land, by sea, but not much by air

The marketing manager generally has several carriers in one or more modes competing for his transportation business. There are five basic modes of freight movement: railroads, motor vehicles, waterways, pipelines, and airplanes.

Table 19–1 shows the annual volume of intercity freight moved in the United States by each mode. Ton-miles carried is the most common method of measuring the importance of various methods of transporta-

Table **19–1** *The intercity freight movement in the United States*

| | Ton-Miles Carried in 1964 | |
	Billions	Percent of Total
Railways	680.0	44%
Motor Vehicles	347.0	23
Inland Waterways	250.0	16
Pipelines	266.0	17
Airways	1.5	..
Total	1,544.5	100

SOURCE: *Statistical Abstract of the United States, 1966*, p. 561.

---

[7] *Ibid.*, p. 55.

tion. A ton-mile represents the movement of a ton of goods one mile. If, for example, 10 tons of sand were carried 10 miles, the total movement would be 100 ton-miles.

Using this measure makes it obvious that railways are the backbone of the U.S. transportation system. Following in consecutive importance are trucks, oil pipelines, and barges. Relatively speaking, airplanes do not yet move a significant volume of freight.

The numbers in the table do not tell the whole story, however. They show total ton-miles, but do not identify the mass of goods that is shipped by trucks, but only for short distances. Information on this subject is sketchy, but it is likely that at least 75 percent of all freight moves by trucks, at least part of the way, from producer to user. Railroads may carry goods for long distances, but trucks haul the bulk of the short-haul movement. The trucking industry slogan, "If you have it, it came by truck," is certainly accurate for consumer goods, although many industrial goods are still delivered directly by railroads or other transportation modes.

The railroad, the workhorse of U.S. transportation, has been impor- **Railroads** tant mainly for carrying heavy and bulky freight such as coal, sand, and steel. By handling large quantities of such commodities, according to standardized methods and in a variety of standardized car types, the railroads are able to transport at relatively low cost. But railroads have had profit difficulties in recent years, in part because trucking firms have set their rates low enough to compete for the more profitable, less bulky items that the railroads were counting on to offset the low rates on the bulky commodities.

The railroads have taken various steps to bring their profits up. Computerization and automation of rail facilities has helped. Catering more specifically to the needs of some target customers has helped, too. By introducing an efficient triple-deck carrier for automobiles, the rails were able to win back from trucks a substantial share of the new-car transport. And the design of special refrigerator cars, tank cars, hopper cars, and cars especially suited for loading and unloading livestock has helped attract and hold business from firms that are willing to pay extra for services tailored to their needs.[8]

Other such services, designed to offset some of the railroads' natural disadvantages and to attract customers, include those discussed in the following paragraphs.

Piggyback service. Operating on the apparent philosophy, "If you can't beat them, haul them," railroads have tried to offer more flexible service by loading truck trailers onto specially designed flatcars and hauling them "piggyback." The trailers are picked up at the producer's location, loaded onto rail flatcars, hauled as close to the customer as rail lines run, then picked up by a truck tractor and delivered to the buyer's

---

[8] "High-Mountain Railroad with Profits to Match," *Business Week,* June 10, 1967, pp. 174–80; "Doubling the Freight Car's Work-Day," *Business Week,* December 18, 1965, pp. 122–26; and *Railroads Unlimited!* (Washington, D.C., Association of American Railroads, no date).

door. Such a service provides all the flexibility of trucking, and on some routes it costs even less. A loaded truck trailer can be shipped piggyback from the Midwest to the West Coast for approximately half the cost of sending it over the highways.

Fast freight. Many of the goods shipped by rail are not particularly perishable or in urgent demand, and as a result, much railroad freight moves more slowly, for example, than truck shipments. But when speed is needed, the train can move.

Some railroads have instituted a "fast freight" service for perishable or high-value items. Such trains, highballing at 60 m.p.h. and stopping only to change crews and load water and ice, can be competitive in speed with trucks, provided the shippers and receivers are located near rail lines.

Pool cars. Railroads are most efficient at handling full carloads of goods. Less-than-carload (LCL) shipments take a considerable amount of handling and rehandling. They usually move slowly, and at a higher price per 100 pounds than carload shipments.

To counter the shortcomings of low speed and high cost and still encourage the business of small shippers, some railroads encourage groups of shippers to cooperate and "pool" their shipments as a full car. This service enables one producer to ship to several buyers in a single area at greater speed and under the lower carload rates. If the buyers of these goods are not located in the same area, the goods may be shipped in a pool car at the carload rate to the first buyer and then broken up for further shipment at LCL rates.

Sometimes local retailers buying from a single area, such as New York City, consolidate their shipments in single cars. Local truckers deliver the goods when they arrive. When various commodities are shipped in the same car, it is called a "mixed car" rather than a "pool car," and the highest rate for any of the commodities applies to the whole shipment.

Diversion in transit. Some railroads allow redirection of carloads already in transit. A carload of California oranges could be shipped toward Chicago or simply eastward toward no specific destination, and as market demand and supply conditions changed, the shipper could change or specify the destination. The railroad would then reroute the car for a small fee.

This service lets a marketing manager get his goods rolling but still stay flexible in his final target market selection.

Transit privilege. Some agricultural or industrial raw materials must be shipped from their original source to a processing plant and then to users. To facilitate this regrouping and processing, some railroads permit shippers to ship commodities away from one source, stop along the way for processing, and then reship them toward the final destination at the "through" rate—as long as the same general direction is maintained. This privilege is especially important in the flour milling industry, where the procedure is called "milling in transit."

Transloading privilege. A more recent innovation, the transloading privilege, speeds delivery of parts of an original carload shipment to two or more destinations. When goods are to be shipped in a car cross-country to customers at several destinations, the railroad does not pull the car from city to city, unloading it bit by bit, here and there. Instead, it moves a full carload of goods to the single point that is closest to the various customers, then reloads parts of the shipment into other cars for the remaining distance to destinations in different directions. Since the transloading privilege makes LCL size deliveries feasible, customers can maintain smaller inventory, shifting the storage function back to the manufacturer or wholesaler. Like the other privileges, transloading gives channel members more latitude in planning marketing strategies and sharing channel functions.

The flexibility of trucks makes them especially suitable for moving small lots of goods short distances. They can travel on almost any road, can serve broad areas without unloading and reloading, and give extremely fast service. Trucks also cause less breakage and rough handling than rails, an important factor because it may permit a reduction in packaging cost. **Motor vehicles**

For short distances and for higher valued commodities, trucks may charge rates that are the same as (or lower than) railroad rates, yet provide much faster service. The way truckers compete with railroads for these high-charge items is somewhat like the way retailers compete in "scrambled merchandising." Pursuing such business is logical for the truckers because it is these smaller high-charge items that trucks are best equipped to handle.

Trucking has opened many new markets and permitted a considerable amount of decentralization by bringing fast, dependable transport to outlying urban areas, smaller towns, and rural areas. Whatever the truth may be about charges that trucks congest traffic and damage highways, it *is* a fact that trucks are indispensable to our present economic and marketing system.

Barges on the internal waterways are used chiefly for bulky, nonperishable products such as iron ore, grain, steel, petroleum products, cement, gravel, sand, coal, and coke. Water transportation is the lowest cost method, but it is also the slowest and most seasonal. When winter ice closes fresh water harbors, alternate transportation must be used. Some shippers, such as those dealing in iron ore, ship their total annual supply during the summer months and store it near their production facilities for winter use. Here, low-cost transportation combined with storage reduces *total cost*. **Waterways**

The availability of ocean transport to the vast industrial and agricultural regions of the inland United States was made possible in 1959 by the completion of the St. Lawrence Waterway System. This 2,342-mile-long waterway opened the Great Lakes to 80 percent of all ocean vessels. Only the very largest ships are excluded.

A recent advance in ocean shipping is the redesign of ships to handle large standard-size containers or "containerized freight," and truck trailers. Now ships combined with trucks can offer a "fishyback"

399

service similar to rail piggyback handling of truck trailers. Door-to-door service is now being offered between the U.S. and European cities.[9]

Pipelines

In the United States, pipelines are used primarily by the petroleum industry to move petroleum liquids and natural gas. Extensive lines in the Southwest bring oil from the fields to refineries. From there, the more flexible railroads, trucks, and ships usually transport refined products to customers.

Ships can transport petroleum products from Texas to the large eastern seaboard markets at less cost than pipelines, but during World War II, two pipelines were built to serve the East Coast because German submarines were sinking the oil tankers. After the war, this traffic returned to the more economical ships, and the pipelines are used today for natural gas.

Airways may cut costs

The most expensive means of cargo transportation yet developed is airfreight—but it also is fast! Trucks took the cream of the railroads' traffic. Now airways are taking the cream of the cream. They also are creating new transportation business by carrying across continents and oceans perishable commodities that simply could not be moved before. Tropical flowers from Hawaii, for example, now are jet-flown to points all over the United States.

The bulk of airfreight so far has been fashions, perishable commodities, and high-value industrial parts for the electronics and metalworking industries.

Airfreight rates normally are at least twice as high as trucking rates, but the greater speed may more than justify the added cost. Although airfreight still is only a small percentage of all freight, the volume of airfreight has been increasing yearly and a real breakthrough may come when the huge flying boxcars, developed originally for the military, become available for civilian service. Some members of the airfreight industry, perhaps optimists, expect these larger planes to be able to compete with trucks over long distances.[10]

An important advantage of air transport is that the cost of packing, unpackaging, and preparing the goods for sale may be reduced or eliminated when goods are shipped by air. One Los Angeles manufacturer of electronic preheaters, who makes all his deliveries beyond 150 miles by airfreight, merely wraps the complex 600-pound machines in heavy wrapping paper. His increased transportation costs are more than offset by the reduction in packaging costs, and he is now competing for business nationally. The speedy service at lower costs has improved the company's marketing mix *and* market position.

Although the *transportation cost* of air shipments may be higher, the *total cost of distribution* for a firm using airfreight may be lower.

[9] See "Containers Widen Their World," *Business Week,* January 7, 1967, pp. 88–90; *Business Week,* February 19, 1966, pp. 76–78; and *Business Week,* November 13, 1965, pp. 198–202.

[10] "Air Space Cargo Sees a Higher Ceiling," *Business Week,* May 13, 1967, pp. 106–10, and 116–20; and "C5A: Lockheed's Path to the Future," *Business Week,* October 9, 1965, pp. 32–33.

Airfreight may enable a firm to reduce its inventory costs by eliminating outlying warehouses. One eastern company had maintained a central warehouse on the West Coast, shipping across the country by rail and then reshipping from the warehouse. Then the company discovered it could save $60,000 annually by doing away with the warehouse and shipping everything direct by airfreight.[11]

Valuable by-products of air transport's speed are the reduction of spoilage, pilferage, and damage. With less time from shipper to customer, goods are exposed to fewer hazards.

Transportation wholesalers

Many marketing managers use freight forwarders to make optimum use of available transportation facilities, especially for the many small shipments that may move by varied transportation services.

Freight forwarders do not own their own transportation facilities, except perhaps pickup and delivery trucks. Rather, they wholesale air, ship, railroad, and truck space. Accumulating small shipments from many shippers, they then reship in larger quantities to obtain lower transportation rates. Their profits mainly come out of the difference in freight rates between small- and large-quantity shipments though they sometimes make special service charges.

Freight forwarders can help the marketing manager who ships many small shipments in many directions. They handle an estimated 75 percent of the general cargo shipped from U.S. ports to foreign countries. More than 90 percent of all exporters, including companies with large shipping departments, use their services; a decisive reason is that the forwarders process all the paper work necessary in overseas shipments.[12]

Should you do it yourself?

To cut transportation costs, some marketing managers provide their own transportation facilities rather than buy from specialists. Trucking has made it easier for a businessman to use do-it-yourself transport. Some large manufacturers own thousands of cars and trucks, and there are iron ore, gypsum rock, and petroleum producers who have their own ships.

The concept of discrepancy of quantity applies here. If there is a great difference between the quantity a firm normally ships and the quantity that carriers find most economical, the firm may have to ship via common carrier or freight forwarder. But if a company normally ships in the same quantities that common carriers find economical, it

This drink and driving did mix

---

[11] For more examples of the advantages to be obtained from shipping by air, see H. T. Lewis and J. W. Culliton, *The Role of Air-Freight in Physical Distribution* (Boston: Graduate School of Business Administration, Harvard University, 1956); and *The Role of Air-Freight in Determining Company Policy* (a report prepared for Emery Air Freight Corporation by Stanford Research Institute, no date).

[12] Paul V. Horn and Henry Gomez, *International Trade Principles and Practices* (4th ed.; Englewood Cliffs, N.J.: Prentice-Hall, Inc., 1959), p. 521.

may save money by using its own trucks and avoiding the cost that common carriers must charge for maintaining a regular schedule or contract carriers must charge against future uncertainties.

If a marketing manager is fairly certain of his future plans, do-it-yourself transportation may be good business. One wholesale wine distributor in New Orleans found that he was paying considerably more to ship wine by rail from California than if he rented a tank truck and hired his own driver for the California run. Because this was a regular and frequent shipment, he bought a truck and operated it

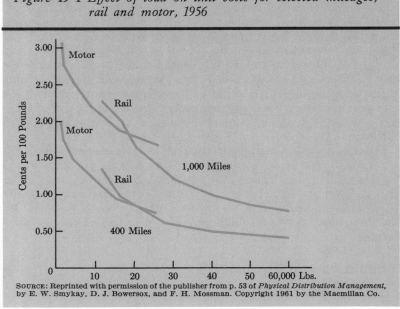

Figure **19–1** *Effect of load on unit costs for selected mileages, rail and motor, 1956*

SOURCE: Reprinted with permission of the publisher from p. 53 of *Physical Distribution Management*, by E. W. Smykay, D. J. Bowersox, and F. H. Mossman. Copyright 1961 by the Macmillan Co.

himself at a large saving. While negotiations with a railroad might have led to a rate reduction, railroads can't always amend their rates.[13]

Which is the best transportation alternative?

It should be apparent by now that picking the lowest cost transportation depends on the commodities, the distances, and the peculiarities of rate structures. But by careful tabulation of the costs of alternate methods, it is possible to evaluate the alternatives using graphs similar to Figure 19–1. This shows the costs for 400- to 1,000-mile shipments of a particular commodity. These cost patterns are found for many commodities.

[13] For a fuller discussion of the advantages and disadvantages of a do-it-yourself approach, see "A Creative Approach to the Question of Private Carriage," *Handling & Shipping,* December, 1962, pp. 38–41.

Least cost is not the only criterion that should be used in selecting the best method, however, because without any analysis we know waterways probably would be least expensive, rail next least expensive, and so on. We must also allow for the services needed, and specify the quantities expected to be shipped.

Note that in Figure 19–1 the cost per 100 pounds overlaps for motor and rail shipments of 15,000 to 20,000 pounds—the full truckload range—and that rail rates do not drop precipitously thereafter. This means that if speed or flexibility in delivery were important for this commodity, trucks might win the business and goods would move in truckload quantities. If speed were *extremely* important and quantities to be shipped were small, perhaps air shipments would be superior, and that cost structure properly would be shown above the others on the graph.

As in buying other services, getting the best transportation demands that someone in the firm—big companies have specialists—first make a critical appraisal of all his firm's needs and then evaluate the available combinations against these needs. More is said on this later in the chapter.

The storing function

Storing is the marketing function of holding goods between the time of production and the time of final use. It provides time utility. **Store it and make money**

Storing is necessary because production does not always match consumption. Some products, such as agricultural commodities, are produced seasonally though they are in demand year-round. If crops could not be stored when they matured or ripened, all the crop would be thrown onto the market at one time, and prices might drop sharply. The consumer might benefit temporarily from this surplus, but later in the year when supplies were scarce and prices high, he would suffer. Storage, therefore, permits price stabilization throughout the consuming period, although prices usually do rise slightly over time to cover storage costs.

Unlike agricultural commodities, some goods—such as film and beachwear—are produced regularly throughout the year in anticipation of demand peaks. Until these goods are consumed, they must be stored somewhere. In contrast, however, to the refrigerated, verminproof storage needed for some food, warehousing for these items does not necessarily increase total costs. In fact, storage of seasonal, nonperishable items may make it practicable for factories to run at a regular rate yearlong, thereby lowering production costs and more than offsetting storage costs.

The practice of storing and therefore withholding products from the market to get better prices is the basic principle behind the U.S. Department of Agriculture's parity program and the occasional stockpiling of commodities such as rubber, coffee, and cocoa beans in other countries. Our federal government has stockpiled metals not only for defense but also to maintain prices. Storing, we can see, may be intimately related to Price as well as to Place.

Using storage, some buyers can purchase in large enough quantities to get quantity discounts. Goods are sometimes stored as a hedge against future price rises, strikes, shipping interruptions, and other disruptions.

Finally, storing goods enables manufacturers and middlemen to keep stocks at convenient locations, ready to meet customers' needs. In fact, storing is one of the major activities of some middlemen.

Remember the rats

As with our excellent transportation system, we in the United States take for granted our storage facilities such as the huge grain elevators throughout the Middle West and at our port cities. In other countries, storage often is inadequate or even nonexistent. India completed its first grain storage elevator in 1957!

Lack of capital is one reason for the lack of storage facilities—but only one reason. There also are differences in outlook. When that first Indian grain elevator was completed in 1957, an observer stated that it would protect the grain from rats. An unimpressed Indian official replied: "We look at it differently. We think the rats also have to eat."[14]

Storing varies the channel system

Most channel members provide the storing function for varying lengths of time. Even final consumers store some things for their future needs. Since storing can be provided anywhere along the channel, the storage function offers several ways to vary a firm's marketing mix and its channel system: (1) adjusting the time goods are held, (2) sharing the storage costs, and (3) delegating the job to a specialized storage facility. This latter variation would mean adding another member to the distribution channel.

Which channel members will store the product and for how long will affect the behavior of all the channel members. If a manufacturer of groceries were to maintain a large local stock, wholesalers probably would maintain smaller inventories, since they would be assured of dependable local supplies. Hawaiian food retailers, for example, maintain four to six weeks' inventory on the items they must receive from the mainland, but they stock only one week's inventory of those goods that are kept in stock locally by a manufacturer or wholesaler. Some manufacturers maintain their own stocks in Hawaii to woo wholesalers and retailers from competitors.

Shifting the cost of storing is a second way a manufacturer may vary his marketing mix. In Hawaii, again, some mainland manufacturers provide storage allowances to encourage Hawaiian wholesalers to maintain stocks beyond their normal needs. This assures adequate local stocks and protects the manufacturers' customer franchises, especially during shipping interruptions.

Specialized storage— collateral for a loan, age for the bourbon

Private or branch warehouses. Private warehouses are those that are owned by individual companies for their own use. Most manufacturers, wholesalers, and retailers have some kind of storage facilities, either in their main buildings or in a warehouse district, often in a

[14] Ralph Westfall and Harper W. Boyd, Jr., "Marketing in India," *Journal of Marketing*, October, 1960, p. 16.

404

Commerce City. Management of a manufacturer's finished-goods warehouse often is the responsibility of a sales manager, especially at sales branches located away from the factory. In retailing, storage is so closely tied to selling that the buyers may control this function.

Private warehouses are used when a large volume of goods must be stored regularly. Owning warehouse space, however, can be expensive, since it is a fixed cost and may limit flexibility in the company's operations. If sales should fall and warehouse stocks decline, the extra space may be hard or impossible to lease, and costs may remain constant while revenue declines.

Public or commercial warehouses. The company that does not need permanent warehouse space may find public warehouses the answer. The customer pays only for the space he uses and may, if he wishes, purchase a variety of additional services.[15] Public warehouses are useful to manufacturers who must maintain stocks in many areas, including foreign countries.[16]

Some public warehouses provide all the services that could be obtained in the company's own branch warehouse or from most wholesalers. These warehouses will receive goods in carload quantities, unload and store them, and later reship them in any size lots ordered by the company or its customers. They will inspect goods, package them, and even invoice customers. They will participate in the financing function by issuing warehouse receipts that can be used as collateral when borrowing from banks. Some public warehouses will provide desk space and telephone service for a company's salesmen. And the public warehouse will be responsible for the risk of damage or the loss of the product in the warehouse.

Public warehouses are located in all major metropolitan areas and many smaller cities. Rural areas also have public warehouses for locally produced agricultural commodities.

General merchandise warehouses store almost every kind of manufactured goods. A special form of general merchandise warehouse is the *bonded* warehouse which is used for storing imported goods or other goods, such as liquors or cigarettes, on which a tax must be paid before the goods are released for sale. If a long storage period is needed, say to age liquor, then these warehouses may lower costs by delaying payment of taxes or duties until the goods are removed. Private bonded warehouses also can provide this latter feature.

Commodity warehouses and *cold-storage* warehouses are designed specifically for storing perishable or easily spoiled products such as apples, butter, and furs. Grain is stored in huge elevators.

The cost of physical handling is a major storage cost. The goods must be handled once when put into storage and again when removed to be sold. Particularly in older, multistoried warehouses, located in

New warehousing is switched on

---

[15] For more details on public warehouses see *Distribution Age,* September, 1962, pp. 53–55; December, 1961, pp. 35–41; February, 1960, pp. 24 ff.; and April, 1960, pp. 52 ff.

[16] "Firm Tells How to Place U.S. Merchandise Closer to the European Consumer," *International Commerce,* July 8, 1963, pp. 14–16.

congested districts, these operations take many man-hours of high-cost labor. Difficult parking, crowded storage areas, and slow freight elevators all delay the process, increasing the cost of distribution.

Today, one-story modern structures are replacing the old multistoried buildings. These new single-level designs eliminate the need for elevators and permit use of power-operated lift trucks, battery-operated motor scooters, roller-skating order pickers, electric hoists for heavy items, and hydraulic ramps to facilitate loading and unloading. Some grocery warehouses even have radio-controlled tractors that order pickers drive by remote control. Most of these new warehouses use lift trucks and pallets (wooden "trays" which carry many cases) for vertical storage and better use of cube space.

One Los Angeles drug wholesaler, through careful planning and use of electronic controls, has now almost eliminated physical handling for most of his repeat business—covering 1,800 items. The system of controls and conveyor belts now assembles in a few seconds the kind of order that an experienced stock clerk formerly spent 20 minutes putting together.[17]

Is storing really needed?

Storage is justifiable only if it helps achieve time utility. Storage is *not* necessary just because there is some discrepancy of quantity or assortment between one channel level and another. If there is a discrepancy *and* time must be used, then perhaps it will make economic sense to regroup and store at the same time. But if time is not needed, then no storage should be provided. This leads us to a whole new idea—the distribution-center concept.

Don't store it, distribute it

The purpose of a distribution center is to *speed* the flow of goods and eliminate unnecessary storage. It is a breaking-bulk operation. Turnover is increased and the cost of carrying inventory is reduced (such cost may run as high as 25 percent a year of the value of the average inventory).

The concept underlying the distribution center is the same one that led to the development of discount houses and mass merchandisers: *Reducing costs and increasing turnover will lead to bigger profits.*

There are many variations of the distribution center. The two following illustrations will help clarify this concept. Both show distribution centers in an integrated operation. Some public warehouses are gearing for this approach, too; it may be possible eventually for a manufacturer to use only 10 or 15 such public warehouse centers and still service the country efficiently and at lower cost than with present methods.[18]

A clothing chain develops 45-minute warehousing

One chain of 124 stores handling women's and children's clothing is trying to reduce its storage operation. This company feels that some warehousing is required, but only because of the inability of industry to

---

[17] "Automation Gets It Wholesale," *Business Week,* March 15, 1958, pp. 157–60.

[18] "Distribution Center—Texas Style," *Distribution Age,* May, 1962, pp. 44–46 ff; Howard E. Way, Jr., "The Role of the Public Warehouse in the Future," *Transportation and Distribution Management,* December, 1962, pp. 20–24.

balance production with sales. Yet because clothing styles change rapidly, it is essential to keep storage time to a minimum.

How can this be done? The chain is trying to make the warehouse an integral part of the whole marketing operation, not just a storage place. To speed distribution, this company uses a complicated conveyor system that enables it to receive goods from its 5,000 suppliers, route them to the appropriate "storage" areas in its warehouse, and from there move the goods out to trucks which take them to each of the firm's 124 stores. Total time: 45 minutes. Final result: Prices are lower, and retail stores get the latest styles sooner.[19]

A grocery manufacturer puts its products where your mouth is

The Pillsbury Co., a large manufacturer of baking mixes and flour, used to move its products in carload lots directly from factory to wholesaler or large retailer. Plants were as near to customers as possible, and each plant, initially, was equipped to produce the whole Pillsbury line. As lines were expanded, however, it became apparent that no plant could produce all the various products. When customers began to ask for mixed carload shipments and faster delivery, Pillsbury found itself adding warehouse space and hauling goods from plant to plant. By 1955, Pillsbury had set up 100 branch warehouses, controlled by 33 sales offices. Each sales office had its own accounting, credit, and other processing operations.

Later, one Pillsbury official was to say of this old system: "Turnover was slow, warehousing costs were high, and there was no effective control over inventories." It was then taking the company one week *just to process an order.*[20]

Today, Pillsbury guarantees its customers "third morning delivery" anywhere in the United States. To make this dramatic advance in efficiency, Pillsbury appointed a director of distribution, equal in rank to the heads of manufacturing and marketing, and established multiple distribution centers. Now, each manufacturing plant specializes in a few product lines, and this permits longer runs. They ship carload lots directly to distribution centers, virtually eliminating warehousing at the factories. The distribution centers themselves are controlled by four regional data processing centers.

The field sales organization at Pillsbury no longer handles physical distribution or inventory. Sales is its only activity, and it has been able to expand its branches from 33 to 52. Sales orders are routed to one of the data processing centers, which immediately determines where and when the goods are to be shipped for that "third morning delivery." Centralized accounting speeds invoices to customers, resulting in quicker payment. And because each distribution center always has adequate supplies, it is possible to route and ship orders directly from that point, by the most economical means.

Before these changes at Pillsbury, neither the production nor sales departments had precise responsibility for what happened to goods

[19] "In and Out of a Warehouse in 45 minutes," *Business Week,* July 6, 1957, pp. 64–70. For a description of a trucker who has developed a somewhat similar system serving many manufacturers and retailers, see "Trucker Tries for Something Extra," *Business Week,* March 4, 1967, pp. 112–18.

[20] "New-fangled Routes Deliver the Goods—Faster and Cheaper," *Business Week,* November 4, 1959, pp. 108–10.

between manufacture and sale. Now the entire physical distribution effort is treated as one system.

Pillsbury salesmen now have something extra to sell—better and faster service. Costs have been reduced and profits increased. Over a four-year period, the new system is credited with boosting the company's ratio of pretax income to sales from 2.9 percent to 4.9 percent.

Physical distribution focuses on total system

We have been looking at the transporting and storing functions as separate activities, partly because this simplifies discussion but also because it is the traditional approach. In recent years, however, attention has turned to the *whole* physical distribution function, not just warehousing and transportation. And this sometimes affects production planning, too, since the business should work as one unit. We just saw this in the Pillsbury case.

Physical distribution, a new idea whose time may come

According to the physical distribution concept, a relatively new business theory, all of the physical handling activities of a business and a channel system should be thought of as part of one system. It may be hard to see this as a startling development, but until just a few years ago even the most progressive companies treated these various functions as separate and quite unrelated activities. Many firms still do.

In some firms, the production department is responsible for warehousing and shipping, and it builds inventories that are related to its production activities rather than market needs. In other companies, inventory may be a separate activity. If those in charge of inventory put little faith in sales forecasts, they may simply adjust stocks according to their own expectations.

Progressive firms, however, are beginning to integrate all their activities, often with the aid of electronic data processing equipment.[21] Although the majority of firms give little evidence of applying the physical distribution concept, considerable interest now surrounds this approach, and it is likely that great strides will be made to implement it in the near future.[22] Certainly the literature has been growing rapidly and shows the way.[23]

[21] For a discussion and examples of how individual firms have and others might integrate, see E. J. McCarthy, J. A. McCarthy, and D. Humes, *Integrated Data Processing Systems* (New York: John Wiley & Sons, Inc., 1966), chaps. ii and xxiii.

[22] R. P. Neuschel, "Physical Distribution—Forgotten Frontier," *Harvard Business Review,* April, 1967, pp. 125–34; J. L. Heskett, "A Missing Link in Physical Distribution Systems Design," *Journal of Marketing,* October, 1966, pp. 37–41; W. M. Stewart, "Physical Distribution: Key to Improved Volume and Profits," *Journal of Marketing,* January, 1965, pp. 65–70; "Bird's-Eye View Helps Win Sales and Savings," *Business Week,* April 8, 1967, pp. 66–69; R. E. McGarrah, "Logistics for the International Manufacturer," *Harvard Business Review,* March–April, 1966, pp. 154–66; and "The Next Place for Paring Costs," *Business Week,* May 1, 1965, pp. 132–36.

[23] E. W. Smykay, D. J. Bowersox, and F. H. Mossman, *Physical Distribution Management* (New York: Macmillan Co., 1961); J. L. Heskett, "Ferment in Marketing's Oldest Area," *Journal of Marketing,* October, 1962, pp. 40–45; J. L. Heskett, R. M. Ivie, and N. A. Glaskowsky, Jr., *Business Logistics* (New York: Ronald Press Co., 1964); J. A. Constantin, *Principles of Logistics Management* (New York: Appleton-Century-Crofts, 1966); and the monthly issues of *Transportation and Distribution Management,* the management-oriented magazine of physical distribution.

The early interest in and concepts about physical distribution can be traced to the military supply forces responsible for getting the right men and material to the right places at the right time. The armed forces were not directly concerned with cost, but they were concerned with an optimum allocation of resources. Transferred to the business world, their approaches lead to lower costs. **Stress has been on total cost approach**

The early efforts to apply logistics to business focused on trying to reduce the cost of physical movement while giving essentially the same level of service. Determining the best, most economical method of physical distribution required comparison of complicated alternatives. To focus on the total cost of the various alternatives was quite logical.

Table 19–2 Comparative costs of airfreight vs. rail warehouse

Total sales = 1,000,000 units or 1,000 tons

	Total Cost	Cost per Ton
Rail and Warehouse		
(2) Interest on inventory, 30-day cycle, 360-day interest year at 6% on $1,500,000 of inventory	$ 90,000.00	$ 90.00
(2) Taxes on inventory	40,000.00	40.00
(2) Warehouse cost	55,200.00	55.20
(1) Transport expense (rail carload)	58,000.00	58.00
Cost via rail and warehouse	$243,200.00	$243.20
Airfreight		
(2) Interest on investment in inventory, 10-day cycle, 360-day interest year at 6% on $500,000 inventory	$ 30,000.00	$ 30.00
(1) Airfreight	120,000.00	120.00
(1) Local delivery	10,000.00	10.00
Cost via airfreight	$160,000.00	$160.00

SOURCE: Reprinted with permission of the publisher from p. 76 of *Physical Distribution Management* by E. W. Smykay, D. J. Bowersox, and F. H. Mossman. Copyright 1961 by the Macmillan Co. (2) indicates fixed and variable expense; (1) indicates variable expense only.

The tools of the cost accountant and economist were applied to this problem. Sometimes the total cost analyses revealed that unconventional physical distribution methods might yield service as good as or better than conventional means, and at lower cost. The following simple examples illustrate the approaches that have been used.

Table 19–2 shows the result of a comparative cost analysis of two alternatives: airfreight with no warehouse versus rail freight with warehouse. The comparison was based on the distribution of 1,000 tons of a particular commodity during a definite period of time. **Rail-and-warehouse combination versus airfreight**

Comparing the final totals showed that using airfreight would be less expensive than the rail-warehouse combination, even though airfreight itself was considerably more costly than rail.

Figure 19–2 presents another cost analysis, this time with five alternatives:

1. Airfreight
2. Motor common carrier
3. Direct rail
4. Rail-warehouse
5. Branch plant

This figure shows the total cost per ton for each of the five alternatives. It is clear that the best alternative depends on the expected sales volume. If the company's sales volume will not exceed 20,000 tons during the given period, then the airfreight system will yield the lowest

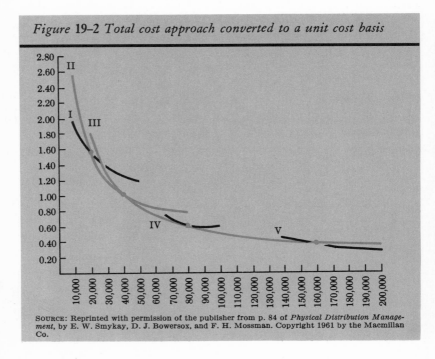

Figure 19–2 Total cost approach converted to a unit cost basis

SOURCE: Reprinted with permission of the publisher from p. 84 of *Physical Distribution Management*, by E. W. Smykay, D. J. Bowersox, and F. H. Mossman. Copyright 1961 by the Macmillan Co.

unit cost. If a 20,000- to 40,000-ton volume is expected, however, the motor freight alternative becomes more economical, and so on.

In any total cost analysis of this kind, all relevant factors must be included and all practical alternatives evaluated and compared. The easiest course is to do things as they always have been done. Yet this could lead to the death of the firm in our competitive economy. It is imperative that all practical alternatives be evaluated and compared.

Sometimes the alternatives are so numerous or complicated that advanced mathematical and statistical techniques, and perhaps a computer, are needed for their analysis.[24]

[24] These techniques are beyond the scope of this book. See the following for leads to the literature: Robert D. Buzzell, *A Basic Bibliography for Mathematical Methods in Marketing* (Chicago: American Marketing Association, 1962).

In evaluating many alternatives, some companies have found it desirable to use a new approach: simulation with a computer. In simulation, the characteristics and costs of the many alternatives are described as carefully as possible, and then the computer tests the alternatives, using a trial-and-error technique.[25] For many applications, however, the straightforward cost analysis discussed previously is practicable and will show whether there is need for a more sophisticated analytical approach.

Although cost reduction tended to be the main focus of early physical distribution efforts, more attention is being directed now toward integrating physical distribution planning into the company's strategy planning. Perhaps by increasing physical distribution costs somewhat, service levels can be so increased that, in effect, a new marketing mix has been created. Larger and broader inventories might be carried to assure prompt delivery *and* adequate supply. Improved packaging and physical handling might cut damages and repairs. This would reduce the time and effort needed for adjusting claims.

Physical distribution not just cost-oriented

In extremely competitive situations, simply increasing the service levels—perhaps through faster delivery or wider stocks—may enable a firm to make significant headway in a market without altering prices or promotion—two changes that are often noticed and easily copied by competitors.

Physical distribution specialists are more interested now in the possible impact of packing and packaging changes on total cost throughout the whole channel of distribution. They are also interested in materials handling methods and in the development of new transportation facilities that will make the whole physical distribution process more effective. While it is true that the traditional specialists in storing and transporting have shared these interests, the physical distribution man adds a desire to integrate all these factors not only within his firm but all along the channel system.

Need for physical distribution manager

Basic company reorganization may be necessary for full acceptance and exploitation of the physical distribution concept. Just adding an executive called a "distribution manager" or a "manager of physical distribution," or simply giving the traffic manager or warehouse manager a new title will not in itself do the job. This might be paying only lip service to the concept of integrating physical distribution activities unless the whole organization also accepted the idea that new methods of production, warehousing, shipping, promotion, and sales may be necessary to achieve this total integration.[26]

---

[25] For a discussion of this approach, see Harvey N. Shycon and Richard B. Maffei, "Simulation—Tools for Better Distribution," *Harvard Business Review*, November–December, 1960, pp. 65–75.

[26] For further discussion, see John F. Stolle, "How to Manage Physical Distribution," *Harvard Business Review*, July–August, 1967, pp. 93–100.

These far-reaching changes may be a long time coming. Many sales and marketing executives still have not realized their responsibility for physical distribution.

One survey found that fewer than 10 percent of top marketing executives were fully responsible for transportation decisions, and only a slightly greater percentage, 10.95 percent, were fully responsible for warehousing. What is worse, in 43 percent of the firms the top marketing executive did not assume any responsibility for physical distribution, and in 35 percent of the firms he did not participate in the discussions concerning this important phase of marketing.[27]

Such separation of storage and transportation from the rest of marketing activities is anachronistic. We recognize now that these functions must be seen together as physical distribution and that this, in turn, must be treated as part of the total marketing system.

A true physical distribution manager would have a big job. He would be concerned not only with physical flows but also with the location of Place facilities through which the flows would move. He might have to become directly involved in the selection of plant locations, warehouses, and retail facilities.

Fortunately, there is a growing body of literature available to anyone interested in this area.[28]

Future physical distribution problems and opportunities

The marketing system of the future, responding to new living patterns and technology, may change drastically in some urban areas. Urban redevelopment programs may cause even more significant shifts of population than we have seen so far. And with mounting population pressure, radical new regulations may be mandatory, such as the exclusion of private automobiles from city streets, either by ordinance or by prohibitively high taxation.

New approaches must be found to mass transportation and urban living. Already, the federal government is subsidizing urban mass transportation systems. There are some limited attempts at developing new residential and commercial building arrangements. France and Sweden have experimented with communities combining residential, working, and recreational facilities in the same center.

Adjustments in transportation rate structures may lead to drastic changes in physical movement patterns. The railroads have seen more and more of their most profitable business go to competitors; if this situation were to be adjusted on a grand scale, the changes in transport might have a profound impact on the whole economy.

Suppose, for example, that the low rail rates charged on bulk commodities such as lumber and coal were raised sharply. This probably would force some producers to relocate nearer their supplies. It might force others to manufacture or use substitutes.

A lumber company in the Northwest, for example, might suffer if

[27] Robert E. Weigand, *Business Topics*, Summer, 1962, pp. 70–71.
[28] In particular, see the textbooks cited in footnote 23.

rail rates for lumber rose. Contractors might shift to other types of building materials. Such a rate increase might even force the whole construction industry to revamp its methods and materials.

Transportation is not one problem but many problems. Any major changes in the existing rate structure will affect manufacturers, wholesalers, retailers, and consumers. So far these adjustments have been made on a piecemeal basis, but a national transportation policy may be coming. The recent formation of a separate U.S. Department of Transportation may bring solutions to some of the problems, but any change comes slowly and is resisted by vested interests.[29]

Planes may race trucks for business

Finally, technological developments, including new materials handling equipment and electronic computers, no doubt will encourage changes in physical distribution. We already have discussed the distribution center concept and the activities of some progressive wholesalers. It also appears that larger and more automated rail facilities will be built. Trucks may travel as large multiunits and be able to handle heavy, bulky loads like railroads do.[30] Larger airplanes may be able to compete with trucks on a cost basis.

As always, the marketing manager who has been able to carve out a target market today will still have to be alert if he wishes to keep it tomorrow.

Conclusion

This chapter has dealt with providing Time and Place utility. We have discussed the various means of transportation and their comparative costs at some length, and also examined the advantages and disadvantages each presents. The railroad rate structure, particularly, seems in need of a drastic overhauling, and this might have a marked impact on our present marketing system.

Storage, the second aspect of physical distribution, was considered, together with the types of warehousing now available. Examples were given of modern techniques which can cut storage and physical handling costs.

Although we discussed transportation and storage separately, it was emphasized that both are related. The distribution center, a new approach in this area, is an attempt to integrate these two activities for the purpose of speeding turnover and lowering handling and storage costs.

The physical distribution concept is concerned with integrating all the physical handling, storing, and transporting activities into a smoothly working system. The total cost approach has been helpful in selecting the most effective physical distribution alternatives. But it focuses on costs, when management often wants to improve service and may select a higher cost alternative to improve its marketing mix. Or the total cost approach may reveal that it is possible *both* to reduce costs and to improve service, perhaps by eliminating warehouses and using airfreight to speed delivery.

Finally, physical distribution should be seen as part of a marketing

[29] "Off on the Wrong Track," *Business Week*, June 24, 1967, p. 39.
[30] "What Shippers Will Be Using in 1973," *Handling & Shipping*, December, 1962, pp. 17–36.

mix. New organizational structures may be needed to achieve the potential benefits of integrating physical distribution activities. But it is still the job of the marketing manager to determine how physical distribution is to be accomplished and how it will be shared with other channel members.

1 Discuss the relative advantages and disadvantages of railroads, trucks, and airlines as transporting methods.

2 What method of transportation would probably be most suitable for the following products (specify any assumptions necessary to obtain a definite answer):

a) Hogs
b) Apples
c) Diamond rings
d) Large tractors or other agricultural machinery
e) Coal
f) Television sets

3 Describe how your college town would be changed if there were no incoming or outgoing transportation except by foot, horseback, or horse-drawn covered wagon.

4 Distinguish between common carriers and contract carriers. What role do the contract carriers play in our economic system? How would our economy be different if there were no common carriers?

5 Distinguish among the following types of railroad rates: class, commodity, and exception rates. If all three rates might apply in a particular situation, which one would probably be the lowest?

6 Explain which transportation method would probably be most suitable for shipment of goods to a large Chicago department store:

a) A 10,000-lb. shipment of dishes from Japan.
b) 15 lbs. of screwdrivers from New York.
c) Three couches from High Point, N.C.
d) 500 high-fashion dresses from the garment district in New York City.
e) 300 lbs. of Maine lobsters.
f) 60,000 lbs. of various appliances from Evansville, Indiana.

How would your answers change if this department store were the only one in a Centertown in Ohio?

7 Indicate the nearest location where you would expect to find substantial storage facilities. What kinds of products would be stored there and why are they stored there instead of some other place?

8 Indicate when a producer or middleman would find it desirable to use a public warehouse rather than a private warehouse. Illustrate, using a specific product or situation.

9 Discuss the distribution center concept. Is this likely to eliminate the storing function of conventional wholesalers? Is it applicable to all products? If not, cite several examples.

10 Clearly differentiate between a warehouse and a distribution center. Explain how a specific product would be handled differently by these marketing institutions.

11 Explain the total cost approach and why it may be necessary to have a physical distribution manager to implement the concept.

12 How would a distribution manager differ from a transportation manager? Would he really be any different than a marketing manager?

Development and management of channel systems

Achannel captain is concerned primarily with the development and management of a channel system. The captain may be a producer, wholesaler, or retailer. Most producers would prefer to handle the whole distribution job themselves. But as we will see, this is not always possible or even desirable.

In an indirect channel, the question of who becomes channel captain depends in part on the relative strength of the various channel members. In this chapter, for convenience of exposition, we will assume that the producer is the channel captain. But this is for convenience only. Middlemen are already dominant in some channels and may be the typical channel captains in the future.

By now you should have a general knowledge of the various types of marketing specialists who have evolved and how they might be combined in channel systems.

Don't memorize what; understand why

We will become specific here about the dominant channels for various kinds of products. You must remember, however, that there may be more than one effective (workable) channel for one kind of product or one target market. You should *not* try to memorize *what is done;* rather, you should try to understand *why* the many alternative channels can and do develop. Your job is to try to anticipate what channels will or should look like in the future, and what role you might play in them.

The best channel system is the one that works best

It may seem platitudinous to say so, but the best channel system is the one that works best in the strategy that the marketing manager develops. The total cost approach discussed in Chapter 19 may be helpful in analyzing the cost of alternative channel systems, but the lowest cost system is not necessarily the best. Ideally, we would like to select the lowest cost channel that does the job. This may turn out to be a relatively high-cost system, but if the customers are satisfied with what it does, then the channel system and the strategy may be profitable.

The market grid concept is applicable here. Some parts of a market might want many services that only an expensive channel system could provide. Some gourmet customers, for example, might want personal service and a large assortment, but they would still buy only in very small quantities. They might be served very well by a high-cost, high-price system composed of manufacturers who sell through small wholesalers to small retailers. Supermarket customers, on the other hand, demand less service, and the volume moving through that channel system allows price reduction. Yet both channel systems may exist side by side and be good channel systems for the different target markets.

What this has to do with the price of eggs

Since the costs of alternate channel systems can be calculated, they may show that some systems have significant cost advantages over others. This may suggest that some prices may drop significantly, if they have not already, or that some channel systems are doomed to failure and will disappear when their plant and equipment wear out and must be replaced.

An analysis of egg production-marketing systems, for instance, showed that when small farmers produce Grade-A large eggs and then move them through the usual middlemen channels to a medium-sized retailer, the cost is about 64 cents a dozen. But when production and distribution are handled through an integrated production-marketing system to large supermarkets, the cost is only about 36 cents a dozen, which is closer to the market price.[1]

This study clearly shows why there has been a movement toward larger integrated production-marketing systems for eggs and why there are similar movements in other agricultural products. Similar cost analyses of other channel systems probably would help explain the trend towards vertical integration and administered channel systems we noted in Chapter 16.

Lower cost, however, may not be the only reason an integrated channel works well. Another reason could be that a better flow of information along integrated or administered channels would enable the channel system to locate and capitalize on new opportunities. This could happen even though not everyone in the channel system were strongly market-oriented. As long as someone, say, the channel captain,

---

[1] E. J. McCarthy and R. J. Williams, "Simulation of Production-Marketing Channels," in Raymond M. Haas (ed.), *Science, Technology, and Marketing* (Chicago: American Marketing Association, 1967), pp. 335–46.

is so oriented, it is possible that he can win the confidence and support of extremely production-oriented firms and make the whole channel work effectively.

Small production-oriented producers in Japan or Hong Kong, for example, may become part of an effective channel if there is a middleman who correctly diagnoses market needs and relays them clearly to his producers. The producers may not even know where their products are going, but the system still can be competitive with other systems.

In ideal terms, a whole channel system of marketing-oriented firms, fully aware of what is happening, would be preferable to a marketing-oriented producer working through rather stodgy middlemen. This, unfortunately, is the position many progressive manufacturers are in, and it is the reason why some have chosen to take over more and more of the distribution job themselves.[2] Remember—the best channel system is the one that satisfies customers' wants, *and* meets the needs of the various channel members.

Don't let stodgy George do it!

Now, let us look at a number of factors that we have not yet considered in the development of effective channel systems, and then go on to describe the channel systems that currently are dominant for various product types.

Factors affecting composition of channel systems

Each marketing manager must reconcile the ideal Place objectives of each channel system with various market realities, including the nature of the target market, special characteristics of the product, the market structure, and his own firm's capabilities and limitations. Often the marketing manager must settle for a channel that is less than ideal. His company may even have to join a channel that is controlled by another firm.

It will be useful to see how some of these market realities might affect channel decisions. While we are examining some of these situations, keep in mind that although a direct channel system has advantages, it also forces the company to incur some more or less fixed overhead expenses (such as the costs of salesmen, office staff salaries, and the expenses of office facilities and warehouses). If the sales potential is not at least large enough to cover these costs, then some kind of *indirect* channel system is clearly indicated.

Size and geographical dispersion affect sales contacts needed. If the sales potential of the target market selected by the marketing manager is large enough, it may be possible for him to go directly to retailers, consumers, or users. This is especially true if the potential target customers are highly concentrated, as are the customers for many industrial goods. For final consumer goods, however, potential custom-

Not all targets look the same

---

[2] For further discussion on this point, see E. J. McCarthy, "Are Effective Marketing Institutions Necessary and Sufficient Conditions for Economic Development?" in S. A. Greyser (ed.), *Toward Scientific Marketing* (Chicago: American Marketing Association, 1964), pp. 393–404.

ers usually are numerous and widely dispersed, and buy in small quantities. Although the total market may be relatively large, it may be split up into small geographical segments, with too little demand in each market grid box to support a direct approach.

Geographical dispersion is a decisive factor in international marketing. Here, middlemen become almost indispensable. Even if world demand is great, direct distribution to individual markets is seldom feasible because of the distance between the producer and the many separate markets.

Value of item and frequency and regularity of purchases. Even low-priced items such as groceries may be handled directly if they are purchased frequently and the cumulative volume is large—as in the case of home-delivered milk and bread. But for products purchased seldom and irregularly—even though purchases are substantial—specialized agencies such as commission merchants, agents, brokers, and other middlemen may be useful. A critical factor is the cost of regularly providing the needed marketing functions in relation to the sales obtained over several months or a year's time.

Customers view some products differently. We have stressed many times that the same physical product may be viewed differently by different target customers. This leads to a different goods classification and, as we would expect, a different channel system might be appropriate. An example from the building materials industry illustrates the point—but also shows that interchannel problems can develop when channels overlap.

Before World War II, most homes were built by small contractors who sold them completely unfurnished. Today, the vast majority of houses are put up by large tract builders who may install washers, dryers, and dishwashers as part of their total product. These large appliances formerly were sold as consumer goods, going from wholesaler to retailer to final consumer. The large tract builders, on the other hand, consider such major appliances as components—that is, industrial goods—and want to buy in quantity at lower prices.

To serve this builder market, some manufacturers have attempted to make adjustments within their present channels.

Others have handled this business directly because their consumer goods distributors were too small to serve the big tract builders; and the manufacturers did not want to disrupt all of the policies they had established for reaching and serving the retail market.

Not unnaturally, this latter approach, sometimes called *dual distribution,* was resented by some of the established middlemen because they saw substantial sales volumes going to competing channels—and in this case, channels set up by their own sources of supply.[3] Resolving such differences is another task of the marketing manager.

Customer preferences. Customer preferences vary even within the same goods classification. Some target customers, especially some industrial customers, have a bias against dealing with middlemen, and even though they may want only small quantities, they may prefer to buy

---

[3] "The Builder's the Hot Market," *Business Week,* February 4, 1961, p. 82.

directly from manufacturers. This may be a nuisance to the manufacturer, but he may tolerate it because the customers occasionally may buy larger quantities.

Other buyers, however, may prefer the convenience of buying through a middleman because they can telephone orders and get immediate action from a local source. Two quite different marketing mixes handled through two channel systems, therefore, may be needed to fully satisfy both types of customers.

Some goods, because of their technical nature, perishability, or bulkiness, require more direct distribution than is implied by their goods classification. **Not all products are the same**

Technical products. Complicated products, such as conveyor systems and electronic data processing equipment, call for a high degree of technical selling knowledge and expert installation and servicing. Wholesalers usually do not wish, nor are they equipped, to provide all these required services.

Perishability. Perishable items, such as cut flowers, milk, and fresh seafood, may have to be handled directly if produced on a small scale, perhaps in an isolated town or in a less developed economic environment. But if many small producers are clustered together, specialists may develop to handle transportation, refrigeration, and storage. Complicated terminal markets, such as those dealing in fresh produce, may develop, along with a host of specialized commission merchants, brokers, merchant wholesalers, and truck wholesalers.

High-fashion items also are perishable, and more direct distribution may be sensible to speed the flow to retailers. Sometimes retailers and final consumers even go directly to the producers to see the latest fashion showings, say in New York and Paris.

Bulkiness. Transportation, handling, and storage costs mount when bulky products are moved about, making it difficult for middlemen to operate. If a producer is unable to make an adequate number of sales contacts when selling bulky items direct, he may decide to use brokers, manufacturers' agents, and especially drop-shippers to make sales contacts and then ship the goods himself directly to the customer. This is another example of function shifting and sharing in a channel system, required in this case because of the nature of the product.

Suitability of available middlemen. The kinds of specialists the marketing manager would like to use may not even be available, especially if the company is a late entrant in the field and his competitors already have tied up the best middlemen. **Not all market and channel structures are the same**

The specific customers already being reached by each proposed specialist are extremely important. If these do not include the marketing manager's target markets, then that middleman doesn't have much to offer. A wholesaler specializing in groceries would have a valuable list for the food business, but it would not be of much value in distributing electronic machinery.

While this example is obvious, errors often are made in more subtle cases.

To expand his sales, a manufacturer of industrial steam traps was considering the appointment of additional distributors in outlying territories. The company assumed that its outlets in large cities were adequate to maintain the present level of sales and that further sales increases in large cities were unlikely. Yet a more careful analysis of its present distributors' customer lists revealed that more wholesalers *were* needed in the cities. The reason: While the steam traps had been handled by distributors catering to the mechanical industries, other distributors were needed to contact the paper and chemical industries where a large share of the potential business was centered. The additional distributors were added, and sales were tripled in a short time.[4]

Strength of traditional arrangements. The market structure may be dominated by traditional arrangements. There may be long-established, highly successful "home-owned" retailers or wholesaler-retailer links based on family or nationality ties. This kind of traditional arrangement is seen in its extreme in tropical Africa, where channels are divided by race and target markets. Large European-owned firms import goods and export domestic production. These Europeans sell to some smaller wholesalers and retailers, but generally Levantines in West Africa and Indians in East Africa serve as middlemen to small retailers who typically are Africans.

There are exceptions to these generalizations, and "breakthrough" opportunities may await those who deviate from the traditional arrangements. But in international markets, the traditional roles of the various groups are long standing and firmly rooted.[5]

The rather freewheeling competition we see in the United States is not typical of international markets. Because of this, the traditional channels of distribution may be the only practicable ones for a new-comer. Innovators may be punished by social sanctions or even legislative restraints aimed specifically at them.[6]

Market coverage of available specialists. The market specialists available in some large metropolitan centers may be highly effective, but such specialists may not be available in outlying areas. This may require two channels to reach both areas—but it may also lead to a dual distribution problem because the agents who might be suitable for outlying areas may also cover the large metropolitan areas. Everyone likes to work where sales are plentiful and easy to make.

Nor does distribution through national or international companies guarantee uniform coverage. For example A&P has a much larger share of the retail grocery market in the East than in the Middle West. Sears, Roebuck has been relatively stronger in the Middle West and West than in other sections. This uneven coverage of marketing spe-

---

[4] R. E. Sessions, "Effective Use of Marketing Channels," in R. M. Clewett (ed.) *Marketing Channels for Manufactured Products* (Homewood, Ill.: Richard D. Irwin, Inc., 1954), p. 415.

[5] Edward Marcus, "Selling the Tropical African Market," *Journal of Marketing,* July, 1961, pp. 27–28; and Alice G. Dewey, *Peasant Marketing in Java* (New York: Free Press of Glencoe, 1962).

[6] Bert C. McCammon, Jr. "Alternative Explanations of Institutional Change and Channel Evaluation," in S. A. Greyser (ed.), *Towards Scientific Marketing* (Chicago: American Marketing Association, 1964), pp. 477–90.

cialists simply means that every channel for every target market must be tailormade.

Financing required in channel system. Adequate credit may be critical in smoothing the flow through a channel system. Some wholesalers enter a channel mainly because they can give financial assistance to the members.

We already have mentioned the role of factors, but some merchant wholesalers also hold a secure position in a channel because of their strong financial condition and ability to meet the financial needs of other channel members. This is especially true in international markets.

In some African markets, the credit cycle from sale to final payment may extend over three years. Since few African businessmen have this much working capital, well-financed European and Chinese importing and exporting firms have been attracted to Africa.[7]

Political and legal environment. Each geographical target market must be studied carefully for special legal or tax requirements that may affect channels. We already have mentioned the controls on exclusive distribution and the anti-merger legislation in the United States. Outside of the United States there are fewer controls of this type, but there are important tax considerations.

In Europe, a major portion of the tax income is collected from sales or "turnover" taxes that are assessed every time title passes from one level of distribution to the next. Partly because of turnover taxes—which may run as high as 25 percent—many European manufacturers sell directly to retailers or users. When they cannot or do not wish to sell directly, they use commission merchants, who make the contacts and sales but avoid taking title.[8] This avoids the turnover tax, but unfortunately, some commission merchants are quite inefficient, and introducing them into the channel reduces the effectiveness of the whole channel system.

In deciding how to work with a channel system, each marketing manager—be he manufacturer, wholesaler, or retailer—must evaluate his own company's capabilities, needs, and potential contributions to a channel. If he is realistic, he may find that his best course is to join a strong system rather than play the role of channel captain himself.

Nature of company itself— is it big, rich, and unprejudiced?

Size of company and width of product line. A company's own size has an important bearing on its place in a channel system because it affects discrepancies of quantity and assortment.[9] A large firm already handling a wide line of food or soap products, for example, may be in a good position to take on an additional product of the same type and handle it the same way, perhaps directly. In contrast, a smaller company or one with narrower lines might suffer from a discrepancy of quantity or discrepancy of assortment or both, and would probably find middlemen more practical. Similarly, a large company going into a

---

[7] Marcus, *op. cit.*, p. 31.

[8] Stewart C. Dalrymple, "Major Pitfalls in Sales and Distribution Methods in the Common Market," *International Trade Review*, January, 1963, pp. 12–13.

[9] Robert E. Weigand, "The Marketing Organization, Channels, and Firm Size," *Journal of Business*, April, 1963, pp. 228–36.

completely unrelated line would lose its advantage, since it would be functioning as the small producer of a new line.[10]

Some industrial goods producers sell enough to overcome the discrepancy-of-quantity problem in *some* of their major markets. There they can use their own branches and warehouses. But the same producer may find middlemen more attractive where markets are smaller or scattered.

Financial strength. A company's financial strength also may be of importance if its customers need financial assistance. Firms not in a position to provide this financing may find specialized middlemen useful. Selling agents, factors, merchant wholesalers, or large retailers, for example, may be in a position to finance a producer or channel members, including users or final consumers. In fact, a channel captain's dominance may depend heavily on his financing capacity.

Executive prejudices. Although the prejudices of company executives should not be a dominant factor, executives are a company resource, and their attitudes may influence channel selection or even be incorporated into company objectives. Some "old-time" sales managers, for example, have strong anti-chain store attitudes which color their thinking. Likewise, some sales managers prefer to control their own sales force rather than work with independent manufacturers' agents who may resist strict direction. Then, top management might specify channel control or direct distribution as an objective, regardless.

Currently dominant channels by product type

We have discussed (*a*) how an ideal channel system might look and perform, (*b*) factors that should be considered in selecting a channel, and (*c*) the kinds of specialists available. Now we will tie all this together in a description of how and why various products typically are distributed.

This discussion, in effect, will be a review, but now we will be using the names of specialists, not the general term "middlemen" in our description. You will want to see whether the material we will discuss jibes with our previous thinking. If it does not, try to determine why not. It may be that you have in mind different target markets, a different size firm, and so on. Or it may be that you have thought of a new system—perhaps a "breakthrough" opportunity for you.

In the following discussion, we will merely describe the *dominant* or *typical* channels. What follows should not be considered "right" but typical.

Convenience goods— get them where the customers are

Staples. Middlemen of various types are commonly employed to handle convenience goods, and especially staples. The wide dispersion of target customers and the typically small size of each purchase encourage the use of several middlemen, especially merchant wholesalers and retailers. Furthermore, there are discrepancies of quantity and assortment between most manufacturers and final consumers. Setting up their own retail outlets would be impractical for the manu-

---

[10] For a description of Philip Morris' distribution system, see "A Machine That Will Sell Anything," *Business Week*, March 14, 1967, pp. 92–104.

facturers, even if they had the financial resources to do so. Finally, most convenience goods are relatively uncomplicated items. They seldom require installation, service, or even much personal selling, and so direct marketing is unnecessary.

Intensive distribution is appropriate for most convenience goods. If a producer promotes his product adequately, the merchant wholesalers and retailers may not need to do much except handle, break bulk, and store the appropriate assortment until it is needed. Such middlemen usually are available.

The producer may be able to arrange for promotional displays by giving promotional allowances or having special salesmen call on retailers for this purpose. Food manufacturers often send their own salesmen into supermarkets to set up promotional displays. Any orders obtained by these salesmen while working on promotion are turned over to the firms in the channel. And food brokers also may be used to promote products in the channels.

Impulse goods. The promotional support for impulse goods must be more aggressive. The manufacturer may have to go directly to retailers with his own salesmen unless aggressive middlemen, such as food brokers, are available.

Emergency goods. Emergency goods must have wide distribution and must be available at times when regular distribution channels might not be open for business. A wide assortment is not necessary. In an emergency, anything that will do the job is acceptable. A variety of outlets cater to "emergency" business—all-night service stations, open-till-midnight grocers, and vending machines.

Target customers for shopping goods, like the customers for convenience goods, are widely dispersed, but shopping-goods customers are willing to make more of an effort to satisfy their needs. The producer needs fewer outlets, and direct-to-retail distribution may be feasible. Direct-to-consumer selling is unlikely, however, because consumers generally want to compare shopping goods.

Shopping goods— the direct route if necessary

Homogeneous shopping goods. Homogeneous shopping goods do not require attractive surroundings or knowledgeable sales personnel—unless, of course, the producer is trying to change the consumer image of his goods. For well-known manufacturers' brands of appliances, for instance, price is important to retail consumers, and they may be willing to patronize back-alley discount houses to buy them.

A manufacturer of homogeneous shopping goods may decide it is too difficult or even impossible to upgrade the consumer image of his product, especially if it is in the latter stages of the product life cycle. He may then abandon any selective distribution efforts and attempt to gain intensive distribution through as many wholesale and retail outlets as possible. Some appliance producers have done just this, encouraging even more scrambled merchandising.

Heterogeneous shopping goods. These goods require more retail display and often more personal selling both to final consumers and to middlemen. Producers frequently prefer to bypass wholesalers because, in any event, they *must* tell the sales story to retailers, sometimes including technical information that must be explained, directly to the retail clerks. Since producers must make the sales calls anyway, they feel they might as well take the orders and deliver the goods themselves.

Fairly direct channels are also encouraged by the willingness of retail buyers to make regular trips to central markets, say for furniture and clothing. Resident buyers in such cities as New York, Chicago, Dallas, or Los Angeles also facilitate the movement of these goods, especially in the style- and fashion-goods markets where new offerings are presented continuously.

If the potential sales volume is fairly large, as in clothing and shoes, large producers may begin to integrate down to the retail level or large retailers may integrate backwards, as we already have seen. This is further encouraged in the case of these products because larger inventories or specialized services may be necessary. Home appliances are an example. If General Electric should move into retailing as prophesied by some marketing analysts, the reason, at least in part, would be GE's desire to do an effective selling job for heterogeneous shopping goods and to keep these goods from being viewed as homogeneous shopping goods.

Specialty goods— ready to handle a plum

These goods normally are distributed through the same channels as those convenience or shopping goods they most nearly resemble. The best middlemen usually are happy to handle them because of the favored position of these goods with consumers.

Unsought goods— need some extra push

A large established firm just introducing an unsought good (but one similar to the firm's other products) may be able to use the rest of its line and its customer franchise to obtain distribution for the new product. A well-known cake mix manufacturer, for instance, felt that on the basis of its reputation it could sell a million cases of a new mix containing only sawdust—just once, of course!

The position of such a manufacturer may enable it to use its typical channels to place the product where similar products are sought. The producer may still have to pay for or supply all promotion, but it *is* able to get distribution—an important and sometimes difficult feat in these days of expanding product lines.

A smaller producer, or a larger one going into a new line may not be so fortunate. It may have to resort to the use of less efficient middlemen, mail-order selling, or aggressive house-to-house selling. Established middlemen sometimes refuse to handle unsought goods until they have achieved some market acceptance.

Installations —the president may turn salesman

Brokers frequently handle sales of used buildings and land rights, since buyers and sellers are only in the market irregularly. These specialized middlemen have a knowledge of the market and can provide a useful service.

New installations normally are sold directly by the contractor's or manufacturer's own salesman, since (1) customers are relatively few and geographically concentrated, (2) the potential sales volume is large, and (3) there is a need for design, technical assistance, and service of a kind that middlemen don't normally provide. Even smaller companies may sell directly, since they are normally in a position to provide the sales and technical assistance required for this type of product. In these companies, the president or executive officers often serve as the sales personnel.

Since technical assistance is required for some accessories, direct sale by the producer is common. For other accessories, however, potential customers are widespread and need frequent contact by experienced sales personnel. For such products, large firms use manufacturers' agents or brokers in less populous areas, and smaller firms use them throughout the country. These agents provide continuous contact, and there is no cost to the producer except when a sale is completed. Since the cost of the agents' regular sales calls is spread over a number of products, the producer may obtain sales coverage without the high overhead sales cost he would incur doing this job for himself for only one line.

Accessory equipment— middlemen often needed

If good agents or brokers are not available, then merchant wholesalers—such as mill supply houses or oil field supply houses—may be used. Relatively little sales effort, however, can be expected from them.

If there is good market potential for the product, the wholesalers may be glad to take it on. But if the potential is not good, the producer may have to choose between going direct and facing the fact that the product cannot be produced and marketed profitably, and should be allowed to die.

The large number of small farmers creates a real discrepancy of quantity and perhaps of assortment. It also makes practical the development of many specialized middlemen. Assemblers are used to gather farm products in rural areas, and commission merchants and merchant wholesalers handle these products in the terminal markets as the products are brought closer to users.

Raw materials— many small farmers, few big producers

Natural products are being produced by fewer and larger firms. There is little or no need for assemblers. Users are not numerous, at least not compared to final consumers. The result is that many of these producers handle distribution themselves, although smaller producers may use brokers or drop-shippers. The smaller firms need practically the same market coverage as the larger firms but have less to sell and, consequently, a smaller sales volume to cover selling costs.

Most components producers are specialized and cater to a relatively small, concentrated group of users. Since technical and design assistance may be required, these producers normally deal directly with their target customers. The executive officers of these smaller producers may do the direct selling, as in the case of installations. If potential customers are numerous and widespread, however, agents may help locate and service new business.

Component parts and materials —dealing face-to-face

Maintenance items. Maintenance items are used widely and are similar in many respects to convenience goods. Customers are fairly widely dispersed, their purchases of each item are relatively small, and little technical assistance or service is required. Since this is an ideal

Supplies— middlemen rank high here

situation for middlemen, merchant wholesalers are common in this field. Mill supply houses and office and stationery supply stores often serve as middlemen for maintenance items. They are contacted directly by the larger producers in the more populous areas and by manufacturers' agents in other areas. The smaller producer may use manufacturers' agents exclusively for his contacts with these merchant wholesalers.

Repair items. Repair items are used widely and, with some exceptions, may be distributed in the same way as maintenance items. Large customers may have complete repair facilities and prefer to buy repair parts directly; smaller manufacturers and contractors more often prefer to have wholesalers carry the parts inventory and perhaps handle the repair service, too.

Operating supply items. Operating supply items, with few exceptions, are similar to maintenance items and are distributed in the same way. The exceptions are some bulky items, such as coal, lubricants, and fuel oil. Direct distribution of these supplies by the producer may be advisable because of technical service considerations (as for lubricants) or the large volume of sales (fuel oil). Drop-shippers commonly act as middlemen for the many small coal producers.

Channel system management must be dynamic

We have been trying to stress the importance of what should and could be in channel systems. This will be your main concern in the future.

If a company has been using the same channel system for more than a few years, the chances are good that it needs to make some changes. Perhaps a new channel should be added, or an existing channel replaced, or specific wholesalers or retailers changed. Perhaps the firm's own sales branches and warehouses should be expanded or modified in line with the modern trend to distribution centers.

To make all this more concrete and show how change might work its way through an industry, we will return to the discussion of the channels in the electrical goods industry which we began in Chapter 15. For a better appreciation of why channel management is a continuing problem, we will investigate how all the variety in that industry developed.

When agents become distributors

Traditionally, merchant wholesalers—called electrical distributors—handled a large share of the business in the electrical goods industry. As product lines increased, however, many manufacturers found that to obtain adequate promotion they had to go direct or establish agents to assist the wholesalers. Some of the manufacturers set up field stocks under their own control or under the control of agents. This ostensibly was to aid the distributors, but in fact the agents made many direct sales. The ready availability of these field stocks also encouraged some small distributors to use drop shipments. This enabled them to cut price because they did not have the cost of handling the goods.

Some manufacturers resorted to the use of brokers because it was the only way they could reach some industrial customers. But these brokers usually would sell only the fast-moving items, on a price basis. This made the market even more competitive. Furthermore, some manufacturers put pressure on agents to obtain business for new lines or less popular lines that distributors would not stock. As a result, some agents assumed the role of distributors and began to solicit all types of orders directly—although these agents dealt in narrower lines than those traditionally handled by the electrical distributors.[11]

All this is very much like the scrambled merchandising we observed in retailing. Here, the small, often production-oriented producers of narrow lines had to resort to various expedients because they could not get complete distribution of their lines through the traditional full-function merchant wholesalers. **No bemoaning, please**

While there is room for doubt as to whether this complexity actually improves the efficiency of electrical supply distribution, this becomes an academic point. This kind of situation typically develops when there are many small, production-oriented manufacturers competing in the latter stages of the product life cycle.

Rather than bemoan his fate, a good marketing manager, faced with stiff competition, should try to find ways to differentiate his product in his channel system. This might require the kind of innovative thinking we have been trying to encourage here. At the very least, he should attempt to develop or become a part of a smoothly flowing channel. This would enable him to reduce his costs as much as possible and obtain a share of whatever profits are possible at his stage in the product life cycle.

Implementation of the channel plan

We have not said much about the selection of individual firms for a channel system and the relations among them. Implementation details of this kind are beyond our scope, but a few general comments are in order. The ongoing management of channels is extremely important and may consume a considerable portion of a marketing manager's or a channel captain's time.

In our general discussion, we will look at the problems of channel systems composed of two or more independent firms, for purposes of simplicity and clarity. We will first view the problem as it develops when a producer is playing the channel captain role, and then when a middleman has this dominant position.

Channel relations are extremely important to a producer because the middlemen are the ones who eventually sell his products, and if this is not done well, he may go out of business. For this reason, producers often attempt to play the channel captain role. **Producers look down the channel**

Before approaching prospective channel members, the marketing

---

[11] E. H. Lewis, "Distributing Electrical Products in a Dynamic Economy," *Electrical Wholesaling,* June, 1958, pp. 83–95.

manager for a producer should have carefully planned his own marketing strategy. Part of this should include his distribution plans. While developing his marketing mix, he should consider how the prospective channel members may react. His mix should provide sufficient incentive to make all of them want to "play the game—hard."

Selecting prospective channel members requires considerable field experience. Marketing research can be useful.[12] A research analyst could determine the availability, size, and market coverage of potential channel members. By interviewing their customers, competitors, and suppliers, the analyst could get a good picture of the reputation and past behavior of these specialists. Experienced sales executives would then interview likely prospects to determine present and probable future sales capacity.

But caution is required here, with checks and double checks.

A middleman's good reputation may be based on the past performance of salesmen now older and less aggressive. Or the good salesmen may have left the company. Investigating the proposed specialist's facilities and talking with his top executives and salesmen can be invaluable.

Once the marketing manager has decided to use a particular firm, he must explain and sell his whole marketing mix, not just to the top executives but to the whole organization. He should make clear exactly what he will do for them and what they in turn will be expected to do for him. It is important that everyone understand at the outset how the team is to operate and how each member will be compensated for his efforts.

It is not enough to sell the channel members initially. They must remain sold. This continuing job, often neglected because it is time-consuming and takes considerable effort, is extremely important in maintaining effective distribution channels. By obtaining and evaluating feedback about the channel, the marketing manager can adjust policies whenever necessary and replace or assist less effective channel members. *The marketing manager and channel captain must be not only an imaginative planner of marketing strategies, but a skillful negotiator and salesman as well.*[13]

Middlemen may not coordinate but dominate

Middlemen may not see themselves as sales arms of producers. Instead, they may follow their own strategies, perhaps including dealer branding.

Strong middlemen often are the channel captains because of the strength of their market position in a particular geographic area. But they may not choose to exercise the coordinating function we are assigning to the channel captain. Instead, they may exert their influence by being more demanding of producers. They may seek lower prices, larger advertising allowances, local manufacturer stocks, fast shipments

---

[12] See Martin D. Steinberg, "Predicting Dealer Success," *Journal of Marketing,* April, 1962, pp. 75–76.

[13] For further discussions, see *Selecting and Evaluating Distributors* (Studies in Business Policy, No. 116 [New York: National Industrial Conference Board, 1965]).

on small orders, and other conditions that enable *them* to operate more effectively.

Some large, strategically located retailers behave this way and some large wholesalers do, too. Their behavior adds weight to the belief of some observers that middlemen may come to dominate marketing.

Other large middlemen, including some large cooperative and voluntary wholesale chains, can see that there are advantages in the whole channel system working together. They have developed more cordial relations with their producer-suppliers. It should be clear, nevertheless, that when a strong middleman, such as Sears, Roebuck, specifies what, when, and how much is to be produced, where it is to be shipped, and what label is to be put on it, then the producer has become *just* that and nothing more—a *producer*.

Most of the important marketing decisions are being made for such a producer, and he is now concerned primarily with production problems. This is not necessarily bad from the standpoint of developing efficient channel systems. But it does mean that there may be less need for a marketing manager in such a firm, unless the company is also catering to other target markets.

Conclusion

This chapter has been concerned with the development of channel systems intended to get the right Product to the target customer—always, of course, at the right Price, with the right Promotion. We have stressed that because each channel system must compete with other channels, a marketing manager of a particular firm must not only consider his own firm's needs and goals but also the needs of others in his channel system.

Although we generally assume that a producer would prefer to sell his product directly to final users or consumers, it is often much more sensible and profitable to use the specialized marketing institutions that are available to do this job. This leads to the possibility of a large number of alternative channel systems and interchannel rivalry.

The most appropriate channel for a given marketing job at any particular time depends upon a great many factors—the nature of the product, the target market, competitive activity, the size and resources of the company, and others.

What may be the "right" channel for one company may be completely impractical for another. Sometimes a single company must use several channels to reach different target markets most effectively.

It is clear that the development of Place policies, while closely related to Place objectives, also must be consistent with the other three P's of the individual marketing manager's firm. The Place policies also must be compatible with the needs and goals of other members of the channel system. We now see that the marketing manager not only must be concerned with the needs and wants and problems of his target customers but also the needs, wants, and problems of his cooperating channel members.

1   Would a direct or some type of indirect channel be most appropriate for the following products? (Utilize the general factors discussed in this chapter and make any assumptions necessary to obtain a definite answer.)

  a) Hedge clippers   d) Fingernail clippers   g) Picture frames
  b) Fly swatters   e) Motor scooters   h) Trucks
  c) Earth-moving ma-   f) Grass seed   i) Fresh apple cider
     chinery

2   For those products in the previous question where indirect distribution was the answer (in light of the assumptions), indicate specifically the kinds of channels which might develop.

3   How would the distribution channels for building materials be changed in 1985 if by that time all new buildings were prefabricated at factories and merely assembled on the job by factory crews?

4   Discuss the competitive situation in the electrical goods industry. Would it be desirable from the consumer viewpoint to legislate against the development of competitive channels? If so, which channels should be eliminated by law?

5   Describe how an electrical tool manufacturer (drills, sanders, etc.) might go about selecting an exclusive distributor in one city. Why might he want to do this?

6   Discuss the promotion a grocery products manufacturer would need in order to develop appropriate channels and move goods through these channels. Would the nature of this job change at all for a dress manufacturer? How about for a small producer of installations?

7   Many persons think of direct sale from the producer to the consumer as "obviously" the most efficient. Why then do we find such complicated channels? Why doesn't everyone buy directly from the farmer or factory and save?

8   Although wholesalers are normally supposed to provide a selling function for the producer, many producers find it necessary to have salesmen call upon the wholesalers' customers. Why? In these cases why doesn't the producer bypass the wholesaler as long as he must provide salesmen anyway? Are these producers' salesmen necessary for all products? If not, why not?

9   Discuss the development of a marketing mix by a truck gardener who lives within 25 miles of a large northern Commerce City. Would the mix change for a farmer capable of growing essentially similar products but located 150 miles from the nearest Centertown or Commerce City?

Promotion— introduction

Promotion is *only* one of the four major variables with which the marketing manager works. A common misconception is that marketing starts and stays with promotion. As we will see, promotion is a vitally important part of marketing, but it is not the whole of marketing.

Nor are advertising and personal selling the whole of promotion. The marketing manager can use publicity, public relations, and various other forms of promotion. The marketing manager should combine all the possible promotional ingredients into a blend which tells target customers that the right product is available at the right place at the right price.

The big push from factory to consumer

We will stress this *blending* of promotion ingredients throughout our discussion of promotion. We will see why one product may need heavy accent on personal selling—encyclopedias are an example. But another, such as cigarettes, may be sold primarily by advertising and sales promotion, with little or no special effort by the salesman at the tobacco counter. Other products will require a mixture between these extremes; various blends of mass and personal selling will be needed to move them from factory to consumer.

In this chapter, we will discuss the basic promotion objectives, methods of implementing these objectives, and ways in which these methods can be blended for effective promotion. The next two chapters will be

431

devoted to personal selling and mass selling, the two basic approaches to promotion.

Basic promotion objectives

The basic, broad objectives of promotion are to *inform, persuade,* or *remind* target customers about the company's marketing mix and the company itself. Agreeing on and stating promotion objectives is critical if the firm's promotion is to be effective, because the right blend depends on what is to be done.

A specific set of promotion objectives would state exactly what and why we want to inform, persuade, or remind. A firm might want to convince customers of its products' virtues in order to create brand preference among target customers, for Brand *A* over both Brands *B* and *C*.

Such clean-cut specific objectives would help guide the promotion effort, and might be accomplished by the specific promotion methods to be discussed in this and the next two chapters. Yet such *specific* objectives are a function of each company's unique product-market situation, and we do not have the space in this text to handle the subject in such detail. Instead, we will work with the more general objectives—informing, persuading, and reminding—to see why these might be our objectives and how we might reach them.

From shout to soft sell
The firm with a distinctly new product may not have to do anything but *inform* consumers about its offering and show them how it works better than all existing products. A peddler in a primitive market might rely on his loud voice to attract attention. In a more complicated society, the firm may have to send out salesmen or advertise to get its message across. But newness and uniqueness in a product may simplify the process and may even get free publicity for the seller.

When others are offering similar products, as is usually the case, the firm has an additional task—not only of informing customers that a product is available but persuading them to buy it from their company. This actually is two different jobs. You cannot persuade potential customers if they have never heard of your product or you. As population continues shifting geographically; as there are more changes in the age, educational, and occupational characteristics of the population; and as more and more competitive products come to the market from more firms, merely reaching and talking to target customers becomes more difficult and expensive. To solve this problem, the firm may place greater reliance on mass communication. It may be more economical for telling a large number of potential customers about the firm's total product.

But even after customers have been attracted and sold once, they are still subject to competitive influences, which force the firm to continue persuading and reminding. As the number of competitors and competitive products have multiplied, this has become simultaneously more necessary and more difficult. Usually a firm must use several promotion methods, all at the same time, to inform, persuade, and remind.

432

Basic promotion methods

The marketing manager normally has several promotion objectives at the same time. He may have to say different things to different target customers. Normally, he uses a blend of three basic promotional methods, namely, personal selling, mass selling, and sales promotion.

Personal selling involves *direct face-to-face relationships between sellers and potential customers.* A salesman can be a very important part of a marketing mix because he can adapt the company's marketing mix to the needs and conditions of each little target market and, in the extreme, to each potential customer. Moreover, face-to-face selling gives immediate feedback, which helps the salesman do this adapting effectively. **Personal selling— flexibility is the biggest asset**

The flexibility offered by personal selling can be absolutely necessary for some products. As we saw earlier when we discussed customer behavior, the needs and preferences of individuals vary greatly; there are group influences, too, and market conditions vary.

Although the wife may do the actual buying for the family, she may be influenced by her husband and children.

An industrial buyer may face pressures from many other executives. Competitive conditions may vary from market to market.

Adjusting to all these target market differences may take the skills of a salesman.

Mass selling is intended to *communicate with large numbers of customers at the same time.* Obviously such a method has less flexibility than personal selling, which can use *immediate* feedback to adjust the presentation for *each* prospect. When the target market is large and dispersed, however, this approach may be much less expensive than personal selling. **Mass selling— reaching millions at a price or even free**

Advertising is the main form of mass selling. *Advertising is any paid form of nonpersonal presentation of ideas, goods, or services, by an identified sponsor.* It involves the use of such media as the following:

Magazines and newspapers
Outdoor posters, signs, skywriting, etc.
Novelties (calendars, blotters)
Cards (bus, train)
Programs and menus
Motion pictures
Direct mail
Store signs
Radio and television
Catalogs, directories, and references
Circulars

Advertising must be paid for by the advertiser. There is, however, another form of mass selling which is "free," and that is publicity.

Effective publicity and public relations efforts can contribute to mass selling at little or no cost. In some cases, it can be more effective than advertising, and the advertising expenditure may "buy" the publicity. Trade magazines, for instance, may write or carry "free" articles about the products of regular advertisers. And this publicity may generate far more inquiries than the company's advertising. These mass selling efforts are too specialized for coverage here, but they can make an important contribution to the promotion effort and probably will become more important in the future as more attention is focused on smaller and more clearly defined target markets.[1]

Sales promotion —tell the customer, show him, sell him

Sales promotion can make both personal and mass selling more effective by coordinating both efforts. Sales promotion personnel may design and arrange for the distribution of novelties, point-of-purchase material and premiums, store signs, catalogs, directory references, and circulars. They may assist in the development of displays, sales demonstrations, trade-show exhibits and other *nonrecurrent* selling efforts. Trade shows are especially important in international marketing.

Sales promotion men often prepare training materials and sales portfolios for the company's own and its customers' salesmen. They may develop "jackpot" or "sweepstake" contests and coupons designed to get customers to try the product—perhaps as part of a pulling policy.

It is difficult to generalize about sales promotion efforts because they are custom-designed and nonrecurring. They can be very effective in moving products, but making them work is a learned skill and not a sideline for amateurs. Consequently, specialists in sales promotion have developed within companies and as consulting firms.[2]

Promotion requires effective communication

Promotion obviously must reach the target audience or it is wasted. What is obvious, however, is not always easily accomplished. Much promotion does not communicate. Recent behavioral science studies indicate that the communication process may be more complicated than we imagined.

That body is not a corpse!

Researchers have demonstrated that the audience evaluates not only the message but also the source of the message in terms of trustworthiness and credibility. These studies have also shown that some persons are more easily persuaded than others. Persuasibility seems to be related to feelings of inadequacy and social inhibitions. While women seem to be more open to persuasion than men, persuasibility does not seem to be related to the level of general intelligence.[3]

[1] See "The World of PR: More Firms Build Big Public Relations Staffs: Bloopers Still Occur," *Wall Street Journal*, November 19, 1962, pp. 1 ff; and "Public Relations Abroad Puts Diplomacy in Marketing," *Printers' Ink*, January 26, 1962, pp. 59–60.

[2] For more discussion on sales promotion activities, see Alfred Gross, *Sales Promotion* (2d ed.; New York: Ronald Press Co., 1961); A. W. Frey, *The Role of Sales Promotion* (Hanover, N.H.: Dartmouth College, 1957), p. 8.

[3] Carl I. Hovland and Irving L. Janis (eds.), *Personality and Persuasibility* (New Haven, Conn.: Yale University Press, 1959), pp. 229–40. See also, other volumes in the Yale Studies of Attitude and Communications: Carl I. Hovland (ed.), *The Order of Presentation in Persuasion; Attitude Organization and Change: An Analysis of Consistency among Attitude Components;* and *Social Judgment: Simulation and Contrast in Communication and Attitude Change.*

Different audiences may perceive the same message in different ways and interpret the same words differently. Such differences are often obvious and to be expected in international marketing, where there are translation problems. General Motors' "Body by Fisher" came out as "Corpse by Fisher" in Flemish.[4]

Semantic problems in the same language may not be so obvious, and yet they must be recognized and solved to avoid giving offense. For instance, a large food company recently discovered that potential women customers didn't like being called "consumers" because they thought the word was too impersonal. They preferred "customers" or "homemakers," and married women, specifically, preferred the term "housewife."[5] These might seem like small differences, but it is just such subtleties that can make the target audience tune out a message, wasting the whole promotion effort.

The communication process can be seen more clearly with the aid of a circular diagram (Figure 21–1).

Talk in circles to be understood

The source shown here is attempting to deliver a message to a receiver, perhaps a potential customer. The source can deliver his

Figure 21–1 The communication process

Source → Encoding → Message Channel → Decoding → Receiver

Feedback

X's = Noise.

message in many ways. The personal salesman does it with his voice and actions, while advertising must do it with mass media, such as magazines, newspapers, handbills, posters, radio, and TV.

A major advantage of personal selling is that the source—the seller—may receive immediate feedback from the receivers. He can judge how his message is being received and adjust the balance of his message accordingly. This gives a real edge to the personal salesman. Mass sellers must rely on marketing research or aggregate sales results to measure what the salesman can see and feel.

The "noise" shown in Figure 21–1 refers to many kinds of things which reduce the effectiveness of the communication process. Perhaps the source cannot agree on what should be said and how, and compromises with a general message. Or the receiver, say a housewife, may be distracted by children when the message comes out of her radio. Or

[4] *Time*, September 20, 1963, p. 93.
[5] *Management Review*, June, 1961, pp. 4 ff.

other advertisers or salesmen may be saying essentially the same thing, and the receiver may become confused or ignore everyone.

The fundamental difficulty in the communication process occurs during encoding and decoding. The source must decide what it wants to say and then try to translate it into terms that will be decoded with the same meaning by the target audience. This can be very tricky because the meanings attached to various words and symbols may differ depending on the frames of reference and experience of the two groups. This can be seen in Figure 21–2. If there is no overlap, communication may be bad or impossible.

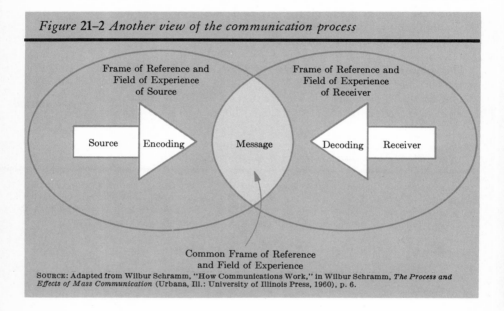

Figure **21–2** *Another view of the communication process*

SOURCE: Adapted from Wilbur Schramm, "How Communications Work," in Wilbur Schramm, *The Process and Effects of Mass Communication* (Urbana, Ill.: University of Illinois Press, 1960), p. 6.

The average car driver, for example, might conceive of the Mustang as a "sports car;" if he constitutes the target audience, then "sports car" terminology should be used in the message. Auto engineers and sports car buffs, however, do not consider the Mustang a true sports car, and they might encode the message in regular "small car" terms, while their average-driver audience wants to hear about ease of handling, acceleration, and racing symbols such as wide tires.

Too frequently, the source—which is familiar with the technical details about a product—is inclined to talk about them and ignore the more general use characteristics the target audience wants to know about. The result is relatively little effective communication.

Further complicating the communications process is the receiver's awareness not only that the message is coming from a sender but that it is coming via some media. Consciously or subconsciously, the receiver may ascribe more virtue to a product if its message comes in a well-respected newspaper or magazine, just as the president of a company might seem more impressive than a junior salesman.

The findings of the behavioral sciences are valuable for a general understanding of the basic communication process.[6] But in planning promotion for a given product, marketing research is often needed to determine the best way to approach specific target customers about particular products.[7] While we cannot discuss these techniques fully in this text, we will cover general guides to strategy planning.

Since most communication is concerned with "selling" new ideas, the behavioral scientists' extensive study of how new ideas are learned, accepted, and diffused can be extremely valuable to us. We discussed the learning process in Chapter 8. Now we will see how the communication theorists have added to our knowledge of *the adoption process*. The adoption process for individuals seems to move through some fairly definite stages, as follows:

Adoption is an achievement, not a happening

> Awareness—The potential customer comes to know about the product but lacks details. He may not even know how it works or what it will do.
> Interest—*If* he becomes interested, he gathers general information and facts about the product.
> Evaluation—He begins to make a mental trial, applying the product to his personal situation.
> Trial—The customer may buy the product so that he can experiment with it in use. A product that is either too costly to try or cannot be obtained for trial may face severe difficulties being adopted.
> Decision—Either adoption or rejection. A satisfactory evaluation and trial may lead to adoption of the product and regular use. According to psychological learning theory, discussed in Chapter 8, reinforcement will lead to adoption.
> Confirmation—The adopter continues to rethink his decision and searches for support for his decision—i.e., further reinforcement.

This last stage may be extremely important to marketing managers because, without this confirmation, the adopter may try something else.[8]

These stages in the adoption process dovetail rather neatly with the four fundamental and interrelated promotion tasks that have been recognized for many years: (1) to get *Attention*, (2) to hold *Interest*,

---

[6] For more discussion of basic studies in the communications area, see David K. Berlo, *The Process of Communication* (New York: Holt, Rinehart & Winston, Inc., 1960); Carl I. Hovland, Irving L. Janis, and Harold H. Kelley, *Communication and Persuasion Effects of Mass Communications* (Urbana, Ill.: University of Illinois Press, 1954); Edgar Crane, *Marketing Communications* (New York: John Wiley & Sons, Inc., 1965); S. H. Britt, *Consumer Behavior and the Behavioral Sciences* (New York: John Wiley & Sons, Inc., 1966); Gerald Zaltman, *Marketing: Contributions from the Behavioral Sciences* (New York: Harcourt, Brace & World, Inc., 1965).

[7] Allan Greenberg, "Is Communications Research Really Worth While?" *Journal of Marketing*, January, 1967, pp. 48–50; M. Dale Beckman, "Are Your Messages Getting Through?" *Journal of Marketing*, July, 1967, pp. 34–38.

[8] Everett M. Rogers, *The Diffusion of Innovations* (New York: Free Press of Glencoe, 1962); E. M. Rogers with F. Schoemaker, *Communication of Innovation: A Cross-Cultural Approach* (New York: Free Press of Glencoe, 1968); and George M. Beal and Joe M. Bohlen, "The Diffusion Process" (Special Report No. 18 [Ames, Iowa: Iowa State University Press, 1962]).

(3) to arouse *Desire,* and (4) to obtain *Action.*[9] (As a memory aid, note that the initial letters of each key word spell out the four-letter word, AIDA, the well-known opera.)

The relationship of the stages of Rogers' adoption process to the AIDA promotion tasks can be seen readily:

Obtaining *attention* is obviously necessary if the potential customer is to become *aware* of the company's offering. Holding *interest* gives the communication a chance to really build the prospect's *interest.* Arousing *desire* is intended to favorably affect the *evaluation* process. And obtaining *action* would include encouraging *trial* and subsequent *adoption.* Continuing promotion is needed to *confirm* the adoption and assure continuing *action.*

This action-oriented AIDA framework will guide our subsequent discussion.

Good communication varies promotional blends along adoption curve

The communication process and the adoption process we have been discussing are focused on individuals. How do you communicate with them? How do you get them to adopt your product?

Most marketing managers must deal not only with individuals but with markets. This complicates matters, because different promotion blends may be needed to communicate effectively with different potential customers. Some prospects already may have become aware of the product and developed considerable interest, while others have never heard of the product. Still others may have adopted the product but are seeking confirmation.

Promotion for innovators is not promotion for laggards

The adoption curve shows how and when different groups accept products, and points up the need for varying the promotional effort through time. The adoption curve is similar to the product life-cycle curve—both are concerned with the rate of acceptance of innovation.

This curve is shown in Figure 21–3. Some of the important characteristics of each of the customer groups are as follows.

Innovators—3 to 5 percent of markets. The innovators are the first to adopt. They tend to be young and, at the same time, high in social and economic status. They are cosmopolites, with many contacts outside their own social group and community. Coupled with this is mobility and apparent creativeness.

Business firms in the innovator class usually are large and rather specialized.

For promotion purposes, an important innovator characteristic is that they tend to rely on impersonal and scientific information sources or other innovators rather than personal salesmen. They often read articles in technical publications or informative advertisements in "respectable" sources to get information.

Early adopters—10 to 15 percent of the market. This group is likely

[9] M. S. Heidingsfield and A. B. Blankenship, *Marketing* (New York: Barnes & Noble, Inc., 1957), p. 149.

438

to be relatively high in social status, probably being opinion leaders. They may be younger and more creative than later adopters, and they may be mobile. But their social relationships are confined to their local group.

Business firms in this category also tend to be specialized.

This group tends to have the greatest contact, of all the groups, with salesmen. Mass media are important information sources, too.

Early majority—about 34 percent of the market. This group consists of those with above average social status. They usually will not consider an innovation until many early adopters have tried it. A long period may elapse between trial and adoption.

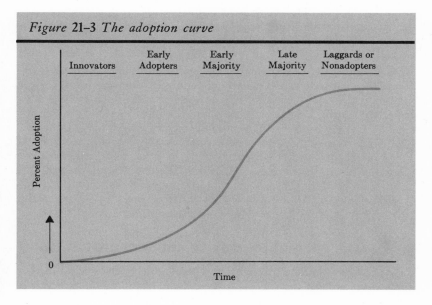

Figure 21–3 *The adoption curve*

Average-sized business firms with less specialization would fit in this category.

The early majority have considerable contact with mass media and salesmen *and* early adopters.

Late majority—34 percent of the market. People in this group tend to be below average in social status and income. They are less likely to follow opinion leaders and early adopters. In fact, some social pressure from their own group may be required before they try the product, but then adoption may follow quickly.

Business firms in this group tend to be smaller sized firms with little specialization.

The late majority make little use of mass media and of salesmen. They tend to be oriented more to other late adopters than to outside sources of information.

Laggards or nonadopters—5 to 16 percent of the market. This group has the lowest social status and income, and tends to be tradition-bound.

The smallest businesses with the least specialization are often in this category.

The main source of information for laggards is other laggards, which certainly bodes ill for marketers who want to reach the whole market quickly or use one promotional method. In fact, it may not pay to bother with this group.[10]

To be
successful,
be talked
about

The adoption curve research reinforces our earlier discussion in Chapter 8 on communicators and the "web of word of mouth." It shows clearly that different target markets seek their information from different sources, and consequently should be approached differently in promotion planning. It shows the crucial importance of selling (1) the innovators, because they help set the example which the early adopters may follow, and (2) the early adopters, because they influence the early majority—and from the early majority the word can spread to many others.

Marketing men are recognizing the prime importance of these interpersonal conversations and recommendations. If the early groups reject the product, it may never get off the ground. But if the early groups accept the product, then what the opinion leaders in each social group say about it may be critical. The web of word of mouth may do the real selling job long before the customer ever walks into the retail store. This points up the importance of trying to reach the opinion leaders (communicators) in various social groups. And because all the communicators are hard to identify—recall from Chapter 8 that different kinds of people may be communicators for different products—mass media may play an important role in carrying the message to them.[11]

Successful promotion may be an economical blend

Once the promotion objectives for a product have been established, a marketing manager may decide to use a blend of promotional methods, since some jobs can be done more economically one way than another. This can be seen most clearly in the industrial goods market, but it is also true with consumer goods.

Industrial
goods
market

While personal selling dominates most industrial goods promotion budgets, mass selling is needed, too. A blend usually is desirable. A personal salesman is nearly always necessary to complete the sale, but it is seldom practical for him to carry the entire promotion load. In 1965, the average cost of an industrial salesman's call was $35.55. This relatively high cost comes from the fact that a salesman has only limited time, and much of what he does is expended on nonselling activities—34 percent of his time is spent traveling and waiting; 20

[10] For further discussion, see Zaltman, *op. cit.,* pp. 45–56 and 23–37.

[11] See W. H. Whyte, Jr., "The Web of Word of Mouth," Fortune, November, 1964, p. 208; Ernest Dichter, "How Word-of-Mouth Advertising Works," *Harvard Business Review,* November–December, 1966, pp. 147–67; Charles K. Ramond, "Must Advertising Communicate to Sell?" *Harvard Business Review,* September–October, 1965, pp. 148–61; and Thomas S. Robertson, "The Process of Innovation and the Diffusion of Innovation," *Journal of Marketing,* January, 1967, pp. 14–19.

percent on reports, paper work, and attending sales meetings; and 5 percent on strictly service calls. Only 42 percent of his time is available for face-to-face selling.

The job of reaching all the buying influences is made more costly and difficult by the continuing turnover of buyers and influencers. An analysis of the circulation records of McGraw-Hill industrial magazines showed that out of every 1,000 paid subscribers in a 12-month period, 304 are replaced, 56 change titles due to promotions and reorganizations, 141 are transferred to different locations with the same or similar type company, and only 499 stay in the same jobs.[12]

An industrial salesman may be responsible for several hundred customers and prospects, with about four buying influencers per company. Clearly, he does not have enough time to get the company's whole message across to every potential customer. The problem was depicted by a McGraw-Hill advertisement that showed a salesman facing an industrial buyer and the buyer's thoughts run:

I don't know who you are.
I don't know your company.
I don't know your company's product.
I don't know what your company stands for.
I don't know your company's customers.
I don't know your company's record.
I don't know your company's reputation.
Now—what was it you wanted to sell me?

As the ad suggests, too much has been invested in a salesman to use his time and skill to answer questions that could be better handled through mass selling. Mass selling can do the general spadework; the salesman should concentrate on answering specific questions and clinching the sale. These mass selling "sales calls" can be made at a fraction of the cost of a personal call. One McGraw-Hill study found a mass selling "call" costing $0.0094 per call; a personal call, $22.[13]

Not all these mass selling calls are effective. Some advertisements will not even be read by the target audiences. When actual audience size decreases, the cost of an effective mass selling call increases. Yet a study indicates that they may still be very economical.

U.S. Steel researchers carefully measured the effectiveness of its ads with one of its major customers, toward which 12 different advertising campaigns, each for a different purpose, had been directed. They found that their advertising resulted in 850 completed calls at a total cost of $128 or 15 cents a call. This was in contrast to the cost of the average U.S. Steel personal sales call—about $30.[14]

These findings by no means indicate that U.S. Steel should or will eliminate its personal salesmen, but rather that the two approaches should be used to complement each other.

Another McGraw-Hill study seems to suggest that for industrial

[12] *The Mathematics of Selling* (New York: McGraw-Hill Publishing Co., Inc., no date).

[13] *Ibid.*

[14] "Ads: U.S. Steel's Penny Salesmen," *Printers' Ink,* May 3, 1963, pp. 32–37.

promotion, at least, relatively high advertising may reduce total promotion cost. This study was based on data supplied by 893 companies with sales ranging from less than $1 million to more than $25 million. The average promotion expense was 10 percent of sales, and the average advertising expense was 21.7 percent of the total promotion expense. When these companies are divided into *"low"* and *"high"* advertisers, total promotion expense rose to 11.1 percent of sales for the low advertisers, but only 8.8 percent of sales for the high advertisers. The researchers concluded that total promotion expense as a percentage of sales may be smaller as advertising assumes a larger part of a promotion blend.[15]

Consumer market

These studies covered the industrial market, where the target customers are less numerous and more concentrated geographically. Although no similar studies are available for consumer goods, it seems logical that mass selling and sales promotion would be more effective with final consumers who are more numerous and widespread. And, in fact, mass selling does tend to be relatively more important in consumer goods promotional blends.

Someone must manage promotional blend

Sales manager manages salesmen

Personal selling usually is the responsibility of a sales manager. Since most sales managers have been personal salesmen, they usually place great confidence in the power of personal contact.

The sales manager may be responsible for implementing Place policies, especially building good distribution channels, and in smaller companies, he often acts as the marketing manager.

Advertising manager works with ads and admen

An advertising manager, on the other hand, is concerned with mass selling effort via television, newspapers, magazines, billboards, and other media. His job is choosing the appropriate media for each purpose and developing the ads. He may manage this effort in the advertising department operated by his firm, especially if he is in retailing, or through an independent outside advertising agency.[16]

Sales promotion manager, a jack of all promotion

The sales promotion manager often fills the gaps between the sales and advertising managers, enhancing their effectiveness. Nearly everything the sales promotion department does could be done by either the sales or advertising departments. But sales promotion activities are so varied that specialists tend to develop.

In some companies, the sales promotion manager works for the sales manager; in others, he is moving toward independent status with responsibility only to the marketing manager.

Marketing manager, talks to all, blends all

Because of differences in outlook and experience, the advertising, sales, and sales promotion managers may have difficulty working with each other as partners or equals, especially when each feels that his

[15] "AIA Told How Ads Cut Cost of Sales," *Advertising Age,* July 1, 1963, pp. 1 ff.
[16] "The Role of the Advertising Manager," *Printers' Ink,* April 14, 1967, pp. 41–45.

approach is the most important. In some companies, they are hardly on speaking terms. It remains the marketing manager's job to weigh the pros and cons of the various approaches and come up with an effective promotional blend, fitting the various departments and personalities into it.[17]

All of these jobs might have to be carried by one man in a smaller company, perhaps with the title of sales manager. In this case, he is responsible for developing an effective promotion blend.

Factors affecting selection of a promotion blend

A food products manufacturer may develop a promotion blend composed of 10 parts advertising to 1 part personal selling. Some producers of paper specialties and industrial equipment may reverse the ratio, putting much more time and money into personal selling. A lawn seed producer might emphasize advertising 4 to 1, and a paint manufacturer might reverse the ratio. Is there some logical pattern underlying these differences?

Each promotion blend is designed to accomplish the firm's overall objectives. But the particular blend selected depends on a number of factors, including (1) the promotion budget available, (2) stage of product in its life cycle, (3) target of the promotion, (4) the nature of the market situation, and (5) the nature of the product.

Small promotion budget can buy big promotion returns

There are some economies of size in Promotion. Network radio or television may reach more people more economically than some combination of local media. Local radio, TV, and newspapers may be more economical than neighborhood media or direct personal contact. But the minimum charge for some alternatives may force smaller firms, or those with small promotion budgets, to use the less economical alternative, in terms of cost per contact. For example, a small retailer might like to use local television, but all he can reasonably afford are handbills and perhaps ads in neighborhood newspapers, together with church and school bulletins.

Some smaller companies, out of necessity rather than choice, use personal selling as their major method of promotion. A personal salesman can be hired for $10,000 a year plus expenses. Sponsorship of a single hour of network television can cost from $50,000 to $100,000. The TV show might bring the firm's message to more people for less per person, but its total one-lump cost might be too high for a small firm.

A small budget, however, need not limit a firm to personal selling. Sales promotion, public relations, and direct mail each have potential value. A small tire manufacturer who wanted to tell potential dealers about his product and was not in a position to compete with the big tiremakers' promotion programs decided instead to use direct mail. His carefully targeted campaign was extremely successful, yielding $196 in new business for every dollar invested.[18] A direct-mail expenditure of

[17] See "Needed: New Ad-Sales Unity," *Printers' Ink,* March 3, 1961, pp. 21–25; and "Creativity vs. Marketing Ability," *Advertising Age,* April 1, 1963, p. 16.
[18] "Direct Mail Puts Jack with Giants," *Printers' Ink,* November 10, 1961, pp. 49–50.

$1,861 brought in 101 new dealers and more than $360,000 of new business.

**Stage of
product in
its life
cycle**
A new product seldom becomes a spectacular success overnight. The adoption curve discussed earlier in the chapter helps explain why. Usually it must go through the several stages discussed in Chapter 14—introduction, market growth, market maturity, and sales decline. During these stages, the promotion blends may be changed to achieve changing promotion objectives, including reaching different social groups at varying stages of the adoption process.

Introduction stage—color TV sets and dishwashers are good. During the introduction stage, the basic objective is to inform. If the product embodies an entirely new idea, the idea must be sold—not just the company's version of it. And the promotion must "pioneer" acceptance of the product idea—not just the company's own brand.

The purpose of this emphasis is to stimulate *primary demand,* a job which may be long and costly. Color TV, portable dishwashers, and skillets with detachable electric units in the handles are examples of new products which required long introductory periods to sell because they were new concepts.

There may be few potential "innovators" during the introductory stage. Personal selling may be very useful, especially for industrial products. Salesmen certainly will be needed to select good channel members and then persuade them to carry the new product. Sales promotion may help draw attention to the product.

Since there are few competitors at this stage, mass selling can concentrate on the basic informing job. Early advertisements might be designed to draw inquiries and uncover new uses. Documented case histories may be used, as this is often a very persuasive type of advertising.

Market growth stage—our color TV and dishwasher are best. In the market growth stage, competitors begin entering the market, and promotional emphasis must shift from stimulating primary demand to stimulating *selective* demand—for the company's own brand. The main job is to persuade customers to buy and stay with the company's own product.

Now that more potential customers are trying and adopting the product, mass selling may become more economical. But personal salesmen must still work in the channels, expanding distribution.

Market maturity stage—you must not miss our color TV. In the market maturity stage, additional competitors have entered the market. Products differ only slightly now because most manufacturers have settled on similar methods of production and have a clear idea of the most attractive form for the product. By now, producers are copying competing features; promotion, beginning to emphasize minor or psychological differences, becomes increasingly persuasive rather than informative.

At this stage, mass selling may dominate the promotion blends of consumer products. Industrial products may require more aggressive personal selling, perhaps complemented by more advertising. The total dollars allocated to the promotion blend may rise as the competitive frenzy rises.

Firms which have achieved a strong customer franchise may be able to use reminder-type advertising, the type that seeks only to remind the customer of the product name, and may be considerably less expensive than more persuasive efforts.

Sales decline stage—let's find those who still want our product. During the sales decline stage, the total amount spent on promotion may decrease as firms attempt to cut costs and remain profitable. Since the product may still be acceptable to some target markets, more specific promotion may be needed to reach these remaining customers. Personal selling may help. The mass selling media must be aimed more carefully. Firms with a strong customer franchise may use reminder-type promotion.

Promotion can be directed to four different groups: final consumers, industrial customers, retailers, and wholesalers. The right promotion blend for each group may be slightly different.

Target of promotion helps set the blend

Promotion to final consumers. The vast number of potential customers practically forces consumer goods manufacturers and retailers to use mass selling in their promotion blends. Mars Candies uses outdoor billboards and magazines to reach as many people as possible. They estimate that, over a one-month period, almost every person over three years of age eats at least one candy bar.[19]

The earlier belief that some personal selling was needed in retailing to make the final sale has given way today to the recognition that for some products, mass selling can establish brand preference to such an extent that little personal selling may be needed. Self-service and discount operations attest to this.

It appears that some consumers do seek information about goods they consider buying. Mass communication may be the way to provide the information. We noted earlier that there are innovators and early adopters, and communicators within social groups, to whom others look for guidance and suggestions. Mass selling is necessary to reach these communicators because they are widely dispersed and it is not possible to identify or approach each one individually.

The predominance of mass selling in promoting to final consumers, however, should not blind us to the spectacular success of some blends which emphasize personal selling. But although some retail sales clerks and door-to-door salesmen can perform this job effectively, this kind of personal salesman usually is hard to find and more expensive. As a result, aggressive personal selling to final consumers usually is found only in relatively expensive channel systems (though a less costly system might not sell the goods at all).

Promotion to industrial customers. Industrial customers are much less numerous than final consumers, and there seems to be more justification for a promotion blend emphasizing personal selling to such customers. Industrial customers may have specific questions or

---

[19] "Mars Candy: The Limitless Market," *Printers' Ink*, July 12, 1963, pp. 40–42.

may need adjustments in the total product. A personal salesman can be more flexible in adjusting his company's appeals to suit each customer. He is also able to call back later and provide the confirmation and additional information that often are necessary in bigger industrial sales. Personal selling becomes more practical as the size of each purchase increases, which is typical in the industrial goods field.

Although personal selling dominates industrial good promotion blends, mass selling *is* used for some jobs. The McGraw-Hill studies showing the economic feasibility of mass selling helps explain why.

Promotion to retailers. As with industrial buyers, the relatively small number of retailers makes it feasible for manufacturers and wholesalers to emphasize personal selling. Sales promotion activities and some mass selling in trade magazines and newspapers are valuable, but the bulk of the promotion effort is by personal salesmen—who can answer retailers' questions about what promotion will be directed toward the final consumer, the retailers' own part in selling the product, and important details concerning price, markups, and promotional assistance.

In other words, promotion to retailers is primarily informative. But since the manufacturer's or wholesaler's salesman cannot *guarantee* the retailer a profit, promotion to retailers must also be persuasive.

The salesman must persuade the retailer that demand for the product exists and that making a profit will be easy. Sometimes persuasion takes the form of extra services—management advice, promotional aids, and demonstrators—special price concessions, advertising allowances, free goods, or some other "extra" that makes the offer more attractive.

Another reason personal selling is so important in dealing with retailers is that marketing mixes may have to be adjusted drastically from one geographical territory to another to meet competitive situations. The mixes in highly competitive urban areas, for example, may tend to emphasize price more than those in outlying areas. Personal salesmen can judge these conditions. We already have seen the development of a specialist—the food broker—to assist producers' salesmen in the extremely competitive grocery industry.

Personal selling is also important in a promotion blend aimed at retailers because part of the selling job is to establish and maintain good channel relationships. The retailer must be shown that the manufacturer or wholesaler has his interest at heart. A channel is a human system and depends on the mutual trust and understanding of channel members which can be built only by personal relations.

Promotion to wholesalers. Promotion to wholesalers is very similar to promotion to retailers except that wholesalers are less numerous and perhaps even more conscious of demand and cost. They respond to economic arguments. They are most interested in the promotion which the producer intends to direct at retailers and final consumers.

Mass selling may play some role here because some wholesalers seem to be impressed by a company which advertises in prestigious national media. In fact, for just this reason, manufacturers may place ads in consumer magazines, such as *Life,* and then distribute copies among present and prospective channel members.

Yet, in the end, personal salesmen are still needed to cement the relationship between producer and wholesaler.

Firms in monopolistic competition may tend to favor mass selling because they have differentiated their product somewhat and apparently have something to talk about. Mass selling may be more economical, especially if they are trying to reach broad audiences. **Nature of market situation requires different promotion**

As the market tends toward pure competition, it is difficult to generalize about what will happen. Competitors in some markets aggressively seek to out-promote each other, using mass or personal selling or both. The only way for a competitor to stay in such a market is to match their promotional efforts—unless, of course, his whole marketing mix can be improved in some other way. We see such vigorous advertising in our daily newspapers all the time.

In markets that are drifting toward pure competition, some companies may resort to price cutting. This will divert funds from promotion and drag price levels down faster. In such a situation, the cash revenues flowing into the business may decline, and all promotion will have to be cut back.

Once a firm is in pure competition, there is little reason to promote the product. But short of this, promotion may be useful. Someone has to get the business, and using persuasive personal salesmen may be the way to get it. For the customer's part, he must buy needed products someplace, and often prefers to buy from friendly salesmen who call regularly.

This condition also exists in oligopoly situations. But there may be sales revenue to support promotional efforts such as entertaining and business gift giving.

The customers' view of the product is the common theme tying together all the variables that must be combined into a marketing mix. Their view of the product affects the promotion blend, too. This was implicit in our discussion of Place objectives in Chapter 16 and of typical channels in Chapter 20. **Nature of product makes a big difference**

Later we will discuss typical promotion blends for the various goods categories. Here, however, we will consider the impact of some general product characteristics on promotion blends.

Technical nature of product. An extremely technical industrial product may require a heavier emphasis on personal selling, preferably by technically trained salesmen. This is the only sure way to make the product understood and obtain feedback on how industry can use it. The technical salesman can meet with engineers, plant people, purchasing agents, and top executives, and can adjust the sales message to the needs and wants of these various influencers within the target market.

Mass selling, on the other hand, is feasible for many consumer goods because there is no technical story to be told. Or, if there are some technical factors—for example, with cars or appliances—they can be offered where there is demonstrated customer interest in them, perhaps in booklets at the dealer's showroom.

Degree of brand preference. If the product has already won a strong brand preference, perhaps after years of satisfactory service in the market, there may be no need for aggressive personal selling. Reminder-type advertising is usually adequate. Indeed, Hershey Chocolate long prided itself on not having to do any advertising! Recently, however, it did begin some advertising and sales promotion to counter increasing competition in the United States. But in Canada, where it is not well established, Hershey has advertised aggressively.

If a firm has not differentiated its product, and does not plan to invest in building a brand name—perhaps because its product is not different—then much heavier emphasis on personal selling is sensible. The major goals then should be building good channel relations and getting distribution in as many outlets as possible. Rather than spending—perhaps fruitlessly—to build a brand name, the firm could invest in Place development.

Typical promotion blends

Many factors affect the selection of a promotion blend, as we have seen. To summarize the interrelation of all these factors, we will tie them to the goods classifications that we have been using throughout the text. As we do so, try to see the "why" of typical blends rather than memorizing "right" answers.

Although the blends shown here are typical, this does not mean they are right for all situations. Some very profitable promotion blends and marketing mixes have departed from the typical to better satisfy some target market.

For the consumer, print it, say it, deliver it

Convenience goods. *Staples* are often in the market maturity stage, with large potential target markets. Promotion, therefore, usually emphasizes mass selling. Brand recognition or brand preference may have been achieved already, but continuing mass selling efforts are needed to reach newcomers and those who regularly switch from brand to brand. The majority of food and drug items are in this category, where much of the total of consumer advertising dollars is spent.

Retailers usually will not voluntarily provide displays or special promotion aids except for their own dealer brands. Consequently, it is necessary for producers and wholesalers' salesmen to promote each product to wholesalers and retailers and to provide any store displays which are required.

Sales promotion departments generally prepare in-store displays and point-of-purchase aids, expecting personal salesmen to make sure they are used to the best advantage in the retail store. Unfortunately, large amounts of such material are wasted because of inadequate follow-through by personal salesmen, perhaps because the promotion blend was poorly planned.

Impulse goods are already accepted by consumers but are not necessarily competing with similar physical products. Instead, they are competing with all the products that could take a part of the consumer's dollar.

Since these items need well-placed displays, they usually require

448

highly persuasive personal selling to the retailer. Consumer advertising may not be essential unless several similar goods are competing in the channels. Then a producer may have to promote his product to final consumers to impress retailers and wholesalers that his product is the best impulse item available.

Retailers may also use local informative advertising by mail or telephone, to encourage impulse buying. Basically, however, promotion of impulse goods is aimed at the channels, relying mainly on personal selling.

Emergency goods are regarded as necessities for special circumstances. Little consumer promotion is needed, except that necessary to remind buyers of its availability when an emergency occurs.

The main promotion job is in the channels—to obtain distribution. An especially persuasive personal selling job may be needed if competitive products are available. Again, as with impulse goods, mass selling may be needed to impress channel members with the firm's offering. Direct mail may develop leads for new outlets, but inquiries probably will have to be followed by personal salesmen. The sales promotion department might develop effective storage racks, posters, or displays for emergency items.

Mass selling methods could be used if a producer wanted to move a product from the emergency goods category—where brands are less important—to another category. Antifreeze manufacturers, for example, advertise to try to get motorists to install *their* brand early in the fall to avoid the last-minute rush. For quite a few years, the major antifreeze makers have been trying to differentiate their product, stressing their brand identity. But despite their efforts, many drivers still wait until the first freeze warning and then pour anything that's available into the radiator. At this point, having widespread distribution is all-important to the producer.

Shopping goods. *Homogeneous shopping goods* may be goods already identified as such by final consumers and then promoted accordingly by producers. Or if the major manufacturers and retailers are advertising similar things, the consumer may come to think of them as interchangeable, especially if the same physical product is available from different retailers.

In either case, the consumer buying these goods is interested primarily in price. He may feel little need for personal salesmen. But the retailer still may use personal selling to try to convert his total product to a heterogeneous shopping good. In addition, the manufacturer and wholesaler may use aggressive personal selling to get the retailer's cooperation in these competitive markets.

Manufacturers and retailers may have to continue mass selling to meet competitors' promotion, but growing promotion budgets may then result in diminishing returns.

Heterogeneous shopping goods are compared by consumers on more bases than price alone. Mass selling may be used to inform customers about the different characteristics of these goods. Consumers searching for the best values often read such ads carefully. Here, advertising can affect consumer understanding of quality, either directly or through opinion leaders—*if* it doesn't contradict the thinking of the various reference groups.

Mass selling by manufacturers may impress middlemen by adding luster to the manufacturer's name and brand. Copies of national advertisements may be distributed to retailers and displayed by them to show customers that they offer nationally advertised products.

Generally, brand promotion is less important here—some manufacturers do little or no advertising, say for clothing and housefurnishings—because the consumers want to compare products in the store. Manufacturers may rely more heavily on informed retail clerks. Retail sales personnel may be paid financial incentives, such as a $5 bonus for each new mattress sold. Personal contacts in the channels, stressing economic arguments and demonstrating effective selling techniques, are essential here.

Specialty goods. Retailers advertising these products may use mass media, such as billboards or newspaper advertisements, simply to remind customers where they are for sale. The favored status of these products makes it relatively easy to promote them to wholesalers and retailers on the basis of profit potential. Even so, the producer's story must be told and told again. Personal salesmen may offer sales promotion aids to retailers to assist their reminder efforts.

Despite their preferred status, specialty goods may require mass selling. Consumers are notoriously fickle. If similar products were being promoted aggressively, the manufacturer would not want to risk losing his customer franchise. New customers are continually entering the market and must be converted to thinking of the product as a specialty good. This mass selling by producers also helps assure middlemen of continued customer acceptance.

Unsought goods. These goods are in the introductory stage of their life cycle. All potential customers must be fully informed about them. Mass selling may be used to reach final consumers, but wholesalers and retailers will need to be convinced of the profit potential of these goods. If they aren't convinced, the goods may never even reach the retail level. This promotion job is becoming increasingly difficult every year as more and more products vie for distribution.

Aggressive and persuasive personal selling will be needed, especially in the channels. But to impress the channel members, it may have to be supported by mass selling—and even a pulling policy. Salesmen may be needed to give demonstrations and to set up displays and point-of-purchase materials. Perhaps the company will need to offer promotional pricing deals. Again, personal salesmen may have to adapt a company's marketing mix to each individual situation.

For the industrial buyer, a handshake and confidence

Unlike consumers, industrial buyers usually do not seek out the goods they will need. By accepted practice, they wait for the seller to present products or ideas. Routine orders may be sent to regular suppliers, but industrial buyers still expect sellers to contact them in person or by telephone.

Mass selling may be used to locate prospects (through inquiry requests) or to develop a well-known brand name. This simplifies the

450

salesman's task. But the promotion blends for most industrial goods emphasize personal selling because the market is relatively limited and concentrated and the selling job is often technical. The specific promotion blend, as with consumer goods, varies with the product.

Installations. Some installations—specific buildings or pieces of property, or custom-made machines—are unique and have special technical characteristics. Promotion must inform target customers about the product and persuade them of its advantages.

Usually personal selling is the most effective method. Advertising may locate prospects and help presell them, but it takes personal selling to complete the sale. Moreover, many of the products in this category remain in the introductory stage indefinitely because of continuous technical improvements.

For some products in this category, however, the buyer has his own specifications or plans, and many competitors may have the capacity to satisfy the demand. Then, personal persuasion becomes even more important.

Accessory equipment. A basic promotion task here is to impart technical information. Mass selling may play a role in achieving some degree of brand preference and in locating prospects, but personal selling is paramount to convince users (or channel members, if they exist) of the merits of buying one company's product rather than another's.

Raw materials. Most of these products have reached the market maturity or even sales decline stages and tend to be standardized. Prices, which usually are widely disseminated, are competitive. Promotion is not unimportant, however. Buyers still must decide from whom they will buy. There are opportunities for considerable persuasive personal selling. The personality of the particular salesman and the company image which he conveys can, in fact, be the deciding factors. Other things being equal, a buyer would prefer to deal with a salesman who is pleasant to deal with and who can assure good quality and prompt delivery.

Component parts and materials. Promotion for these products must inform the prospective buyer about technical details as well as price, quality, and delivery dependability.

Personal selling is the chief means of promoting component parts and materials. Some components and materials are custom-made for specific applications, and personal salesmen are vital to assure that both buyer and seller are aware of each other's needs and capabilities. Salesmen also are important because many competitors can offer the same technical service or even identical products, and much personal persuasion is needed. Again, given essentially homogeneous products and price, the competence and personality of the salesman play an important role.

Supplies. *Maintenance and Operating Supplies.* For these goods, the producer's main promotion job is personal selling in the channel.

So many products that are essentially homogeneous are available in this category that the chief differences the industrial buyer sees are in price and ready availability. Since industrial buyers are likely to telephone their local wholesalers, or wait for their calls, a manufacturer's problem is to get distribution. Well-known brands and some mass selling to users may be desirable to encourage wholesalers to stock his products.

The wholesaler's job is to inform and persuade buyers to patronize his outlet because of the availability of all necessary products at reasonable prices. Personal salesmanship, perhaps including business lunches and entertaining, also may be important to underline the advantages of a friendly relationship with a dependable supplier.

Most of these products are in the market maturity stage. For a new product requiring some pioneering, the normal channels may not be able to promote the product adequately. The producer then may have to resort to direct-to-user promotion to do the job properly, using both mass and personal selling.

Repairs. Since most repair parts come directly from the original manufacturer, the main promotional task is to inform buyers of their availability. This is especially true if branch outlets have been established to offer better service. These products have a "captive market," and persuasion is not necesssry. If the market, however, is large enough to attract competitors, as in the automotive and electrical goods fields, then persuasion must be used, too. The main promotional appeals are faster, more dependable service. Mass selling might be adequate to tell this story, but personal selling may have to be used anyway, to meet competition.

Services. Since most service businesses have relatively undifferentiated products, their promotional task usually is persuasive in nature. The emphasis is on personal selling.

When a service is new, information about price, availability, and dependability is important. But competitors usually enter a profitable field quickly, and personal persuasion is then needed to hold customers. Persuasion will continue to be necessary if prices are forced down by competition. This situation is seen in the highly competitive industrial towel and cleaning service markets.

How some promotion budgets have been allocated

There is no "right" promotion blend for all situations. Each must be developed as part of a total marketing mix. But to round out our discussion of typical blends, it will help to see how various companies have allocated their promotion budgets.

Figure 21–4 shows the variation observed in one careful study of promotion blends. The lines show the variation in ratios of advertising expenditures (including sales promotion) to personal selling. Do *not* read the lines as measures of total expenditures. A short line merely means that the expenditures for advertising and personal selling were roughly equal.[20]

Figure 21–4 shows that the ratio of advertising to personal selling varied from over 10 to 1, to 1 to 10. The 10-plus-to-1 ratio for one food product represented an instance in which the company was selling a

---

[20] Edwin H. Lewis, "Sales Promotion Decisions," *Business News Notes* (Minneapolis: School of Business Administration, University of Minnesota, November, 1954), p. 2.

452

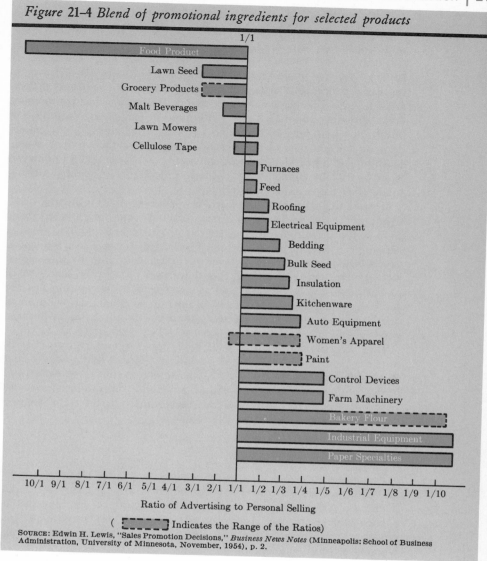

Figure 21-4 *Blend of promotional ingredients for selected products*

Ratio of Advertising to Personal Selling

([- - - - -] Indicates the Range of the Ratios)

SOURCE: Edwin H. Lewis, "Sales Promotion Decisions," *Business News Notes* (Minneapolis: School of Business Administration, University of Minnesota, November, 1954), p. 2.

staple convenience good with heavy emphasis on brand identification. Practically no personal selling was done, even in the distribution channels.

A lawn seed producer used a ratio of 3–4 to 1 in favor of advertising. This lawn seed was highly differentiated, and considerable emphasis was placed on brand promotion, although some personal selling was necessary in the channels. In contrast, promoting bulk lawn seed represents an almost reverse situation. Little brand identification is involved, and most of the promotional effort is directed through salesmen to the channel members to assure distribution and dealer support.

453

Major emphasis is placed on brand advertising to a mass market, rather than personal selling, for malt beverages, grocery products, and some consumer flour products.

Interestingly, however, when flour is sold in large quantities as bakery flour, the basic nature of the product changes. It becomes an industrial component material, and greater emphasis is placed on personal selling. The bakery flour market is extremely price competitive, and the main promotional effort is limited to persuading customers to buy from a particular company on a service or friendship basis. Bakery flour buyers understand the technical qualities of the product, where most of the housewives buying consumer flour do not. Housewives want to buy by brand to be assured of dependable quality, making brand advertising more important.

Most of the other products cited in Figure 21–4 are industrial products, and heavier emphasis on personal selling would be expected there. Two of the three remaining consumer products, bedding and wearing apparel, are heterogeneous shopping goods; for these, again, we would expect heavier weighting in favor of personal selling. In the sale of kitchenware, personal selling also dominates. There are many small competitors in this industry, and aggressive brand promotion has not yet been undertaken. The stress instead is on obtaining widespread distribution, as many of these items are probably purchased as impulse goods anyway.

Two companies cited in Figure 21–4, one a manufacturer of lawn-mowers and the other of cellulose tape, had advertising-to-personal-selling ratios of 1 to 1. The reason is that these companies have a wide range of both consumer and industrial products. Heavier advertising emphasis on the consumer products is offset by heavier personal selling on the industrial products.

Conclusion

Promotion is a vital factor in any marketing mix. Most consumers and intermediate customers can choose from among many products. To be successful, a manufacturer must not only offer a good product at a reasonable price but also must tell potential customers about his product and where it can be purchased. The producer must tell wholesalers and retailers in the channel about his product and his marketing mix. These middlemen, in turn, must use promotion to reach their customers.

Various promotion methods can be used. Among them are personal selling, mass selling, and sales promotion. Personal selling is done face-to-face. Mass selling primarily involves advertising. Sales promotion activities consist of many special-purpose and nonrecurring promotional activities, such as the design and distribution of novelties, store signs and catalogs, and the development of displays for trade shows and international expositions.

Finally, the marketing manager must blend these methods into one promotion effort for each marketing mix. Special considerations which may affect the promotion blend are the size of the promotion budget, stage of product in its life cycle, the particular target customers who must be reached, the nature of the market situation, and the nature of the product.

In this chapter, we have considered some typical promotion blends. In the next two chapters, we will treat personal and mass selling in greater depth.

<hr>

Questions and problems

1 Relate the three basic promotion objectives to the four tasks (AIDA) of the promotion job, using a specific example.
2 Discuss the potential conflict among the various promotion managers.
3 Discuss the communication process in relation to a manufacturer's promotion of an accessory good, say a portable air hammer used for breaking up concrete pavement.
4 Explain how an understanding of the way individuals adopt new ideas or products (the adoption process) would be helpful in developing a promotion blend. In particular, explain how it might be desirable to change a promotion blend during the course of the adoption process. To make this more concrete, discuss it in relation to the acceptance of a new sport-coat style.
5 Discuss how our understanding of the adoption curve should be applied to planning the promotion blend(s) for a new, small (personal) electric car.
6 Discuss the nature of the promotion job in relation to the life cycle of a product. Illustrate, using household dishwashing machines.
7 Promotion has been the target of considerable criticism. What specific types of promotion are probably the object of this criticism?
8 Might promotion be successful in expanding the general demand for: (a) oranges, (b) automobiles, (c) tennis rackets, (d) cashmere sweaters, (e) iron ore, (f) steel, (g) cement? Explain why or why not in each case.
9 Indicate the promotion blend which might be most appropriate for manufacturers of the following established products (assume average- to large-sized firms in each case) and support your answer:

a) Candy bars.
b) Men's T shirts.
c) Castings for automobile engines.
d) Car batteries.
e) Industrial fire insurance.
f) Inexpensive plastic raincoats.
g) A camera which has achieved a specialty goods status.
h) A completely new home permanent-wave concept packaged in a convenient kit.
i) A contracting service, capable of bidding on projects up to large dams.
j) Lumber.
k) Production tools for finishing furniture.
l) Glass for window repair.

Personal selling

Promotion is communication with potential customers. Often a personal presentation is the best way to do the communicating. While face-to-face with the prospect, a salesman can get more attention than an advertisement or a display. He can adjust the presentation as he goes along, in line with prospect feedback, and if (and when) the prospect indicates that "this might be a good idea," the salesman is there to close the sale and take the order.

In this chapter, we will discuss the nature of the personal selling job and the sales management decisions that are needed to make it an effective part of a promotion blend and a marketing mix.

Importance of personal selling

We already have seen that personal selling is important in some promotion blends and vital in others. Some of its supporters feel that personal selling is the dynamic element which keeps our economy going.

Without question, our economy does need and use many salesmen. Census Bureau statistics show that almost 10 percent of the total U.S. labor force is in sales work. Keeping in mind that the Bureau is inclined to place many persons who are primarily personal salesmen into other classifications, it is likely that *at least* 10 percent of the nation's labor force, or about 7 million people, are engaged in personal selling. Contrast this with less than half a million people working in

456

advertising. Any activity that engages so many people and is so important to the economy, deserves study.

Personal selling is vital to the survival of many businesses. Until something is sold to the wholesaler, and the retailer, and ultimately the consumer, those employed in manufacturing, agriculture, mining, etc., cannot depend on a job or an income. Sales work is taking on a number of the characteristics of a profession in some businesses. Many high-caliber salesmen believe in the importance and values of personal selling. They subscribe to codes of ethics. They see their customers' satisfaction as a better test of their accomplishments than volume of sales or personal income. Some are engaged in what is called *systems selling,* so termed because they are no longer selling just products but whole systems. These systems are designed to meet customers' needs, solve their problems, and enable them to operate more productively. In short, we are seeing the development of a new kind of salesman.[1]

Birth of a salesman

Nature of selling job

Increasingly, good salesmen are not trying to *sell* the customer but, rather, are trying to *help him buy* by presenting both the advantages and disadvantages of their products and showing how they will satisfy his needs. They find that this helpfulness results in satisfied customers and long-term relationships. This new approach recognizes the growing sophistication of buyers, especially industrial buyers.

Helping to buy is good selling

The old-line salesman with the funny story and the engaging grin is being replaced by the salesman who has something concrete to contribute. The smiling "bag of wind" with the big expense account is headed toward extinction. Many such salesmen are still around, but it is difficult for them to compete against the modern breed. Purchasing agents may still be civil to them, but more and more the people in purchasing are placing their orders with those salesmen who can see a way to apply the right product in the right way and get results for the buyer.

As evidence of this change in thinking, some companies now give their salesmen such titles as field manager, market specialist, sales representative, or sales engineer. Just as important, the salesman is increasingly recognized as a representative of the whole company, responsible for explaining its total effort to target customers rather than just moving products.

A salesman is expected to do much more than just bring in new business, though this certainly is an important part of his job. But in terms of the communication process discussed earlier, he must both get action—the adoption of the product—and then continue to work with customers to help them confirm their decision and continue

The salesman is both transmitter and receiver

---

[1] Carl Rieser, "The Salesman Isn't Dead—He's Different," *Fortune*, November, 1962, pp. 124–27 ff; "How To Raise the Prestige of Salesmanship: Keep It Professional, or Recognize Everybody," *Printers' Ink*, May 4, 1962, pp. 56 ff.

buying. This may take the form of regular follow-up calls to be sure the customer is satisfied with his last purchase.

At the same time, the salesman may gather feedback data to enable the company to do a better job in its subsequent planning. Recall that a feedback function is an integral part of both the communications process *and* the basic management process of planning, executing, and controlling.

The salesman, in other words, not only serves to communicate the company's story to customers but also feeds back customer reaction to the company. He is a vital link both in the communication and marketing processes.

Good salesmen are taught, not born

The idea that good salesmen are born has some truth in it, but it is far from the whole story. A *born* salesman—if that term refers to a gregarious, aggressive kind of individual—may not do nearly as well when the going gets rough as his less extroverted colleague who has had solid and usually specialized training. Experiments have shown that it is possible to train any alert person to be a good salesman. Much of this training is grounded on basic steps that each salesman should follow. These include:

1. Search out or meet prospective buyers.
2. Select appeals especially adapted to the particular buyer.
3. Help him to make a selection—that is, help him to buy.
4. Give the prospect advice.
5. Answer individual questions and objections.
6. Assure buyers when they have doubts about a particular point.
7. Show samples and demonstrate the use of the product.
8. Help indecisive buyers to make up their minds.
9. Close the sale—that is, ask for the order.
10. Make suggestions for additional or complementary items.
11. Follow up with buyer after sale to assure satisfaction.

These steps may seem logical and even obvious, but what is obvious in theory may not always be practiced. Many salesmen fail, or are mediocre in performance, because they don't apply the fundamental rules. Others have never even been taught them in the first place. And many orders are lost simply because the salesman does not have enough information about the product or doesn't ask for the order.

New salesmen often are hired and immediately sent out on the road or the retail selling floor with no grounding in the basic steps and no information about his product or the customer—just a price list and a pat on the back. This isn't enough.

It is up to sales and marketing management to be sure that the salesmen have adequate training.

It's more than "Get rid of the product"

In discussing some of the fundamentals of selling, from the standpoint of marketing management, we will assume that the rest of the marketing mix the salesman is to sell is reasonably good.[2] But in

---

[2] The details of salesmanship are beyond the scope of this book. For more detailed treatment, see C. A. Pederson and M. D. Wright, *Salesmanship: Principles and Methods* (4th ed.: Homewood, Ill.: Richard D. Irwin, Inc., 1966); F. A. Russell, F. H. Beach, and R. Buskirk, *Textbook of Salesmanship* (7th ed.; New York: McGraw-Hill Book Co.,

fairness to salesmen and salesmanship, this is not always the case, and a salesman should not be expected to compensate completely for his firm's failings. Production-oriented businessmen often are inclined to feel that it is the salesman's job to "get rid of the product," whether it is good or not. But if the salesman can see that he doesn't have much to sell, it is easy to understand why his morale might slip and the whole promotion job would suffer. He may or may not be to blame.

Finding prospective buyers is not as easy as reading census reports. While there are about 200 million final consumers and 11 million intermediate customers in the United States, only a fraction of these are "live" prospects—prospective buyers for a particular product at any one time. What the salesman needs are methods to locate prospects.

The big buyer who wasn't there

The market analysis techniques discussed earlier can be helpful. The market grid concept is useful, too, since making a cold call on John Smith is expensive. Even on industrial calls, when it is known that a company needs a product, it may be difficult to locate the specific person who would be the prospective buyer or who will influence the purchase. One study found that 64 percent of industrial calls are made on the wrong person.[3] Another showed that since retail organizations frequently rearrange their organizational structure and buying responsibilities, continuous and detailed customer analysis is needed.[4]

Knowing how to handle individual customers, once they are located, is aided by the findings of psychology and sociology. But the behavioral sciences are not advanced to the point that they can tell us exactly which stimuli to use on a specific person.

Deal with emotions, remember economics

Salesmen know that some customers react to emotional appeals— remember the emotional motives—but also want economic justification for their buying decisions. This leads most salesmen to key their sales presentation to emotional appeals, and also provide an economic basis for buying. Eventually, experienced salesmen develop a "sense" of how to vary the blend of appeals, depending upon the feedback they receive during the course of the presentation.

Salesmen make sales presentations, which usually follow, at least roughly, the activities listed on page 458. The AIDA concept discussed in Chapter 21 is a useful framework for seeing what a salesman needs to do in a sales presentation, and why.[5]

Using AIDA to plan sales promotions

1963); P. H. Nystrom, *Marketing Handbook* (New York: Ronald Press Co., 1958), Section 18; and Steven J. Shaw and Joseph W. Thomson (eds.), *Salesmanship—Modern Viewpoints on Personal Communication* (New York: Holt, Rinehart & Winston, 1960).

[3] "64 Per Cent of Industrial Calls Are on the Wrong Man," *Sales Management*, February 6, 1959, pp. 53–56.

[4] E. B. Weiss, "Giant Retailer's Organization Table Upsets Selling Apple Cart," *Advertising Age*, April 1, 1963, pp. 90–91.

[5] The view presented here fits with our stress on marketing strategy planning—selecting a target market and designing a mix, including personal selling, for it. Some people view an AIDA approach as rather mechanical, because some sales managers responsible for "getting rid of" whatever was to be sold have had their salesmen memorize AIDA-inspired speeches which work fairly well. A modern view would reject this in favor of the needs-satisfying approach discussed below, but this mechanistic approach does work in some cases, being better than no preparation at all.

Attention. There is no prescribed, sure way to get a prospect's attention. Much depends on the salesman's instincts and his originality, as well as his knowledge of his customers. If a salesman calls on the same customers frequently, he will want to use a new approach each time. If each call is on a new prospect, a few successful attention-getters will suffice.

At the first stage of his meeting with a customer, the salesman's main purpose is to distract the potential customer from his current thoughts and begin a conversation. He might do this by just introducing himself or saying, "Hello, can I help you?" as a retail clerk might. Or a statement about the plans of the prospect's competitors might get attention. Other attention-getting devices can range from a movie or slide projector to a model of the product or even a colorful hat or necktie.[6]

Whatever is used, the attention-getter should be casual, not elaborate, so that the salesman can move quickly, naturally, and logically into the next step—creating interest. Otherwise, attention may be followed by a letdown.

Interest. Creating interest takes more time. It usually is desirable to probe for the prospect's basic needs or problems, especially ones which the salesman might be able to solve. A furniture store salesman should not go into a prepared speech about rugs every time a customer comes in—some might want lamps, sofas, and so on. Getting the customer talking begins a dialogue and gives the salesman the all-important feedback which guides his subsequent effort. Theoretically, he should select prospects from among the target customers of the marketing strategy he is implementing. Therefore, he should know roughly what they want and have a marketing mix that has been designed specifically for them. His job is to show how and why it does fit their needs, in order to close the sale.

If the salesman has correctly selected his prospect, he may be able to use some visual aids which were specifically designed to hold interest and avoid having the presentation cut short. A slide or movie projector might communicate the kinds of things the salesman's company sells or does. Or to appeal to his senses, the potential customer might be given a product or model to handle or, in the case of food, a sample to taste.

Desire. Arousing desire requires an even more persuasive effort. It is imperative at this stage for the salesman to determine exactly what his prospect's problems are. This will enable the salesman to show how his product fits the need, counter any objections, and prepare for closing the sale. This feedback is vital to his sales presentation and is an important advantage of personal selling.

Knowing the prospect's specific needs, the salesman can explain *specifically* how the product could be used in the customer's factory or how it would be purchased by the buyer's customers.

One goal at this stage is to encourage the prospect to make a mental trial of the product to see how it could fit in with his needs. The salesman might show a grocer, for example, the statistics and testimonials on successes of the product in other stores.

---

[6] "Opening the Door with an 8mm Film," *Sales Management,* April 5, 1963, pp. 73–75.

Action. Finally, the salesman will try to summarize the important points he has made, tailor his arguments to the customer's needs and interests, and try to close the sale. It is interesting to note that one of the most frequent reasons for the loss of a sale is that the salesman never *asks* for the order. Perhaps this is because he does not want to be refused. A direct request for the order is all too easily answered with a "No."

There are ways, however, to avoid this awful word. The experienced salesman knows how to avoid a direct confrontation with human inertia and reluctance to make a decision. Without asking for a direct yes or no, they may begin to write up the order or ask which of various delivery dates would be preferable. He may inquire about the quantity the customer would like to try in a new display. This may lead the customer into taking action without consciously having to make a direct decision—an extremely difficult step for some people.

A good salesman not only must be able to make a good sales presentation but also must be able to locate live prospects. Effective prospecting might even be thought of as more important than making a good presentation, especially if the company's marketing mix is basically strong. But all of the promotion tasks are important in selling, and it is helpful to think of the typical sales call as requiring PAID-A —Prospecting and AIDA.[7]

The name of the game is PAID-A

Defining the kinds of sales jobs

One of the difficulties of discussing selling is that each sales job is different. While the engineer or accountant can look forward to rather specific duties, the salesman's job is constantly changing. He must do far more than merely talk to interested customers, play golf, and go to lunch.

Two salesman's job descriptions prepared by the management of two companies illustrate the variations in the salesman's duties.

No small-time operator, he

The first covers the activities of a retail salesman for the Scott Paper Co., the well-known paper products manufacturer. These products— convenience goods requiring intensive distribution—are sold through wholesalers to retail outlets. The retail salesman's job is to call directly on retailers, less to sell than to assure the company of adequate distribution. Scott wants good merchandise display. It cannot depend on the wholesaler's salesman to accomplish this objective. As is customary in this business however, any orders obtained by the retail salesman are filled by the normal wholesale channels.

ANALYSIS OF SCOTT RETAIL SALESMAN'S JOB[8]

I. *Making the Sale on Scott Products*
   A. Sells new orders to retail outlets.
   B. Sells repeat orders to retail outlets.

---

[7] This idea should be attributed to Professor F. Mauser of Wayne State University.

[8] D. M. Phelps, *Sales Management Policies and Procedures* (Homewood, Ill.: Richard D. Irwin, Inc., 1953), pp. 545–46.

II. *Service on Scott Products*
    A. Renders merchandising advice and assistance to retail outlets.
       1. Builds displays.
       2. Plans and conducts demonstrations.
       3. Distributes dealer helps related to Scott products (including visual aids such as special display stands, price cards, and folders).
       4. Delivers merchandise where required.
    B. Secures newspaper and handbill advertising and other tie-in promotions from indirect customers (coordinates trade features with company advertising campaigns).
    C. Counsels with retail customers on most advantageous Scott resale prices. (Those that produce profits yet largest possible volume of repeat business.)
III. *Routine Duties*
    A. Records daily calls and results, and mails this report to divisional office daily.
    B. Maintains selective selling records on our products and on leading competitive brands, and summarizes these periodically, upon completion of each route coverage.
    C. Sends orders to divisional office daily.
IV. *Executive*
    A. Plans his daily and long-range work program.
    B. Helps in training of younger retail salesmen.
    C. Observes facts in his territory that have a bearing on the sale of his products.
    D. Works out new ideas and mails suggestions to superiors.
    E. Studies and keeps abreast of merchandising and marketing in other fields. Discusses some of these problems with other salesmen and his superiors.
V. *Creating Goodwill toward Himself and His Company*
    A. Sell Scott Paper Co., its concepts and policies to retail dealers.
    B. Offers retail dealers constructive merchandising ideas not related to Scott products.
    C. Distributes dealer helps not specifically related to Scott products.
    D. Continually strives to maintain and improve friendly relationship with retail customers.

The second illustration of a salesman's job description is from an industrial goods manufacturer who sells record control systems for business and industry. It sells not only machines and devices for processing a firm's paper work but also the specialized forms used by the machines. While the company is primarily interested in the sale of the forms, the whole system—including the machines—must be sold initially. This amounts to selling two products: a systems installation, plus supplies on a continuing basis.

The company describes the tasks the salesmen are to perform as follows:

Job Description for Salesmen[9]

1. Must deal with executive-type personnel.
2. Prepares approach material by gathering, through various sources, information as complete as possible about prospects concerned before calling. Select proper sales tools for making the first call.

---

[9] *Ibid.*, pp. 546–47.

3. Makes a detailed survey of a selected system or group of systems presently in use by the prospect.
4. Flow-charts all procedures in present system.
5. Applies principles of work simplification to improve present procedures. Designs . . . Company business forms to fit the revised procedure.
6. Prepares written proposal to present to prospect.
7. Explains proposals and flow-charts quite often to a group of executives in prospective concerns.
8. Communicates details of the orders to the home office and draws copy for the business forms as they are to be printed.
9. Arranges and holds clinics for executives from different companies, or for executives within one company, on the subject of work simplification as applied to office paper work.
10. Maintains three different types of personal sales records.
11. Must be familiar with principles and mechanical specifications of 20 or more different business machines.
12. Must be thoroughly familiar with printing specifications.
13. Spends 20 percent of his time in personal selling. Eighty percent of his time is devoted to methods study, office work, detail work.
14. Calls on customers for soliciting repeat order business where the question is largely that of handling the details in writing up orders and specification sheets.

Clearly, there is more to selling than talking. The salesman must bring to each selling job an overall yet detailed view of what his company is offering and what his customer needs. This requires planning, continuous prospecting, and follow-through as well as effective sales calls.

The industrial salesman's job is neither simple nor limited. The salesman today, in effect, must play the role of manager in his own territory or in his own retail department. Some beginning salesmen are responsible for larger sales volumes than are achieved by average or even large-sized retail stores.

All selling is divided into three parts

Not only is every salesman's job unique but the tasks of any salesman continually change. These tasks vary with company objectives, with market conditions, and not the least, with the preferences of each individual customer.

There are, however, three basic sales tasks that are found in any sales *organization*. Although one salesman may have to do all three tasks, management must recognize that these essentially different activities are being performed by one man. Among other things, the method of compensating salesmen should be based on the blend of these three sales tasks.

These tasks are: (*1*) *order getting,* (*2*) *order taking,* and (*3*) *supporting.* For convenience we will designate salesmen by these terms, referring to their primary task.

As the names imply, order getters and order takers are order-oriented. They are specifically interested in obtaining orders for their company. In contrast, supporting salesmen are not directly interested in taking orders. Their function is to help the order-oriented salesmen.

While it is true that specific men—with certain abilities, interests, and training—are best suited for specific jobs, note that there is a place in personal selling for nearly everyone.

Order getters— develop new business

Order getting is concerned with developing new business. *Order getting, sometimes called "creative selling," entails aggressively seeking out potential buyers with a well-organized sales presentation which is designed to sell a product, service, or idea.*

Order getters may sell complete lines or only a single line, in which case they may be called specialty salesmen. They may be interested in selling the advantages of buying from one company rather than from another, or shifting the share of purchases from others to the salesman's company, or finding completely new customers and even entirely new markets.

An order getter must have complete confidence in his abilities, his company, and his product, since his attitude shows through to customers. He must be patient with the potential customer's employees, doing a thorough selling job throughout the potential customer's organization. The order getter must be a teacher and counselor, not just a contact man, and must inspire confidence by his manner and performance. But most important, he must be aggressive and confident—ready, willing, and able to face (and control) new faces and new situations.

Order-getting salesmen work for manufacturers, wholesalers, and retailers.

Manufacturers' order-getting salesmen. Manufacturers of all kinds of goods, but especially industrial goods, have a great need for order getters. They are needed to locate new prospects, open new accounts, visualize new opportunities, and help establish and build channel relationships.

High-caliber order getters are essential in sales of installations and accessory equipment, where substantial sums are involved and top-level management participates in the buying decision. Such salesmen must be especially knowledgeable and persuasive, but not extremely aggressive in the manner of the typical door-to-door consumer goods salesmen.

Top-level customers are more interested in ways to save or make more money than in technical details, and a good order getter caters to this interest. He sells concepts and ideas rather than physical products. The products are merely the means of achieving the ends desired by the customer.

In selling other industrial goods—such as raw materials, components, supplies, and services—skilled order getters also are necessary. Yet in these fields they may be required only for the initial contacts. Since many competitors offer nearly the same product in this area, the salesman's crucial selling job here is getting his company's name "on the list." Persuasion of the highest order and sometimes deliberate social cultivation of top-executive prospects may be necessary, perhaps at the local country club.[10]

---

[10] For a story of how one top-level order getter deliberately cultivated the acquaintance of a railroad executive, see "The Personal Touch Clinched the Sale," *Printers' Ink*, March 27, 1959, p. 70.

Many industrial goods order getters are required to help solve the customers' problems which continually arise in the course of production. To supply themselves with technically competent order-getting salesmen, firms often give special technical training to business-trained college graduates. Such salesmen then can deal intelligently with their specialist customers. In fact, they may be more technically competent in their narrow specialty than anyone they are likely to encounter and so may be able to provide a unique service.

"Worms," Said the Salesman. The crucial need for technical training and an interest in service and problem solving can be seen in an incident in the career of a young salesman who was selling Ralston-Purina hog feed, (a component material) to hog raisers. This salesman had worked at Ralston Purina Co.'s huge—26,000 animals—experimental farm which that firm uses as a training school for its salesmen. After training at this school, a salesman knows about the care and feeding of animals because he has fed and weighed many animals and recorded their gains in weight.

One day he called on a hog raiser—one of the biggest buyers of hog feed in that part of the state. The farmer was not interested in Purina products. While our young salesman was talking with him, one of his hogs lay down and died in the mud right in front of them. "Worms," said the salesman. "No such thing!" said the farmer. *"I've had my hogs tested for worms and they don't have any."* "Give me a sharp knife and let's see," suggested the newly graduated youngster. So he performed an autopsy on that porker and revealed that it was full of worms.

His next step was an offer of *service.* He said, "Now let's de-worm the rest of your hogs before you lose any more of them. I'll hang around and help you do it." He spent the best part of three days helping with this rather unpleasant chore, then made bold to suggest that the farmer would be wise to put a solid floor on his pens so that the hogs could live under cleaner conditions. By this time, the hog raiser was somewhat humbled and genuinely grateful; so he promised to make this improvement. Then, without being asked, he came across with the startling proposition: "Young fellow, you know hogs. You know things that I had never learned. I'd like your advice on how I should feed my hogs."

Of course, he became one of the biggest buyers of Purina hog feed and, through his influence, almost an assistant salesman to our young friend.[11]

He Must Know Other Men's Business. Business training also is important to enable the manufacturer's salesman to visualize the needs and potentials of particular prospects and to discuss prices and long-run business conditions with purchasing agents.

The Kaiser Aluminum Co. expects its industrial salesmen to know "financial rating and background, raw-materials usage, plant locations, names of key persons, policies as to buying and use of aluminum, status of company's orders, delivery schedule, pattern of aluminum buying, and developments which might involve the use of aluminum."[12]

Manufacturers need order getters to make at least the initial contacts

---

[11] F. A. Russell and F. H. Beach, *Textbook of Salesmanship* (6th ed.; New York: McGraw-Hill Book Co., 1951), pp. 113–14.
[12] Russell and Beach, *op. cit.,* p. 59.

with wholesalers and retailers and to convince prospective channel members that they should take a chance with a new product or new line.

In recruiting other channel members, the order getter ought to know how they should be running their business, how his product will help them, and what objections they may have to his product. He must be extremely self-confident, sure of the proposition he is offering and able to radiate this mood to his prospects.

Order getting is a big job and manufacturers' order getters normally are well paid. Many earn more than $25,000 a year.

Wholesalers' order-getting salesmen—hand it to the customer, almost. We have seen already that progressive wholesalers are developing into counselors and store advisers rather than just order takers. In some situations, routine orders are simply handled by mail or telephone, with wholesalers' salesmen functioning as "partners" of retailers in the job of moving merchandise from the wholesale warehouse through the retail store to consumers.

The emphasis here is on *through*. Modern wholesalers are attempting to cooperate with retailers rather than merely stocking them. The philosophy here is that nothing is really sold until the final consumer or user buys it.

Such salesmen truly are in the order-getting class. Many have found it much more profitable to do an extremely good job with few accounts rather than contacting large numbers of retailers but selling little to each of them. These order getters practically become a part of the retailer's staff, helping to check stock, write orders, conduct demonstrations, and plan advertising, special promotions, and other retailing activities.

Wholesalers probably would employ even more order getters if so many small retailers didn't seem to shun help. The more aggressive wholesalers avoid dealing with such retailers, as evidenced in this statement by a successful wholesale salesman: "I can't afford to waste my time calling on the grippers and the men who do nothing to help themselves. There are too many other retailers with whom I can work . . . merchants, not storekeepers. Men who want to improve their stores and their sales . . . who have open minds, not closed minds."[13]

The wholesalers calling directly on intermediate customers often are order getters, particularly in the case of the more aggressive manufacturers' agents and brokers and some limited line and specialty wholesalers. These face the same tasks as manufacturers' order getters.

Retail order-getting salesmen—visionaries at the storm window. Order getters are necessary for unsought goods and desirable for some shopping goods.

Unsought Goods. Convincing customers of the merits of products they have not seriously considered takes a high degree of personal salesmanship. Encyclopedia salesmen, for example, must convince prospects that $300 or $400 is a small price for a lifetime of literate happiness.

---

[13] "The Salesman's Changing Role," *Hardware Retailer,* May, 1958, p. 35.

Order getters may have to visualize how a particular product will satisfy existing needs now being filled by something else. Early salesmen for aluminum storm windows and other aluminum and plastic home improvements faced the difficult task of convincing skeptical prospects that these materials were not only durable but would save money and take less maintenance in the long run. Similar problems were faced by the early refrigerator salesmen in the 1920's and air-conditioning salesmen in the 1930's (but encyclopedia salesmen will probably face them from now until doomsday).

Without order-getting salesmen, many of the products we now accept as part of our standard of living—such as refrigerators and window air conditioners—might have died in the introductory stage. Most people reject or wait for others to accept new ideas. It is the visionary order getter who helps bring products out of the introductory stage into the market growth and market maturity stages. It is the order getter who sells enough customers to get the web-of-word-of-mouth going. Without sales and profits in the early stages, the product may fail and never be offered again.[14]

Low Pressure Keeps the Foot Out of the Door. Some of the order getters selling unsought goods are the high-pressure, "born" salesmen, who have given some aspects of selling a bad name. Low-priced appliances, especially washing machines, are now being introduced aggressively in Britain by such salesmen.[15] But some of today's companies have found it more desirable to use a lower pressure approach with better trained and more mannerly salesmen. For these companies, customers are responding favorably, and in some lines, house-to-house selling is attaining a new respectability.

Give Her the Bird—and the Instructions. Order-getting salesmen are desirable for selling *heterogeneous* shopping goods. Consumers shop for many of these items on the basis of price *and* quality, and they welcome useful information. Automobiles, furniture and furnishings, power tools, cameras and photographic supplies, paints, and fashion items can be sold effectively by an aggressive, helpful order-getting salesman. Friendly advice, based on thorough knowledge of the product and its alternatives, may help consumers and bring profits to the salesman and retailers through the trade it attracts.

Many specialty shops and limited-line stores have developed a following because of the assistance offered by the stores' salesmen. Some stores notify their regular customers when they have special offerings. They frequently will advise a customer *not* to buy a particular product because it will not fit his needs, even though they do not have a suitable substitute. The store may lose an immediate sale, but this type of assistance in buying is profitable to retailers seeking loyal customers and repeat business.

Well-trained order-getting salesmen can help retailers compete with low-markup mass sellers. A pet shop owner, for instance, emphasizes that customers ask his advice on what pet to select, how to feed it, and

[14] Robert C. Brooks, Jr., "Relating the Selling Effort to Patterns of Purchase Behavior," *Business Topics,* Winter, 1963, pp. 73–79.

[15] "Good Show—But Is It Cricket?" *Business Week,* January 5, 1963, pp. 42–44.

how to care for it. If a customer wanted "just a parakeet," she could buy it at department stores, variety stores, or even discount houses at about half the pet shop price.

This retailer feels his is selling not just birds, but pets *plus* the instructions and supplies to care for them properly—just as the good industrial salesman is selling more than nuts, bolts, and castings.[16]

Order takers— keep the business coming

Order takers complete the bulk of all sales transactions. After the customer has been interested in the products of a specific firm—either by an order-getting salesman, a supporting salesman, or through advertising or sales promotion—then an order taker may be necessary to answer any final questions and complete the sale.

Order taking, which is defined as the routine completion of sales made regularly to the same or similar customers, makes up much of personal selling. Most wholesaling and retailing transactions require some order taking.

The term "order taker" should not be considered derogatory. Sometimes sales managers or customers will use the term in a snide way when referring to salesmen, but such usage is often inaccurate and highly colored with prejudice. A salesman may perform so poorly that criticism of him is justified. But it is a mistake to downgrade the *function* of order taking. Order taking is extremely important whether handled by human hands or machines.

The order-taking function *can* sometimes be reduced to taking money mechanically and delivering the product, as by vending machine. Computers may take over many routine buying and selling transactions in the industrial goods area; companies can now buy supplies in this way.[17] But there are many aspects of order taking that demand the human touch.

Manufacturers' order takers—sales by the carload. After the order getters have opened up industrial, wholesale, or retail accounts, it is necessary to follow through on a day-in and day-out basis. Someone is needed to explain all the details, make adjustments, handle complaints, and keep the customer informed on new developments. In selling some products to manufacturers, it may be necessary to train the company's employees in the use of the machines or products. In sales to dealers, it may be necessary to train the wholesalers' or retailers' salesmen. All these activities are part of the order taker's job.

Usually these salesmen have a regular route with many calls, which they may make at fixed times. To handle these calls well, they must have considerable physical energy, persistence, enthusiasm, and a friendly personality that wears well over time.

Many times the order taker must set up displays, or place the company's sales promotion materials. He must continually explain the company's marketing mix to his customers. As it changes, he will have to negotiate new prices, allowances, guarantees, credit terms, cooperative advertising, and other aspects of the mix.

[16] *The Pet Dealer,* March, 1961, p. 39.

[17] "The Computer," *Sales Management,* April 5, 1963, pp. 44–46; and "Electronic Salesman at Customer's Elbow," *Systems Management,* March, 1963, pp. 14–15.

Sometimes jobs that are basically order taking are used to train potential order getters and managers, since they may offer order-getting possibilities. This can be seen in the following description of his job by a young Colgate salesman, who moved rapidly into the ranks of sales management:

Over many months, I worked carefully with Gromer's Super Market in Hammond, Ill. It was an aggressive young store. After a few calls, I felt I had built up a warm friendship with the store personnel. They came to trust me and, more frequently than not, after I straightened shelves, checked out-of-stocks and did the usual dusting and rearranging, I gave them an order blank already filled in.

It got to be a joke with big, husky Paul Gromer, the owner, and his hard-working manager-brother. They kept asking, "Well, what did we buy today?" and they signed the order book without checking.

Naturally, I worked at that order like it was my own business, making certain that they were never stuck with dead stock or over-orders. They were making continual progress, though nothing sensational.

Finally, Colgate came out with a good deal. I knew it was right for Gromer's and I thought the store ought to double its weekly order to 400 cases. I talked to Paul Gromer about it and, without any reason that I'm able to think of today, I said, "Paul, this is a hot deal and I think you're ready for a carload order."

He looked at me for just a moment. I braced myself for an argument. Then he said, "Sure, why not? You've always been right before. Just ship it."

It was the biggest order of soap Gromer's had ever taken—and the store soon became a regular carload buyer.[18]

Normally, order takers need not be as aggressive as the order getters who open accounts. But this type of job does offer considerable challenge and is satisfying to many men. While not nearly as wearing on the physical and nervous system, it can yield very satisfactory financial returns.

Wholesalers' order takers—not getting orders, but keeping them. While manufacturers' order-taking salesmen handle relatively few items or perhaps even a single item, wholesalers' order takers may handle 125,000 items or more. In this circumstance, they obviously cannot be much more than order takers in the narrow sense of the word. In fact, the term often applies specifically to wholesalers' salesmen.

Most such salesmen just sell out of their catalog, having so many items that they cannot possibly give aggressive sales effort to very many of them, except perhaps newer or more profitable items. But once a new product has been featured, it is unlikely that the order taker will give it much attention for some time, if ever again. He just has too many items to single any out for special attention. The order taker's strength is his wide assortment rather than detailed knowledge of individual products. Even if shown that he could substantially expand sales of particular items, he probably would not do it.

To show such wholesalers' salesmen that the market potential for a

[18] Michael F. Lennon, "Don't Limit Customer's Horizon," *Printers' Ink,* June 30, 1961, p. 43.

small accessory tool was worth pursuing, a manufacturers' agent spent one week in one city and personally sold more tools than were sold by all the merchant wholesalers in the surrounding six-state area during the previous three-months' period. This performance did not change the methods of the order takers, however, and probably should not have. This kind of selling should be handled by a different kind of salesman and a different kind of wholesaler.

The wholesale order taker's main function is to keep in close contact with his customers, perhaps once a week, and fill any needs that have developed. Sometimes such a salesman gets very close to industrial customers or retailers. Some retailers permit him—like the Colgate soap salesman—to take inventory and write up his own order. Obviously this position of trust cannot be abused. After writing up the order, this salesman normally checks to be sure his company fills the order promptly and accurately. He also handles any adjustments or complaints and generally acts as a liaison between his company and his customers.

Such salesmen are usually of the low-pressure type, friendly and easygoing. Usually these jobs are not as high paying as the order-getting variety but are attractive to many because they are not as physically taxing. Relatively little traveling is required, and there is little or no pressure to develop new accounts.

Retail order takers—often they are poor clerks. Order taking is the most mechanical at the retail level. Most retail clerks selling convenience and specialty goods (and sometimes, unfortunately, even heterogeneous shopping goods) are poor order takers. They are compensated accordingly, and it is sometimes difficult to know which came first, the low salary or the poor order taking.

For most convenience goods and for specialty goods which have already been thoroughly presold, little needs to be done except to fill the customer's order, wrap it, and make change. As a result, retail clerks often are expected to concentrate on setting up and arranging stock—and sometimes they seem to be annoyed even with having to complete sales. Many are downright rude.

One survey of retail outlets, selling both convenience goods and shopping goods, indicated overwhelmingly that:

Most salesclerks are indifferent to customers.
Very few clerks know much about the merchandise they are selling, and many are of no help at all to the customers seeking information.
Most salespeople apparently assume a customer is presold.
If a store doesn't have an item a customer asks about, rarely does the salesman try to sell the prospective buyer anything else.
The ratio was 1 alert, interested clerk to every 10 who were lackadaisical and unconcerned.

This survey, and others like it, suggests that many retail order-taker salesmen are not good at their basic function.[19] It is understandable that

---

[19] "Crisis in Selling: What Can Salesmen Do to Win Back Discouraged Customers?" *Printers' Ink,* August 1, 1958, p. 22; "Retailers: Weak Link in Marketing?" *Printers' Ink,* March 9, 1962, pp. 51–53; Allen F. Jung, "Are Retail Salesmen Selling?" *Journal of Retailing,* Summer, 1962; and "Unhappy Customers," *Wall Street Journal,* December 4, 1961, pp. 1 ff.

more and more merchants are turning to self-service selling. This reduces the need for order takers but increases the need for other types of promotion.

It would appear that although many retail order getters and order takers are needed, there may be far fewer such jobs in the future as manufacturers and wholesalers make adjustments in promotion to offset poor sales personnel at the retail level.

There are two types of salesmen who *support and assist the order-oriented salesmen, but do not themselves try to secure orders*. These two types are *missionary salesmen and technical specialists*. Their activities, naturally, are directed toward obtaining sales, at least in the long run. For the short run, however, they are ambassadors of goodwill who provide specialized services. Almost all supporting salesmen work for manufacturers or are middlemen specialists who do this supporting work for manufacturers.

Supporting salesmen —inform and help the source of business

Missionary salesmen. A missionary salesman is employed by a manufacturer to work with his distributors and his distributors' customers. His usual purpose is to develop goodwill and stimulate demand, help or induce the distributor to promote sales of his employer's goods, help the distributor train his salesmen to do so, and often take orders for delivery by such distributors.[20]

Sometimes missionary salesmen are called *merchandising salesmen*. They are especially useful, and sometimes absolutely necessary, if the manufacturer uses merchant wholesalers to obtain widespread distribution and yet requires aggressive personal selling. They may be used to give an occasional shot in the arm to the company's regular wholesalers and retailers.

Usually these jobs do not require order-getting talents, but often men with such talents do this work when the job is used as a training ground for new salesmen. Normally, missionary selling takes less imagination than order getting, and the missionary salesman may get a good deal of supervision.

A special kind of missionary salesman is the *detail man*. He is used in the drug industry to call on doctors, dentists, pharmacists, and nurses, as well as drug wholesalers and retailers. Men who have had some science training frequently hold these jobs, since they must be able to talk to the professional people both knowledgeably and convincingly. They leave professional samples and explain possible uses for new products. They are normally selling the reputation of the company and the quality of its products rather than any particular product. The goal is to encourage these professional people to recommend or use the company's products and, in the case of doctors, to write prescriptions specifying the company's brand names.

Technical specialists. These men are usually scientists or engineers who have relatively little interest in sales. Instead, they are people with technical competence, plus the ability to explain the advantages of the company's product. Since they normally talk to the customer's technical people, there is little need for a high order of salesmanship. Prior to the

[20] "Report of the Definitions Committee," *Journal of Marketing,* October, 1948, p. 211, and *Marketing Definitions* (Chicago: American Marketing Association, 1960), p. 17.

specialist's visit, an order getter probably has stimulated interest. Then the technical specialist can provide the details.

Frequently, it is the order getter's job to get past the purchasing agent or other company executives who serve as a screen for the company's engineering or technical personnel. The order getter locates a problem and suggests that his technical people can solve it. Then it is up to the technical specialist. The order getter probably will consummate the sale, but only after the customer's technical people give at least tentative approval. Some of these technical specialists eventually become fine order-getting salesmen, but the majority are more interested in establishing the technical excellence of their product than working closely with people to persuade them to buy it.

Most selling takes the right blend of all three

We have isolated and described three sales tasks—order getting, order taking, and supporting. You should understand, however, that a particular salesman might be given at least two of these tasks and perhaps all three. Ten percent of a particular salesman's job may be order getting, 80 percent order taking, and the additional 10 percent supporting. Another salesman may have the same title but a far different blend of sales tasks.

The type of man required for a given sales position and the level of compensation will depend largely on which sales tasks are required and in what combination. This is why job descriptions for salesmen's positions are so important.

A careful job description should be written for each sales job as part of the marketing strategy planning effort. This, in turn, can guide implementation.

To see this more clearly, turn back to the two job descriptions presented earlier in the chapter and try to determine which of the three sales tasks, or what combination of the three, is needed for each of these jobs. You will see that these job descriptions provide fairly clear guidelines to the kind of salesmen who should be selected, the amount and kind of training that will be needed, how much they will have to be paid, and how they should be paid. These matters are discussed below.

Sales management must be planned, too

Marketing strategy planning must include some consideration of how the personal selling job will be carried out—in particular, how the job of selecting, training, compensating, and controlling salesmen will be handled. Otherwise, the planning may be unrealistic. We will not cover in detail the sales management function, but we will discuss briefly the sales manager's major tasks.[21]

Hiring by blood lines or psychological tests

It is extremely important to obtain *good, competent* salesmen. But since these descriptive terms mean different things to different compa-

[21] For further treatment, see W. J. Stanton and R. H. Buskirk, *Management of the Sales Force* (rev. ed.; Homewood, Ill.: Richard D. Irwin, Inc., 1964); and D. M. Phelps and J. Howard Westing, *Marketing Management* (3d ed.; Homewood, Ill.: Richard D. Irwin, Inc., 1968).

nies, a careful job analysis and job description should be used as the basis for the selection process.

The selection of salesmen in most companies is a hit-or-miss affair, normally attempted without any job analysis or serious thought about exactly what kind of man is needed. Friends and relations or people who are available may be used because many people feel that the only qualifications for sales jobs are friendliness and a presentable appearance. This approach has contributed to poor sales and high personnel turnover for many companies.

Progressive companies have attempted to use more scientific procedures in hiring, including multiple interviews with various executives, and psychological tests. The personality and characteristics of an applicant may be compared with those of successful salesmen in the job.

Unfortunately, none of these techniques can guarantee success—but experiments have shown that using some kind of selection method brings in better personnel than using no selection aids at all. Psychological tests particularly have caused a great deal of controversy; as in the case of motivation research, many proponents have oversold the technique. But used with care, such tests can be valuable aids to management judgment

The market grid concept may have to be given greater recognition in the selection of salesmen. Behavioral science research seems to indicate that the effectiveness of salesmen depends upon the kinds and personalities of the company's customers. Insurance salesmen, for example, seem to be more successful when dealing with individuals similar to them in age, height, income, religious affiliation, education, politics, and even smoking habits.[22]

Logically, this would mean that the sales manager should know as much as possible about his various target markets before selecting salesmen. He may need to hire a wide variety of men to meet different kinds of customers. As applied psychology and sociology are developed further, firms probably will be able to select and manage their sales forces more scientifically.[23]

A sales organization can't be successful unless its salesmen know how to reach the goals of the organization. This information can be imparted in a sales training program. Such a program should cover the following fundamental areas: (1) company policies and practices, (2) product information, and (3) selling techniques.

Training salesmen is never ending

Company policies and practices. Since the salesman may be the only

[22] Franklin B. Evans, "Selling Is a Dyadic Relationship—A New Approach," *American Behavioral Scientist*, May, 1963, p. 79.

[23] For more discussion on this, see G. Zaltman, *Marketing: Contributions from the Behavioral Sciences* (New York: Harcourt, Brace & World, Inc., 1965), pp. 116–21; S. M. Stevens, "The Application of Social Science Findings to Selling and the Salesman," in S. H. Britt and H. W. Boyd, Jr., *Marketing Management and Administrative Action* (New York: McGraw-Hill Book Co., 1963), pp. 601–10; M. S. Gadel, "Concentration by Salesmen on Congenial Prospects," *Journal of Marketing,* April, 1964, pp. 64–66; and James E. Stafford and Thomas V. Greer, "Consumer Preferences for Types of Salesmen: A Study of Independence-Dependence Characteristics," *Journal of Retailing,* Summer, 1965, pp. 27–33 ff.; and J. A. Belasco, "The Salesman's Role Revisited," *Journal of Marketing,* April, 1966, pp. 6–8.

company representative that a customer ever sees, he ought to be thoroughly familiar with the company's policies on credit, size of orders, dating of invoices, delivery, transportation costs, returned-goods privileges, and pricing. He should thoroughly understand his firm's requirements concerning reports expected of him, expenses and their control, and attendance at sales meetings. And he should understand internal procedure so that he can assist his customers in expediting orders, securing adjustments, and generally making it easier for them to deal with his company.

Product information. The amount of product information a salesman needs depends on the type of sales job he has and the complexity of the product line. We have discussed these matters already in Chapter 21 and in other sections of this text that deal with the classification of products and customer buying motives and habits. The important thing is that the salesman have enough information to be able to satisfy his customers—considerable information for some accessory and shopping goods, for example, but less for convenience goods.

Selling techniques. The ability to handle a selling situation is basic. Some companies are finding it more profitable to train salesmen in the specific selling methods they wish them to use. They rely less upon the old fashioned "born salesman," because he frequently does not do well when competition gets tough.

At the same time, however, it is ironic and unfortunate that training in selling techniques has lagged in most companies because these firms feel that selling techniques are something innate in all people—or at least in those who are hired as salesmen.

More progressive companies are finding that salesmanship can be taught effectively by observing senior salesmen, making trial demonstrations and sales presentations, and by analyzing why present customers buy from the company, why former customers now buy from competitors, and why some prospects remain only prospects. This training is started in the classroom and often supplemented by on-the-job coaching by sales managers. Time for this training must be included in the promotion blend, or the whole promotion effort may suffer.

Length of training period. Some sales training programs are as long as three years, though most last only a few weeks. The length of the initial training period should be in almost direct proportion to the difficulty of the salesman's task as shown by the job description.

Sales training, as such, however, should go on indefinitely. For this ongoing training, many companies use weekly sales meetings, annual or semiannual conventions, regular weekly or biweekly newsletters, and a regular program of sales supervision. Many salesmen tend to get set in their ways and can profit greatly from additional training. This training also provides additional opportunities for evaluating and selecting men for greater responsibilities.

Compensating and motivating

While it is true that public recognition, sales contests, and simple personal recognition for a job well done may be highly effective in stimulating greater sales effort, most companies use monetary spurs to sales personnel.[24] Our primary emphasis here, too, will be upon monetary stimulation.

Two basic decisions must be made in developing a compensation plan: (1) determine the level of compensation and (2) set the method of payment.

Level of compensation. The job description makes possible a careful appraisal of the salesman's role in the total marketing mix. This description shows whether any special skills or responsibilities are required that suggest higher pay levels.

To make sure that it can afford a given type of salesman with a certain set of responsibilities, the company should estimate, at the time this description is being written, how valuable such a salesman will be. A good order getter might be worth over $50,000 a year to one corporation, but only $5,000 to another company, simply because it does not have enough to sell. In the latter case, the company probably will have to redraft its job specifications or completely reshape its promotion plans, since the going compensation level for such salesmen is far higher than $5,000 a year.

To attract and retain men, most companies must at least meet the going market wage for salesmen of a particular caliber. Order getters are paid more than order takers. Some retail store clerks, basically low-level order takers, may not even be paid the federal minimum wage.

If there are particularly difficult aspects to a job, such as extensive traveling, aggressive pioneering, or contacts with less pleasant kinds of customers, the compensation may have to be increased. The salesmen's compensation level should correspond at least roughly with the pay scale of the rest of the firm, normally running higher than the compensation of the office or production force but seldom exceeding that of the executives who supervise them.

Method of payment. Once the general level of compensaion has been determined, then the method of payment must be set. There are three basic methods of payment: (1) *straight salary,* (2) *straight commission,* or (3) a *combination plan.*

Straight salary normally supplies the maximum security for the salesman and straight commission, the maximum incentive. Because these two represent extremes, and most companies want to offer their salesmen some balance between incentive and security, the most popular method of payment is a combination plan which includes some salary and some commission. Bonuses and other goal-directed incentives are becoming more popular, too. Pensions, insurance, and other fringe benefits may be included, too, but straight salary and straight commission methods are basic to most combination plans.[25]

What determines the choice of the pay plan? Four standards should be applied: control, incentive, flexibility, and simplicity.

---

[24] "The Sales Incentive: Booster or Fringe Benefit?" *Sales Management,* September 21, 1962, Part 1 of two parts, p. 41.

[25] For further discussion, see *The Conference Board, Incentives for Salesmen* (Experiences in Marketing Management, No. 14 [New York: National Industrial Conference Board, 1967]).

Control. A sales manager's control over a salesman tends to vary directly with the proportion of the compensation which is in the form of salary. The straight salary plan permits the maximum amount of supervision, while the man on commission tends to be his own boss. The salesman on straight salary earns the same amount regardless of how he spends his time or which products he pushes. If the sales manager wishes the salesman to spend substantial time on order taking, supporting sales activities, repair work, or delivery services, then the salaried salesman can be expected to do these activities without complaining. The company is paying for the use of his services for a set period of time, and he should expect to work as needed.

Since the sales manager must give more supervision when there is a straight salary or large salary element in the compensation plan, a compensation plan which included some commission or even a straight commission with built-in direction should be used if such personal supervision would be difficult.

A poorly designed commission plan can lead to lack of control. A manufacturer of industrial fabrics which paid its salesmen a straight commission on sales volume found his plant was swamped with a large quantity of small-yardage orders. Furthermore, the plant was continually receiving requests for bids on highly competitive low-margin items. This was unsatisfactory, since the company's objective was the development of new markets, rather than obtaining immediate business. In this case, the sales compensation plan was directing the salesmen toward the wrong objective.[26]

Incentive. An incentive plan can range anywhere from an indirect incentive (a modest sharing of company profits) to a direct incentive, where a salesman's income is strictly a commission on his sales. The incentive should be large only if there is a direct relationship between the salesman's effort and results. If the relationship is less direct, as when a number of people are involved in the sale—engineers, top management, or supporting salesmen—then each one's contribution to the total results is less clear-cut and greater emphasis on salary may be appropriate.

Strong incentives are normally offered order-getting salesmen when a company wants to expand sales rapidly. Strong incentives may be used, too, when the company's objectives are shifting or varied. In this way, the salesman's activities and efforts can be directed and shifted as needed. One trucking company, for example, has a sales incentive plan that pays commissions on business required to balance the freight movement, depending on how heavily traffic has been moving in one direction or another. At any one time, commissions are paid only on traffic moving in one direction.

Flexibility. Flexibility is probably the most difficult standard to maintain in the pay plan. One major reason that combination plans have become more popular than straight salary or commission plans is that they offer a way to meet varying situations. Four major kinds of flexibility will be considered.

---

[26] D. J. Wilson, "Common Characteristics of Compensation Plans for Industrial Salesmen," in R. L. Clewett (ed.), *Marketing's Role in Scientific Management* (Chicago: American Marketing Association, 1957), p. 168.

476

1. Flexibility in selling costs. This is important for most small companies. With their limited working capital and uncertain markets, small companies like the fixed selling costs (as a percent of sales) aspect of straight commission, or at least combination plans with a large commission element. When sales drop off, costs do, too. This feature is often overriding in selecting a method of sales compensation.
2. Flexibility among territories. Different sales territories present different potentials. Unless the pay plan allows for this fact, the salesman in a growing territory might have rapidly increasing earnings for the same amount of work, while the salesman in a poor area has little to show for his effort. Such a situation is not fair and can lead to considerable dissatisfaction and high salesman turnover. The star salesman may be the one who through luck or a family relationship has managed to obtain the best territory.
3. Flexibility among men. Most companies use salesmen at varying stages of their professional development. Trainees and new salesmen usually require a special pay plan with considerable emphasis on salary.
4. Flexibility among products. Most companies make several different products which have different profit potentials. Unless this fact is recognized, the salesmen may emphasize the sale of those products which sell easiest without respect to the overall company profit. A flexible commission system may more readily adjust to changing profit potentials as demand conditions warrant.

Simplicity. A final consideration is the need for simplicity as a standard to be maintained in the pay plan. Complicated plans are hard for salesmen to understand and costly for the accounting department to administer. Considerable dissatisfaction may result if salesmen cannot see a direct relationship between their effort and their income.

Simplicity is best achieved with straight commission. A predetermined commission is paid on the amount of the sale. There is no need to adjust salary levels for the age and experience of salesmen, the changes in demand and supply conditions in the personnel market, the size and potentials of the various territories, and so on.

It is also true, however, that in practice it usually is better to sacrifice some simplicity to gain some flexibility, incentive, or control. The actual combination of these factors must depend on the job description, the marketing mix, and the company's objectives.[27]

There are, unfortunately, no easy answers to the compensation problem. A strong incentive compensation plan might have been suitable when a company was small and growing and had a great need for order getters. But this plan might be entirely unsuitable just a few years later when there is more need for order *takers*.[28]

The sales manager in cooperation with the marketing manager must develop a good compensation plan. The sales manager's efforts must coordinate with the whole marketing plan because he can accomplish

Sales management must coordinate with marketing management

[27] For more discussion, see F. E. Webster, Jr., "Rationalizing Salesmen's Compensation Plans," *Journal of Marketing,* January, 1966, pp. 55–58; and R. L. Day and P. D. Bennett, "Should Salesmen's Compensation Be Geared to Profits?" *Journal of Marketing,* October, 1962, pp. 6–9.

[28] Kenneth R. Davis, "Salesmen's Compensation: Two Basic Problems," *Management Aids for Small Manufacturers* (Washington, D.C.: Small Business Administration, September, 1958).

his goals only if adequate funds can be allocated to this task. As already noted, it is the marketing manager's job to balance the promotion blend. The expected cost and performance of the sales force is only one of the many variables he must consider in making the final decision. To make these judgments, the marketing manager must know what a sales force should consist of, what its goals should be, and what it should cost.

Once the sales manager's basic plan and budget have been accepted, his job becomes one of implementing the plan, including directing and controlling the sales force. This would include the determination and assignment of sales territories and the evaluation of performance.

More is said on this in Chapter 30; but it should be noted that the sales manager has more to do than fly about the country entertaining customers. A sales manager is deeply involved with the basic management tasks of planning and control, as well as the ongoing execution of the personal selling effort.

Conclusion

In this chapter, we have discussed the importance and nature of personal selling and reviewed the variety of personal selling jobs. It can be seen that almost any person could fit into some personal selling job.

The first step in determining the type of salesman required in a particular situation is to develop a detailed job description. Three *basic* kinds of sales tasks were isolated: (1) order getting, (2) order taking, and (3) supporting. Most sales jobs are a combination of at least two of these three tasks, and the nature of the job (and the level and method of compensation) depend in large part on the blend of these tasks.

We noted that personal selling is achieving a new status, almost professional, because of the competence and degree of personal responsibility required of some salesmen. The day of the grinning glad-hander is passing in favor of the specialist who is ingenious, industrious, persuasive, knowledgeable, and highly trained. Many companies now have training programs that last several weeks or months, during which time the salesman does no productive work except preparing to serve the company's customers.

Salesmen of this caliber are usually welcome at a buyer's office because they are in a position to help the buyer. This type of salesman always has been, and probably always will be, in short supply. And the demand for high-caliber salesmen is continually growing.

There is a real challenge to sales management to select, train, compensate, and control this growing army of salesmen. Sales efforts in the past too often have been poor or even slipshod, in part because the need for salesmen was so pressing and sales management was not always the best. This situation is changing rapidly as marketing and sales management improves its techniques and adapts the tools and findings of cost accounting, statistics, economics, psychology, and sociology.

The sales manager is becoming a real manager of men, not just an older salesman. His efforts, however, still must be part of a promotion blend as well as a total marketing mix.

478

1 Ideally, the salesman's job might be to help explain how his company's **Questions** "really good" marketing mix was designed for and fits the customer's **and** needs. Cite three examples where you feel the salesman has a different **problems** role. Also, cite an example of a salesman who is using the AIDA approach rather mechanically to "get rid of a product."

2 Write a job description for a college textbook salesman. Does it make any difference whether the salesman knows anything about the material in the books he is selling? What kind of a salesman is he?

3 What kind of salesman is required to sell the following products? If there are several selling jobs in the channel for each product, then indicate the kinds of salesmen required. (Specify any assumptions necessary to give definite answers.):

a) Soya bean oil   d) Handkerchiefs   f) Corn
b) Costume jewelry   e) Mattresses   g) Cigarettes
c) Nuts and bolts

4 Distinguish among the jobs of manufacturers', wholesalers', and retailers' order-getting salesmen. If one order getter is needed, must all the salesmen in a channel be order getters? Illustrate.

5 Distinguish between merchants and shopkeepers as far as promotion is concerned. Are there any other differences? Illustrate.

6 Refer to the two detailed job descriptions in the chapter, and estimate what proportion of each salesman's time would be expended for order-getting, order-taking, and supporting activities (estimate in minutes for one day and then convert to proportions, making any assumptions necessary). Which of the two would probably receive the higher compensation and why? What compensation plan would be most appropriate for each job? Where might such salesmen be recruited and how should they be selected? What type and how much training would seem appropriate?

7 Explain how a straight commission system might provide flexibility in the sale of a line of women's clothing products which continually varied in profitability.

8 Explain how a compensation system could be developed to provide incentives for older salesman and yet make some provision for trainees who have not yet learned their job.

9 Discuss the role of the manufacturers' agent in the marketing manager's promotion plans. What kind of salesman is he?

10 Discuss the future of the specialty shop if manufacturers place greater emphasis on mass selling because of the inadequacy of retail order-taking.

11 Describe the operation of our economy if personal salesmen were outlawed. Could the economy work? If so, how; if not, what is the minimum personal selling effort necessary? Could this minimum personal selling effort be controlled effectively by law?

Mass selling

Mass distribution, needed to make our mass production economy run, is facilitated by mass selling. Personal face-to-face selling alone cannot provide the promotion required to move the huge variety of goods produced by our modern farms and factories.

Although a marketing manager might prefer to use personal selling exclusively, it can be expensive on a per-sale basis. Mass selling is a way around this road block. It is not as pinpointed as personal selling, but it does permit the communication of ideas or information to large numbers of potential customers at the same time. Today, most promotion blends contain both personal and mass selling.

Primary emphasis in this chapter will be on the use of advertising as a mass selling tool. The need for *advertising objectives,* reaching target customers (via media), and communicating with target customers (with messages) will receive extensive treatment. The management and control of advertising also will be discussed.

Importance of advertising

By the bicentennial, $30 billion in ads

We saw in Chapter 21 that advertising can get results in a promotion blend. It may help a marketing manager differentiate his product or even carve our a separate little target market for his firm. It may even help obtain product and brand acceptance to the point that customers will willingly pay substantial price premiums for advertised brands.

Good advertising results are obtained at a cost, of course. Expenditures in the U.S. for advertising have been growing continuously since World War II, and more growth is expected. In 1946, they were slightly more than $3 billion; by 1966, they topped $16 billion—and it is predicted that by 1976 the total annual advertising expenditure will be $30 billion.[1]

While total advertising expenditures are large, the advertising industry itself employs relatively few people. The major expense is for media time and space. And in the U.S., the largest share of this—almost 30 percent—goes for newspaper space. Television takes almost 17 percent of the total and direct mail, about 15 percent.[2]

It's all done by less than half a million

Fewer than 500,000 people work directly in the U.S. advertising industry. This would include all people who help create or sell advertising for advertising media, such as radio and television stations, newspapers, and magazines, as well as those in advertising agencies and those working for retailers, wholesalers, and manufacturers who handle their own advertising. The sometimes glamorous and often maligned 3,000 U.S. advertising agencies, however, employ only about 50,000 persons. Among these, not many are large, most employing fewer than 10 persons.[3]

U.S. corporations invest an average of only about 1½ percent of their sales dollar in advertising. This is relatively small compared to the aggregate cost of marketing—perhaps 50 percent of the consumer's dollar—and the 20 to 50 percent gross margins with which we have been dealing at various channel levels.

Advertisers aren't really spending that much

In reviewing overall U.S. advertising expenditures, however, it is important to note that the figures reported as totals and averages may at times be misleading. For example, according to the most recent annual Internal Revenue Service data, some industries spend a considerably larger percentage of sales for advertising than the average of 1½ percent. Soap and related products manufacturers spent 14.2 percent, drug manufacturers 11.05 percent, and tobacco manufacturers 6.06 percent. At the other extreme, coal mining companies spent only 0.09 percent, construction companies 0.10 percent, dyers and finishers of textiles 0.15 percent, men's and boys' clothing 0.11 percent, aircraft manufacturers 0.13 percent, and wholesalers and retailers in the aggregate 1.05 percent.[4]

Likewise, advertising expenditure figures must be read carefully because the amount spent by a particular firm or industry may not be a true total. The reason is that many firms sell to others who advertise farther along in the channel. And when this channel advertising is included, the total bill is somewhat higher. In 1966, total advertising

---

[1] *Advertising Age,* September 18, 1967, p. 2; and Jules Backman, *Advertising and Competition* (New York: New York University Press, 1967), p. 179.

[2] *Ibid.,* p. 188.

[3] Exact data on this industry is elusive. For the most recent estimates available from a good industry source, see "How Many People Work in Advertising?" *Printers' Ink,* December 6, 1957, p. 88. See also, John J. Humpal and H. G. Meyer-Oertel, "Measuring Change in the Advertising Agency Business," *Journal of Marketing,* January, 1967, pp. 56–59.

[4] *Advertising Age,* September 18, 1967, pp. 77–78.

expenditures accounted for 2.24 percent of gross national product and 3.56 percent of personal consumption expenditures.[5]

Clearly, advertising is an important factor in certain markets, especially the consumer goods markets. Nevertheless, we must keep in mind that in the aggregate it costs much less than personal selling.

Advertising objectives tied to marketing strategy

We have emphasized throughout this text the importance of setting and following specific objectives, including overall company, marketing, and promotion objectives.

You get what you ask for

Every advertisement and advertising campaign should be seeking clearly defined objectives. But we also have noted that objectives frequently are not stated explicitly, if at all. As a result, it is not surprising to find that many advertisers merely turn this task over to their advertising agency with instructions to "promote the product," having no idea themselves exactly what they want done. The agency then must shift for itself.

They may face-lift the previous campaign or develop what appear to be reasonable objectives. Or they may develop objectives which, although reasonable, allow the agency to experiment with new approaches or to plan campaigns that *will win awards within the advertising industry.*

Progressive companies are realizing that without clearly defined objectives, preparing an advertising campaign is guesswork, and measuring the effectiveness of the advertising is difficult or impossible. They are beginning to state their objectives more specifically. This gives them standards against which to measure performance.

Some firms—and their agencies—are most eager to evaluate advertising effectiveness. The Campbell Soup Co. and its agency have even agreed to tests by a third party to help evaluate how effectively the advertising agency's plans will accomplish the objectives set by Campbell advertising executives. This approach has a useful by-product. It forces both the company and the agency to specify very clearly their objectives.[6]

If you want half the market, say so!

Advertising objectives must be extremely specific, probably much more specific than personal selling objectives. One of the advantages of personal selling is that the salesman can shift his presentation to meet customers' needs. Each advertisement, however, is a specific communication that must be effective not just for one customer but for thousands or millions of target customers. Moreover, each advertisement in a continuing advertising campaign may seek to accomplish different objectives. It is essential, therefore, to specify not only the objectives of the whole campaign but of each individual advertisement.

Specific advertising objectives should include, (1) the customer reaction sought by the campaign or individual advertisement and (2) the

---

[5] Backman, *op. cit.,* p. 182.

[6] "Getting the Most Ad for the Money," *Printers' Ink,* September 27, 1963, pp. 27–30; and "Ad Roles Shifting for Agencies and Clients," *Business Week,* December 8, 1962, pp. 53–56.

role played by the campaign or advertisement in the overall promotion blend—and in the larger framework, as part of the marketing mix.

More specifically, an advertisement or advertising campaign might work toward the following *advertising objectives:*

1. Aid in the introduction of new products to specific target markets.
2. Assist in the expansion or maintenance of market share.
3. Help obtain desirable dealer outlets.
4. Prepare the way for salesmen by presenting the company's name and the merits of its products.
5. Tell about the availability of new products and the possible uses of other products.
6. Provide contact with the target customers even when the salesman is not available.
7. Sell the company "brand image."
8. Obtain immediate buying action.
9. Help a buyer confirm his purchasing decision.
10. Develop goodwill for the company itself.

Even these objectives, however, are not specific enough as a basis for measuring the effectiveness of advertising. An advertisement which sought (as in No. 5) to tell about the availability of a new product could, for example, be judged successful if market research results showed that *any* customers were now aware of the existence of the new product. But would a 1 percent awareness be impressive? Not if the advertiser had been hoping for a 50 percent awareness!

Two examples show the interrelation of specifying goals and measuring results.

Aim for the target, count the score

1. Rather than just telling about the availability of a particular new product, the specific advertising objective might be "to increase the awareness of Product X by 20 percent, over a one-year period, among housewives between the ages of 25 and 40 years in the 212 U.S. Standard Metropolitan Statistical Areas."

This objective would give the advertising agency something to work toward. It clearly specifies some actions and eliminates others. For example, it is clear that no effort would need to be made to increase awareness in rural areas. It also is clear that a test of *current* awareness would be needed as a bench mark, to be able to measure the *increase* in awareness.

2. A general promotional objective, "To assist in the expansion of market share," could be rephrased more specifically, "To increase traffic in our cooperating retailer outlets by 25 percent during the next three months."

Such a specific objective obviously has an impact on implementation plans. Advertising that might be right for building a good image among communicators might be entirely wrong for getting customers into the retailers' stores. Here we might use contests or tie-in sales. And the media used would be more pinpointed to help particular dealers, perhaps including local newspapers and billboards rather than national consumer magazines.[7]

---

[7] For further discussion on this, see Russell H. Colley, *Defining Advertising Goals for Measured Advertising Results* (New York: Association of National Advertisers, Inc.,

Objectives determine kinds of advertising needed

The advertising objectives selected will largely determine which of two basic types of advertising to use—*product* or *institutional.*

Product advertising, as the name implies, is concerned with *informing about and selling a product.* It may be aimed at final users or consumers, or to channel members.

Institutional advertising, on the other hand, does not involve a product but rather a company or even an industry. It is intended primarily to *develop goodwill toward the company or industry.* The long-run goal is to improve sales and relations with the various publics with whom the company deals. This includes not only consumers but current and prospective channel members or component suppliers, shareholders, etc.

Product advertising —meet us, like us, remember us

Product advertising is of three kinds: pioneering, competitive, and reminder advertising.

Pioneering advertising—builds primary demand. Pioneering advertising is aimed at developing primary demand for a product category rather than a specific brand. It is needed in the early stages of the adoption process to inform potential adopters about a new product or concept.

Pioneering advertising is used in the introductory stage in the product life cycle and might be appropriate for use with several general advertising objectives (No's. 1, 3, 4, and 5, for example). Its basic job is to inform, not persuade.

Pioneering advertising need not mention the brand or specific company at all. A producer of military reconnaissance cameras found it first had to sell the concept and value of reconnaissance to the military—and then cameras.[8] The California olive industry promoted olives as olives, not certain brands. This was so successful that after only five years of promotion, the industry's surpluses had become shortages, and it diverted promotional funds to horticultural research to increase production.[9]

Competitive advertising—emphasizes selective demand. Competitive advertising is intended to stimulate selective demand by selling a specific brand rather than a general product category. In 1963, for instance, the United Fruit Co. gave up its almost 20-year-long advertising of bananas as the fruit that should not be refrigerated and turned to selling its own "Chiquita" brand. It launched a $4 million nationwide advertising campaign with the theme, "We've put a seal on our peel." The reason for the change was simple. During nearly two decades, while single-handedly promoting bananas as such under the Chiquita name and symbol, United had slowly lost its own market share to competitors. The competitive advertising program was launched to avoid further competitive inroads.[10]

1961), Part 2, and *Setting Advertising Objectives* (Studies in Business Policy No. 118 [New York: National Industrial Conference Board, 1966]).

[8] "Battle Stories Win Military Sales," *Printers' Ink,* March 3, 1961, pp. 39–40.

[9] *Business Week,* November 17, 1962, p. 68.

[10] "Chiquita, United Fruit's 'Banana Girl,' to Narrow Her Field of Sales," *Business Week,* May 25, 1963, p. 108.

Competitive advertising is useful when the product has reached the market growth and especially the market maturity stage. It may work with a product differentiation policy—stressing physical or psychological differences. It may be either direct or indirect, however.

The *direct type* is aimed at immediate buying action.

The *indirect type* is intended to point out product virtues so that when the customer is ready to buy, he will buy *that* product.

Much airline advertising is of the competitive variety. The various airlines are bidding for patronage, either immediately—in which case the ads are of the direct-action type with prices, timetables, and phone numbers to call for reservations—or eventually, in which case the ads are of the indirect-action type, suggesting that you mention their name when talking to your travel agent.

Reminder advertising—reinforces earlier promotion. Reminder advertising may be useful when the product has achieved a favored status, probably in the market maturity or sales decline stage. The advertiser mainly wants to keep his product's name before the public and will use soft-sell ads that merely mention the name as a reminder. Much Coca-Cola advertising has been of this variety in the past.

Institutional advertising focuses only on the name and prestige of a company or industry. It may be seeking to inform, persuade, or remind. A well-known Texas retailer, Neiman-Marcus, uses some institutional ads that have reminder aspects. It does not expect the majority of its ads to pay for themselves immediately, but rather to continue to present its image to the public.

Institutional advertising —remember our name in St. Louis, Seattle, Charleston . . .

A persuading kind of promotion is sometimes used by large companies with several divisions. General Motors Corp., for example, does considerable institutional advertising of the GM name, emphasizing the quality and research behind *all* GM products. These are often keyed to GM's "Mark of Excellence."

Some large companies, such as General Motors and Du Pont, use institutional ads to emphasize the value of large corporations. Their ultimate goal is developing a favorable political and legal environment in which to work.

Sometimes an advertising campaign may have both product and institutional aspects because the federal government has taken an increasingly dim view of institutional advertising. The Internal Revenue Service has limited tax deductions on institutional advertising. And defense contractors are specifically barred from including advertising expenditures as a cost of doing business with the government.[11]

The discussion above might suggest that mainly producers do product or institutional advertising. This is not true, of course, but they may affect the advertising done by others. Sometimes a manufacturer knows what promotion job or advertising job he wants done but finds that it can be done more effectively or more economically by someone further

Put your money where it buys more

11 "Will Defense-Contractor Ads Run into New Snags in Washington?" *Printers' Ink,* January 4, 1963, p. 7; and Nugent Wedding, "Advertising Mass Communication, and Tax Deduction," *Journal of Marketing,* April, 1960, pp. 17–22.

along the channel. In this case, he may offer *advertising allowances* to buy the promotion he feels is needed by the channel system. In other cases, he advances only some of the money, and the middlemen are expected to add the balance—this is called *cooperative advertising*.

Cooperative advertising helps the manufacturer get more promotion for his advertising dollar because media rate structures usually are set up to give local advertisers lower rates than national firms. The retailer is committed to follow through where he is paying a share of the cost. Such cooperative efforts encourage more local effort from salesmen or salesclerks.[12]

Media reach target customers

For effective promotion, specific customers on the market grid must be reached. Unfortunately, not all potential customers read all newspapers, magazines, or other printed media, or listen to all radio and television programs. So not all media are equally effective.

What is the best medium for fur coats and pediatricians?

There is no simple answer to the question, "What is the best medium?" This depends upon (1) the promotion objectives, (2) the funds available to accomplish the objectives, (3) the target markets, (4) the market coverage of each medium, (5) the life of messages in each medium, and (6) the environment in which the ads will appear.

Relatively little would be gained by advertising women's fur coats in the humor magazine of an all-male university. The use of men's magazines such as *Esquire* and *True* to reach doctors would be highly inefficient. Medical journals and direct mail are the most effective advertising media for telling doctors about new drugs.[13] And if the product is for children, a specialized journal such as *Pediatrics* might be the best medium.

On the other hand, if the "mass market" is the target—including women fur-coat buyers, men, doctors, etc., etc.—then the mass media such as network radio and television and *Life* magazine may be most economical.

The need for comparing different types of media—such as magazines, which must be read, with radio and television, which must be heard and seen—makes the selection task even harder. Furthermore, it is difficult to know:

Do people read each page of a magazine?
How many are listening to each radio or television set?
How many read a particular magazine or listen to a particular program over a period of time (cumulative audience)?
What will be the editorial or program environment in which the advertisement appears in a given issue or on a specific program?

Figure the cost per something

To guarantee good media selection, the advertiser first must clearly specify his target markets, a step necessary for all our marketing

[12] R. L. Hicks, "Can You Buy Distribution with Your Cooperative Advertising?" *Sales Management*, September 5, 1958, p. 58.
[13] *Advertising Age*, February 28, 1958, p. 24.

strategy planning. Next, media must be chosen that are heard, read, or seen by these target customers.

This is the major stumbling block to effective media selection, because it is not always certain who sees or hears what. To be sure, most of the major media have used marketing research to develop profiles of the people who buy their publications or live in their broadcasting area. Some have broken down their "audience" by sex, age, income, education, occupation, place of residence (such as farm or nonfarm), by ownership of various appliances or automobiles, and by ownership of homes or other articles of particular relevance. But they cannot be as definite about who actually reads each page or sees or hears each show. Furthermore, there has been little standardization of audience measurement among competing media, and some media buyers distrust media research, expecting bias. In most foreign countries, even these audience profiles are usually not available.

In the face of all these subjective uncertainties, there is one measure that is not subjective—cost. Until better audience data becomes available, media buyers will probably continue to evaluate media in terms of *cost per something.* Media buyers typically choose media that they think may do the needed job and then compare the costs of alternative media.

Newspapers—inch by inch. Most media costs are expressed as cost per unit—per line, per page, or per minute. Newspapers, for example, quote their rates in terms of a line $\frac{1}{14}$-inch deep and one column wide; usually there is a minimum allowable linage.

But these line rates tell little about the value offered by a particular paper. A high rate per line might be a good buy in a large-circulation publication, a poor one in a smaller medium. To make allowance for this, a special yardstick is applied to newspaper rates. This yardstick, "milline rate" is computed as follows:

$$\text{Milline rate} = \frac{\text{Line rate} \times 1,000,000}{\text{Circulation}}$$

The milline rate converts the cost per line to a common standard—the cost per line per 1 million circulation. Using milline rates instead of actual line rates frequently reveals that the seemingly higher cost paper actually offers a significantly lower cost because of its larger circulation.

Magazines—page by page. Magazines also charge by space and circulation size. Their rates usually are quoted by the page or fraction of a page. Their yardstick is a cost per page per thousand circulation or more commonly, "cost per thousand." This formula is:

$$\text{Cost per thousand} = \frac{\text{Page rate} \times 1,000}{\text{Circulation}}$$

To compare media effectiveness if the target market were teen-agers or upper income families, the total circulation figures in the formulas can be replaced with the total for the groups in question. Or if the

487

pass-along audience were significant to the advertiser, it might be better to insert total number of *readers* rather than circulation.

Outdoor advertising—you have to see it to believe it. The audience for outdoor advertising, including billboards, posters, and car cards in transit vehicles, is measured on a slightly different basis, namely, the number of cars passing the billboards or the number of people riding on the vehicles. These measures, too, are subject to criticism concerning how many and what types of customers actually do see and receive the message.

Radio and television—minute by minute. Radio and television are sold on a time basis. An advertiser may buy time on a number of specific stations or cover the entire nation by paying for network time.

It is possible to compute a cost per commercial minute per thousand viewers or listeners for TV or radio. The weak link in such computations, however, is the figure for audience size. At present, there are relatively few reliable measures of audience size. There are too many variations by time of day, program, audience, etc., because it is so easy to use the on-off switch and tuning dial.[14]

New media selection methods may force better perspective

In view of the difficulty of evaluating competing media, it is easy to see why a media analyst resorts to the use of whatever objective measures are available, and especially measures of the milline or cost-per-thousand variety. Yet this may result in cost, and only cost, becoming the overriding concern of the analyst and lead him into ignoring the varying characteristics of his target markets. He may even become mesmerized by the relatively low cost per something of a mass medium when, in fact, a more specialized medium might be a much better buy, since its readers might have more interest in the product, or more money to spend, or more willingness to buy, etc.[15]

It is humanly impossible to evaluate fully all the potential media that might be considered. But within the last several years, some advertising specialists have been attempting to apply a mathematical technique called "linear programming" to media selection. Theoretically, this technique, with the aid of a computer, can evaluate all the many possibilities that a media analyst should consider and then pick the best media to reach the objective.[16] The major obstacle to the use of linear programming has been the poor quality or complete lack of audience data.

As greater use is made of this potentially powerful tool, the various media will be forced to supply better audience descriptions. Marketing managers and agencies, in their turn, will have to more carefully specify their target markets.

The growing acceptance of a more analytical approach to media selection will not replace the human media analyst. But it certainly will

[14] E. Crane, A. Talbott, and R. Hume, "Time Use Profiles and Program Strategy," *Journal of Broadcasting,* Fall, 1961, pp. 335–43.

[15] "The Cost per Thousand Home Worshippers and the Error of Their Ways," *Advertising Age,* April 1, 1963, pp. 86–87.

[16] For references to texts on the technique, see Robert D. Buzzell, *A Basic Bibliography on Mathematical Methods in Marketing* (Chicago: American Marketing Association, 1962).

488

force him (or more typically, "her") to be more analytical and more efficient. The idea that "everyone is our market" is certainly not always true, and more advertisers and media buyers are recognizing this.[17]

According to the market grid concept, any market may consist of many smaller markets. We increasingly find more attention directed to reaching smaller target markets. Many magazines now offer regional editions to meet special needs. *Life* magazine offers 26 regional markets and 20 SPOT city markets. *Time* offers not only seven regional editions and eight metropolitan editions but also has special editions for college students, educators, and doctors.

Specialized media help zero-in on target markets

Many magazines serve only special-interest groups, such as fishermen, radio and television enthusiasts, homemakers, religious groups, and professional groups. Many trade associations and labor unions have their own magazine or newspaper, and there may be a number for each trade or line of business. There are trade magazines in countless fields, such as chemical engineering, electrical wholesaling, farming, and the defense market. *Standard Rate and Data* provides a guide to the thousands of magazine media available. For those especially interested in the industrial market, *Industrial Marketing* magazine publishes the *Media Market Planning Guide*.

Radio suffered at first from the inroads of television. But now, like a number of magazines and newspapers, it has become a more specialized medium. Some stations cater to particular nationality, racial, and religious groups, such as Puerto Ricans, Negroes, Catholics, etc., while others emphasize Western, popular, or classical music.

Perhaps the most specific medium is direct-mail advertising. The purpose of this medium is to go directly to the reader via his mailbox. The method is to send a specific message to a carefully selected list of names. There are organizations that specialize in providing these names in the form of mailing lists, ranging in number from hundreds to millions of names. The diversity of these lists is shown below and indicates the importance of knowing specifically the firm's target market or markets:[18]

Quantity of Names	*Name of List*
425	Small Business Advisors
40,000	Social Register of Canada
5,000	Society of American Bacteriologists
500	South Carolina Engineering Society
2,000	South Dakota State Pharmaceutical Association
250	Southern California Academy of Science
12,000	Texas Manufacturing Executives
720	Trailer Coach Association
1,200	United Community Funds of America
50,000	University of Utah Alumni
19,000	Veterinarians

---

[17] Media selection models are not panaceas, however. See F. M. Bass and R. T. Lonsdale, "An Exploration of Linear Programming in Media Selection," *Journal of Marketing Research,* May, 1966, pp. 179–88.

[18] Available from Walter Drey, Inc., New York and Chicago.

Messages carry the message

Some messages communicate poorly

Once the objectives of the advertising campaign determine generally what is to be communicated, then the key problem is how to develop messages—both copy and illustrations—to communicate it.

Advertising must use general appeals, which is one source of difficulty. It must communicate with large numbers of target customers who are constantly changing their attitudes, outlooks, and desires. Our understanding of the communication process helps guide message planning, but adapting specific messages to the many potential target markets is not easy. As we saw in Chapter 21, common frames of reference and experience are desirable for good communication.

Some advertisers realize the complexity of the communication process and use research to help them as much as possible. Others rely almost exclusively on their own "creative genius." This is at the root of many poor campaigns. Some are brilliant and others are miserable failures. Sometimes copywriters feel their audience is much more sophisticated than it is; at other times, they talk down to it.

Much advertising emanates from agencies in New York City, and one advertising manager has deplored advertising "conditioned by our New York sophistication." His experience has taught him that "New York's price of being New York is loss of perspective; New York is not America."[19]

A study by the American Association of Advertising Agencies indicated that the majority of consumers felt advertisers considered them "stupid," and almost half chose the word "gullible." Interestingly, however, the consumers did not seem to be particularly offended by being talked down to or considered stupid. They just ignored or discounted advertising which did this.[20]

Bottoms up in New York, thumbs down in L.A.

Advertising innovators find that successful ad approaches are copied quickly by competitors, just as products are copied. Whether this makes competitive sense has not been demonstrated. Perhaps it simply shows that there are few really "creative" people. In any case, some advertisers seem to feel that if you can't beat competition, you should at least meet it.

There are relatively few tried-and-true rules in message construction. Everything we see and every new way we see it changes us, the viewers. An idea that may have worked a year ago may fail today. A highly successful advertising program that sold much beer in the New York area flopped in Los Angeles.[21] And one industrial advertiser received more inquiries as it *reduced* the size of its ads.[22]

Let AIDA help guide message planning

How should we plan messages to assure access to the customer's eye, ear and, hopefully, pocketbook?

Greater dependence on marketing research as well as greater interest in the findings of the social sciences may help. We will, however, need

---

[19] *Advertising Age,* May 27, 1963, p. 90.
[20] "Advertising: Its Own Worst Enemy," *Sales Management,* May 17, 1963, pp. 19–20.
[21] "More Than Ads Sell Rheingold," *Business Week,* September 21, 1957, p. 70.
[22] "How to Advertise *Not* by The Book," *Printers' Ink,* September 6, 1963, pp. 47–48.

specific research in each individual case, since basic social science research can only isolate general principles—while most advertisers should cater to specific target markets.

We will again use the AIDA concept: getting Attention, holding Interest, arousing Desire, and obtaining Action. This approach is general, but these four steps can be a framework within which we can discuss the important problem areas requiring specific research.

Attention. Getting attention is the basic job of an advertisement. If this is not done, it doesn't matter how many people can or do see it. Many readers leaf through magazines and newspapers, seeing few or no advertisements. Many listeners or viewers run errands or get snacks during the commercials on radio and television.

The devices for catching the customer's attention are numerous. A large headline, newsy or shocking statements, pictures of pretty girls, babies, cartoon characters—or anything that is "different" or eye-catching—may do the trick. But . . . the attention-getting device must not distract from the next step—holding interest.[23]

Interest. Holding interest is another matter. A pretty girl may get attention, but once you've seen her, then what? A man will pause to appreciate her, women will look at her. But if there is no relation between the girl and the product, readers of both sexes will move on.

More is known about holding interest than getting attention. The tone and language of the advertisement must be compatible with the field of experience and attitudes of target customers and their reference groups. A food advertisement featuring persons in riding costumes, for example, might be noted but passed over by many potential customers who do not ride to the hounds. An ad aimed at farm families using obviously city-bred models and city language could not expect to hold as much interest among farmers, especially those with lower incomes.

The need to consider the cultural training of the target market is vital. Perfume has long been considered feminine, but male cosmetics makers, by carefully avoiding feminine appeals and stressing the "maleness" of their products, have been successful. Shaving lotion would have the same utility if it contained only its base material, alcohol. But by adding perfume and coloring, the manufacturers have developed a profitable product. The words and ideas used in shaving lotion advertising, however, are entirely different from those used in female perfume advertising.[24]

In addition to speaking the target customer's language, the advertising layouts should look right to the customer. The illustrations and copy should be arranged so that the eye is encouraged to move smoothly through the ad, perhaps from the upper left-hand corner to the signature or brand name at the lower right-hand corner. Advertisements having this natural flowing characteristic are said to encourage *gaze motion*.[25]

[23] Alfred Politz, "The Dilemma of Creative Advertising," *Journal of Marketing*, October, 1960, pp. 1–6.

[24] I. S. White, "The Functions of Advertising in a Culture," *Journal of Marketing*, July, 1959, pp. 10, 12.

[25] Advertising practitioners have found many rules useful for holding interest. While these are beyond our scope, many textbooks are devoted to these matters. See Otto Kleppner, *Advertising Procedure* (New York: Prentice-Hall, Inc., 1950); C. H. Sandage

Desire. Arousing desire to own or use a particular product is one of the most difficult jobs of an advertisement. It requires that the advertiser be successful in communicating with the customer. To communicate effectively, the advertiser should understand how his target customers think, behave, and make decisions.

To be successful, an advertisement must convince the customer that the product can meet his needs. *Pioneering* advertising may be useful to develop primary demand and show how the whole product class would satisfy latent wants. Later, in the market growth and market maturity stages, *competitive* advertising may be needed to show how a particular brand will satisfy particular wants.

An advertisement also may have the function, especially during the market growth and market maturity stages, of supplying the words that the customer can use for rationalizing his desire to buy. For although products may satisfy certain emotional wants, in our society many consumers find it necessary to justify their purchases on an economic or even moral basis. Desire may develop around emotional motives, but economic motives must also be reinforced.

Action. Getting action is the final job, and not an easy one. We now know, from communications research, that the potential customer must be encouraged to try the product before he adopts it. The prospective customer must be led beyond considering how the product might fit into his life to actually trying it or letting the company's salesman come in and show him how it works.

Getting action with advertising is especially difficult because it must appeal to broader audiences than a personal salesman.

Strongly felt customer needs might be pinpointed in the ads to communicate more effectively. Careful research on the attitudes and wants in the various market grid boxes may help uncover such strongly felt unsatisfied needs.

Appealing to them may get more action and also provide the kind of information the actual buyer seeks to confirm his decision. We are beginning to see that this may be one of the important roles of advertising. Some customers seem to read more advertising *after* the purchase than before. What is communicated to them may be very important if they are to start or keep the web of word of mouth going. The ad may supply the words they use to tell others about the product.

Advertising director directs mass selling

Most companies have an advertising manager, so identified either by title or function. His job is to develop the advertising campaign within the framework of the promotion blend and the overall marketing mix.

Many advertising managers, especially those working for retailers, have their own advertising departments that plan the specific advertising campaigns and carry out the details, including copy and artwork preparation, purchase of art work and printing, hiring of radio and

and V. Fryburger, *Advertising Theory and Practice* (7th ed.; Homewood, Ill.: Richard D. Irwin, Inc., 1967); and H. G. Wales, D. L. Gentry, and M. Wales, *Advertising Copy, Layout and Typography* (New York: Ronald Press Co., 1958).

television talent, production of programs and commercials, media selection, preparation of advertising schedules (timing of placement), space and time buying, and many details of shipping ad materials to media, issuing direct-mail items, and monitoring presentation of ads by media.

Considerable technical skill is involved in handling all these details, and largely for this reason, many advertising managers delegate much of the advertising task to specialists—advertising agencies.

Advertising agencies often do the work

Advertising agencies are specialists in handling the mass selling details we have been discussing. Agencies play a useful role because they are independent of the advertiser and have an outside viewpoint. They bring broad experience to bear on the individual client's problems because they are working for many other clients having different products, selling in different markets, and using other channels of distribution and media. In addition, the agencies become specialists in the various phases of technical preparation and placement of advertising, and often can perform these functions more economically than a company's own department. And the agency discounts in the media rate structure help cover some or all of the costs of their services for national advertisers (a term used to distinguish this class of advertisers from *local* advertisers).

Evolution of agencies

Historically, advertising agencies started as space salesmen (brokers) working for a commission *from the media*. The amount of the commission paid to space salesmen has varied, but until recently it was about 15 percent of the charge paid by national advertisers.

In the early days, space salesmen earned their income by selling empty time or space. As competition grew, these salesmen helped their customers fill this time or space by writing the advertisements. In time, the advertisers became even more demanding, and the original space or time salesmen have moved closer to customers than to media. Nevertheless, the commission system has continued. It is ironic to note that many media now find it necessary to hire salesmen to call on the advertising agencies, who ostensibly are selling space for them.

As they moved closer to the space buyers, advertising agencies took on more and more functions. Agencies sometimes handle overall marketing strategy planning as well as marketing research, product and package development, and the development of sales promotion aids. Some agencies make good marketing partners and almost assume the role of the firm's marketing department.[26]

One of the ad agency's virtues is that the advertiser is free at any time to cancel the arrangement. This gives extreme flexibility. Some companies even use their advertising agency as a scapegoat—whenever anything goes wrong, it's the advertising agency's fault, and they seek a new one. But a more fundamental advantage of the agency is that it is normally able to use specialists more effectively and continuously than

---

[26] "Why Ad Agencies Make Good Marketing Partners," *Printers' Ink,* November 11, 1960, pp. 68–69.

individual advertisers. For this reason, it may be able to do a better job at less cost.

Loyalties may be split

A major deficiency of advertising agencies is related to the way their compensation system has evolved; it is inherent in the agency commission system. Generally, agencies get most of their income from selling advertising time and space. There is a natural temptation to recommend maximum expenditures on time and space, while limiting other activities for which they frequently do *not* receive any extra income, such as research, other supporting services, and sales promotion.

It's the way they are paid

The major users of advertising agencies are manufacturers or national distributors, because of the media rate structure in the industry. Normally, the media have two prices: one for national advertisers and another, lower one, for local advertisers such as retailers. The agencies earn their discount, usually 15 percent, only when time or space is purchased at the higher national rate. National distributors or manufacturers have a real incentive to use advertising agencies because the 15 percent discount is allowed to any authorized agency they choose, but it is not available to them. Retailers, who are entitled to the lower local rates, seldom use agencies.

There is a growing resistance to the present method of agency compensation. The chief complaints are that the agencies receive the flat 15 percent commission, regardless of work performed, and also that the commission system makes it hard for the agencies to be completely objective about low-cost media or promotional campaigns that use little advertising space or time.

Not all agencies are satisfied with the present arrangement, either. Some would like to charge additional fees as they see rising costs and advertisers demanding more services.

The commission system is most favored by those accounts, such as producers of industrial goods, that require extensive service but buy relatively little advertising. These are the firms the agencies would like to, and sometimes do, charge additional fees.

The commission system is generally opposed by very large consumer goods advertisers who do much of their own research and planning, requiring only basic services from their agencies. Some of these accounts may be very profitable for the agencies working on such accounts, and naturally these agencies would prefer the fixed-commission system.

Fifteen Percent No Longer Required. The Federal Trade Commission worked for many years to change the method of advertising agency compensation. Finally, in 1956, the American Association of Advertising Agencies signed a consent decree with the Justice Department, indicating that by joint action they would no longer require the maintenance of the 15 percent commission system. This opened the way to discounts and other changes in compensation methods.[27]

---

[27] "Fee Is Pay for Actual Services: Elliott to 4A's," *Advertising Age*, November 11, 1963, pp. 1 and 77; and "How Should Agencies Be Paid for Test-Marketing Programs?" *Printers' Ink*, September 6, 1963, p. 8.

Some of the criticism of the commission system probably can be traced to the work of less efficient agencies who, under the umbrella of the 15 percent, were able to obtain business primarily through social contacts rather than their business ability. Advertising is no business for incompetents with good contacts. Many of the large agencies have grown large because they truly have done a better job for their clients. These agencies understand marketing and seek to improve their clients' marketing mixes. They probably will continue to play an even larger role in the future.

Measuring advertising effectiveness is not easy

It would be convenient if we could measure the results of advertising by a simple analysis of sales. Unfortunately, this is not possible. The total marketing mix, not just promotion generally or advertising specifically, is responsible for the sales result. The one exception to this rule, as it concerns advertising, is direct-mail advertising. If it doesn't produce immediate results, it is considered a failure.

Total sales results, the sum of all parts of the mix

Still, advertising literature is filled with success stories that "prove" advertising has increased sales.[28] Sometimes statistical analysis of sales over time in relation to advertising seem to show that advertising is more or less directly related to sales.[29] But these general approaches tend to give all the credit for improved performance to advertising, when the total marketing mix is involved.

Ideally, management should pretest advertising before it is run rather than relying solely on the judgment of "creative" people or advertising "experts," who too frequently judge solely on the basis of originality or cleverness of the copy and illustrations. Management people may be no better, if as good, at divining how "good" an ad will be.

It's great —but will it communicate?

Some progressive advertisers are now demanding laboratory or market tests to evaluate the effectiveness of the ads. In addition, before they are run, opinion and attitude research is sometimes used. Researchers try to evaluate consumers' reactions to particular advertisements or parts of advertisements, using the basic marketing research techniques discussed earlier as well as psychological and sociological scaling procedures and laboratory-type devices which measure skin moisture or eye reaction.[30]

After the advertisements have been run, researchers may attempt to measure how much is recalled about specific products or advertisements. Inquiries from customers may be used as a measure of the effectiveness of particular advertisements.

Hindsight may lead us to foresight

[28] The pages of *Printers' Ink* regularly carry such stories. See, for example, "Proving Business Papers Produce," *Printers' Ink*, June 29, 1962, pp. 29–36.

[29] "More Proof That Ads Build Sales," *Printers' Ink*, May 25, 1962, pp. 25–50; and "Westinghouse: Too Little Advertising," *Printers' Ink*, June 21, 1963, pp. 21–25.

[30] "Research Must Predict Ad's Effects, Says Coulson—And He Cites Examples of How It's Done," *Advertising Age*, September 30, 1963, pp. 89–98; and "Burnett Men Get Fast Test Results via Busy Creative Research Workshop," *Advertising Age*, September 10, 1962.

The response to radio or television commercials may be estimated, using various survey techniques to check the size and composition of audiences (the familiar Hooper, Crosley, Nielsen, and similar ratings), implicitly assuming that larger audiences lead directly to greater purchases.

These specific measurements are applicable only when the advertiser knows what measurable level or degree of performance he is trying to reach. When such advertising objectives are set, research can provide feedback on the effectiveness of the advertising.

While such advertising research techniques are far from foolproof, they are probably far superior to reliance on pure judgment by advertising "experts."

The director of research of one large advertising agency, while calling for more basic research on the communication process, said: "The truth is that none of us knows nearly enough about how advertising works. And we do not know, except in certain circumstances, how to measure scientifically and with any exactness just what our campaigns individually accomplish. It is extremely important that we learn."[31]

Mathematicians and statisticians may be able to provide more help in evaluating advertising in the future. Operations researchers, in particular, have been working in this area. Du Pont researchers have used a mathematical model to measure what is going on in the marketplace and how the company's advertising will affect it.[32]

Until more effective advertising research tools are developed, however, the present method of carefully defining specific advertising objectives and then selecting media and messages to accomplish these objectives would seem most fruitful.[33] The traditional marketing research techniques—applied with imagination—seem to be the best way to find these targets and the ways to communicate with them, too.

Conclusion

Theoretically, it is relatively simple to develop a mass selling program. The target customers must be selected and advertising objectives set. Then media must be picked and messages must be developed.

Yet this is no simple process. There are many complications, and specialists—advertising agencies—have evolved to handle some of them. Specific objectives must be set, or the advertising may have little

---

[31] Donald R. Longman, "Competitive Pressures Are Corrupting Market Research: More Stress Needed on Fundamental Inquiry: Longman," *Advertising Age*, December 1, 1958, p. 61; and Arthur Koponen, "Uses and Abuses of Copy Research," *Tide*, December, 1958, pp. 46–51.

[32] M. H. Halbert, "A Practical and Proven Measure of Advertising Effectiveness," in S. H. Britt and H. W. Boyd, Jr., *Marketing Management and Administrative Action* (New York: McGraw-Hill Book Co., 1963), pp. 749–59.

[33] D. B. Lucas and S. H. Britt, *Measuring Advertising Effectiveness* (New York: McGraw-Hill Book Co., 1963); H. D. Wolfe, J. K. Brown, and G. C. Thompson, *Measuring Advertising Results* (Studies in Business Policies, No. 102 [New York: National Industrial Conference Board, 1962]); Harry D. Wolfe *et al., Pretesting Advertising* (Studies in Business Policy No. 109 [New York: National Industrial Conference Board, 1963]); and Howard L. Gordon, "Yes, Virginia, Research Helps Make Better Advertisements," *Journal of Marketing*, January, 1967, pp. 64–66.

direction and will be almost impossible to evaluate. Media and message planning may need to rely on considerable marketing research. When specific tasks are outlined in this way, it is then much easier to measure the effectiveness of the advertising effort and to compare the actual performance against goals.

Ultimately, effective advertising should affect sales. But the whole marketing mix affects sales, and the results of advertising cannot be measured by sales changes alone. Advertising is only a part of promotion, and promotion is only a part of the total marketing mix that the marketing manager must develop to satisfy target customers.

Questions and problems

1 How would retailing promotion be affected if all local newspapers went out on strike for several months? Would there be any impact on total sales? If so, would it probably affect all goods and stores equally?
2 Present three examples where advertising to middlemen might be necessary. What would be the objective(s) of such moves?
3 What does it mean to say that "money is invested in advertising"? Is all advertising an investment? Illustrate.
4 Find advertisements to final consumers which illustrate the following types of advertising: (*a*) institutional, (*b*) pioneering, (*c*) competitive, (*d*) reminder. What objective(s) does each of these ads have? List the emotional and economic motives utilized in each of these advertisements.
5 A movie producer was comparing the cost of advertising in two magazines. He was planning to purchase a full-page ad in either one of the two magazines. The page rate in the first magazine was $2,000 and in the second magazine, $9,500. The circulation of the first magazine was 1 million in total and 300,000 teenagers. The second magazine had a circulation of 5 million persons in total and 1 million teenagers. Which would be the better buy? Which would be the better buy if the objective were to reach teenagers only? Would these magazines appear to be a good buy in view of this latter objective?
6 List the mass selling media which might be utilized by the advertising department of a large department store in a Commerce City. Then list the media which might be utilized by a small specialty shop in the same city. Would your answers be any different if these stores were located in a relatively small Centertown?
7 Describe the type of media which might be most suitable for promoting: (*a*) tomato soup, (*b*) greeting cards, (*c*) an industrial component material, (*d*) playground equipment. Specify any assumptions necessary to obtain a definite answer.
8 Discuss the use of testimonials in advertising. Which of the four AIDA steps might testimonials accomplish? Would they be suitable for all types of products? If not, for which types would they be most suitable?
9 Discuss the future of independent advertising agencies now that the 15 percent commission system is not required.
10 Does mass selling cost too much? How can this be measured?

Price and pricing objectives

Price is one of the four major variables that the marketing manager usually controls. His Price decisions affect, in turn, the firm's sales and profits.

Uniqueness of the product, creative promotion, or simple availability may be more important than Price in some cases. But Price can never be ignored when developing a marketing mix. Although customers sometimes behave as though they were ignoring Price—on impulse items, for example—price always is a consideration. Many customers treat a 25-cent bag of potato chips as an impulse item. They want it and casually put down the quarter. But price that bag at $1 or $2, and not many people will buy so casually. For purchases such as these, price may not be the *determining* factor, but it is a *qualifying* factor, since the price must remain within a reasonable range.

We went over demand and supply analysis in Chapter 10, but we did not define Price nor discuss price determination. In the following five chapters, we will discuss these matters together with the development of pricing objectives and policies and the impact of legislation on these policies.

What is price?

Everyone has had experience with prices, so the answer to this question may seem obvious. In Chapter 10, we casually referred to "market price" and "equilibrium price" as these terms are traditionally used by the economist. Yet it is not quite so easy to define Price in real-life situations. Price, as we shall see, has many dimensions. It gives the alert marketing manager another opportunity to tailor his marketing mix to his target markets.

If you were offered a current model Ford station wagon for $1,000, **I'll tell you** would this be a good price for an automobile that normally sells for **what I'm** over $3,000? Or if you were offered bananas at a penny a pound that **gonna** normally sell for 15 cents a pound in the supermarkets, would this be a **do . . .** good price? Or if you were offered a 21-inch television set for $100 when they normally sell for $200, would this be a good buy?

In each case, the first reaction would be an enthusiastic "Yes!" But wait a minute. It might be wiser to investigate the matter further. The $1,000 for the Ford station wagon might be the price of a wreck worth only a few hundred dollars at the scrap yard. The penny-a-pound for bananas might be the price of bananas in large bunches—green bunches hanging on trees in South America, rather than at your local supermarket.

The $100 for the TV set might be a reasonable price for all its components in a parts bin at the factory. If you wanted these assembled, you would have to pay $25 extra. If you were interested in buying the cabinet, it would be an additional $25. But if you wanted a quality guarantee, there might be an added charge of $50.

These examples emphasize that when a price is quoted, it is related **The price** to *some* assortment of goods and services. *Any transaction in our* **equation:** *modern economy can be thought of as an exchange of money—the* **Price =** *money being the price—for "something."* **Something**

This *something* can be the physical product in various stages of completion, with or without the services normally provided with such products; with or without quality guarantees; with or without installation and instruction services and the assurance of repair facilities; and with or without packaging. And this "product" may or may not be conveniently available to you.

If the product is being made available to channel members instead of final users or consumers, the price may be set so that each of the channel members has a chance to cover his costs and make a profit when he sells it at a higher price.

The nature and extent of this *something* will determine the amount of money to be exchanged. Final consumers or users may pay the suggested "list price," or they may be able to obtain significant discounts or allowances because something is *not* provided. The possible variations are summarized in Figure 24–1 for consumers or users and in Figure 24–2 for channel members. Some of these variations are discussed in the following pages to help make the point that price is a multidimensional variable.

First, however, we should note that not everyone gets merely his money's worth in a sales transaction. The "price" we are talking about is an equilibrium price related to demand and supply forces. You will recall that the demand curve which we discussed in Chapter 10 was

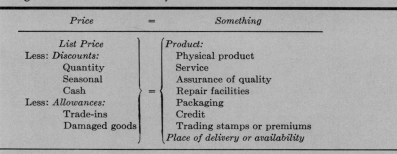

Figure 24–1 Price as seen by consumers or users

Price	=	Something

List Price
Less: *Discounts:*
    Quantity
    Seasonal
    Cash
Less: *Allowances:*
    Trade-ins
    Damaged goods
	=	*Product:*
		  Physical product
		  Service
		  Assurance of quality
		  Repair facilities
		  Packaging
		  Credit
		  Trading stamps or premiums
		Place of delivery or availability

generally downsloping and that some of the demand curve was above the equilibrium price. This is simply a graphic way of showing that *some* customers would be willing to pay more than the equilibrium price if they had to. In effect, some of them are getting a "bargain" by being able to buy at the equilibrium price. Economists have traditionally called these bargains the "consumer surplus."

There may be several list prices

Most price structures are built around *list prices*. How these list prices come to be determined is the subject of Chapters 25 and 26. For the moment, however, we must understand that there may be several list prices.

Basic list prices   Basic list prices are the prices that final consumers (or industrial customers) normally are asked to pay for goods. These prices may

Figure 24–2 Price as seen by channel members

Price	=	Something

List Price
Less: *Discounts*
    Quantity
    Seasonal
    Cash
    Trade or Functional
Less: *Allowances*
    Damaged goods
    Advertising
    Push Money
	=	*Product*
		  Branded—well known
		  Guaranteed
		  Warranted
		  Service—repair facilities
		  Convenient packaging for
		    handling
		Place
		  Availability—when and
		    where
		Price
		  Price-level guarantee
		  Sufficient margin to allow
		    chance for profit
		Promotion
		  Promotion aimed at cus-
		    tomers

change when the firm decides to change its price level. But here, we are concerned with the list price structure, not with these price-level changes. Unless otherwise specified, the term "list price" here will refer to "basic list price."

Some list prices are not changed over a period of time and may have little relation to market prices. They may have been set years ago with the expectation that continual adjustment would be needed. When price changes must be made, the add-ons or discounts are simply changed. The new current prices are calculated by adding or subtracting specific dollar or percentage amounts from the unchanging list prices. Since this method of changing prices avoids constant catalog revisions, it is often used in industries where frequent price changes are necessary. Rather than printing a complete new catalog, the firm can simply publish a new list of discounts or increases, applicable item by item or by broad product categories.

Unchanging list prices —an administrative convenience

This method of changing prices does *not* give the marketing manager another way of varying his mix. It is merely an administrative device to reduce the cost of announcing price changes. It is important to know about such "list" prices, however, because firms may offer extremely impressive discounts from these so-called list prices. These prices are the ones some discount house customers are shown as the "costs" below which prices cannot be cut!

Sometimes, especially at the final consumer level, what might be called *phony list prices* are published so that the customers can be shown that the price they are to pay has been discounted from "list." Most businessmen, Better Business Bureaus, and government agencies frown upon this practice. But many customers, by equating discounts with value and savings, have encouraged the use of these jacked-up list prices. Some customers, in fact, seem more interested in the size of the purported discount than the price itself, and they may wind up paying more than the competitive market price.

Phony list prices for bargain hunters

List price may depend on who pays transportation costs

Retail list prices often include free delivery. Or free delivery may be offered to some customers as an aid to closing the sale. In short, what is included (or not included) in the retail list price may not be formally published; this helps the retailer adjust his marketing mix to the situation.

Deciding who is going to pay the freight is more important on sales to intermediate customers and industrial users than to final consumers. Usually purchase orders specify place, time, method of delivery, freight costs, insurance, handling, and other incidental charges. There are many possible variations here for an imaginative marketing manager, and a number of specialized terms have developed. A few are discussed below.

501

F.O.B. the customer's doorstep

F.O.B. is a commonly used term regarding transportation. It means "free on board" some vehicle at some place, and typically is used in conjunction with *some named point,* that is, the location of the seller's factory or warehouse, as in "F.O.B. Detroit," "F.O.B. Chicago," etc. It means that the seller pays the cost of loading the merchandise onto some vehicle, usually a common carrier such as a truck, railroad car, or ship. At the point of loading, title to the goods passes to the buyer, who pays the freight and assumes responsibility for damage in transit, except as covered by the transportation agency.

Variations are made easily, however, by changing the *some named point* part of the terms. If the marketing manager wanted to pay the freight for the convenience of his customer, he could use: "F.O.B. delivered" or "F.O.B. buyer's factory" (or warehouse). In this case, title would not pass until the goods were delivered. If he did want title to pass immediately—but still wanted to pay the freight bill (and then include it in the invoice)—he could use: "F.O.B. seller's factory— freight prepaid."

In international marketing, the *some named point* must be specified even more carefully. Commercial practices vary among countries, and even competing carriers' rates can vary, so it may be desirable to specify which carrier is to be used and how the shipment is to be routed.[1]

These terms help clarify the "something" that is being offered for the quoted list price. If the buyer is paying the freight, the quoted price can be lower. If the buyer is to be responsible for damage in shipment—or at least for negotiations with the transportation agency in case of damage—then the seller's marketing manager can offer lower prices. Some marketing managers have strengthened their marketing mix by adjusting terms to the wants of their target markets.

List price may depend on currency

The currency used in a price quotation in international trade is an important but technical matter that is beyond the scope of this text.[2] The problem is a complex one, since not all currencies are convertible to all others without restriction. Moreover, exchange rates fluctuate continually. A price quotation of $100 in U.S. currency may mean a Canadian firm will have to pay $110 in Canadian currency one day and $109.50 the second day later. Thus, just a change in the exchange rate between U.S. and Canadian dollars may change the product's price in Canada and affect sales. Alternately, the U.S. firm could quote prices in Canadian dollars and expect varying dollar returns, depending on the exchange rate.

Quoting prices in U.S. dollars may be easier and advisable if the buyer's government will release dollars, but quoting in the local cur-

---

[1] For more extensive details on terms in foreign shipments, see Paul V. Horn and Henry Gomez, *International Trade Principles and Practices* (4th ed.; Englewood Cliffs, N.J.: Prentice-Hall, Inc., 1959), chaps. xxi–xxiv; *Exporter's Encyclopedia* (annual; New York: Thomas Ashwell & Co.); and *Revised American Foreign Trade Definitions,* National Foreign Trade Council, 1951.

[2] See Horn and Gomez, *op. cit.,* chaps. xiv, xxi, and xxii.

502

rency and three-way or barter arrangements may bring in sales that would be lost otherwise. Here is another opportunity for the imaginative businessman.

Some customers get discounts off list

Discounts are reductions from the list price that are granted by a seller to a buyer who either *foregoes some marketing function or provides the function for himself*. Discounts may be highly useful tools in marketing strategy planning.

In the following discussion, consider what function the buyer is foregoing or providing for himself when he obtains each of these discounts.

Sellers offer quantity discounts to *induce customers to purchase in larger quantities*. This enables the seller to get more of a buyer's business or shift some of the storing function to the buyer or reduce shipping and selling costs, or all of these. These discounts are of two kinds, cumulative and noncumulative.

Cumulative discounts apply to purchases over a given period—such as a year—and normally increase as the quantity purchased increases. Cumulative discounts are intended to encourage buying from a single company by reducing the price for additional purchases.

Noncumulative discounts are quantity discounts that apply to individual shipments or orders only. Such discounts encourage larger orders but do not tie a buyer to the seller beyond that one purchase.

Quantity discounts may be given in a number of ways. Some common methods are:

Quantity discounts are designed to encourage volume buying

1. Based on the *dollar value* of the entire order.
2. Based on *number of units purchased*. Men's shirts are sometimes sold at three for $10 or $4 each. One manufacturer of materials handling equipment quotes prices subject to the following discounts:

Units	Discounts
1–24	45 percent off list price.
25–49	48 percent off list price.
50 or more	51 percent off list price.

3. Based on the *size of the package purchased*. One drug wholesaler offers retailers a 40 percent discount when purchase is made in "shippers" (shipping cartons), but only 36 percent discount when purchases are made in less than "shippers." This encourages orders that permit the wholesaler to reship in original containers.

Quantity discounts usually are given in money—a reduction in the price—but sometimes they are given as free or bonus goods. In this case, customers receive one or more units "free" with the purchase of a specified quantity.

Quantity discounts may be a very useful variable for the marketing manager. Customers are eager to get them. But marketing managers must use quantity discounts, and especially cumulative quantity discounts, with care to avoid price discrimination. The Robinson-Patman Act states that quantity discounts must be based on actual cost savings, yet it is sometimes difficult to show these cost savings to the satisfaction of government officials. The impact of legislation on pricing is discussed more fully in Chapter 28.

Seasonal discounts are designed to encourage earlier buying

Seasonal discounts are especially important within channels. They induce buyers to stock earlier than immediate customer demand would necessitate. This discount tends to shift the storing function farther along in the channel. If seasonal discounts are substantial, channel members may pass them along to their customers. In coal sales, seasonal discounts are given in the spring and summer all the way through the channel to final consumers and users.

Besides shifting the storing function, seasonal discounts may gain new business by tapping additional target markets during slack periods. By using seasonal discounts to win new business, even at a lower price, the marketing manager may help pay the overhead when business is slow.

Seasonal discounts are given to offset a reduction in the "something" offered the buyer. The cost of carrying inventory—sometimes a high cost—which otherwise would be handled by the seller now must be assumed by the buyer. The buyer also must bear the risk of price changes during the longer storage period. Seasonal discounts may run to 5 or 10 percent of the usual list price to offset the burdens being assumed by the buyer.

The special price reductions (or "free" goods) offered by grocery stores, gasoline stations, and department stores during their slow periods are a type of seasonal discount. Many such businesses find a distinct seasonal pattern within each week, month, and the year. Although such price reductions may not be announced as seasonal discounts, the concept is the same. The marketing manager is attempting to make more effective use of his fixed facilities.

Cash discounts should encourage prompt payment

Final consumers often delay payment at a cost. Most retail transactions, at least those involving small nondurable items, are on a cash or credit (with no charge) basis; no discounts for prompt payment are given. Such charge accounts are usually payable in full each month. Charge accounts often are provided as a convenience so that customers will not have to carry cash.

For major purchases of, say, clothing or expensive durable goods which last for several years, the regular monthly payment charge account with all payments due in 30 days is less practical. To pay for a new Easter outfit, a new car, or a living room furniture suite in one month is out of the question for many customers. Many merchants and sales finance companies, therefore, have set up plans to make it easier for consumers to buy more costly items. Payments, usually due monthly, may be stretched to 36 months at interest rates of 6 to 8 percent or more per annum on the *initial* balance. Since the balance owed declines as the payments are made, the effective rate of interest amounts to 12 to 16 percent or more.

504

These seemingly high rates are needed to cover the cost of borrowing money and the collection and repossession process. For some merchants, granting credit can be a profitable business, perhaps more so than their basic business. Clearly, customers get a substantial "discount" by paying immediately or within the 30-day "free" period.

How cash discount terms look to channel members. Most sales to channel members and final users are made on credit. The seller issues an invoice, and the buyer sends it through his accounting department for payment. Many channel members come to depend on other members for temporary working capital, and therefore it is extremely important for both sides to clearly specify the terms of payment, including the availability of cash discounts. The following terms of payment frequently are used:

Net means that payment for the face value of the invoice is due immediately. These terms are sometimes altered to "net 10" or "net 30," which mean payment is due within 10 or 30 days of the date of the invoice.

1/10 net 30 means that 1 percent discount off the face value of the invoice is permitted if the invoice is paid within 10 days. Otherwise, the full face value is due within 30 days. And it usually is implied that an interest charge will be made after the expiration of that 30-day free credit period.

The due date for payment usually is based on the date of the invoice. This often is the date the goods are shipped, but a convenient alternate way for the seller to offer additional credit without changing his basic terms is to *advance* the date of the invoice. This practice is called "forward dating" and is sometimes used in extremely competitive situations. If a firm frequently forward dates its invoices, this practice may be formalized by stating the additional terms discussed below. All these special terms could be used in conjunction with basic terms such as *net 30* or *1/10 net 30*.

E.O.M. means end of month and gives free credit to the end of the month, when other terms apply. The terms 2/10 net 30 E.O.M. would mean that the invoice should be treated as though it were dated the first of the month following the date on the face of the invoice. In other words, if some goods were purchased on January 7, the invoice date might be January 7, but the 2 percent cash discount could be taken until February 10, more than a month after purchase.

Another type of special dating terms is *R.O.G.* or *A.O.G.* (receipt of goods, or arrival of goods). Under these terms, the discount period begins the day the purchaser receives the goods. These terms would also be in conjunction with basic terms, such as 2/10 net 30 R.O.G.

R.O.G. terms are especially useful when a marketing manager is attempting to sell throughout a large geographical area because the terms could meet the objections of distant purchasers who don't want to pay for goods before they are received.

Why cash discounts are given and should be taken. A marketing manager may use cash discounts to obtain his money more quickly, to reduce his credit risk, or to reduce his credit and collection staff.

Cash discounts are used chiefly to encourage buyers to pay their bills promptly, and smart buyers take advantage of them. A discount of *2/10, net 30* may not look like very much, but any company that passes it up is missing a good financial opportunity because it would be money ahead to borrow at a bank to pay such invoices.

The 2 percent discount is earned for paying the invoice just 20 days sooner than it would have to be paid anyway. And if it is not taken, the company in effect is borrowing at an annual rate of 36 percent. That is, assuming a 360-day year and dividing by 20 days, there are 18 periods during which the firm could earn 2 percent—and 18 times 2 equals 36 percent a year.

In some trades, the cash discount is even more attractive and may run as high as 10 percent if the bill is paid within 10 days. These extremely attractive cash discounts are more like price cuts, since they probably cannot be justified for encouraging prompt payment.

While the marketing manager can use the cash discount as a marketing variable, in some cases a specific cash discount may be so firmly established in his industry that he cannot change or use it to suit his needs. He must grant the customary terms, even if he has no need for cash. Purchasing agents are aware of the attractiveness of cash discounts and will insist that the marketing manager offer the same terms normally offered by his competitors. In fact, some buyers automatically will deduct the accepted cash discount from their invoices regardless of the invoice terms.

Cash terms are different in international trade. Financial resources usually are in shorter supply outside the United States, and you might expect to find more use of cash discounts abroad. This is not the case. Sellers in foreign countries are more concerned about collecting than prompt payment. They may be willing to extend credit up to 180 days for normal shipments, but usually will make financial arrangements through domestic and foreign banks to insure payment. On shipments requiring even longer credit terms, the marketing manager may seek a government guarantee against nonpayment or expropriation.[3]

Trade or functional discounts make channels work

A trade or functional discount is a list price reduction given to channel members in anticipation of a job they are going to perform.

A manufacturer, for example, might allow his retailers a 30 percent trade discount from the suggested retail list price to cover the cost of their retailing function and their profit. To cover similar costs, the manufacturer might allow wholesalers a *chain discount* of 30 percent and 10 percent off the retail price. In this case, the wholesalers would be expected to pass the 30 percent discount on to retailers.

As an example, suppose the suggested retail price were $100. The wholesaler's selling price would be $70 (70 percent of $100), and the manufacturer's selling price would be $63 (90 percent of $70).

The wholesaler, according to our percentages, would be allowed only $37 off the retail list price. It is important to note that a chain discount of 30 and 10 percent is not the same as a 40 percent discount, just as a

---

[3] Clarence J. Ruethling, *Financing Export Sales,* Management Aids for Small Manufacturers No. 149, February, 1963.

chain discount of 50 percent and 50 percent does not represent 100 percent but, rather, 75 percent off the retail list price.

Trade discounts offered to wholesalers and retailers vary by trades, but they are based roughly on the operating expenses of each particular trade. The usual turnover rate of the specific merchandise and the required selling effort are important factors. One drug manufacturer gives 30, 10, 5, and 4 percent discounts to his wholesale customers—30 percent for the retailers, and the rest for the wholesaler involved as follows: 10 percent for handling costs and 5 percent for profit, and 4 percent for selling effort.

Other examples of trade discounts offered by manufacturers illustrate the wide variation in discount practice. The discounts shown here are "off list," that is, they are deducted from list price:

1. A heating equipment manufacturer offers discounts on parts as follows: 50 percent to distributors on orders of $200 or more, and only 45 percent on orders under $200 (a combination trade and quantity discount).
2. An electrical equipment manufacturer offers 50 percent to electrical supply distributors and 60, 10, and 10 percent to radio parts distributors.
3. An automotive accessories manufacturer offers 50 percent to wholesalers, 40 percent to dealers, and 30 percent to chain stores and industrial users.

Trade discounts might seem to offer the marketing manager great flexibility in varying his marketing mix, but in fact they may limit him greatly. The customary trade discount may be so well established that he has to accept it in setting his prices. More will be said about this in the next chapter.[4]

Some customers get allowances off list

Allowances are similar to discounts. They are given to final consumers or users for accepting less of "something," or adjusting for variations in "something." Or they are given to channel members for providing a service, perhaps additional selling effort.

Bring in the old, ring up the new

Trade-ins give the marketing manager a convenient way to reduce his price to the customer without reducing list price. An automobile buyer may be able to get a substantial discount by trading in his old car. But although he may pay less than the list price for his new car, the "something" has varied. Once the deal is completed, he no longer has his old car.

Proper handling of trade-ins is especially important for the marketing manager who is selling durable goods, both to final consumers and intermediate customers. Customers buying machinery or buildings, for example, are buying long-term satisfaction, say, in terms of more manufacturing capacity. If the list price less the trade-in discount and

---

[4] This discussion on discounts is based on G. E. Larson and M. N. Poteat, *Selling the United States Market* (Domestic Commerce Series No. 29 [Washington, D.C.: U.S. Government Printing Office, 1951], pp. 73–76.

the old equipment does not offer greater satisfaction or value—as the customer sees it—then no sales will be made.

Many firms replace machinery slowly, perhaps too slowly, because they value their old equipment more highly than the firm selling the new equipment. This same situation seems to apply to new cars. Customers want higher trade-ins for their old cars than their current market valuation. This prompts the use of high, perhaps "phony," list prices so that high trade-in allowances can be given.

Damaged-goods allowances —less for less

Frequently, prices to both final consumers and intermediate customers may be reduced because the goods they have bought or wish to buy were delivered soiled or damaged. To complete the transaction, the marketing manager may make a damaged-goods allowance, since the *something* is not as originally specified. (A damaged-goods allowance should be distinguished from a lower price offered on goods known to be "seconds." Such lower prices for "seconds" are offered as the original list price for an entirely different marketing mix.)

Advertising allowances —something for something

Manufacturers frequently give price reductions to firms farther along in a channel to encourage them to advertise, display, or otherwise promote goods locally. General Electric has given a 1.5 percent allowance to its distributors of housewares and radios who, in return, are expected to provide something—in this case, local advertising. Often manufacturers expect the middlemen to match their allowance in a joint effort called *cooperative advertising*.

P.M.'s— push for cash

"Push money" or "prize money" allowances are similar to advertising allowances. They are given to retailers by manufacturers or wholesalers to pass on to the retailers' salesmen in return for aggressively selling particular items or lines. The P.M. allowances usually are reserved for new merchandise, slower moving items, or higher margin items, and are especially common in the furniture and clothing industries. A salesman, for example, might earn an additional $5 for each new type of mattress sold.

Brokerage allowances —may be illegal

While brokerage allowances probably should be included under trade or functional discounts, they are treated separately because of their special legal status. Brokers normally are allowed a trade discount for their services. But sometimes large organizations, such as grocery chains, act as their own brokers and request that they be granted the broker's trade discount in the form of a brokerage allowance. Under the Robinson-Patman Act, such brokerage allowances for buyers or buyers' representatives are now illegal. In highly competitive fields, however, the marketing manager may feel he has to grant such an allowance, perhaps calling it an advertising allowance but without any expectation of obtaining additional promotion. In effect, competitive pressures are pushing prices downward. This has been seen in the low-profit-margin grocery retailing industry where the buyer's ability to win extra allowances and favorable cash discounts may make the difference between profit and loss.

508

The "something" obtained by final consumers may vary

The "something" in our price equation really consists of the rest of the marketing mix—all of the nonprice aspects. This "something" varies from one marketing strategy to another. So far we have discussed the major variables in the marketing mix, noting how interrelated they are, but there is one "something" we have not yet examined—trading stamps.

Trading stamps frequently are used in lieu of price competition. For this reason, although they are sometimes considered an addition to the product or a promotional device, we will discuss trading stamps under pricing.

Trading stamps may add that important "something"

Retailers usually buy trading stamps from trading-stamp companies or set up their own plans and distribute stamps to customers at a cost of about 2 to 3 percent of the retail sales dollar. Customers can then redeem stamps for merchandise premiums or cash or goods at the merchant's own store.

There has been much controversy about the value and desirability of stamp plans, particularly concerning their effect on prices. It is difficult to generalize about this, since so many factors are involved, including the degree of competition and past market history.

Stamps have been most popular recently in grocery retailing, where the net profit margin is approximately 1 to 2 percent of sales. A stamp plan costing the retailer 2 to 3 percent of his sales would seem inevitably to push prices up. Yet this is not always the case. The increased cost of the stamps may be offset by reduced promotional expenditures or by a substantial increase in sales—both resulting from customers' eagerness to buy goods and get stamps. In the food business, however, it usually is necessary for sales to increase 10 to 15 percent before a stamp plan begins to be profitable.[5]

Saving stamps has become almost a rite for many consumers, who feel they are getting something for nothing. It may be more accurate to say that they are getting something, but they *are* paying for it.

Stamps seem here to stay

The early users of stamps in a community seem to gain a competitive advantage, but when competitors also start offering stamps, the advantage may be canceled. This is similar to competition in the product life cycle where innovators are copied and profits are squeezed.

Trading stamps have been spreading to other countries, too, and are received with mixed feelings by some businessmen abroad just as in the United States.

Many small businessmen, such as some filling station operators in the United States and some small shopkeepers in Britain, are vigorously opposed to using stamps. The executive secretary of the Petroleum

---

[5] Albert Haring and Wallace O. Yoder (eds.), *Trading Stamps Practice and Pricing Policy* (Indiana Business Report 27, Bureau of Business Research [Bloomington: Indiana University, 1958]), p. 301.

Congress (U.S.) calls stamps "a cancerous business practice."[6] And a spokesman for the 12,000-store Multiple Grocers Association in Britain says, "We have had the advantage of seeing what happened with stamps in the U.S. You have an initial competitive advantage; then your rivals have stamps and you lose the advantage. But you're stuck with the stamps."[7]

There have been efforts to outlaw stamps, just as there are continuing efforts to outlaw various other promotional devices and certain kinds of advertising. It seems, however, that the larger and stronger stamp companies will likely continue for many years to come. The oldest one has operated since 1896.[8]

Stamp plans may be thought of as an addition to the marketing mix, perhaps in lieu of a price reduction, as well as a sometimes effective promotional tool. But discount grocery operators now claim they can save their customers from 3 to 7 percent by not giving stamps.[9] Perhaps stamps will continue to be used by conventional retailers, and this may encourage new—and extremely price-competitive—distribution channels.

The "something" for channel members may vary, too

For channel members, it's the whole mix

The "something" for channel members is the entire marketing mix. For the money they pay, channel members receive a product, perhaps well branded, guaranteed, and specially packaged for easy handling. They may receive service or repair facilities. There may be promotional assistance from others in the channel, most often the producer. Channel members may be offered national or regional advertising support, plus an advertising allowance for local promotion. And the channel captain may offer a price structure with enough margin to give each channel member an opportunity for profit.

Although pricing considerations are only part of the total mix, they are an important part. Much more is said about pricing in the following chapters, but here two additions to the "something" for channel members will be covered: price guarantees and profit guarantees.

A price is a promise

Marketing managers or channel captains sometimes give assurances to the various channel members that the price structure will not change in the near future. Such assurances, called price guarantees, free channel members from one of the risks of distribution.

Price guarantees are especially valuable when channel members, to provide their function effectively, must buy goods six months to a year in advance of sale. If they normally operate on a margin of 1 or 2 percent profit on sales, then any price decrease can quickly lead to

---

[6] *Time*, October 26, 1962, p. 64.

[7] *Time*, May 17, 1963, p. 114.

[8] "Trading Stamps Start to Look More Like Money," *Business Week*, April 1, 1967, p. 68; "Are Trading Stamps Losing Their Punch?" *Business Week*, September 4, 1965, pp. 66–68.

[9] *Time*, October 26, 1962, p. 64.

losses—especially if competitors get supplies at the new lower prices. If there is any possibility of imminent price reductions, many channel members balk at carrying out their normal accumulating function, and movement through the channel is slowed. A marketing manager may be able to improve the operation of a whole channel by giving a price guarantee.

Sometimes price guarantees take the form of an assurance that goods can be returned at their original prices or that rebates will be made if prices decrease. No such problem arises if prices increase. In this case, inventory stocks appreciate in value.

Guarantees against price decreases, however, are not always completely satisfactory. Once the granter announces such a guarantee, he may hold his list prices constant while market prices are declining. He avoids making good on a guarantee, even though the channel's competitors are cutting their prices and he is losing any goodwill he had achieved. Generally, though, a price guarantee would be valued by channel members and could be a useful addition to a marketing mix.

A variation on the price guarantee is the profit guarantee. This may take the form of an assurance that a certain volume will be sold at a given markup—or the channel member will be paid an equivalent profit. **A profit you can bank on**

A quality frozen-food manufacturer guaranteed profits to grocery stores that agreed to buy at regular prices and display practically its full line of products for a 90-day trial period. The manufacturer's purpose was to get distribution of his full line without giving special price concessions. Instead, he guaranteed certain minimum financial returns.

Pricing objectives guide pricing policies

Pricing has many facets, and pricing objectives should be clearly specified to guide pricing policies and price determination. This sounds very logical, but actually the setting of pricing objectives and related policies is neglected in many companies.

It is possible to develop a pricing policy—such as "always price below competitors"—without consciously considering the purpose of such a policy. Some companies even mistake a policy for an *objective*. Perhaps this is because they do not have definite or written policies. One study showed that only 4 out of 155 leading industrial companies had *written* price policies. This study also showed that even in the best managed companies, an understanding of price determination was comparatively rare.[10]

Ambiguity about pricing policies may be due to a lack of pricing objectives or uncertainty about which ones the company does have. **Intelligent planning or luck?**

[10] J. E. Anderson and E. C. Gassenheimer, *Pricing Arithmetic for Small Business Managers* (Management Aids for Small Manufacturers No. 100 [Washington, D.C.: Small Business Administration, February, 1959]), p. 1.

Table 24-1 *Pricing goals of 20 large industrial corporations*

Company	Principal Pricing Goal	Collateral Pricing Goals	Rate of Return on Investment (After Taxes) 1947–55 Average	Range
Alcoa	20% on investment (before taxes); higher on new products (about 10% effective rate after taxes)	(a) "Promotive" policy on new products (b) Price stabilization	13.8	7.8–18.7
American Can	Maintenance of market share	(a) "Meeting" competition (using cost of substitute product to determine price) (b) Price stabilization	11.6	9.6–14.7
A & P	Increasing market share	"General promotive"(low-margin policy)	13.0	9.7–18.8
Du Pont	Target return on investment—no specific figure given	(a) Charging what traffic will bear over long run (b) Maximum return for new products—"life cycle" pricing	25.9	19.6–34.1
Esso	"Fair-return" target—no specific figure given	(a) Maintenance market share (b) Price stabilization	16.0	12.9–18.9
General Electric	20% on investment (after taxes); 7% on sales (after taxes)	(a) Promotive policy on new products (b) Price stabilization on nationally advertised products	21.4	18.4–26.6
General Foods	33⅓% gross margin: "⅓ to make, ⅓ to sell and ⅓ for profit"); expectation of realizing target only on new products	(a) Full line of food products and novelties (b) Maintaining market share	12.2	8.9–15.7
General Motors	20% on investment (after taxes)	Maintaining market share	26.0	19.9–37.0
Goodyear	"Meeting competitors"	(a) Maintain "position" (b) Price stabilization	13.3	9.2–16.1
Gulf	Follow price of most important marketer in each area	(a) Maintain market share (b) Price stabilization	12.6	10.7–16.7
International Harvester	10% on investment (after taxes)	Market share: ceiling of "Less than a dominant share of any market"	8.9	4.9–11.9

Company objectives often are not stated or they are so general as to be platitudes. Or they may not be compatible with each other. One study of 20 of the largest corporations in the United States found that although many did *not* have *written* pricing objectives, they did have pricing objectives—sometimes several simultaneously. Multiple and sometimes conflicting objectives were found by interviewing different executives! The relative importance of any one objective depended on the point of view of the man interviewed![11]

This seeming confusion about pricing objectives and pricing policies should emphasize the importance of careful study of price. Price is one of the marketing manager's four major variables, and haphazard or

---

[11] Robert F. Lanzillotti, "Pricing Objectives in Large Companies," *American Economic Review,* December, 1958, pp. 921–40. This was a continuation of the study by A. D. M. Kaplan, J. P. Dirlam, and R. F. Lanzillotti, *Pricing in Big Business* (Washington, D.C.: Brookings Institution, 1958).

Table 24–1—Continued

Company	Principal Pricing Goal	Collateral Pricing Goals	Rate of Return on Investment (After Taxes) 1947–55 Average	Range
Johns-Manville	Return on investment greater than last 15-year average (about 15% after taxes); higher target for new products	(a) Market share not greater than 20% (b) Stabilization of prices	14.9	10.7–19.6
Kennecott	Stabilization of prices		16.0	9.3–20.9
Kroger	Maintaining market share	Target return of 20% on investment before taxes	12.1	9.7–16.1
National Steel	Matching the market—price follower	Increase market share	12.1	7.0–17.4
Sears, Roebuck	Increasing market share (8–10% regarded as satisfactory share)	(a) Realization of traditional return on investment of 10–15% (after taxes) (b) General promotive (low margin) policy	5.4	1.6–10.7
Standard Oil (Ind.)	Maintain market share	(a) Stabilize prices (b) Target return on investment (none specified)	10.4	7.9–14.4
Swift	Maintenance of market share in livestock buying and meatpacking		6.9	3.9–11.1
Union Carbide	Target return on investment	Promotive policy on new products; "life cycle" pricing on chemicals generally	19.2	13.5–24.3
U.S. Steel	8% on investment (after taxes)	(a) Target market share of 30% (b) Stable price (c) Stable margin	10.3	7.6–14.8

SOURCE: Robert F. Lanzillotti, "Pricing Objectives in Large Companies," *American Economic Review*, Vol. XLVIII, No. 5 (December, 1958), pp. 921–40.

unimaginative handling of this variable is not likely to lead to maximum profits or any other specific objective—except by dumb luck.

Generally, pricing objectives should flow from overall company objectives. Indeed, the two may be synonymous, depending on how specifically the overall objectives are stated. For our purposes, we will not try to distinguish between the two. Rather, we will discuss some objectives that have definite pricing implications under three headings: profit-oriented objectives, sales-oriented objectives, and status quo objectives.

The pricing objectives of the 20 large corporations mentioned earlier are presented in Table 24–1 and used below to make our discussion more concrete. Most of the following discussion will center around the objectives of larger companies because this is the only area where formal research has been done. Still, the evidence is scanty even here, since the companies that have specified objectives consider them private and have no reason to publish this information.

Profit-oriented objectives

**By their
target
returns
know them**

Seeking a target return is a common objective. The target may be a certain percentage return on sales or on investment or a fixed dollar amount of profit. The new target may be equal to or slightly above last year's return. Targets may be set for the short or long run.

The size of the short-run target return depends partly on industry or market practice, and partly on competition. Some companies deliberately set a relatively moderate objective to discourage potential competitors. But if little competition is expected, the company may set extremely high targets for the short run. The style or novelty of goods may be a factor in such a case.

In relatively stable or slowly expanding markets, a target return objective may have the desirable effect of leading to stable or slowly growing profits. A firm may select a target return that is consistent from year to year; if its competitors have similar objectives and use similar methods of price determination, then all may obtain their objectives. Their profits will tend to be stable through the years unless demand shifts markedly. When all the firms in a market have this objective, both profits and prices may be stable, and there will be little price competition. Instead, competition may shift to the other three P's.

Long-run targets are used by companies that have carved out markets for themselves or that are, at least, leaders in their fields, such as Alcoa, Du Pont, General Motors, International Harvester, and U.S. Steel.

For such companies, a long-run target return objective makes considerable sense. These companies might be considered public utilities. They are well aware that the public and governmental eye is upon them. They frequently play the role of price leaders and wage setters, and the public seems to expect them to follow a policy that is popularly referred to as being "in the public interest."

The pricing practices of large companies after World War II gave clear evidence of long-run target return pricing and a consciousness of public reaction. The large pent-up demand for goods coupled with the inadequate supply easily could have led to extremely high prices on products such as steel, building materials, and automobiles. The automobile manufacturers did raise prices, but not nearly so much as demand might have permitted. It was, instead, individual new-and used-car dealers who took advantage of the situation. Some raised prices considerably, often with mandatory extras. Some new-car dealers funneled new cars to "used-car" dealers who could obtain even higher prices without incurring the wrath of the manufacturers.

Stay out of the courts and in business. The size of the target return that is set varies considerably, as can be seen in Table 24–1. The average of the targets was 14 percent, after taxes. Only one was below 10 percent, and the highest was 20 percent.

The most frequent justifications for seeking a particular return were (1) fair or reasonable return in relation to risk—the public utility concept applied using past price and volume relationships, (2) desire to equal or better the previous returns, (3) desire to get what they

514

thought they could get in the long run, something close to maximum profit, and (4) a means of stabilizing industry prices—if competing firms have a similar target return objective, this may lead to essentially the same prices and a condition of stability.[12]

A target return objective has another advantage in a large company. It simplifies measuring and controlling the performance of the many divisions and departments, all of which are using capital. Some companies will eliminate divisions or drop products not yielding a certain predetermined rate of return on investment. Naturally, then, managers use target return pricing, trying to hit this desired figure. It isn't easy. Too large a return may invite government action. Too small a return may put the division out of business.

Does high morality mean low profits? Objectives seeking to maximize profits might be stated as a desire to achieve profit growth and rapid return on investment or, more bluntly, "all the traffic will bear."

Profit maximization has its supporters

Profit maximization objectives seem to be found more frequently among smaller firms, especially small merchants and manufacturers who are out of the public limelight or who have successfully carved out their own market.[13]

One small industrial tool manufacturer, for example, is well aware that the demand for his product is highly inelastic, and he acts accordingly. He gives attractive margins to channel members and sets his own price to allow for substantially more than a 100 percent markup on his production cost. But such profits may lead to competition, as the small tool manufacturer now knows. Even though he has fairly strong patent protection on his basic product, the company has had to improve it continually and use aggressive promotion to maintain its profit position among the many competitors its success has attracted. Examples such as this one make some economists feel that such competition encourages a dynamic economy and economic growth.

Some business executives seem reluctant to admit that they hold a profit maximization objective. Not all hold the strong beliefs of the president of Cummins Engine Company, who says: "The idea that the highest morality brings the lowest profit does not necessarily apply. If we concentrate on giving the consumer what he needs at a price favorable to him, profits roll in as a by-product."[14] And the president of Armour & Co. has set out to convert his managers to an almost single-minded pursuit of profits. He says: "Everybody at Armour [formerly] was an operating man. Plant managers thought of themselves as killers of cattle and hogs, of producers of great tonnages of beef and pork. I wanted them to think of themselves as managers of money, responsible for a portion of the company's capital."[15]

High profits need not mean high prices. The public, and many businessmen, have come to associate a profit maximization objective

---

[12] Much of this section is based upon Lanzillotti, *op. cit.*

[13] W. Warren Haynes, *Pricing Decisions in Small Business* (Lexington: University of Kentucky Press, 1962).

[14] *Time,* September 29, 1961, p. 86.

[15] *Wall Street Journal,* January 25, 1962, p. 1.

with high prices and monopolies. Many people feel that anyone attempting to maximize profits is operating contrary to the public interest. In the United States, public fear of a profit maximization objective probably has its origins historically in the pricing behavior of some companies who obtained a public utility type of monopoly during the late 1800's. Railroads, in particular, are frequently cited.

Economic theory, however, does not support this reaction. Profit maximization does not necessarily lead to high prices. True, if competition cannot offer effective substitutes, then demand and supply *may* bring extremely high prices. But this happens *if, and only if,* demand is highly inelastic. If demand is highly elastic, it probably would be in a monopolist's interest to charge relatively low prices so that sales will be expanded.

Most markets with extremely inelastic demand curves have been regulated, as in the case of the transport systems and utilities. Aside from these, relatively few monopolies exist today. Most firms have direct competitors within their own industry, and industry and target market boundaries are not rigidly fixed. Other firms are always trying to offer substitutes. Even steel, often cited as a near-monopoly, has intraindustry competition and also interindustry competition from substitute materials such as aluminum and plastics.

Please do squeeze the profits. Profit maximization can have desirable results for both business and consumers. Profit can be viewed as a return for efficiency. If the customer is served poorly, no profit may be earned at all. If he is served more adequately, profit may be larger. A firm should be allowed to reap the benefits of its efficiency. Competitors will see its high profits and want to emulate it. In this way, competition—even the monopolistic competition variety—will eventually reduce profits (and probably prices, too).

In the long run, profits are squeezed until there is just enough profit to encourage enough efficient firms to stay in the business. We saw this process at work in Chapter 14 in the rise and fall of profits during the life cycle of a product. Contrary to common belief, a profit maximization objective may be desirable from a social viewpoint.[16] Much of our discussion on price determination will be aimed at implementing this objective.

After the entrepreneurs, just satisfaction

Although the pricing study just cited did not find any firms admitting that their goal was *satisfactory* profits, some management theorists maintain that this is the level of profit sought by some businessmen today. To be sure, they are working for profits, but they aren't nearly as aggressive as they might be if they were seeking maximum profits. They do want to convince stockholders of their competence and assure the firm's survival, but as long as profits are *satisfactory* for these purposes, they will have achieved their ends.

"Satisficing" may be a characteristic of present-day administrators as

---

[16] For a more extensive discussion of these ideas, see Claude Robinson, *Understanding Profits* (Princeton, N.J.: D. Van Nostrand Co., Inc., 1962).

distinct from the original entrepreneurs of the business world.[17] It is clear that the administrator whose goal is satisfactory profits might find it easier to pursue several pricing objectives than the administrator who is seeking a specific target return or maximum profits.

Sales-oriented objectives

Some business executives seem more concerned about growth in sales than in profits. One economist states that "the typical large corporation in the United States seeks to maximize not its profits but its total revenues, which a businessman calls his sales."[18]

Does big growth mean big profit?

One reason advanced for the popularity of the sales growth objective is the tendency to equate growth with profitability. Yet the two are not always corollaries. Since World War II, major corporations have faced a continuing profit squeeze while sales have grown. Average returns on investments have dropped to the 5 to 10 percent level, depending on the industry and line of trade. Excessive emphasis on sales growth has been partly responsible. More recently, however, this fallacy has been recognized, and some companies now are trying to determine whether growth does, in fact, lead to more profit.

Another explanation of the popularity of growth-oriented objectives is that the administrator's salary may be more closely related to sales than to profits.[19] As noted in Chapter 22, compensation systems should be used to get desired results. Here it seems that compensation systems may have had a bearing on the selection of corporate objectives rather than vice versa.

Maintaining market share—the percentage of the market you are "entitled" to because of your size and reputation—seems to be extremely important to some business executives. Maintaining market share is such an important objective to some larger companies, especially grocery manufacturers, that they seem willing to forego other objectives to reach this highly measurable goal.

Getting your share, getting enough

It is fairly easy to determine by surveys whether a company has maintained its percentage of the market. This is much easier to measure than whether profits are being maximized. Consequently, as long as some profit is returned, the managers seem to prefer emphasizing market share instead, especially if promotions are based on market share performance!

Note, however, that some large companies do not want more than a certain percentage of the market. Why? The reasons vary among firms.

Don't rile justice; do be offensive

Some companies don't want to rile or arouse the U.S. Department of Justice. Some observers feel that General Motors is not as aggressive as it could be in certain markets because it doesn't want to get substan-

[17] For more discussion of the behavior of satisficers, see Herbert A. Simon, *Administrative Behavior* (2d ed.; New York: Macmillan Co., 1961).

[18] W. J. Baumol, "On the Theory of Oligopoly," *Economica,* August, 1958, p. 187.

[19] Joseph W. McGuire, John S. Y. Chiu, and Alvar O. Elving, "Executive Incomes, Sales and Profits," *American Economic Review,* September, 1962, pp. 753–61.

tially more than 50 percent of the market. One GM executive, commenting on his corporation's share of the market, stated: "Yes, it's a little better. Our market penetration in March was under 53 percent. In February, you remember, we took more than 57 percent."[20]

Viewed from another standpoint, some managers want only a relatively small percentage of a market because they would rather be on the offensive, trying to gain an additional share or maintain their share, than to achieve a temporary success and then be on the defensive. Johns-Manville and General Electric officials indicate that, for this reason, they would prefer to have 20 to 25 percent of a market than 50 percent.[21] This is like the rationale leading to the sales expansion objectives and may result from the compensation system used.

Aggressive and especially smaller companies often emphasize an objective of *increasing* their market share or even dominating a market. In some businesses, economies of scale can be gained by larger operations, and a firm may work both to increase market share and maximize profits. In other cases, however, firms blindly follow the market expansion goal, and this leads to pricing goods practically at cost in order to get more of the market. These growth tendencies sometimes lead to profitless prosperity, where slight miscalculations may lead to bankruptcy.

Status quo objectives

More time for golf or aggression elsewhere

These might be described as *don't-rock-the-boat* objectives. The purpose of these objectives is stated variously as "meeting competition," or "avoiding competition," or "stabilizing prices."

Often a status quo objective is held by a conservative management that wishes to minimize the risk of loss, preferring instead a comfortable way of life and some assurance of profit. Maintaining stable prices may forestall competition and eliminate the need for hard decisions. There may be more time for golf.

On the other hand, status quo pricing objectives can be part of an extremely aggressive marketing mix. The *pricing* objective may seem conservative, but the intention may be to avoid price competition in favor of aggressive action on one or more of the other P's. If a company chooses to hold a status quo objective regarding pricing, it should have either aggressive objectives in one or more of the other P's or an extremely strong customer franchise. Otherwise, the continuing pressure of time along the product life cycle will lead to poor results. A firm may de-emphasize price in its marketing mix, but it cannot de-emphasize marketing generally and hope to survive.

A number of the large firms listed in Table 24–1 admitted to status quo objectives, yet they are aggressive in other respects. Examples include American Can, Esso, General Electric, Goodyear, Gulf, Johns-Manville, Kroger, Standard Oil (Ind.), and U.S. Steel.

---

[20] *Wall Street Journal,* April 18, 1962, p. 1.
[21] Lanzillotti, *op. cit.*

Conclusion

The Price variable has many facets and offers an alert marketing manager many possibilities for varying marketing mixes.

Most price structures have a basic list price from which varying discounts and allowances are subtracted. Among the discounts discussed in this chapter are quantity, seasonal, cash, and trade or functional discounts. We also discussed trade-ins, and damage, advertising, and brokerage allowances. Special terms, such as F.O.B., specify more clearly the nature of the "something;" which party is to assume the freight and other charges, and where and when the title is to pass.

The "something" that is offered for a price really represents the total marketing mix (except Price) being developed for a particular target market. It may even include such things as trading stamps or profit guarantees.

How prices are set and which prices are set depends on pricing objectives. We examined profit-oriented, sales-oriented and status quo–oriented objectives. We saw that some companies have multiple objectives, perhaps because different executives hold different objectives. Ideally, objectives should be clearly stated and *written,* because they provide direction for subsequent pricing policies.

Pricing objectives should be consistent with the company's overall objectives. A company might choose rather conservative status quo pricing objectives while holding very aggressive overall objectives. The purpose would be to de-emphasize the highly visible and easily imitated price variable in favor of other elements of a marketing mix.

Throughout this chapter, we have assumed that a list price had already been established. We have placed primary emphasis on what may be included (or specifically excluded) in the "something" and what objectives a firm might have in its pricing policies. The critical matter of price determination itself was not discussed. We will cover this in the next two chapters, showing ways of implementing the various pricing objectives.

---

1 Indicate what the final consumer really obtains when he (she) pays the list price for the following "products": (*a*) an automobile, (*b*) a portable radio, (*c*) a package of frozen peas, (*d*) a lipstick in a jeweled case. **Questions and problems**

2 Explain what the retailer gets for the products in Question 1 when paying the wholesale price. Explain what the wholesaler obtains from the manufacturer when paying the manufacturer's price for the same products.

3 Explain how a marketing manager might change his F.O.B. terms to make his otherwise competitive marketing mix more attractive.

4 Some critics have suggested that the manufacturer ought to be responsible for all guarantees and warranties on his products and include the cost of this service in his price. How would this affect our marketing

structure? What role would wholesalers and retailers play in such a system? Would promotion be more or less important? What would happen to prices?

5   Are seasonal discounts appropriate in agricultural businesses (which are certainly seasonal)?

6   What are the "effective" annual interest rates on the following cash discount terms: (*a*) 1/10 net 60, (*b*) 1/5 net 10, (*c*) net 30, (*d*) 1/10 net 30 E.O.M. for goods bought on November 20, (*e*) 3/10 net 30 R.O.G. (goods shipped on November 15 and received on December 15).

7   What is the manufacturer's selling price if he grants trade discounts of 30, 20, and 10 percent off a list price of $200 per unit? What might these discounts be allowed for?

8   Evaluate the use of trading stamps. In what lines or in what situations would they be most appropriate? Would they have any value for use among middlemen? Why or why not?

9   How might a company's pricing objectives vary depending on the point of view of the price maker? Consider the objectives which might be held by the: Production Manager, Controller, and Sales Manager.

10 If Alcoa's pricing objective is a 10 percent return on investment after taxes, how can its average return of 13.8 percent for the period 1947–55 be explained? Note that its range during this period was from 7.8 to 18.7 percent.

11 In view of A&P's policy of low-margin selling, how can a return on investment after taxes of 13 percent be explained, when Kroger, a company which has not pursued a low-margin policy, had a rate of return of only 12.1 percent during the same period (1947–55)?

12 Which of the 20 large corporations seem to be consciously following a profit maximization policy?

13 Discuss the implementation of General Foods' objectives.

14 How would the acceptance of a profit-oriented, or a sales-oriented, or a status quo–oriented pricing objective affect the development of a company's marketing strategy?

Price determination—
cost-oriented

In the previous chapter, we accepted the fact that a list price can be established in a number of ways. Now we will go on to see how a list price might be set by an individual firm.

Although in practice there are many ways of arriving at a price, these can be reduced, for simplicity, to two basic methods: (1) cost-oriented and (2) demand-oriented price determination. We will discuss the cost-oriented approach in this chapter and the demand-oriented approach in Chapter 26.

Cost-oriented pricing is quite commonly used because most accounting systems accumulate costs, and profit-and-loss statements show very clearly that they must be covered. Moreover, costs provide a floor below which prices cannot go (for long, anyway), and it is only logical that prices should be built on seemingly precise cost data. **Neither simple nor foolproof**

As we will see, however, cost-oriented pricing is not as simple or foolproof as it might seem at first glance. We will begin our discussion by examining how retailers, wholesalers, and producers set cost-oriented prices.

Pricing by wholesalers and retailers

Most retail and wholesale prices are determined by a cost-oriented markup approach, using the traditional markups taken in those types of trades. The markup is normally the trade or functional discount **A case can be made for tradition**

521

allowed by the previous channel members. Using this method, the retailer or wholesaler adds a markup to the delivered cost of his goods.

Generally, the trade discounts or traditional markups are applied rather mechanically. Some retailers or wholesalers, in fact, use the same markup for all of their goods—which, if nothing else, certainly simplifies their pricing procedure. Other retailers (and sometimes wholesalers) may take a higher markup on some items because of their apparent quality or their slow turnover. Or they may take a lower markup to meet competitive prices because of their estimate of how consumers will accept a price set by using the traditional markups. In general, though, wholesalers and retailers use the traditional markups. This is true especially in larger firms where management may be reluctant to delegate the pricing job to a large number of retail clerks who may have relatively little experience.

Considering the large number of items the average retailer and wholesaler carries and the small sales volume of any one item, this cost-oriented markup approach to pricing seems both reasonable and practical. Spending the time and effort to determine the best price to charge on every item in stock, day to day or week to week, probably would not pay for itself.

It will be helpful to understand how retailers usually determine a selling price, and a discussion of this follows. Wholesalers follow essentially the same procedure.

There are two kinds of markups

Suppose a dealer buys an article for $1. To make a profit the dealer obviously must sell this article for more than its cost. If the dealer adds 50 cents to the selling price of the article to cover his operating costs and provide a profit, we say that he is marking up the item 50 cents.

Markups, however, generally are expressed as percentages rather than dollar amounts. And this is where the difficulty begins. Is a markup of 50 cents on a cost of $1 a markup of 50 percent? Or should the markup be computed as a percentage of the selling price—$1.50—and therefore be 33⅓ percent? A clear definition is necessary.

We will use the following definition: Unless otherwise specified, *markup means "percentage of selling price."* By this definition, the 50-cent markup on the $1.50 selling price is a markup of 33⅓ percent.

The reason markups are related to selling price is convenience. For one thing, the markup on selling price is roughly equivalent to the gross margin,[1] which is computed in relation to total sales. Most businessmen have a full appreciation of the concept of gross margin because they continually see gross margin data on their profit-and-loss statements. They know that unless there is an adequate gross margin, there will not be any profits left at the end of the period. For this reason, businessmen readily accept traditional markups that are close to their gross margins.

Relating markups to the selling price also is consistent with our emphasis on the consumer rather than internal considerations, such as

---

[1] The ratio of sales and administrative expenses plus profit to net sales—usually expressed as a percent. See Appendix on Marketing Arithmetic at the end of the book.

cost. There is nothing wrong, however, with the concept of markup on cost. The essential thing is to clearly indicate which markup we are using, to avoid confusion. Some dealers use the term "mark-on" to indicate a markup based on cost, but this is by no means common. In the everyday world, the terms are often interchanged rather haphazardly.

Some retailers frequently need to convert a markup on cost to one based on selling price, or vice versa. Conversion tables have been developed for this purpose, but they are not essential because the calculations are simple.[2]

A chain of markups can set the price structure in a whole channel. A markup is figured on the selling price at each level of the channel—by producers (if they use this approach to pricing), wholesalers, and retailers. The producer's marked up selling price to the wholesaler becomes the wholesaler's cost; the wholesaler's marked up selling price to the retailer becomes the retailer's cost; and his marked up cost

Markup chain may be used in channel pricing

Figure 25–1 Example of a markup chain

		Selling Price = $50.00 = 100%
	Selling Price = $30.00 = 100%	Markup = $20.00 = 40%
Selling Price = $24.00 = 100%	Markup = $ 6.00 = 20%	Cost = $30.00 = 60%
Markup = $ 2.40 = 10%	Cost = $24.00 = 80%	
Cost = $21.60 = 90%		
MANUFACTURER	WHOLESALER	RETAILER

---

becomes the retail selling price. Each markup is expected to cover the expenses of selling and administration and to leave a profit. Figure 25–1 shows how a markup might be used at each level of a channel system.

This illustration starts with a production cost (factory cost) of $21.60. In this case, the producer is taking a 10 percent markup and sells the goods for $24. The markup is 10 percent of $24 or $2.40. The producer's selling price now becomes the wholesaler's cost—$24. If the wholesaler is accustomed to taking a 20 percent markup on selling price, his markup is $6, and his selling price becomes $30. The wholesaler's selling price of $30 now becomes the retailer's cost. And if the retailer is accustomed to a 40 percent markup, he adds $20 and the retail selling price becomes $50.

Final consumers often are shocked by a retail markup of 50 or 60 percent. They immediately think of this as "price gouging" to make exorbitant profits. Yet some retailers and wholesalers strive in vain for larger profits with higher markups. The truth is, however, that if they were primarily concerned with increasing their total profit or return on

Fallacy of seeking high profits through high markups

---

[2] See "Markup Conversion," in the Appendix on Marketing Arithmetic.

investment they probably should be more concerned about the profit achievable with various markups than about the size of the markup itself. Full appreciation and use of this idea helps account for the spectacular success of the mass marketers. Why?

The fallacy of seeking high profits through high markups can be seen by an extreme example. A 90 percent markup on selling price may not be nearly as profitable as a 10 percent markup on selling price! This apparent paradox is easy to understand if we assume an extreme condition in which no units are sold at the high markup, but a very large number are sold at the low one. The key is *turnover*. You cannot earn much if you don't sell much, regardless of the size of the markup. Nevertheless, many retailers and wholesalers seem more concerned with the size of their markup than with their total profit.

Markup varied, turnover faster, profits up

Not *all* retailers and wholesalers, however, are enamored with the traditional markups. Some are concerned with speeding turnover to increase profit, even if this means reducing the markup. They see themselves running an ongoing system that is incurring costs of operation as a function of time and the volume of goods handled. If they can sell a much greater volume of goods in the same time period, they may be able to take a lower markup on such items and still have a higher profit at the end of the time period.

An important concept in this connection is the stockturn rate—the number of times the average inventory is sold in a given time period, such as a year. Various methods of computing a stockturn rate are used, but they are all concerned with how many times the average inventory is sold.[3] If the stockturn rate is low, this probably will be undesirable for profits.

At the very least, a slow stockturn will increase cost by tying up working capital. If the stockturn were 1 (once per year) rather than 5, annual sales of $100,000 would require $100,000 rather than $20,000 in working capital just to carry the necessary inventory. Turnover is obviously important in profit and financial planning and may determine whether a particular firm can afford to operate in a certain line. Newcomers to retailing often appear not to understand turnover, and their lack of capital forces narrow assortments and then bankruptcy when the goods fail to move quickly.

What constitutes a "high" and "low" stockturn depends on the industry. For instance, an annual rate of 1 or 2 might be expected in the retail jewelry industry, while 40 to 50 would be typical for fresh fruits and vegetables. Comparisons for a given period within a firm, however, can help spot troubles. Comparison among firms within an industry will indicate whether a particular firm is turning over its stock as rapidly as competitors.

Living too high on the markup

The use of high, inflexible markups can have a damaging impact on the image and subsequently on the profits in an industry. Hardware retailers, for example, have been especially inflexible about markups and this has led to real difficulties.

---

[3] See "Computing the Stockturn Rate," in the Appendix on Marketing Arithmetic.

524

A study by the National Retail Hardware Association, a trade association of hardware retailers, found that fewer than 100 items in the average hardware store were bought on the basis of price. Since many hardware retailers traditionally have marked up all items 50 percent *on cost,* consumers have felt that hardware stores were high priced and have traded there only to get items unobtainable elsewhere. This has meant relatively low total profits for hardware retailers. For thousands of their items, the turnover is so low that even the normal 50 percent markup yields no profit.

To convince its members of the cause-effect relation of turnover and profit, the National Retail Hardware Association has developed a *Turnover Handbook* which strongly urges the abandonment of the practice of marking up all goods by 50 percent of cost. Instead, it suggests classifying about 5,000 different items into six categories, on the basis of demand sensitivity.

In the "A" category are goods that should be sold competitively. The markup for these items vary from a 45 percent markup in a small town to only 10 percent in a large city where there is greater competition. The "A" category includes only a relatively small number of items but involves the store "image"; it is important that the store be competitive on these items.

The *Handbook* suggests that goods in the other five categories be marked up progressively, the last group to more than 100 percent of cost. The items for which the highest markups are suggested are (1) those carried as a community service—low-priced items with a low turnover—and (2) high-priced items that require extensive product knowledge to sell.[4]

Grocery supermarket operators have shown that they understand the importance of turnover. They have been more flexible than the hardware retailers and many smaller grocers, too. The big grocers put only small markups on fast-selling items such as sugar, shortening, soaps and detergents, canned milk, soups, desserts, beverages, baby foods, pet foods, bleaches, flour, and canned vegetables. Sugar, for example, may carry a margin of 8 percent; shortening, 9 or 10 percent; soaps and detergents, 10 or 11 percent. **Grocers run a fast company**

Since supermarket expenses average about 15 percent of sales, some people feel that many of these items are carried at a loss. But since the 15 percent figure is a storewide average, this need not be true.

Fast-moving goods generally are less expensive to stock and sell. They occupy valuable space for shorter periods, are damaged less, and tie up less working capital. Lower markups will cover the costs of these items and make a profit too. With lower markups, the goods may turn even faster, and a small profit per unit will be earned more frequently.

One extensive supermarket study, covering a three-month period, showed that this low-markup and fast-turnover approach was quite profitable. The 150 items carrying margins averaging 10 percent or less earned more than twice as many dollars per item as the average of the

[4] "Handbook Teaches Dealers How to Sell," *Printers' Ink,* March 27, 1959, pp. 65–69.

higher margin items. These 150 items earned an average gross profit of $1.14 a week, while the remaining items averaged only 48 cents gross profit a week.

The higher returns were obtained because of higher turnover. The average turnover in the grocery department in this study was 14 times a year. Yet sugar turned over 31 times, beverages 28 times, shortening 23 times, and soups 21 times.

It should be noted here that the high-margin items were not necessarily unprofitable. They simply were not as profitable *per item* as some of the low-margin items.[5]

Varied markups may imply demand consideration

The use of varied markups and careful attention to stockturn rates implies an interest in demand. If turnover is rapid, profits may be greater even while margins are smaller. High or inflexible markups may slow turnover and decrease profits. Elasticity of demand is involved here, if only implicitly. If demand is extremely elastic, for example, a price cut will expand sales substantially and the turnover rate will rise.

Nevertheless, some of the retailers and wholesalers using varied markups do so from custom or habit, not because they have analyzed the demands of their target markets.[6] Firms which are using varied markups and have a full recognition of demand seem to be the exceptions, not the rule.

Some small firms seem to be less rigidly tied to cost-oriented pricing than larger firms, perhaps because of the administrative red tape and the need for definite policies in the larger companies.[7] But size need not lock a firm into inflexibility.

Some department stores have been using sales and cost analysis procedures to determine the prospective profit contribution of any *item* of merchandise, given various markups. This, however, is difficult to do in a large retail establishment handling many items; as an alternative, some stores have developed cost patterns for *groups of* similar products.[8]

Pricing by producers

It's up to the captain to set the list price

Some markups eventually become customary in a particular trade whether retailers and wholesalers use a common markup for all items or whether they vary their markups. Most of the channel members will tend to follow a similar markup process, adding a certain percentage to the previous price. Who determines price in the first place?

The basic list price usually is determined by the channel captain—a

---

[5] *Super-Valu Study* (New York: *Progressive Grocer,* 1957), p. S–4–7.

[6] "Colorado Seedsmen Admonished for Obsolete Pricing Methods," *Western Feed & Seed,* January, 1963, p. 37; and "Pricing Practices of American Enterprise," *Business Record,* September, 1958.

[7] W. Warren Haynes, *Pricing Decisions in Small Business* (Lexington: University of Kentucky Press, 1962), p. 152.

[8] See a special issue of the *Journal of Retailing* devoted exclusively to merchandise management accounting, Spring, 1958; and "Pinning Down Retailing Costs," *Business Week,* October 19, 1957, pp. 134–38.

large retailer, a large wholesaler, or often the producer. Here we are concerned with the pricing approach of such firms, and for convenience we will call them "producers."

Producers commonly use some cost-oriented approach. They may start with a dollar-cost-per-unit figure and add a markup, perhaps a customary percentage, to obtain the selling price. They may be guided by a rule-of-thumb formula such as: *production cost* $\times$ *3* $=$ *selling price*. In the electronics industry, a customary formula is: *price* $=$ *material cost* $+$ *direct labor cost* $+$ *100 percent of direct labor for overhead* $+$ *120 to 180 percent of direct labor for all other costs*.[9]

Each producer usually develops his own rules and markups in the light of his own costs and objectives. Yet even the single step of selecting the appropriate cost per unit to build on is no simple matter. So we must discuss several approaches to see how cost-oriented price determination really works.

One simple and common approach consists of adding a "reasonable" markup to the cost per unit. The cost per unit is found by assuming that all the inventory has been sold during a specific period, such as the past month, then taking the total cost for that period and dividing this figure by the number of units produced and sold in the same period. **Naïve, simple, and dangerous**

If the total cost of the latest month were $5,000 for labor and materials and $5,000 for fixed overhead expenses (such as selling expenses, rent, and executive salaries), then total cost would be $10,000. If the company produced 10,000 items in the previous month, the average cost was $1 a unit. To get the price, the producer decides how much profit markup per unit seems "reasonable," then adds this figure to the cost per unit. If 10 cents were considered a reasonable profit for each unit (perhaps they had a target return of $1,000 a month), the new price would be set at $1.10.

The chief merit of this approach is its simplicity. This is also its weakness. To see why, we will observe this firm further.

If in the next month, only 5,000 units are produced and sold, the firm may be in trouble. Five thousand units sold at $1.10 each would yield a total revenue of $5,500. The overhead would still be fixed at $5,000, and material and labor costs probably would amount to $2,500, for a total of $7,500. This would mean a loss of $2,000 or 40 cents a unit. The method that seemed to allow for a profit of 10 cents a unit instead would cause a loss of 40 cents a unit.

It is apparent that this naïve cost-plus method does not adjust for cost variations at different levels of output. Since all costs do not behave the same way as sales expand or contract, the average cost per unit may change considerably as output rises or falls. The following paragraphs explain these variations.

One reason the naïve cost-plus approach fails is that total cost includes a variety of costs, and each of these changes in a different way as output changes. Any method that uses costs as the basis for determin- **Many costs make one price**

[9] "Management Problems in the Electronics Industry," *Management Research Summary,* Small Business Administration, November, 1962, p. 3.

ing prices must make allowance for these variations. The more realistic approach described below does so.

To fully understand this method, however, it will be desirable first to define and illustrate six types of cost. An understanding of the differences among these costs is important because these differences are at the root of the problems many companies have with pricing.

Total fixed cost is the sum of those costs that are fixed in total regardless of output level. Among these fixed costs are rent, depreciation, executive salaries, property taxes, and insurance. Such costs must be paid even if production stops temporarily. Over a period of years, fixed costs can change—the factory may be expanded or sold; new executives may be hired or fired. But in the short run, total fixed cost is set.

Total variable cost, on the other hand, is the sum of those variable expenses that are closely related to output level—expenses for components, wages paid to workers, packaging materials, outgoing freight, and sales commissions.

At zero output, total variable cost is zero. As output increases, so do variable costs. If a dress manufacturer doubles his output of dresses in a year, his *total* cost of cloth would also roughly double (ignoring quantity discounts), although the cost of cloth *per dress* would remain about the same.[10]

Total cost is the sum of total fixed and total variable costs. The rate of growth of total cost depends upon the increase in total variable cost, since total fixed cost, by definition, is already set.

The pricing executive usually is more interested in cost per unit than total cost because prices in the marketplace usually are quoted per unit. Costs per unit are called "average" costs, and there are several types.

Average cost per unit is obtained by dividing total cost by the related quantity.

Average fixed cost is obtained by dividing total fixed cost by the related quantity.

Average variable cost is obtained by dividing total variable cost by the related quantity. We commonly assume that average variable cost is *constant per unit* over a short production range. Actually, average variable cost usually decreases as a firm gains some economies of scale levels out for a while, and then it begins to rise again at still higher levels of output if the firm must use less efficient machines or workers, pay overtime wage rates, or pay higher prices for materials when expanded sales cause shortages.

The assumption that average variable cost is constant for short ranges is reasonable only in certain cases—but when appropriate, it simplifies analysis. This assumption is used in the following example.

A Cost Structure Example. In Table 25–1, cost data is presented for one firm; it is based on the assumption that average variable cost is constant for each unit. Notice how average fixed cost decreases steadily as the quantity increases and how, although the average variable cost

---

[10] Some expenditures have both fixed and variable components and are called semifixed or semivariable costs. To simplify this discussion we will omit this refinement.

Table 25–1 Cost structure of a firm

Quantity	Total Fixed Costs (TFC)	Average Fixed Costs (AFC)	Average Variable Costs (AVC)	Total Variable Costs (TVC)	Total Cost (TC)	Average Cost (AC)
0	$30,000	$	$ 0	$ 0	$ 30,000	$
10,000	30,000	3.00	0.80	8,000	38,000	3.80
20,000	30,000	1.50	0.80	16,000	46,000	2.30
30,000	30,000	1.00	0.80	24,000	54,000	1.80
40,000	30,000	0.75	0.80	32,000	62,000	1.51
50,000	30,000	0.60	0.80	40,000	70,000	1.40
60,000	30,000	0.50	0.80	48,000	78,000	1.30
70,000	30,000	0.43	0.80	56,000	86,000	1.23
80,000	30,000	0.38	0.80	64,000	94,000	1.18
90,000	30,000	0.33	0.80	72,000	102,000	1.13
100,000	30,000	0.30	0.80	80,000	110,000	1.10

remains constant, total variable cost increases when quantity increases. Average cost decreases continually. This is because average variable cost is constant and average fixed cost is decreasing. Figure 25–2 graphs the behavior of the three average-cost curves.

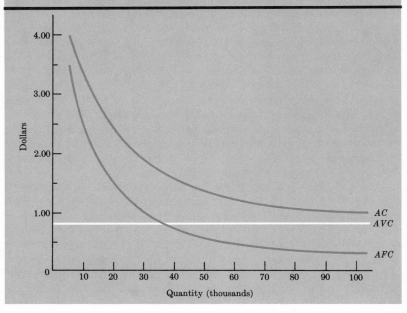

Figure 25–2 Typical shape of cost (per unit) curves when AVC is assumed constant per unit

The pricing executive could set prices using a graph such as that in Figure 25–2. Assuming that the average-cost curve includes a provision for profit (either a fixed total amount included in total fixed cost or a fixed amount per unit included in average variable cost), then all he has to do is decide how many units the firm is going to sell. If he expects to sell 50,000 units, then by referring to the average-cost curve shown here, the price could be determined. It would be $1.40. If he plans to sell 80,000 units, the price suggested by the average-cost curve would be $1.18.

Those using this approach often estimate the quantity to be sold by assuming that new sales will approximate the volume of the last period.

Assuming the firm will sell a quantity similar to past sales, the average-cost method works easily. The "average-cost" price is along the *AC* curve at that previous quantity. This seems to assure that all the fixed costs will be covered. The fixed costs covered by each unit are easily calculated. And it is an easy next step to develop pricing formulas to insure that on each item that amount of fixed cost is covered.

Various cost-oriented pricing formulas might be invented but the intent would be the same—to cover all the costs. The formulas suggested earlier in the chapter illustrate the possibilities.

Cost-oriented pricing of this type is used in calculating bid prices for industrial goods and for government business. The major task is assembling all the costs, including the variable costs and the fixed costs that should apply to each order. This may sound relatively straightforward, but in actual practice thousands of cost components may have to go into a complicated bid.

Thousands or even millions of dollars have been spent just developing cost-oriented bids for large industrial or government orders. To assure that all costs are included in a given order, computers often are used to help accumulate the costs.[11] Great care is essential in developing such bid prices. The omission of an important cost item might make the firm the low bidder—but cause it to lose money on the contract.

As long as actual sales do not vary too much from the previous period, this cost-oriented approach will produce fairly good results. As with the naïve approach, however, losses may result if actual sales are much *lower* than in the previous period because the fixed costs will not be covered as completely as was expected. But if actual sales are much *higher* than in the past, then profits will be excellent.

This approach does not jibe with the demand theory discussed in Chapter 10, however. The cost-oriented approach indicates that if increased sales are expected, the selling price should go down. Or if sales are expected to drop, the price should go up. But the demand theory says that if increased demand is expected (i.e., the demand curve is moving to the right), more could be sold at the same price and perhaps even at a higher price. Depending on demand elasticity, perhaps prices should be raised rather than lowered if demand is expand-

---

[11] "Estimating Bids by Computer," *Business Week*, November 23, 1963.

ing—and vice versa. Clearly, pricing along the average-cost curve leaves something to be desired when market conditions are changing.

Target return pricing, seeking a target return objective, has become popular in recent years. With this approach, the price setter seeks to obtain (1) a percentage return (say 10 percent per year) on his investment or (2) a specific total dollar return.

Target return pricing scores . . . sometimes

The method is basically the same as the average-cost method described previously, since the desired target return is added into total cost. An example illustrates the method: 12,000 units were sold last year, and it is hoped the same quantity will be sold this year.

Executive salaries, general administrative overhead, and other fixed expenses total $600,000.

Total investment is $300,000.

Target return is a 10 percent return on investment.

Therefore . . . *total fixed cost*—including the 10 percent target return—is $630,000.

This total, divided by 12,000 units, yields a fixed cost and target

Table 25–2 Results of target return pricing

	10,000 Units Sold		20,000 Units Sold	
Total revenue.............		$ 925,000		$1,850,000
Total cost				
Total fixed cost..........	$600,000		$600,000	
Total variable cost.......	400,000		800,000	
		1,000,000		1,400,000
Profit (loss)...............		($75,000)		$ 450,000
Return on investment.......	$\left(\dfrac{-75,000}{300,000}\right) = -25\%$		$\left(\dfrac{450,000}{300,000}\right) = 150\%$	

return per unit figure of $52.50. If the variable cost per unit is $40, the price that apparently should be set to bring a 10 percent return on investment is $92.50.

This approach suffers from the same deficiency as the average-cost approach. If the quantity that actually is sold in a given period is less than the quantity used in setting the price, then the target return is not achieved, even though it seems to be an integral part of the price structure. To see more clearly how this happens, look at the results when either 10,000 or 20,000 units are sold (see Table 25–2).

If only 10,000 units are sold, there is a 25 percent *loss* on investment instead of a 10 percent return. If 20,000 units are sold, there is a 150 percent return on investment instead of only a 10 percent target return. Target return pricing clearly does not guarantee that the target objective will be achieved.

Executives in some larger and more stable firms, wanting to achieve long-run target return objectives, perhaps covering five or more years, have adopted another cost-oriented approach. Instead of estimating the

Hitting the target in the long run

quantity they expect to produce in any one year, they assume that during several years' time their plants will produce at, say, 80 percent of capacity. They use that quantity in their pricing.

No reference at all is made to current demand when setting current prices. Demand was estimated when the plant was built. Some demand and cost factors had to be considered at that time, and in reality it was the decision to build a plant of a certain size that determined subsequent prices.

Companies taking this longer run view assume that there will be recession years when sales drop below 80 percent of capacity, and the target return won't be earned, but also there will be other years when the plant operates at a higher level and betters the target return. Over the long run, the target return will be achieved. If business is consistently good, it would be expected that such firms would consistently earn higher than their target figure. Of the large companies whose objectives we discussed in the last chapter, those with target return objectives made profits in the prosperous 1947–55 period that were higher than their target levels for that period.

This long-run approach to target return pricing sounds simple. But like pricing in general, it cannot be approached mechanically. For example, "capacity" is a rather flexible concept, perhaps referring to a five-day, single-shift operation or a seven-day, three-shift operation.

Long-run target return pricing, consequently, need not lead to a unique price or a stable price. Typically, however, companies using target return pricing tend to have more stable prices.

Break-even analysis may be helpful in seeing profitability of possible prices

Some businessmen use break-even analysis in an attempt to bring prospective revenue (and perhaps demand) into a cost-oriented pricing approach.

Break-even analysis is especially useful for considering the relation of revenue and cost. A break-even chart can be drawn showing the total revenue which would be received at various levels of output when selling *at an assumed price*. This total revenue curve can then be related to the total cost curve to find where the company would break even. This intersection is called the break-even point (*BEP*).

At this point, total revenue and total cost are equal; beyond it, at a greater output level, the company will begin to make a profit on each unit; below it, the company incurs a loss. Figure 25–3, a break-even chart, shows these profit and loss areas.

In most break-even analysis, *average variable cost is assumed to be constant per unit. Total cost is segregated into fixed and variable costs. And a single price is assumed when drawing the total revenue curve.*

In a situation that is correctly described by break-even analysis, the obvious conclusion is to try to sell as many units as possible. The big question is: Will break-even analysis help find the right price? Before answering this question, let us look at the details of this analysis.

Computation of break-even point. The *BEP* may be computed in terms of units or dollar value of units. In units, the *BEP* can be found by using the following formula:

$$BEP \text{ (in units)} = \frac{TFC}{FC \text{ contribution per unit}}$$

The *fixed-cost contribution per unit* is equal to the selling price per unit minus the variable cost per unit. Variable cost *should* be covered on each item or there is no point in producing the item. Total fixed cost, however, does *not* have to be covered because it would continue even if the plant were temporarily shut down. In fact, it is sometimes better to continue production for a time, even without a profit, if all the variable costs and at least some of the fixed costs can be covered.

To illustrate the formula, let us use the cost data for the firm in

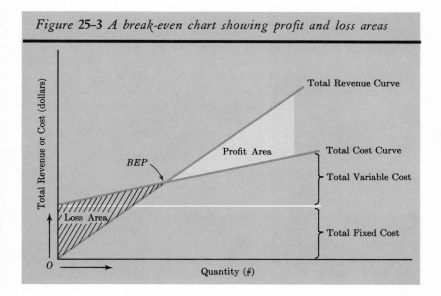

Figure 25–3 *A break-even chart showing profit and loss areas*

Table 25–1, and assume a selling price per unit of $1.20. Using the following values:

Total fixed cost = $30,000
Variable cost per unit = $0.80
FC contribution ($1.20 − $.80) = $0.40

and substituting in the formula:

$$BEP = \frac{30,000}{0.40} = 75,000 \text{ units}$$

From this it is evident that if this firm sells 75,000 units, it will cover exactly all its fixed and variable costs. If even one more unit is sold, then it will begin to show a profit—in this case, 40 cents.

The *BEP* can also be figured in terms of dollar value:

$$BEP \text{ (in dollars)} = \frac{TFC}{1 - \dfrac{VC/\text{Unit}}{\text{Selling price}/\text{Unit}}}$$

Using the figures above, we obtain:

$$\frac{\$30,000}{1 - \dfrac{\$0.80}{\$1.20}} = \$90,000$$

To check our result, we can multiply the selling price ($1.20) times the *BEP* in units (75,000): $1.20 times 75,000 equals $90,000, the *BEP* in dollars.[12]

The results of the foregoing analyses can be graphed as shown in Figure 25–4. The definiteness of this graph and the probable growth of profits beyond the break-even point certainly make it appear that the pricing problem is solved, at least if we are sure of being able to sell more than the break-even quantity. It appears that the more optimistic we are about exceeding the break-even point, the more satisfaction we can feel, since profits will grow as volume expands.

Helpful, yes—but not a pricing solution

Break-even analysis is useful for comparing pricing alternatives. The break-even points of various assumed prices can be calculated and evaluated to see how reasonable they are—that is, is it likely the *BEP*'s will be exceeded? The assumed prices may have been developed by other cost-oriented approaches, and a check of their respective *BEP*'s might quickly eliminate some of them.

Yet, helpful as it is for evaluating the impact of various *assumed* price levels, break-even analysis does *not* solve the pricing problem. Break-even analysis can be done without relating the assumed price to potential demand. In fact, many assumed prices can be analyzed in break-even analysis without any relation to market reality. But although the graph, with its straight-line total revenue curve makes it appear that any quantity might be sold at the assumed price, this usually is unrealistic. This is equivalent to assuming the existence of a perfectly horizontal demand curve at that price; if demand is perfectly elastic, there is no need for pricing analysis because the pricing executive would have no pricing decision to make.

At the end of this chapter we will evaluate the effectiveness of break-even analysis, along with other cost-oriented approaches. For now, though, we can see that our pricing problem is not solved.

---

[12] Students familiar with algebra may find the following approach more meaningful. Where *x* equals *BEP* in quantity, and we solve for the intersection of the *TR* and *TC* lines.

$$\begin{aligned}
\text{(Price) } (x) &= TFC + VC\ (x) \\
1.20x &= 30,000 + .80x \\
.40x &= 30,000 \\
x &= 75,000 \text{ units}
\end{aligned}$$

and $1.20 (75,000) = $90,000 = *BEP* in dollars.

Figure 25–4 Break-even chart for a particular situation

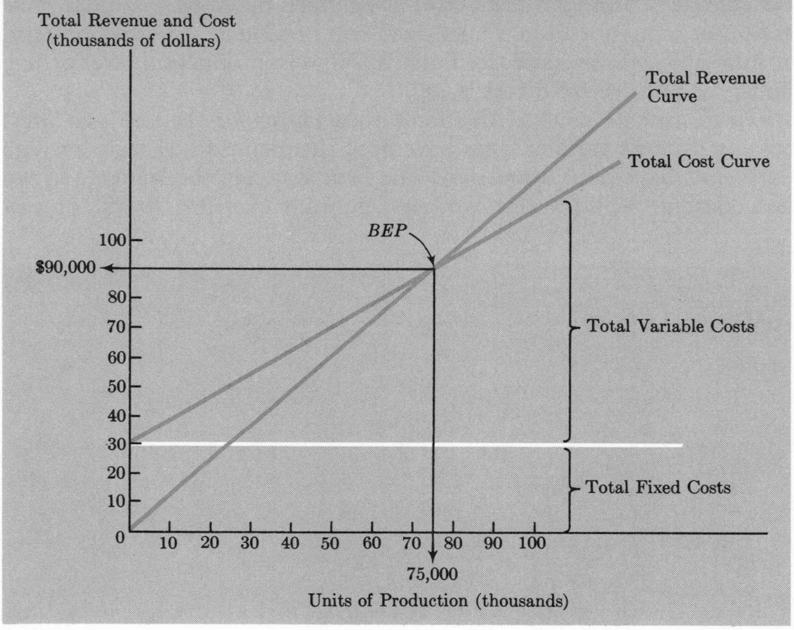

Total Revenue and Cost
(thousands of dollars)

Total Revenue Curve

Total Cost Curve

BEP

$90,000

100
80
70
60
50
40
30
20
10
0

Total Variable Costs

Total Fixed Costs

10 20 30 40 50 60 70 80 90 100

75,000

Units of Production (thousands)

By now we know that various kinds of costs behave differently and that there is no single type of cost that should be the basis for setting the price in all situations.

The cost of just one more may help in special cases

In some special pricing situations, however, there is another cost that may be useful. This is marginal cost, *the change in total cost that results from producing an extra unit.*

The subject of marginal cost will become especially important in the next chapter on demand-oriented pricing. In anticipation of this use, we will introduce a new set of cost data to illustrate the concept of marginal cost. See Table 25–3.

According to the marginal cost concept, if it costs $275 to produce 9 units of a product and $280 to produce 10 units, then marginal cost is $5 for the 10th unit. In other words, marginal cost contrasted to average cost per unit is the additional cost of producing one more *specific unit,* while average cost is the average for *all units.*

Table 25–3 indicates how all of these costs could vary for an individual firm. You should fill in the missing numbers on this table. Notice that variable cost no longer is assumed constant per unit in Table 25–3. In this situation, we use the more realistic assumption that variable costs will decline for a while and then rise.

In Table 25–3, several important points should be noted. *First,* total fixed costs do not change over the entire range of output, but total variable costs increase continually as more and more units are produced. It is obvious, then, that total costs—the sum of total fixed costs and total variable costs—will increase as total quantity increases.

535

Second, average costs will decrease over most of the range of production, since average costs are the sum of average fixed costs and average variable costs, and total fixed costs are divided by more and more units as output mounts. Given a total fixed cost of $200 at a production level of four units, the average fixed cost is $50; at a production level of five units, the average fixed cost is $40.

Third, average costs in this table start rising for the last two units because average variable costs have been increasing faster than average fixed costs have been decreasing. The firm may have been forced to use less efficient facilities and workers, go into overtime work, or pay

Table 25-3 Cost structure for individual firm

Quantity Q (1)	Total Fixed Cost TFC (2)	Total Variable Cost TVC (3)	Average Variable Cost AVC (4)	Total Cost (TFC + TVC = TC) TC (5)	Average Cost (AC = TC ÷ Q) AC (6)	Marginal Cost (per unit) MC (7)
0	$200	$ 0	$ 0	$200	Infinity	
1	200	96	96	296	$296	$ 96
2	200	116	58	316		20
3	200			331	110.33	
4	200			344		
5	200	155	31		71	11
6	200	168			61.33	13
7		183				15
8		223				
9		307		507	56.33	
10		510	51	710	71	203

higher prices for the materials it needed. This turn-up of the average cost curve happens frequently.

How little can keep us in business?

The *marginal cost* column in Table 25-3 is the most important column for our purposes. It shows specifically what each extra unit costs, and therefore indicates the minimum extra revenue we should get for each additional unit. Like average cost, marginal cost drops, but it begins to rise again at a lower level of output than average cost.

Total fixed costs do *not* affect marginal cost computations. Although average cost per unit is going down over most of the quantity range, marginal cost *starts up earlier* at five units. Figure 25-5 shows the behavior of the *average-cost, average variable cost,* and *marginal cost* curves. Note that the marginal cost curve intersects the average variable cost and average-cost curves from below *at their low points,* and then rises rapidly thereafter. This is how this curve typically behaves.

The marginal cost curve shows the *extra* cost of producing each extra unit. This cost may be extremely relevant when the marketing manager is trying to find a low price at which his plant can operate in depressed times—and still not lose money. Or he may want to use marginal cost when pricing a promotional item. The lower the price the better, short of giving the item away.

Marginal cost pricing is often used during short-term price wars, or to attract business a company would not ordinarily get during seasonal slack periods, or for other short-run objectives.

In the long run, we should aim to cover fixed costs, and pricing at marginal cost would not be wise. But in these special short-run situations, pricing at the average-cost level might not be wise, either, because the actual out-of-pocket costs—the marginal costs—might be considerably higher than average costs. This could cause out-of-pocket losses.

Figure 25–5 Per unit cost curves

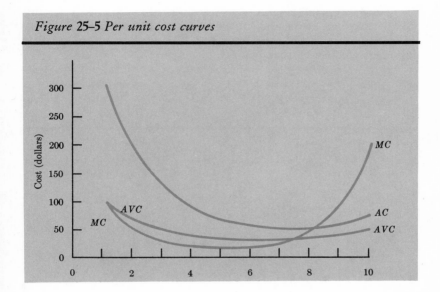

Cost-oriented price determination has major deficiencies

If a company is to base its pricing on costs, it must be able to make some estimate of the quantity to be sold in the coming period. But unless this estimated quantity is related to price—that is, unless demand is considered—the pricing executive may set a price that either does not maximize profits or, worse, does not even cover total costs. Such a possible predicament can be seen in a simple illustration of a firm with a total fixed cost of $90,000 and a variable cost of $40 per unit. This firm's demand curve is shown in Figure 25–6. Remember—customers' demands are still relevant, whether management takes time to analyze the demand curve or not.

In this example, whether management sets the price at $100 ($60 markup) or $50 ($10 markup), it will incur a loss. At $100, 1,000 units will be sold, but the *BEP* is 1,500 units. At $50, 6,000 will be sold but the *BEP* is 9,000 units! In both instances, the firm has a loss. **Simple in theory, crude in practice**

If management made some attempt to estimate the demand curve, however crudely, the price probably would be set in an intermediate range, say at $70, where the *BEP* is 3,000 units. At this price, 4,000 units would be sold at a profit of $30,000, that is, $280,000 less $160,000 TVC less $90,000 *TFC* equals $30,000 profit.

In short, a cost-oriented approach to price determination is simple in theory but often very crude in practice. In static situations, prices set in this manner may yield profits—but not necessarily maximum profits. And interestingly, such prices may be higher than the prices that could maximize the firm's profits, as shown in Figure 25–6.

First the customer, then the price
Typically, demand is ignored in cost-oriented approaches to pricing. To be sure, some estimate of quantity may be included in the calculations, but this quantity may set a price that may be far higher than customers will pay for that quantity.

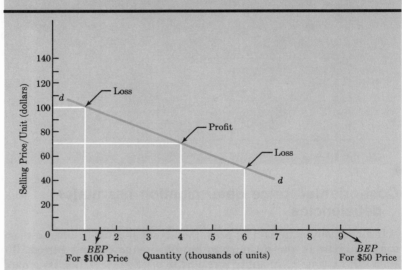

Figure 25–6 Evaluation of various prices along a firm's demand curve

It has become almost axiomatic in this book that the *customer must be considered before anything is done.* This certainly applies to pricing. It means that when management is setting the price, it must consider the prices customers will be willing to pay.

In the next chapter, we will discuss methods of estimating demand curves and demand-oriented pricing.

Conclusion

In this chapter, we considered various methods of cost-oriented price determination. Generally, retailers and wholesalers use traditional markups that they know will yield a reasonable rate of profit. Some retailers and wholesalers use the same markup on all of their items;

538

others have found that varying their markups may increase turnover and profit. And demand may enter here implicitly!

Cost-oriented pricing seems to make sense for retailers and wholesalers because they handle small quantities of many items. Perhaps they are not maximizing profit on each item, but the extra cost of more analysis might actually reduce total profit.

We found that it is less desirable for a producer or channel captain to use traditional markups. A common alternative, the naïve cost-plus approach, ignores demand completely and is not the answer. A more realistic cost-plus approach using average-cost curves requires some forecast of sales. Such a forecast often amounts to assuming that sales in the next period will be roughly the same as in the last period.

Given such an assumption, the average-cost pricing method enables the pricing executive to determine a price. But this price *may or may not* cover all costs and yield the desired rate of profit. It depends on how accurately the pricing executive has estimated the quantity which will be sold. Estimating sales is the crux of the problem in the average-cost and target return methods of pricing. Using these methods, the quantity estimate may be set without regard to the price, although in fact the quantity demanded by customers *varies* with the price. This can be seen on a demand curve.

Cost-oriented pricing frequently yields a price that is "too high." This causes slow turnover and low profit or even losses. The first concern of too many businessmen is an "adequate" margin. They do not like to take the risk of lower prices in anticipation of increased sales and possibly greater profits. Their reluctance results both from their cost orientation and an absence of demand analysis.

Although the break-even approach can bring various prices into the analysis, it can also lead to less than optimum results unless the prices used in the analysis are related to demand.

Chapter 26 shows that it is possible to bring demand into price determination.

Questions and problems

1 Many retailers mark up their goods by more than their gross margin. Explain how this can be if the gross margin is the difference between selling price and the cost of the goods.

2 Why do department stores seek a markup of about 40 percent when some discount houses operate on a 20 percent markup?

3 A manufacturer was selling an item for $120. What would be the final price to the consumer if the wholesaler took a markup of 20 percent and the retailer took a markup of 40 percent?

4 A buyer for a department store was computing the price he should charge for an item that cost him $72. In order to cover his expenses of 36 percent and still secure a profit of 4 percent, what retail price should be placed on the item?

5 A manufacturer of household appliances distributed its products through wholesalers and retailers. The retail selling price was $250, and

the manufacturing cost to the company was $100. The retail markup was 40 percent and the wholesale markup 25 percent.

    a) What was the cost to the wholesaler? Retailer?

    b) What percentage markup did the manufacturer take?

6 Does it make any difference in which order a chain of markups is taken? Illustrate your answer.

7 Relate the concept of stock turnover to the rise of discount houses. Use a simple example in your answer.

8 If total fixed costs are $100,000 and total variable costs are $200,000 at an output of 10,000 units, what are the probable total fixed costs and total variable costs at an output of 20,000 units? What are the average fixed costs, average variable costs, and average costs at these two output levels? Determine the price which should be charged. (Make any simplifying assumptions necessary to obtain a definite answer.)

9 Explain how target return pricing differs from average cost pricing.

10 Construct an example showing that mechanical use of a very large or very small markup might still lead to unprofitable operation while some intermediate price would be profitable. Draw a graph and use break-even analysis.

11 The Apex Co. wishes to use break-even analysis. Its fixed costs for the year are estimated at $100,000, the variable costs are usually about 70 percent of sales. Sales for the coming year are expected to reach $380,000. What is the break-even point? Expected profit? If sales were forecast at only $200,000, should the Apex Co. shut down operations? Why?

Price determination— demand-oriented

T he marketing concept stresses the importance of the customer, and nowhere should the customer be in sharper focus nor more carefully scrutinized than at the point of determining price.

The previous chapter showed the difficulty of trying to set prices without recognizing potential customer demand. In this chapter, we will bring demand explicitly into the analysis, discussing several demand-oriented approaches to pricing and several ways of estimating demand curves.

Flexible break-even analysis considers demand

Demand *can* be brought into the pricing picture through the use of break-even charts. Instead of using only one straight-line total revenue (*TR*) curve at a time as we did in the previous chapter, many such total revenue curves can be used. Each of these total revenue curves may be arbitrary, of course, since they are based on *assumed* prices. If high prices are assumed, the total revenue curves are sharply upsloping. If lower prices are assumed, the total revenue lines become flatter. (See Figure 26–1 for an illustration of five such *TR* lines for various prices.)

Each of these hypothetical total revenue lines, however, still has no connection with potential demand. This demand factor is considered when the exact quantity that customers would demand at each of the assumed prices is determined and plotted on each of the total revenue curves. These quantities are assumed to be the points D^1, D^2, D^3, D^5, in Figure 26–1. Connecting these points develops a potential total revenue curve (like a demand curve). This is not a demand curve in the usual sense, however, since it indicates the *total revenue* that will be received at various prices and quantities.

More common way to find the best price
The most profitable output is indicated by the point on the potential total revenue curve that is at the greatest vertical distance above the total cost curve. Of the five prices represented on this figure, the most profitable price would be the one which was used to draw line TR_3. Clearly, the most profitable quantity associated with this price is greater than the related *BEP*—that is, the quantity indicated at the intersection of TR_3 and TC.

Figure 26–1 Flexible break-even chart

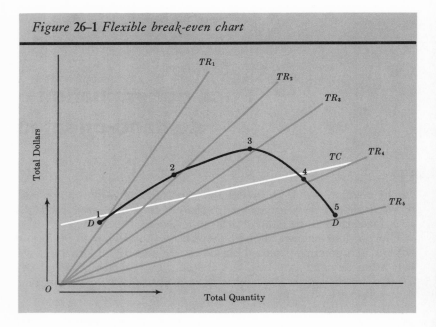

Management men who are accustomed to using break-even analysis can easily understand this flexible approach. For this reason, a marketing manager might choose this approach to illustrate how potential demand could and should be considered in price determination.

But the more common method of finding the most profitable price consists of using demand and supply curves to show price and cost *per unit* rather than as totals.

The balance of this chapter follows this more traditional method. Remember, however, that the flexible break-even approach and the following approach are similar except in method of graphic presentation.[1]

---

[1] This idea was developed by E. R. Hawkins. See Edward R. Hawkins, "Price Policies and Theory," *Journal of Marketing,* January, 1954, p. 234.

Traditional demand and supply analysis shows how to maximize profits

In Chapter 10, we saw that most demand curves are downsloping and most supply curves are upsloping. The intersection of these demand and supply curves would seem to determine price and, therefore, take care of demand-oriented pricing for the firm. Unfortunately, reality is not quite that simple.

Although such analysis may be appropriate for whole industries, some refinements are necessary in applying it to the individual firm seeking to maximize profits.

In the following pages, we will discuss these refinements, concentrating on price determination in the large majority of situations in which demand curves are downsloping—that is, monopolistic competition situations. In these situations, the firm has carved out a little market for itself and does have a pricing decision to make. By contrast, in the pure or nearly pure competition situation, the marketing manager has little difficulty with the pricing decision. He simply uses the market price.

Not just profit but the biggest profit

Our discussion also will focus on how to maximize profits, not just seek some profits. This has been the traditional approach of economic analysis, and it is a reasonable one. If you know how to make the biggest profit, you can always adjust to pursue other objectives.

Most monopolistic competitors—and these apparently constitute the vast majority of business firms[2]—have a downsloping demand curve. With such a curve, the marketing manager must consider the effect on total revenue of any price change. If he reduces his price along a demand curve to sell extra units, *all* his customers are offered lower prices. If he raises price, he must expect to lose some business. Either action will affect his revenue, both total and marginal.

Is selling just one more really worth it?

Marginal revenue is the change in total revenue which results from the sale of one additional unit of product. Since the firm's demand curve is downsloping, this extra unit can be sold only by reducing the price of all items. The total revenue that would be obtained if price were cut might still be positive, but the marginal revenue—that is, the extra revenue—gained might be negative.

Table 26–1 indicates the relationship between price, quantity, total revenue, and marginal revenue in a hypothetical situation.

If four units could be sold for $420 and five units for $460, then marginal revenue for the fifth unit is $40. Considering only revenue, it would be desirable to sell this extra unit. But Table 26–1 shows that negative marginal revenues may occur at lower price levels. Obviously, the way in which marginal revenue changes may be relevant to pricing.

The marginal revenue curve is always below a downsloping demand curve, as can be seen in Figure 26–2 where the data in Table 26–1 is

[2] W. Warren Haynes, *Pricing Decisions in Small Business* (Lexington: University of Kentucky Press, 1962), p. 152.

plotted. The fact that the demand curve and the marginal revenue curve are different in monopolistic competition is quite significant. We will use both of them when finding the best price and quantity, but for different purposes.[3]

Make the marginal cost curve the supply curve

We introduced the marginal cost curve in the previous chapter because we were considering cost-oriented ideas, and marginal cost has special applications there. It is even more useful, however, in relation to maximizing profits because it reflects what is happening to costs the manager can control. As we saw in the previous chapter, the marginal cost curve might be going up while the average-cost curve was going down at larger quantities. Clearly, we should not plan to increase the

Table 26–1 Marginal revenue and price

Quantity q (1)	Price p (2)	Total Revenue (1) × (2) = TR (3)	Marginal Revenue MR (4)
0	150	0	
1	140	140	140
2	130	260	120
3	117	351	91
4	105	420	69
5	92	460	40
6	79	474	14
7	66	462	−12
8	53	424	−38
9	42	378	−46
10	31	310	−68

quantity we will offer unless the sales return will at least cover the extra costs we will incur. The marginal cost curve shows these costs.

Computing most profitable price and quantity

We see now that a firm should not supply additional units unless it can obtain at least a marginal revenue equal to the marginal cost of those extra units. From this we can derive the following rule for

[3] The data for drawing a marginal revenue curve always can be derived by calculating changes in the total revenue curve, but a simple graphical shortcut is available if straight-line demand curves are being used. Although the demand curve within the relevant range normally may not extend all the way to the horizontal and vertical axes, it can be extended to these axes. The marginal revenue curve is then obtained by drawing a line running from the intersection of the demand curve with the vertical (price) axis down to the point on the quantity axis bisecting the segment from 0 to the point where the demand curve extension intersects that axis. This marginal revenue curve also can be extended below the quantity axis to obtain the negative marginal revenue values. The only relevant part of the marginal revenue curve is that part directly below the relevant range of the demand curve.

When working with curved demand curves, tangents to the curve can be drawn at several places to obtain the general shape of the MR curve. Readers familiar with calculus probably will recognize that the marginal revenue curve is simply the derivative of the total revenue curve, and they can use this approach in finding the marginal revenue curve.

544

maximizing profit: *The firm should produce that output where marginal cost is just less than or equal to marginal revenue.*[4]

The selling price for this optimum quantity is determined by referring to the demand curve, which shows what price customers are

Figure 26–2 *A plotting of the demand and marginal revenue data in Table 26–1*

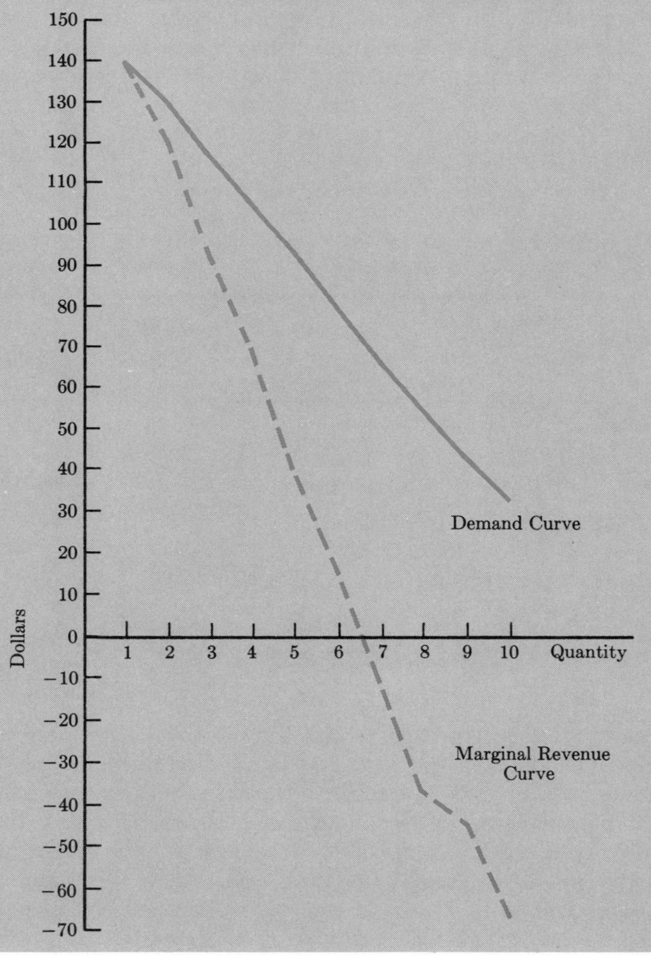

willing to pay for the optimum quantity. The optimum price is *not* found on the marginal revenue curve.

This method of finding the most profitable price and quantity is a

[4] This rule applies in the typical situations where the curves are shaped similarly to those discussed here. Technically, however, we should add the following to the rule for maximizing profit: *The marginal cost must be increasing at a greater rate or decreasing at a lesser rate than marginal revenue.*

useful tool for the marketing manager. To assure full understanding of the approach, we will illustrate its application. To make doubly sure that this approach is fully explained, we will calculate the most profitable price and quantity using total revenue and total cost curves first, and then show that the same answer is obtained with marginal curves. This will give us a check of the method as well as perspective on how the marginal revenue–marginal cost method works.

Pricing with total revenue and total cost curves. Table 26–2 provides illustrative data on total revenue, total cost, and total profit for this firm. Figure 26–3 simply graphs the total revenue, total cost, and total profit relationships. It is clear from the graph of the total profit curve that the most profitable quantity is six—this is the quantity where we find the greatest vertical distance between the *TR* curve and the *TC* curve. Table 26–2 shows that the most profitable price is $79 and a quantity of six will be sold.

Table 26–2 Revenue, cost, and profit for individual firm

Quantity q (1)	Price p (2)	Total Revenue TR (3)	Total Cost TC (4)	Profit $(TR - TC)$ (5)	Marginal Revenue MR (6)	Marginal Cost MC (7)	Marginal Profit $(MR - MC)$ (8)
0	150	0	200	−200			
1	140	140	296	− 156	140	96	+ 44
2	130	260	316	− 56	120	20	+100
3	117	351	331	+ 20	91	15	+ 76
4	105	420	344	+ 76	69	13	+ 56
5	92	460	355	+105	40	11	+ 29
6	79	474	368	+106	14	13	+ 1
7	66	462	383	+ 79	− 12	15	− 27
8	53	424	423	+ 1	− 38	40	− 78
9	42	378	507	−129	− 46	84	−130
10	31	310	710	−400	− 68	203	−271

The similarity of this approach to the flexible break-even analysis should be obvious. The *TR* line is similar to the curved total revenue curve we saw there. The total cost curve, however, is curving and more accurately reflects the nature of fixed and variable costs. It is clear that beyond a quantity of six, the total profit curve declines; the marketing manager would not be interested in selling more than this number. This is *not* apparent with a simple break-even analysis. In fact, as already noted, simple break-even analysis often suggests that profits will grow and grow beyond the break-even point!

Pricing using marginal curves. Now we can apply the rule we developed earlier for maximizing profit using marginal curves. The same best quantity and price are obtained, as is shown in Figure 26–3 based on the data for marginal revenue and marginal cost in Table 26–2.

In Figure 26–4, the intersection of the marginal cost and marginal revenue curves occurs at a quantity of six. This is the most profitable quantity. But the best price must be obtained by going up to the demand curve. It is *not* at the *MR–MC* intersection. Again, the best price is $79.

The graphic interpretation is supported by the data in Table 26–2. At a quantity of six, marginal revenue equals $14 and marginal cost is $13. There is a marginal profit of $1, and this suggests that it might be profitable to offer seven rather than six units. This is not the case, however. The marginal cost of the seventh unit is $15 while its mar-

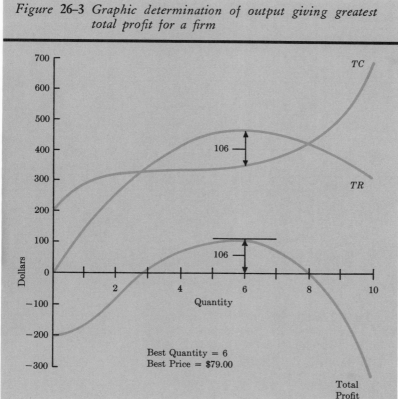

Figure 26–3 *Graphic determination of output giving greatest total profit for a firm*

Best Quantity = 6
Best Price = $79.00

ginal revenue is actually negative. Offering to sell seven units (instead of only six) will reduce profit by $27.

It is important to realize that marginal revenue can actually become negative. This simply means that the *total* revenue curve is declining, as shown in Figure 26–3.

It also is important to realize that *total* profit is *not* near zero when *MR* equals *MC*. *Marginal profit* (the extra profit on the last unit) is near zero, but that is exactly why the quantity obtained at the *MR–MC* intersection is the most profitable. Marginal analysis indicates that the firm should continue producing and selling units as long as the last unit yields any *extra* profit.

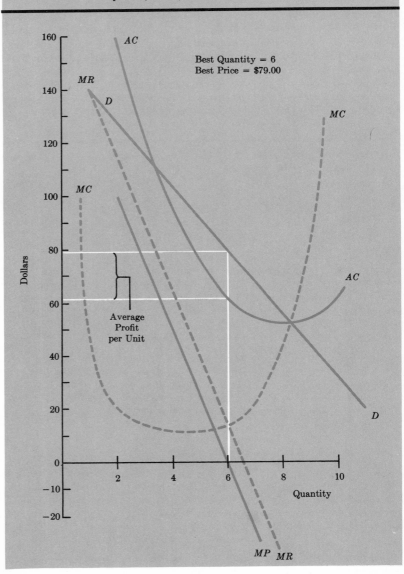

Figure 26–4 *Alternate determination of most profitable output and price for a firm*

Best Quantity = 6
Best Price = $79.00

How to lose less, if you must

This approach to determining the most profitable output also will determine that output which will be least unprofitable when market conditions are so poor that the firm must operate at a loss.

If sales are slow, the marketing manager may even have to consider suspending operation. When making this decision, he should ignore fixed costs, since these will continue whether or not production is maintained. Some fixed costs may even involve items that are so "sunk" in the business that they cannot be sold for anything near the cost shown on the company's records. The special-purpose buildings and machines of an unsuccessful company might be next to worthless to anyone else.

Marginal costs are another matter. If the firm cannot recover marginal costs, it should suspend operations temporarily or go out of business. The only exceptions are mitigating social or humanitarian considerations, or the fact that the marginal costs of closing temporarily are high and stronger demand is expected *soon*. But if marginal costs can be covered in the short run, even though fixed costs are not, the firm should remain in operation, at least until fixed facilities such as plant and machinery wear out. This will earn at least some contribution to fixed costs.

The marketing manager caught in a pure-competition situation also can apply the methods just discussed. He does not have a price decision, but he does have an output decision. The demand curve facing him is flat, and this means that the marginal revenue curve is also flat at the same level. He could equate that marginal revenue curve, therefore, with his own unique marginal cost curve to determine his most profitable (or least unprofitable) output level. A little experimentation will show that the marginal cost approach might lead to a different output decision than the average-cost approach. In general, a marginal approach is the most dependable if you are seeking to maximize profits or if it is necessary to minimize losses.

Getting the most in pure competition

We have been seeking the most profitable price and quantity, but in a dynamic world this is an elusive goal. Fortunately, this optimum is surrounded by a profitable range.

A profit range is reassuring

Note that in Figure 26–3 there are *two* break-even points rather than a single point, which was the case when we were discussing break-even analysis. The second break-even point falls farther out because total costs turn up and total revenue is turning down.

These two break-even points are important to note because they define the range of profitable operations. Although we are seeking to find the point of maximum profit, we know that this point is an ideal goal rather than a realistic possibility. What is essential is that the marketing manager knows there is a range of profit that includes an optimum. This should provide greater assurance that pursuing the optimum is a wise policy.

How some businessmen see demand curves

For the firm interested in profits, demand-oriented pricing obviously makes considerable sense. The use of marginal analysis provides a convenient technique for incorporating demand into a profit-oriented pricing procedure. Yet relatively few firms use this approach. Why? Demand estimation is not a simple task. A demand curve represents

549

the summation of a considerable number of variables, including potential customers' reactions to the firm's planned marketing mix. It is easy to imagine but harder to pin down.

Yet we do find businessmen setting prices as though they believe certain types of demand curves are present. And pricing research indicates they are. It is clear that some prestige, odd-even, psychological, and market segmentation pricing efforts do consider demand. Even some retailers appear to be involved—a fact that manufacturers working through them must recognize in their own pricing. In addition, as

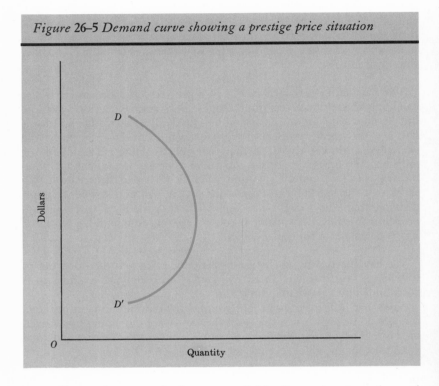

Figure 26–5 Demand curve showing a prestige price situation

we will see later, methods are available for estimating demand curves—and some firms are using them.

Prestige pricing— make it high and not too low

To some target customers, relatively high prices seem to mean high quality or high status. If prices are dropped a little bit, these customers may see a bargain. But if the prices begin to appear "cheap," they start worrying about quality and may stop buying.

Such target customers present the marketing manager with an unusual demand curve. Instead of a normal downslope, the curve slopes down for a while, and then bends back to the left again (see Figure 26–5). The marginal revenue curve for such a demand curve would drop sharply and show minus marginal revenues over most of the course.

550

Marketing managers dealing with this kind of demand—such as jewelry and fur retailers and nightclub owners—typically set high prices, sometimes called "prestige prices."

Some marketing men also feel that the notion of a smooth demand curve oversimplifies the case. They feel that consumers will react more favorably to prices ending in certain numbers, usually the odd numbers. Retail studies show that merchants *do use* certain prices more frequently than others.[5]

For merchandise selling under $50, prices ending with 95—such as

Odd-even pricing . . . it's $5.95, but watch the profits

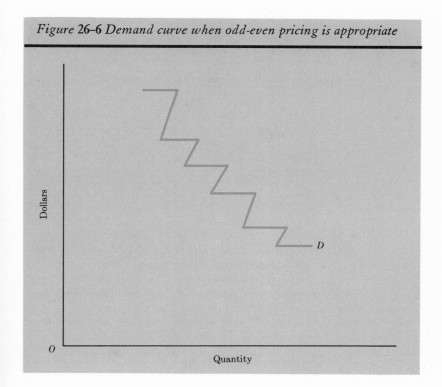

Figure 26–6 Demand curve when odd-even pricing is appropriate

Dollars

O

Quantity

D

$5.95, $6.95, and so on—are common. In general, prices ending in nine are most popular followed by prices ending in five and three.[6] For merchandise selling over $50, prices that are $1 or $2 below the even-dollar figure are the most popular.[7]

Marketing men using these prices seem to assume that they have a rather jagged demand curve; that consumers will buy less for a while as prices are lowered and then more as each "magic" price is approached. This kind of demand curve is shown in Figure 26–6.

---

[5] See Eli Ginsberg, "Customary Prices," *American Economic Review,* May, 1936, p. 296.
[6] Dik W. Twedt, "Does the '9 Fixation' in Retailing Really Promote Sales?" *Journal of Marketing,* October, 1965, pp. 54–55.
[7] H. J. Rudolph, "Pricing for Today's Market," *Printers' Ink,* May 29, 1954, pp. 22–24.

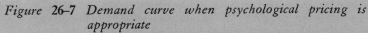

Figure 26-7 Demand curve when psychological pricing is appropriate

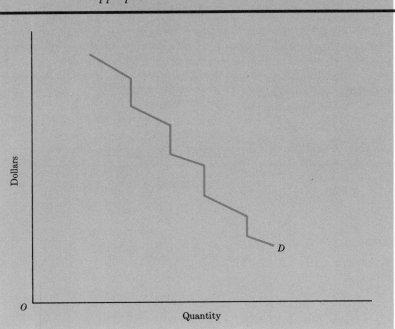

It is debatable whether these odd prices are effective. They apparently were adopted by some retailers to force their clerks to make change. Then they would have to record the sale, and could not pocket the money. Today, however, it is not always clear why these odd prices are used and whether they are effective. Perhaps consumers have been "trained" to expect more favorable offers at certain prices and they do work. Or perhaps it is done simply because "everyone else does it"; if so, it may lead to rigidities in the price structure that actually may reduce profits.

Psychological pricing—some prices just seem right

So-called psychological pricing has no real basis in psychological research. Some businessmen simply feel that certain prices for certain products are psychologically appealing. Between these prices are whole ranges where customers perceive prices as roughly equivalent. Price cuts in these ranges would not increase the quantity sold. Below such a range, customers would buy more for a while, and then the quantity demanded would not increase again.

The kind of demand curve that seems appropriate in this case is shown in Figure 26-7. Vertical drops mark the price ranges which customers see as equivalent. Some pricing research indicates that there do seem to be such demand curves.[8]

---

[8] E. R. Hawkins, "Price Policies and Theory," *Journal of Marketing,* January, 1954, p. 236.

Pricing neckties at various levels—say, $1.50, $2.50, $3.50, and $5—may be an attempt to price as nearly as possible to the top of such ranges. This conception of demand underlies the price-lining policy we will discuss more fully in the next chapter.

Throughout this text, we have discussed various approaches to segmenting markets. We have assumed that each such market had its own demand curve, and often this is the case, especially if distinctly different needs have been isolated. In other cases, however, businessmen seem to see a general demand curve for a product type and then develop slightly different qualities for different segments of the market. We

Some markets are segmented —class, mass, and fighting

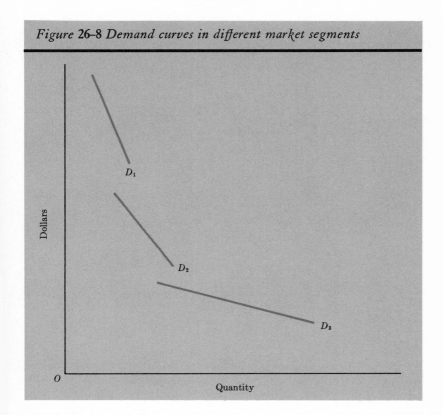

Figure 26–8 Demand curves in different market segments

D_1

D_2

D_3

Dollars

O

Quantity

already have noted that appliance and car manufacturers, for example, may develop a prestige product for the top of the market, a mass market product, and a "fighting" brand at lower prices.

The demand-oriented thinking behind such moves can be seen as an effort to segment a general demand curve into three distinct segments, as shown in Figure 26–8. Actually, the segments may not be so neatly separated; it may be possible, for instance, to "trade up" a customer from one segment to the other. But it does add clarity to our marketing strategy planning to think of each market as having different demand curves.

How to estimate demand curves

Businessmen obviously have some knowledge of the demand in their target markets and often seem to behave accordingly. Sometimes they may make only rough judgments, but even these may be better than nothing. As we saw earlier, even rough estimates of the elasticity of demand may be helpful in estimating the nature of the market situation and sometimes even the direction that price changes should take.

Ideally, we would like to have a quantitative estimate of the demand curve because this would enable us to use marginal analysis. Let's consider some of the ways we can derive demand curves.[9]

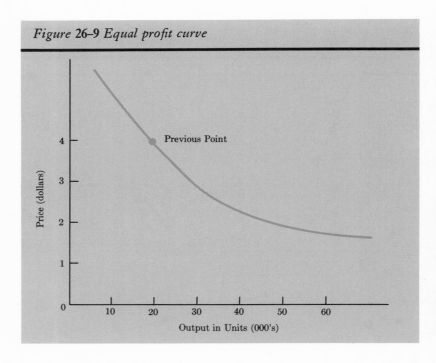

Figure 26–9 Equal profit curve

Demand analysis using equal profit curves

This easy-to-use approach is suitable only for products with which the marketing manager has had recent experience. Basically, he attempts to determine whether demand has changed enough since the last period so that a new price would lead to a greater profit. This approach seeks only to improve the profit position and not necessarily to maximize profits. In other words, if the marketing manager knows what quantity he sold recently (for example, last year) at a particular price and expects future conditions to be somewhat similar, he can think of that price and quantity as one point on his unknown demand curve. The question then is, should he use the same price again—or is there a more profitable price?

[9] For additional discussion, see Edward R. Hawkins, "Methods of Estimating Demand," *Journal of Marketing*, April, 1957, pp. 428–38.

First, the marketing manager must construct an equal profit curve showing the various prices which could be charged and the quantities which would have to be sold to make the same profit he made during last period. Figure 26–9 shows an equal profit curve. It shows that the profit obtained last period, when 20,000 units were sold at $4 each, also could have been obtained if he had sold 30,000 units at $2.75, 50,000 units at $2, and so forth.

Given an equal profit curve, the marketing manager might ask others intimately familiar with the market whether they think the company can sell more than 20,000 units at $4 each. There might be similar questions about sales at less and more than $4, but still along the equal profit curve. In other words, could he sell more than 25,000 units at $3.50 and more than 17,000 units at $4.50? If mixed "Yes" and

Figure **26–10** *Equal profit curve and estimated demand curve*

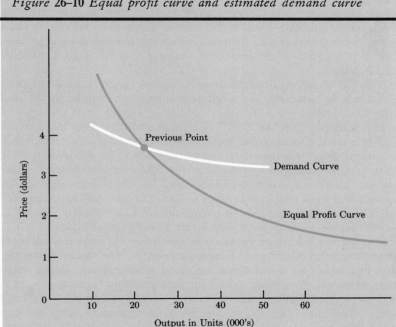

"No" answers are obtained to several such questions, the equal profit curve probably would be a reasonable approximation of the demand curve. This would mean that any price along this curve would be equally profitable, and there probably would be little reason to change the $4 price.

If, however, very emphatic "Yes" or "No" answers are obtained, the demand curve would be either above or below the equal profit curve. The course of action should be clear. For instance, if it appears that the demand curve would be somewhere above the equal profit curve at lower prices, then it might be desirable for the firm to drop its price to increase profit. Such a demand curve is illustrated in Figure 26–10.

How far prices should be lowered would depend in part on the strength of the pricing executive's feelings about the shape of the curve.

As noted earlier, this procedure does not assure profit maximization, but it is certainly better than ignoring demand. It brings management judgment regarding demand to bear on pricing decisions.[10] And price changes suggested by the analysis should increase profit and thus tend toward the maximum profit position.

Judging where demand curves go

It is possible to "guesstimate" where a demand curve is. The marketing manager (or other executives knowledgeable about the probable reaction of the market to price changes) can answer questions using their educated judgment. And these answers can lead to rough-and-ready, yet quantitative, demand estimates.

What is needed is a whole demand curve, not just the small portion above and below the current price level that we sought with the equal profit curve approach. Concern with small changes may be useful in fairly static situations, but it also can be misleading because it often gives the impression that demand is inelastic around current prices—probably because of the inertia of customers' psychological attitudes and habits.

When we are seeking the most profitable price, substantial price shifts may be necessary, and a different approach to estimating demand may be desirable.

Just a simple "Yes" or "No." This approach to estimating demand curves is similar to the equal profit curve approach. Managers are asked questions about whether they expect they would be able to sell more than certain quantities at specific prices. They are *not* asked to make specific numerical estimates. Only "Yes" or "No" responses are required. For most people, it is easier to say "Yes" or "No" to a suggested price than to conceive their own numbers.[11] Despite their interest in prices, people seem to have little exact knowledge of them.

The approach is to ask experienced executives: "Could you sell more than (a specific quantity) at (a specific price)?" The specific quantities and prices that are asked about are along a cost-per-unit asking curve that serves as a floor below which the firm probably would not want to sell anyway. By asking the executives several questions, eventually some "Yes" and "No" points are found in succession along the cost curve, and this suggests that the demand curve crosses this cost curve somewhere nearby. By connecting two such crossing points, it is possible to determine a workable approximation to the relevant demand curve. See Figure 26–11 where a straight line is used to connect the crossing points. More questions can be asked along this line to be sure it fits with management judgment.

---

[10] This analysis is developed in Wilford J. Eiteman's, *Price Discrimination in Oligopolistic and Monopolistic Situations* (Michigan Business Reports No. 33 [Ann Arbor: Bureau of Business Research, University of Michigan, 1960]).

[11] This approach is somewhat similar to Schlaifer's use of questions about different "bets" to extract subjective probability distributions from businessmen. See R. Schlaifer, *Probability and Statistics for Business Decisions* (New York: McGraw-Hill Book Co., 1959), chaps. i and ii; and for an example of the use of subjective probabilities in pricing strategy, see Paul E. Green, "Bayesian Decision Theory in Pricing Strategy," *Journal of Marketing,* January, 1963, pp. 5–14.

This subjective approach to quantifying management's feelings about demand appears to get the pricing executives within striking distance of the best price and quantity. It gives them a quantitative summarization of their attitudes—a demand curve—and if the price obtained through marginal analysis differs from their intuitive feel of the price they should charge, it may force them to recheck their thinking and subsequently to change their pricing decision.

In one case, for example, marginal analysis following the development of such a demand curve indicated that the producer's retail price should be 42 cents. The current price level was about 39 cents. At this

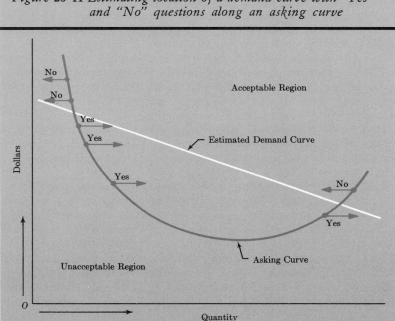

Figure **26-11** *Estimating location of a demand curve with "Yes" and "No" questions along an asking curve*

time, the producer was the industry price leader. He was seriously considering a price cut in reaction to price dealing and free goods given away by his competitors.

When marginal analysis indicated that he should raise his price rather than lower it, this industry leader decided to hold his general price level constant, while meeting the price cutting in extremely competitive areas. Further marginal analysis showed that selective price cuts in some areas would actually help cover overhead rather than lose money—as his accountants had figured! This led to the development of different strategies for different target markets.[12]

---

[12] For further discussion on this method, see "Determining a Subjective Demand Curve," in E. J. McCarthy, *Basic Marketing: A Managerial Approach* (rev. ed.; Homewood, Ill.: Richard D. Irwin, Inc., 1964), pp. 799–804.

Various methods discussed in Chapter 4 ("Gathering Marketing Information") can be used for estimating demand. Surveys, for example, can be used, but with care. Questions such as: "What would you pay if . . . ?" must be interpreted cautiously. But if survey results suggest little interest in price—perhaps because of strong brand loyalty or simple indifference—it may be reasonable to conclude that demand is inelastic. Then, perhaps, prices can be raised substantially.

Industrial goods buyers may be more aware of prices and the impact costs have on their firms' operations. Their answers about possible reactions to price changes may be quite meaningful.

Market tests also may be useful, either in trial areas or as general experiments. In recent years, many airlines have attempted to expand demand and reach new target markets by offering special reduced rates for no-reservation service, tourist flights, weekend flights, and special prices for couples, senior citizens, and young people willing to stand by at the airport for the first vacancy available.

Two classic cases of market tests are worth noting.

The long-play phonograph record industry long resisted price reductions. At last, one price cut was tried, and demand was found to be quite elastic. This brought about greatly increased sales and profits for all members of the industry.

Henry Ford's Model T was another famous experiment. He cut prices dramatically because he anticipated a much larger consumer demand, and in so doing, greatly expanded the automobile industry.

Historical data can be and has been subjected to statistical techniques to estimate demand. This approach is less valuable to us, however, because historical records are available only for essentially homogeneous commodities, such as farm, mine, and forest products, and these usually are sold in almost purely competitive markets anyway.

The real need for demand estimates is in markets where conditions are shifting and where products are continually changing. As seen in our discussion of product life cycles, changing conditions are inevitable. Analysis of historical data not only may be difficult but dangerous in these situations. Entirely different market situations may exist at different points in time, while statistical analysis of historical data must work with homogeneous data—and mechanical misuse of these methods may lead to invalid estimates. Statistical techniques are most useful for developing industry demand estimates for commodities, rather than the differentiated products with which we are most concerned in this text.[13]

Conclusion

Flexible break-even analysis and traditional supply and demand analysis provide analytical tools that enable a marketing manager to develop the *most profitable* price per unit. "Most profitable" is empha-

---

[13] For more details on estimating with this approach—basically a "least squares" approach—see Richard S. Watt, *A Method of Analyzing Demand for General Commodities, a Case Study of Salt* (U.S. Department of the Interior, Bureau of Mines, Information Circular 8057, 1962), p. 35.

sized because cost-oriented pricing often will yield a profit but *not* necessarily the maximum profit. Sometimes, in fact, even with a high unit price, cost-oriented pricing will result in losses.

Demand and supply analysis utilizes the concepts of marginal revenue and marginal cost in the determination of the *most profitable quantity to produce.* The most profitable quantity is found graphically at the intersection of the marginal revenue and marginal-cost curves. To determine the *most profitable price,* the pricing executive takes his most profitable quantity to the firm's demand curve to determine what price target customers will be willing to pay for this quantity.

The major difficulty in using marginal analysis is determining a demand curve. It is clear from observing the behavior of businessmen that they do have opinions about demand. This is reflected in prestige, odd-even, and psychological pricing.

Several ways of estimating demand were presented. The equal profit curve approach is useful when the marketing manager has had recent experience with the product and when market conditions are fairly stable. Using the previous price as a starting point, he tries to determine whether prices should be changed to increase profit.

Another approach uses "Yes" or "No" questions to estimate a complete demand curve. These questions should be asked of someone who is intimately familiar with the market and can predict probable reaction to the planned marketing mix. Market tests or other marketing research techniques also can be used to estimate demand.

Our discussion of price determination has been intentionally critical of cost-oriented approaches. Too many firms seem to ignore demand and depend almost blindly on cost-oriented pricing. This is often the case in firms where pricing is controlled by financial or accounting officers who have not yet accepted the importance of customers.

Deriving demand curves is not easy nor will estimated curves be perfectly accurate. Nevertheless, experienced executives—aided perhaps by marketing research—should make estimates of the nature of demand for their product. Such estimates, even if they are inexact, are useful, since prices are usually changed in discrete steps, and an absolutely accurate demand curve, therefore, is not necessary.

It is clear that the marketing manager should make use of the analytical tools at his disposal to estimate customer demand, because the firm's demand curve does not cease to exist simply because it is ignored. Some information is better than none at all.

Questions and problems

1 Explain the difference between a flexible break-even chart and a regular break-even chart. Relate flexible break-even analysis to demand and supply analysis.

2 Distinguish among marginal revenue, average revenue, and price.

3 Draw a graph showing a demand and cost situation where marginal analysis would correctly indicate that the firm should continue producing even though the profit and loss statement shows a loss.

4 How would a prestige pricing policy fit into a marketing mix? Would exclusive distribution be necessary?

5 Explain the basic difference between estimating demand using equal profit curves and subjective demand curves.

6 Discuss the idea of drawing separate demand curves for different market segments. It seems logical because each target market should have its own marketing mix. But won't this lead to a considerable number of demand curves and possibly prices? And what will this mean with respect to functional discounts and varying prices in the marketplace? Would this be legal? Would it be practical?

7 In June, 1959, *Life* magazine cut its newsstand price from 25 cents to 19 cents. The company expected that the circulation would increase from 6 million copies to 6.5 million copies by February, 1960. Assuming that *Life* obtains 50 percent of the retail selling price on retail copies (assume no subscription copies), was this price cut a wise move?

8 Evergreen Pea Company has been enjoying a profitable year. Their product sells to wholesalers for 20 cents a can. After careful study, it has been decided that a 60 percent gross margin should be maintained. Their manufacturing costs are divided in this manner: material, 50 percent of cost; labor, 40 percent of cost; and 10 percent of cost goes for overhead. Both material and labor costs experienced a 10 percent increase. Determine the new price per can based on their present pricing methods. Is it wise to hold fast to a 60 percent margin, if *a price increase* would mean lost customers? Answer using graphs and MC-MR analysis. Show a situation where it would be most profitable to (1) raise price, (2) leave price alone, (3) reduce price.

Pricing policies

Although pricing objectives can serve as a general guide to price determination, it is desirable to develop a set of pricing policies that spell out what the marketing manager will do in various pricing situations. These policies would state, in particular, how flexible his prices will be; at what level they will be set; how he will handle pricing during the course of the product life cycle; and what will be the relation of prices for a single product to those for whole product lines.

In competitive situations, it is vital to have specific pricing policies on these and other questions. Otherwise, the marketing manager must reexamine his strategy every time a customer asks for a price. This not only would be a drain on executive time, but customer goodwill easily could be lost if quoted prices did not seem to follow a logical pattern.

Positive price policies are fundamental in most sectors of our dynamic economy—even in areas where government or industry discourages active price competition. These policies lead to consciously set prices aimed at reaching the firm's pricing objectives. Rather than letting daily market forces determine their prices, most firms (including those in monopolistic competition) set their own prices, perhaps holding them steady for long periods of time (depending on competitive market forces). For this reason, most prices are called *administered prices*.

They don't leave prices to market forces

Administered prices usually are developed out of a set of pricing

561

policies involving a number of factors. These policies are the subject of the balance of this chapter.

Price flexibility policies

One of the first decisions the marketing manager must make is whether he will adopt a policy of one price or flexible prices.

One-price policy

A one-price policy consists of offering the *same price to all customers* who purchase goods under essentially the same conditions and in the same quantities. A majority of U.S. producers adopt a one-price policy, mainly for administrative convenience and to maintain goodwill among customers. Most food stores, department stores, and even the modern discount houses use a one-price policy, too.

A marketing manager could change his price every day and still be following a one-price policy, because the frequency of change is not involved here. Neither is the question of whether the price is at the right level. The policy simply means that the same price is offered to all customers at the same time.

Long-established prices, sometimes called *customary prices,* are extreme examples of a one-price policy. Some companies have consistently maintained a 5-cent price for candy bars and chewing gum. Sometimes the quantity or package size are changed as costs change, but a single price is maintained because the consumer has become used to it.

Although the retail price may not change, however, prices in the channel might. The producer might raise his price to middlemen because the degree of brand insistence for his product assures him that middlemen will *have* to carry it. Still, as long as the higher price is charged to everyone, the producer has a one-price policy.

A one-price policy may make pricing easier for the seller, but the marketing manager must be careful to avoid rigid adherence to a one-price policy. For such a policy could amount to broadcasting a price which his more aggressive competitors then could undercut—especially if his prices were somewhat high. One reason discount houses arose is that conventional retailers applied traditional margins and rigidly stuck to them.

Flexible-price policy

Under a flexible-price policy, the same products and quantities are offered to *different customers at different prices,* depending on their bargaining ability, family relationship, or other factors.[1]

Flexible pricing was most common when businesses were small, products were not standardized, and bargaining was traditional. These conditions still exist in most foreign countries. But in the United States, the one-price policy is more common, especially at the retail level, since it facilitates mass selling efforts.

Flexible pricing does have advantages, however. It allows a salesman to make adjustments for competitive conditions rather than refusing an

---

[1] For an interesting discussion of the many variations from a one-price system in retailing, see Stanley C. Hollander, "The 'One-Price' System—Fact or Fiction?" *Journal of Retailing,* Fall, 1955, pp. 127–44.

order. An aggressive salesman can first try to emphasize the quality of his product rather than its price. He may charge a higher price to those customers who will pay it and cut the price to those who will not. Some firms are willing to grant discounts or to make adjustments for "salesmen's errors" when competitive conditions require it or when highly elastic demand conditions exist in certain segments of the market grid.

Flexible prices also may enable a marketing manager to adjust more readily to the different jobs to be done in different channels of distribution or in different territories. In some places, his products may be well accepted; in others, he may have to "buy" distribution by offering lower prices.[2]

This use of lower prices can cause legal difficulties, however, because he may be attempting to reach different target markets with his flexible prices—but some middlemen customers may be competing with each other in the same markets. This might make his flexible prices illegal under the Robinson-Patman Act because this act prohibits charging different prices to *competing* buyers for the same goods under the same conditions, unless the prices are necessary to *meet competition*. In practice, this last clause *encourages* a considerable amount of price flexibility, at least for small companies.

A flexible pricing policy has other disadvantages, too. The customer who finds that others have obtained lower prices for what he feels is the same marketing mix is not going to be happy. The time used bargaining may increase, and the cost of selling may rise as buyers become aware that this may be profitable to them. Finally, some salesmen may let the practice of offering price cuts become a habit. This could eliminate price as a competitive tool and lead, instead, to a new and lower price level.

Price-level policies

When a marketing manager administers his prices—as most do—he must consciously make another policy decision: Will his prices be set below the market, at the same level as competition, or above the market? If the firm is in pure competition, of course, no policy is really necessary; to offer goods above or below the market price would be foolish. We will be concerned, therefore, with those less than purely competitive situations in which the marketing manager does have a choice.

Retail discounters and mass merchandisers of both soft and hard goods, and more recently of foods,[3] have consistently offered goods below the prices of conventional retailers. Even some conventional retailers use this approach. R. H. Macy & Co., in its main midtown Manhattan store *only,* has followed a policy of always selling below

Below the market—but below may not be below

---

[2] Martin R. Warshaw, "Pricing to Gain Wholesalers' Selling Support," *Journal of Marketing,* July, 1962, pp. 50–54.

[3] E. W. Cundiff and R. C. Anderson, "Competitive Food Pricing of Discounters," *Journal of Retailing,* Spring, 1963, pp. 15–17.

competitors' prices. It is obvious that this policy successfully appeals to some target markets—perhaps the economic shoppers.

Some manufacturers emphasize below-the-market prices in their marketing mix. This is most effective when the firm is not large in relation to the total industry, making competitive retaliation less likely. It helps, too, if the firm or product has a reputation for dependable quality which, at a lower price, makes for a good value.

The Elkhart (Indiana) Paint Co., a small industrial paint supplier, recently held its prices steady when its large competitors raised theirs. An Elkhart official observed that Elkhart paint customers charged fixed prices for their own products and "We feel they will appreciate our stand and favor us as their paint supplier so long as we continue to give them good products at a good price and good service."

A major example of a large company attempting to price under the market is the Dynacolor Corp., a major producer and processer of photographic films, which attempted to compete with Eastman Kodak in 8–mm and 35–mm color film by selling at lower prices. Dynacolor hoped to capture 35 percent of the color film market "before Eastman steps in with lowered film prices."[4]

One critical question here was whether potential customers would perceive that Dynacolor's price was lower. Another was whether customers really would consider Dynacolor film and processing identical to Kodak film and processing. Perhaps they would see the two physical product offerings as identical and appreciate the lower price. Or they would feel that Dynacolor's product was "almost as good," and "worth buying at the lower price." Actually, the company is not doing as well as it hoped, in part because it has not been able to get and hold distribution.

The important point here is that if some customers *do* perceive differences in the physical product, or in the whole marketing mix, then what we really are talking about are different marketing strategies, not different price levels. Seemingly lower prices are merely lower prices in different marketing mixes. This raises the question, are any prices truly below the market? Ultimately, this depends on the attitudes of the various target customers. The same price might be seen as below the market in some market grid boxes and merely "the price" in other boxes.

Meeting competition —sense for a few nuts

A firm with a unique marketing strategy might not have to worry much about meeting competition. It might even be difficult to define exactly what the competition is. Most firms, however, must set their prices within a range determined by the prices of nearly direct competitors and substitutes. They have some latitude in their pricing—but not complete freedom.

A meet-competition policy might be employed by a busy executive who did not wish to disturb the pricing status quo, either in his own company or among competitors. Prices are highly visible competitive

---

[4] *Business Week,* July 30, 1960, p. 33.

weapons and are more easily matched by competitors than any of the other marketing mix components.

In highly competitive markets, all firms must of necessity meet competition—the market price. Even the large oil companies, such as Standard Oil Co. of New Jersey and Standard Oil Co. of Indiana must meet competition. They may attempt to set price to get a target return on investment, but there are usually so many competitors, both large and small, that they are not able to rely strictly on cost-based pricing.

Smaller firms often will sell at anything above variable cost, especially when the market becomes flooded. Then the larger firms must meet competition whether they like it or not. As one Citgo official said: "We would not have this situation [price cuts] if a few nuts got some sense into their heads."[5]

Meeting competition in oligopoly situations. Meeting competition may be the only sensible policy—following either a target return or profit maximization objective—in *oligopoly* situations.

Oligopoly situations are special market situations which develop when a market has several basic characteristics. In oligopoly situations there are:

Essentially homogeneous products, such as basic industrial chemicals or gasoline.

Usually relatively few sellers, or a few large firms and perhaps many smaller ones who follow the lead of the large ones.

Usually fairly inelastic industry demand.

The marketing manager sees that cutting prices under such oligopolistic conditions may lead to ruinous competition, and raising prices may be pointless because there is no assurance that competitors will follow.

When demand goes kinky. The demand curve for each firm is particularly interesting in such a situation. Although the industry demand curve may be inelastic throughout the relevant range, the demand curve facing each individual oligopolistic competitor looks "kinked," as shown in Figure 27–1. The current market price is at the kink.

Each marketing manager must expect that raising his price above the market for such a homogeneous product would cause a substantial loss of sales; his demand curve would be relatively flat above the market price, since few, if any, competitors would follow his price increase. But if he lowers his price, he must expect competitors to follow. Given inelastic industry demand, his own demand curve would be inelastic at lower prices. Since lowering prices along such a curve is clearly an unprofitable move, he probably would not do so.

The dashed marginal revenue line in Figure 27–1 shows that marginal revenue drops precipitously at the kinked point. This means that if the supply curve crosses the *MR* curve any place along this drop, it would be sensible for the firm to hold its price at the kinked price level. Reducing price below the kink would actually reduce total revenue and profit.

---

[5] *Time,* October 6, 1961, p. 82.

Saving the great steel face. Most of the firms in an oligopoly situation are aware of the economics of the situation, at least intuitively. A price leader usually sets a price, perhaps to maximize profits or to get a certain target return on investment. Then, without any collusion, the other members of the industry follow his price, and it may be maintained for a long period or at least as long as all of the members of the industry continue making a reasonable profit.

The price leader might try to lead others to higher levels if basic industry conditions seem to warrant, perhaps if labor costs have increased. But this must be done carefully. The others may not follow, and the leader may have to retreat, perhaps losing face in the industry.

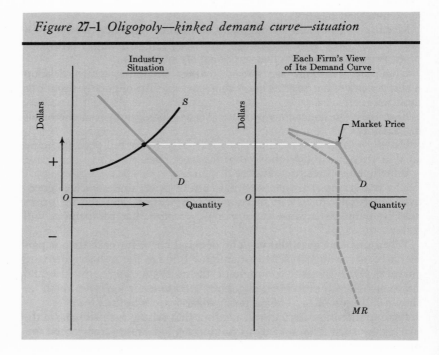

Figure 27–1 Oligopoly—kinked demand curve—situation

U.S. Steel's effort to raise prices in 1962 ran into both government and industry opposition. As an aftermath, the American Iron and Steel Institute set out to repair the damage to the industry's image, and some members openly expressed dissatisfaction with the leadership of U.S. Steel.[6]

Either you need sulfur or you don't—at our price. Price adjustments downward may be painful. If demand decreases considerably, as in a recession, or if large new supplies become available, then the industry may readjust its price by trial and error. Another firm may become the price leader or at least lead prices downward until an acceptable level is found. In some cases, if prices are cut too much, a dominant firm may resort to a price war to bring the others into line.

---

[6] "Steel Moves to Repair the Damage," *Business Week,* June 2, 1962, pp. 32–33.

The U.S. sulfur industry was long a classic oligopoly example. A few large sulfur producers maintained a similar price through good and bad times. They assumed that demand was inelastic and that the industry price didn't need to be lower. Although the price probably could have been higher, the industry apparently was following a target-return-on-investment objective.

Then a major new source of supply, Mexican sulfur, became available at lower prices. This upset the kinked-demand-curve situation and set off a round of price cuts. Some of the industry members deplored the price cutting and pointed to the inelastic demand situation. They said, "The price cut won't cause increased consumption. Either a person uses sulfur or he doesn't."[7] Yet prices stayed at a lower level, and profits decreased—as would be expected.

Usually oligopoly situations are fairly stable as long as all competitors' prices remain close to the leader's price, and competitors do not change market shares too much by other marketing tactics. But when the market is upset, as it was by the lower priced Mexican sulfur, the situation can degenerate into a price war.

More recently, demand has increased significantly in the world sulfur market and prices have moved up—all of the U.S. producers moving up at about the same time, as would be expected in an oligopoly situation.[8]

Oligopoly fairly common—often leads to price cutting. In recent years, we have seen price cutting and price wars among oligopolists in electrical equipment, aluminum, and synthetic fibers. Recently the price of polyester fibers, such as Du Pont's "Dacron," was cut 25 percent at one time. This was caused, in part, by production capacity that already exceeded demand and was scheduled for future expansion.[9]

The homogeneous products involved in such price cutting may be produced all over the world. Changes in one country or area may set off price changes elsewhere. This is a current problem in the chemical and steel industries, and it probably will continue.

Enough final consumers seem to think of gasoline as homogeneous to create oligopoly conditions in some areas where a few retail service stations share the business. Periodic gasoline price wars are common at the retail level. These usually start when some dealer-brand price discounter(s) successfully attracts "too much" business, perhaps by price cutting 1 cent a gallon below his usual price. The war proceeds for a time, until one of the dealers calls a meeting and suggests that they all "get a little sense." Sometimes these price wars will end immediately after such a meeting, with prices returning to a "reasonable and proper" level. Usually this is a level where all costs are covered and *some* profits are earned, although in the specific case of gasoline retailing, profits traditionally have not been too attractive.[10]

---

[7] "Sulphur Heads into Price War," *Business Week,* September 28, 1957, p. 50.

[8] "Unlocking a Rich Store of Sulphur," *Business Week,* April 22, 1967, pp. 60–66; and "Price Wrangle Approaches a Climax," *Business Week,* June 18, 1966, pp. 126–30.

[9] *Business Week,* June 24, 1967, p. 85.

[10] For further discussion on oligopolistic pricing, see Robert L. Knox, "Competitive Oligopolistic Pricing," *Journal of Marketing,* July, 1966, pp. 47–51.

Unless they are offering a better product or better service, marketing managers cannot consistently or for long charge prices that are above the market. Vigorous promotion may enable a firm to obtain a premium above essentially similar physical products, perhaps because of implied or stated product guarantees or the greater psychic satisfaction that customers receive because of the advertising. But here a new product has been created, and its price may *not* be above the market. Rather, a new price is set for a new marketing mix or even a new marketing strategy.

Even top management may not clearly understand the concept that a different price may be required, or at least be possible, for a different marketing mix or marketing strategy. Zenith Radio Corp. executives proudly claim that their prices start well above those of competing models and that one of the reasons for their outstanding success in recent years is that while other companies cut prices and skimped on quality, Zenith consistently maintained high quality. In marketing strategy terms, however, Zenith prices were not above the market, but rather were higher prices for higher quality. Some customers want quality more than they want low price, and Zenith benefited by satisfying these target markets.

Product life-cycle pricing

The life cycle of a product (discussed in Chapter 14) must be considered when developing pricing policies. You will recall that profits generally rise during the early stage of a product's life and then decline as competitive products enter the market. In the early stages, the firm is more likely to have a strong monopolistic competition situation, approaching monopoly; later in the product life cycle, its market situation may tend toward pure competition.

The price policy the firm adopts will significantly affect how fast the product moves through the cycle. The initial price may be especially important. A high price, for example, will tend to encourage competitors because they will see more opportunity for profit at the this price level.

The specific prices used will depend somewhat on the company's pricing objectives, but there are two extremes that should be considered in pricing a new product. Should the firm use a *skimming* or a *penetration* price? Both elasticity of demand in the target market(s) and competition will affect this decision.

A skimming policy is aimed at taking the "cream" of the market (the top of the demand curve) at a high price before catering to the more price-sensitive segments of the market. Skimming frequently is practiced to maximize profits on new products—particularly in the product introductory stage when demand is fairly inelastic, at least in the upper price ranges.

Skimming is useful for feeling out demand. It is easier to start with a high price that customers can refuse and then reduce it, than to start with a low price and then try to raise it. When the top of the market is insensitive to price and willing to pay what is asked—when the demand curve is inelastic—a skimming policy will produce more income in the early stages of the product life cycle. This provides funds for expansion into new markets and for repaying research and development costs quickly.

A skimming policy may lead to slowly reducing the price in a step-down or "cascading" process. This helps the marketing manager to get information about the shape of the demand curve that he can use in setting the best price for the mass market. The "step-down" technique, however, must be viewed as part of a dynamic process. As the prices are lowered, new target markets are sought. New place and promotion policies may be needed, too. In short, a skimming pricing policy may involve changing prices through a succession of marketing strategies during the course of the product life cycle.

A penetration policy is the opposite of a skimming policy. It may be used where there is no "elite" market. This means that the whole demand curve is fairly elastic, even in the early stages of the product life cycle.

Penetration pricing—get the business even at a loss

A penetration policy may be even more attractive if it appears that as volume expands, substantial economies of scale will reduce costs, or if the firm seriously expects strong competition *very soon* after introduction. Such a low penetration price may be called a "stay-out" price since it may be intended to discourage large competitors from entering the market.

A penetration price might slow down the speed of the product life cycle and enable the firm to hold the same price for a longer time. The firm might have to accept some losses in the early stages, however, while the product is gaining customer acceptance.[11]

Penetration prices also might be used to help build a market by popularizing a product. For example, some of the special promotional fares offered by airlines to special groups, such as families and the youth market, are designed to sell air travel as such and thus broaden the base of future travelers. For the present, however, these reduced fares often result in losses on this business.[12]

Product-line policies

Our emphasis has been, and will continue to be, on the problems of pricing a single item, mainly because this simplifies our discussion. But most marketing managers actually are responsible for more than one product. In fact, their "product" may be the whole company line. This

---

[11] Joel Dean, *How to Price a New Product* (Management Aids for Small Manufacturers, No. 62 [Washington, D.C.: Small Business Administration, April, 1955]), pp. 1 and 2; and "Pricing Policies For New Products," *Harvard Business Review*, November, 1950, pp. 45–53.

[12] "Long-Term Gain Can Produce Short-Term Loss, Eastern Finds," *Marketing Insights*, April 17, 1967, p. 7.

added complication does not invalidate our discussion, but points up again that handling the pricing variable is not a simple task.

Full-line pricing— costs are not much help

Many companies offer a complete line (or assortment) of products. All the products in the line may be aimed at the same target market or different products may be aimed at different target markets, with several market grid boxes being involved. Which of these two strategies is being followed makes a great deal of difference in pricing.

In the first case—say a TV manufacturer selling a whole line to retailers, or a forklift truck producer offering various sizes to large manufacturers, or a grocery retailer with his thousands of items—customers see the prices of the whole line, and the firm must consider their view of this full line of prices. In the second case, however—say a chemical manufacturer of a wide variety of organic compounds—customers in the different target markets may not see or consider the other items in the line, and each product should be priced separately. To do otherwise suggests a product- or cost-based production orientation rather than a customer orientation.

Costs are not much help to the marketing manager in full-line pricing. There is no single correct way to allocate a company's total fixed costs to each of the products. Many ways are used in practice, but all are arbitrary. And if such a method is carried through without regard to demand, it may lead to extremely unrealistic prices.

The marketing manager's job is to try to recover all the costs on the whole line, perhaps pricing quite low on competitive items and much higher on less competitive items. It is vital for the marketing manager to be able to judge demand for the whole line as well as demand for each individual product in each target market.

Markups make the image

A marketing manager usually attempts to price products in the line so that the prices will seem logically related and make sense to potential customers.

Most customers, especially industrial customers, feel that prices should be somewhat related to cost, and this must be considered in developing price lines. They usually realize that small production runs are likely to be more costly, and they may willingly pay higher prices for items which they know have a small market.

With these factors in mind, the marketing manager may accumulate directly variable costs on the many items in his line for the purpose of calculating a floor under which he won't price. To this, he will add a "reasonable" markup based on his assessment of the quality of the product, the strength of the demand for the product, and the degree of competition he faces. Then he must consider the image projected by the markups.

A few prices that are out of line with competitive products may project a high-price image which will carry over to other items in his line on which comparison is more difficult if not impossible. This should be avoided. The marketing manager would be better advised to deliberately price his competitive items low—not only to meet competition but also to help establish a low-price image for his entire line.

570

The marketing manager should be especially careful about price competition from the competitor with a shorter line who tries to offer "low" prices to offset his lack of a complete line. The full-line competitor's approach would be to meet such competition by lowering prices where necessary and raising prices on items facing less competition.

It is difficult for the marketing manager to judge just how important to customers is the completeness of a line of products. As a result, lines sometimes become long and cumbersome, the marketing manager wanting to have something for everyone. It is true that some target customers do value a wide assortment and prefer to deal with suppliers who can offer them what they want, but this can be expensive.

A sharper focus on smaller market grid boxes shows that sometimes shorter product lines are suitable *and* more profitable. Some companies have made great savings in costs and expanded profits rapidly when they began pruning product lines.

Price lining is similar to full-line pricing in that prices are developed for more than one product at a time. But here the focus is on prices at the retail level.

Price lining is an application of the psychological pricing discussed in Chapter 26. It is the policy of setting a few price levels for given classes or lines of merchandise and then marking all items at one of these established prices. There are no prices at the intermediate points. Exactly how does price lining work?

It would be reasonable to presume that most men will pay between $1.50 and $5 for a necktie. In price lining, there will *not* be many prices in this range; there will be only a few. Ties will *not* be priced at $1.50, $1.65, $1.70, $1.75, $1.95, $2.05, etc. They will be priced in perhaps four levels at $1.50, $2.50, $3.50 and $5.

The main advantage of pricing lining is that for both clerks and customers it lessens the confusion caused by a multiplicity of prices. Some customers may consider goods in only one price catetory. The major decision then becomes *which* item to choose at that price. Price no longer is a question unless the goods at that price are unsatisfactory. Then perhaps the salesclerk can trade the customer up to the next price level.

For the retailer, price lining has several advantages. Sales may increase because he can offer a larger assortment in each price line, and because it is easier to get customers to make decisions within one price line. Stock planning is simpler because demand is larger at the relatively few prices. Price lining also can reduce expenses because total stock requirements are lessened even though ample stocks are carried in each line. Price lining results in greater turnover rates, fewer markdowns, quicker sales, and simplified buying procedures.

Care must be taken with price lining for shopping goods. Most such items cover a wide price range, often making it difficult for a retailer to "trade up" the customer because each jump means a sizable increase. If the price lines for men's slacks are set at $10, $15, and $20, the customer who is considering a pair at $10 may not be willing to jump all the way to $15. But if more lines are available, say at $12.50 and $17.50, he might be moved up one line. When the jump is too great, the customer may look elsewhere, and the retailer may lose a sale.

Another potential price-lining difficulty is the adjustment of prices when costs are raised or lowered. Consider the retailer carrying two price lines, say $9.95 and $13.50, with costs of $5.89 and $8.00 respectively. A 10 percent wholesale price rise would be a problem for the retailer. His costs on the $9.95 retail line would rise to $6.48, but the $13.50 price would be too high to be competitive. Yet if he kept the goods at $9.95 retail, his gross profit would fall from $4.06 to $3.47.

One solution to this problem would be to establish a new price line. But as other price changes followed, this might confuse customers and even destroy the image of the store.

This problem often can be prevented in the first place by manufacturers who know their retail market. When manufacturing costs increase, instead of increasing their price, they reduce the size of the package or cheapen the product so that established prices can be maintained. In other words, these producers use demand-backward pricing.

Demand-backward pricing facilitates price lining. Demand-backward pricing is commonly used by producers of final consumer goods, especially shopping goods such as women's and children's clothing and shoes and other things like toys or gifts for which the customer will spend a specific amount because he is seeking "a two-dollar or five-dollar gift." Here, a sort of reverse cost-plus pricing process is used, inspired by the availability of demand at various price levels. It has been called "market-minus" pricing.

The producer starts with the retail price for a particular price line and then works backward, subtracting the typical margins which channel members expect. This gives him the approximate price he should charge. Then, he deducts from this price his typical or planned marketing expenses to estimate the allocation for the production cost of each item. What kind of a product he can offer at this price depends on the nature of his cost structure and the expected sales volume.

Obviously, demand estimates are necessary if demand-backed pricing is to be done effectively. Since competitors can be expected to make the best product possible, marginal analysis might be helpful to determine the optimum amount to be spent on manufacturing costs. By increasing marginal costs slightly, the product might be so improved in consumers' eyes that the firm would sell many more units. But if consumers are not quality conscious, but only seeking novelty, additional quality might not increase the quantity demanded and should not be offered.

Retailer still has pricing decision. Some retailers seem to feel that adopting price lines eliminates the need for pricing decisions. This is not true.

The retailer must first decide which price lines will best appeal to his customers. Then he must decide what quality of goods to buy for these price lines.

Theoretically, the more a retailer pays for an item to be sold in a particular price line, the greater the quantity he should sell. That is, the

572

better the value he offers his customers, the greater should be his turnover. The question is: How small a margin should he take to increase his turnover and profit? This is a profit-maximizing process requiring serious consideration of prices—both his own and competitors'—and costs.[13]

Promotional pricing policies

Trading stamps, as we have seen, are involved in both pricing and promotion. Now we will consider several other possible pricing policies that also have promotional value.

Multiple-unit pricing is primarily a consumer goods phenomenon. It is something like a quantity discount, designed to increase sales. Three units, a six-pack, or a case of any item may be offered at a lower price per unit. Multiple packs of soft drinks and other beverages are attractive to many customers, mainly because of their convenience but sometimes also because of a lower price. Not all multiple packs are sold at a unit discount, however.

Some customers—note the market grid concept again—seem to be impulsive quantity buyers. Multiple-unit offerings, even at *higher* prices, may actually sell better than cheaper single units. For example, when a manufacturer's brand of apricots regularly selling at 29 cents a can was offered at 3/89 cents, the stockturn rate improved rapidly.

Multiple-unit offerings may be merely "borrowing" sales from future periods, but in some cases they do seem to increase consumption, especially if the size of the pack fits with typical consumer usage patterns. Few families buy or use one soft drink at a time, for example, and a multiple-pack offer may actually increase sales of the product because availability at the point of consumption may encourage greater consumption—to "finish off" the carton.

Multiple-unit pricing— sell more, pay more, use more

Leader pricing is commonly used to get customers into retail stores. Certain products are picked for their promotional value and priced low. In food stores, the leader prices are the "specials" that are run and advertised regularly to communicate an image of low prices. Large stocks of these low-priced items are sold.

The leader-priced items are bona fide bargains priced very low for the sole purpose of getting customers into the store. Leader pricing usually is restricted to well-known, widely used, branded items on which customers will recognize a bona fide price cut. Ideally, the leader item should be chosen from items that are reasonably expensive, so that customers have something to gain, but not so expensive that they would have limited appeal. A 40 percent cut on a candy bar, from 5 cents to 3 cents, might not seem important enough to customers to bother with but, on the other hand, 40 per cent off a $15 or $18 Virginia ham might still yield a higher price than many customers would want to pay.

Leader pricing— boost sales but don't play football

[13] For a fuller discussion of product-line pricing, see A. R. Oxenfeldt, "Product Line Pricing," *Harvard Business Review,* July–August, 1966, pp. 137–44.

Leader pricing usually is restricted to goods that customers will not stock heavily—butter, coffee, cigarettes, and similar items. The intention is to attract customers, not sell large quantities of the leaders. And to avoid hurting the firm's own profits, it may be desirable to use items that are not directly competitive with major lines, as in the sale of bargain-priced cigarettes at a gasoline station.

Leader items usually are sold above cost but below the normal price level. For consumers, leader pricing is desirable because money that might have been spent on promotion is used to cut prices. For manufacturers, leader pricing may mean something else.

Some manufacturers are extremely unhappy when retailers choose their product as a price leader. They feel their product then becomes a "price football" that customers will only buy at a discount. They also fear that established channel relationships will suffer and that eventually the sales of their product will decrease. For well-known brands of established quality, however, their fear seems exaggerated, unless the low price should be maintained for a considerable length of time. Generally, it is not. The novelty and promotional value of a price cut is quickly lost, and most drugstores and grocery stores that regularly use leader pricing switch continually from one item to another. They want to attract business, not lower some manufacturer's price level.

Bait pricing— offer for a pittance, but sell under protest

Bait pricing, like leader pricing, is used to attract business. But unlike leader pricing, the seller *does not* plan to sell much merchandise at the low price.

This procedure is commonly used in the retail furniture trade. To attract customers, an extremely low price is offered on an item which the trade considers "nailed down." Then, once customers are in the store, the salesmen are expected to point out the disadvantages of the lower quality item and to switch customers to higher quality and more expensive products. Customers can buy the bait item, but only with great difficulty.

This policy attempts to attract "bargain hunters" or customers on the very low end of the demand curve and not normally part of the market. If bait pricing is successful, customers may be traded up, and the demand for higher quality products will expand. But extremely aggressive and sometimes deceptive bait-pricing advertising has brought this method into disrepute. The Federal Trade Commission considers bait pricing a deceptive act and has prohibited its use in interstate commerce. Still, some retailers, operating solely within one state, continue to advertise bait prices.

Introductory price dealing— okay, get in there and fight!

Outright price cuts do attract customers. Retailers or producers offering new products, therefore, often use *temporary* price cuts to speed their entry into a market. These temporary price cuts should be distinguished from low-penetration prices, however, because the intention is to raise prices as soon as the introductory offer is over.

Established competitors often choose not to meet this introductory price dealing, as long as the introductory period is not too long or too successful. But realizing that customers may shift their loyalties if they try competitors' products, some aggressive competitors do meet such introductory price cuts, perhaps with a price cut of their own or combination offers such as a "free" toothbrush with toothpaste at the regular toothpaste price.

Once price dealing gets started in a market, it may continue for some time—perhaps with "cents-off" offers—especially if the basic product type is late in the market growth stage or in the market maturity stage. Profits may be declining at the same time that newcomers are trying to enter the market with price deals. Some firms will associate the dealing with their declining profits and retaliate, thereby contributing to the vigorous competition which is typical as the life cycle moves on.

It is clear that when a marketing manager is setting pricing policies he must have a full appreciation for the product life-cycle concept, understanding how long it is likely to run and knowing where his products are in the cycle.[14]

Geographic pricing policies

Another major pricing policy that the marketing manager must set is who is to pay the freight or how it is to be split between buyer and seller.

In Chapter 24, we discussed the commonly accepted terms, such as F.O.B., that are used to specify these relationships. And in Chapter 19, we explained that an alert marketing manager or channel captain might maintain a traffic department to help suppliers and customers ship most economically, and thereby improve his own channel position. But choosing which terms to use and how to share transportation expenses requires more consideration.

Although quoting prices on an F.O.B. factory basis may simplify the seller's pricing problem, it may also cause another problem. Since the delivered cost of the goods will vary, depending on the buyer's location, this variation may limit the size of the seller's territory. A customer located farther from the seller must pay more for his goods. F.O.B. pricing also may limit a potential buyer's market, because he would have difficulty incorporating a higher cost product into his finished product and then shipping it back for sale near to the original seller's plant.

F.O.B pricing— the closer the cheaper

This is one reason why so many producers operate plants near their basic material suppliers. Heavy industry, which consumes large quantities of steel, a high-freight-cost item, is concentrated in Milwaukee, Chicago, Detroit, Cleveland, Pittsburgh, and Philadelphia, near to the biggest steel mills. A location close to his basic material suppliers enables a manufacturer of a final product to compete over a wider area.

---

[14] For more discussion on price dealing, see Charles L. Hinkle, "The Strategy of Price Deals," *Harvard Business Review,* July–August, 1965, pp. 75–85; H. J. Claycamp, "Dynamic Effects of Short Duration Price Differentials on Retail Gasoline Prices," *Journal of Marketing Research,* May, 1966, pp. 175–78; and W. F. Massy and R. E. Frank, "Short Terms Price and Dealing Effects in Selected Market Segments," *Journal of Marketing Research,* May, 1965, pp. 171–85.

Zone pricing is intended to reduce the variation in delivered prices and to simplify charging for transportation. Under zone pricing, an average freight charge is made to all buyers within certain geographical areas. The seller pays the actual freight charges and then bills the customer for an average charge. The United States might be divided into five zones, for example, and all buyers within each zone would pay the same freight charge. Buyers nearer to the factory really would be subsidizing those farther away, but if freight charges are not too high, it makes little difference to the buyers.

Zone pricing also may tend to stabilize prices within an area, since all buyers will pay the same basic price before quantity or other discounts. Such stabilized prices may be especially important when there is pricing rivalry between middlemen in adjacent geographic territories.

The zone approach often is used by manufacturers of hardware and food items, both to minimize the possibility of price competition in the channels and to simplify the computation of the transportation charges they must make to the thousands of wholesalers and retailers they serve.

Uniform delivered pricing—sometimes called "postage stamp pricing"—is simply an extension of zone pricing. An entire country may be considered one zone, and the average cost of delivery is included in the price. It is most often used when transportation costs are relatively low and the manufacturer wishes to sell his product in all geographic areas at one price, perhaps one which is nationally advertised.

Freight
absorption
pricing—
on equal
ground in
somebody
else's
territory

When all the firms in an industry use F.O.B. factory pricing, there is a tendency for a firm to do well near its plant or shipping point but not so well farther away. As salesmen solicit business at greater distances, delivered prices rise, and they find themselves priced out of the market.

This situation does not always benefit the consumer or business firms. Since competitors have difficulty competing in someone else's home market, the home-market seller is faced with less competition and may raise his own price. Without competition, the home-territory seller may also let quality slip.

Freight-absorption pricing enables manufacturers and wholesalers to compete in larger territories—which on the whole increases competition. When a marketing manager decides to penetrate a new territory, he generally absorbs freight cost so that his delivered price will meet the nearest competitor's. This amounts to cutting his price to appeal to new market grid segments.

Using freight absorption pricing, the only limit on the size of his marketing territory is the amount of freight cost the marketing manager is willing to absorb. These absorbed costs cut net return on each sale, but the new business may raise total profit.

Freight absorption pricing is commonly used when firms have high fixed costs and low variable costs. These conditions dictate that the company achieve good volume. Actually, a company could absorb freight costs until its net return was barely above variable cost and such business still would be desirable. On the matter of legality, absorbing freight costs for the purpose of reaching into more distant regions is not considered illegal unless the members of an industry arrive at a common method through conspiracy.

Basing-point pricing policies benefit a company uniquely by reducing or eliminating the need for freight absorption.

Basing-point pricing

To see how basing-point pricing might develop, assume that all plants in a new industry are located together and have the same production costs. Each producer might start out selling F.O.B. his plant. Delivered prices in distant markets would be considerably higher than near the home market, and these higher prices would encourage competitive plants to develop in outlying markets. When they did, what prices would be charged in these markets?

Single-basing-point system. This was precisely the situation during the early days of the steel industry. Steel offers the outstanding example of a single-basing-point system.

Originally steel was produced in the United States in the Pittsburgh area and sold F.O.B. Pittsburgh. As additional plants developed in Cleveland and Chicago, for instance, there was a question of what price to set. If the Chicago producer, for example, had identical production costs and set his price F.O.B. Chicago, then he might eliminate Pittsburgh sellers from the Chicago market and other markets where he had a freight advantage. Pittsburgh sellers could absorb freight cost, but this would reduce their profits.

To solve this problem, the steel industry leaders decided that all steel in the country would be sold, regardless of where it had been produced, *as if it had come from Pittsburgh*—the single basing point for prices.

The advantage to the Pittsburgh sellers was obvious, but why did the Chicago area sellers agree? The answer is simple: it was extremely profitable for them.

Their total sales might be reduced by Pittsburgh competition, but in return, the system permitted them to charge their Chicago customers freight from Pittsburgh. If the basic steel price were $50 a ton in either Pittsburgh or Chicago, and the transportation charge from Pittsburgh to Chicago were $10 a ton, then the Chicago producer collected a $10 "phantom freight" charge on all steel sold in the Chicago area. See Figure 27–2 for a pictorial view of how basing-point pricing works.

Basing-point pricing systems have been found in basic industries,—such as steel, cement, and building materials—that are characterized by oligopoly, high transportation costs relative to the goods' price, and high fixed costs relative to variable costs. In such situations, it is desirable to expand sales volume, yet inelastic demand has made this difficult. A basing-point plan was an industry reaction to a difficult market situation.

Basing-point pricing, however, was so obviously at variance with the consumer interest that the Federal Trade Commission, as early as 1921, took action against the U.S. Steel Corp. and other steel companies. As a result of this FTC action, the steel industry, beginning in 1924, shifted to a multiple-basing-point system which was not nearly as detrimental to the consumer. This system used several steel production centers as basing points. But since not all steel centers were considered basing points, some phantom freight still was being charged. The FTC opposed this multiple-basing-point system too, and finally, in 1945 and 1948, the U.S. Supreme Court ruled against *any* industry-wide system involving phantom freight.[15]

Multiple basing points. Something resembling basing-point pricing is still used in some industries. Now, however, all the major producing points usually are considered basing points. The practical result is that all the competitors set their prices to compete with the nearest producing point, absorbing whatever freight cost is necessary.

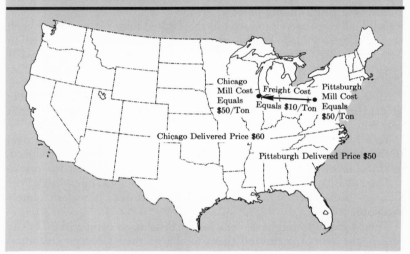

Figure 27-2 A single-basing-point system with Pittsburgh as the base gives Chicago producers $10 in phantom freight in the Chicago market

Under these conditions, alert purchasing agents are continually looking for new or closer producers. When they find one, they exert pressure on their suppliers to treat this new source as a basing point, too, and so there is little likelihood of phantom freight charges lasting for long.

Present legal status of geographical pricing

There are two points of view about what constitutes geographical price discrimination under the Robinson-Patman Act. According to one view, the delivered price should be the same to all buyers. According to the other, the factory price should be the same to all buyers.

The first view would permit a considerable amount of freight cost absorption to enable the seller to broaden his territory, perhaps allow-

---

[15] In cases against Corn Products Refining Co. and A. E. Staley Co. in 1945 and against the Cement Institute in 1948.

ing him to expand his factory and operate at a more efficient level—assuming that economies of scale are possible.

The second view, by contrast, insists on F.O.B. pricing even if this might encourage the development of monopoly areas around each firm's plant or plants.

The second view has long been favored by the FTC and is gaining acceptance in the courts. Currently, however, although basing-point systems involving phantom freight are illegal, freight absorption systems are legal as long as there are no agreements or conspiracies.[16]

Channel pricing policies

In our discussion of price determination, we have focused on the pricing decisions an individual marketing manager must make for his firm. We have largely neglected channel-oriented pricing decisions.

It should be clear by now that channels compete with channels, and that the prices set by competing channels should be competitive—or at least their marketing mixes should be competitive. If we view a channel as a unit, then all the analytical tools and policies discussed above could be applied to the channel as a unit. For example, if the channel sought to maximize profits, marginal analysis could be used.

The channel captain could use the demand curve facing the whole channel to derive the channel's marginal revenue curve. He could obtain the channel's cost by adding all the markups typically taken by channel members plus the basic production costs. Then, equating marginal revenue and marginal cost would enable him to derive the optimum quantity to move through the channel at the optimum list price.

Pricing hits the channel where it lives

This approach would maximize profits for the channel as a whole, but how would the profits be shared among the channel members?

The best present answer is that their traditional markups should include adequate profits. If markups are directly related to services performed, this approach should work.

The problem of setting prices within the channel is similar to determining costs as a product moves from one factory department or operating division to the next. There is no single "right" answer. Intrafirm pricing may be determined arbitrarily by an executive or committee; the whole issue may be avoided by transferring products at their direct or variable costs; or if there are comparable market prices, they may be used.

Pricing within a firm is a serious matter, sometimes leading to heated arguments. The profitability of the various departments may determine the bonuses or salary increases in those departments, and profitability *is* affected by how costs are allocated.

The same stresses apply to channels composed of independent mem-

---

[16] For a more extensive discussion of geographical pricing policies, see Jules Backman, *Price Practices and Price Policies* (New York: Ronald Press Co., 1953), pp. 174–208; and E. F. Pegrum, "The Present Status of Geographic Pricing," *Journal of Marketing*, April, 1951, p. 425.

bers. The way in which channel prices are determined directly affects the profits of each individual business! The channel captain may set prices or negotiate prices with various members, but this only underlines the fact that each situation must be resolved separately. The only rules flow from the supply and demand of the particular situation.

Be a strategist, be a salesman

It is the job of the channel captain to try to insure that everyone feels adequately rewarded. In the absence of a clearly superior way to allocate potential profits, it is easy to understand the middlemen's traditional attachment to the traditional markups and long-established channel arrangements, including trade discounts. The channel captain must try to lead them, remembering that they do have the option to quit (or not join) his channel. But if a channel captain develops a drastically new approach, it behooves all channel members to reassess how profits are shared—remembering that faster turnover, not just high markups, affects profitability.

A successful marketing manager and channel captain must be both strategist and salesman, able to develop good strategies and to sell them to his prospective colleagues in the channel system.

Conclusion

In this chapter, we have considered the many pricing policies that the marketing manager must set, guided by the framework of the company's overall objectives and specific pricing objectives. We have seen that the marketing manager must be concerned with decisions about price flexibility—Will the firm use one price or flexible prices? And price levels—Will they be below, at, or above the market?

Product life cycles move on and may require different pricing policies at different stages. For new products in particular, the marketing manager must decide whether he is going to "skim the cream of the market" or use a penetration policy to ward off competition and perhaps lengthen the life cycle.

Companies having more than one product must make a decision with respect to full-line pricing. Retailers see this in terms of price lining; producers catering to such retailers often use demand-backward pricing to facilitate price lining.

Direct price cuts obviously have promotional value, but other pricing policies have promotional impact, such as multiple-unit, leader, and bait pricing, and introductory dealing.

In all cases, a decision must be made about who will pay transportation charges and from what point. We discussed various possible geographical pricing policies and evaluated their present legal status.

Finally, we considered the problem of pricing within a channel system. Clearly, a channel can operate as a unit in competing with other channels, perhaps using marginal analysis if the objective of the channel is to maximize profits. Traditional margins may or may not be adequate—or prove workable. Enlightened self-interest among members in a system probably should guide negotiations on how jobs, costs,

580

and potential profits should be shared, remembering that the marketing mix of their channel system must compete with the mixes of other systems.

1 Distinguish between one-price and flexible-price policies. Which would be most appropriate for a supermarket? Why?
2 Cite a local example of an oligopoly. Discuss how stable price has been in this oligopoly.
3 Cite two examples of continuously selling above the market price. Describe the situations.
4 Explain the types of market situations which might lead to a "meeting competition" price policy.
5 Is a full-line pricing policy available only to producers? Cite local examples of full-line pricing. Why is full-line pricing important?
6 Distinguish between leader pricing and bait pricing. What do they have in common? How can their use affect a marketing mix?
7 What pricing objectives would a skimming pricing policy most likely be implementing? Could the same be true for a penetration pricing policy? Which policy would probably be most appropriate for each of the following products:
    a) A new type of home lawn-sprinkling system.
    b) A new low-cost meat substitute.
    c) A new type children's toy.
    d) A faster electronic computer.
8 What type of geographical pricing policy would seem most appropriate for the following products (specify any assumptions necessary to obtain a definite answer)?
    a) A chemical by-product (no fixed costs charged to it).
    b) Nationally advertised candy bars.
    c) Rebuilt auto parts.
    d) Tricycles.
9 Explain how the prohibition of freight absorption (that is, requiring F.O.B. factory pricing) might affect a producer with substantial economies of scale in production.
10 Specifically, what basic pricing decisions are required when a producer selling to middlemen is developing a price structure?
11 Identical items often can be purchased at lower cost out of a Sears, Roebuck catalog than from one of its own retail stores. The difference amounts to about 10 percent. How can this discrepancy in prices be explained? What price policy is being used?

The influence of legislation on pricing

We have covered price determination and pricing policies in previous chapters but have made only scattered references to their legality. Because of its importance, we must now consider in more detail the legal framework within which the marketing manager must make pricing decisions.

Get a feel for pricing legislation

From our general treatment of legislation in Chapter 3, you might get the impression that companies have little latitude in pricing or may even need government approval for their prices. There are restrictions, to be sure, but they are not nearly this limiting.

At the same time, price legislation is a complex field. There are seldom neat answers that apply wholly to all similar situations; you should not be discouraged by apparent ambiguities. Even legal authorities cannot assure their clients of clear-cut advice in all pricing matters. In part this is because several of the most important U.S. Supreme Court decisions concerning pricing have been almost evenly divided.[1]

Your primary concern should be getting a "feel" for pricing legislation and for the thinking of legislators and the courts. This will help you to anticipate and evaluate future rulings in an ever changing field. U.S. legislation is stressed so that we can be more specific, but other countries offer similar pricing constraints.

---

[1] W. David Robbins, "A Marketing Appraisal of the Robinson-Patman Act," *Journal of Marketing,* July, 1959, p. 15.

After a discussion of pricing legislation and its impact on pricing policy, we will review the pricing policies available to a marketing manager, considering these policies within the context of two basic approaches: (1) de-emphasizing price in the marketing mix, and (2) using price as an active variable.

How legislation affects pricing policy

The Unfair Trade Practice Acts which have been passed in more than half the states are designed to put a floor under prices, especially at the wholesale and retail levels. Wholesalers and retailers are normally required to take a certain minimum percentage markup over their merchandise-plus-transportation costs. The most common markup figures are 6 percent at retail and 2 percent at wholesale. The specific provisions of these state laws and the strictness of their enforcement will vary from state to state and from time to time.

Some control over minimum prices

If a specific wholesaler or retailer can show that his operating costs are lower than the minimum required figure, then he may be permitted to offer merchandise at lower prices. But he must prove conclusively that he does have lower costs, and this usually is quite difficult if any fixed costs are involved. As we have already seen, several kinds of costs—average cost, average variable cost, and marginal cost—might be used as a basis for pricing. The various state control boards normally require the use of average cost, allocating fixed cost over all the items handled or sold.

The practical effect of these laws is to protect some limited-line food retailers, such as dairy stores, from the kind of "ruinous" competition that full-line stores might offer if they chose to sell a dairy item as a leader at below cost for some time. For other than food lines, however, the 2 or 6 percent markup is so low that significant price reductions from normal levels could be made without approaching the floor.

Most of these laws were enacted during the 1930's, when the distressed economic conditions caused a considerable amount of variable-cost pricing. Unless we have another depression, it is unlikely that these laws will again become important. Even the most vigorous discounters know enough about their costs to seek larger markups than these minimums.

Price fixing is generally prohibited under the Sherman Act and more specifically under the Federal Trade Commission Act. There are special cases, however, in which collusion and price fixing are specifically permitted by law.

Permits some price fixing

"Fair trade" (or "resale price maintenance") laws permit price fixing by manufacturers *who choose to do so*. These state laws, for example, would permit a manufacturer to sue retailers for not adhering to the 79-cent retail price set by the maker for a tube of toothpaste.

Too much competition for small retailers. These price-fixing laws were a product, again, of the depression of the 1930's. The mass migration of low-income families into California made price cutting an

583

attractive sales stimulant. In an effort to control this sometimes drastic price cutting, California passed an act in 1931 to permit manufacturers or wholesalers to set retail prices for trademarked goods—the ones commonly discounted—by signing price-fixing contracts with their retailer customers.

This act was not particularly effective at first, since it did not bind nonsigners, but this was changed in 1933 with the passage of a "nonsigner's clause." This clause bound all retailers in the state if one retailer signed a price-fixing contract.

Wholesalers and retailers in other states, seeing the success of the California law, lobbied for such legislation, and eventually 45 states passed them. In fact, the legislators in seven states—Arizona, Iowa, Louisiana, New Jersey, New York, Pennsylvania, and Tennessee— were so responsive to this prodding that in their haste they incorporated in their legislation a stenographic error from the original California act that made one part of the original and all its imitators meaningless.[2]

Fair trade across state lines.   All of this legislation was alike in being limited to *intra*state trade. The question remained whether price-fixing agreements in *inter*state commerce were legal. In 1937, the Miller-Tydings Act was passed by the U.S. Congress, allowing manufacturers in interstate commerce to make such agreements in states which had fair-trade laws, without violating federal antitrust legislation. This was an enabling act, since it permitted such agreements only in states that already had such laws.

The Miller-Tydings Act, however, did not specifically contain a provision for the nonsigner's clause. In a court test of this loophole, precipitated by Schwegmann Brothers, a large supermarket chain in New Orleans, the U.S. Supreme Court ruled (1951) that the Miller-Tydings Act applied only to signers. This decision led to a rash of price cuts on fair-traded merchandise throughout the country. The following year, 1952, Congress passed the McGuire Act, which said in effect that Congress had intended the nonsigner's clause to be in the Miller-Tydings Act.

With the previous ambiguity cleared up, fair trade became effective again in those states having such laws. Schwegmann Brothers again violated the law as a test case and lost, and the Supreme Court refused to review a lower court's decision against the New Orleans firm. Fair traders have not had free sailing, however, since some states have repealed their laws. About half still have such legislation.

The tide moved against fair trade on a large scale when General Electric capitulated to the discounters in 1958. General Electric had staunchly adhered to fair trade on small appliances, even though aggressive discounters in New York and other markets made this extremely difficult. Finally, when Masters, Inc., of New York, a discounter, won a court fight with General Electric over the right to sell by mail in fair-traded New York from nonfair-traded Washington, D.C., General Electric gave up. A wave of price cutting began on GE

---

[2] Jules Backman, *Price Practices and Price Policies* (New York: Ronald Press Co., 1953), p. 420.

appliances—and other appliance manufacturers gave up on fair trade, too.[3]

Fair trade supporters continue to offer fair trade bills in various state legislatures, but in recent years they have not had much success.

A new approach for accomplishing roughly the same objective as fair trade is known as "quality stabilization." Proponents of quality stabilization legislation allegedly are trying to insure that consumers are offered quality products—*at fixed prices*. So far, these efforts have not succeeded, but it is likely that supporters will continue to press for a federal law permitting price fixing rather than relying on the Miller-Tydings Act, which only permits price fixing where individual states take action.

Fair trade may be a useful managerial tool. Fair trade has been used effectively for well-differentiated products with relatively inelastic demands and with manufacturing costs that represent a small percentage of the price. Drug and cosmetics products are examples.

For drug items such as aspirin, there is relatively little relationship between production cost and retail price. Yet significant price reductions would create little expansion in demand and would therefore decrease total revenue.

Retail druggists have found fair trade an effective managerial device to maximize profits on inelastic demand curves—the very thing that some large companies are discouraged from doing by the current legal and political environment. Druggists, however, have been able to keep their fair-trade prices. Why?

One reason is that they have been able to maintain their position legally, in part because they are numerous and have considerable influence in state legislatures. Another factor is that consumers have not been too concerned because each fair-traded item represents only a relatively small part of their total expenditure.[4]

Advocates of fair trade sometimes argue that such laws are in the consumer interest because, so they say, (1) without fair trade, small retailers would go out of business, and consumers would not have the convenience of nearby stores, (2) consumers would be further penalized without fair trade because price cutters would have to make up for lost margins by raising prices on other items, and (3) consumers might be inconvenienced when seeking items that discounters have used as price leaders—because some small retailers drop the items.

To the retailer and wholesaler who is fair-trade minded, these laws make sense because they help assure a "fair" percentage of the price to cover their costs. They feel they are entitled to this percentage and if they do not get it, they will not choose to be a member of the channel team.

To the manufacturer, fair trade sometimes makes sense because discounters frequently will provide a place for a product and emphasize

[3] "Bargain Hunters Have a Heyday as G.E. Gives Up on 'Fair Trade,'" *Business Week,* March 18, 1958, pp. 26–28.

[4] For a comprehensive examination of the history and effects of resale price fixing, see E. T. Grether, *Price Control under Fair Trade Legislation* (New York: Oxford University Press, Inc., 1939); also E. R. Corey, "Fair Trade Pricing: A Reappraisal," *Harvard Business Review,* September–October, 1952, pp. 47–62.

price but ignore promotion. They will use only three of the four P's, skimming the cream by dealing only with customers who are presold or easily sold, and ignoring the balance of the market.[5]

But may not make economic sense. Although fair trade has some attractive features, 90 to 95 percent of all retail goods never were fair traded because manufacturers, wholesalers, and some retailers realized that such activity would merely provide a price umbrella and that short-run profits would encourage the entry of more retailers and manufacturers.

From the consumer viewpoint, there probably is little justification for fair trade. Its main purpose is to stabilize or increase the price level. The exact effect has been subject to considerable controversy, but "most disinterested consumers seem to believe that Fair Trade has tended to narrow the range and raise the average level of prices."[6]

One analyst has concluded that the breakdown of fair trade results more from economic factors than legal setbacks.[7] If the retailer's task costs only 15 to 20 percent of the retail price, then trade discounts larger than this will encourage price cuts by discounters. Many so-called ethical or legitimate sellers have not recognized changing conditions in retailing. They are still geared to give their normal service in return for relatively high 30 to 40 percent margins—even though manufacturers no longer require nor do consumers really want such a selling job.

Another factor contributing to the decline of fair trade is that legislation is normally permissive rather than mandatory. A manufacturer does not have to use fair-trade pricing, but if he chooses to, then the burden of policing is upon him. Yet effective policing can be expensive. It involves court cases, and often there is difficulty in securing prompt injunctions against discounters. And the relatively small penalties awarded to the producer together with the ill will generated among channel members concerned in the dispute may overbalance the benefits of fair-trade pricing.

On balance, it is easy to see why a relatively small share of consumer goods have been fair traded and why fair trading has declined in importance. Modern marketing men are finding much more imaginative and more positive approaches to improving the effectiveness of their marketing mixes. Now, they are adopting offensive rather than defensive tactics. Instead of trying to block competitive activity, they

---

[5] For further discussion see Louis W. Stern, "Economic Factors Influencing Manufacturers' Decisions Concerning Price Maintenance," *Journal of Retailing,* Spring, 1965, pp. 30–37, 55.

[6] Stanley C. Hollander, *Retail Price Policies* (East Lansing: Bureau of Business and Economic Research, Michigan State University, 1958), p. 5; also, M. Frankel, "The Effects of Fair Trade: Fact and Fiction in the Statistical Findings," *Journal of Business,* July, 1955, pp. 182–94; S. M. Lee, "The Impact of Fair Trade Laws on Retailing," *Journal of Retailing,* Spring, 1965, pp. 1–6; and Charles J. Stewart, "Mandatory Resale Price Maintenance of Distilled Spirits in California," *Journal of Marketing,* April, 1954, p. 370.

[7] Stanley C. Hollander, "Is Fair Trade Finished?" *Challenge,* June–July, 1958, pp. 48–52; see also, S. C. Hollander's discussion of the U.S. Fair Trade movement in B. S. Yamey, *Resale Price Maintenance* (Chicago: Aldine Publishing Co., 1966), pp. 65–100. The experience in other countries is also discussed in this text.

are initiating new systems and making their present systems more effective.

The legislative concern about price discrimination culminating in the Robinson-Patman Act of 1936 was discussed in Chapter 3. You will recall that the Robinson-Patman Act makes unlawful, in interstate commerce, any price discrimination between different purchasers of "commodities of like grade and quality" which may *tend to injure competition*. This law does permit some price differentials, but they must be based on cost differences or the need to "meet competition." Both buyers and sellers are liable to prosecution if they knowingly enter into discriminatory arrangements.

Prohibits price discrimination unless . . .

How many Robinson-Patman Acts are there? The major difficulty with this potentially powerful law is that it is confusing, to say the least. As the U.S. Supreme Court observed, "Precision of expression is not an outstanding characteristic of the Robinson-Patman Act."[8] While one chairman of the FTC felt that "its substance is both sound and clear," a respected legal authority called it "an extremely poorly drafted statute."[9]

Although the wording of the original act has not changed, W. David Robbins feels that because of changing interpretations of the courts and the Federal Trade Commission, there have been, in effect, three different Robinson-Patman Acts.

The first "act" was applied during the period of limited enforcement from 1936 until the middle of the 1940's. In the middle and late 1940's, there was another "act" marked by enforcement ranging from strict to radical. Practically all price differentials were illegal during this period. During the 1950's, the courts and the Commission became more temperate in their interpretation of the act, reverting back to "injury to competition" as opposed to "injury to competitors."[10]

A later analyst felt Robbins was being too optimistic in his depiction of increasing clarity and temperance of Robinson-Patman enforcement.[11] Currently the Robinson-Patman situation is still not absolutely clear.[12]

It is clear that the FTC is concerned with protecting competitors. As one FTC official sees it, "The primary thrust [of the act] was protection of businessmen, one from the other." Yet the same official admits that the FTC has not always been clear about what this means and how it is to be accomplished.[13]

Lack of criteria for investigation certainly is obvious. As Lowell

---

[8] 346 U.S. 6173 Supreme Court 1017.

[9] "Robinson-Patman Act: It Demands a Close Look Now," *Printers' Ink*, October 20, 1961, pp. 22–27.

[10] Robbins, *op. cit.*, p. 15.

[11] Brian Dixon, *Price Discrimination in Marketing Management* (Michigan Business Studies, Vol. 15, No. 1 [Ann Arbor: University of Michigan, 1960]), pp. 98–99.

[12] See Charles C. Slater and Frank H. Mossman, "Positive Robinson-Patman Pricing," *Journal of Marketing*, April, 1967, pp. 8–14.

[13] Daniel J. Murphy, "The Federal Trade Commission of the 1960's," *Journal of Marketing*, April, 1963, pp. 1–2.

Mason, a former FTC commissioner says, "Nowhere is institutional whim more apparent and more deadly than in the choice of defendants the FTC sues under the Robinson-Patman Act."[14]

Unfortunately for businessmen, the FTC is responsible not only for investigation but for enforcement. It is not only investigator and prosecutor, but judge. The FTC's rulings, however, can be and often are, appealed to the federal courts and finally the U.S. Supreme Court. Litigation is often extensive, with one court reversing the other, sometimes on close votes.

What does "like grade and quality" mean? The Robinson-Patman Act permits a marketing manager to use price differentials if the products are not of "like grade and quality."

It might seem that many price differentials for products could be justified by offering a different "something," even if the same physical product were involved. If customers feel this "something" makes a difference and are willing to pay for it, then there is a difference.

This view, however, is not acceptable to the FTC, which is concerned primarily with the physical characteristics of products.

The FTC view was upheld in a 1966 U.S. Supreme Court ruling against the Borden Co. The court held that a well-known label *alone* does not make a product different from one with an unknown label. The issue was rather clear-cut in the Borden case because the company acknowledged that the canned milk it sold at different prices under different labels was essentially the same.

Although the Supreme Court agreed with the FTC in the Borden case with respect to "like grade and quality," it sent the case back to a U.S. Court of Appeals to determine whether the price difference injured competition. In 1967 this court found no evidence of injury and further noted that there could be no injury unless Borden's price differential exceeded the "recognized consumer appeal of the Borden label." How "consumer appeal" is to be measured was not spelled out and may lead to further litigation.[15]

Eventually, what the consumer thinks about the product may be determining. For now, however, it would appear safer for producers wishing to sell several brands or dealer brands at lower prices than their main brand to offer actual and genuine physical differences. It appears further that it would be advisable to make differences that are genuinely useful to various buyers, not merely decorative or trivial. Another possibility for differentiation that has won some support in the courts is packaging differences.[16]

---

[14] "Robinson-Patman Act: It Demands a Closer Look Now," *Printers' Ink,* October 20, 1961, p. 24. For a more extensive discussion, see Robert C. Brooks, Jr., "Businessmen's Concepts of 'Injury to Competition'," *California Management Review,* Summer, 1961, pp. 89–101; Lawrence X. Tarpey, "What About the Good-Faith Defense?" *Journal of Marketing,* July, 1960, pp. 62–65; "Indirect Price Discrimination and Robinson-Patman," *Journal of Marketing,* January, 1963, pp. 68–71; and Earl W. Kintner, "Avoiding Price Discrimination," *Business Topics,* Winter, 1962, pp. 18–28.

[15] Jacky Knopp, Jr., "What Are 'Commodities of Like Grade and Quality'?" *Journal of Marketing,* July, 1963, p. 63; and Frederick D. Buggie, "Lawful Discrimination in Marketing," *Journal of Marketing,* April, 1962, p. 1; "Price Differentials on Brands Upheld," *Business Week,* July 29, 1967.

[16] T. F. Schutte, V. J. Cook, Jr., and R. Hemsley, "What Management Can Learn from the Borden Case," *Business Horizons,* Winter, 1966, pp. 23–30.

Can cost analysis justify price differentials? Justifying cost differentials is a difficult task, since fixed costs usually must be allocated to several products, perhaps arbitrarily. It is easy, however, to raise objections to whatever allocation method is used. The Federal Trade Commission successfully won a quantity discount case against the Morton Salt Co. for this reason. Morton had to change its quantity discount schedule, partly because it was not able to justify its case on the basis of cost, but probably more because of the possible injurious effect on competitors.[17]

At the very least, it appears that costs should be segregated to show the cost of servicing different homogeneous target markets. This is difficult and expensive, and the courts may decide that the group is not homogeneous enough. In the extreme, each outlet of each customer might have to be treated separately, and the cost of doing all this might be more expensive than it would be worth.[18]

Even when cost differentials can be shown, quantity discounts may be allowed only to a certain extent. The FTC has sought to control the size of quantity discounts on the grounds that big discounts, although justified on a cost basis, may be unfair to small competitors.

The FTC ruled against Thompson Products, Inc., for selling certain replacement parts to the Big Three automobile makers—for their own use and resale to car dealers—at prices lower than Thompson's own distributors were being charged. Thompson argued, unsuccessfully, that it was able to produce the large orders in special production runs and ship without warehousing.[19]

How do you legally meet competition? "Meeting competition" is permitted as a defense in price-discrimination situations under the Robinson-Patman Act, although the FTC normally has taken a rather dim view of this tactic.

In a significant 5–4 decision in 1956, the U.S. Supreme Court said that "meeting competition" in "good faith" is a permissible defense if it can be shown that the price discrimination occurred as a *defensive* rather than an offensive action. The dissenting justices saw the implications and suggested that this ruling "crippled the enforcement of the act." They added that if price cutting should begin generally, the majority decision could permit a considerable amount of price cutting—*perhaps to the detriment of less efficient outlets.*[20]

More recently, a new and potentially confusing twist has been added by another Supreme Court decision. In 1967, the Court ruled in favor of the Utah Pie Co., a small company that had entered an established market with a low-price appeal. This company's success led to a downward spiral of prices, including sales below cost by the larger national companies. The Court ruled, 6 to 2, that regional price cutting

---

[17] Peter G. Peterson, "Quantity Discounts in the Morton Salt Case," *Journal of Business of the University of Chicago,* April, 1952, pp. 109–20.

[18] Robert A. Lynn, *Price Policies and Marketing Management* (Homewood, Ill.: Richard D. Irwin, Inc., 1967), pp. 262–264; and "Is the Cost Defense Workable," *Journal of Marketing,* January, 1965, pp. 37–42.

[19] *Business Week,* April 26, 1958, p. 57.

[20] *Business Week,* February 1, 1958, p. 53.

by a national manufacturer is illegal where it involves "persistent sales below cost." In this judgment, the cost considerations seemed to take precedence over the defensive meeting of competitive prices.[21]

This decision could have important implications for national distributors, perhaps encouraging regional specialists. As the two dissenting justices noted, in this case the smaller firm did not lose money, and the market share it won by price cutting declined from 66 percent to 45 percent only because it was challenged by lower prices. Yet the defensive price cutters—the big national firms—who felt they were "meeting competition" in "good faith" were found guilty!

Are functional discounts discriminatory? Can functional discounts be considered price discrimination? Legislation is not completely clear on this, but court decisions seem to have settled the matter with emphasis on functions provided.[22] At the root of this matter is the distinction between wholesalers and retailers, since wholesalers are entitled to certain discounts from producers.

Generally, the courts have felt that the identification of a firm as a wholesaler or a retailer depends not on the quantity he buys or handles but on the nature of the service he provides. A producer could legally refuse to give a wholesale discount to a large retail grocery chain, although the chain might handle a much larger volume than some small wholesalers. The justification is that functional discounts are imperative for the small wholesaler if he is to cover his costs and still sell to retailers at prices low enough to permit the retailers to be competitive.

A chain probably would not have to pay the same price offered a small retailer, however. A special functional discount could be set up for chain stores. As long as a functional discount seems to reflect the nature of the job required in the channel, the courts probably would consider it legal.

Special allowances may not be allowed. Some firms have violated the Robinson-Patman Act by providing PM's (push money), demonstrators, advertising allowances, or other promotional aids to certain customers and not others. The act specifically prohibits such special allowances unless they are made available to all customers on "proportionately equal" terms. No proof of injury to competition is necessary, and the FTC has been fairly successful in prosecuting such cases.

The need for such a rule is clear, once price regulation begins. Allowances for promotional aid could be granted to retailers or wholesalers without expectation that any promotion would actually be undertaken. This plainly would be price discrimination in disguise.

The provision does work hardships, since it sometimes is difficult to provide allowances on "proportionately equal" terms to both large and small customers. The Robinson-Patman Act does not state clearly whether a small store should be allowed the same dollar advertising

---

[21] "Court Raps Price Cuts," *Business Week*, April 29, 1967, p. 50; and *Journal of Marketing*, October, 1967, p. 74.

[22] *FTC* v. *The Mennen Company*, and *National Biscuit Company* v. *FTC*.

allowance as a large one or an allowance in proportion to sales. The latter probably would not buy the same promotional impact.

"Equal price" equals no wrath. In general, the FTC seems more concerned about the protection of small competitors, regardless of cost to consumers or variations in total marketing mixes. The Commission is following what has been called the "equal price theory"—that all competitors should obtain equal prices. This tends to guarantee that small middlemen will have a place in the channel even though larger firms might be served at lower cost.

An alternate approach, called the "equal profit theory," would require price differentials to reflect cost differences—to avoid price discrimination. This might lead to substantially lower prices to some customers, especially larger customers, who might be much more economical to serve.

Distribution cost accountants have the capacity to implement this theory and suggest that its use might substantially reduce the economy's total distribution costs.[23] For now, however, any considerable deviation from the "equal price" approach is likely to incur the FTC's wrath.

How to avoid discriminating. One way to avoid discriminating is to avoid price differentials. Until this potentially powerful but confusing law is clarified, many business executives probably will continue to feel that it is wise to de-emphasize price as a marketing variable. They have concluded that the safest course is to offer few or no quantity discounts, and to offer the same cost-based prices to *all* customers.

As long as the FTC seems to favor "equal" prices, marketing managers probably will tend to avoid active price competition. This shifts competition to areas that are more difficult both to measure and to copy. It also may lead to other behavior condemned by the FTC, such as conscious parallel action, discussed subsequently.

It is clear that today many companies are carefully avoiding active price competition. It would be unfortunate if all price competition were eliminated, ostensibly in the public interest but actually more to the benefit of individual competitors. Prices probably would rise, and the total cost of distribution would, too, because of the restriction on the free operation of the economy.[24]

Strictly speaking, there is no legislative rule against price increases. But in recent years, concern about inflation has led to wage-price guideposts developed by the President and his advisors. Compliance has been encouraged by sometimes not-so-veiled threats of antitrust investigations. The episode in the spring of 1962 between President Kennedy and the U.S. Steel Corp. is probably the most dramatic example. But President Johnson had a similar confrontation with the

Government may discourage price increases

[23] See Slater and Mossman, *op. cit.*
[24] For further discussion, see Corwin D. Edwards, *Maintaining Competition* (New York: McGraw-Hill Book Co., 1949), pp. 161–62; and Dixon, *op. cit.*, pp. 107–16.

Aluminum Co. of America in 1965, and since then the oil industry, among others, has also felt the power of the federal government.[25]

Besides such eyeball-to-eyeball confrontations, federal pressure on prices can be exercised through sales from stockpiles, the authorization of additional subsidized production (of copper, for example), or the adjustment of import and export curbs and quotas.

The potential impact of the federal government on Price reemphasizes the importance of continual study of the political environment.

When the price isn't the price— deceptive pricing

Now we will turn to deceptive pricing and advertised prices which are designed to create price confusion. Phony "preticketed" prices, "factory" or "wholesale" prices, and half-price, 50 percent off, "two-for-one," and 1-cent sales are found mostly at the retail level. The Federal Trade Commission has sought to control such deceptive pricing as an "unfair or deceptive act in commerce."

In the late 1950's, deceptive pricing was used commonly as a competitive device, not only by back-alley discount houses but by major retailers. Television sets advertised at $309.95 might be sold "on sale" for $249.95, but might be available elsewhere for a nonadvertised price of $215.

The situation worsened as regular retailers attempted to compete with discounters; soon, few advertisers' prices made any sense at all. Yet Better Business Bureaus found that all the blame for tricky practices could not be placed on retailers. The vice president of the Chicago Better Business Bureau said, "The customer wants to think he drove a hard bargain. The retailer helps him kid himself. And the retailer and the manufacturer get together to back up their inflated price."[26]

In 1958, the Federal Trade Commission finally stepped into the chaos caused by these phony prices and established its "Guides Against Deceptive Pricing." These were clarified in 1964 to protect advertisers, especially national advertisers, from being responsible for what happened in the channels, beyond their control.

The FTC guides said that manufacturers, distributors, and retailers "must in every case act honestly and in good faith on advertising a list price, and not with the intention of establishing a basis . . . for a deceptive comparison in any local . . . trade area." This was designed to reduce collusion on pricing along the channel. At the retail level, it is expected that the retailer will have a good grasp of competitive prices and not advertise so as to create a false impression of the value being offered.[27]

The Better Business Bureaus encouraged compliance with the FTC Guides. Many manufacturers were also willing and anxious to go

[25] Charles A. Bliss, "Flaw in the Wage-Price Guideposts," *Harvard Business Review*, May–June, 1966, pp. 73–78; Michael C. Jensen, "Gamesmanship with the Guideposts," *Harvard Business Review*, November–December, 1966, pp. 168–83; and "Oilmen Get the Word on Prices," *Business Week*, February 25, 1967, p. 142.

[26] *Time*, November 10, 1958, p. 78.

[27] "War on Phony Bargain Prices," *Business Week*, October 18, 1958, p. 34; or "Guides Against Deceptive Pricing," Federal Trade Commission, October 10, 1958, and January 8, 1964.

along, since it enabled them to stop practices which many felt forced into by competitive action.

Pricing as part of marketing mixes

In the preceding few chapters, we have emphasized manipulation of the pricing variable. But we also have indicated that less use is being made of Price because of the impact of various state and federal laws.

In their efforts to protect the consumer, the FTC and the courts have tended to protect competitors and to discourage aggressive and efficient organizations from cutting price. Even "meeting competition" is construed as collusive by some government officials, as, for example, in price leadership situations. And recently price rises initiated by key firms in an industry have been severely questioned unless they were cost based. **The price is right —if the law says so**

The marketing manager clearly must consider the political and legal environment when developing Price policies that can be combined compatibly with the other three P's.

We have discussed many pricing policies in this text. To summarize our discussion and focus on action implications, we will consider two extremes: (1) de-emphasizing price in a marketing mix, and (2) using price as an active variable.

The three basic ways of de-emphasizing price in a marketing mix are (1) nonprice competiton, (2) price control via legal or administrative devices, and (3) price leadership. **De-emphasizing price in a marketing mix**

Nonprice competition. Nonprice competition involves the conscious use of the other three variables—Product, Place, and Promotion—so that the marketing manager can carve out a market for himself and escape a competitive price situation. This requires careful analysis of the market grid and the selection of marketing mixes appealing to distinct target markets.

Through policies of product differentiation or market segmentation, the marketing manager attempts to obtain his own downsloping demand curve. Ideally, he would like demand curves that are as far to the right and as inelastic as possible. But as long as he caters to somewhat separate markets, he may be able to maintain an extremely profitable position without worrying too much about others' prices.

Under these conditions, because of the uniqueness of his marketing strategies, there is less need for direct price competition. Prices, nevertheless, cannot deviate too far from similar products because few products are truly without substitutes; the marketing manager has latitude but not license in manipulating the pricing variable. The more he caters to distinct target markets and differentiates his marketing mixes, the less attention he needs to pay to competitors' prices.

Over the years, nonprice competition may lead to rising prices as more costly improvements are added. This has been true in the automobile industry, where more powerful engines, better suspension sys-

593

tems and brakes, new power accessories, and varied safety features have caused a steady rise in the total dollar price of cars.

But nonprice competition—or at least competition where price is not considered an important variable—can lead to lower prices, too, as the product moves through the product life cycle and some of the economies of mass production are achieved. Examples are the falling prices of refrigerators, television sets, and other appliances.

In nonprice competition, the marketing manager does have to set prices. Every marketing mix contains a price. The major point is that in nonprice competition, a marketing manager does not rely on a lower price to carry his mix. Instead he, and perhaps his fellow competitors, carefully avoid aggressive pricing moves to avoid provoking others to follow. Each competitor may price near the "competitive" level and then do his best to bring out a better product at this price level, advertise more effectively, build better relations within his channels, and so on.

No collusion need be involved. Each of the competitors simply wants to avoid direct price competition, since Price is so easily and quickly copied—and can hit profits hard.

They are well aware that a price war may lead to lower price levels, squeezing margins and profits to the extent that there will be little money later to pay the cost of nonprice competition. Then, the only remaining course may be additional price cuts. The product may be doomed to a profitless future, unless the market expands greatly at the lower prices or competitors grow discouraged and leave the field.

Price control. As the market situation approaches pure competition or oligopoly, the marketing manager may have real problems controlling price, especially if firms in his own or in competing channels place heavy emphasis on price in their marketing mixes.

Several approaches can be used to control a price or those in the channel.

Fair trade, or resale price maintenance, may effectively control retail prices in states where use of this tool is legal. If the retail price is fixed, this may lead to less pricing ferment in a channel and among competing producers. Then emphasis can shift to nonprice competition.

This approach may be useful in the short run, but it seems to encourage the development of new dealer brands and new manufacturers' brands. The price fixing applies only to each manufacturer's product. Although the manufacturer may be able to fix *his* prices, he must consider the prices of substitute products that may become available at substantially lower prices. In effect, his higher fair-trade prices may provide a price umbrella for the dealer branders, assuring them of no price competition. And the higher price may provide the retailers carrying lower priced dealer brands with an easy way to show that they are providing good values.

Exclusive or selective distribution might be used, choosing distributors and retailers who can be relied on to maintain prices. When small-appliance fair-trade pricing collapsed in 1958, for example, the Sunbeam Corp. and the Dormeyer Corp. drastically reduced the number of wholesalers and retailers handling their lines in an effort to obtain price stability.[28] Wholesalers, granted both wholesale and retail functional discounts, can offer substantial price cuts to final consumers if they choose.

Careful planning of functional discount structures avoids price cutting by leaving no room for the cuts. Each job in the channel is carefully defined. A discount is offered that should cover the cost of providing that function plus the necessary profit.

Such tight planning is basic to effective, smoothly operating channel systems. It is especially important when there are many target markets, and some channels serve the same, as well as different, markets. Different channels may have different requirements and need different discounts, but if too large a discount is allowed someplace, then it is likely to lead to price cutting at the most competitive points of the competing channel systems.

Tight planning is possible, however, only if the company offers something unique that the good middlemen will be eager to handle. As we have noted already, middlemen do not always see themselves as selling arms of those above them in the channels. Further, many are tradition-bound and may insist on the traditional markups. Any effort to change the system may be resisted.

While the development of a reasonable and acceptable functional discount structure is difficult, greater information on the cost of providing all the functions needed by the *many* different target markets will be helpful. Today, computers make it increasingly easy to keep track of such details.

Leasing rather than selling the product to customers may enable a producer to retain control over price because all contracts then are directly between the producer and the final customer. Middlemen might be used to handle the local selling, as, for example, in car leasing. But the prices and terms of the lease would be specified by the producer.

Leasing also may change the marketing mix to such a degree that price is de-emphasized. When a computer is leased, for example, its high purchase price is not too relevant. Neither is its operative life-span, if the supplier has agreed to replace it when a new model is available. In such cases, price in relation to basic hardware characteristics becomes less relevant than the service it will provide, availability for delivery, and sales and service backup.

Leasing tends to change the purchase from a capital to an expense item, and as we have already seen, this tends to change the buying procedure. Perhaps for these reasons some of the office equipment manufacturers, including IBM and Xerox, apparently have set their prices to encourage leasing rather than buying.

Consignment selling consists of selling the product to the final user or consumer only. The manufacturer retains ownership of the goods until the final transaction, and any channel members act merely as agents in arranging the transaction.

---

[28] *Business Week,* June 28, 1958, p. 76.

Consignment selling has been used in the distribution of electrical conduit, plumbing piping, caskets, bicycles, electric light bulbs, bread, magazines, and newspapers. It is a rather complicated procedure, usually requiring that the seller have considerable financial resources—unless rapid turnover minimizes inventory problems, as in the case of bread, newspapers, and magazines.

Consignment selling may attain new attractiveness following a 1967 Supreme Court ruling involving Arnold Schwinn & Co., the bicycle maker. The Court held that while companies may not impose restraints on dealers who buy their products outright, they may—as Schwinn was doing—set conditions for sales made on consignment.[29]

Price fixing by collusion is mentioned as a method here only because some businessmen have conspired to fix prices, often in desperation. Aside from fair trading, all price fixing is illegal. In highly competitive and oligopolistic situations, some marketing managers have been so unsuccessful in differentiating their marketing mixes that the only remaining variable available to them is pricing. Yet price cutting may lead to ruinous competition.

It is interesting to note that the industries in which price fixing actually or allegedly has arisen have been primarily in the industrial goods market where product differentiation and branding are difficult and, consequently, less developed. These industries include carbon dioxide, railroad wheels, pipe flanges, steel rings, brazing alloys, carbon sheet steel, toilets, bathtubs, sinks, aluminum cable, asphalt, salt, and electrical equipment.[30] In the electrical equipment industry price-fixing case, some executives went to jail for their violations of the law.[31]

The predisposing conditions for the development of price fixing should be understood. Price fixing can develop if the marketing manager has failed to differentiate his product effectively or has been unduly hamstrung by company objectives or other company policies. It may be that he is not even a marketing manager in the full sense of the word, having little control over any company policies *except* selling and prices. If he doesn't meet sales goals, he may be fired.

Regardless of the pertinent circumstances or excuses, however, price fixing is illegal in the United States. An interesting question, though, is, Who should go to jail for it?

Should it be the sales manager who actually conducts collusive activities or should he share the guilt with (1) the production and financial executives who should have been well aware of the market

---

[29] "High Court Hits a Softer Tone," *Business Week,* June 17, 1967, p. 40; "G. E. Challenged on Bulb Prices," *Business Week,* October 1, 1966, p. 50.

[30] *Wall Street Journal,* February 1, 1967, p. 1; *Business Week,* October 15, 1966, p. 43; *Business Week,* September 25, 1965, p. 38; *Business Week,* October 9, 1965, p. 42; the (Lansing, Michigan) *State Journal,* March 11, 1967, p. 1; *Wall Street Journal,* November 15, 1961, p. 3; and *Business Week,* December 9, 1961, p. 38 and April 6, 1963, p. 36.

[31] *Time,* February 17, 1961, pp. 84–85; *Business Week,* April 20, 1961, p. 28; *Wall Street Journal,* September 26, 1962, p. 6, January 10, 12, and 13, 1961, pp. 1 ff. and January 2, 1962, p. 1. For a general discussion of price fixing, see Walter Jensen, Jr., and Harold A. Wolf, "A Legal and Economic Note on Price-Fixing," *Business Topics,* Spring, 1962, pp. 55–65; "Climbing Toll for the Price-Fixers," *Business Week,* August 29, 1964, pp. 96–102.

situation and what the sales manager had to do to keep the plant working and the revenue flowing in, or (2) the top executives who presumably are integrating the firm's whole business system?

In world markets, price fixing is viewed quite differently. Price fixing and cartel arrangements are more common and may become more so as production capacities grow.[32] Price fixing is sanctioned or even encouraged by some foreign governments. Some latitude is permitted U.S. firms operating abroad to enable them to compete successfully in foreign trade.[33]

Mergers can reduce competition by eliminating competitors. Reducing competition would seem to be an attractive way to control prices, but this is one of the very reasons for federal anti-merger legislation. And since the federal government may prohibit or undo mergers, this no longer can be thought of as an effective way to control prices.

Procter & Gamble has been required by the federal government (1967 Supreme Court ruling) to sell Clorox Chemical Co., which it acquired in 1957, because the government decided that P&G's great marketing and advertising power—it is one of the largest advertisers—would upset the competitive balance in the laundry-bleach field, and probably lessen competition. The P&G dissolution did not even involve a competitor buying out a direct competitor but rather, a large firm buying into another industry.[34] Unfortunately, the final court ruling came 10 years after the merger, which is one reason companies planning mergers often seek a preliminary Justice Department opinion.

Price leadership. In oligopoly situations, the marketing manager of a firm may be able to assume the role of price leader and discourage active use of price. We have noted that each individual firm sees a kinked-demand-curve situation and generally is not eager to cut price. So the best way of avoiding active price competition is to be sure that the price at the kink is suitable for all potential competitors. This does not mean that all competitors must make equal profits, but that they should make reasonably acceptable profits. This would require careful analysis of the price leader's own cost structure, estimation of his competitors' cost structures and pricing objectives, and analysis of industry demand.

Setting too high a price also may lead to difficulty. Additional competitors may be attracted into the market by the high price. This often leads to trouble later, when capacity has expanded, unless demand keeps growing.

Setting too low a price, on the other hand, may lead to action from antitrust officials who become concerned about the plight of small competitors.

An optimum price may be one which is just high enough to support

---

[32] *Business Week,* March 30, 1962, p. 50, June 8, 1963, p. 62 and April 6, 1963, pp. 96–99; and Norman B. Obbard, "The Common Market and Its Relationship to the United States Steel Industry," *Iron and Steel Engineer,* December, 1962.

[33] Under the Webb-Pomerene Law, passed in 1918, or under specific commodity agreements.

[34] "P&G Is Told It Must Sell Clorox," *Business Week,* December 21, 1963; *The Detroit News,* April 13, 1967.

the marginal firm—the least efficient company whose production would be needed to meet peak long-run demands.[35]

Whatever analytical approach is used, if the price leader chooses a price that the others can accept profitably, they may follow without any necessity for agreement. This is called "conscious parallel action." It is a policy the FTC and the Justice Department deplore, but it still has not been declared illegal. Indeed, it is hard to see how it could be, because the only logical alternative is for the government to set individual prices in substantially the same manner.

The price leader must take his responsibility seriously. If the followers are not able to make a reasonable profit at the market price, then they may try "secret" price cuts to expand sales without incurring retaliation. If very much of this takes place, the price leader will lose a considerable volume of business, and the situation may degenerate into a violent price war. Or there may be a temptation to collude, as we have seen. Lacking an effective leader, the market may be unstable, and price cutting may be a continual threat.

Using price for all it's worth

Although some marketing managers de-emphasize the pricing variable, others find pricing useful in their marketing mixes. They may rely on product development and promotion programs to help make their marketing mixes as attractive as possible and, in this way, shift the demand curve to the right and make them more inelastic than they might be otherwise. Then these managers may use price actively by (1) making fuller use of demand, and (2) using price cutting along the present demand curve.

Full use of demand in market grid boxes. Leader and bait pricing attempt to draw in customers and, in effect, expand the demand for the total line—for the retailer, all of the products of a store. These policies are related to full-line pricing and price lining in that they are intended to affect both the demand for individual products in the line and the full line itself.

With full-line pricing, there usually are "fighting brands" at the bottom of the producer's line. These low-priced items can be promoted as leaders to get the business at the low end of the market, where the demand curve may be quite elastic. Higher priced items will appeal to other target markets that may offer less elastic demand curves. In fact, the marketing manager may add prestige products to the top of the line, simply to attract customers who may not want to buy these premium-priced items but who do want to buy from a firm that offers them.

In short, by selling several items in a line, the firm attempts to satisfy various segments of the market grid. Each of these may have a demand curve with different demand elasticities.

Except for leader pricing and bait pricing, active pricing does not

---

[35] For more extensive discussion, see J. Howard Westing and Jon G. Udell, "Pricing and the Anti-Trust Laws," *Michigan Business Review,* November, 1962, pp. 6–11; Marcus Alexis, "Marketing Laws and Marketing Strategy," *Journal of Marketing,* October, 1962, pp. 67–70; John J. Scanlon, "How Much Should a Corporation Earn?" *Harvard Business Review,* January–February, 1967, pp. 4–21; and J. G. Van Cise, "Regulation—By Business or Government?" *Harvard Business Review,* March–April, 1966, pp. 53–63.

necessarily mean emphasizing low prices. Certainly pricing a full line to take advantage of the different demands in different market grid boxes is not a low-price policy. Neither is a skimming policy. Odd-even and psychological pricing policies do not always yield low prices. Even leader and bait pricing use low prices merely to draw potential customers to a wider assortment of items.

An interesting case of using price actively is the introduction of "sub-regular" brands of gasoline at slightly lower prices than "regular." These brands, suitable for lower horsepower engines have been marketed by major oil companies. Gulf Oil's Gulftane brand is probably the best known. They are offered at 1 to 2 cents lower than regular, putting major brands in direct competition with dealer brands which usually sell at 2 cents a gallon below the major companies' regular.[36] Here, consumers can see that the product is different, but not so different that it is an unsuitable substitute for dealer or unknown brands of regular offered at the same price.

This move has caused sporadic gasoline price wars, and each one has been settled only as a temporary truce. More ferment can be expected in gasoline marketing.

Price changing along the present demand curve. Straight price changes, either increases or decreases, take the demand curve as given and try to make the best of it. Here, we are concerned with price changes on established products. New product prices should be set to minimize the need for correction. But if conditions change, the prices may have to be changed, too.

Price increases are not easy to make unless the firm's marketing mix is significantly better than the competition's. Customers don't like price increases and may temporarily stop buying or look for new sources. But if the firm's marketing mix is truly unique and if its demand curve is inelastic upward from the present prices, a price increase probably will increase profits once customers have adjusted to the new price.

If the firm must worry about competitive reaction, and recently has faced raw material or labor cost increases, perhaps it can attempt to play the price leader role by publicly announcing why it is increasing prices. This might attract followers if the industry demand is inelastic.

Price cuts are easier to make, either as offensive moves or in an effort to relieve pressure on the other three P's—especially Promotion. Both simple price cutting and a conscious below-the-market price policy are efforts to expand sales by moving down the demand curve that already exists for the product.

In highly competitive markets, price cutting is frequently used as an active variable. The tendency, of course, is to slowly push the price level down, and down again. As the price level drops, the original cutters may achieve some short-run gains, although in the long run all the industry members may be in worse condition.

Industry price cutting may be effective only if the general demand for the product is fairly elastic, because then total revenue will increase if the price is cut. Price cutting can be useful in a marketing mix, but it

---

[36] "New Gasolines Stir Up a Storm," *Business Week*, November 25, 1961, pp. 83–86.

must be used only after careful analysis of demand and cost. At the extreme lower end of a demand curve, demand still may be expandable, but costs may begin to rise, and further price cutting may be unprofitable.

Late in the product life cycle, too, it appears that when there is competition from new products, further price cutting no longer expands demand. It may be desirable then to simply drop that product and devote its monies to the development and promotion of other more profitable products.[37]

Conclusion

In this chapter, we have discussed the legal framework within which the marketing manager sets prices. Theoretically, at least, he has a great deal of latitude as long as he avoids collusion and price discrimination. In some states, he may even be allowed to fix prices.

Generally, however, there is legislation which controls minimum prices at the wholesale and retail levels. Government officials occasionally may discourage price increases. Moreover, if he meets competition, this may be taken as a sign of collusion.

The legal environment is somewhat confused because, although most pricing legislation ostensibly was designed to protect competition and consumers, "competition" has been narrowly interpreted as meaning "competitors." Although the guidelines laid down by legislation and court cases are dim and uncertain, there are good reasons for the marketing manager to heed them.

Finally, the marketing manager must develop a set of price policies. Two basic approaches were isolated (1) de-emphasizing Price, and (2) treating Price as an active variable.

Pricing can be de-emphasized by stressing nonprice competition. Various price control measures may also be useful, such as fair trading, exclusive or selective distribution, planned functional discount structures, leasing and consignment selling. Pricing can be further de-emphasized by statesmanlike price leadership which considers the welfare of the rest of the industry and the dangers of a too-low or too-high price.

Using Price as an active variable involves catering to different target markets on the market grid and then pricing in line with the demand and cost situations in each of the market grid boxes. Or straight price cuts can be used to expand the quantity demanded along a demand curve.

Whether Price is used actively or de-emphasized, Price is one of the four major variables the marketing manager works with. It should be based on well-defined policies. Lack of policy really represents policy, too. It would seem more desirable to set policies consciously, in the light of the competitive and legal environment in each target market.

---

[37] Charles L. Hinkle, working paper on "Market Response to Sales Promotion," Marketing Science Institute, to be published by Allyn & Bacon, Inc.

1 Discuss Unfair Trade Practices acts. To whòm are they "unfair"?

2 Discuss the thinking behind Fair Trade acts. To whom are they "fair"?

3 How would our marketing structure be changed if manufacturers were required to specify Fair Trade prices on *all* products sold at retail and *all* retailers were required to use these prices? Would this place greater or lesser importance on the development of the manufacturer's marketing mix? What kind of an operation would retailing be in this situation? Would consumers receive more or less service?

4 Would it be price discrimination if a company sold gasoline to taxicab associations for 2½ cents a gallon less than charged to retail service stations? What happens if the cab associations resell gasoline not only to taxicab operators, but to the general public as well?

5 Discuss the economic forces or situations which might lead to deceptive pricing. Why might some marketing organizations include deceptive pricing in their marketing mixes? In what lines of trade or for what types of products would such pricing be more likely?

6 If a company did not wish to use price as an active variable, what policy (or policies) might be appropriate for each of the following products? (Specify any necessary assumptions in order to obtain a definite answer.)

a) Cough syrup
b) Lipstick
c) Men's ties
d) Electric shavers
e) Cuff links
f) Industrial paint products
g) Nickel
h) Electronic measuring instruments for paper production
i) Automobiles
j) Passenger tires

7 Why is active price competition always a possibility, even in oligopoly situations? Illustrate why active price competition might be attractive to a marketing manager. Would active price competition seem to be in the public interest? If so, why is it frequently looked upon with disfavor by the courts and legislatures?

8 Discuss the problem of granting P.M.'s and other promotional allowances within the provisions of the Robinson-Patman Act. How can these allowances be made on "proportionately equal terms" when stores are of varying size and importance to the producer or wholesaler? Should all retailers be allowed a sufficient allowance to run the same size advertisement or should it be on some basis such as percentage of sales? In the latter case, would the small retailer make as effective use of such allowances in view of the fact that there are substantial economies in purchasing large blocks of advertising?

9 In view of down-sloping demand curves, price cutting at the retail level would mean expanded sales volume for producers. Why then do some manufacturers support Fair Trade legislation?

Integrating a
marketing program

In recent years, an increasing number of producers, wholesalers, and retailers have adopted the marketing concept and have seen the parallel importance of viewing the business as a total system of action.

These companies have traveled the long, evolutionary road from the days when the overwhelming consideration of manufacturers and middlemen was producing or stocking products. We discussed this process in the early chapters and have seen its application throughout this text. Now we will round out our discussion and show why an individual firm should see each of its internal activities as well as its relations with outsiders as part of a total system of action.

Our major stress so far has been on developing parts of, and whole, marketing strategies, but usually we have been discussing this in terms of one product or market at a time. Now we will see that a marketing manager must develop a marketing program—a set of marketing strategies which seek to reach the firm's goals by making the most effective possible use of the firm's resources.

Need for a total system view

In Chapters 1 and 2, we discussed the growing acceptance of the marketing concept and the importance of its wholehearted adoption by top management *and* the whole organization. Some company reorganization may be necessary (and sometimes is essential) to implement the marketing concept and effectively run a total system of action. But without the enthusiastic support of top management, organizational changes may be only window dressing.

The typical business executive, and especially the one with a functional specialty—such as sales, production, accounting, or finance—has tended to view his firm from his own vantage point. He tends to see the rest of the business working around him. He often expects the other executives to adjust their activities to make his plans work well. **Step across the line . . . to do a better job**

When all the executives of the firm follow this same path, we sometimes see chaos, or at the very least, a system with many malfunctions. This is why reorganization may be needed if the marketing concept is *really* adopted.

Departmental or functional "empires" may have been necessary when the flows of information between and among departments were slow. Now, however, with the growing use of data processing equipment, we see that the traditional departmental approach is not only unnecessary but may be quite ineffective. Furthermore, when the whole business is seen as a system, tasks that formerly seemed to require considerable management judgment can now be assumed by computers.

General Electric's system illustrates the possibilities. It demonstrates why an internal business system should be seen as a system, crossing traditional functional lines wherever necessary.

General Electric has developed a computer-oriented system that ties together its widely dispersed manufacturing and distribution facilities. This computer system links together 65 customer service centers (sales offices) located in 49 states, 18 distribution warehouses in 11 states, and 40 product departments with 53 manufacturing plants in 21 states. If, for example, a customer wanted to place an order for a truckload of lamps *on the condition that shipment be made promptly,* he could call one of the GE local sales offices and place his order tentatively, assuming that GE could, in fact, meet his conditions. **Ask the computer, wait 15 seconds**

If he telephoned the order to the local sales office, the salesman there could enter the required data into the GE computer system while the potential buyer was still on the phone. The computer system then would check to see if GE wanted to sell to him (a credit check) and if the item were in stock at a convenient location. If the answer to both questions were yes, the system would (*a*) issue an order to ship, (*b*) bill the customer, (*c*) update the inventory records, (*d*) generate the records that are reviewed periodically so that orders are issued automatically to factories to replenish inventory at the various distribution points, and (*e*) relay the message back to the GE salesman that the customer's order is on the way. And all of this would take less than 15 seconds!

The speed of this system is remarkable—but the most remarkable achievement is the integration of the system. By looking at the GE operation as a total system, the following activities that often have been handled by separate departmental or functional entities now are assumed by the computer: credit checking, inventory control, production **No mourning for the passing of boundaries** scheduling, shipping control, billing, order entry procedure, and all the bookkeeping that formerly occupied many clerks.

This system also allows random inquiry for specific management information and regularly produces special and exception reports for management.

Clearly, then, the traditional functional departmental boundaries make little sense in such an integrated system.[1]

The total system reaches out

The external as well as the internal affairs of any business should be viewed as part of a total system of action. The production-oriented businessman sometimes feels his job is done when the salesmen have somehow "gotten rid of" the company's products. But as we have seen in many places throughout this text, a firm must view itself as part of a channel system. It will prosper only as the whole channel system functions well. Even so small a matter as a packing decision on the production line may have to be based on a consideration of how wholesalers and retailers will handle the product in their warehouses and stores.

Such total system thinking may be annoying to those who would prefer to focus on their own problems, but it is necessary for survival of entire companies in our competitive world. As we have already noted, product life cycles are shortening and competition is stiffening in many markets. The standardized, homogeneous products which production-oriented people prefer to produce are often not profitable in head-on competition with similar products.

Who should organize and run the total systems?

Top management is responsible for developing and running a total system of action—designed to satisfy target customers, for a profit. Ideally, the whole company becomes customer-oriented, and all the company departments pull together to reach its objectives. We still see departments, because there are advantages in job specialization. But the former battles to protect "empire" boundaries are reduced because the total system is (or should be) supreme. To be sure, there may be disagreements over strategy. The production department might question whether the consumer really does want, and is willing to pay for, products which are practically custom-made. But rather than resort to an internal power struggle, a marketing-oriented system would do some marketing research, perhaps run some market tests, and calculate potential costs and company (not departmental) profits for alternate strategies. Then it would decide what is best for the firm (or channel), not just what is best for the strongest department or coalition of departments.

In such a system, the marketing manager would help develop this total system attitude within his firm and his channel system. He must work regularly with the external system as well as the internal system

---

[1] For more details on this system, see Clint DeGabriell, "Design Criteria for an On-Line Nation-Wide Order Processing System," *Disc File Applications* (Detroit: American Data Processing, Inc., 1964), pp. 71–75. Westinghouse Electric has a similar system in operation. See *Systems,* April, 1965, p. 10. See also, E. J. McCarthy, J. A. McCarthy, and D. Humes, *Integrated Data Processing Systems* (New York: John Wiley & Sons, Inc., 1966).

and is in an ideal position to keep the system working. In a sense, he is a coordinator and integrator—as well as a liaison man between the final customers of the channel system and the executives in his own company.

Need for innovative strategy planning

Important as organizing the total system is, however, organization as such is not enough to guarantee success in our increasingly competitive marketplace. Competent execution of poor or obsolete strategies may lead to poor results. The system must be innovative. It is here that wholehearted acceptance of the marketing concept is essential.

Too many businesses have been concerned with obtaining a larger share or maintaining their share of their *current* market, rather than trying to find new markets or expanding the current market. *They are essentially competitive rather than innovative.* This helps account for the declining profit rates we see in some industries and firms.

Make it new, make it better, or you may not make it

Although investments in plant and equipment have been growing, it appears that profits no longer can be bought simply with increased investments. Moreover, domestic and foreign competition threatens those who do not create more satisfying goods and services. New markets, new customers, and new ways of doing things must be found if companies are to operate profitably in the future.[2]

The importance of aggressive, imaginative marketing strategy planning was discussed in Chapter 2 and summarized in the General Foods hypothesis. The intervening chapters should have given you greater perspective on the implications of this hypothesis. In particular, it may mean that less attention should be paid to finding ways to use a company's present resources more fully—a typical production-oriented concern—and more attention should be paid to locating wholly new market opportunities which may obsolete your own or competitors' strategies.

Market grids are revealing

Firms may find tremendous new opportunities while trying to locate unsatisfied target markets. Research in the watch industry, for instance, showed that there were three distinct groups of watch customers and that only one was being catered to by present strategies.

Consumers in the first two segments were primarily concerned with economic factors. The first group was interested in paying the lowest price possible for a watch that worked reasonably well. Consumers in the second segment were willing to pay higher prices for product features that added longer life, greater durability and accuracy, or more attractive style. Consumers in the third segment, on the other hand, were more concerned with emotional values. They usually purchased a watch as a gift and wanted it to have symbolic value.

This research showed that 23 percent of the market was in the first

[2] Peter G. Peterson, "Conventional Wisdom and the Sixties," *Journal of Marketing,* April, 1962, pp. 63–67; and J. B. McKitterick, "Needed: New Thinking on Market Strategy and Investment," *Advertising Age,* July 23, 1962, pp. 73–76.

segment—those who buy at the lowest price; 46 percent was in the second segment—those who want durability and general excellence; and 31 percent was in the third segment—those who buy a symbol for some important occasion. It was clear that the better-known watch companies were aiming at the third segment almost exclusively. They were producing primarily expensive watches and stressing their suitability as gifts. Their promotion was heavily concentrated around Christmas and graduation time, when many watches are purchased as gifts.

Find a market, sell to it

This commonly accepted strategy of the major watch companies left the first two segments unsatisfied. The U.S. Time Co. successfully filled this void with its "Timex" watches. This emphasis on market segmentation has made the U.S. Time Co. the world's largest watch company.[3]

It is important to note that the major companies previously had been seeking to compete with lower priced foreign competition, and they were using essentially the same marketing mixes as their competitors. U.S. Time completely upset the watch industry, both foreign and domestic, by not only offering a good product (with a one-year unconditional guarantee) at a lower price but also by using new channels of distribution. Its watches are widely available at department stores, drugstores, discount houses, and nearly any other retailer who will carry them.

Such drastic shifts in strategy may be startling to the conventional production-oriented businessman. But they are becoming much more frequent in industries where some or all firms have accepted the marketing concept. Such new marketing stretegies often cannot be met by competitors through a simple price cut. In effect, the innovators carve out their own little market, at least for a short period and perhaps for longer. This search for unsatisfied target markets seems not only desirable but absolutely necessary for survival in a marketing-oriented age.

Need for marketing programs

In our introductory treatment of marketing strategy planning, we tended to focus on particular target markets and products. But most companies aim at several target markets and may offer them quite different marketing mixes. The clock keeps moving, so we should have *a plan for* adjusting *each strategy* as the product life cycle moves on. And in turn, each of these *plans must be merged into* a total *marketing program* which then becomes the responsibility of the business firm, working as a total system of action.

Taking the time to plan each strategy

It is impractical to change a marketing strategy every day or every week. Strategy must be implemented during the course of a planning period of some duration. This may be only a month or two in some

---

[3] Daniel Yankelovich, "Psychological Market Segmentation," in Jack Z. Sissors (ed.), *Some Bold New Theories of Advertising in Marketing* (Evanston, Ill.: Northwestern University, Jack Z. Sissors, 1963), pp. 23–25.

cases, as when style and fashion are extremely important. Or the strategy-planning period may go on for several years, perhaps covering the course of the product life cycle or at least the early stages of the product life cycle.

Business planning may be done for monthly or quarterly periods but most commonly covers annual periods. While there is nothing inherently superior about an annual period, accounting statements usually are prepared at least annually; the monies budgeted to the various marketing functions usually are related to time periods such as a year; and since seasons affect production and/or sales in most companies, the yearly period makes sense. As a result, in the absence of good reasons to the contrary, marketing plans usually cover a year, or a year as part of a longer period.

We could question the wisdom of forcing a company's operating management to adjust its planning and reporting to an arbitrary time cycle, but we will not take up that matter now. The use of such established time cycles is current practice, and our discussion will be within the framework of current practice. Logically, however, a marketing manager's plans might better cover periods shorter than or, more frequently, considerably longer than a year. This period will vary in length depending on the nature of the product and the market situation, the current product life cycle stage, and many other factors we have been discussing throughout this text. The 20- to 40-year planning periods, however, which have been traditional for evaluating investments in plant and equipment, probably are too long in the face of shortening product life cycles. In a less dynamic age, 20- to 40-year cycles may have been suitable, but now they seem more to reflect the regulations of the Internal Revenue Service than the realities of the marketplace. Some companies already have recognized this by keeping one set of books for tax purposes and another to reflect more realistically what is happening in the business.

Figure 29–1 indicates why it is essential to develop a strategy for the course of a planning period. Figure 29–1 shows the way in which basic marketing variables typically change through the course of the product life cycle.

Planning for a changing strategy

This should be a fruitful review. For example, you will see that as the product life cycle moves on, the marketing manager should *expect* to find more products entering "his" market and pushing the market situation closer to pure competition. At the same time, he might want to shift from a selective to an intensive distribution policy *and* move from a skimming to a penetration pricing policy.

His original plan for implementing his strategy should include these probable adjustments and the probable timing involved. If it is likely that the cycle will move very quickly, then he may have to select a less-than-optimal plan early in the product life cycle, knowing that he will not be able to change the plan fast enough later. Regarding his distribution structure, for example, he might choose intensive rather than selective distribution because he knows this is what he is going to need and want one year down the planning period.

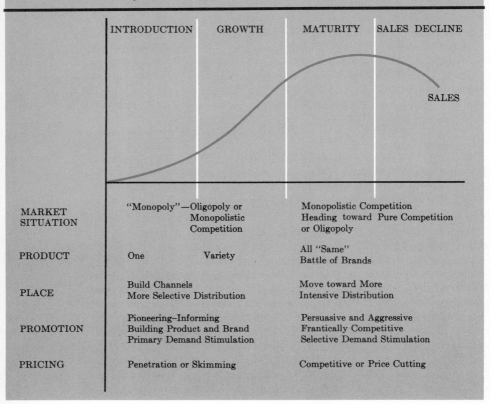

Figure 29–1 *Typical changes in marketing variables over the course of the product life cycle*

	INTRODUCTION	GROWTH	MATURITY	SALES DECLINE

SALES

MARKET SITUATION	"Monopoly"—Oligopoly or Monopolistic Competition	Monopolistic Competition Heading toward Pure Competition or Oligopoly
PRODUCT	One Variety	All "Same" Battle of Brands
PLACE	Build Channels More Selective Distribution	Move toward More Intensive Distribution
PROMOTION	Pioneering–Informing Building Product and Brand Primary Demand Stimulation	Persuasive and Aggressive Frantically Competitive Selective Demand Stimulation
PRICING	Penetration or Skimming	Competitive or Price Cutting

A plan for implementation of a strategy must have a timetable. The various tasks that are to be accomplished through the course of time should be itemized, along with the expected sales and profit results at various stages in the plan. This gives the marketing manager and other company executives a clearer view of what is to be accomplished by the plan and the resources needed to accomplish it. It also helps them measure, control, and if necessary, change the plan later. More is said about this below.

A program consists of a set of strategy plans

Most companies are carrying on several plans at the same time. They may have different products aimed at different target markets or the same products may be part of different strategies offered in different geographical or product-user markets. Yet the company is responsible for manning and running the whole program, not just individual plans. It is necessary for planners of the business system to keep this whole program in mind in their planning and allocation of resources.

The dynamics of this ongoing market-programming effort are illustrated in the marketing activities of the Agricultural Division of American Cyanamid Co., which has thoroughly accepted the marketing

608

concept. This division alone (there are 10 other operating divisions in the company) markets more than 300 different agricultural products, including drugs, pharmaceuticals, fertilizer products, insecticides, fumigants, weed killers, industrial nitrogen products, and chemicals for the food industry—all industrial goods. It realizes that agriculture is not a single industry but a collection of dozens of heterogeneous sub-industries, each with its own market grid.

Each of the division's marketing mixes contains the four P's as ingredients. But because of the complexity of the agricultural market and the wide product line offered, the marketing mixes vary from sales territory to sales territory and from product to product. This diversity of mixes is well described by the Agricultural Division's director of marketing:

There are times when we use across-the-board national media and promotion, but usually our programs are pin-pointed to individual agricultural industries and areas. A case in point would be our TV Farm Newsreel which was carried on more than 50 television stations in high income farm areas. During the past year all the commercial messages have been tailored to local needs. The majority of our print advertising is directed to specific segments of the agricultural industry through schedules in specialized horizontal publications serving the feed milling industry, veterinarians, cattle growers, broiler producers or various other agricultural sub-industries. We also run heavy schedules in state and local publications and on local radio and television stations. Our promotions (sales promotions) are also tailored to individual agricultural industries or geographic areas.

We have no pat marketing mix formula. I will use four of our products and product lines as examples of how our marketing mixes vary. First come our *Aurofac* animal feed supplements. These are various strengths and formulations of *Aureomycin* which are used as ingredient products by feed manufacturers in their feed products. *Aurofac* maintains livestock health and promotes livestock growth. The *Aurofac* marketing mix primarily depends on a large technically trained sales force and sharing the top position in the *Aurofac* marketing mix is our technical service by scientists. These scientists, working in close relationship with the technically trained sales force, provide research and consultation on feeding problems. They prepare and supply to the trade highly specialized bulletins on the use of *Aurofac* in feeding problems. They conduct field trials and demonstrations using the most advanced methods of statistical control. In conjunction with professional motion picture producers, these scientists have prepared and are continually enlarging an extensive library of films which in simple language document the benefits of *Aurofac* to animal health and growth—animal industry by animal industry.

Next in importance are advertising and public relations. Our *Aurofac* trade advertising is for the purpose of supporting our technically trained sales force and our scientists in their relationship with feed manufacturers. It tells the feed manufacturer how *Aureomycin* will benefit him and benefit his customers. Our *Aurofac* advertising to the livestock grower is designed to support the feed manufacturer in the sale of his products containing *Aureomycin*. Our advertising to the farmer tells him that having *Aureomycin* in his feeds is profitable and insures against disease loss and promotes animal growth. To the farmer we sell a concept. To the feed manufacturer we sell a product.

Packaging and promotion come next. Good packaging is necessary, but it is not of primary importance. Our *Aurofac* promotion is not extensive and here again its purpose is to make it easier for the feed manufacturer to sell his products containing *Aureomycin.*

The next example is *Aureomycin* Mastitis Suspension which cures mastitis, a high incidence disease among dairy cows. Although this product's basic ingredient is chlortetracycline, which is also the basis of *Aurofac,* the two marketing mixes are substantially different. In this case, primary emphasis goes to a large sales force trained in merchandising. *Aureomycin* Mastitis is sold through many types of wholesalers and distributors and about 25,000 farm supply outlets. Getting and holding distribution, controlling inventories, displaying the merchandise and educating the trade are the salesmens' primary tasks. Sharing top position in its marketing mix are advertising, promotion and packaging. Here our advertising sells *our* specific product. Special promotions are utilized at three distinct links in the marketing chain, namely, the wholesale, retail and ultimate user levels. Our packaging must include identification, imagery and impulse appeals not too unlike those of a convenience goods manufacturer, but it must also educate the user and make it easier for him to utilize the product in a highly specialized use situation.

Technical service by scientists occupies a subordinate position in the marketing mix mainly because we do not have to send a scientist with every order as is sometimes the case with *Aurofac.* This product was developed for a specific mass market so the vast majority of technical problems was licked in the development stage. Our scientists, however, supply research and consultation where needed, technical bulletins, educational films, and are continually running field trials and demonstrations. The scientists take second place in the marketing of this product.

Then come our Phosphate and Nitrogen Products which fall roughly into two groups. One group consists of ingredient concentrates which are sold to fertilizer manufacturers who formulate them into finished fertilizer products. The second group compromises finished fertilizer products which we sell through farm supply channels. The most important part of our phosphate and nitrogen fertilizer marketing mix is a special technically trained sales force. Again, as in the case of *Aurofac,* the sales force works in close cooperation with our technical service men. The second ingredient in our fertilizer marketing mix is an item which ordinarily would not be considered part of a marketing mix but because fertilizers are heavy tonnage, relatively low priced products, the location of our production facilities is very important in the marketing mix. Strategic advertising, public relations, and promotion are used, but not nearly to the extent that they are in the majority of products in our line.

The fourth example is our Cyanamid Special Grade Defoliant, a product based on our original Cyanamid compound which was developed 51 years ago. This product defoliates cotton prior to mechanical picking. It is a packaged item and is sold through farm supply channels. Defoliants are used by cotton farmers only when there has been rainfall just before picking time. This rainfall causes fresh new growth and the resulting green leaves stain the cotton when it is mechanically picked if they are not removed prior to picking. Since the product is useful only when there is fresh new growth, the most important ingredient in Cyanamid Special Grade Defoliant's marketing mix is availability when and if needed. The hardest job is to have it on hand at the right time, the right place and in the right quantity. Advertising, public relations, promotion and packaging are relatively unimportant for this product. The advertising we do is highly localized and conveys the message that the defoliants are available in the locality.

610

I mentioned earlier that our total product line is a long one. We don't have a distinctly different marketing mix for every product in this line, but we do have several dozen product sub-groups with significantly different marketing mix requirements. Add to this the variations in marketing mix caused by geographic differences and special area problems, and I believe you will see why we say we have no pat formula for developing marketing mixes.[4]

The Agricultural Division regularly uses marketing research to aid in the definition of its marketing mix problems. In addition, to improve future mixes, it uses accounting expense controls and marketing research to analyze the effectiveness of its various mixes. The guiding influence here is the concept that "the business of business is the creating and fulfilling of product user needs at a profit."

Flexible as far as the dollar stretches

While the marketing manager does have to be flexible, willing to change his plans as market or customer needs direct, he must work with plans and a complete program. He has some flexibility within each plan, but his resources are always limited. He cannot launch a plan to pursue every promising opportunity he sees or simply spend some more money on advertising because it "looks as if it might pay off." Instead, limited resources always force him to make hard decisions between alternative plans when developing and implementing his program. To see this more clearly, let's investigate a systematic approach to developing a marketing program.

Systematic approach for developing a marketing program

Defining areas of interest

To be certain that the development of his marketing program is practical, the marketing manager should clearly define what kind of product-market possibilities he will consider. We discussed this in Chapter 3, emphasizing that a company in defining its objectives should determine what business it wants to be in. Otherwise, a search for new opportunities could range all over the map, with considerable time and resources wasted simply pursuing interesting possibilities.

The area of interest should not be defined too narrowly, such as only what the company is doing now. On the other hand, it should not be so broad that the marketing manager is forced to evaluate ways to satisfy *all* human needs. A watch manufacturer, for example, probably should not think only of satisfying the needs for time measuring; it should also include consumer desires for gifts, status, ego boosting, pride in personal possessions and appearance, and economy. This broader view would involve many more possibilities, yet would limit the analysis to ones which might be provided within the firm's present resources. An example of the result of such an analysis is the experience of U.S. Time Co. with its "Timex" watches.

The British paint manufacturer we discussed in Chapter 2 also

---

[4] Adapted slightly from Burton S. Bowman, "The Utility of Marketing Tools and the Accomplishment of Marketing Objectives," speech to the 41st National Conference of the American Marketing Association, Chicago, December 29, 1958.

followed this approach. He defined his area of interest as the home-decorating field, then developed his marketing strategy and program accordingly.

Find market dimensions, then subdivide by groups

The qualitative and quantitative research discussed in Chapter 4 would be used to discover what people are doing in your area of interest, say in home decorating. You would attempt to identify *what* people are doing and *why,* and relate this to socioeconomic characteristics, such as age, income, and so on, for which there already is considerable published data. Remember that the British paint manufacturer did this in the process of isolating the Cost-Conscious Couple.

Make up market grids— using socioeconomic data to estimate size of boxes

Here, market gridding is used, and the available socioeconomic data is employed to estimate the number of people in the various boxes. You will recall that the paint manufacturer was able to estimate that about 10 percent of the total "home-decorating-with-paint" market was in each of the four corner markets he had isolated.

At this point, we begin evaluating the economic potential of alternate marketing strategies and plans, including present plans. We should evaluate this potential over a reasonable planning period, not necessarily the one-year period typically used in the accounting cycle. If a product life cycle is likely to last about three years, then it is possible that the strategy will not be profitable during the first six months to a year. On the other hand, if the plan is evaluated over the projected three-year life-span, then the plan may look quite attractive.

Evaluate boxes for economic potential

The evaluation of the potential of each box should include forecasts of potential revenue during the course of the evaluation period as well as forecasts of the projected costs of implementing the marketing mix associated with the plan. This is merely an extension of the total cost and total profit analysis of alternatives discussed in Chapter 19 on Physical Distribution. In other words, all the aspects of each plan—including potential revenue and cost—should be evaluated together. Those managing the business system should think of each plan as one integrated effort.

The prospects for each strategy might be evaluated over a five-year planning period, with monthly and/or annual estimates of sales and costs. This is illustrated graphically in Figure 29–2. Note that the product life cycle can be incorporated in this analysis through the shapes of the sales and cost curves. There is nothing sacred, however, about the five-year period.

In a market free from extreme competition, it might be safe and realistic to think in terms of 10- or 20-year horizons. The British paint manufacturer felt safe with such a long view because he did not expect his competitors to move into his "low-quality" and therefore "low-status" market. Not many American manufacturers can expect such placid competition.

Finally, after an evaluation of alternate strategies and plans, the marketing manager must face up to the fact that because the company's

612

resources are limited, some plans must be selected and others rejected or phased out.

How do you find the best program? There is no one best way of comparing various plans. A great deal of reliance must be placed on management judgment. Yet some calculations are helpful, too. If a five-year planning horizon seems to be realistic for the firm's product markets, then the expected profits over the five-year period could be calculated for each plan.

Assuming the company had a profit-oriented objective, the more profitable plans could be considered first, both in terms of the potential

Match potential and resources— by trial and error

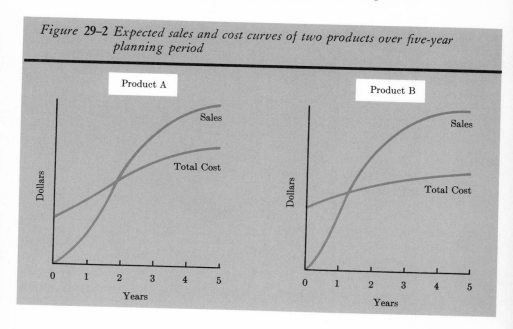

Figure 29–2 Expected sales and cost curves of two products over five-year planning period

profit and of the resources they would use. Also, the impact on the entire program should be evaluated. One profitable-looking alternative might not be a good first choice because it might use up all the company's resources and preclude the pursuit of several plans which together would be more profitable.

Some juggling among the various plans in relation to profitability versus resources needed and available would tend to move the manager towards the *most profitable* program.

This trial-and-error approach might be replaced with a computer program if a great number of alternatives had to be evaluated. Actually, however, the computer would merely perform the same function—trying to match potential revenues and profits against available resources.[5]

---

[5] For further discussion on evaluating and selecting alternate plans, see W. I. Little, "The Integrated Management Approach to Marketing," *Journal of Marketing,* April, 1967, pp. 32–36; and Leon Winer, "A Profit-Oriented Decision System," *Journal of Marketing,*

Allocating budgets for marketing programs

Once the overall marketing program and five-year (or so) plans have been set, shorter term plans also must be worked out. Typically, companies use annual budgets both to plan what they are going to do and to provide control over various functions. Each department may be allowed to spend its budgeted amount, perhaps by months, for each of their departmental functions. As long as the departments stay within their budgets, they are allowed considerable (or complete) autonomy. But expenditures beyond the budget are considered deviations from the general plan and require considerable discussion and approval at a higher level.

Budgeting for marketing? —50%, 30% or 10% is better than none

The most common method of budgeting for marketing expenditures is to compute them as a percentage of either past or forecasted sales. The virtue of this method is its simplicity. A similar percentage can be used rather automatically each year, eliminating the need to repeatedly evaluate the kind and amount of marketing effort that is needed and its probable cost. It enables those executives who are not too sympathetic with marketing to "write off" a certain percentage or number of dollars, and at the same time control the amount spent. When a company's top executives have this attitude, they often get what they expect from their marketing activities—less than top performance.

Some marketing executives find this percentage-of-sales approach convenient. It assures them of a reasonable budget. It should be clear, however, that the users of this approach do not fully understand the interrelation of the ingredients of a marketing mix, the need to blend them into a strategy, and in turn, the need to develop sets of strategy plans as part of a whole marketing program for a total system of action.

Find the task, budget for it

Mechanically budgeting a certain percentage of past or forecasted sales leads, ironically, to expanding marketing expenditures when business is good and sales are rising, and contracting them when business is poor. It may, in fact, be desirable to increase marketing expenditures when business is good, though it is questionable whether this should be in a direct ratio. But when business is poor, the most sensible approach is to be *more,* not less, aggressive!

There are other methods of budgeting for marketing expenditures. Some of these are as follows:

April, 1966, pp. 38–44. This latter reference discusses discounting the future flow of profits to provide a more realistic appraisal of the value of alternate plans. This procedure can be used for equating the profit flows for different time periods, that is, a five-year profit flow would be compared with a 10-year profit flow by discounting all the future flows to their present value. See also, S. C. Brandt, "Dissecting the Segmentation Syndrome," *Journal of Marketing,* October, 1966, pp. 22–27; F. H. Mossman and M. L. Worrel, Jr., "Analytical Methods of Measuring Marketing Profitability," *MSU Business Topics,* Autumn, 1966, pp. 35–45; and W. J. E. Crissy and R. M. Kaplan, "Matrix Models for Marketing Planning," *MSU Business Topics,* Summer, 1963, pp. 48–66.

In attempting to develop more profitable programs, some firms may find it useful to use computer simulations of their own and competitors' potential strategies to evaluate the attractiveness of various plans. For more discussion on simulation, see Harold Weitz, "The Promise of Simulation in Marketing," *Journal of Marketing,* July, 1967, pp. 28–33; and P. Kotler, "The Competitive Marketing Simulator—A New Management Tool," *California Management Review,* Spring, 1965.

1. Match expenditures with competitors.
2. Set the budget as a certain number of cents or dollars per sales unit (by case, by thousand, or by ton), using the past year or estimated year ahead as a base for computation.
3. Set aside all available funds. Companies willing to sacrifice current profits for future sales may use this approach, i.e., *invest* in marketing.
4. Base the budget on the number of new customers desired or the amount required to reach a predetermined sales goal, as when entering new territories, increasing volume, or seeking other objectives. This method is frequently called the "task method."

In the light of our continuing discussion about marketing strategy and its part in a total system of action, the most sensible approach to budgeting marketing expenditures would seem to be this last approach, the *task method*.

The amount budgeted using this method might be expressed ultimately as a percentage of sales, but the route for arriving at this shorthand description would be much more involved than picking up a past percentage. It would require a careful consideration of the five-year plans discussed previously and the specific tasks that are to be accomplished this year as part of each of these five-year plans. The costs of these tasks then would be totaled to determine how much should be budgeted for marketing and the other business functions provided for in the one- and five-year plans. If a careful five-year planning procedure has been used and accepted by top management, then the budget should be assembled directly from these detailed plans, rather than looking at historical patterns or ratios.

After the marketing department has received its budget for the year, it could, presumably, spend it any way it saw fit. But if the previous planning-budgeting procedure has been followed, it would be reasonable to continue allocating expenditures within the marketing function according to the plans in the marketing program. **Spending without agony**

Again, everyone in the marketing department and in the business should view the company as a system of action and plan accordingly. If this is done, then it will be possible to eliminate some of the traditional planning-budgeting decisions which have been so agonizing because, in the nature of things, one executive often was pitted against another and one department against another.[6]

Our discussion of an organized planning-budgeting process using the task method makes budgeting for marketing sound so simple. In fact, however, it is not. The procedures we have been describing set the framework, but considerable management judgment and marketing research still may have to be employed to weigh the relative effectiveness of the four P's in various target markets. Marginal analysis of the potential effectiveness of alternative variables often is useful.[7] **Decisions still must be made**

[6] For more discussion on budget allocation, see C. E. Eldridge, "The Marketing Budget and Its Allocation," *Printers' Ink*, May 12, 1967, pp. 35–44.
[7] For a more detailed discussion of how to spend or budget parts of the total marketing budget more effectively, see R. L. Mela, "Sales Budgeting for Controlled Growth

Much research is being done and will continue to be done on such subjects as the relative impact of advertising versus personal selling. But in the end, the marketing manager and top management will have to weigh and evaluate the past and present sales and cost data, marketing research data, and their expectations for the future.

Because he's out on the breakthrough frontier

The procedures we have discussed can be helpful as guides, but the ultimate responsibility for developing a profitable marketing program rests with management. And typically much judgment is required, because future market conditions must be forecasted. This is why we stressed earlier the importance of looking for real "breakthrough opportunities" rather than merely trying to patch up or improve present marketing strategies. It is relatively easy to decide between one strategy that probably will yield a 30 percent return on investment in the next two years and one that will yield only 10 percent during the next year. Finding a new strategy that will return 50 percent the first year is more difficult, but makes strategy selection even easier.

As we see it, one of the marketing manager's important roles is helping to find such breakthrough opportunities. And this role falls to him especially, because such opportunities are more likely to be found in the market—through finding unsatisfied customer needs—than through cost savings in the plant, warehouse, or store.

Coordinating marketing programs

We have assigned the role of coordinating the whole marketing program to the marketing manager. The title of the executive responsible for this function, however, may differ from company to company. The point is that *someone* in each firm must be responsible for planning and then implementing an integrated marketing program.

Many of the topics we have discussed in this book will be helpful in

Objectives," *Journal of Marketing Research,* May, 1965, pp. 133–40; Joel Dean, "Does Advertising Belong in the Capital Budget?" *Journal of Marketing,* October, 1966, pp. 15–21; J. S. Schiff and M. Schiff, "New Sales Management Tools: ROAM," *Harvard Business Review,* July–August, 1967, pp. 59–66; J. G. Udell, "How Important Is Pricing in Competitive Strategy?" *Journal of Marketing,* January, 1964, pp. 44–48; C. L. Hinkle, "The Strategy of Price Deals," *Harvard Business Review,* July–August, 1963, pp. 75–85; M. Schiff, "The Use of ROI in Sales Management," *Journal of Marketing,* July, 1963, pp. 70–73; M. J. Margolis, "How to Evaluate Field Sales Promotion," *Journal of Marketing,* July, 1963, pp. 42–46; P. E. Green, M. H. Halbert, and P. J. Robinson, "A Behavioral Experiment in Sales Effort Allocation," *Journal of Marketing Research,* August, 1966, pp. 261–68; J. R. Katzenbach and R. R. Champion, "Linking Top-Level Planning to Salesman Performance," *Business Horizons,* Fall, 1966, pp. 91–100; D. S. Tull, "The Carry-Over Effect of Advertising," *Journal of Marketing,* April, 1965, pp. 46–53; J. L. Simon, "A Simple Model for Determining Advertising Appropriations," *Journal of Marketing Research,* August, 1965, pp. 285–92; P. E. Green, P. J. Robinson, and P. T. Fitzroy, "Advertising Expenditure Models: State of the Art and Prospects," *Business Horizons,* Summer, 1966, pp. 73–80; Joel Dean, "How Much to Spend on Advertising," *Harvard Business Review,* January–February, 1951, pp. 65–74; W. J. Semlow, "How Many Salesmen Do You Need?" *Harvard Business Review,* May–June, 1959, pp. 126–32; C. Freeman, "How to Evaluate Advertising's Contribution," *Harvard Business Review,* July–August, 1962, pp. 133–45 and 148; and M. H. Halbert, "A Practical and Proven Measure of Advertising Effectiveness," in S. H. Britt and H. W. Boyd, Jr., *Marketing Management and Administrative Action* (New York: McGraw-Hill Book Co., 1963), pp. 749–59.

both integrating the effort and carrying it out. The overall company objectives and then the specific Product, Place, Promotion, and Pricing objectives determine what is to be accomplished. Job specifications, advertising campaign plans, pricing policies, and so on should be designed to meet specific problems as they arise during the course of the implementation.

Some marketing managers and analysts have found it helpful to draw flow charts or diagrams of all of the interrelated tasks that must be accomplished on schedule. In recent years, some firms have successfully applied such flow-charting techniques as CPM (critical path method) or PERT (program evaluation and review technique). These techniques were originally developed as part of the United States' NASA space program to insure that the various contractors and subcontractors' efforts would stay on schedule and reach their goals as planned. **Flow charts point the way**

The detailed flow charts used in these approaches describe which marketing activities must be done in sequence and which can be done concurrently. These charts also show the time allotments needed for various activities. By totaling the time allotments along the various chart paths, the most critical (the longest) path, as well as the most desirable starting and ending dates for the various activities within the project, will be shown.

The flow-chart approach is credited with helping Diamond Alkali Co. avoid a difficult situation when introducing a new product. By spending a few days flow charting their plans for this product, Diamond Alkali found that they would spend about 76 weeks introducing it—although their predetermined schedule had allotted only 36 weeks for the introduction. By rearranging their plans with the aid of the flow-chart technique, they did squeeze the effort into 36 weeks. Now the use of flow charts is mandatory for all Diamond Alkali new product introductions.[8]

Marketing managers often make decisions based almost wholly on their judgment and on very little hard information. Yet when data is or could be available, it is pointless to take the risks that such blind-flying decisions entail. **Knowing must come before deciding**

To improve the quality and quantity of decision-related information available, progressive firms are expanding the role assigned to their marketing research departments, turning them into marketing *information* centers. In other companies, it appears that this new function may be separated into a new department because management, regarding the information process as extremely important, wants to assure that it does not get buried in the ongoing activities of the marketing research department.

---

[8] "Applying Advanced Science to Marketing and Ad Plans," *Printers' Ink,* September 24, 1963, pp. 15–21; see also, "Pioneering with PERT, How to Speed Entry into a New Market," *Business Management,* September, 1967, pp. 66–74; and W. Dusenbury, "CPM for New Product Introductions," *Harvard Business Review,* July–August, 1967, pp. 124–37.

Careful analysis of data already available to the company could lead to more effective planning and implementation, helping the marketing manager in his coordinating role. Routine sales analysis, for example, could be organized to determine whether the firm's various target markets were, in fact, purchasing the product.

If management has made its plans carefully, it ought to be able to test continuously whether these plans are working out and the firm is moving toward its objectives. This control activity is discussed at greater length in the next chapter, but here it should be noted that the control activity could do much more than merely assure that the various functional activities will stay within their budgets.

Finding new customers, feeding back data

Routine sales analysis might also reveal surprising new opportunities, perhaps showing that the original target market is not buying but that new and better markets have shown interest.

At Ford Motor Co., sales analysis indicated that more doctors ordered the Thunderbird than men in any other profession. Although doctors had typically driven larger and more formal cars—by tradition, a dark-colored Buick—the sales results indicated they were changing their buying habits to buy the Thunderbird, a sporty personal car. As a result, another strategy was added. Special promotion was aimed directly at the medical profession, with good results.

At the very least, a marketing information system would provide the data needed to control the whole marketing program and the feedback which helps management plan new programs. More is said on this in the next chapter.[9]

Conclusion

In this chapter, we have emphasized the role of marketing management as an integrating force in company management. The marketing concept says that *all* the activities of a company should be directed toward satisfying customers—at a profit. This may require the elimination of the conflicting departmental "empires" often found within a company. But only when a company operates as an integrated system, and as a part of an effective channel system, can it compete most effectively in the marketplace.

Throughout this text, we have stressed marketing strategy planning. In this chapter, we have seen that a marketing manager should develop a plan for carrying out each strategy and then, in turn, coordinate a set of plans into a marketing program.

We described a systematic approach for developing a marketing program. If the planning has been effective, the allocation of budgets to particular functions should be relatively simple.

The development of a marketing program can make use of the total

---

[9] For more discussion on these ideas, see D. F. Cox and R. E. Good, "How to Build a Marketing Information System," *Harvard Business Review*, June, 1967, pp. 145–54; P. Kotler, "A Design for the Firm's Marketing Nerve Center," *Business Horizons*, Fall, 1966, pp. 63–74; G. Albaum, "Information Flow and Decentralized Decision Making in Marketing," *California Management Review*, Summer, 1967, pp. 59–70; and E. B. Weiss, "A Revolution in Communication," *Marketing Insights*, November 14, 1966, pp. 16–18.

cost and total profit approaches for evaluating alternate opportunities. Evaluation should not be limited to one year at a time, however, but should cover some reasonable time period, depending primarily upon the length of the product life cycle and the nature of competition in the firm's target markets. In some extremely competitive markets, a few months may be a reasonable planning cycle. In other markets, 5 to 20 years might be appropriate.

Finally, it is the marketing manager's job to coordinate the whole marketing program and provide liaison within his firm, and between his firm, the channel system and target customers.

1 Explain why a firm should view its internal activities as part of a "total system of action." Illustrate your answer for (*a*) a large grocery products manufacturer, (*b*) a plumbing wholesaler, and (*c*) a department store chain.

2 Does the acceptance of the marketing concept almost demand that a firm view itself as a "total system of action"?

3 When we view a channel as a "total system of action," is there any company executive at any level in the channel who should obviously be considered for the channel captain role? Is it a role which logically falls to someone or some company? Is it a role which could be sought?

4 Consider how the job of the marketing manager becomes more complex as he must develop and plan *several* strategies as part of his marketing program. Be sure to discuss how he might have to handle different strategies at different stages in the product life cycle. To make this more concrete, consider the job of a marketing manager for a sporting goods manufacturer.

5 Discuss how a marketing manager could go about choosing among several possible marketing plans, given that he must because of limited resources. Do you feel that the job would be easier in the consumer goods or in the industrial goods areas? Why?

6 Illustrate how you would go about seeking new and potentially profitable opportunities in your local community if you had $10,000 to $15,000 to invest, your present knowledge and training, and a willingness to work. Become quite specific about how you would proceed, steps you would take, data you would look for, whom you would talk to, and so on.

7 Explain why the budgeting procedure is typically such an agonizing procedure, usually consisting of extending past budgets, perhaps with small modifications for current plans. How would the budgeting procedure be changed if the marketing program planning procedure discussed in the chapter were implemented?

8 Explain how flow charting might be helpful to a marketing manager in coordinating his implementation efforts. In particular, explain how flow charts might be used to help him plan the implementation of his strategies on a week-by-week and month-by-month basis. Sketch what one such flow chart might look like.

9 Discuss the potential importance of a company information center to the marketing manager. In particular, would it be more helpful in his implementation efforts or in his planning efforts? Should he participate

Questions and problems

in the development of such a center, recognizing that usually he is already swamped with other responsibilities?

10 The marketing concept seeks to satisfy customers, but does this mean that marketing management should seek to satisfy the customer in all respects if this entails a reduction in profit? What should guide the efforts of the marketing manager in this respect?

11 Who might be expected to lead the movement toward the marketing concept in manufacturing organizations producing the following products?

a) Dog food   e) Electronic machinery controls
b) Garden tractors   f) Industrial conveying machinery
c) Shovels   g) Industrial lift trucks
d) Cake mixes
Why?

12 Explain why the marketing concept may be even more important to a firm as it expands into worldwide operations. Would such an expansion seem desirable? Or should it be thought of as a necessity? Does it make any difference what products the company is making?

Controlling marketing programs

So far, our main emphasis has been on marketing strategy *planning*—with good reason, as we discussed in Chapter 2. Better results may be achieved by finding unsatisfied target markets and developing good marketing mixes for them.

In fact, if you can do something unique, you may not have to worry too much about how effectively you do it. It is for this reason that we have de-emphasized the details of implementation and of control. Now, however, we want to show that attention to control is very important, both in running an ongoing business system and in discovering new opportunities.

In this chapter, we will discuss methods and techniques for evaluating whether our strategies are being carried out effectively—or if they are even good strategies. In particular, we will focus on sales analysis, performance analysis, and cost analysis.

Control requires feedback

The basic management process consists of planning, execution, and control. For effective management, the executive must receive feedback on the effectiveness of his plans and of their execution. Sales and cost analyses help provide this feedback, showing what has happened and comparing these actual results with what the manager expected would happen or had planned for.

If extreme discrepancies have developed, these are reported back to management as exception reports. This not only permits control of the ongoing process but also aids in planning for the future. A good manager, for example, would want to know more than which products' sales are highest. He would want to know why, and whether they are profitable, so that he could base his judgment on hard facts in developing better plans for the future.

Sales analysis shows what is going on

A detailed breakdown of the company's sales records can be especially illuminating the first time it is done. Too often managers who have moved up in the business are not aware of specific changes that have taken place since they were in the field. This is especially true of managers who have assistants to handle details. Yet the broad marketing decisions for which they are responsible are made on the basis of their knowledge of the business, however outdated or incomplete this may be.

Know who's giving you the business

Some managers hold out against sales analysis, or any analysis for that matter, because they do not fully appreciate how valuable it can be to them. One large producer of consumer products made no attempt to analyze his sales, even by geographical area. When asked why, he replied: "Why should we? We're making money!"

But today's profit is no guarantee of tomorrow's. In fact, this attitude toward sales analysis can lead to poor decisions today. One manufacturer carried on extensive national advertising on the premise that the firm was, in fact, selling nationally. A simple sales analysis, however, revealed that the vast majority of its customers were within a 250-mile radius of the factory. Obviously, the firm was wasting most of the money spent on national advertising. Shortly after the analysis, the advertising manager was fired and the promotion blend readjusted, followed by significantly better sales results.

Routine sales analyses prepared each week, month, or year provide up-to-date data and also may show trends. These analyses also permit members of management to check their hypotheses and assumptions—for example, about the probable responsiveness of various market grid boxes to certain products, package sizes, and store preferences. This may reveal new opportunities, as discussed in Chapter 29 when we saw how the Ford Motor Co. quickly added another strategy when it discovered that physicians were buying the Thunderbird automobile.

The facts are often buried in the invoices

It is hard to overstate the value of careful, ongoing sales analysis. Most of the major auto manufacturers, for example, have installed large-scale electronic computers to analyze their daily sales, according to style and model. Their concern points up the interrelationship of sales and production. It emphasizes the logic of the marketing concept and the treatment of a business as a total system.

Slow sales analysis in the auto business can have severe repercussions on production planning and on profits. One day's overrun of fenders may cause a loss of a least $10,000. In the days before production was

622

tied closely to sales analysis, overruns of several days and sometimes several weeks were common.

Unless definite arrangements are made for sales analysis, however, valuable sales data is buried in sales invoice files after the usual accounting functions are completed. Manual analysis of such records is so lengthy and burdensome that it is seldom undertaken. Today, however, with electronic data processing equipment, effective sales analysis can be done easily and at comparatively small cost—if marketing management wants it done.

Actually, the possibility of getting detailed sales analyses is one of the strongest talking points of data processing salesmen. Sales analysis is usually one of the first EDP applications, since it can be obtained as a by-product of the basic billing and accounts receivable procedures. While the data for these functions is being collected, additional identifying information on the territory, salesmen, and so on, can be recorded easily on punched cards or some other medium. With this data as input to data processing equipment, various sales analyses can be run separately from the accounting function.

Enough reports to drown a manager

There is no one best way to analyze sales data. One or several breakdowns may be appropriate, depending on the nature of the company, its products, and which strategies are being tested or evaluated. Common breakdowns include:

1. Geographical region—states, counties, cities, salesmen's territories, etc.
2. Product, package size, grade, or color.
3. Customer or customer size.
4. Customer type or class of trade.
5. Price or discount class.
6. Method of sales—mail, telephone, or direct salesman.
7. Financial arrangement—cash or charge.
8. Size of order.
9. Commission class.

While this data is a considerable improvement over little data, provided too late for action, such detailed sales breakdowns can easily "drown" a manager in reports. To avoid this, most managers move on to a slightly more sophisticated type of analysis, called performance analysis.

Performance analysis looks for differences

Performance analysis seeks exceptions or variations from planned performance. In simple sales analysis, the facts and figures are merely listed, with no attempt to measure them against standards. In performance analysis, however, comparisons are made. One territory might be compared against another, against the same territory's performance last year, or against the expected performance based on a sales forecast.

The purpose of performance analysis is to improve operations. The salesman, territory, or other units showing poor performance can be identified and singled out for detailed analysis and remedial action. Or especially outstanding performances can be analyzed to see whether these successes can be explained and made the general rule.

Performance analysis need not be concerned only with sales. Other data can be analyzed and compared, too. This data might include miles traveled, number of calls made, number of orders, or the cost of various tasks.

Some performance analyses are done in terms of tons or numbers of units shipped, numbers of salesmen, and other nondollar amounts because the continual fluctuation of prices and costs may make analysis of dollar data misleading. In the meat-packing industry, for example, tonnage shipped is a more significant variable than dollars worth of meat products shipped, because market price levels fluctuate continuously.

How to organize a flood

Much of our discussion of strategy planning was concerned with setting objectives, policies, and tasks to be accomplished. If a firm has expressed these in specific terms, performance analysis can be used routinely to determine whether the plans have been carried out.

Salesmen's call reports contain a great deal of timely and often vital information. But they continue to flood into the home office, and frequently their sheer bulk renders them useless unless the data is quickly transferred into machine-processable form *and* processed. This information may be quite revealing of differences, as is evident in the following example.

An illustration —salesman analysis

A manufacturer of industrial products sold to wholesalers through five salesmen, each serving a separate territory. Total net sales for the year amounted to $1,193,000. Compensation and expenses of salesmen came to $99,000. This yielded a direct-selling expense ratio of 8.3 percent—that is, $99,000 divided by $1,193,000, times 100.

This information, drawn from a profit-and-loss statement, was interesting but did not explain what was actually taking place from one territory to another. To obtain a clearer picture, the analyst segregated and compared the sales results with other data from each territory. See Tables 30–1 and 30–2.

Table **30–1** *Comparative performance of salesmen*

Sales Area	Total Calls	Total Orders	Sale— Call Ratio	Sales by Salesman	Average Salesman Order	Total Customers
A	1,900	1,140	60.0%	$ 456,000	$400	195
B	1,500	1,000	66.7	360,000	360	160
C	1,400	700	50.0	280,000	400	140
D	1,030	279	27.1	66,000	239	60
E	820	165	20.1	31,000	187	50
	6,650	3,784	44.8	$1,193,000	$317	605

SOURCE: Charles H. Sevin, "Analyzing Your Cost of Marketing," *Management Aids for Small Manufacturers* (Washington, D.C.: Small Business Administration, June, 1957), p. 2.

Table 30–2 *Comparative cost of salesmen*

Sales Area	Annual Compensation	Expense Payments	Total Salesman Cost	Sales Produced	Cost— Sales Ratio
A	$11,400	$ 5,600	$17,000	$ 456,000	3.7%
B	10,800	7,200	18,000	360,000	5.0
C	10,200	5,800	16,000	280,000	5.7
D	9,600	12,400	22,000	66,000	33.3
E	10,000	16,000	26,000	31,000	83.8
	$52,000	$47,000	$99,000	$1,193,000	8.3%

SOURCE: Charles H. Sevin, "Analyzing Your Cost of Marketing," *Management Aids for Small Manufacturers* (Washington, D.C.: Small Business Administration, June, 1957), p. 2.

The salesmen in sales areas D and E obviously were not doing well. Sales were low, and marketing costs were high. Perhaps salesmen with more "push" could have done a better job, but the number of customers suggests that the potential might be low.

The figures themselves, of course, do not provide the answers—but they do reveal the areas that need remedial action.[1] This is the main value of performance analysis. It is up to sales management to provide the remedy.

Performance indices simplify human analysis

As a supplement to this simple performance analysis, the marketing manager could evaluate personally the variations among salesmen in an effort to explain the "why." This is time-consuming, however, and sometimes the truth is that "poor" performances actually are not so bad as the bare figures may seem to indicate. There may be adverse or uncontrollable factors in a particular territory which automatically lower the sales potential. Or it may be found that a territory did not have good potential to begin with.

A better check on the effectiveness of performance is obtained when the marketing manager is able to compare what "ought to have happened" with what did happen. At first, this may seem akin to looking into a crystal ball, but it need not be.

When the marketing manager develops his plans and forecasts, he should break these down into their components so that when the figures are in, he can compare actual performance against expected performance. If the regular planning procedure does not require such detailed breakdowns, then it may be fruitful to prepare them anyway. As the basis for such breakdowns, he can use such measures as population in each salesman's territory, the number of last year's orders, or another logical quantitative measurement. While not all significant factors can be quantified, this is a good start.

When the company is selling a product that should appeal to all consumers, the size of population in each territory might be useful for breaking down a product sales forecast. But if the marketing mix is

[1] Charles H. Sevin, "Analyzing Your Cost of Marketing," *Management Aids for Small Manufacturers* (Washington, D.C.: Small Business Administration, June, 1957), p. 2.

directed to very specific target markets, their particular characteristics should be used. If the product were aimed specifically at high-income groups, for example, population size might be modified by income to develop an accurate estimate of potential. Going a step further, if the product were aimed mainly at higher income groups in particular areas, such as suburbs, additional modifications should be made. Data for this type of analysis can be obtained from the Census Bureau or from such private sources as *Sales Management's* "Survey of Buying Power," discussed in Chapter 5.

How are the salesmen batting. When standards have been developed—that is, quantitative measures of what "ought to have happened"—it is then a relatively simple matter to develop a *performance index*. This is merely a number, such as a baseball batting average, which shows the relation of one value to another.

Table 30–3 Development of a measure of sales performance (by regions)

Regions	(Col. 1) Population as Percent of U.S.	(Col. 2) Expected Distribution of Sales Based on Population	(Col. 3) Actual Sales	(Col. 4) Performance Index
Eastern	25	$ 250,000	$ 150,000	60
Southern	20	200,000	250,000	125
Midwestern	25	250,000	300,000	120
Mountain	10	100,000	100,000	100
Western	20	200,000	200,000	100
Total	100	$1,000,000	$1,000,000	

Baseball batting averages are computed by dividing the actual number of hits by the number of times at bat (the possible number of times the batter could have had a hit). A sales performance index is computed by dividing actual sales by expected sales for an area (or salesman, product, etc.) and then multiplying this figure by 100 to eliminate decimal points. If a salesman is "batting" 82 percent, the index is 82.

Now, that's where the problem is. The development of a performance index is illustrated in the following problem, which assumes that population provides an adequate measure of sales potential.

In Table 30–3, the population of the United States is broken down by regions as a percentage of the total population. The regions in this case are the Eastern, Southern, Midwestern, Mountain, and Western.

This firm already has achieved $1 million in sales and now wants to evaluate performance in each region. The actual sales of $1 million, broken down in proportion to the population in the five regions, are shown in column 2. This is how sales should have been distributed if population were a good measure of future performance. The third column in Table 30–3 shows the actual sales for the year for each region. The fourth column shows measures of performance (perform-ance indices), which are column 3 divided by column 2, multiplied by 100.

Note that population in the Eastern region was 25 percent of the population, and expected sales (based on population) were $250,000. Actual sales, however, were only $150,000. This means that the Eastern region's performance index was only 60—actual sales were much lower than would be expected on the basis of population.

If population is a sound basis for measuring expected sales (which is an important *if*), then the explanation for poor sales performance will have to be traced further. Perhaps the salesmen in the Eastern region are not doing as well as they should. Perhaps promotion in this region is not as effective as elsewhere. Or competitive products may have entered the market in this region. It may be that there are some other problems.

Whatever the cause, it should be understood that performance analy-sis does not solve problems. It pinpoints problems—and it does this well.

Use the data that is best

Data processing equipment can quickly calculate performance in-dices, and then it is a relatively simple matter for the manager to skim these and look for extremely high or extremely low performances. He no longer has to look through all the detailed data and try to determine whether each item has deviated from some reasonable expected figure.

Performance analysis is quite flexible. If an aggregate sales forecast had been developed in the example just discussed, it could have been broken down as in column 2 and the performance indices developed by comparing actual sales with a breakdown of forecasted sales. If a detailed sales forecast had been made for each region, then this data could have been inserted in column 2.

The basic concept is to compare actual to anticipated performance, and obviously the manager would want to use the best data available.

Performance analysis can find the real problem

Routine performance analysis can enable a marketing manager to probe and discover whether the firm's marketing activities are working properly and, if not, to correct the problems. This may require a series of performance analyses as shown in the following example.

To get an impression of the passage of time, follow this example carefully, one table at a time. Try to anticipate the marketing manag-er's decision.

The case of Stereo, Inc. Stereo's sales manager found that sales for the Pacific Coast region were $130,000 below the quota of $14,500,000 (that is, actual sales were $14,370,000) for the January–June, 1967, period. The quota was based on forecasted sales of the various types of stereophonic sound equipment which the company manufactures. Spe-cifically, the quota was based on forecasts for each product type in each store in each salesman's territory.

The sales manager felt this discrepancy was not too large (1.52 percent) and was inclined to forget the matter, especially since forecasts usually err to some extent. He was considering sending a letter, however, to all salesmen and district supervisors in the region, a letter aimed at stimulating sales effort.

The overall story of what was happening to Stereo's sales on the Coast was told in the following district sales figures. What should the manager do?

Sales performance—Pacific Coast region, January–June, 1967 (in thousands of dollars)

District	Quota	Actual	Plus or Minus	Performance to Quota
Los Angeles	$ 4,675	$ 4,765	Plus $ 90	102%
San Francisco	3,625	3,675	Plus 50	101
Portland	3,000	2,800	Minus 200	93
Seattle	3,200	3,130	Minus 70	98
	$14,500	$14,370	Minus $130	99%

Before writing an exhortatory letter, the sales manager decided to analyze the performance of the four salesmen in the Portland district, which had the poorest sales. A breakdown of the Portland figures by salesmen is shown below. What conclusion or action is suggested?

Sales performance—Portland district, January–June, 1967 (in thousands of dollars)

Salesmen	Quota	Actual	Plus or Minus	Performance to Quota
Johnson	$ 750	$ 780	Plus $ 30	104%
Smith	800	550	Minus 250	69
Jones	790	840	Plus 50	106
Carson	660	630	Minus 30	95
	$3,000	$2,800	Minus $200	93%

Since Smith had been the top salesman, the sales manager wondered if Smith were having trouble with some of his larger accounts. Before making a drastic move, he obtained the following analysis of Smith's sales to five large accounts. What action could he take now? Should Smith be fired?

Smith's sales in all the large stores were down significantly, although his sales in many small stores were holding up well. It would seem that Smith's problem was general. Perhaps he was simply not working. One other aspect which the sales manager decided to investigate was Smith's sales of the four major products. The following data was obtained. What action is indicated now?

628

Sales performance—Selected stores of Mr. Smith in Portland disitrict, January–June, 1967 (in thousands of dollars)

Stores	Quota	Actual	Plus or Minus	Perform- ance to Quota
1	$140	$ 65	Minus $ 75	46%
2	110	70	Minus 40	69
3	105	60	Minus 45	57
4	130	65	Minus 65	50
5	205	150	Minus 55	73
Others	110	140	Plus 30	127
	$800	$550	Minus $250	69%

Sales performance—Mr. Smith in Portland district, January– June, 1967 (in thousands of dollars)

Product	Quota	Actual	Plus or Minus	Perform- ance to Quota
Tape recorders	$ 70	$ 80	Plus $ 10	114%
Portable phonographs	430	160	Minus 270	37
Console phonographs	150	150	0	100
Speakers	100	110	Plus 10	110
Others	50	50	0	100
	$800	$550	Minus $250	69%

Smith was having real trouble with portable phonographs. Was the problem Smith or the phonographs?

Further analysis by product for the whole region indicated that everyone on the Pacific Coast was having trouble with portable phono- graphs because a regional competitor was cutting prices, but higher sales on other products had hidden this fact. Since phonograph sales had been doing all right nationally, this problem was only now coming to light. Clearly, this is *the* major problem.

Since overall company sales were going fairly well, many sales executives would not have bothered with this analysis. They might or might not have traced the problem to Smith. But without detailed sales records and performance analysis, the natural human reaction of a Smith would be to blame business conditions or aggressive competition or to seek some other handy excuse.

Stay home and use the computer. This case shows that aggregate figures can be deceiving. Marketing managers should not jump on the first plane or reach for the telephone until they have all the facts. The home office should have the records and facilities to isolate problem areas, then rely on the field staff for explanations and assistance in locating the precise problem. The field sales force and those in charge of execution may not be familiar with all details. A salesman may know only generally what products are ordered by his customers, especially if the customers send orders directly to the company. Even if the salesman gets copies of the invoices, it is not a simple task to summarize mentally all of the details on many invoices and to draw accurate conclusions.

Even worse than rushing to the scene would be a rash judgment based on inadequate information. Some students have wanted to fire Smith after the store-by-store data was presented in the third table. Continuing analysis usually is fruitful, as this case shows. With EDP equipment, this can be done routinely and in great detail, *provided marketing management requests it.*

The "iceberg" principle

One of the most interesting conclusions to be drawn out of the Stereo illustration is the "iceberg" principle.[2] Icebergs, as everyone knows, show only about 10 percent of their mass above the water level, the other 90 percent being below the water level—and not directly below, either. The submerged portion almost seems to be searching out ships that come too near.

The same is true of much business and marketing data. Since sales volumes may be large and overall company activities so varied, difficulties or problems in one area may be submerged below the surface. All may appear to be calm and peaceful, yet a more careful analysis may reveal jagged edges which may severely damage or even "sink" the business. The lesson to be learned is that averaging and summarizing data can be helpful to the business executive, but he had better be wary that his summaries do not hide more than they reveal.

The Stereo, Inc., case dramatically illustrates what results can be obtained from careful sales and performance analysis. The analyses presented earlier in Tables 30–1 and 30–2 also illustrate the iceberg principle. In that case, the direct selling expense ratio of 8.3 obtained from the profit and loss statement did not reveal any of the underlying problems.[3]

Marketing cost analysis

So far we have emphasized sales analysis. But sales are obtained only at a cost. And costs can and should be analyzed and controlled.

Detailed cost analysis has been highly useful in the factory, but much less has been done with marketing cost accounting.[4] Many accountants,

---

[2] Richard D. Crisp, *Marketing Research* (New York: McGraw-Hill Book Co., 1957), p. 144.

[3] For further discussion on these matters, see Allan Easton, "A Forward Step in Performance Evaluation," *Journal of Marketing,* July, 1966, pp. 26–32; *Sales Analysis* (Studies in Business Policies No. 113 [New York: National Industrial Conference Board, 1965]); and *Measuring Salesmen's Performance* (Studies in Business Policies No. 114 [New York: National Industrial Conference Board, 1965]).

[4] See "Norton Helps Distributors in Cost Analysis," *Industrial Marketing,* March, 1958; "15,800 More Sales Calls per Year," *Sales Management,* December 5, 1958, pp. 48–55; James R. Snitzler, "How Wholesalers Can Cut Delivery Costs," *Journal of Marketing,* July, 1958, pp. 25–31; William F. Peters, "Control of Stocks in Grocery Retailing," *Journal of Marketing,* October, 1957, pp. 148–53; Leo V. Aspinwall, *Are Your Merchandise Lines Paying Their Rent?* (Small Marketers Aids No. 30 [Washington, D.C.: Small

unfortunately, have shown little interest in the marketing process. Many think of salesmen as "gay blades" who wine-and-dine the customers, play golf all afternoon, and occasionally pick up orders. In this situation, they feel it is impossible to allocate the wide-ranging costs of selling to particular products or customers. Many accountants have felt, too, that advertising is almost a complete waste of money—and that there is no way of tracing it to particular sales. They have wound up treating it as a general overhead cost, then forgotten about it.

Careful analysis of most marketing expenditures, however, shows that the money is spent to accomplish a specific purpose—either to prepare or promote a *particular product* or to serve *particular customers*. It is reasonable, then, to seek ways to allocate costs to specific customers or to specific products. Expected costs then can be compared to actual costs, and performance indices can be computed as we did with sales data. **Marketing costs have a purpose**

There are two basic approaches to cost analysis—the full-cost approach and the contribution-margin approach. We will discuss each of these in turn.

First, however, it is important to note that marketing cost analysis usually requires a new way of classifying accounting data. We want to use not "natural" accounts but "functional" accounts.

Natural accounts are the categories to which various costs are charged in the normal accounting cycle. These accounts include salaries, wages, social security, taxes, supplies, raw materials, auto, gas and oil expenses, advertising, and other such categories. These accounts are called "natural" because they bear the names of their expense categories. **Natural versus functional accounts**

This is not the approach to cost analysis used in factories, however, and it is not the one we will use. In the factory, functional accounts are set up to indicate the *purpose* for which the expenditures are made. Factory functional accounts include shearing, milling, grinding, floor cleaning, maintenance, and so on. Frequently, factory cost accounting records are so organized that the cost of particular products or jobs can be developed from them.

Various marketing jobs are done for specific purposes, too. With some foresight and analysis, the costs of marketing also can be allocated to specific categories, such as customers and products.

The first step in marketing cost analysis is to reclassify all the dollar cost entries in the natural accounts into functional cost accounts. The many cost items in the natural *salary* account might be allocated to functional accounts with the following names: storage, inventory control, order assembly, packing and shipping, transportation, selling, **Marketing cost analysis finds no-profit Jones**

Business Administration, December, 1957); "Cost Accounting, Wholesalers Must Learn Which Departments Make—or Lose—Money," *Hardware Retailer,* May, 1958; and of course the basic texts in this area—Donald R. Longman and Michael Schiff, *Practical Distribution Cost Analysis* (Homewood, Ill.: Richard D. Irwin, Inc., 1955), and J. Brooks Heckert and Robert B. Miner, *Distribution Costs* (2d ed.; New York: Ronald Press Co., 1953).

advertising, order entry, billing, credit extension, and accounts receivable. Similarly, the entries in the natural *supplies* account would be allocated to the functional accounts for which those supply expenditures were made. The same would be true for rent, depreciation, heat, light, power, and other natural accounts.

The method of reallocating natural to functional accounts is not fixed. It depends on the method of operation of the particular firm. If a company were making only one product and selling its entire output to a single customer, then it could assign all of its marketing costs to that product or customer. But since most companies serve a diverse market with a large number of products, a more detailed classification is necessary.

After the firm's method of operation has been studied, specific cost items can be distributed to functional cost groups by means of time studies, space measurements, actual accounts, and managerial estimates.

The costs allocated to the functional accounts would equal in total those in the natural accounts. They are merely organized in a different way. But instead of being used just to show total firm profitability, they can now be arranged to show the profitability of territories, products, customers, salesmen, price classes, order sizes, methods of distribution, methods of sale, or any other breakdown desired.

The next step is to reallocate the functional costs to those things or customers for which the costs were incurred. The most common reallocation of functional costs is to products and to customers. After all of the costs are allocated to each product and each customer, then these detailed totals can be recombined in any way desired, for example, by product or customer class, region, and so on.

Illustrative example. These ideas can be seen more clearly in the following hypothetical example. In this case, the usual accounting approach—with natural accounts—showed that the company made a profit of $938 last month. The profit and loss statement was as follows:

Sales		$17,000
Cost of goods sold		11,900
Gross Margin		5,100
Expenses		
Salaries	$2,500	
Rent	500	
Wrapping supplies	1,012	
Stationery and stamps	50	
Office equipment	100	
		4,162
Net Profit		$ 938

When a question is raised about the profitability of the company's three customers, the above statement is of no help. The marketing manager decides to use marketing cost analysis because he wants to know whether a change in marketing methods might improve profit.

First, the costs in the five natural accounts are distributed to four

632

functional accounts—sales, packaging, advertising, and billing and collection (see Table 30–4)—according to the functional reason for incurring the expenses. Specifically, $1,000 of the total salary cost was for salesmen who seldom even come into the office, since their function is to call on customers; $900 of the salary cost was for packaging labor; and $600 was for office help. It is estimated that the office force split its time about evenly between addressing and mailing advertising and other material, and the billing and collection function. So the $600 is split evenly into these two functional accounts.

The $500 for rent was for the entire building, but 80 percent of the floor space was used for packaging and 20 percent for the office. Thus $400 is allocated to the packaging account. The remaining $100 is divided evenly between the advertising and billing accounts because these functions used the office space about equally. The stationery and stamps, and office equipment charges are allocated equally to the latter

Table 30–4 Spreading natural accounts to functional accounts

Natural Accounts		Functional Accounts			
		Sales	Packaging	Advertising	Billing and Collection
Salaries	$2,500	$1,000	$ 900	$300	$300
Rent	500		400	50	50
Wrapping supplies	1,012		1,012		
Stationery and stamps	50			25	25
Office equipment	100			50	50
	$4,162	$1,000	$2,312	$425	$425

two accounts for the same reason. Charges for wrapping supplies are allocated to the packaging account because all of these supplies were used in packaging. In another situation, different allocations and even different accounts might be appropiate, but these are workable here.

Now we are in a better position to calculate the profitability of the company's three customers. But additional information is needed before we can allocate these functional accounts to customers or products. It is presented in tabular form in Table 30–5 for convenient reference.

Table 30–5 shows that the company's three products vary in cost, selling price, and sales volume. The products also have different "bulks," and so the packaging costs are unrelated to the selling price. For example, product C is six times bulkier than A. When packaging costs are allocated to products, this must be considered. This is accomplished by computing a new measure—a packaging "unit"—which is used to allocate the costs in the packaging account. Packaging units take into consideration relative bulk and the number of each type of product sold. While only 10 units of product C are sold, it is bulky and requires 10 times 6, or 60 packaging units. This will cause relatively

Table 30–5 Basic data for cost analysis example

A. PRODUCTS

Products	Cost/Unit	Selling Price/Unit	No. Units Sold in Period	Sales Volume in Period	Relative "Bulk" per Unit	Packaging "Units"
A	$ 7	$ 10	1,000	$10,000	1	1,000
B	35	50	100	5,000	3	300
C	140	200	10	2,000	6	60
			1,110	$17,000		1,360

B. CUSTOMERS

Customers	No. of Sales Calls in Period	No. of Orders Placed in Period	No. of Each Product Ordered in Period		
			A	B	C
Smith	30	30	900	30	0
Jones	40	3	90	30	3
Brown	30	1	10	40	7
	100	34	1,000	100	10

more of the costs in the packaging account to be allocated to each unit of product C.

Table 30–5 also shows that the three customers require different amounts of sales effort, place different numbers of orders, and buy different product combinations.

Jones requires more sales calls. Smith places many orders which must be processed in the office, with increased billing expense. Brown seems to be an attractive customer, since he placed only one order—accounting for 70 percent of the sales of high-valued product C.

The basic computations for allocating the functional account amounts to the three customers are shown in Table 30–6. There were 100 sales calls in the period. With no reason to assume that any calls were more time-consuming than others, it is logical to derive the average cost per call by dividing the $1,000 sales cost by 100 calls, giving an average cost of $10. Similar reasoning is used in breaking down the billing and packaging account totals. Advertising during this period was for the benefit of product C only, and this cost is split among the units of C sold.

Table 30–6 Functional cost account allocations

Sales calls =	$1,000/100 calls	= $10/call
Billing =	$425/34 orders	= $12.50/order
Packaging unit costs =	$2,312/1,360 packaging units	= $1.70/packaging unit or
		$ 1.70 for product A
		$ 5.10 " " B
		$10.20 " " C
Advertising =	$425/10 units of C	= $42.50/unit of C

634

Now we can compute a profit and loss statement for each customer, allowing for his purchases and the cost of serving him. This is done in Table 30–7. A statement is developed for each customer, and of course the sum of each of the four major components (sales, cost of goods sold, expenses, and profit) is the same as on the original statement. We have merely rearranged and renamed the data, for analysis purposes.

The explanation of this procedure is in Smith's statement in Table 30–7. Smith bought 900 units of A at $10 each and 30 units of B at $50 each for the respective sales totals ($9,000 and $1,500) shown in Table 30–7. Cost of goods sold is computed on the same basis. Thirty sales calls at an average of $10 each were made on Smith. Total sales calls cost $300. He placed 30 orders (at an average cost of $12.50 each time)

Table 30–7 Profit and loss statements for customers

	Smith	Jones	Brown	Whole Company
Sales				
A....................	$9,000	$ 900	$ 100	
B....................	1,500	1,500	2,000	
C....................		600	1,400	
Total Sales..........	$10,500	$3,000	$3,500	$17,000
Cost of goods sold				
A....................	$6,300	$ 630	$ 70	
B....................	1,050	1,050	1,400	
C....................		420	980	
Total Cost of Goods Sold.............	$ 7,350	$2,100	$2,450	$11,900
Gross Margin....	$ 3,150	$ 900	$1,050	$ 5,100
Expenses				
Sales calls ($10 each).......	$ 300	$ 400.00	$ 300.00	
Order costs ($12.50 ea.).....	375	37.50	12.50	
Packaging costs				
A....................	1,530	153.00	17.00	
B....................	153	153.00	204.00	
C....................		30.60	71.40	
Advertising..............		127.50	297.50	
	2,358	901.60	902.40	4,162
Net Profit (or Loss)....	$ 792	$ (1.60)	$ 147.60	$ 938

for a total ordering cost of $375. And total packaging costs amounted to $1,530 for A (900 units purchased times $1.70 per unit) and $153 for B (30 units purchased times $5.10 per unit). There were no packaging costs for C because Smith did not buy any of product C. Neither were any advertising costs charged to Smith, since all costs were spent promoting product C, which he did not buy.

We see now that Smith was the most profitable customer—yielding over 75 percent of the net profit.

This analysis shows that Brown was profitable, too, but not as profitable as Smith, because Smith bought three times as much. Jones was unprofitable because he bought too little and required one third more sales calls.

It is clear that the "iceberg" principle is operating again here. Although the company as a whole is profitable, customer Jones is not profitable. Before taking any drastic action, however, the marketing manager should study his figures and methods of operation very carefully. Perhaps Jones should be called on less frequently, or perhaps he will grow into a profitable account. The marketing manager many also want to analyze his advertising costs against results, since this is a heavy expense against each unit of product C.

Cost analysis is not performance analysis

This cost analysis is not performance analysis, of course. If the marketing manager had budgeted various costs to various tasks, it would be possible to extend the cost analysis to a cost performance analysis. This would be a logical and perhaps a desirable extension, but few companies have moved this far as yet.

As the cost of computer-oriented record keeping drops further, we may see some companies accumulating detailed data on the cost of servicing various customers. They could then compute fairly realistic profit and loss statements for individual customers, just as some factory cost accounting systems can develop fairly realistic cost estimates for products.

Cost analysis can be quite sophisticated

It is clear that cost analysis can be an aid in spotting troubles—if management is willing to reallocate costs from natural to functional accounts, and then to products and customers. Our simple example emphasizes the concepts. A more realistic example would involve much more detail, but the ideas and approach are the same.

To show the detail that might be needed in a real situation, the 12 functional accounts used by one company are presented in Table 30–8 together with the bases for allocating the functional account totals to products and customers.

Note that some cost groups show bases of allocation to both products and customers. Obviously, a functional cost group will not be allocated to both at the same time. If the analysis is by products, all the expenses that logically can be allocated directly to specific products will be carried there. The remainder of the functional cost groups will be allocated to *all* products on some logical basis, such as dollars of sales or numbers of units.

If the analysis were to be by customers, all the functional costs would be allocated to customers if possible. Others would be allocated to products. Then these product-oriented costs could be charged to customers on the basis of the volumes of each product sold to each customer.

We have discussed the general principles, but the matter of allocating costs is a sticky one. Some costs are likely to be fixed for the near future, regardless of what decision is made. And some costs are likely to be *common* to several products or customers, making allocation difficult.

There are two basic approaches to handling this difficult problem—the full-cost approach and the contribution-margin approach.

Full-cost approach

In the full-cost approach, all functional costs are allocated to products, customers, or other categories. Even fixed costs (those that do not vary in the short run) are allocated in some way, as are common costs.

Table 30-8 *Functional cost groups and possible bases of allocation to products and customers*

Functional Cost Groups	Bases of Allocation To Products	Bases of Allocation To Customers
1. Investment in finished goods	Average inventory value.	(Not allocated)
2. Storage of finished goods	Floor space occupied.	(Not allocated)
3. Inventory control, finished goods	No. of invoice lines.	(Not allocated)
4. Order assembly (handling)	No. of standard handling units.	No. of invoice lines.
5. Packing and shipping	Weight or no. of shipping units.	Weight or number of shipping units.
6. Transportation	Weight or no. of shipping units.	Weight or no. of shipping units.
7. Selling	Time studies.	No. of sales calls.
8. Advertising	Cost of space, etc., of specific product.	Cost of space, etc. of specific customer advertising.
9. Order entry	No. of invoice lines.	No. of orders.
10. Billing	No. of invoice lines.	No. of invoice lines.
11. Credit extension	(Not allocated)	Average amount outstanding.
12. Accounts receivable	(Not allocated)	No. of invoices posted.

SOURCE: Charles H. Sevin, "Analyzing Your Cost of Marketing," *Management Aids for Small Manufacturers* (Washington, D.C.: Small Business Administration, June, 1957), p. 3.

Full-cost approach—everything costs something

The full-cost approach is used to determine the profit for particular products or customers, or the total cost of various alternatives. This usually requires that some costs that are difficult to allocate be apportioned on some such basis as dollars of sales or numbers of units.

The assumption here is that the services provided for those costs were equally beneficial to customers, to products, or to whatever group they are allocated. Sometimes this is done rather mechanically, but often logical reasoning can support the allocation providing that we accept the idea that marketing costs are incurred for a purpose. Advertising costs, for example, that are not directly allocatable to specific customers or products, *might* be allocated to all customers on the basis of their purchases. The theory is that this advertising has helped bring in the sales.

Full cost finds a poor strategy

The full-cost approach allocates all costs to some groups, and so it is possible to relate these costs to the revenue received from these groups and determine each one's profitability. An evaluation of this profitability and the effort expended may help determine the effectiveness of various strategies and lead to the development of new ones, as the following example illustrates.

When product "I" was added to a company's line, it was promoted vigorously because of its high gross margin. Many businessmen automatically associate a high gross margin with a high net profit!

The company's sales executives were enthusiastic about the new product because they felt it could be added to a family of products at little additional cost. A subsequent analysis, however, indicated that the new item was not really in the same product family. There were differences in physical characteristics, handling, and volume per sale. But more important, the new product appealed more strongly to a different target market.

Table **30–9** *Margins, distribution costs, and profits, by product groups during one year's operations*

Product Group	Gross Margin per Unit of Product	Distribution Cost per Unit of Product	Profit or Loss per Unit of Product	Volume per Item Percent of Average	Volume per Sales Call Percent of Average
A	$0.46	$0.43	$0.03	178	219
B	0.45	0.53	−0.08	119	109
C	0.24	0.42	−0.18	186	150
D	0.99	0.64	0.35	52	56
E	1.08	0.58	0.50	77	82
F	0.76	0.42	0.34	158	151
G	0.71	0.79	−0.08	63	56
H	0.96	0.72	0.24	52	56
I	1.31	1.25	0.06	15	21
Averages or totals, entire business......	$0.74	$0.65	$0.09	100	100

SOURCE: Charles H. Sevin, *How Manufacturers Reduce Their Distribution Costs* (Economic Series No. 72, U.S. Department of Commerce), Case 44.

The analysis which developed as a part of their control operation is shown in Table 30–9. A detailed cost allocation approach of the kind shown in Table 30–8 was used in this case.

The company found that product "I" was contributing a small profit but far less than was expected from the high gross margin. More detailed analysis indicated that the product was sold and consumed in small quantities, and found its largest market in small stores (which are generally more expensive to serve). It appeared that it would be difficult to change customers' buying habits. Demand appeared to be quite elastic, but because of the relatively high expense of serving this target market, a price cut did not appear profitable.

To solve this problem, the firm reallocated promotional effort away from product "I" and toward the faster moving products. In one year, the marketing costs for the firm's average unit had dropped from 65 cents to 59 cents and the profit per unit had climbed from 9 to 17 cents. The cost of distributing product "I" had declined so that its profitability was about average. It appeared that this new strategy would be continued until better use could be made of the company's resources.[5]

When we use the contribution-margin approach, it is not necessary to consider all costs in *all* situations. What is the value of this?

Contribution margin ignores some costs to see results

When various alternatives are being compared, it may be most helpful for management to consider only the costs which really are directly related to particular alternatives. Variable costs are particularly relevant here, as we saw when we discussed break-even analysis in Chapter 25.

The contribution-margin approach focuses the attention of management on variable costs rather than on total costs, which may include either some fixed costs, which do not change in the short run and can safely be ignored, or some common costs, which are more difficult to allocate.[6]

Table **30–10** *Profit and loss statement by department for the year 196X*

	Totals	Depart- ment 1	Depart- ment 2	Depart- ment 3
Sales	$100,000	$50,000	$30,000	$20,000
Cost of goods sold	80,000	45,000	25,000	10,000
Gross margin	$ 20,000	$ 5,000	$ 5,000	$10,000
Other expenses				
Selling expenses	5,000	2,500	1,500	1,000
Administrative expenses	6,000	3,000	1,800	1,200
Total Other Expenses	$ 11,000	$ 5,500	$ 3,300	$ 2,200
Net Profit or (Loss)	$ 9,000	$ (500)	$ 1,700	$ 7,800

SOURCE: Robert K. Jaedicke, "A Method for Making Product-Combination Decisions," *Business News Notes* (Minneapolis: University of Minnesota, April, 1958), pp. 1–2.

The distinction between the full-cost approach and the contribution-margin approach is not academic. Different decisions may be suggested by the two approaches. These are contrasted in the following example. Table 30–10 shows a profit and loss statement, using the full-cost approach, for a department store with three operating departments.

[5] Charles H. Sevin, *How Manufacturers Reduce Their Distribution Costs* (Economic Series No. 72, U.S. Department of Commerce), Case 44.

[6] Technically, a distinction should be made between variable and direct costs, but we will use these terms interchangeably. Similarly, not all common costs are fixed costs and vice versa, but the important point here is to recognize that some costs are fairly easy to allocate, and other costs are not.

Table **30–11** *Profit and loss statement by department for the year 196X if Department 1 were eliminated*

	Totals	Department 2	Department 3
Sales	$50,000	$30,000	$20,000
Cost of goods sold	35,000	25,000	10,000
Gross margin	$15,000	$ 5,000	$10,000
Other expenses			
Selling expenses	2,500	1,500	1,000
Administrative expenses	6,000	3,600	2,400
Total Other Expenses	$ 8,500	$ 5,100	$ 3,400
Net Profit or (Loss)	$ 6,500	$ (100)	$ 6,600

The administrative expenses, which represent the only fixed cost in this particular case, have been allocated to departments on the basis of percentage of sales volume of each department—a typical method of allocation. In this case, some executives argued that Department 1 was clearly unprofitable and should be eliminated because it showed a net loss of $500. Were they correct?

To find out, see Table 30–11 which shows what would happen if Department 1 were eliminated.

Several facts immediately become clear. The overall profit of the store would be reduced if Department 1 were dropped. Fixed costs amounting to $3,000, now being charged to Department 1, would have to be allocated to the other departments; this would reduce net profit $2,500, since Department 1 previously covered $2,500 of the $3,000 fixed costs charged. This shifting of costs would then make Department 2 unprofitable.

Table **30–12** *Contribution-margin statement by departments for the year 196X*

	Totals	Dept. 1	Dept. 2	Dept. 3
Sales	$100,000	$50,000	$30,000	$20,000
Variable costs				
Cost of goods sold	80,000	45,000	25,000	10,000
Selling expenses	5,000	2,500	1,500	1,000
Total variable costs	$ 85,000	$47,500	$26,500	$11,000
Contribution margin	15,000	2,500	3,500	9,000
Fixed costs				
Administrative expenses	6,000			
Net Profit	$ 9,000			

SOURCE: Robert K. Jaedicke, "A Method for Making Product-Combination Decisions," *Business News Notes* (Minneapolis: University of Minnesota, April, 1958), pp. 1–2.

A contribution-margin income statement for the department store is shown in Table 30–12. Note that each department has a positive contribution margin. Here the Department 1 contribution of $2,500 is obvious. This actually is the amount that would be lost if Department 1 were dropped. (This example assumes that the fixed administrative expenses are *truly* fixed—that none of them would be eliminated if this department were eliminated.)

A contribution-margin income statement shows the contribution of each department more clearly, including its contribution to both fixed costs and profit. As long as a department or other unit has some contribution margin—and as long as there are no better alternative uses for the resources invested in it—then the department or salesman or product or other variable in the particular analysis should be retained.

Contribution margin versus full cost— choose your side

The full-cost approach often leads to controversy within the company. Any one method of allocation tends to make some products or customers appear less profitable than another allocation method would.

Allocating all common advertising costs to customers, based on their purchases, can be supported logically. But it also can be criticized on the ground that it may make large-volume customers appear less profitable than they actually are, especially if the marketing mix which is aimed at the larger customers focuses more on price than on advertising.

Those in the company who are interested in having the smaller customers look more profitable will argue for this allocation method on the grounds that general advertising helps "build" good customers because it affects the overall image of the company and its products.

In one sense, such arguments are futile, since the only goal of allocation is to clearly identify expenses and their sources and to give the firm a better picture of its operations.

The argument about allocation methods may be deadly serious, however, because which of the allocation methods is used may determine the apparent performance of various company executives and subsequently their salaries and bonuses. The product managers, for example, would be vitally interested in how the various fixed and common costs were allocated to products. Each, in turn, might like to have costs shifted to his colleagues' products.

Arbitrary allocation of costs also may have a direct impact on salesmen morale. If salesmen see their variable costs "loaded" with additional common or fixed costs over which they have no control, they may decide, "What's the use?"

To avoid this problem, the contribution-margin approach is frequently used in marketing cost analysis. It avoids many of the problems of arbitrarily allocating fixed or common costs. It is especially useful for evaluating alternatives, and it is also useful for showing operating executives and salesmen how they are performing. The contribution-margin approach shows what they have actually contributed to the general overhead and profit.

Top management, on the other hand, often finds full-cost analysis more useful. In the long run, some product, department, or customer must bear the fixed costs. Full-cost analysis has its place here.[7]

Planning and control combined

We have been treating sales and cost analyses separately up to this point. But often management will combine them to help keep a running check on its activities—to be sure that the plans are materializing or to see when and where new strategies are needed.

Let us see how this works at the XYZ Hardware Co., a typical hardware retailer.

This firm netted $7,750 last year. Expecting no basic change in the competitive situation and slightly better local business conditions, the manager set this year's profit goal at $8,150, an increase of about 5 percent.

Next, he began developing tentative plans to show how this higher profit could be made. He estimated the sales volumes, gross margins, and expenses—broken down by months and by the departments in his store—which would be necessary to net $8,150.

Table 30–13 is a planning and control chart which the XYZ manager developed to show the contribution which should be made each month by each department. At the bottom of Table 30–13, the plan for the year is summarized. Notice that space is provided to insert the actual performance and a measure of variation, allowing both planning and control functions to be implemented with this table.

Table 30–13 shows that XYZ's manager is focusing on the monthly contribution by each department. The purpose of monthly estimates is to get more frequent feedback and to enable more frequent adjustment of plans. Generally, the shorter the planning and review period, the easier it is to correct problems before they become emergencies.

Here, we concentrate on the contribution of each department and on profit. A modified contribution-margin approach is being used, since some of the fixed costs can be allocated logically to particular departments. On this chart, the balance left after direct fixed and variable costs are charged to departments is called "Contribution to Store." The hope is that each department will contribute to covering *general* store expenses, such as top-management salaries and Christmas decorations, and to net profits. In Table 30–13, note how the monthly operating profit is computed.

The contribution from each of the four departments is totaled, then

---

[7] For further discussion on these methods, see Charles H. Sevin, *Marketing Productivity Analysis* (New York: McGraw-Hill Book Co., 1965); R. D. Buzzell *et al., Product Profitability Measurement and Merchandising Decisions* (Boston: Division of Research, Graduate School of Business Administration, Harvard University, 1965); *Cost Analysis for Product Line Decisions* (Management Services Technical Study No. 1 [New York: American Institute of Certified Public Accountants, 1965]); *Cost Analysis for Pricing and Distribution Policies* (Management Services Technical Study No. 2 [New York: American Institute of Certified Public Accountants, 1965]); C. G. Baumes, *Allocating Corporate Expenses* (Business Policy Study No. 108 [New York: National Industrial Conference Board, 1963]); and J. L. Goldstucker, "Allocating Costs In International Operations," *Business Horizons,* Winter, 1965, pp. 75–84.

the general store expenses are subtracted to obtain the operating profit for each month.

Table 30–14 shows a similar planning and control chart for a single XYZ department, Department B. In this table, actual results have been entered for the month of January. An unfavorable deviation is revealed

Table **30–13** *XYZ Hardware Company planning and control chart*

1960	Contribution to Store				Total	Store Ex-pense	Op-erating Profit	Cumu-lative Operat-ing Profit
	Dept. A	Dept. B	Dept. C	Dept. D*				
January								
Planned	1,350	450	200	−50	1,950	1,200	750	750
Actual								
Variation								
February								
Planned	1,000	325	125	−50	1,400	1,200	200	950
Actual								
Variation								
November								
Planned	1,600	375	125	0	2,100	1,200	900	5,325
Actual								
Variation								
December								
Planned	3,150	625	200	450	4,025	1,200	2,825	8,150
Actual								
Variation								
1960								
Planned	15,800	3,500	3,450	−200	22,550	14,400	8,150	8,150
Actual								
Variation								

* The goal of minus $200 for this department was established on the same basis as the goals for the other departments, i.e., it represents the same percentage gain over 1959, when Department D's loss was $210. Plans call for discontinuance of the department unless it shows marked improvement by the end of the year.

between planned and actual sales performance (−$700), and gross profit (−$85).

Now, the marketing manager must determine why actual sales were less than projected, with a view to making new plans. Possible hypotheses are that (1) prices were too high, (2) promotion was ineffective, (3) the product selection was not satisfying the target customers, and (4) errors might have been made in marking the prices or in tallying sales.

Corrective action could take either of two courses, namely, improvement of implementation or development of new, more realistic strategies.

Table 30–14 *XYZ Hardware Company planning and control chart—Department B*

| 1960 | Sales | Gross Profit | Direct Expense | | | Contribution to Store | Cumulative Contribution to Store |
			Total	Fixed	Variable		
January							
Planned	3,000	900	450	300	150	450	450
Actual	2,300	815	415	300	115	400	400
Variation	−700	−85	35	0	35	−50	−50
February							
Planned	2,500	750	425	300	125	325	775
Actual							
Variation							
November							
Planned	3,500	1,050	675	500	175	375	2,875
Actual·							
Variation							
December							
Planned	4,500	1,350	725	500	225	625	3,500
Actual							
Variation							
1960							
Planned	30,000	9,000	5,500	4,000	1,500	3,500	3,500
Actual							
Variation							

SOURCE: Wallace O. Yoder and Clarence E. Vincent, "Control Methods for Hardware Dealers," *Management Research Summary* (Washington, D.C.: Small Business Administration, May, 1961), pp. 2–3.

Implementing the control process

All of this analysis could be implemented by manual methods. They may be best on small or nonrecurring jobs. But when the sales volume and complexity of the business have grown, mechanical methods not only may be faster and more accurate but may be the only way to handle the control procedure.

A crucial capture by the marketing manager

Punched card systems and computer systems are commonly used for data analysis in larger companies. Increasingly, smaller companies have access to computing capabilities through time-sharing systems offered by computer manufacturers and service bureaus.

But this kind of analysis is not possible unless the sales and other performance data is in machine-processible form, so it can be sorted and analyzed rapidly. At this point, the marketing manager can play a crucial role, by insisting that the data he wants is collected. If the data he wishes to analyze is not captured as it comes in, this information will be difficult if not impossible to obtain later.

Practically, the only limitation on more effective and revealing data analysis is the imagination of the marketing manager, now that machines can handle the drudgery. But he must see the interrelation of the planning and control process, and be sure the data he wants to use will be available when needed. Then he can confidently ask the data processors to produce the reports he needs.[8]

Ongoing data analysis may even go beyond analyzing the firm's own data. As we have seen earlier, some manufacturers and wholesalers, trying to develop a smoother flow through the channel system, are currently keeping inventory records for some of their wholesalers or retailers. With the growing capabilities of electronic data processing, we may see much more of this.[9]

Analysis crosses company boundaries

The marketing audit

The analyses we have discussed so far are designed to help a marketing manager plan and control his own operations. They can help him do a better job. Often, however, the control process tends to focus on only a few critical elements, such as sales variations by product in different territories—and it misses such considerations as the appropriateness of various marketing strategies and the effectiveness of various mixes in alternate strategies.

While crises pop, marketing goes on

The marketing manager usually is responsible for the day-to-day execution function as well as the planning and control functions, and seldom has the leisure to casually contemplate the effectiveness of his efforts. Sometimes, crises are popping in several places at the same time, and a good deal of his concern must be focused on adjusting marketing mixes or shifting strategies in the short run.

To insure that the whole marketing program is properly evaluated on an ongoing basis, therefore, marketing specialists have developed a new concept that is gaining popularity—the marketing audit. It is similar to the accounting audit or the personnel audit, both of which have been accepted by business for some time.

The marketing audit has been defined as "A systematic, critical, and unbiased review and appraisal of the basic objectives and policies of the marketing function and of the organization, methods, procedures, and personnel employed to implement the policies and achieve the objectives."[10]

A marketing audit would take a big view of the business and evaluate the whole marketing program. It might be conducted by a separate department within the company. Or to avoid bias, it might be desirable to have it conducted by an outside organization such as a management consulting firm.

It shouldn't be necessary

[8] For further discussion on the development of data processing systems, see E. J. McCarthy, J. A. McCarthy, and D. Humes, *Integrated Data Processing Systems* (New York: John Wiley & Sons, Inc., 1966).

[9] See Felix Kaufman, "Data Systems that Cross Company Boundaries," *Harvard Business Review*, January–February, 1966, pp. 141–55.

[10] A. R. Oxenfeldt, "The Marketing Audit as a Total Evaluation Program," in *Analyzing and Improving Marketing Performance: Marketing Audits in Theory and Practice* (New York: American Management Association, 1959), p. 26.

Ideally, a marketing audit should not be needed. A good manager should attempt to do his very best in planning, executing, and controlling and should attempt to continually evaluate the effectiveness of his operation.

In practice, however, managers often become identified with certain strategies and persistently pursue them when alternate courses might be more effective. Since an outside view may give needed perspective, we may see greater use of the marketing audit in the future.[11]

Conclusion

In this chapter, we have tried to show how sales and cost analysis can help a marketing manager control his marketing program, and that the control procedures can be useful for aiding his planning. Controls lead to feedback that can be incorporated into subsequent planning.

Simple sales analysis merely gives a picture of what has happened. But when sales forecasts or other data showing expected results are brought into the analysis, it is possible to evaluate performance, using performance indices.

Cost analysis also can be useful, providing costs are reallocated from natural to functional accounts and then to customers and products. There are two basic approaches to cost analysis—full cost and contribution margin. Using the full-cost approach, all costs are allocated in some way; using the contribution-margin approach, only the variable or direct costs are allocated. Both methods have their advantages and special uses.

Ideally, the marketing manager should arrange for a continual flow of data that can be analyzed routinely, preferably by machine, to enable him to control and subsequently plan new strategies. A marketing audit program may assist him in this ongoing evaluation. Perhaps either a separate department within the company or an outside, objective organization might conduct this audit.

Whichever evaluation procedure is used, however, it is clear that a marketing program must be controlled. Good control helps the marketing manager locate and correct weak spots, while at the same time finding strengths which he may be able to turn to his own advantage and apply throughout his marketing program. Control works hand in hand with planning in a total system of action.

Questions and problems

1 Various breakdowns of sales are suggested for sales analysis in certain situations, depending upon the nature of the company and its product. Describe a situation (one for each) where each of the following breakdowns would yield useful information. Explain why.

---

[11] For further discussion on the marketing audit, see *Analyzing and Improving Marketing Performance: "Marketing Audits" in Theory and Practice* (Management Report No. 32 [New York: American Management Association, 1959]).

a) By geographical region.
b) By product.
c) By customer.
d) By size of order.
e) By size of salesman's commission allowed (on each product or product group.

2 Explain carefully what the "iceberg principle" should mean to the marketing manager.

3 Explain the meaning of the comparative performance and comparative cost data in Tables 30–1 and 30–2. Why does it appear that eliminating sales areas D and E would be profitable?

4 Most sales forecasting is subject to some error (perhaps 5 to 10 percent). Is it proper to conclude then that variations in sales performance of 5 or 10 percent above or below quota are to be expected? If so, how should such variations be treated in evaluating performance?

5 Develop appropriate functional cost accounts for a house-to-house selling organization. First list logical natural expenses and show how they would be allocated to functional accounts. It is planned to allocate the costs in these functional accounts to various customer types in an effort to determine the profitability of calling on different kinds of customers. (Specify any assumptions necessary to obtain a definite answer.) To make this more concrete, assume the company is selling encyclopedias at $150 a set.

6 Explain why there is a controversy between the advocates of the "net profit approach" and the "contribution margin" approach to cost analysis.

7 The profit and loss statement for June for the Tempting Food Co. is as follows:

	Retailers	Hospitals and Schools	Total
Sales			
80,000 units at $0.70	$56,000		$56,000
20,000 units at $0.60		$12,000	12,000
Total	$56,000	$12,000	$68,000
Cost of goods sold	40,000	10,000	50,000
Gross margin	$16,000	$ 2,000	$18,000
Sales and administrative expenses			
Variable	$ 6,000	$ 1,500	$ 7,500
Fixed	5,600	900	6,500
Total	$11,600	$ 2,400	$14,000
Net profit (loss)	$ 4,400	$ (400)	$ 4,000

If competitive conditions make price increases impossible, and management has cut costs as much as possible, should the Tempting Food Co. stop selling to hospitals and schools? Why?

8 Explain why it is so important for the marketing manager to be directly involved in the planning of control procedures.

9 Explain why a marketing audit might be desirable even in a well run company. Discuss who or what kind of an organization would be the best one to conduct a marketing audit. Would a marketing research firm be good? Would the present C.P.A. firms be most suitable?

Does marketing cost too much?—An evaluation

Many people feel quite strongly that marketing costs too much. This may be partly because it is human to look for quick and easy solutions to pervasive problems, such as the continuing unemployment and rising prices. Marketing activities are especially susceptible to public criticism. They are continuously exposed to the public, and people get emotionally involved when their pocketbooks are hurt.

Moreover, many consumers have definite feelings about the "tremendous markups" taken by wholesalers and retailers. They are quick to point to the large discounts offered by "discount houses" as proof that these excessive markups exist.

Although most of this criticism is based either on theoretical analysis or a few unhappy experiences, the criticism is widespread. The marketing manager must recognize this and be realistic about the environment in which he must operate, in order to deal effectively with it.

At various places in this text, we have referred to criticism of marketing and to the effects of business practices on consumer welfare. But we have *not* attempted to answer the general and underlying question of whether marketing costs too much, thinking instead that you needed background to develop an answer for yourself.

This book has tried to provide this necessary background, which is primarily an understanding of the job of the marketing manager. Now that you have a better appreciation of the marketing process, you should be able to give this question thoughtful consideration.

The answer is extremely important. Your own business career and the economy in which you will live will be affected by your decision and by that of the public generally.

In this chapter, we will consider the criticism of marketing and try to reach a conclusion regarding the effectiveness of marketing, particularly in the American economy.

What's wrong with marketing: some charges

It is often said that distribution is too expensive relative to the cost of production. As we saw in Chapter 1, 50 percent of the consumer dollar may be spent for distribution.

"Distribution costs are just too high . . ."

Housewives are especially sensitive concerning the price of food. During the period from 1947–49 to 1964, there was a reduction of 18 percent in the farm value of a typical market basket of farm foods—but an increase of 12 percent in the retail price of this market basket.[1] Since the activities between the farmer and consumer are presumed to be marketing functions, the housewife often blames "the middlemen" for the rising cost of food in the store, especially as the price paid to the farmer falls.

In addition to the complaint that costs and prices are too high, many critics have specific comments about products. Complaints usually center around how expensive the product is in relation to quality. Sometimes there is the implication that businessmen, in their greed, make the cheapest product possible.

"Models change too often, products are too numerous . . ."

Critics often cite policies of planned product obsolescence to back up their arguments. The examples they mention to support their charges are the regular model changes of automobiles, appliances, and household furnishings, and rapid changes in fashions, especially in women's clothing.

Complaints also center on the similarity of merchandise offered under different brand names. It has been estimated, for example, that there are as many as 10,000 brands of wheat flour, 4,500 brands of canned corn, 1,000 brands of canned peaches, 1,000 brands of canned salmon and peas, 500 brands of mustard, and 300 brands of pineapple.[2] The critics feel that there obviously cannot be that many physical variations in products. This multiplicity of brands, whatever its cause, further confuses the consumer, who already has a hard enough time determining product quality.

Another major area of criticism is the complexity of distribution channels. One sore spot is the sheer number of wholesalers and retailers. Another is the belief that their practices and methods are inefficient. Many wholesalers, for example, operate in older central districts of cities which were designed for horse-drawn carts, trains, and ships rather than modern trucks. This often leads to additional handling, so

"Too many middlemen adding to the cost . . ."

[1] Economic Research Service Publication No. 226, April, 1965, U.S. Department of Agriculture, Washington, D.C.

[2] S. H. Slichter, *Modern Economic Society* (New York: Henry Holt & Co., Inc., 1951), p. 552.

that costs rise without adding to the value of the product. Sometimes it seems that inadequate middlemen lead to the development of additional wholesalers in order to get the job done.

Many farmers have been particularly unhappy about the way their products are handled and the costs which are added. They know what they are paid for a product and what the customer finally has to pay. They frequently feel that they receive far too little of the final consumer price. This has led some farmers to try cooperative marketing, to avoid middlemen.

"Too much advertising of the wrong things for the wrong reasons . . ."

Probably most of the criticism of marketing is leveled at advertising and sales promotion. One factor is advertising expenditures, which have been rising continually and, as of 1966, totaled more than $16 billion. The main complaint about advertising, however, is that it stimulates people to buy unnecessary products even when they have other more pressing needs. The critics often cite examples that "prove" this charge.

One husband was sued for divorce because he bought himself an electric train for Christmas while his three children had to depend on a charity organization for Christmas presents. In another case, among 200 homes in an industrial town in England, it was found that only three had bathtubs, six had hot water, and four had their own toilets, while *125 had television sets.*[3]

A best seller of a few years ago, *The Hidden Persuaders,* claims to show how advertising and public relations people are "manipulating" consumers.[4] This very readable book probably gives too much credit to the abilities of the advertising and public relations professions, but is significant reading for marketing men because it is a book that many critics of marketing use for ammunition.

The Waste Makers, by the same author, focuses on the alleged wastefulness being promoted by industry to sell its huge output of products.[5]

In many respects, these books are similar to critical works of the early 1930's which appeared under the titles of *Your Money's Worth* and *100,000,000 Guinea Pigs.*[6] They tried to show that most marketing activities were concerned with cheating and defrauding the public.

The earlier books helped to stimulate and crystallize consumer thinking about some of the aggressive and sometimes harmful marketing practices—especially concerning patent medicines and their advertising—which had developed during the 1920's. Increasing public concern led to the development of private testing and rating agencies for consumer goods, such as Consumers Research, Inc., and Consumers Union. These organizations attempt to evaluate and rate new products. Although some consumers find such aids helpful, probably only a few

[3] *Time,* October 6, 1958, p. 96.

[4] Vance Packard, *The Hidden Persuaders* (New York: Pocketbooks, Inc., 1958).

[5] Vance Packard, *The Waste Makers* (New York: David McKay Co., Inc. 1960).

[6] S. Chase and F. J. Schlink, *Your Money's Worth* (New York: Macmillan Co., 1931), and A. Kallek and F. J. Schlink, *100,000,000 Guinea Pigs* (New York: Vanguard Press, Inc., 1932).

million people ever see the magazines published by these organizations.

The well-known historian, Arnold Toynbee, recently joined the attack against advertising and, even more broadly, against our business system. He called for a reform of our way of life and suggested that personal consumption expenditures could be limited to the level of present-day American monks and nuns. Then, he said, "The balance of our productive capacity could be diverted to supplying elementary needs of the poverty-stricken three-quarters of the human race."[7]

Many critics of advertising feel that it creates a demand for trivial goods, urges false standards on people, and builds up consumer preferences for products that are not very different from others available. Furthermore, it is charged, advertising tends to create a monopoly for a particular producer by creating a situation where sellers can avoid price competition. Finally, other critics say that advertising is merely shuffling demand from one brand to another, rather than stimulating the new demand that is basic to the vitality of a free economy.

"Consumer credit is a misused market technique . . ."

Liberal credit is frequently decried, especially the "no-down-payment" and "easy-terms" type, on the basis that it may encourage some consumers to overextend themselves. Critics feel this may lead to neglect of truly necessary expenditures, and indebtedness with all its depressing effects on the family. Some firms are so lax in their credit checks and so anxious to make sales that there have been instances of consumers being sold so many goods that the monthly payments totaled more than their income.

Mortgaging a consumer's future income for a home is now accepted practice, but many persons remain critical of letting consumers commit themselves for less durable goods. They feel "easy credit" is mainly a marketing technique to get rid of more goods.

"Retail service is deteriorating rapidly . . ."

Most consumers at one time or another have received poor service from some retail store, even though they had to pay a high retail markup. Critics feel that people have little choice but to patronize such high-cost, poor-service outlets, and that is just another proof of the high cost and inefficiency of marketing. They claim that in recent years the personal service in large department stores—and in retail stores generally—has deteriorated considerably.

"Wrong kinds of goods are produced . . ."

Critics of marketing are concerned with what is produced in the economy. If advertising or other marketing activities encourage consumers to want or buy the "wrong kings of goods," then the businessmen will produce these goods—and thereby allocate the economy's resources to the "wrong ends." An example might be a television set in a home where there is too little food or clothing . . . or no toilet.

---

[7] Is It Immoral to Stimulate Buying?" *Printers' Ink*, May 11, 1962, p. 43; "The Real Enemy?" *Time*, September 22, 1961, p. 112; "James Webb Young on Toynbee: 'Adrift on Uses of Advertising,' " *Printers' Ink*, October 20, 1961; and "Are Thought-Leaders a Threat?" *Printers' Ink*, April 26, 1963, pp. 54–56.

"Marketing makes men materialistic . . ."

Some critics, as noted in the reference to Toynbee, also decry what they consider Americans' materialistic orientation. They usually imply that advertising has created or encouraged this supposed materialism. They note that some men moonlight and some housewives work, and they attribute this to a desire for more goods. Some critics from abroad say they are concerned because what they see as American materialism seems to be spreading to other areas. Youth throughout the world, they say, seem to want more goods *now*. This is upsetting some social-economic systems—and the "establishment" naturally looks for someone to blame."[8]

"Controlled markets restrict income and employment . . ."

It is charged that businessmen attempt to create their own market (or monopoly) through product design and promotion, which enables them to raise prices and to restrict output and employment. Sometimes it is argued that there is only a certain amount of income to be spent. If prices are raised on some goods, consumers in total will be able to buy fewer goods. This, in turn, may mean fewer workers will be needed, and the national output and income will decrease.

"The big incomes go to the hornswog-glers . . ."

Following the previous argument, if marketing activities enable the firm to obtain higher prices and perhaps higher profits, these higher profits may be diverted to those who are good promoters rather than good producers. In other words, the total income of the economy will be split in favor of the marketing people. It is frequently assumed that marketing people are paid fabulous salaries for their ability to horn-swoggle the public.

How effective is marketing?

The question is, WHICH marketing?

Although it isn't apparent at first glance, these criticisms of marketing actually divide into two fundamental and separate areas.

Some criticisms are aimed at marketing as a *business operation*—that is, the way specific firms operate. Other criticisms concern marketing as an *economic institution*—the general economic process of producing goods and allocating them to the members of a free enterprise economy. Criticisms of this second type are criticisms of our economic system in general.

Evaluating these two different aspects of "marketing" requires different techniques. It also requires some agreement on the purpose of an economic system. Unless we agree on the objective of an economy, little can be accomplished through dialogue.

Let the buyer be the chooser

We have emphasized the importance of the customer in planning marketing strategies because we have assumed that the basic objective of our economy is meeting consumers' needs *as they, the consumers, see them*. This is no more than an acknowledgment, in economic terms, that in a free society free men have a right to live as they choose.

---

[8] See John K. Galbraith, *The Affluent Society* (Boston: Houghton Mifflin Co., 1958). For further discussion of criticisms, see R. M. Farmer, "Would You Want Your Daughter to Marry a Marketing Man?" *Journal of Marketing*, January, 1967, pp. 1–3.

652

This is no place for an extensive discussion of the merits of this objective. Philosophers, politicians, and others can (and should) dissect this subject; perhaps eventually, such a dialogue will lead to a change in our economic goals.

It is sufficient here to note that different economies have different objectives. Totalitarian states, for example, may be concerned mainly with satisfying the needs *of the political elite.* In a socialist state, the objective might be to satisfy needs *as seen by social planners*—perhaps equal division of wealth. In still other economies, the objective may be to build up the country militarily or economically, perhaps for the *long-run good of all consumers (the people), but as evaluated by the state.*

In all of these economies, a business system would be required, but it might operate quite differently because of the difference in objectives.

In the following paragraphs, our primary concern will be with evaluating the operation of marketing in the American economy where the objective is to satisfy consumers' needs *as consumers see them.* That is the essence of our system, and the business that ignores this fact does so at its own peril.

Since consumer satisfaction is our economic goal, the efficiency of marketing must be measured by *the extent of this satisfaction.* Unfortunately, however, we cannot quantitatively measure this satisfaction and, therefore, marketing. While there are a number of approaches to such measurement, none is fully satisfactory. **What do you measure to get the measure?**

We can, for example, measure marketing "inputs," such as the number of traveling salesmen and how many boxcars are moved. But what about marketing "outputs?"

Some analysts attempt to measure the value of marketing in terms of the value of the inputs, but this does not measure consumer satisfaction—and because it equates cost with value, marketing analysts are not satisfied with it. Our evaluation of marketing as an economic institution, therefore, will have to be subjective.

Measuring the efficiency of individual business operations also is difficult, but here the relative profitability of various firms is helpful as a measure. Within a firm, comparison of costs and profits of alternate products, channels, media, and so on, may be useful. Marketing cost analysis and marketing research techniques may be useful, too. In the final analysis, however, every company uses slightly different marketing strategies, and it is up to each customer to decide how effectively individual firms satisfy his needs.

In view of the difficulty of measuring the effectiveness of marketing, it is easy to see why reasonable men might have different views on the subject. If the objective of the economy is clearly defined, however, and the argument is stripped of emotion, the question probably can be answered. **Not gospel, but arguments**

This chapter will argue that marketing as a business operation frequently does cost too much, but that marketing as an economic institution does not cost too much, given the present objective of the economy—consumer satisfaction.

These views should not be accepted as "gospel" but rather as arguments. In the end, you, the student of marketing, will have to make your own decision.[9]

Marketing as a business operation *does* cost too much

Many new products, old businesses fail

Our focus throughout the text has been on what marketing managers should or could do to run a business more efficiently. But it must be acknowledged that the majority of firms are still production-oriented.

Many firms are not nearly as efficient as they might be. We have noted already that at least four out of five new products fail. New and old businesses fail regularly, too. The main reason for such failure is poor management or just plain managerial incompetence. One survey of 15,782 failures found that more than 90 percent were caused directly by incompetent or inexperienced management. Other surveys have obtained similar results.[10]

Incompetence and bad management lead to higher costs of operation and tend to reduce the effectiveness of the business system in general. Generally speaking, business inefficiencies are due to one or more of three reasons:

1. Lack of interest or understanding of the sometimes capricious customer.
2. Improper blending of the four P's, caused, in part, by an overemphasis on production and internal problems as contrasted with a customer orientation.
3. Lack of understanding of, or adjustment to, uncontrollable factors.

The company can get in the way of the customer

Serving the customer is plainly the function of marketing, yet some business managers seem to feel that customers are avidly awaiting any product they produce. So they turn instead to what they consider the first task of management, namely, internal problems. They do not see a business as a "total system" focused on satisfying customer needs.

The production manager, for example, may be primarily interested in designing products that are easy to make or can be made readily on the company's present machines. The production people usually want long production runs of standardized products because this helps to lower costs. Or the production department may want new equipment for prestige reasons, whether the end product sells at a competitive price or not.

Sometimes the production department emphasizes low-cost produc-

---

[9] For an extensive discussion of the problems and mechanics of measuring the efficiency of marketing, see R. S. Vaile, E. T. Grether, and R. Cox, *Marketing In The American Economy* (New York: Ronald Press Co., 1952), chaps. xxxii and xxxiii, and T. N. Beckman, H. H. Maynard, W. R. Davidson, *Principles of Marketing* (6th ed.; New York: Ronald Press Co., 1957, chap. xxxv; and Stanley C. Hollander, "Measuring the Cost and Value of Marketing," *Business Topics,* Summer, 1961, pp. 17–26.

[10] *Time* June 21, 1963, p. 86; Merchant's Service, National Cash Register Co., *Establishing a Retail Store,* p. 3.; and National Retail Merchants Association.

tion mainly because it "sells" its products to the sales department at a fixed price and, therefore, can make a good showing with long, low-cost runs. Yet this may force the use of costly promotion to try to move less desirable goods.

Similarly, accounting or financial departments, being responsible for effective use of money, try to cut costs by reducing raw material or finished-product inventory, even though this may not serve customers well. It may require more expensive hand-to-mouth buying, or lose sales because of lack of stock.

Perhaps lack of concern with the customer is most noticeable in the ways the four P's are combined—or sometimes are forced—into a marketing mix. This can happen in many ways, as the following discussion shows.

The high cost of poor marketing mixes

Product—forget the customer, full speed ahead! Some researchers, engineers, and production men apparently develop a company's product less to meet the needs of some target customers than to satisfy some concept held by themselves or their friends. They sometimes produce products too high or too low in quality, or too complicated for many target markets. Then, to compound these errors, the packaging people frequently put this ill-conceived product in a container that is easy to make and use, but not protective or appealing to the customer.

These poorly designed, poorly packaged products then are turned over to the sales department for it to "get rid of." Sometimes these products cannot be moved off the counter or can be moved only with overly aggressive (or even fraudulent) promotion. This sort of promotion can be expensive and may become more common unless businesses become more customer-oriented.

A study of more than 22,000 salesmen from 1960 to 1966 showed that their attitude toward the products they sell dropped from an 86 percent favorable rating in 1960 to 63 percent in 1966. Unless quality improves, it is likely that this pattern of decline will continue, inevitably leading to poor performance and costly turnover of salesmen.[11]

Place—don't rock the boat, or sell to chains. Sales managers seldom make adjustments in channels as frequently as might be desirable, partly because of their personal relationships in their channel and partly because, being human, they prefer not to rock the boat. Yet such inflexibility can be extremely costly, especially in view of the "scrambling" we saw in the distribution structure.

Some old-timer salesmen are so tied to the idea of small independent wholesalers and retailers that they even refuse to sell to chain stores or large organizations. Their personal relationships with their old customers may make business more pleasant, but do not necessarily contribute to efficiency. The continued use of possibly obsolete and overly expensive channels may give substance to the charge of "too many" wholesalers and retailers. Or, from another standpoint, if a large chain is forced to open a new production plant to get a source of supply at a time when the established plants have unused capacity, is this efficient?

[11] "Salesmen's Product Faith Down," The (Lansing, Michigan) State Journal, June 20, 1966, p. C–4.

Price—pick a price, any high price. Prices frequently are set by the production, finance, or accounting department on a cost-plus basis. This is analogous to putting the choice of products in the hands of the production-oriented people.

This method of pricing may ignore customer demand and lead to unnecessarily high (and less profitable) prices. Many businessmen consider both margin and expected volume in pricing goods, but margins are definite, while volume is only predictable. These businessmen, therefore, choose high margins, and these may lead to high prices and reduced volume. Firms faced with elastic demands, however, perhaps should set lower prices, since they would be appreciated by the customer—and might be more profitable for the seller.

Promotion—in spite of the advertising geniuses and star salesmen. If a product is poorly or improperly designed, or if inadequate channels are employed, or if cost-plus pricing is used, it is easy to see why promotion may be costly. Aggressive selling may be needed to overcome previous miscalculations or errors. Perhaps it is understandable that some sales and advertising managers would feel they had to resort to tricks (including unethical ones) to sell goods.

Even if a good job is done on the other three P's, however, Promotion sometimes is inefficient and costly. As already noted, the sales manager and the advertising manager may not cooperate, each feeling that his own technique is most effective and does not need the support of the other. In some companies, the advertising manager and sales manager do not communicate at all.

Until recently, only lip service was paid to the value of customer research in some firms. Some advertising executives still feel that all a promotional campaign needs is their creative genius. And the difficulty of checking advertising results makes it hard to tell whether ad men are talking to the customers or to themselves.

Sales management also has its problems. There are many types of sales jobs. Recruiting the right person for each is difficult. Furthermore, the very nature of the sales job makes it difficult to measure sales performance.

Careful analysis and management are necessary to build a productive sales force at a reasonable cost. Unfortunately, many sales managers, although former "star" salesmen, are not up to this management task.

When competition gets tough —for the customer

Some business managers have a poor appreciation or none at all for the marketing concept. They develop weak, undifferentiated marketing strategies, then try to use aggressive implementation to make them work in the competitive marketplace.

Competition is by nature a give-and-take process, and sometimes it gets extremely rough. Products may be copied rapidly; selective or exclusive distribution may be used by large competitors to tie up desirable dealers; price-cutting may be used selectively to discourage competitors; and personal selling and advertising may be used to oppose competitors in test areas or new territories.

Aggressive efforts are part of the competitive business game, and competition is expected to benefit the consumer in the long run.

Supposedly, various competitors will offer a continually better product to win more business, providing consumers with a better value.

For the short run, however, head-on competition with relatively undifferentiated products may be expensive for competitors and may not really benefit the consumers. Additional brands may be added and promoted, but because they are like goods already on the market, contribute little to consumers. Marginal wholesale and retail outlets may open and subsequently fail. Advertising may be bought for awhile on a grand scale to promote a new product. All these activities are costly and in the spirit of vigorous competition, but it is not clear that they increase customer satisfaction.

Such competition may even hurt consumers. Vigorous price competition on appliances during the late 1950's, especially through discount houses, apparently led some manufacturers to so cheapen their products that they needed frequent repairs. Some manufacturers, finally deciding this was foolish, planned to rebuild their price structure and emphasize quality in future years.[12]

Company objectives may force higher cost operation

Top-management decisions on company objectives significantly affect the cost of marketing. A decision to pursue growth for growth's sake, for example, might mean big spending for promotion. Or working to expand market share, again for its own sake, might be accomplished only by aggressive, costly promotion.

Diversification for its own sake could require the development of costly new arrangements for Place. Or if the established firms already had developed and protected basic ideas, perhaps obtaining solid customer franchises, the firm might be forced to turn out second-rate products. And even if the company *had* a competitive physical product, the Place and Promotion tasks might be overwhelming.

For these reasons, it is imperative that the marketing manager both be alert to the possibility of such pitfalls and dilemmas and participate fully in shaping the firm's objectives. Recognizing the importance of marketing, many progressive firms have given marketing management a greater voice—and sometimes the dominant voice—in determining company objectives. Unfortunately, though, in many more firms, marketing is still looked upon as the department that "gets rid of" the product.

Keeping competitors down may push prices up

Many small retailers have lobbied for laws ostensibly designed to protect competition. Some of these laws, as we have discussed, have not been designed to protect competition but to protect competitors. Sometimes there is a vast difference between the two.

To protect an inefficient competitor may be injurious to competition. Yet some aspects of the Robinson-Patman Act, the Miller-Tydings and McGuire Acts, some state unfair practices acts, and some court decisions concerning the Sherman Act seem intended to protect competitors. It is obvious that the state anti-chain store laws are intended more

---

[12] "Crisis in Buying: Sales Suffer as Quality Slips, Service Stops," *Printers' Ink*, December 19, 1958, pp. 20–24.

to hamstring competitors than protect price competition, since most surveys indicate that the large chain stores already offer goods at low or the lowest prices.[13]

Legal restrictions that protect the small or inefficient firm naturally have their effect on total marketing costs. That effect probably is to increase them, because it is difficult to adjust efficiently when the guidelines are so vague and confusing.

Concerning legislation on competition, a well-known economist, Professor Kenneth E. Boulding, once said, "Mr. Bumble's ass seems to have developed a remarkable ability to ride off in several directions at once. The A&P is condemned for being too competitive; the tobacco and cement companies are condemned for not being competitive enough."[14]

But the customer is coming into view

It appears that marketing, as a business operation, does cost too much. Marketing mixes often are put together by departments and executives who have interests other than serving customers; the customer, in effect, is the last factor considered in company planning. Moreover, when the production, accounting, finance, and sales departments are all working toward their own departmental goals instead of toward the single goal of satisfying some customers, it is probable that marketing will cost too much.

But all marketing efforts should not be condemned out of hand. Admittedly some inefficiencies are caused by members of the business, political, and legal communities. But the trend is toward elimination of unnecessary costs, through more effective business management.

Distribution channels are continually shifting as new ways are found for doing the marketing job more effectively. Limited-function wholesalers have developed in many lines. Discount houses have eliminated many small, conventional retail stores which did not recognize changing customer demands. Wholesalers who have not adopted the new methods of storing and transporting have been bypassed.

One encouraging sign is the end of the notion that just anybody can run a business successfully. This never was true, and today the growing complexity of business is drawing more and more professionals into business. This includes not only professional business managers but psychologists, sociologists, statisticians, and economists.

The professional business managers who adopt the marketing concept as a way of business life will do a better job. This concept provides that all the activities of the business will be integrated into one "total system of action," which will be oriented toward the one objective of serving the customer, at a profit. If this is done effectively, both businesses and the customers will benefit. Then *marketing as a business operation* will *not* cost too much.

---

[13] Werner Z. Hirsch, "Grocery Chain Store Prices—A Case Study," *Journal of Marketing*, July, 1956, p. 9; and Charles F. Stewart, "Mandatory Resale Price Maintenance of Distilled Spirits in California," *Journal of Marketing*, April, 1954, p. 70.

[14] "A Pricing System that Works Only One Way—Up," *Business Week*, June 15, 1957, p. 190.

Marketing as an economic institution does *not* cost too much

Many criticisms of marketing are directed against marketing not as a business operation but as an economic institution. These criticisms suggest that advertising and promotion in general are socially undesirable; that marketing causes an improper allocation of resources, restricts income and employment; and that marketing practices lead to an improper distribution of income. Most of these criticisms imply that many marketing activities should not be permitted, and because they are, marketing costs too much.

Give customers complete freedom and no freedom

Much of this criticism comes from those who have their own version of the ideal way of running an economy. Some of the most severe critics of marketing are theoretical economists who use the pure-competition model as their ideal. They would give consumers free choice in the market, presuming that consumers have perfect knowledge of all the available offerings and have only economic motives (i.e., the "economic man"). Other critics are those social planners who would rather substitute their own values for those of individual consumers. These different viewpoints should be kept in mind when evaluating criticism.

In the following discussion, the word "business" probably could be substituted for "marketing" in most instances. Marketing is the most exposed arm of business, but it is nearly impossible to separate this arm from the rest of the body. A criticism of marketing usually implies a criticism of our business system and suggests that another system would be more effective.

Although the objective of marketing is service to the customer, one of the major criticisms of marketing is that the allocation of resources to marketing functions actually reduces consumer "welfare."

Is pure competition the welfare ideal?

The allocation-of-resources argument is concerned with how the economy's wealth is allocated to producing and distributing goods. These critics usually maintain that scarce resources could be better spent on the production of goods than on marketing of goods.

The pure-competition economists, for example, see little need for any advertising except purely informative ads that would advise their "economic men" about the availability of products. They feel that emotional and persuasive advertising discourages the economic comparison needed for their ideal pure-competition economy, where, they assume, all competitive products are alike and there is no need to explain and persuade about differences.

Such critics of the way resources are allocated in a marketing-oriented economy assume that pure competition is the ideal for maximizing consumer welfare.

Theoretical economic analysis can show convincingly that pure competition will provide greater consumer welfare than monopolistic competition—provided all of the conditions and assumptions of pure competition are met. It is for this reason that the pure-competition

659

proponents feel that advertising, personal selling, and marketing in general—any activities causing deviations from pure competition—should be condemned on welfare grounds.

It is important that we evaluate this view.

Different people want different things. At the outset, we can say that our present knowledge of the complexity of human behavior and peoples' desire for different products pretty well demolishes the economists' "economic man" assumption, and therefore the pure-competition ideal.[15] The pioneer in monopolistic competition analysis, E. H. Chamberlin, also argues logically against the pure-competition ideal. He observes that people, in fact, are different and that they do have different demands. He translates these differences into demands for different products. Given this type of demand (downsloping demand curves), monopoly elements naturally develop. He concludes that "monopoly is necessarily a part of the welfare ideal. . . ."[16]

Once it is acknowledged that not all consumers know everything and that they have varied demands, then the need for many marketing activities becomes clear.

It is certainly true that marketing activities may lead to a different allocation of resources than would be found in a pure-competition economy. It takes more time and effort to satisfy varied demands than to make one product for everyone, take it or leave it. But this allocation of resources probably results in greater consumer welfare. People are getting what they want.

Advertising can make the whole marketing process work better. It can, says another economist, be a powerful influence in the elimination of ignorance and the disseminator of price information, making the whole searching process more economical.[17]

Creating demand does not misallocate resources

It would seem, then, that just satisfying customers' demands certainly does not lead to a misallocation of resources. Giving individuals what they want, after all, is the purpose of a free enterprise economic system. But there is still another issue that concerns some critics. They ask, "Is it right to influence consumers' demands?"

We already have seen that psychologists view consumers as a bundle of needs and drives, some of which are innate but most of which are learned. Some critics feel that promotion not only stimulates people's needs and drives toward a particular product, but often teaches entirely new wants—and that this violates, if only subtly, the individual's control of his own actions.

Behavioral scientists find that it *is* possible to change attitudes and behavior. But an important question is, How basic are the needs which might be created? If we think of promotion for a new recreational gadget as "creating new demands," there can be no argument. Promo-

---

[15] F. M. Nicosia, *Consumer Decision Processes* (Englewood Cliffs, N.J.: Prentice-Hall, Inc., 1966), p. 39.

[16] E. H. Chamberlin, "Product Heterogeneity and Public Policy," *American Economic Review*, May, 1950, p. 86.

[17] George J. Stigler, "The Economics of Information," *Journal of Political Economy*, June, 1961, p. 213.

tion can do it. But to state more broadly that promotion can create a wish for (or pleasure in) recreation, distinctiveness, or emulation, is another matter. It is likely that the human being already has learned these needs.

Take the bikini, for example. It is difficult to think of any new product for which an entirely new set of basic needs or drives had to be created. Even the exaggerated, up-again-down-again styles of women's clothing meet some women's need to be distinctive, to be style leaders. Yet some new feminine styles do not sell even with extensive publicity. Consider the bikini and topless bathing suits, for most women.

Don't be pigheaded—swim downstream! Rather than seeking to create entirely new basic needs, which would be extremely difficult and expensive, business firms seek to stimulate or direct those needs or drives which already are held. They find it is "easier to swim with the current than against it."[18] Marketing research is used to test the current.

Marketing research helps management discover what target customers want or would like, so that the four P's can be tailored to their desires. Instead of just "guessing" what might be wanted, then working at expensive hit-or-miss development of new products, the modern marketing man seeks to assure maximum customer satisfaction by analyzing the customers' needs, drives, and likely behavior.

Once these are known, marketing follows an intelligent course—not selfish, pigheaded, or diabolical. It gives the customer what he wants. In return, the customers give the company what it wants: profits. This customer-oriented procedure also reduces the need to rely on heavy promotion to differentiate a product or try to create basically new demands.

Promotion also has been criticized for creating and serving "false" standards, and thereby leading to an improper allocation of resources. But this standard has never been precisely defined. What is "false" apparently depends on the critic's point of view. **"False" standards according to whom?**

One critic of the two-car-family advertising which started in 1959 was a New York television critic who found even *one* car an inconvenience in crowded New York City.[19] To the suburban housewife, however, who is marooned perhaps miles from public transportation while her husband has *the* car, the advertisers are not creating any need at all. She has been thinking about this for some time. The historical truth is that the two-car ad campaign came *after* the fact. It grew out of consumer research showing that many suburban families, especially those with teen-agers, already were developing into two-car and in some cases, three-car families.

The critics of "false" standards are either unwilling to accept or truly unaware that other people may prefer standards different from those the critics like. They see judgment or taste measured on an absolute scale, ranging from "good" at the top—where they are—to "bad" at the bottom, and they do not want the lower end of the scale served.

[18] George Katona, in a seminar at the University of Notre Dame during 1962.
[19] John Crosby, "One-Car Captivity Now Brand of Poor," *South Bend Tribune,* April 17, 1959, p. 51.

Regarding the serving of "false tastes," a well-known economist, George Stigler, said:

The marketplace responds to the tastes of consumers with the goods and services that are salable, whether the tastes are elevated or depraved. It is unfair to criticize the marketplace for fulfilling these desires, when clearly the defects lie in the popular tastes themselves. I consider it a cowardly concession to a false extension of the idea of democracy to make sub rosa attacks on public tastes by denouncing the people who serve them. It is like blaming the waiters in restaurants for obesity.[20]

Sometimes it's the little things that count

Criticism of promotion which focuses on minor product differences has been common, especially among the very "rational." Sociological and psychological research, however, indicates that promotion actually may create *new* values for these products—new psychological values that may be of greater value to the buyer than the physical product itself.

How does this value-creation process work? Consider an extreme example, the placebo or sugar pill that a doctor uses for his hypochondriac patients to give reassurance that, yes, they are being medicated. The doctor's advice (promotion) that the pill will do some good frequently gets very desirable results when, in fact, the only value of the pill is psychological, not medicinal.

In a similar way, promotion sometimes does enable marketers to satisfy better the many varied demands of consumers without an expensive physical variation of the product. With a little help from an ad copywriter, women can imagine all sorts of desirable consequences of using a particular perfume or lipstick—and if they believe it, it may come true. (Value has been added!)

Marketing expands output through innovation

Some critics feel that marketing helps create monopoly, or at least monopolistic competition, and that this in turn leads to higher prices, the restriction of output, and a reduction in the national income and employment.

The basis for this criticism is economic analysis showing that profit-maximizing firms in monopolistic competition should choose a lower level of output and higher price than would prevail in pure competition. This criticism is valid if pure competition is, in fact, the ideal economic situation. But again the critics miss the main point—that consumers differ. As long as this is true, there will be demand for varied products; this will lead to downsloping demand curves and monopolistic competition, as described previously.

Monopolistic competition brings innovation, innovation brings barnacles. Given the monopolistic competition situation, it is quite true that use of the Product, Place, and Promotion variables does cause a shifting of demand curves and in some cases even makes demand curves inelastic. The exact effect of this on output and prices, however, is indefinite. It depends on the shape of the cost curves and the extent to which the demand curves are shifted. If the new curves are extremely

---

[20] "Intellectuals Should Re-Examine the Marketplace; It Supports Them, Helps Keep Them Free: Prof. Stigler," *Advertising Age,* January 28, 1963.

elastic, prices might be lower with output increased considerably. But it is not possible to generalize on the effect of marketing activities for all situations.[21]

There is no arguing that producers in a marketing-oriented economy make a real effort to carve out separate monopolistic markets for themselves. This approach may have the short-run effect of restricting output (depending upon the shape of the new demand and supply curves) and raising prices on *that particular new product.*

Customers are not taken advantage of in the short run, however. They do not have to buy the new product unless they feel it is a better value. The old products are still available. Ironically, the prices even may be lower on the old products to meet the new competition, and yet their sales may decline because customers are shifting to the new product.

Over several years, the profits of the innovator may rise—but the rising profits also act as a spur to further innovation by competitors. This leads to new investments, which contribute to economic growth, raising the level of national income and employment.

Here, the increasing profits attract competition. The profits then begin to drop as competitors enter and begin producing somewhat similar products. Recall the rise and fall of industry profit during the life cycle of a product.

Monopolistic competition, it is clear, provides a dynamic element in the economy and breeds its own competition. The innovators also pave the way for the coming of the "barnacle" brands, so called because they attach themselves to the successful market established by the innovators. They are offered at lower prices and for this reason are accepted as bargains in the latter stages of the product life cycle.[22]

Output pie not fixed in size. Some critics argue that there is only a certain amount of income to be spent and that higher prices, which sometimes accompany effective market segmentation or product differentiation, could lead to a reduction in the level of income or employment. Most economists consider this a naïve view of the economy. The economic pie is not fixed in size. The levels of income and employment appear to be more directly related to the level of expenditures of consumers, business, and the government.[23]

Advertising didn't concentrate them. Some critics are concerned that promotion may lead to greater concentration of industry—that is, a few large firms dominating each industry. This seems an illogical objection, since there was much concentration of industry before promotion became widespread in the 1920's and 1930's.

The most recent analysis of the available statistical data shows that industrial concentration was not caused by advertising, but rather by the availability of economies through large-scale production and distribution and the potential for financial advantage in larger units.

---

[21] E. H. Chamberlin, *The Theory of Monopolistic Competition* (Cambridge, Mass.: Harvard University Press, 1936), pp. 166–67.

[22] Jules Backman, *Advertising in Competition* (New York: New York University Press, 1967), p. 44.

[23] See Chapter 5 on national income forecasting.

There appears to be no relationship between the intensity of advertising and the trend to concentration.[24]

Large firms are vigorous, customers are benefiting. Another objection to marketing is that supposedly it will aid the growth of large organizations, thus further restricting entry and reducing competition, output, and employment. In recent years, though, the reverse seems to be true. Many firms have grown quite large, but this growth has been primarily because of diversification into many different fields.

In most industries, competition (using all four P's) is extremely vigorous among a number of large, well-diversified organizations. They have the money to undertake basic research, resulting in true innovation. These firms can afford the extensive market research and careful planning of marketing mixes needed to compete effectively with their large competitors. They can underwrite and carry a new product until volume permits economies of scale and lower prices.[25]

These large firms may compete aggressively, true, but out of this may come better service to the public than is offered by small firms which take refuge in guild-like behavior, following the "accepted customs of the trade."[26]

A well-known economist, John Maurice Clark, cites the home-building industry and small retailing as illustrations of areas in which the existence of many small firms has not led to especially good results. He concluded that consumer interests often are best served by companies that are strong and well financed.[27]

Marketing men get their fair share of income

The main concern about distribution of income is that marketing may divert a large share of the national income to marketing people because of the greater profitability of firms which have successfully sold their products. Such criticism does not seem justified, however, if the purpose of a free economy is to satisfy consumers and if marketing does that job successfully. Logically, the marketing segment of the economy should then be entitled to its higher incomes and higher profits.

Incomes in marketing *are* high for certain types of jobs, especially order-getting salesmen and some advertising and sales promotion people. But it also is true that many of the order takers, especially retail salespeople, have low incomes—in many cases below the federal minimum wage. These salaries probably reflect fairly accurately the contribution of each to the economy.

Does marketing cost enough?

The question, "Does Marketing Cost Too Much?" has been answered by one well-known financial officer with another question, "Does distribution cost enough?"[28] His analysis showed that marketing is an important and integral part of the business system.

---

[24] Backman, *op. cit.,* pp. 113–14.

[25] J. B. McKitterick, "What Is the Marketing Management Concept?" in Frank M. Bass (ed.), *The Frontiers of Marketing Thought and Science* (Chicago: American Marketing Association, 1957), pp. 71–82.

[26] Backman, *op. cit.,* pp. 79–81 and 112–14.

[27] "How U.S. 'Giants' Compete," *Business Week,* February 3, 1962, pp. 104–5; and John Maurice Clark, *Competition as a Dynamic Process* (Washington, D.C.: Brookings Institution, 1961).

[28] Paul M. Mazur, "Does Distribution Cost Enough?" *Fortune,* November, 1947.

He suggested that perhaps even more should be spent on marketing, since "distribution is the delivery of a standard of living"—that is, the satisfaction of consumers.

The role of business is to satisfy the consumer. Production cannot do it alone, nor can marketing. It makes little sense to think of production and marketing as truly separate entities. They are different sides of the same coin. Mass production requires mass distribution. If the *total cost* of mass production *and* marketing is less than before, then the system is more efficient regardless of how much marketing *alone* costs.

The market system provides for a fairly automatic operation of the economy. Many competitors in a relatively free market serve the needs of millions of consumers far better than central economic planning could serve them.

Market system is automatic and effective

In the planned Soviet economy, it usually has been necessary to tolerate a gray or black market and free-economy-type brokers to make the economy work. Now the Soviets are coming to see that product differentiation, branding, and advertising actually may help to facilitate the operation of a planned economy. They find that when customers recognize products by advertised brand, this permits self-service, speeds selling and cuts its cost. Requiring that each plant succeed in the market with its own brand acts as an automatic control on quality. Bureaucratic control, using standards and inspectors, would be increasingly difficult or impossible to accomplish now that the economy of the U.S.S.R. is offering more heterogeneous products.[29]

Certainly we do not now have the economists' "ideal"—pure competition—but the monopolistic competition situation that is typical of our economy is the result of customer preferences, not manipulation of markets by businessmen. Monopolistic competition may seem costly at times, but it seems to work fairly well in serving the welfare of consumers who have many and varied demands.

Consumers ask for it, consumers pay for it

Many consumers, for example, use material possessions as a means of differentiating themselves from their fellows. The newness of products is one measure of their distinction, and consumers may insist upon newness for this reason alone.

Many consumers want extensive services, such as credit, returned-goods privileges, and delivery services.

Many wish extensive product variety and immediate service at retail outlets. Large numbers may want this service at the same time of the day or week, and may be particularly insistent on service at Thanksgiving, Christmas, or Easter. But in the middle of the week or the middle of the summer, these consumers may leave the required facilities almost idle.

All these consumer demands add to the cost of marketing. Yet do these costs, when totaled, make marketing cost too much? *If the role of business is to serve the consumer, then the cost of whatever services*

---

[29] "Making the Soviet Future Work," *Business Week,* June 10, 1967, pp. 128–34; and Marshall I. Goldman, "A New Perspective of Product Differentiation and Advertising: The Soviet View," *Business Review*, Boston University, Spring, 1962, pp. 3–12.

consumers demand cannot be considered excessive. They are merely the cost of serving the consumer.

Social planners wonder if consumer should be king

Some critics are concerned with an economy that treats the consumer as king, allowing each to choose what he wants to buy for himself. To be sure, some may not use their income wisely by others' standards, but we do not yet have (*a*) ways of measuring consumer satisfaction, or (*b*) provisions for allowing one citizen to impose his choice of "correct" purchases on another citizen.

Planners often make such choices in totalitarian or socialist states. But it is axiomatic in democracies with free enterprise economies that individual consumers *are* the best judges of what will satisfy them most. This system has its deficiencies and some consumers make mistakes, but it is generally considered to be better than letting someone else decide for you. The college student might better appreciate this by reflecting on whether he would rather have someone else—his parents, for example—make all of his decisions for him.

It is only fair to note, however, that not *all* critics of marketing wish to substitute their own judgment for the consumer's. Rather, they want merely to give potential customers more information about the bewildering array of goods and services on the market.

Properly motivated efforts to inform the customer better are to be commended; it sometimes is most difficult to evaluate the increasingly technical offerings. Educating consumers to the real cost of interest on credit purchases is a good example of filling the need for better customer information. Another is better product information on packages.

At the same time, it may not be desirable to arbitrarily restrict the kinds of offerings that can be made, because it is difficult to draw other than minimum specifications for some products. As noted, the Soviets have discovered this the hard way.[30]

Marketing must keep satisfying customers

To repeat, marketing as an economic institution does *not* cost too much. Business has been assigned the role, by consumers, of satisfying their needs. Consumers have found it satisfactory—even desirable—to permit businessmen to cater to them and even to stimulate wants. As long as consumers are satisfied, marketing as an economic institution will not cost too much, and business will be permitted to continue as a profit-making venture.

Yet make no mistake. Business in a free economy enjoys no special privilege. Its role is neither God-given nor royally sanctioned nor bureaucratically protected. The right to do business is a right given by individuals in their capacities as consumers, through continued patronage, and as citizens, through their votes. At any time, the right to engage in business can be revoked by the consumer-citizen. Many businesses fail for lack of customers. More drastically, consumers may revoke private business's right to operate, and turn the activity over to public authorities.

This has happened in such cases as power plants taken over by

---

[30] Louis L. Stern, "Consumer Protection via Increased Information," *Journal of Marketing,* April, 1967, pp. 48–52.

municipalities; establishment of the postal service, TVA, and school systems; and government operation of defense plants.[31]

It must always be remembered that business exists at the consumers' discretion, and it is only by satisfying the consumer that a particular business firm and our private enterprise system can justify its existence and hope to perpetuate itself.[32]

Conclusion

Marketing as an economic institution certainly does *not* cost too much. It provides a necessary function in our economy, which is keyed to serving the consumer. By the decisions of many consumers and businesses, rather than a few planners, the needs and desires of consumers are satisfied.

In carrying out this role granted by consumers, however, the implementation of marketing is not always as effective as it might be.

Many businessmen do not understand the marketing concept nor the roles that either marketing or business play. Furthermore, many businessmen are not as competent as they should be. In this sense, marketing does cost too much. This situation is being improved, however, as training for business expands and as more competent people are attracted to marketing and business generally.

The efficiency of business and marketing would be increased greatly if more business managers understood and accepted the marketing concept—that the primary purpose of the whole business is to satisfy the customer. Acceptance of this philosophy forces an integration of all the activities of a business into a total system of action. This integration and the direction of all activities toward a specific goal can only lead to more effective business management.

The techniques and philosophy presented in this book indicate how acceptance of the marketing concept would encourage more efficient operation of business as well as whole economies, both underdeveloped and advanced.[33]

---

[31] James W. Culliton, "A Marketing Analysis of Religion," *Business Horizons,* Spring, 1959.

[32] Marketing men are paying much more attention to ethics and the place of marketing in our society. See Robert Bartels, "A Model for Ethics in Marketing," *Journal of Marketing,* January, 1967, pp. 20–26; Earl A. Clasen, "Marketing Ethics and the Consumer," *Harvard Business Review,* January–February, 1967, pp. 79–86; James M. Patterson, "What Are the Social and Ethical Responsibilities of Marketing Executives?" *Journal of Marketing,* July, 1966, pp. 12–15; J. Irwin Miller "Business, Education, Society," *Business Horizons,* Spring, 1967, pp. 21–30; A. W. Lorig, "Corporate Responsibilities," *Business Horizons,* Spring, 1967, pp. 51–54; *Ethics and Marketing* (Graduate School of Business Administration, University of Minnesota, 1966); and Robert Bartels, (ed.) *Ethics in Business* (Columbus, Ohio: Bureau of Business Research, College of Commerce and Administration, The Ohio State University, 1963).

[33] For a more thorough discussion of this point, see J. P. Austin, "World Marketing as a New Force for Peace," *Journal of Marketing,* January, 1966, pp. 1–3; Peter F. Drucker, "Marketing and Economic Development," *Journal of Marketing,* January, 1958, pp. 252–59; E. J. McCarthy, "Are Effective Marketing Institutions Necessary and Sufficient Conditions for Economic Development?" and J. C. Abbott, "Marketing Studies, Organization, Methods and Services of Development and Settlement Areas," in *Proceedings* of 1963 Winter Conference of the American Marketing Association.

1 What distinction can be made between marketing and production? Of what use is this distinction?

2 It appears that competition sometimes leads to inefficiency in the short run. Many people argue for monopoly in order to eliminate this inefficiency. Discuss this solution to the problem of inefficiency.

3 How would officially granted monopolies affect the operation of our economic system? Specifically, consider the effect on allocation of resources, the level of income and employment, and the distribution of income? Is the effect any different than if a monopoly were obtained through winning out in a competitive market?

4 Discuss the merits of various economic system objectives. Is the objective of the American economic system sensible? Do you feel more consumer satisfaction might be achieved by permitting some sociologists or some public officials to determine how the needs of the lower-income or less-educated members of the society should be satisfied? If you approve of this latter suggestion, what educational or income level should be required before an individual is granted free choice by the social planners?

5 Discuss the conflict of interests among production, finance, accounting, and marketing executives. How does this conflict contribute to the operation of an individual business? Of the economic system? Why does this conflict exist?

6 Why does the text indicate that the adoption of the marketing concept will encourage more efficient operation of an individual business? Be specific about the impact of the marketing concept on the various departments of a firm.

7 What impact does legislation have on the efficiency or inefficiency of marketing?

8 Should the goal of our economy be maximum efficiency? If your answer is yes, efficiency in what? If not, what should the goal be?

9 Cite an example of a critic using his own value system when evaluating marketing.

10 Is there any possibility of a pure competition economy evolving naturally? Could legislation force a pure competition economy?

11 Comment on the following statement: "Ultimately, the high cost of marketing is due only to consumers."

Appendix:
Marketing arithmetic

The beginning business student must become familiar with the essentials of the "language of business." Businessmen commonly use accounting terminology when discussing costs, prices, and profit. So it is essential for the student to have an understanding of this terminology if the use of accounting data is to become a practical tool in analyzing marketing problems.

The following discussion introduces the basic ideas underlying the operating statement, some commonly used ratios relating to the operating statement, markups, and the markdown ratio which is frequently used in retailing. Other analytical techniques are introduced at various parts in the text and so are not treated separately here.

The operating statement

An operating statement for a wholesale or retail business, commonly referred to as a profit and loss statement, is presented in Figure 1. A complete and detailed statement is presented so you will see the framework throughout the discussion, but the amount of detail on an operating statement is by no means standardized. Many companies present financial statements in considerably less detail than that shown. Their emphasis is placed on clarity and readability, rather than detail. To understand an operating statement, however, one must be aware of the items of which it is composed.

The operating statement is, in fact, only a simple description—or model—of the company's operations. It presents a summary of the financial results of the operations of the company over a specified period of time. Some beginning students may object that the operating statement is not simple in its description or summary of ordinary business operations, but as we shall see, this is not the case. *The primary purpose of the operating statement is the determination of the net profit figure, and presentation of data to support that figure.*

Figure 1 Operating statement for XYZ Company for the (year) ended (December 31, 196X)

Gross sales............................			$54,000
Less: Returns and allowances..............			4,000
Net sales..............................			$50,000
Cost of goods sold			
Beginning inventory at cost................		$ 8,000	
Purchases at billed cost...................	$31,000		
Less: Purchase discounts.................	4,000		
Purchases at net cost.....................	$27,000		
Plus freight-in..........................	2,000		
Net cost of delivered purchases............		29,000	
Cost of goods available for sale.............		$37,000	
Less: Ending inventory at cost.............		7,000	
Cost of goods sold.......................			30,000
Gross margin (gross profit).................			$20,000
Expenses			
Selling expenses			
Sales salaries...........................	$ 6,000		
Advertising expense.....................	2,000		
Delivery expense........................	2,000		
Total selling expense............		$10,000	
Administrative expense			
Office salaries...........................	$ 3,000		
Office supplies..........................	1,000		
Miscellaneous administrative expense.......	500		
Total administrative expense......		4,500	
General expense			
Rent expense...........................	$ 1,000		
Miscellaneous general expenses............	500		
Total general expense............		1,500	
Total expenses.........................			16,000
Net profit from operation..................			$ 4,000

Only three basic components   The basic components of an operating statement are sales, which are derived from the sale of goods or services; the costs which are incurred in the making and selling process; and the balance (called profit or loss), which is merely the difference between sales and costs. So there are only three basic facts in the statement: *sales, costs, and profit.*

Time period covered may vary   There is no single length of time which an operating statement covers. Rather, statements are prepared to satisfy the needs of a particular business. This may be at the end of each day or at the end of each

670

week. Usually, however, an operating statement summarizes results of transactions over a period of one month, three months, six months, or a full fiscal year. Since this time period does vary with the company preparing the statement, this information is included in the heading of the statement, as follows:

Operating Statement
for
XYZ Company
For the (period) ended (date)

Before proceeding to a more detailed discussion of the elements of our operating statement, note some of the uses for such a statement. A glance at Figure 1 reveals that a wealth of information is presented in a clear and concise manner. With this information, management can readily determine the *percentage of its net sales* represented by the cost of goods sold, by the gross margin, by expenses, and by the net profit. *Opening and closing inventory figures* are available, as is the amount spent during the period for the *purchase of goods for resale*. The *total expenses* are classified for the purpose of comparison with previous statements and control of these expenses. **Management uses of operating statements**

All of this information is of vital interest to the management of a company. Assume that a particular company prepares monthly operating statements. It should be obvious that a series of these statements represents a valuable tool for the direction and control of the business. By comparing results obtained from one month to the next, management can uncover adverse trends in the sales, expense, or profit areas of the business, and take corrective action.

Let us refer to Figure 1 and begin to analyze this seemingly detailed statement. The intention at this point is to acquire first-hand knowledge of the composition of the operating statement. **A skeleton statement gets down to essential details**

As a first step, suppose we take all the items that have dollar amounts extended to the third, or right-hand, column. Using these items only the operating statement looks as follows:

Gross sales	$54,000
Less: Returns and allowances	4,000
Net sales	$50,000
Less: Cost of goods sold	30,000
Gross margin	$20,000
Less: Total expenses	16,000
Net profit (loss)	$ 4,000

Is this a complete operating statement? Note that the skeleton statement differs from Figure 1 only in the matter of supporting detail. It is obvious that we have a complete operating statement, because all of the basic elements are included. In fact, the only items we *must* list to have a *complete* operating statement are:

Net sales	$50,000
Less: Costs	46,000
Net profit (loss)	$ 4,000

671

These three items are the *essence* of an operating statement. All other subdivisions or details are merely useful refinements.

Meaning of "sales"

The next step is to define and explore the meaning of the terms that are used in the skeleton statement.

The first item is sales. But just what do we mean by sales? The term *gross sales,* as used in this discussion, is the total amount of original billing to all customers. It is inevitable, however, that there will be a certain amount of customer dissatisfaction, or just plain errors in ordering and shipping goods. This results in *returns and allowances.*

A return is the act of a customer bringing or sending back goods he has purchased. The company either refunds the purchase price or allows the customer an equal amount in credit or exchange goods.

An allowance occurs when a customer is not fully satisfied with the purchased goods for some reason, and the company grants a price reduction on the original invoice but the customer keeps the goods.

These refunds and reductions must be taken into account when the sales figure for the period is computed. We are only interested in the revenue which the company manages to retain—that is, the actual sales dollars received or which will be received. Therefore, all reductions, refunds, cancellations, and so forth—made because of returns and allowances—are deducted from the original total (gross sales) to give us the net sales figure. This may be illustrated as follows:

Gross sales	$54,000
Less: Returns and allowances	4,000
Net sales	$50,000

Meaning of "cost of goods sold"

The next item appearing in the operating statement, cost of goods sold, shows the total value (at cost) of all the goods sold during the period. We will discuss the computation of *cost of goods sold* later. Meanwhile, merely note that after the cost of goods sold figure is obtained, it is subtracted from the net sales figure to get the amount of gross margin.

Meaning of "gross margin" and "expenses"

Gross margin, or gross profit, may be defined as the funds available to cover the cost of selling the goods and managing the business (and hopefully, to provide a profit after these expenses have been met).

Selling expense commonly is the major expense below the gross margin. It should be noted that in Figure 1 all expenses are deducted from the gross margin to arrive at the net profit figure. The expenses, in this case, are the selling, administrative, and general expenses. Notice that the cost of goods purchased and sold is not included in this total expense figure—it has been deducted previously from net sales to determine gross margin.

The net profit figure at the bottom of the statement shows what the company has earned through its operations during this particular period. It is the amount left after the cost of goods sold and the expenses have been deducted from net sales.

672

Detailed analysis of sections of operating statement

The cost of goods sold section includes details which are used to determine the cost of goods sold ($30,000), which is placed in the third column. But just what do we mean when we say cost of goods sold? By this term we mean *the cost value of goods sold—that is, actually removed from the company's control—and not the cost value of goods on hand at any given time.*

In Figure 1, it is obvious that beginning and ending inventory, purchases, purchase discounts, and freight-in are all necessary in the computation of cost of goods sold. If we pull the cost of goods sold section from the operating statement, it appears as follows:

Cost of goods sold for a wholesale or retail concern

Cost of goods sold		
Beginning inventory at cost.........		$ 8,000
Purchases at billed cost............$31,000		
Less: Purchase discounts.......... 4,000		
Purchases at net cost.............$27,000		
Plus: Freight-in................. 2,000		
Net cost of delivered purchases......	29,000	
Cost of goods available for sale.......	$37,000	
Less: Ending inventory at cost.....	7,000	
Cost of goods sold................		$30,000

The inventory figures merely indicate the cost of merchandise on hand at the beginning of and at the end of the period the statement covers. These figures may be obtained by a physical count of the merchandise on hand on these dates, or they may be estimated through a system of perpetual inventory bookkeeping which would show the inventory balance at any given time. Variations in inventory are of considerable importance to marketing people. The methods used in determining the inventory should be as accurate as possible, since these figures have a decided effect upon the cost of goods sold during the period, and consequently upon the net profit realized.

The net cost of delivered purchases must take into account freight charges incurred and purchase discounts received, since these items affect the cash actually spent to procure the goods and bring them to the place of business. A purchase discount is merely a reduction of the original invoice amount agreed upon at the time the goods were purchased, or which is given in consideration of prompt cash payment of the amount due. The total of such discounts is subtracted from the original invoice cost of purchases to determine the *net* cost of purchases. To this figure we add the freight charges for bringing the goods to the place of business. This gives the net cost of *delivered* purchases. When the net cost of delivered purchases is added to the *beginning* inventory at cost, we have the total cost of goods available for sale during the period. If we now subtract the *ending* inventory at cost

673

from the cost of the goods available for sale, we obtain the cost of goods sold.[1]

Cost of goods sold for a manufacturing concern

Figure 1 illustrates the way the proprietor of a wholesale or retail business would arrive at his cost of goods sold. Such a business would *purchase* finished goods and resell them. In a manufacturing concern, the purchases section of this operating statement would be replaced by a section called "cost of goods manufactured." This section would then take into account purchases of raw materials and parts, direct and indirect labor costs, and factory overhead charges (such as heat, light, and power) necessary in the production of the finished goods. The cost of goods manufactured would be added to the beginning inventory, just as the net cost of delivered purchases has been, to arrive at the cost of goods available for sale. Frequently, a separate cost of goods manufactured statement is prepared, and only the total cost of production is shown in the operating statement. See Figure 2 for an illustration of the cost of goods sold section of an operating statement for a manufacturing concern.

Expenses

Expenses typically appear below the gross margin. They usually include the costs of marketing, and administering the business. They do not include the cost of goods, either purchased or produced.

There is no specific method for classifying the expense accounts or for arranging them on the operating statement. They might just as easily have been arranged alphabetically, or according to amount, with the largest being placed at the top, and so on down the line. In a business of any size, though, it is desirable to group the expenses in some manner and to use subtotals by groups for analysis and control purposes. This was done in Figure 1.

Summary on operating statements

The statement presented in Figure 1 contains all of the major categories in an operating statement, together with a normal amount of supporting detail. Further detail could be added to the statement under any of the major categories without changing the nature of the statement. The amount of detail normally is determined by the use to which the statement will be put. A stockholder may be presented with a sketchy operating statement, while the one prepared for internal company use may incorporate a great amount of detail.

We have already seem that the elimination of some of the detail in Figure 1 did not affect the essential elements of the statement—net sales, costs, and net profit. Whatever further detail is added to the statement, its purpose is to help the reader to see how these three figures have been determined. A very detailed statement might easily

---

[1] One important point should be noted in connection with cost of goods sold. Inventory valuation methods vary from one company to another, and these different methods may cause large relative differences in the operating statements of these companies. Consult any basic accounting textbook for descriptions of the various inventory valuation methods.

Figure 2 Cost of goods sold section of an operating statement for a manufacturing firm

Cost of goods sold		
Finished goods inventory (beginning).............	$ 20,000	
Cost of goods manufactured (Schedule 1)............	100,000	
Total cost of finished goods available for sale.........	$120,000	
Less: Finished goods inventory (ending).............	30,000	
Cost of goods sold..........................		$ 90,000

Schedule 1. Schedule of Cost of Goods Manufactured			
Beginning work in process inventory..................			$ 15,000
Raw materials			
Beginning raw materials inventory..................	$ 10,000		
Net cost of delivered purchases.....................	80,000		
Total cost of materials available for use.............	$ 90,000		
Less: Ending raw materials inventory...............	15,000		
Cost of materials placed in production..........	$ 75,000		
Direct labor....................................	20,000		
Manufacturing expenses			
Indirect labor............................	$4,000		
Maintenance and repairs..................	3,000		
Factory supplies.........................	1,000		
Heat, light, and power....................	2,000		
Total manufacturing expenses........		10,000	
Total manufacturing costs...................			105,000
Total work in process during period..........			$120,000
Less: Ending work in process inventory........			20,000
Cost of goods manufactured.................			$100,000

Note: Last item, cost of goods manufactured, is used in the operating statement to determine the cost of goods sold, as above.

run to several single-spaced pages, yet the nature of the operating statement would remain the same.

Computing the stockturn rate

A detailed operating statement can provide the data which is needed to compute the stockturn rate. This is a measure of the number of times the average inventory is sold during a year. Note, the stockturn rate is related to the turnover during the course of a *year, not* the length of time covered by *any* operating statement.

The stockturn rate is an especially important measure because it shows how rapidly the firm's inventory is moving. Some lines of trade typically have slower turnover than others, but a decrease in the rate of turnover in a particular business can be very alarming. For one thing, it may mean that the firm's assortment of goods is no longer as attractive as it was. Also, it may mean that more working capital will be needed to handle the same volume of sales. Most businessmen pay considerable attention to the stockturn rate, attempting to achieve more rapid turnover.

Three methods, all basically similar, can be used to compute the stockturn rate. Which method is used depends somewhat on the data which is available. These three methods are shown below and usually give approximately the same results.[2]

$$1. \quad \frac{\text{Cost of goods sold}}{\text{Average inventory at cost}}$$

$$2. \quad \frac{\text{Net sales}}{\text{Average inventory at selling price}}$$

$$3. \quad \frac{\text{Sales in units}}{\text{Average inventory in units}}$$

The computation of the stockturn rate will be illustrated for the first method, since all are similar. The only difference is that the cost figures used in the first formula are changed to a selling price or numerical count basis in the other two methods. It is necessary, regardless of the method used, to express both the numerator and denominator of the formula in the same terms.

Using the first formula, the average inventory at cost is determined by adding the beginning and ending inventories at cost and dividing by 2. This average inventory figure is then divided *into* the cost of goods sold (expressed in cost terms) to obtain the stockturn rate.

For example, suppose the cost of goods sold for one year were $100,000. Beginning inventory was $25,000 and ending inventory $15,000. Adding the two inventory figures and dividing by 2, we obtain an average inventory of $20,000. We next divide the cost of goods sold by the average inventory ($100,000 divided by $20,000) and get a stockturn rate of 5.

Further discussion of the application of the stockturn rate is found in Chapter 25.

Operating ratios help analyze the business

The operating statement data is also used for a number of other purposes. In particular, many businessmen calculate what are called "operating ratios" from their operating statements and compare these ratios from one accounting period to another, as well as comparing their own operating ratios with those of competitors. Such competitive data is often available through trade associations. Each firm may report its results to the trade association, and then summary results are tabulated and distributed to the members. These ratios help management to analyze their operations and also are often used for control purposes. If some expense ratios are rising, for example, those particular costs are singled out for special attention.

Operating ratios are calculated by dividing net sales into the various operating statement items which appear below the net sales level in the

---

[2] Differences will occur because of varied markups and nonhomogeneous product assortments. In an assortment of tires, for example, those with markups might have sold much better than those with small markups, but with formula 3 all would be treated equally.

statement. Net sales is used as the denominator in the operating ratio, because it is this figure with which the businessman is most concerned—that is, the revenue actually received and retained in the business.

We can see the relation of operating ratios to the operating statement if we think of there being an additional column to the right of the dollar figures in an operating statement. This additional column would contain percentage figures, using net sales as 100 percent. This idea may be illustrated as follows:

Gross sales.............................	$540.00	
Less: Returns and allowances.........	40.00	
Net sales..............................	$500.00	100%
Cost of goods sold....................	350.00	70
Gross margin..........................	$150.00	30%
Expenses..............................	100.00	20
Net profit............................	$ 50.00	10%

The ratio of gross margin to net sales in the above illustration shows that 30 percent of the net sales dollar is available to cover sales expenses and the administration of the business, and to provide a profit. Note that the ratio of expenses to sales, plus the ratio of profit to sales, equals the 30 percent gross margin ratio. The net profit ratio of 10 percent indicates that 10 percent of the net sales dollar is left for profit.

The usefulness of percentage ratios should be obvious. The percentages are easily derived, and much easier to work with than large dollar figures. With net sales as the base figure, they provide a useful means of comparison and control.

It should be noted that because of the interrelationship of these various categories, only a few pieces of information are necessary and the others can be derived easily. In this case, for example, knowledge of gross margin percent and net profit percent would enable the derivation of expense and cost of goods sold percentages. Furthermore, the inclusion of a single dollar amount would enable the calculation of all other dollar amounts.

Markups

A markup is the amount a firm adds to its cost to obtain its selling price. The gross margin is similar to the markup, as it is the margin available to cover the costs of selling and the management of the business, as well as to provide a profit. Gross margin and the concept of markup are related because the amount added onto the unit cost of a product by a retailer or wholesaler is expected to cover the selling and administrative expenses, and to provide a profit.

The markup approach to pricing is discussed in Chapter 25, so it will not be discussed extensively here. A simple example will illustrate the idea, however. If a retailer bought an article which cost $1 when delivered to his store, then obviously he must sell it for more than this cost if he hopes to make a profit. He might add 50 cents onto the cost of the article in order to cover his selling and other costs and, hopefully, to provide a profit. The 50 cents would be the markup.

It would also be the gross margin or gross profit on that item *if* it is sold, but it should be emphasized that it is *not* the net profit. His selling expenses might amount to 35 cents, 45 cents, or even 55 cents. In other words, there is no assurance that the markup will cover his costs. Furthermore, there is no assurance that the customers will buy at his marked-up price. This may necessitate markdowns, which are dis- cussed later.

Markup conversions
Sometimes it is convenient to talk in terms of markups on cost, while at other times markups on selling price are useful. In order to have some convention, unless otherwise specified, markup (without any clarifying comment) will mean percentage of selling price. By this definition, the 50-cent markup on the $1.50 selling price is a markup of $33\frac{1}{3}$ percent.

Some retailers and wholesalers have developed markup conversion tables so they can readily convert from cost to selling price depending on the markup on selling price they desire. To see the interrelation, we present below two formulas which can be used to convert either type of markup to the other.

1. Percentage markup on selling price =
$$\frac{\text{Percentage markup on cost}}{100\% + \text{percentage markup on cost}}$$

2. Percentage markup on cost =
$$\frac{\text{Percentage markup on selling price}}{100\% - \text{Percentage markup on selling price}}$$

In the previous example, we had a cost of $1, a markup of 50 cents, and a selling price of $1.50. We saw that the markup on selling price was $33\frac{1}{3}$ percent, and on cost, it was 50 percent. Let us substitute these percentage figures into formulas 1 and 2 to see the process of conver- sion of markup from one basis to another. Assume first of all that we only know the markup on selling price, and want to convert to markup on cost. Using formula 2 we obtain:

$$\text{Percentage markup on cost} = \frac{33\frac{1}{3}\%}{100\% - 33\frac{1}{3}\%} = \frac{33\frac{1}{3}\%}{66\frac{2}{3}\%} = 50\%$$

If we know, on the other hand, only the percentage markup on cost, we could convert to markup on selling price as follows:

$$\text{Percentage markup on selling price} = \frac{50\%}{100\% + 50\%} = \frac{50\%}{150\%} = 33\frac{1}{3}\%$$

These results can be proved and summarized as follows:

Markup $0.50 =	50% of cost or	$33\frac{1}{3}\%$ of selling price
Cost $1.00 =	100% of cost or	$66\frac{2}{3}\%$ of selling price
Selling price $1.50 =	150% of cost or	100% of selling price

It is essential to see that the percentage figures alone have changed, while the monetary figures of cost, markup, and selling price remained the same. Notice, too, that when the selling price is used as the basis for the computation (100 percent), then the cost percentage plus the markup percentage equal 100 percent. But when the cost of the product is used as the base figure (100 percent), it is obvious that the selling price percentage must exceed 100 percent (by the markup on cost).

Markdown ratios help control retail operations

The ratios we discussed earlier were concerned with figures on the operating statement. Another important ratio, the markdown ratio, is an analytical tool which is used by many retail merchants to measure efficiency of various departments and their whole business. But note, it is not directly related to the operating statement. It requires special calculations.

A *markdown* is simply a retail price reduction which is often required because the customers will not buy some items at the originally marked-up price. This refusal to buy may be due to a variety of reasons—soiling, style changes, fading, damage caused by handling, or an original markup which was too high. To dispose of these goods, the merchant offers the merchandise at a lower price.

Markdowns are generally considered to be due to "business errors," perhaps because of poor buying, too high original markups, and other reasons. Perhaps the goods were damaged or soiled on display, but this, too, may have been due to poor buying or display. Regardless of the cause, however, markdowns are reductions in the original price and are important to managers who want to obtain some measure of the effectiveness of their operations.

Markdowns are similar to allowances in that price reductions have been made. Thus, in computing a markdown ratio, markdowns and allowances are usually added together and then divided by net sales. This markdown ratio is computed as follows:

$$\text{Markdown } \% = \frac{\$ \text{ Markdowns} + \$ \text{ Allowance}}{\$ \text{ Net sales}} \times 100$$

The 100 is multiplied times the fraction to reduce the handling of decimal points.

Returns are *not* included in the calculation of the markdown ratio. Returns are considered as "consumer errors," not business errors, and therefore are *not* included in the computation of this measure of business efficiency.

Retailers who use markdown ratios maintain a record of the amount of markdowns and allowances in each department and then divide the total by the net sales in each department. Over a period of time, these ratios gives management a measure of the efficiency of the buyers and salespersons in the various departments.

It should be stressed again that the markdown ratio has nothing to do with the operating statement. It is not calculated directly from data on the operating statement, since the markdowns take place before the goods are sold. In fact, some goods may be marked down and still not sold. Even if the marked down items are not sold, the markdowns—that is, the reevaluations of their value—are included in the calculations in the period when they are taken.

Note again that the markdown ratio would be calculated for the whole department and not individual items. What we are seeking is a measure of the effectiveness of the whole department, not how well the department did on individual items.

1 Distinguish between the following pairs of items which appear on operating statements:
 a) Gross sales and net sales.
 b) Purchases at billed cost and purchases at net cost.
 c) Cost of goods available for sale and cost of goods sold.
2 How does gross margin differ from gross profit? From net profit?
3 Make a list of 10 expense items that could be classified as selling or distribution expenses, and 10 items which could be classified as administrative or general expenses.
4 Why are percentage ratios figured using net sales rather than gross sales as a base figure?
5 Explain the similarity between markups and gross margin. What connection do markdowns have with the operating statement?
6 What are the essential items on an operating statement? What is an operating statement? Of what use is an operating statement to management?
7 How is gross margin obtained? What is its significance?
8 Compute the net profit for a company with the following data:

Beginning inventory (cost)	$ 15,000
Purchases at billed cost	33,000
Sales returns and allowances	25,000
Purchases at billed cost	33,000
Rent	6,000
Salaries	40,000
Heat and light	18,000
Ending inventory (cost)	25,000
Freight cost (inbound)	9,000
Gross sales	125,000

9 From the following data, draw up a retail operating statement.

Gross sales	$500,000
Purchases at net cost	325,000
Markdowns	50,000
Opening inventory at cost	120,000
Returns and allowances	50,000
Closing inventory at cost	125,000
Expenses	115,000

680

10 Construct an operating statement from the following data.

Returns and allowances	$ 15,000
Expenses	20%
Closing inventory at cost	60,000
Markdowns	2%
Inward transportation	3,000
Purchases	100,000
Net profit (5%)	30,000

11 Construct an income statement on the basis of the following data and compute the gross margin percentage, the net profit percentage, and the markdown percentage.

Salary expense	$ 40,000
Inward transportation	5,000
Average inventory at cost	50,000
Closing inventory at cost	40,000
Purchases at billed cost	200,000
Markdowns	40,000
Other expense	10,000
Customer returns	10,000
Gross sales	420,000
Rent	30,000
Supplies	5,000
Advertising	15,000

12 Gilberts men's store bought 100 suits to sell at $90; 50 suits sold at the original retail; 20 were marked down $10 from the original price; the remainder were marked down $20 from the original price. Compute the markdown percentage. The cost of the suits to Gilberts was $54 each.

13 Data given:

Markdowns	$ 5,000
Gross sales	100,000
Returns	8,000
Allowances	12,000

Compute net sales and percent of markdowns.

14 a) What percentage markups on cost are equivalent to the following percentage markups on selling price: 20, 37½, 50, and 66.67?
   b) What percentage markups on selling price are equivalent to the following percentage markups on cost: 33⅓, 20, 40, and 50?

15 What net sales volume is required to secure a stockturn rate of 10 times a year on an average inventory at cost of $100,000, with a gross margin of 30 percent?

16 If the beginning inventory at cost is $50,000 and the ending inventory is $100,000, what net sales volume is required to secure a stockturn rate of 7 if the company normally has a gross margin of 40 percent?

17 Explain why markdowns are not included in operating statements? What value are they if they are not in the statement?

18 Explain how the general manager of a department store might use the markdown ratios computed for his various departments? Would this be a fair measure? Of what?

19 Explain why operating ratios may be of greater use to management than the actual dollar and cents data.

Cases*

---

* See "Guide to the use of these cases" on page 684.

Guide to the use of these cases*

Cases can be used in many ways. And the same case may be fruitfully considered several times, for different purposes.

The following cases are organized under several headings to suggest when they might be used for the first time. The basic criterion for placement, however, was *not* whether the subject matter of the case fit best there, but rather whether any text principles or technical terminology to be covered later in the text were needed to read the case meaningfully. Some early cases might require some consideration of Price, for example, and might be used twice. But cases listed under Price can be treated more effectively after the Price chapters have been covered.

* Some of these cases are rewritten or edited versions of cases written by my students. I want to thank the following for their creative efforts: J. Stubbs, R. Moscote, J. Speer, D. Payeur, P. Nelson, S. Flaster, J. Helmer, C. L. Jones, J. Genung, J. Devona, E. Young, W. Supernaw, C. B. Jones, D. Polson, P. Abelson, D. Metz, and R. Wright.

Introduction to marketing management

National is a large manufacturer of bicycles, bowling alley equipment, golf clubs, bakery equipment, sewing machines, and cigarette-making machines. Its experience with various kinds of equipment led it into the development of a completely automated restaurant system. In 1962, National created the Automeal Division to handle the development and marketing of this new concept.

An Automeal system automatically handles order taking, food preparation, order assembly, and billing for a "hamburger" or "drive-in" type operation. Each system consists of several component machines (hamburger, beverage, milkshake, french fry, and entrée) connected by a system of conveyers and controlled by an electronic order and billing machine. One Automeal system would require only three persons to operate the entire setup: an operator, an assembler, and a maintenance man. It could produce up to 625 meals per hour.

From its beginning in 1962, the Automeal Division grew to 130 employees by 1967, including a vice president and various executives in charge of engineering, manufacturing, and field operations.

National executives take great pride in the development of the Automeal system and believe that its long-run potential justifies the multimillion-dollar investment. They believe that installation of an Automeal system would result in substantial savings to restaurant owners. Although no studies have been conducted on (1) the acceptance or need for this type of system by restaurant owners or managers, or (2) consumer reaction to food prepared by this system, the company's researchers have estimated that it can cut labor costs by 34 percent and food costs by 20 percent. They see it as economically feasible for any restaurant or institution that is serving over 250,000 limited-menu meals annually. (Limited menu is defined as less than 51 items.) Typically, this type of restaurant uses conventional equipment produced by any of hundreds of manufacturers and employs at least ten food-preparation people.

There are no competitors to Automeal. As a result, when the system was introduced in 1966 it received considerable publicity in national magazines (e.g., *Newsweek* and *Business Week*). Advertising was also undertaken in trade magazines (magazines aimed at those in the food-preparation business). These ads appeared unproductive, however, and were dropped. Promotion now emphasizes displays at trade shows, and personal calls on prospective customers. Four salesmen who formerly worked with one of National's other divisions are employed under the direction of a sales manager.

The total cost of the basic system is about $150,000. In response to initial price resistance, a leasing plan was developed shortly after the introduction. In the 18 months following the introduction, three systems were leased and five others were started with partial financial support from National. The results thus far have been disappointing. The three leased operations and one of the joint projects have been closed because they were unprofitable. Further, there is doubt whether the remaining systems can be successful if the current policies are followed.

In an effort to improve the division's performance, the vice president has changed the role of the marketing department. Its primary purpose had been to gather data to demonstrate the economic potential of the Automeal system to prospective buyers. Advertising and sales had been separate from the marketing department. Under the new organization, sales remain the responsibility of the sales manager, but the position of advertising director was eliminated. The marketing department has been given the task of "searching for new applications for present Automeal equipment."

Discuss what the Automeal Division has been doing and what it might do to improve its situation.

2

Mid-State Manufacturing Company

Mid-State Manufacturing Co. is a large manufacturer of basic chemicals and polymer resins located in Pensylvania.

Bob Zicuti, a bright young engineer, has been working for Mid-State as a research engineer in the polymer resins laboratory. His job is to do research on established resins to find new, more profitable applications for resin products.

During the last five years, Bob has been under intense pressure from top management to come up with an idea that would open up new markets for the company's foamed polystyrene.

Two years ago, Bob developed the "spiral dome concept," a method of using the foamed polystyrene to make dome-shaped roofs and other structures. He described the procedure for making domes as follows:

The construction of a spiral dome involves the use of a specially designed machine which bends, places, and bonds pieces of plastic foam together into a predetermined dome shape. In forming a dome, the machine head is mounted on a boom, which swings around a pivot like the hands of a clock, laying and bonding layer upon layer of foam board in a rising spherical form.

According to Bob, polystyrene foamed boards have several advantages:

1. Foam board is stiff, but capable of controlled deformation and can be bonded to itself by heat alone.
2. Foam board is extremely lightweight and easy to handle. It has good structural rigidity.

3. Foam board has excellent and permanent insulating characteristics. (In fact the major use for foamed board is as an insulator)
4. Foam board provides an "excellent" base on which to apply a variety of surface finishes.

With his fine speaking and reasoning abilities, Bob had little trouble convincing top management of the soundness of the idea.

According to a preliminary study carried out by the marketing department, the following were areas of construction that could be served by the domes:

1. Bulk storage.
2. Cold storage.
3. Educational construction.
4. Industrial tanks (covers for).
5. Light commercial construction.
6. Planetariums.
7. Recreational construction (such as a golf course starter house).

The study was based on uses for existing dome structures. Most of the existing domes are made out of concrete or some cement base material. It was estimated that considerable savings would be realized by using foam boards, due to the reduction of construction time.

Because of the new technology involved, the company decided to do its own contracting (at least for the first four to five years after starting the sales program). It felt this was necessary to make sure that no mistakes were made by inexperienced contractor crews. For example, if not applied properly, the plastic may burn.

After building a few domes to demonstrate the concept, the company contacted some leading architects across the country. Reactions were as follows:

It is very interesting, but you know that the Fire Marshal of Detroit will never give his OK.

Your tests show that foamed domes can be protected against fires, but there are no *good* tests for unconventional building materials as far as I am concerned.

I like the idea, but foam board does not have the impact resistance of cement.

We design a lot of recreational facilities and kids will find a way of sawing holes into the foam.

Building codes around L.A. are written for wood and cement structures. Maybe when the codes change.

After this unexpected reaction, management did not know what to do. Bob still thinks the company should go ahead. He feels that a few reports of well-constructed domes in leading newspapers would go a long way toward selling the idea.

What should Mid-State do? Why did it get into the present situation?

R. R. Tank Cars, Inc., is a division of a large corporation in the transportation industry. This division manufactures railroad tank cars and dry bulk carriers, either for sale to outsiders or to the leasing division of the corporation.

Last year, the division accounted for almost one fourth of the corporation's net profit of $25 million, on a production of over 3,000 railroad cars.

The industry consists of a total of five producers of railroad tank cars, with R. R. Tank Cars, Inc., being the largest by far in terms of sales and production capacity. This advantage has forced the competitors to become extremely vigorous, especially in product innovation. But the R. R. Tank Cars engineers have always been able to place a close substitute or a superior version on the market soon after a competitive innovation.

The sales staff for the division is completely separated from the manufacturing department, with sales offices in all major transportation centers. The sales staff is extremely active and effective in terms of sales contacts, customer relations, dispersion of product information, and obtaining sales. Whenever a need arises for a new type of car, or a modification to an existing model, the sales staff contacts the design engineers at the manufacturing plant. The design engineers supply a preliminary design and cost estimates to the sales staff, so that specific details on capacity, size, cost, and so on may be shown to a potential customer.

The design engineering department is manned by a staff of very competent engineers versed in the various technical areas needed to design railroad cars. The department is responsible to the manager of the manufacturing department. As of late, this manager has received numerous complaints from the engineering department about the methods of the sales staff.

The problem came to a peak recently when the sales staff returned with a rather large order for a radically new type of tank car. The engineering department had previously provided preliminary designs and cost estimates to the sales staff, but the sales staff announced that what they had sold had little relation to the preliminary designs. Instead it was completely different from such designs.

The complaints of the engineering department can be summarized as follows:

The sales staff comes in here and asks us for a preliminary design for a new car, and we break our backs to provide them with such information on very short notice. Then they have the gall to come back and tell us that they have sold a completely different car, for which we have done no work. It seems to me that they will sell anything the market wants, instead of what we design for them.

Another point of irritation to the engineers is the sales staff "habit" of bargaining on the prices of cars with each customer. The engineers' comment on this practice was: "Hasn't anyone around here ever heard of a standard price?"

Evaluate the engineers' views. What should be done?

4

Toni's Restaurant

Toni's was a fairly large restaurant, covering about 20,000 square feet of floor space, located in the center of a small shopping center which was completed early in 1958. In addition to this restaurant, other businesses in the shopping center included a bakery, a beauty shop, a liquor store, and a meat market. There was room for several cars in front of each of the stores.

The shopping center was located in a residential section of a growing suburb in the East. The center was situated along a heavily travelled major traffic artery. The nearby population was composed largely of middle-income families, and although the ethnic background of the residents was fairly heterogeneous, a large proportion of Italians were represented in the neighborhood.

Toni's Restaurant, which deals primarily in full-course dinners (no bar), is operated by Anthony Rocco, a neat-appearing man who was born in the community in 1910, of Italian parentage. He graduated from a local high school and a nearby university and had been living in this town with his wife and two children for many years. He had been in the restaurant business (self-employed) since his graduation from college in 1933. His most recent venture, prior to opening this restaurant, was a large restaurant which he operated successfully with his brother, from 1951 to 1957, at which time he sold out because of illness. Following his recovery, he was anxious for something to do and opened the present restaurant in April, 1958.

Toni felt that his plans for the business and his opening were well thought out. He had even designed his very attractive sign three years before. When he was ready to go into this business, he inspected several possible locations before finally deciding on the present one. He said: "I looked everywhere, and this is one of the areas I inspected. I particularly noticed the heavy traffic when I first looked at it. This is the crossroads from north to south for practically every main artery statewise. So obviously the potential is here."

Having decided upon the location, Toni attacked the problem of the new building with vigor. He tiled the floor; put in walls of surfwood; installed new plumbing and electrical fixtures, and an extra washroom; and purchased the necessary restaurant equipment, all brand new. All this cost him $29,000—which came from his own cash savings. He then spent an additional $600 for glassware, $1,500 for his initial food stock, and $455 to advertise his opening in the local newspaper. The local newspaper covered quite a large area so the $455 purchased only three quarter-page ads. These expenditures also came from his own personal savings. Next, he hired five waitresses at $40 a week and one chef at $65 a week. Then, with $6,000 cash on hand, he was ready to do business. Reflecting his "sound business sense," Toni realized the necessity of having a substantial cash reserve to fall back on until the business had had time to get on its own feet. He expected this to take about one year. He did not have any expectations about "getting rich overnight."

The business opened in April and by August he had achieved a weekly gross revenue of only $800. Toni was a little discouraged with this, but he was still able to meet all his operating expenses without investing any "new money" in the business. However, he was concerned that he might have to do so if business did not pick up in the next couple of months. It had not by September, and Toni did have to invest an additional $800 in the business "for survival purposes."

Business had not improved in November and Toni was still insisting that it would take at least a year to build up a business of this nature. In view of the failure to "catch on rapidly," Toni indicated that he had intensified his advertising to see if this would help the business any. In the last few weeks, he had spent $150 of his own cash for radio advertising—ten late evening spots. Moreover, he was planning to spend even more during the next several weeks for some newspaper ads.

By February, 1959, business had picked up very slightly—about a $20–$30 increase in the average weekly gross.

By April, 1959, the situation had begun to improve and by June his weekly gross was up to between $1,200 and $1,300. By March in the following year, the weekly gross had risen to about $1,600. Toni increased the working hours of his staff 6 to 7 hours a week and added another man to handle the increasing number of customers. Toni was more optimistic for the future. He had not put any new money into the business since the summer of 1959 and expected business to continue to rise. He had not yet taken any salary for himself, but indicated that he was in a position to do so if he wished. Instead, he planned to put in an air-conditioning system at a cost of $5,000 and was also planning to use what salary he would have taken for himself to hire two new waitresses to handle his ever-increasing volume of business.

In explaining the successful survival and growth of his business, Toni said: "I had a lot of cash on hand, a well-planned program, and the patience to wait it out."

Evaluate Rocco's marketing strategy. How might he have improved his chances for success and achieved more rapid growth?

Customer behavior

State Camera Co. is located in a large, midwestern city near a major university. It sells high-quality still and movie cameras, accessories, and projection equipment, including 8 and 16MM movie projectors, 35MM slide projectors, opaque and overhead projectors, and a large assortment of projection screens. Most of the sales of this specialized equipment are made to area school boards for classroom use, to industry for use in research and sales, and to the university for use in research and instruction.

State Camera also offers a wide selection of film and a specialized film-processing service. Rather than processing film on a mass production basis, however, each roll of film is given individual attention to accentuate the particular features requested by the customer. This service is used extensively by local industries who need high-quality pictures of lab or manufacturing processes for analytical and sales work.

To encourage the school and industrial trade, State Camera offers a graphics consultation service. If a customer wishes to construct a display, whether large or small, professional advice is readily available. Along with this free service, State Camera carries a full line of graphic arts supplies.

State Camera employs four full-time store clerks and two outside salesmen. These salesmen make calls on industry, attend trade shows, make presentations for schools, and assist both present and potential customers in their use and choice of visual aids.

The people who make most of the over-the-store-counter purchases are serious amateur photographers and some professional photographers who buy in small quantities. Price discounts of up to 25 percent of the suggested retail price are given to customers who purchase more than $500 worth of goods per year. Most regular customers qualify for the discount.

About a year ago, Eastman Kodak introduced the Kodak Instamatic Camera. This camera comes in several models, each offering selected features and ranging in price from $11.95 to $140. Kodak has had great success with this camera, especially in the low-price range. The features which are especially appealing are cartridge loading ("just drop it in and shoot"), no rewinding (this is done by a spring motor), and no adjustments (camera is completely automatic). The most popular film for the Instamatic is the 35MM, 2 + 2 slide film.

The camera's major appeal is to those people who typically have had difficulty with more complicated cameras, but still enjoy taking their own pictures. Kodak claims "You get a perfect picture every time."

Because the Instamatic camera is available in discount houses, drugstores, department stores, and nearly every other possible outlet, State

Camera does not carry it. However, it does sell the film cartridges, which come with a mail-in processing envelope.

Andrew Machey, the manager of State Camera, felt that with so many people taking 35MM slide pictures there ought to be a good demand for some way of viewing them. Therefore, he planned a special pre-Christmas sale of inexpensive slide projectors, viewers, and home-sized projection screens. Hoping that most of these would be purchased as Christmas gifts, Machey selected some products which offered good value and discounted the prices to competitive levels, e.g., projectors at $29.95, viewers at $3.95, and screens at $11.95. To promote the sale, large signs were posted in the store windows and ads were run in a Christmas gift suggestion edition of the local newspaper. This edition appeared each Wednesday during the four weeks preceeding Christmas.

At these prices and with this promotion, Machey hoped to sell at least 150 projectors and screens, and 200 viewers. When the Christmas returns were in, total sales were 22 projectors, 15 screens, and 48 viewers. He was most disappointed with these results, especially because trade estimates suggested that sales of projection equipment in this price and quality range were up 300 percent over last year.

Evaluate what happened. What should Mr. Machey do in the future?

6

Inland Steel Company

Inland Steel Company is one of the two major producers of wide flange beams in the Chicago area. The other major producer is the U.S. Steel Corp. (USS), which is several times larger than Inland as far as production capacity on this particular product is concerned. Bethlehem Steel Company and USS have eastern plants which produce this product. Also, there are some small competitors in the Chicago area and foreign competition is sometimes a factor. Generally, however, U.S. Steel and Inland Steel are the major competitors in the Chicago area because typically the mill price charged by all producers is the same and the customer must pay freight from the mill. Therefore, the large eastern mills landed price would not be competitive in the Chicago area.

Wide flange beams are one of the principal steel products used in construction. They are the "modern" version of what are commonly known as "I-beams." USS rolls a full range of wide flanges from 6 inches to 36 inches. Inland entered the field about 15 years ago when it coverted an existing mill to the production of this product. This mill is limited to flanges up to 24 inches, however. At the time of the conversion it was estimated that customer usage of sizes over 24 inches was likely to be small. In the past few years, however, there has been a very pronounced trend toward the larger and heavier sections.

The beams produced by the various competitors are almost identical since the customers buy according to standard dimensional and physical property specifications. In the smaller size range, there are a number of competitors, but above 14 inches only U.S. Steel and Inland compete in the Chicago area. Above 24 inches, U.S. Steel has not had any competition.

All the steel companies sell these beams through their own sales forces. The customer for these beams is called a structural fabricator. This fabricator typically buys unshaped beams and other steel products from the mills and shapes them according to the specifications of his customer. The fabricator's customer is the contractor or owner of a particular building or structure which is being built.

The structural fabricator typically sells his product and services on a competitive bid basis. The bidding is done on the basis of plans and specifications which are prepared by an architectural or structural engineering firm and forwarded to him by the contractor desiring the bid. Although several hundred structural fabricators compete in the Midwest, relatively few account for the majority of wide flange tonnage. Since the price is the same from all producers, they typically buy beams on the basis of availability (i.e., availability to meet production schedules) and performance (reliability in meeting the promised delivery schedule).

Several years ago, Inland production schedulers saw that they were going to have an excess of hot-rolled plate capacity in the near future. At the same time, a new production technique was developed which would enable a steel company to weld three plates together into a section with the same dimensional and physical properties and almost the same cross section as a rolled wide flange beam. This technical development appeared to offer two advantages to Inland: (1) it would enable Inland to use some of the excess plate capacity, and (2) larger sizes of wide flange beams could be offered. Cost analysts showed that by using a fully depreciated plate mill and the new welding process it would be possible to produce and sell larger wide flange beams at "competitive" prices, i.e., at the same price charged by USS.

Inland executives were excited about the possibilities because they thought customers would appreciate having a second source of supply. Also, the new approach would allow the production of up to a 60-inch depth of section and an almost 30-inch width of flange. With a little imagination, these larger sizes could offer a significant breakthrough for the construction industry.

Inland decided to go ahead with the new project. As the production capacity was being converted, the salesmen were kept well informed of the progress. They, in turn, promoted this new capability, emphasizing that soon they would be able to offer a full range of beam products. Several general information letters were sent to the trade, but no advertising was used. Moreover, the market development section of the sales department was very busy explaining the new possibilities of the process, particularly to fabricators at engineering trade associations and shows.

When the new line was finally ready to go, the reaction was disappointing. In general, the customers were wary of the new product. The structural fabricators felt they could not use it without the approval of their customers, because it would involve deviating from the specified rolled sections. And, as long as they could still get the rolled section, why make the extra effort for something unfamiliar, especially with no price advantage. The salesmen were also plagued with a very common question: "How can you take plate which you sell for about $121 per ton and make a product which you can sell for $122?" This question came up frequently and tended to divert the whole discussion to the cost of production rather than the way the new product might be used.

Evaluate Inland's present situation. What should it do to gain greater acceptance for its new product?

7

The "New" Arnold Constable

Arnold Constable, a large New York City women's specialty store, was founded in that city in 1825. At the turn of the century, it was considered an exclusive fashion store, catering to leading society figures.

Isaac Liberman, now chairman of the board, became president of the store in 1925. After that time, the store continued to alter its pricing policies to the point where it became and remained a popular- to medium-priced speciality store which no longer manufactured any of its own fashions. Newspaper ads began to put major emphasis on price rather than fashion.

In the early 1960's, yearly sales were declining. Also, there was heavy turnover in executive positions, with the exception of the presidency, which was held by Merwin Bayer, Mr. Liberman's nephew.

In 1963, Mr. Bayer attempted to sell Arnold Constable to a discount house, Vornado Brothers. Despite extensive negotiations, the sale was never consummated. Then, in 1964, management embarked on a program to create a "new" Arnold Constable.

Mr. Bayer made heavy investments in refurbishing the store, following a current trend toward creating many boutiques, or small shops, within a larger store. Since the store is located in a major downtown shopping district near the 42nd Street business area, with countless young businesswomen working nearby, such investments were thought to be both warranted and what was needed to attract younger customers.

The store's third floor, where dresses were sold, was transformed into approximately ten small shops. The inventory in each shop was strictly divided on the basis of price and broad classification of garments. Shoppers did not have to (and could not) look at $18 and $23 dresses at the same time, nor cocktail and casual garments of the same price range. The new arrangement necessitated larger inventories. Management met this by stocking heavy assortments of the merchandise of well-known manufacturers who sell to nearby department stores, rather than stocking smaller selections of more unusual clothing.

694

The most exciting boutique, for more expensive ready-to-wear, was placed at the rear of the main floor, clearly visible from the "down" escalator and impossible to miss as women were leaving the store. In neighboring main floor departments, new functional open display cases were used to create self-selection buying arrangements. Many less expensive brands were introduced, but traditional markup structures were maintained.

Little change was made in promotion. A new logo, "The New Arnold Constable" was added to the usual advertising format. But the new store arrangements were not announced.

In 1964, Arnold Constable sustained a net loss of $480,000, which rose to $944,000 in 1965. For the first six months of 1966, the loss was $964,680. An outside study of the operating results of 84 U.S. retailers found that the majority were enjoying all-time prosperity.

Mr. Bayer attributed his store's operating loss to one-time expenses of remodeling. However, between 1964 and 1965, there was an 8.5 percent decrease in Arnold Constable's sales volume (from $27.9 million to $25.5 million), a trend which continued in the first six months of 1966. Also, the company's net worth fell from $8.3 million in 1964 to $7.3 million in 1965.

Evaluate what has been going on. What should Mr. Bayer do?

The Great Lakes Nursery Corporation, based in Wisconsin, is developing a network of franchised Christmas tree farms. They will produce trees near urban areas, thereby making it easier for buyers to select and cut their own trees. In 1967, the company already had a network of 200 franchised tree farms and its goal by 1975 was 1,000 franchise holders. If this idea were successful, it would obsolete the present production-marketing patterns of the $225 million a year Christmas tree industry. Currently, producers in the northern states and Canada cut trees and then ship them throughout the United States.

8

Great Lakes Nursery Corporation

The Great Lakes Nursery Corporation is aiming for 15 percent of the market within the next few years. Its present strategy is to sell franchises to farmers and others with at least 15 acres of land. The company supplies the trees, and all the technical know-how and training needed by the franchise holder. In addition, Great Lakes will help them sell the products, either at wholesale or retail. If the franchisee decides to sell the trees at the retail level, Great Lakes will provide promotional assistance. A cooperative advertising program is to be financed with 10 percent of gross sales receipts. Wholesale contacts have already been made with large national retailing concerns, such as Sears, Roebuck.

The company has already started making money on the sale of franchise rights, but the big return will come only if the franchisees succeed. The company will receive 25 percent—33⅓ percent of the franchisee's gross sales. In 1967, the revenue from this source was only $25,000 while the revenue from the sale of franchise rights was $250,000. By 1972, the company expects to receive over $1 million as its share of sales. And it expects that this figure will continue rising thereafter. Much depends, however, on the success of the company's franchise holders' sales.

Discuss Great Lakes' strategy and how it can assure that its franchise holders will be successful.

Product

9

Eastern Chemical Company

The Eastern Chemical Company is a large producer of industrial chemicals. Research, development, and technical service have been the backbone of Eastern's growth. In 1961, as several of its competitors became active in producing new consumer products, Eastern sensed profitable opportunities for expansion in this area. Company executives felt they ought to be able to incorporate some of their technical know-how into new consumer products.

Choosing the housewife as a target market, Eastern commissioned a major research project to study this particular market. They wanted to find a need that could be filled by introducing a new product concept. After spending $500,000 for this research, they found that the job housewives dreaded most was cleaning their dirty ovens.

To date, the market leader in oven cleaners was a product that did a good job. But it was messy to use. Further, it could cause serious chemical burns as well as remove paint, floor wax, and so forth on contact. To clean her oven with this product, a housewife had to wear rubber gloves, put newspapers on her kitchen floor, and use extreme caution during application.

Eastern decided to introduce an aerosol oven cleaner that could be used without rubber gloves. Work on the new product began in 1962. In 1963, a preliminary product use test was made. Then, after making necessary changes and improvements, the product was ready to be test marketed. Three geographical regions were chosen to be representative of the total national market. Since the product would eventually be introduced nationwide, the typical grocery wholesalers and retailers it expected to use later were selected in the test market regions. The product was advertised on local television, informing the public of the new concept in oven cleaning. A relatively high price (double the price of the leader) was set as Eastern felt that the new concept would be worth it to the housewife and would also provide a higher return on investment. In June of 1963, the results of the three-month market test

696

indicated excellent acceptance of the new concept. Sales rates were far higher than those needed for success.

Full-scale production facilities were set up. The nationwide launch was finally made in April of 1964. Television and nationally distributed household magazines were used as the primary advertising media. As proved most successful during the market test, the advertising informed the housewife of the new aerosol, no-gloves-needed concept. The high price was maintained, since it did not seem to inhibit sales in the test market.

At just about the same time, several other companies also began launching their own aerosol oven cleaners at lower prices. The total sales of these products rose rapidly, all except Eastern's. Although Eastern's oven cleaner was superior in performance and Eastern spent more on advertising than all the others put together, the company's sales of this product during the first year were considerably below even the most pessimistic expectations.

What happened? What should Eastern do? Why?

The Perlick Company, of Milwaukee, Wisconsin, has been in business for 50 years, manufacturing a line of brass and copper fittings used in the production and dispensing of beer. The product line consists of valves, casings, and connectors which are used in breweries, as well as tapping equipment which is used in taverns and restaurants. Their products are sold by several of their own salesmen who call directly on breweries, taverns, and restaurants.

10

The Perlick Company

Several years ago, the salesmen reported an opportunity to offer better quality refrigeration equipment for chilling bottled and tap beer in restaurants and taverns. Following some preliminary market and engineering research, the company decided to expand its product line in this direction. It set up a "Cabinet Division" to manufacture a high-quality line of all-metal beer coolers and glass chillers. The company offered four different sizes of refrigerator cabinets, but all were basically the same style and color (black).

The same salesmen who were selling the other Perlick products had considerable success selling the new products to current customers. The salesmen had correctly seen that some of their customers' equipment had depreciated to the point where they would be very interested in new equipment. The salesmen also received some business from those setting up new establishments. But this business was more difficult to obtain because the salesmen traveled widely and were not always aware when and where new businesses were being organized. Some inquiries came to them from small ads which were placed in trade magazines appealing to restaurant and tavern operators. All such inquiries were followed up immediately by the salesmen, and the high quality of Perlick's product helped close many sales.

The cabinets were well designed from an engineering standpoint and technically superior to similar products available from competitors. (In particular, they were built more solidly. It was expected that they would outlast competitive products by four to six years. They also chilled beer faster, were more compact, and had a longer lasting finish). This higher quality enabled the cabinets to be sold for 10 to 15 percent more than competitors' products; prices ranged from $300 for the smallest size cooler to $2400 for the largest unit.

Perlick was enjoying considerable prosperity for the first two years, since production was easily standardized on the four sizes it was producing. Further, Perlick was concentrating its sales effort in the Upper Midwest to keep its selling costs low—90 percent of sales were made in Wisconsin, Illinois, Indiana, and Michigan. This also had the effect of reducing customers' delivered costs, because typically customers paid transportation costs from the factory. Most of Perlick's competitors sold on a nationwide basis, and many were located in other parts of the country.

Some units were sold by Perlick outside its normal selling area. These orders came in response to the small ads which were placed in leading trade magazines. The salesmen did not follow up these inquiries personally, but occasionally the telephone was used to handle closing details.

Two years after Perlick entered this business, its sales began to slip. Competitors began offering a wider variety of styles, colors, and sizes to suit the tavern and restaurant owners. Competitors' cabinets became available in black, white, blue, grey, and brown. Up to 15 different sizes were offered to meet customers' space limitations. Formica and plastic finishes were offered to supplement the metal exteriors already available. Perlick countered these offerings by extending a 10-year guarantee on the refrigeration unit, in addition to the free installation and service already provided. Sales failed to increase, however, and the sales manager recommended that the company meet the demands of customers.

The production manager maintained, however, that increasing variety in the product line would greatly increase cost. Perlick was currently producing 15 cabinets per working day, after reaching a high of 20 cabinets a day before the sales decline. The production manager estimated that if the product line were expanded as the sales manager recommended, the company would have to produce and sell an average of 45 cabinets per day to hold down its costs, while keeping quality constant.

The production manager felt that the sales manager should expand his market coverage, and perhaps also should find distributors in the present territories who could provide continuing representation, thereby supplementing the efforts of the salesmen. Basically, he felt that Perlick had developed an efficient production system, and a relatively small increase in sales would enable them to continue profitably with their present operation. He estimated that a doubling in capital investment would be required to expand to the higher volume. This was risky, and he felt that more attention should be paid to expanding sales

698

of the present line rather than investing in more plant and equipment to offer a wider line and greater variety.

The sales manager, on the other hand, claimed that Perlick had to remain competitive in the market place or the sales decline would continue. He felt that simply expanding the territory would only add to cost and not result in a significant improvement in sales. Further, he noted that the company's financial condition was good. It had the resources to increase production as he recommended and he felt that now was the time to take action. He wanted to go on the offensive rather than wait to see what happened. Specifically, he wanted permission to expand the sales force to develop a nationwide selling program and generate the sales which would keep the expanded production facilities going. To begin with, he wanted the addition of three more salesmen and the company's commitment to expand the product line. Otherwise, he felt the morale of the salesmen would continue to decline and conditions would continue to deteriorate.

Evaluate the present situation and explain what Perlick should do.

Dow Chemical Company is one of the larger chemical companies in the United States, making a diversified line of organic and inorganic chemicals, plastics, bioproducts, and metals. Research has played a vital role in the company's growth.

11

Dow Chemical Company

Recently, Dow's research laboratories developed a new product in the antifreeze line—Dowtherm 209. Much research was devoted to the technical phase, involving various experiments concerned with the quality of the components in the new product.

The antifreeze commonly used now is ethylene glycol. If it leaks into the crankcase oil, it forms a thick pasty sludge that can produce bearing damage, cylinder scoring, or a dozen other costly and time-consuming troubles for both the operator and owner of heavy-duty equipment.

Dow Chemical believed that Dowtherm 209 would be very valuable to the owners of heavy-duty diesel and gasoline trucks as well as other heavy equipment owners. Chemically, Dowtherm 209 consists of methoxy propanol, as distinguished from the conventional glycol and alcohol products. It cannot prevent leakage, but if it does get into the crankcase, it will not cause any problems.

Dowtherm 209 has been proven in the laboratory to prevent seizing of rod and main bearings, pistons, rings, and piston pins which are common with glycol leakage. The new product will not remain in the engine oil and will cut down on the sludge residue.

At first, Dow thought it had two attractive markets for this product: (1) the manufacturers of heavy-duty equipment, and (2) the users of heavy-duty equipment. Dow salesmen have made numerous calls and so far neither type of customer has been very interested. The manufacturers are reluctant to show interest in the product until it has been proven in actual use. The buyers for construction companies and other firms using heavy-duty equipment have also been hesitant. Some felt the price was far too high for the advantages offered. Others didn't understand what was wrong with the present antifreeze and dismissed the idea of paying extra for "just another" antifreeze.

The price of Dowtherm 209 is $7.98 per gallon, which is about twice the price of regular antifreeze. The higher price is a result of higher costs in producing the product and an increment for making a better type of antifreeze.

Explain what has happened so far. What would you do if you were responsible for this product?

12
Smile Toothpaste

The Block Pharmaceutical Company is a well-known manufacturer of high quality cosmetics and ointments. A little over a year ago, Mr. Fine, the president of Block, was scanning the income statements for the last three quarters and did not like what he saw. At the next board meeting he stated that Block should be showing a larger profit. It was generally agreed that the reason for the profit decline was that the firm had not added any new products to its line during the last two years.

Management was directed to investigate this matter and remedy it if possible.

Mr. Fine immediately requested a report from the product planning group and found that it had been working on a new formula for a toothpaste that might be put into production immediately if a new product were needed. Mr. Archer, the head of the research department, assured Mr. Fine that the new ingredients in this toothpaste had remarkable qualities. Clinical tests had consistently shown that the new, as yet unnamed, dentifrice cleaned teeth better and prevented decay significantly more efficiently than the many toothpastes furiously battling for prominence in the market. Based on these tests, Mr. Fine concluded that perhaps this product was what was needed and ordered work to proceed quickly to bring it to the market.

The marketing research department was asked to come up with a name that was pleasing, and a tube and carton design. The results were reported back within two months; the product was to be called "Smile" and the package would emphasize eye-pleasing pastels.

The marketing department decided to offer Smile along with its other "prestige" products in the drug stores which were carrying the rest of Block's better quality, higher priced products. Block's success had been built on moving quality products through these outlets, and management felt that quality-oriented customers would probably be willing to pay a bit more for a significantly better toothpaste. Block was already well established with the wholesalers selling to these retailers and experienced little difficulty obtaining distribution for Smile.

It is now six months after the introduction of Smile and the sales results have not been good. The established wholesalers and retailers carried the product, but relatively little was purchased by final consumers. And now many retailers are requesting that Block accept returns on Smile because obviously it is not going to catch on with consumers, despite the extremely large (matching competitors) amounts of advertising which have supported Smile.

Mr. Fine has requested the marketing research department to analyze the situation and explain the disappointing results thus far. An outside survey agency interviewed several hundred consumers and has tabulated its results. These are pretty well summarized in the following quotes:

"The stuff I'm using now tastes good. Smile tastes terrible!"
"I never saw that brand at the supermarket I shop at."
"I like what I'm using . . . why change?"
"I'm not going to pay that much for any toothpaste . . . it couldn't be *that* much better!"

What recommendation would you make to Mr. Fine? Why?

Compagnie Marcel Mayer (CMM) was one of the pioneer firms in the French food processing industry, and now is one of the largest canned food producers. Specializing in canned vegetables, it has the largest share of the canned asparagus and carrot markets in France, and the largest share of the canned beet market in Germany. CMM also has substantial sales in most of the other Common Market countries.

13

The Marcel Mayer Company (Compagnie Marcel Mayer)

In the years before World War II, Marcel Mayer was *the* firm in the canned vegetable market of France, but in postwar years, many competitors have entered the market and CMM's share of market of several vegetables has fallen considerably.

All CMM products are marketed under the Marcel Mayer family brand in similar packages, and management's traditional objective has been to gain a dominant share of the canned vegetable market, utilizing low prices to aim specifically at low- and middle-income consumers. Recent independent research revealed some interesting data. First, despite the market position of CMM products, the brand in the consumers' minds was associated with canned vegetables and not canned foods in general. When questioned specifically about the MM brand, typical replies were "it's one of the oldest brands." Consumers also noted that MM canned vegetables were the cheapest in the market and did not speak too enthusiastically about the quality of MM products, although most considered them "a good buy for the money."

About two years ago, Mr. Jacques Mayer, son of the company's founder and currently president of CMM, heard of a Canadian firm which had perfected and patented formulas and processes for the manufacture of canned baby foods. This product was a relative novelty in France at the time, and after discussing the matter with Mr. Renaud, CMM's marketing manager, the two decided that the new product would make a good addition to their line. After considerable negotiation with the Canadian company, CMM was granted an exclusive license to manufacture and sell the baby foods in the Common Market countries.

New production facilities for the baby foods are almost complete and management is now faced with the problem of choosing a brand name for the new products. Two major opinions have been set forth and heated discussion is taking place.

Some of the executives, led by Mr. Renaud, want to sell the baby foods under a new name. They argue that at the moment there is confusion about the quality of product the MM brand stands for, and that the addition of a new line which will not fit into either the low or low-medium price ranges will confuse the issue still further. Besides, the "cheap-price" image of MM might have detrimental effects on the baby food line. They believe that the baby foods should not be packaged with the regular CMM green labels. Renaud recommends that the new name for the baby foods be "Joie des Anges" (literally, "nectar of the angels; babies are frequently referred to as "anges"), and that the name be printed in white on a powder-blue background. He sees this name as the overall brand for what could possibly lead to a full line of baby food products.

Mr. Mayer, continuing in his father's tradition, wants to further strengthen the MM family brand. He and his supporters stress that the MM brand was originally conceived of by the company as covering all canned foods. Other points stressed are that continuing with a single brand name will help to concentrate advertising expenditures on building the image of one brand, since the adoption of a new brand would divide such expenditures and spread them too thin. Finally, they argue that the addition of the new product would upgrade the total line of MM products, and that the traditional colors would not cause any problems with the sale of the baby foods. Hence they favor the retention of the existing brand name and labeling the cans (or jars) as "MM Nourriture pour Enfants" (MM Baby Food).

Which approach should CMM select? Why?

Place

Gold and Company is a full-line department store located in Lincoln, Nebraska. In 1963, the family-owned firm was purchased by Brandeis, Incorporated. Brandeis is a high-quality department store operation in Omaha, Nebraska, with a large downtown location and several suburban stores in successful shopping centers. It is by far the most successful store in Omaha, a position similar to that Gold's held in Lincoln before the purchase was completed.

Nathan Gold founded Gold's around the turn of the century and maintained a high quality operation, catering to the middle and upper classes of Lincoln. Because of his long reputation as a civic leader, Nathan Gold was a respected and popular citizen. For many years he was "the man behind the city government in Lincoln."

Following the purchase by Brandeis, Gold's sales dropped considerably. In some departments, sales in 1966 were one half those of 1962. On the average, sales declined 20 percent under the new management—i.e., from 1963 to 1966.

Following the purchase by Brandeis, the entire credit function was transferred to Omaha. Only a few clerks were left at the Lincoln store. Brandeis credit cards were issued to all charge customers, replacing the former cards which were good at seven downtown Lincoln stores. Monthly statements come from the Omaha credit office and bear "Brandeis Omaha" as a return address.

For many years the store had given trading stamps, and the local S&H Green Stamp Redemption Center was located on the fourth floor of Gold's. Stamps were discontinued almost immediately after the purchase, and S&H built a new redemption center.

Miller and Paine, the main competitor of Gold's, gives local trading stamps and has picked up much of Gold's lost sales. One advertising slogan used by Miller and Paine is: "Lincoln's only home-owned department store."

Another factor which may contribute to Gold's present situation is its downtown location. In the mid 1950's, a major shopping center was built in an outlying area of Lincoln and many of the downtown stores opened branches there. The Gateway Center became an immediate success, in part due to the fact that it was located near to the major middle-class residential areas. This shopping center contained two department stores (Miller and Paine, and Montgomery Ward), several higher quality shops, a large grocery store, and a large drug store. Gold's did not locate in the center, in part because Nathan Gold had recently died and the management was merely continuing the former policies.

Parking had become quite a problem in the downtown area in the last few years. In recognition of this, Gold's just recently began offering one hour free parking with any purchase. It was hoped that this would make downtown shopping more attractive and help reverse the declining sales trend.

Gold's local manager has become increasingly concerned about his situation and has requested that customers' comments and complaints about Gold's or Gold's service be referred to him. The first returns from this request include the following:

"They have my charge account mixed up all the time and nobody here can straighten it out."

"I don't want to send my money to Omaha."

"Prices at Miller and Paine are the same and I can get stamps, too."

"They didn't lower their prices a bit when they quit their stamps."

Analyze how Gold's has evolved to its present situation. What would you do if you were the manager of this store?

15

Bailey Company

John Bailey graduated in business from a large midwestern university in 1962. After a year as a car salesman, he decided to go into business for himself. In an effort to locate new opportunities, John placed several advertisements in his local newspaper—in Toledo, Ohio— explaining that he was interested in becoming a sales representative in the local area. He was quite pleased to receive a number of responses. Eventually, he became the sales representative in the Toledo area for three local manufacturers: the Sampson Drill and Press Company which manufactured portable drills; the J. C. Peterson Company which manufactured portable sanding machines; and the Gilbert Lathe Company which manufactured small lathes. All of these companies were relatively small and were represented in other areas by other men like John Bailey.

Bailey's main job was to *call* on industrial customers. Once he made a sale, he would send the order to the respective manufacturer who would, in turn, ship the goods directly to the particular customer. The manufacturer would bill the customer, and Bailey would receive a commission varying from 5 percent to 10 percent of the dollar value of the sale. It was Bailey's responsibility to pay his own expenses.

Bailey called on anyone in the Toledo area who might use the products he was handling. At first, his job was relatively easy and sales came quickly because there was little sales competition. There are many national companies making similar products, but at that time they were not well represented in the Toledo area.

In 1964, John Bailey sold $150,000 worth of drills, earning a 10 percent commission; $50,000 worth of sanding machines, also earning a 10 percent commission; and $75,000 worth of small lathes earning a 5 percent commission. He was most encouraged with his progress and was looking forward to expanding sales in the future. He was especially optimistic because he had achieved these sales volumes without overtaxing himself. In fact, he felt he was operating at about 70 percent of his capacity.

Early in 1965, however, a local manufacturer with a very good reputation—the Porter Electrical Equipment Company—decided to manufacture a line of portable drills. It had a good reputation locally, and by April of 1965 Porter had captured approximately one half of Sampson's Toledo drill market by charging a substantially lower price. Porter was using its own sales force locally and it was likely that it would continue to do so.

The Sampson Company assured Bailey that Porter could not afford to continue to sell at such a low price and that shortly Sampson's price would be competitive with Porter's. John Bailey was not nearly as optimistic about the near term prospects, however. He began looking for other products he could handle in the Toledo area. A manufacturer of hand trucks had recently approached him, but he was not too enthusiastic about this offer because the commission was only 2 percent on potential annual sales of $150,000.

Now John Bailey is faced with another decision. The Howard Paint Company in Cleveland, Ohio, has made what appears to be an attractive offer. They heard what a fine job he was doing in the Toledo area and felt that maybe he could help them out of their present problem. Howard is having difficulty with its whole marketing effort and would like John Bailey to take over.

The Howard Paint Company has been selling primarily to industrial customers in the Cleveland area and is faced with many competitors selling essentially the same product and charging the same low prices. Howard Paint is a small manufacturer. Last year's sales were $80,000. They would like to increase this sales volume and could handle at least double this sales volume with ease. They have offered Bailey a 12 percent commission on sales if he will take charge of their pricing, advertising, and sales efforts in the Cleveland area. John was flattered by their offer, but he is a little concerned because there would be a great deal more travelling than he is doing at present. For one thing, he would have to spend a couple of days each week in the Cleveland area, which is 110 miles distant. Further, he realizes that he is being asked to do more than just sell. But he did have some marketing courses in college and thinks the new opportunity might be challenging.

What should John Bailey do? Why?

In the early 1950s, the village of Arlington Heights, Illinois, was just beginning to feel the effects of the exodus of Chicagoans to the suburbs. Built along a railroad commuter line, Arlington had been until then just another small town with traditional retail outlets. These were built along both sides of the railroad tracks which went through the heart of the town. Although Arlington's principal stores were of the dry clean-

16

The Reignbeaux

ing, drug, and dime store variety, several small shops catering to special groups had developed as more middle-class suburbanites moved into the area. Among this group was the Reignbeaux.

Operated by Mr. and Mrs. John Graham, the Reignbeaux had established itself as the only "really nice" store for women's clothing and accessories in this town of 20,000 population. Since the nearest shopping center, and the Chicago shopping area were both nearly an hour's driving time away, the Graham's store had been able to capture a great deal of the new suburbanite trade in Arlington Heights. Although most new residents had never heard of the shop, its location adjacent to the A&P and Woolworth stores was such that everyone soon knew of its presence.

By 1959, Arlington Heights had grown to over 32,000 population. To keep pace with its affluent clientele, the Reignbeaux underwent continuous renovation. A charge plan was added, the store front and fixtures were modernized, and more expensive lines of clothing were added. Although popular brand names were retained in lingerie and blouses, the Grahams began to place greater emphasis on more expensive dresses and accessories.

Mr. Graham, realizing that he had now narrowed down his clientele to the upper-middle class, soon began advertising in the local weekly newspaper. Although each ad would generally describe a newly arrived fashion in the $175 range, the primary emphasis was on the store's plush decor, the experienced salespeople, and the store's convenient location. Judging from the size of the store's credit accounts, Mr. Graham was quite certain that the "new image" was paying off.

In 1961, the area's first large shopping center opened. Although it contained the same basic types of stores which were already present in "downtown" Arlington, Arlington Plaza also contained a Goldblatt Department Store. Although this store had traditionally catered to lower classes, John Graham discovered that many of Goldblatt's items were very competitive with those in his store. After observing no sales decline in these items, however, Graham considered his position as quite stable with respect to the "shopping center threat."

In early 1962, the Grahams negotiated a six-year lease on a larger building, formerly occupied by the local bank. Located only a half block from their old location, the Grahams felt that the additional interior room and parking facilities would more than compensate for the higher rent and remodeling costs. By October of 1962 the new shop was in operation and, by the end of the year, the Reignbeaux had recorded another record sales year.

In mid-1963, the area's second major shopping center opened. Located about four miles from the Reignbeaux, Randhurst was one of the "new generation" shopping centers. Besides having four major department stores and a dozen or so specialty shops for women, the center also housed an array of 120 other shops, all enclosed under an all-weather mall. Although the Reignbeaux had been offered rental space in mid-1962, the Grahams could neither afford such a venture, nor did they feel that the new center would seriously harm its established trade.

As the Christmas season approached in 1963, the Reignbeaux experienced a drastic slowdown in sales. October and November sales were barely half of what they were one year before. Most of the sales were in the lingerie, sweater, and blouse lines. Most disturbing, however, was the absence of the store's most loyal and regular customers. Although he was certain that the new shopping center had caused this slowdown, John Graham was unable to pinpoint the reason why. Furthermore, when sales failed to pick up after the holidays, the Grahams were completely baffled as to what had happened.

The Grahams realized that they still had five years to run on their lease so they did not give serious thought to moving. Instead, most of their discussion focused on how they could attract their former customers back and hopefully attract new customers, perhaps from a wider area. They were also considering changing the kind of lines carried, as well as their pricing policy. The more they talked about it the more discouraged and confused they became. What they had been doing before seemed to have worked so well and now any change was problematical. Further, one change might require adjusting several things. One approach, for example, was to advertise more aggressively in local media, perhaps with a slightly lower price emphasis or lower price for the same quality. Another approach was to concentrate more heavily on the lingerie, sweaters, and blouses which had been selling well recently, while deemphasizing and eventually going out of the more expensive dress and accessory lines.

Evaluate the strategy the Graham's have been using and explain what they should do now.

The Mullenkamp Cooperative Association is an organization of greenhouse vegetable producers located in southwestern Ohio. The Association has a membership of approximately 40 members, most of whom specialize in producing greenhouse tomatoes. The other major crop is lettuce. All members belonging to the co-op must sell all of their output through the same wholesaler, who is under contract with the Association. The wholesaler's responsibility is to sell the producers' output to other produce wholesalers and chain retailers. The wholesaler arranges for pickup and delivery of the produce and attempts to match the producers' supply to current demand.

17

The Mullenkamp Cooperative Association

The wholesaler operates primarily in the local area but faces major competition from Florida producers who ship large quantities of "green wrap" tomatoes into the area. "Green wrap" is a term referring to tomatoes that are picked from the vine while still green, shipped to their destination, and then ripened with ethylene gas in banana ripening rooms. These tomatoes are typically sold in attractive consumer packages, each containing three medium-sized tomatoes.

The greenhouse tomatoes produced by members of the Association, on the other hand, are partially ripened on the vine and then packed in 8-pound cartons. These cartons enable the consumer to inspect and select each tomato before purchasing. Many consumers seem to believe the greenhouse tomato has a superior taste to that shipped from Florida and sometimes premium prices are obtained for this reason. Often, however, supermarkets selling the Association's tomatoes have mixed the Florida tomatoes with the greenhouse tomatoes. To counteract this practice, the Association decided to offer its tomatoes with the green stem attached. To attempt to communicate this to final consumers, an advertising program was launched in the Cincinnati, Ohio, area. Advertisements were run on billboards, buses, and a television program. This promotion campaign was soon stopped when the members saw no immediate success. Further, the Florida competition began shipping tomatoes into the area with the stem on their tomato too.

The Association also considered improving the packaging, but this move was blocked by some of the older members of the Association who said, "My father sold tomatoes in this carton. If it was good enough for him, it's good enough for us."

But business has not been "good enough" in the last few years. Some of the older, small-volume members are considering going out of business. At the same time, several of the younger, large-volume producers are considering organizing a new group and selling through another wholesaler. Such drastic moves are considered because demand has not been meeting supply in the last few years. Market prices have generally been no greater and often less than the average post–World War II prices. At the same time, production expenses have risen. The average market price of greenhouse tomatoes in the southwestern Ohio area is shown in the following table:

Year	Average Market Price (per 8-pound carton)
1930	$ .58
1940	.90
1950	2.05
1955	2.20
1960	1.90
1965	1.75

Discuss the situation the members of the Association find themselves in. What would you do if you were one of the younger, large-volume producers?

Promotion

Mrs. Ann Alden has been operating the Sunnyside
Furniture Co. for 10 years and has slowly built the
sales to $200,000 a year. Her store is located in the
downtown shopping area of a Midwestern city of
150,000 population. This is basically a factory town
and she has deliberately selected "blue-collar" workers as her target market. She carries some higher priced furniture
lines, but places great emphasis on budget combinations and stresses
easy credit terms.

18

**Sunnyside
Furniture Co.**

Mrs. Alden is most concerned because she feels she has reached the
limit of her sales potential; at least it would seem that way because sales
have not been increasing during the last two years. Her newspaper
advertising seems to attract her target customers but many of these
people come in, shop around, and then leave. Some of them come back,
but the majority do not. She feels her product selections are very
suitable for her target market and is concerned that her sales personnel
do not close more sales with potential customers. She has discussed this
matter several times with her sales personnel. They respond that they

Table 1* In shopping for furniture I found (find) that:

| | Socioeconomic Groups | | | | Marital Status | |
| | Group A | Group B | Group C | Group D | Newly-weds | Married 3–10 Yrs. |
			(Percent)			
I looked at furniture in many stores before I made a purchase	78%	57%	52%	50%	66%	71%
I went (am going) to only one store and bought (buy) what I found (find) there	2	9	10	11	9	12
To make my purchase I went (am going) back to one of the stores I shopped in previously	48	45	39	34	51	49
I looked (am looking) at furniture in no more than three stores and made (will make) my purchase in one of these	20	25	24	45	37	30
No answer	10	18	27	27	6	4

* *The New Consumer: Cautious or Confident?*, Report #2, 1963, conducted for Kroehler Mfg. Co. by
the Institute for Motivational Research.

feel they ought to treat all customers alike, the way they personally would want to be treated—that is, they feel their role is merely to answer questions when asked, and not to make suggestions or help customers arrive at their selections. They feel that this would be too high-pressure.

Mrs. Alden feels her sales personnel's attitudes are interpreted as indifference by the customers who are attracted to the store by her advertising. She feels that customers must be treated on an individual basis—and that some customers need more encouragement and suggestion than others. Moreover, she feels that some customers will actually appreciate more help and suggestion than the salespeople themselves might. In support of her opinion, she showed her salesmen the accompanying table and sample design explanation from a recent study about furniture store customers and tried to explain to them about the differences in socioeconomic groups, and that her store was definitely trying to cater to specific groups. She tried to point out that they (the salesmen) really had different attitudes than their target customers and that as a result the salesmen ought to cater to the needs and desires of their customers and think less about how they would like to be treated.

Table 2 The sample design

SOCIOECONOMIC STATUS

Upper Class (Group A) 13% of sample
   This group consisted of managers, proprietors, or executives of large businesses. Professionals, including doctors, lawyers, engineers, college professors and school administrators, research personnel. Sales personnel, including managers, executives, and upper-income sales people above level of clerks.
   FAMILY INCOME OVER $10,000
Middle Class (Group B) 37% of sample
   Group B consists of white-collar workers including clerical, secretarial, sales clerks, bookkeepers, etc.
   It also includes school teachers, social workers, semiprofessionals, proprietors or managers of small businesses; industrial foremen and other supervisory personnel.
   FAMILY INCOME BETWEEN $5,000 AND $10,000
Lower Middle Class (Group C) 36% of sample
   Skilled workers and semiskilled technicians were in this category along with custodians, elevator operators, telephone linemen, factory operatives, construction workers, and some domestic and personal service employees.
   FAMILY INCOME BETWEEN $5,000 AND $10,000
   NO ONE IN THIS GROUP HAD ABOVE A HIGH SCHOOL EDUCATION
Lower Class (Group D) 14% of sample
   Nonskilled employees, day laborers. It also includes some factory operatives, domestic and service people.
   FAMILY INCOME UNDER $5,000
   NONE HAD COMPLETED HIGH SCHOOL; SOME HAD ONLY GRADE SCHOOL EDUCATION

Evaluate Mrs. Alden's thinking and suggest implications for her promotion.

The Morefiber Wire Rope Company produces wire rope and cable ranging from ½ inch to 4 inches in diameter. The Chicago-based company produces and sells on a national basis. Principal users of the products are manufacturing firms employing cranes and various other overhead lifts in their operations. Lately, ski resorts have become customers, as cables are used in the various lifts. However, the principal customers are still cement plants, railroad and boat yards, heavy equipment manufacturers, mining operations, construction companies, and steel manufacturers.

19

Morefiber Wire Rope Company

Morefiber employs its own sales specialists to call on the purchasing agents of potential users. All the men are qualified engineers who go through an extensive training program covering the different applications, strengths, and other technical details concerning rope and cable. Then they are assigned a region or district, the size depending on the number of customers.

Charles Roste went to work for Morefiber in 1942, immediately after receiving a civil engineering degree from Purdue University. After going through the training program, he was assigned, along with one other representative, to the Ohio, Indiana, and Michigan region. His job was to service and give technical assistance to present customers of rope and cable. He was expected to solicit new customers when the occasion arose. But his primary duties were to: (1) supply the technical assistance needed to use rope or cable in the most efficient and safe manner, (2) handle complaints, and (3) provide evaluation reports to customers' management regarding their use of cabling.

Charles Roste became one of Morefiber's most successful representatives. His exceptional ability to handle customer complaints and provide technical assistance was noted by many of the firm's customers. He also brought in a considerable amount of new business, primarily from the automobile manufacturers and ski resorts in Michigan.

Roste's success established Michigan as Morefiber's largest volume state. As a result, Michigan was designated as a separate district, and Charles Roste was assigned as the representative for the district in 1949.

Although the company's sales in Michigan have not continued to grow in the past few years, the replacement market has been steady and profitable. This fact is primarily due to the ability and reputation of Charles Roste. As one of the purchasing agents for a large automobile manufacturer mentioned, "When Charles Roste makes a recommendation regarding use of our equipment and cabling, even if it is a competitor's cable we are using, we are sure it is for the best for our company. Last week, for example, a cable of one of his competitors broke and we were going to give him a contract. He told us it was not a defective cable that caused the break, but rather the way we were using it. He told us how it should be used and what we needed to do to correct our operation. We took his advice and gave him the contract as well!"

Four years ago, Morefiber introduced an expensive wire sling device for holding cable groupings together. The sling makes operations around the cable much safer and its use could reduce hospital and lost-time costs due to accidents. The profit margin for the sling is high, and Morefiber urged all its representatives to push the sling.

The only man to sell the sling with any success has been Charles Roste. Eighty percent of his customers are currently using the wire sling. In other areas, sling sales are negligible.

As a result of his success, Morefiber is now considering forming a separate department for sling sales and putting Charles Roste in charge. His duties would include traveling to the various sales districts and training other representatives in how to sell the sling. The Michigan district would be represented by a new man.

The question confronting Morefiber management is: Should they gamble losing profitable customers in Michigan in hopes that sling sales will increase?

What would you advise? Why?

20

The American Bank of Meadville

The American Bank of Meadville, Missouri, was organized in 1898 and has been in continuous operation since that time. The bank is located in a community of about 6,500 people, which is situated 35 miles south of Kansas City. Being in Scott County, Meadville is considered to be part of the Greater Kansas City metropolitan area. The county has been experiencing rapid population growth, particularly in its northern sectors. The 1960 Census gave Scott County a population of 60,000. Projected population for 1970 is 145,000. Meadville's 1960 population was 5,400. The community has four local factories which employ about seven hundred. All other local employment is in service businesses, such as clothing, grocery, drug and hardware stores. A significant number of people commute to Kansas City to work. Four buses now shuttle workers to jobs at three Kansas City plants.

Meadville is the primary retail trade center for southern Scott County. Market studies have shown that it has an effective trade radius of about eight miles. The American Bank has been the only bank serving the community since the early 1930's when the Farmers and Merchants Bank was liquidated. American's footings in 1966 were about $10,000,000, a growth of about $1,500,000 over 1964.

The largest bank in the county, with footings of $11,000,000, is located 10 miles northeast of Meadville in the town of Hempstead. Immediately adjacent to Hempstead is its twin city of Anderson. Both communities have a combined population of about 14,000 people. The Anderson State Bank's 1966 footings were about $7,000,000. The Bank of Scottsdale, located at the county seat six miles northwest of Meadville, has footings of about $3,500,000. The American Bank has no other banking competition for a distance of 25 miles to the southwest, south, and southeast.

The American Bank is controlled by a prominent local physician, Dr. Yokum. He also controls the local savings and loan association and owns much real estate in the community. He exerts considerable influence upon the operating policy of the American Bank and has seen to it that American has had a very conservative image. Likewise, he has not been a strong advocate for community growth. As recently as 1960 he said that "I'm very happy with Meadville just the way it is."

The American Bank now employs about 23 people and has 5 operating officers. The executive vice president and cashier, Mr. Martin, is about 48 years old and came to American 10 years ago from The Commerce Bank of Kansas City. The assistant to the vice president is Sam Yokum, Dr. Yokum's son, a recent political science graduate of a small men's college. The three assistant cashiers are Mr. Smith (age 54), Mrs. Conti (age 60), and Mr. Sanders (age 26). Mr. Smith handles the consumer loan department and is noted in the community for his sour disposition. Mrs. Conti handles the real estate loan department and has been experiencing some health problems the past six months. In recent years an increasing proportion of Meadville's real estate financing has been handled by Piedmont Federal Savings and Loan, located 30 miles to the south in the town of Stapleton. Mr. Sanders supervises the bookkeeping department and is noted in the community for his enthusiasm and drive. He graduated from the local high school and went to work as a teller at American. Since that time, he has taken 60 hours of accounting and similar subjects in night school at the University of Kansas City.

American occupies a large two-story building which was remodeled in 1964. In 1966 it opened a new drive-in-walk-up facility in a shopping center on North Main Street. This facility represented an investment of about $175,000 and many in the community were surprised that "old Doc Yokum" had been persuaded to go into this venture. Hours at the bank and drive-in are similar to those of other banks in the county. And the bank offers a full line of services common to banks in the area. Its interest rates and charges are now the same as other county banks.

The officers of American can always be found in the bank. No formal plan exists for its officers to make regular visits to businesses in the community. Mr. Martin tries to get out and about town, but he has found that he must spend considerable time instructing Sam Yokum in banking matters. Both Sam's and Mr. Martin's memberships in Rotary are paid by the bank, but only Mr. Martin belongs to any other community organizations. These include the local industrial development board and the Chamber of Commerce. All bank employees are encouraged to participate in church activities and Mrs. Conti is particularly active.

The American Bank advertises in two papers having concentrated circulation in the Meadville area. The bank also advertises in an "ad" paper printed at the county seat. This paper has free countywide distribution, and all of its costs are borne by its advertisers. American has no road signs of any type and does not advertise over the county's one radio station. Recent promotional efforts have included the distribution of American Bank calendars, telephone book covers, and sending congratulation messages to area high school and college graduates. In addition, a large meeting room on the bank's second floor is made available to various local organizations. No charge is made for the use of this room. This service has not been pushed, however, and only six meetings were held in this room in the past year.

Early in 1967, a group of local business and professional men were granted a state charter to establish and operate The First State Bank of Meadville. The new bank building will be 1½ blocks north of the American Bank. The Board of Directors of First State have announced, through local news media, that they will aggressively pursue an energetic and progressive banking policy—to give the people of Meadville the outstanding financial services needed by a rapidly growing community.

Discuss American Bank's past strategy and what they should do now.

21

The Idaho Potato Industry

The state of Idaho has long been recognized as one of the greatest, if not the greatest, potato producing areas in the United States. Idaho has the advantage of plenty of land and water. It also has hot days and cool nights in the summer, which helps to improve the quality of the potato grown there.

The Idaho potato industry has been foremost in the development of advanced harvesting techniques. The industry has also led the way in new processing developments such as frozen potato products, dehydrated mashed potatoes, and dehydrated chips. Idaho potatoes have a good reputation and preference in many markets.

The Idaho potato industry has the disadvantage of being far from most large consuming areas. It is true that the population center has been moving west in recent years, but for the most part the population still resides further east. This distance causes a great disadvantage in freight rates for Idaho potato products.

According to trend projections, 213 million hundredweight of potatoes were needed in 1965, 240 million hundredweight will be needed by 1970, and 272 by 1975. Based on projections of the population trend, we will need 12.7 percent more potatoes in 1970 than we had in 1965 and 28 percent more in 1975 than in 1965.[1]

Further, the trend is away from fresh potatoes and toward processed potatoes. Processing will bypass fresh consumption by the 1972–73 crop year.

A superior potato and a good reputation have helped Idaho produc-

---

[1] W. Smith Greig, "Population, Transportation, Irrigation, and Potato Economics" presented at the 16th National Potato Utilization Conference, Colorado State University, Fort Collins, Colorado, July 27, 1966.

ers do well until now, in spite of high freight rates for fresh potatoes. But now it appears that the industry may be headed for trouble. Processed potatoes are becoming more important in the industry and processing will tend to eliminate the quality differential of the potatoes, especially as processing techniques become more sophisticated. When someone opens a box of frozen french fried potatoes, he may not care whether the potatoes were originally Idaho "bakers" or Michigan potatoes. He will only be interested in the taste of the potatoes he has purchased, and it may not make any difference in the quality of the product, assuming good processing in both cases. This obviously would have a direct effect on the demand for Idaho potatoes.

In 1966, Idaho was shipping about twice the volume of frozen potato products as was its nearest competitor, Maine. And this was even in the face of some freight disadvantage. Table 1 shows the marginal freight disadvantage of the five major potato producing areas in the United States with respect to frozen products which would be shipped under an optimal distribution system.[2]

Table 1

State of Origin	Marginal Freight Cost
Michigan	$.00
Maine	.15
Red River Valley (Minn., etc.)	.18
Washington	.78
Idaho	.87

Table 1 is interpreted as follows: A processor of raw potatoes could save $.87 per hundred pounds if the product were processed in Michigan rather than in Idaho. This obviously would suggest that if a producer could buy potatoes at about the same price in Michigan or Idaho, he should locate his processing facilities in Michigan, and save the extra cost of shipping the finished product.

This freight rate differential is not nearly as great for dehydrated potato products, but Michigan is still the lowest cost location and Idaho is the highest by a difference of $.40 per hundred pounds.

The issue facing Idaho producers might be phrased as follows: "How can Idaho maintain its share of the market in view of the declining usage of fresh potatoes, increasing demand for processed potatoes, and a natural freight rate disadvantage?" It seems likely that some processors will build their plants closer to population centers such as Ore-Ida Foods, Inc., did recently when it built a plant in Greenville, Michigan.

Assess the Idaho potato industry situation. Will prestige alone maintain Idaho's position in the potato market?

---

[2] *Ibid.*

As the general sales manager of the Bonded Abrasives Division of the Carborundum Company, you must make a decision shortly about how to, or whether to, meet the competitive move of the Norton Company. Norton's action seems to threaten a long-established distribution and pricing setup and you will have to say or do something, soon.

Bonded abrasives and grinding wheels are used in almost all manufacturing operations. Of approximately $250 million annual industry-wide sales, the Norton Company's grinding wheel division accounts for approximately 35 percent, the Carborundum Company's bonded abrasives division accounts for approximately 25 percent, and the Bay State abrasives division of AVCO gets approximately 10 percent. The remaining 35 percent is divided among almost 60 small producers.

The three large companies are characterized by their full-line activity and excellent facilities for giving customers technical assistance. The majority of smaller producers specialize in only one commodity line (e.g., only course-grained resinoid wheels; no fine-grained wheels, no vitrified products, no diamond products, etc.) and most give no technical assistance to customers, selling only standard items to only a few industries.

The "Big 3" sell through selected industrial supply distributors (most of whom are members of one of the two major trade associations, NIDA or SIDA) who generally are specialists in material removal and finishing. Salesmen for these distributors usually are competent to handle most problems that arise. They are supported by sales representatives from the Big 3 producers, who give technical training and sales support to the distributors, as well as call on end-use customers directly. Almost all sales except to the federal government are made through distributors, regardless of who calls on the customer. The smaller producers, on the other hand, sell mostly through their own salesmen, agents, or full-line mill supply houses.

The Big 3 distributor system has evolved to meet a need. While some target markets are like the Milwaukee, Wisconsin, area with only 135 customers (most of whom are in one industry—foundries casting iron, steel, and non-ferrous metals), or like Pittsburgh, with over 90 percent of sales to the basic steel industry, most markets are quite the opposite. Detroit, Michigan, with its major automobile producers and many supporting components manufacturers and their supporting "job-shops" or sub-subcontractors, has over 15,000 customers. New York, with its diversified industries, has almost 30,000 customers. These customers may use anywhere from $500 to $100,000 worth of bonded abrasives per year, with most using under $2,500. It would be prohibitively expensive for a factory representative to call on all these customers. Over the years, very close associations have grown between the Big 3 and their better distributors to fill the needs of these target markets.

The nature of the distributor setup used by the large producers has a direct bearing on the price structure. Basically, quantity discounts are given, and by combining the orders of a number of his customers, the distributor can gain additional quantity discounts while charging each customer the price which is appropriate for the quantity he is buying. The prices of various kinds of grinding wheels run all the way from as low as 50 cents to over $1,500, but the dollar value is not used directly in computing the appropriate quantity discounts. Instead, discounts are based on a system of units, with price breaks occurring at intervals of 1, 2, 5, 10, and 25 units. Each unit has a net value of somewhere between $50 and $80 depending on the item. In other words, a very large grinding wheel might be considered as many units when computing the appropriate price discount. The quantity breaks are identified by letters; i.e., a customer may buy at the A price if he purchases one unit at a time, but at C price if he purchases 5, and so forth.

The average distributor discount is 10 percent off the final customer discounted price. But, as noted above, a distributor may combine his purchases in order to entitle him to a larger discount. For example, an order combining five C quantity purchases, or an order combining three C quantity purchases and one D quantity purchase, would entitle the distributor to the E quantity price on *all* the items purchased. His customers would only be entitled to the C or D prices, however. Therefore, if a distributor were able to forecast his total sales accurately and then carry out a warehousing and bulk-breaking function, he might be able to earn up to a 45 percent discount on all of his purchases. This would occur if he catered primarily to small customers who would normally be buying A quantity while he bought at E prices. This extreme is certainly not always possible, but many distributors do earn an average 30 percent discount. This discount is considerably higher than the average that this kind of distributor would earn on his other business. Thus it is understandable why distributors would prize large volume (E quantity) customers, even though they can make only a 10 percent discount on sales to them. For each purchase a distributor would make for an E customer, he could add on all his other small purchases and obtain E prices for all.

The many smaller competitors of the Big 3 have not used the same pricing system. They are not as interested in supporting a distributor system and provide little technical and selling assistance. To offset this lack of service, they have offered significantly lower prices, often as much as 20 percent lower than the larger companies. This substantially lower price is *the* important selling point in those target markets where "rough-grinding" is adequate and there is a high volume of repetitive operations. Of the 35 percent of the total market held by the smaller producers, about one half is made up of sales to companies who do not need the specialized products and technical service offered by the larger companies. Some of these companies might like to buy from the larger producers, but they cannot afford the 10–20 percent price differences which are built into the price structure to cover the cost of the variety of products and services offered.

In an effort to become more appealing to some of this high-volume repetitive business, the Norton Company announced the "Norton

Plan" on March 1, 1965. Under the terms of this plan, customers who buy a large annual volume of one single item (size, grade, or shape) may purchase directly from Norton at a special low price, low enough to beat the price competition of the small competitors.

The terms of the plan are as follows:

1. To qualify on a "per item" basis, the minimum annual purchase requirement shall be five times E quantity (125 units).

2. No individual purchase shall be less than the minimum order quantity, computed by Norton to be the most economical manufacturing quantity (usually $\frac{1}{6}$ to $\frac{1}{8}$ the annual requirements of the customer).

3. All shipments will be direct from the Norton factory to the customer. Norton will do no warehousing of "Plan" items.

4. The customer is required to reorder whenever his inventory reaches a "reorder point" computed by Norton. This consists of the estimated "usage during delivery" stock plus a "reserve for contingencies" stock.

5. No prices will be published. Items will be priced individually by the Norton office, and price will be determined in part by quantities produced. All customers using identical items in all respects will receive identical prices.

6. Any price increases will take effect after 90 days notice. Price reductions will be effective immediately.

7. If it is determined that the customer's purchase will not total the minimum annual requirement, Norton may cancel the contract after 60 days' notice.

8. The customer may cancel the contract for any reason after 30 days' notice to Norton. He must, however, accept all work in process at time of notice. Norton may cancel the contract for any reason after 90 days' notice. Norton will fill all orders up to day of cancellation.

In the week since the plan was announced, Norton's sales force has been explaining the plan to its current large-volume customers. They have not yet had time to try to reach firms that are not now buying from them in quantity, so reaction here cannot be determined. But their distributors have expressed great dissatisfaction with the "Norton Plan." Several large distributors (over $500,000 sales per year of grinding wheels, or over $1,000,000 per year of total abrasive sales for Norton) have threatened to drop the entire Norton line. Some have already contacted Carborundum and Bay State representatives.

Distributor's feelings may be reflected in the articles and editorials in *Industrial Distributor,* the weekly trade paper published jointly by the National Industrial Distributor's Association and the Southern Industrial Distributor's Association. The initial reaction here is that Norton has completely disregarded its network of distributors and unilaterally taken away a great "lever" for combining purchases. They feel that this move may start a trend towards downgrading or eliminating the role of the distributor and they plan to fight it. Already they are starting to prepare advertising materials and brochures stressing the importance of the functions carried out by industrial distributors, both for manufacturers and their customers.

It is now March 8, 1965, one week after Norton's announcement. You are the general sales manager, bonded abrasives division of the Carborundum Company. In the past week, you have been called at least once by nine of your best distributors, all either current or former members of Carborundum's Distributor Advisory Board. They all caution against any type of "me too" action on the part of Carborundum. You also have been asked by *Industrial Distributor* for a statement.

What would you do? Why?

Wire Specialties Company, located in Minneapolis, Minnesota, is a custom producer of industrial wire products. The company has had a great deal of varied experience bending wire into many shapes, and has as well the facilities to chrome or gold-plate finished products. The company was started ten years ago, and has slowly built its sales volume to $1 million a year. Just one year ago, Mr. Robert Thomas was appointed sales manager of the consumer products division. It was his responsibility to develop this division as a producer and marketer of the company's own branded products, as distinguished from custom orders which the industrial division produces for others.

Mr. Thomas has been working on a number of different product ideas for almost a year now, and has developed several unique designs for letter holders, flowerpot holders, key and pencil holders, and other novelties. His most promising product is a letter holder in the shape of a dog. It is very similar to one which the industrial division produced for a number of years for another company. In fact, it was experience with the seemingly amazing sales volume of this product which interested the company in the consumer market and led to the development of the consumer products division.

Mr. Thomas has sold hundreds of units of his various products to local chain stores and wholesalers on a trial basis, but each time the price has been negotiated and no firm price policy has been established. Now he is faced with the decision of what price to set on the dog-shaped letter holder which he plans to push aggressively wherever he can. Actually, he has not yet decided on exactly which channels of distribution he will use, but the trials in the local area have been encouraging, and, as noted above, the experience in the industrial division suggests that there is a large market for the product.

The manufacturing cost on this product is approximately 5 cents if it is painted black and 10 cents if it is chromed or gold-plated. Similar products have been selling at retail in the 50 cents to $1.50 range. The sales and administrative overhead to be charged to the division would amount to $15,000 a year. This would include Mr. Thomas' salary and some office expenses. It is expected that a number of other products will be developed in the near future, but for the coming year it is hoped that this letter holder will account for about half the consumer products division's sales volume.

Evaluate Mr. Thomas' marketing strategy. What price should he set?

Happy Hills State Park is located on the shores of one of the Great Lakes. Facilities for camping, picnicing, hiking, and swimming are operated and maintained by the State Conservation Department. The concession at Happy Hills is operated privately and is secured on a bid basis. The contract is up for bid every five years and the bid is usually stated as a percentage-of-sales, although this is not required. The present contract was won with a bid of 28 percent of sales; i.e., the present operator pays the state 28 percent of his sales for rent of the facilities.

The concession presently has two major operations: (1) renting baskets (for checking clothes) and umbrellas; and (2) selling snacks, souvenirs, and supplies that are needed at the beach or for picnicing. (See Table 1.)

Table 1

Concession Items	Price*
Snacks	
Soft drinks	$.10–$.20
Hot dogs	$.30
Hamburgers	$.35
Potato chips	$.15
Popcorn	$.15
Cotton candy	$.15
Candy bars	$.05–$.15
Ice cream bars	$.10
Popsicles	$.10
Frozen malts	$.30
Slush	$.05–$.15
Souvenirs†	
Happy Hills trinkets	Varied
Postcards	$.05, 6 for $.25
Pennants	$.35
Miscellaneous†	
Can openers	$.15
Suntan oil	$1.25
Sun glasses	$1.25
Sun hats	Varied
Beach balls	$1.25
Beach toys	Varied
Film	Varied
Insect repellent	$1.00
Charcoal	$.70
Lighter fluid	$.70
Playing cards	$.75
Rentals	
Baskets	$.25/day
Umbrellas	$.35/hr.

* All prices are subject to written approval by the State Conservation Department.
† Maximum allowed price is cost plus 100 percent (50 percent markup).

The majority of sales (approximately 90 percent) are food items. Food prices are established with approval of the State Conservation Department after review of costs of goods to be sold. Nonfood items can be sold at the maximum markup. Prices are usually higher inside than outside the park.

The daily volume typically ranges from $150 to $300 during the week and $400 to $1,000 on weekends. Sales drop by as much as 50 percent during rainy or cold weather.

Joe Mark, a local businessman, is considering a bid on the concession contract, which is coming up soon. He believes he can expand sales (which now run around $30,000 per season) by 20–30 percent by widening the lines and giving better service to the customers. His plan would require him to spend about $3,000 to obtain additional equipment.

What should Joe bid on the concession? Why?

On January 20, 1964, the Aluminum Co. of America announced that it would maintain its price of aluminum ingot at 23 cents a pound in the face of price increases in its own and other industries.

25

Alcoa

Alcoa is the country's largest aluminum producer and this immediately raised the question whether the other producers would rescind a one cent a pound increase announced the previous week. Those increasing prices were Reynolds, Kaiser, Consolidated Aluminum, and Aluminium, Ltd. Interestingly, Aluminium, Ltd., a Canadian firm, had announced that its new price would affect its ingot sales only in the United States.

The reason given by Alcoa for its action was that there had been no increase in the price of aluminum in Canada or other foreign countries and without such an increase, foreign producers could sell at lower prices in the United States without violating antidumping laws. Further, Alcoa said that because of the higher price in this country, American producers could not effectively or lawfully compete in foreign markets. Alcoa felt that without a better cost-price relationship for fabricated products and without the likelihood of a corresponding increase in the ingot price in world markets, an increase in ingot price in the United States was neither justified nor realistic.

Alcoa did note however, that increases in the prices of extrusions and roofing products recently announced by other producers were warranted and were being put into effect by Alcoa.

Evaluate Alcoa's pricing strategies.

26

**Kyle & Evans
Manufacturing
Company***

In 1942, Henry Kyle and Sidney Evans, then in their mid-30's, resigned their positions as superintendents in a small construction company to form their own company. They had both spent their entire business lives in the construction industry and so it was logical for them to plan to produce construction equipment and parts, such as bulldozer blades, and to do repair work on heavy construction equipment.

By 1960, the company's sales volume had grown substantially. The volume had fluctuated between $1 million and $1,700,000 during the past few years. Unfortunately, however, recent profits had been quite small. In 1959, the company actually suffered a loss of $6,600 on sales of over $1,700,000 and there was real concern about the cause of this situation. Balance sheets, income statements, and selected data for some recent years are presented in Exhibits 1, 2, and 3.

Part of the difficulty seemed to stem from organizational problems. In 1958, Mr. Kyle died after suffering a lingering illness and the management of the day-to-day operations of the company was turned over to Mr. Armstrong who had been brought into the organization in 1950. Mr. Evans had acquired a personal fortune of over $1 million in a number of outside interests such as real estate and construction. As a result, he was less interested in this business. "Mr. Evans is quick to delegate responsibility," observed one of the officers, "but we are not too sure just what our authority is and how far it goes."

Over the years, the product line had broadened to include concrete batching plants, heavy-duty truck trailers such as those used for hauling large construction equipment, and a variety of steel fabricated items which were made to order for the construction industry. Employment had increased to 50 men in the shop and 22 in the office. Also, a steel warehousing division had grown rapidly over the last few years and now accounted for $550,000 of the company's total sales.

Mr. Armstrong held the title of executive vice president and had come with the company in 1950 after working one year as a salesman for a dealer in heavy equipment for road construction. Prior to that time he had spent a number of years as salesman for the Midwest Rolling Mill Co., a large integrated steel company. His duties with Kyle & Evans included general administration and, in addition, he did about 80 percent of the purchasing of materials and supplies used by the company. He was in his mid-50's, about the same age as Mr. Evans.

Mr. Stout, the comptroller, was 48 years of age and had been with the

* This case was adapted from John B. Kline and John T. Doutt, *Case Problems of Small Business in the Rocky Mountain West,* prepared by the Bureau of Business Research, University of Colorado, under a grant from the Small Business Administration, Washington 25, D.C., 1961, pp. 58–72.

Table 1 Balance sheets for the fiscal years*: 1954–1955–1956–1957–1958 and 12/1/58 through 5/31/59

ASSETS	1954	1955	1956	1957	1958	12/1/58 5/31/59
Current Assets						
Cash on hand and in bank	12,745	10,055	3,821	82,482	8,564	7,909
Accounts receivable	85,578	51,114	94,480	132,119	305,846	256,510
Contracts receivable	6,222	—0—	15,530	28,779	22,578	18,781
Notes receivable	2,595	—0—	—0—	—0—	—0—	—0—
Interest receivable	228	—0—	2,187	2,501	2,808	2,191
Inventories						
Warehouse stock and finished goods	156,460	184,050	199,951	357,877	397,693	424,155
Work in process	29,381	109,872	45,438	27,818	88,302	95,033
Total Inventories	185,841	293,922	245,389	385,695	485,995	519,188
Prepaid Expenses	1,397	3,465	3,888	3,498	4,126	1,554
Total Current Assets	294,606	358,556	365,395	635,074	829,917	806,133
Fixed Assets						
Autos and trucks	3,669	50,550	53,104	60,892	64,440	74,981
Machinery and equipment	48,049	53,586	64,197	70,471	86,634	91,031
Office furniture and fixtures	6,828	7,404	10,787	11,169	12,297	13,974
Leasehold improvements	8,458	9,514	9,514	9,514	9,424	9,424
Total Fixed Assets	67,003	121,053	137,602	152,046	172,795	189,410
Less: Reserves for depreciation and amortization	29,395	44,025	73,186	84,745	107,043	119,343
Net Book Value	37,608	77,028	64,416	67,301	65,752	70,067
Other Assets						
Cash value of life insurance	—0—	3,250	4,600	5,900	7,250	7,250
Miscellaneous assets	991	1,002	999	381	1,231	1,181
Total Other Assets	991	4,252	5,599	6,281	8,481	8,431
Total Assets	333,205	439,836	435,310	708,656	904,150	884,631
LIABILITIES						
Current Liabilities						
Accounts payable	15,056	77,182	34,702	55,878	114,671	195,869
Notes payable	84,000	74,000	40,000	265,162	385,000	260,000
Contracts payable	—0—	34,176	22,140	35,000	25,605	13,095 .
Accrued payroll and payroll taxes	8,317	6,634	6,124	6,462	10,098	11,921
Accrued income taxes	6,418	9,221	44,105	31,000	15,786	19,361
Other accrued items	6,136	8,390	6,042	5,069	7,309	15,617
Total Current Liabilities	119,927	209,603	153,113	398,571	558,469	515,863
Deferred Income						
Prepaid interest	24	9	2,187	—0—	1,935	1,200
Capital						
Stock outstanding	140,000	140,000	140,000	140,000	140,000	140,000
Earned surplus	73,254	90,224	140,010	170,085	203,746	227,568
Total Capital	213,254	230,224	280,010	310,085	343,746	367,568
Total Liabilities and Capital	333,205	439,836	435,310	708,656	904,150	884,631

* Compiled from audited financial statements.

Table 2 Selected data from the income statements—1953–59

	1953	1954	1955	1956	1957	1958	1959
Sales	$1,452,742	$573,012	$711,465	$1,644,690	$1,127,893	$1,210,988	$1,736,378
Inventories	151,742	185,840	293,922	245,389	385,695	485,995	437,728
Net operating profit	64,778	21,779	31,553	97,936	66,816	49,881	13,190
Warehouse salaries	12,190	7,593	8,851	14,439	17,939	34,565	56,947
Admin. expense	116,170	91,291	86,457	124,173	141,360	169,313	192,495
Selling expense	9,000	1,222	1,244	36,304	43,778	48,800	33,000
Accounts receivable	98,151	85,577	51,114	93,833	156,813	305,700	134,413
Interest paid	2,993	3,854	4,612	8,990	10,644	13,647	16,779
Net profit or loss (before tax)	62,968	20,526	27,913	49,786	30,075	40,643	(6,692)

Table 3 Kyle & Evans selected financial data for year ended November 30

	1953	1954	1955	1956	1957	1958	1959
Sales	$1,452,742	$573,012	$711,465	$1,644,690	$1,127,893	$1,210,988	$1,736,378
Inventories	151,742	185,841	293,922	245,389	385,695	485,995	437,728
Percent of sales	10%	24%	41%	15%	35%	40%	25%
Warehouse salaries	12,190	7,593	8,851	14,439	17,939	34,565	56,947
Percent of sales	0.8%	1.3%	1.2%	0.9%	1.6%	2.9%	3.3%
Administrative expense	116,170	91,291	86,457	124,173	141,360	169,313	192,495
Percent of sales	8%	16%	12%	5%	9%	14%	11%
Interest paid	2,993	3,854	4,612	8,990	10,644	13,647	16,779
Percent of sales	0.2%	0.7%	0.6%	0.5%	0.9%	1.1%	1.0%
Operating profit	64,778	21,779	31,553	97,936	66,816	49,881	13,190
Percent of sales	4.4%	3.8%	4.4%	6.0%	5.9%	4.1%	0.8%
Net profit before taxes	62,968	20,526	27,913	49,786	30,075	40,643	(6,962)
Percent of sales	4.3%	3.7%	3.9%	3.0%	2.7%	3.4%	(0.4)
Sales Breakdown*							
Manufacturing				N.A.	$ 848,000	$ 811,000	$1,186,000
Warehouse				N.A.	280,000	400,000	550,000

* Comptroller's estimates.

company 5 years. His past experience included systems work with an insurance company, 3 years with a C.P.A. firm, 6 years in the Air Force doing systems work, and 11 years as the business manager of a small college in the East. While Mr. Armstrong regarded him as an invaluable aide, describing him as probably the only man in the organization with whom he could discuss policy matters, Mr. Stout had a narrower view of his job. "A comptroller in a construction company is like a fifth wheel," he observed. "Records and reports are regarded as a necessary evil, and while there is much that could be done by way of improved records and procedures, it isn't too likely that I will ever get the chance to work them in." The size of the comptroller's division had doubled since his coming, now having three clerks employed full time in the processing of records and accounts. But despite the fact that he held the title of "Comptroller," it was not expected that he would analyze the various facets of the company's operations with a view to reducing cost or correcting unsatisfactory situations.

Mr. Stout felt that "organization" was the chief problem of the company. "There has never been the required supervision and control exerted for a business as large as ours. People are allowed to go their own way. As a result, we have experienced a certain amount of internal 'empire building.' These problems are sure to get worse if we try to grow any more." He felt the problem was especially acute with respect to the warehousing division. Lax procedures had allowed such problems to develop as the warehouse division selling to the manufacturing division at actual costs, despite the fact that the warehouse did its own ordering, storing, and handling of materials. Mr. Stout felt this was hardly fair in assessing the value of the warehousing division. Further, failure of the manufacturing personnel to fill out records and requisitions adequately often meant that overcharges resulted for raw materials because credits were not given by the warehouse when small pieces were returned at the end of a manufacturing job. Further, he felt that warehouse inventory would be reduced by at least $100,000 if the warehouse division were eliminated. Nuts and bolts alone accounted for $60,000 worth of the total stock carried, and these were not a large requirement for the fabricating division of the company.

In 1959, warehouse sales of steel stock, bolts and nuts, accounted for $550,000 of the company's total sales. Of the remaining volume, fabrication of steel items for the construction industry accounted for approximately 60 percent. In general, design work for this business was done by the customer himself, the chief problem being the pricing of estimates and bids in what was generally regarded as a disorganized market. From the past cost records, it was possible to develop a fairly accurate estimate of the direct material and direct labor costs for a given job. To this figure, 150 percent of direct labor was added for overhead. The item was then priced with the goal of achieving 20 percent profit (before taxes) on the bid.

According to Mr. Steck, the Chief Engineer, it was impossible to observe any pattern in the bids of competitors, so they went ahead on their own and bid as systematically as they could. Despite this approach, they found that their profits on fabrication jobs tended to vary widely. Mr. Stout felt that this resulted from the varied amount of engineering in each job and the inflexible policy of charging a flat 150 percent of direct labor on all estimates.

It was commonly accepted in the industry that fabrication work tended to be the least profitable type of work because of the presence of

725

small producers who did not know their costs or would, on occasion, bid unreasonably low just to keep their shops open. Mr. Armstrong felt that most customers for fabricated steel work were primarily concerned with price, and so he felt that a more flexible system of bidding might be necessary in a market as competitive as steel fabrication.

Aside from an occasional truck trailer made for heavy equipment, the balance of the company's business was in the area of concrete batching plants, screening units for sand and gravel plants, and accessory items such as belt conveyors, screw type conveyors, bucket elevators, and concrete buckets. It was estimated that about half of these accessory items were sold as a complete package and about half were sold piece by piece for replacement, repair, or batching plant modification. While virtually all of the parts and items going into a batching plant tended to be of a standardized nature, Kyle & Evans sold 90 percent of their batching plants in custom-type applications. Mr. Steck estimated that 80 percent of the demand for batching plants was for standardized plants and only 20 percent for the custom-type installation in which Kyle & Evans specialized. Their specialization was due in part to the fact that they were not directly competitive pricewise with large Eastern and local manufacturers of standardized batch plants, their prices running about 20 percent higher than others. This was due in part to the fact that others used pricing practices which were set to yield a 10 percent profit (before taxes) on large jobs and 40 percent profit (before taxes) on small units. On custom-type installations, Kyle & Evans' prices tended to run about twice as much as other producers, but in the opinion of Mr. Steck, there was no real comparison between the end products. Other custom builders were building inferior plants which they would sell for $12,500. The $25,000 figure charged by Kyle & Evans could, in his view, be easily justified. He believed that quality was the proper emphasis in selling a batching plant.

Only one salesman, Mr. Andrews, was responsible for the sale of fabricated items. Mr. Andrews was 36 years of age and had spent 9 years as a truck salesman prior to joining this company in 1959. He was expected to sell the entire line of the company's products, although much of the heavy equipment business came to them from previously established contacts. Mr. Armstrong felt that he had a good personality and knew how to make contacts. He was paid a base salary of $400 per month, plus the privilege of a company car. In addition he was paid a commission of 3 to 4½ percent on sales of fabricated items.

Mr. Bimpson was in charge of the warehouse division. He estimated that about $425,000 of the $550,000 of warehouse sales were made on the "outside" to customers in the immediate area, who purchased small quantities of steel, bolts, and trailer parts. Of the total, sales of bolts and nuts accounted for $125,000 and steel stock for $300,000. In 1953 when the warehouse division was begun, there had been only Mr. Bimpson and two warehousemen, but by 1959 when the warehouse sales accounted for more than 25 percent of the sales volume of the company, there were three clerks in the office in addition to Mr. Bimpson and a total of five warehousemen.

The warehouse division was in direct competition with four other warehouses located in the same city. Price levels were set by the large distributors located throughout the Midwest and the only way the warehouse division could make more money was to expand its sales volume. All prices for steel products were standardized on both the selling and buying side, but with increased volume additional discounts were allowed.

The company had the reputation of having the largest stock of nuts and bolts in this part of the country. This reputation helped expand its sales. This growth was also reflected in the increase in trucking charges. In 1953 these amounted to $11,000, while in 1959 the figure was $65,000. The warehouse had one salesman, Mr. Head, who specialized in selling warehouse items to the various users in the immediately surrounding area.

In Mr. Bimpson's opinion, it was necessary to order about one quarter of a year ahead on steel requirements. Otherwise, the mills might not be able to deliver steel stock of the shape and size needed for a particular job, and the profit on a fabricating order might be lost because the company had had to purchase steel from another warehouse at full price. Consequently, he proceeded to order such steel as he felt might be needed in the future, although he did not place dollar figures on the requisitions, nor did he know the financial position of the company when such orders were made out. In other words, Mr. Bimpson was in charge of buying, selling, and storing all warehouse items. In addition, he was expected to have steel stock for the use of the fabricating division on hand at all times and was expected to keep adequate records on the day-to-day transactions of the division.

Commenting on the warehousing operation, Mr. Armstrong stated, "A number of us have the feeling that the warehouse operation taken as a whole is not a profitable undertaking. But our accounting records do not show just how much money they make and how much they cost to operate. We feel that if it could be set up as a separate division and allowed to charge us what would be a fair and reasonable price for what we get from them, we could then know more about its profitability. But Mr. Bimpson is hard to approach on this subject. He has built up a sizable division there and regards our suggestions with some suspicion. And until Mr. Evans says so, we don't want to make any specific move that would dislocate the operations of the organization even more than they are." Probably one reason that the fabricating division has not pushed this point more is that it now has considerable flexibility in drawing from the warehouse division's stock. For example, if a piece of steel 8 feet long is needed for a job on the production floor, the production division may requisition this 8-foot piece on the usual form. But the workman actually sent to get the piece may have to take a "mill length" piece 20 feet long with the understanding that the balance will be returned to stock. Frequently, however, he will fail to return the balance to the warehouse, simply pushing it off to one side of the production floor.

What are the objectives of this firm? Evaluate its marketing strategy and consider how its operations might be improved.

27

**Beaver Ranch
Supply Company***

John Roth, the owner of Beaver Ranch Supply Co., was a franchised dealer of farm implements for the David Harris Co., a major manufacturer of farm implements. He bought the business in 1954 for $45,000. In 1959 he said, "If I could sell out for half that much, I'd do it tomorrow. This business is never going to be the same again, what with competition from other David Harris dealers, the soil-bank program, and the uncertainties of the weather."

Beaver Ranch Supply Co. was located in the rural community of Beaver. Beaver was located in the western part of Nebraska, in an area which specialized in wheat and cattle. The population of 1,800 did not accurately reflect the great activity in Beaver, as it was a junction for two railroads and a crossroads for three major highways. Two other villages that were smaller in size were located about 15 miles away, and Rockmont, a city of over 100,000, was located approximately 75 miles away.

John Roth had been a wheat and livestock farmer in Iowa for 17 years before moving to Beaver. After selling his farm, Mr. Roth had $45,000 clear which he paid to Claude Remington, who had been operating the David Harris agency in Beaver for a number of years. This figure covered only the inventories, fixtures, and office and shop equipment of the business. Terms of the sale were inventory at cost, and when the actual count was made, they were found to be $10,000 higher than Mr. Remington had thought. Consequently, he took a personal note from Mr. Roth in the amount of $10,000. Mr. Roth signed a lease with Remington for $250 a month for 6 years for the brick showroom, the quonset-type building adjoining it, and the acre of ground on which the buildings were situated.

An arrangement was made whereby Mr. Remington was to have use of office space in the showroom to sell a sizable stock of used farm machinery which he had accumulated during his years in business. After several weeks, considerable strain developed between Mr. Roth and Mr. Remington. It soon became apparent to Mr. Roth that the sale of used farm machinery by Mr. Remington was injurious to his own business. Moreover, a little experience in the business had led Mr. Roth to believe that the sales figures Mr. Remington had shown which had induced him to purchase the business had been misrepresented and that many of the sales recorded had been on the "black market" to nonfranchised dealers in other states, who then proceeded to sell the equipment at a discount. While the David Harris Co. made every effort to stop this practice, it was being carried on by some dealers in 1954 when Mr. Roth bought the business.

Finally, the note for $10,000 which Mr. Roth had understood would

---

* This case was adapted from John D. Kline and John T. Doutt, *Case Problems of Small Business in the Rocky Mountain West,* 1961, prepared by the Bureau of Business Research, University of Colorado, under a grant from the Small Business Administration, Washington 25, D.C., pp. 95–100.

be held by Mr. Remington until the business got "on its feet," had instead been discounted at the Beaver National Bank on a 90-day basis. At the end of that period the bank presented the note for payment, and if it had not been for the resources of a friend of the family who paid off the loan and made a new loan to Mr. Roth, he might have had to go out of business.

Mr. Remington was ousted from his office in the building, but his departure did not end the troubled relationship between the two men. He continued to hurt the business by sending local customers for David Harris equipment across the state line to a friend of his, who gave good prices to these out-of-state people. These low prices were based upon a number of factors: (1) the merchandise could be sold with little thought for future servicing, (2) a 5 percent volume discount was granted by the David Harris Co. to all franchised dealers who met their quota, and (3) the elimination of the state sales tax. Presumably, this merchandise was caught at the ports of entry located on the main highways leading from one state to another, but it was Mr. Roth's opinion that some farm equipment got into the state without ever having a sales tax levied on it.

Other sources of competition, by 1959, were four other implement dealers in Beaver, three dealers in the two nearby villages, none of which was a David Harris dealer, and a David Harris dealer in Rockmont. The Rockmont dealer was quite wealthy, having money from other sources, and was simply seeking ways of putting his money to good use. One of the most convenient ways he could find was the financing of farm machinery at 8 percent per annum. He reasoned that he could sell his merchandise at cost and still obtain 13 percent on sales, after allowing for the 5 percent David Harris volume discount.

One unique thing about this farm implement business was the relationship between the manufacturer and the dealer. In the fall of each year, each David Harris dealer was expected to draw up a contract for the farm machinery that he thought he would need during the coming year, but he did not have an obligation to take delivery until he actually ordered a piece of machinery. He was then given 16 months from the time of the order-release until the payment was due. In the event that only part of the order was sold, the balance owed could be extended for another 16-month period. For example, if an order-release calling for two tractors was dated March 15th, actual payment for the tractors was due July 15th of the following year. In the event that only one of the tractors was sold within this 16-month period, an adjustment would be made lengthening the time until payment for the second tractor was due.

It was important to attempt to draw up an accurate contract list, because it was difficult to get machinery during the peak spring and summer season unless it was on the contract list. Some trading was done among the David Harris dealers and was expedited by the David Harris regional representative that called every two weeks, but this was not a reliable source. Mr. Roth felt that it was impossible for the David Harris Co. to know all of the differences that existed from one region to another, and this was their way of shifting some of the risk of "out-guessing" the market onto the dealer. It did have the effect of limiting a dealer somewhat, however, because if a number of his sales efforts were especially successful, then he might have difficulty obtaining delivery. On the other hand, if he overestimated his sales possibilities, then he would not be eligible for the 5 percent volume discount.

The David Harris Co. was willing to finance part of a dealer's inventory in trade-in machinery, but the total amount extended to any one dealer was dependent in part on whether he was keeping up-to-date on his new machinery payments. In Mr. Roth's case, it was felt that he had already exceeded his limit, and as a result, they would grant him no further financing on used machinery until the new machinery account was cleared up. This seriously hampered the sale of new machinery, as most of it involved trade-ins. Local bank connections were, in the opinion of Mr. Roth, "cattle-minded," and not "machinery-minded," and the possibility of financing new sales through this channel seemed unlikely.

"The farm implement market is definitely changing," stated Mr. Roth. "We have a lot more custom-cutters[1] up here this year than we had last year. That means we sell more parts but fewer pieces of equipment. They buy their equipment down in Texas where the dealers go for high volume and low markup, but we just can't do that here because our volume isn't big enough and can't be made big enough. *Life* magazine ran a story last winter about the custom-cutter and all the profits he makes, and we have certainly seen the results up here this year. Many of our local ranchers never even oiled their machines. They just let the custom-cutter come in and do it for them."

"Then there is the question of the small- and medium-sized ranch. There aren't many ranches that can afford an $8,000 combine, but some people buy them anyhow. The trend in the future is going to be towards larger farms that can utilize a major investment in machinery. And they won't be buying their equipment from a small dealer like me. These people will shop around several states before they buy. They want the best price they can get. Some implement manufacturers will sell direct to a large customer, and even though David Harris will not do this themselves, this type of competition hurts me. It's bad enough already. We get men in here from as far away as 100 miles. I had a man in here last week from Corinth, which is over 80 miles north. He wanted to buy two drills and I priced them to him at $2,000. He said he could get them in Corinth for $2,000, and that he thought he should have at least $100 discount for traveling all that way. I told him to go back to Corinth and buy them. I am not putting any money into Corinth, but his local dealer of Harris equipment is. He ought to buy in his own community and boost it."

"Yesterday I had a man in here that wanted a 30 percent discount from list price. I told him I just couldn't do it because I was only allowed 20–25 percent, depending on the item. Finally, I took him to

---

[1] The term "custom-cutter" refers to men who own combines and travel through the area, cutting wheat for the land owner at some agreed price.

my files and showed him exactly what the merchandise cost me, and the freight I had to pay on it. He was really surprised. He thought I had a much higher markup on the equipment. So we talked it over for a while and I cut my usual markup right in half. He took it. All they want is price.

"One of the problems of a place like this is getting the right kind of help. My parts man left me last week, and I am filling in until I find someone. Right now we don't need anyone, as slow as business is. He went down the street to one of the other implement dealers. Then my mechanic got a phone call from a David Harris agency up in Logan City. I don't know if he'll go or not. You've got to have a service department to build traffic; otherwise I think I'd turn it over to some independent garage here in town.

"I sometimes wonder if I'm making any money or not. My accountant says that I am just using up my principal. You never know how much you are making until you sell your used machinery and get your money out of that. We carry it at trade-in value on our monthly statements, although we try to be realistic about it on our annual reports."

Sales of new David Harris equipment have been averaging about $11,000 per month during the last few years but inventories of new equipment have been rising, from about $40,000 in 1957 to $70,000 in 1959. Sales of used machinery have been averaging only a few thousand dollars a month, but these inventories have been rising too, from about $15,000 at trade-in value in 1957 to about $30,000 in 1959. Usually the used machinery had to be sold at lower than the trade-in price. In 1957, the business showed a net profit of almost $20,000 on total sales of $217,000, including all kinds of equipment and parts. In 1958, approximately $19,000 net profit was earned on total sales of $285,000. Mr. Roth's salary of about $6,000 was included in expenses each year. The amount owed David Harris Co. has risen from an average of about $40,000 in 1957 to approximately $90,000 in 1959. It appeared that 1959 sales would be about the same as 1957.

The organization of the Beaver Ranch Supply Co. consisted of the bookkeeper, one heavy equipment mechanic who was paid $100 per week, a delivery man paid $80 per week who also helped out in the garage, a parts man who earned $75 per week, a part-time setup man paid $1.10 per hour and a full-time salesman who was paid a 5 percent commission on both new and used machinery and who was guaranteed $75 per week.

Evaluate John Roth's marketing strategy. Should he have been more "flexible" about price discounting?

The Seifert Manufacturing Co. was set up in 1935 when the Mid-Continent Wholesale and Distributing Co. purchased a small clothing manufacturer in order to supply it with some of the items it sold. Both the wholesale establishment and the manufacturing firm were located in Denver, Colorado. The wholesaling firm had been formed in 1909 by Samuel Seifert and two cousins. Both companies are still basically family operations.

Joseph Seifert, the 37-year-old secretary-treasurer and general manager of the Seifert Manufacturing Co. has been operating the company seven years, since 1952, and has helped improve the firm's condition. He added a sales force and new product lines so that by 1959 the manufacturing and the wholesaling firms were in no way interrelated or interdependent except through common ownership. In fact, in certain lines the two companies compete almost directly, although Joe Seifert feels that his firm seeks a slightly higher priced market. Looking into the future, Joe Seifert feels that the problem which will concern him most is that of increasing sales and developing an adequate sales force.

Seifert Manufacturing Co. offers a number of lines of men's and women's clothing. The Deseret brand is a line of women's specialty wear consisting of such things as women's cotton blouses and jeans. The Plainsman line consists of men's car coats and some sport shirts. The American Beauty line includes sweaters, skirts, sportswear, and denim jeans. Most of these garments are in the medium-price range. The company makes all items in their lines except sweaters and sports shirts. They have found that these are specialized items which some firms can make as economically as they can. Therefore, these garments, which consist of about 25 percent of their sales, are subcontracted.

Seifert has close to national distribution and faces strong competition in all areas. The company is represented by a total of 10 salesmen—4 who sell exclusively for Seifert and 6 manufacturers' agents who sell one or more additional lines. Sales are made directly to retail stores and, in most cases, salesmen are given credit for a sale in their territory whether it was a mail-order sale or a sale solicited personally by the salesman.

They try to cater to the medium-priced field. Mr. Seifert said that: "The secret in the garment business is to find a niche in the market and then fill that niche. That is what we have tried to do." Part of his basic philosophy is stated as follows:

Back in New York City, they produce a type of merchandise that can be in a price range below ours, but the styling and quality are not always what is desired in stores where the "casual feeling" is desired. The finish

---

* This case was adapted from John B. Kline and John T. Doutt, *Case Problems of Small Business in the Rocky Mountain West*, prepared by the Bureau of Business Research, University of Colorado, under a grant from the Small Business Administration, Washington 25, D.C., 1961, pp. 6–26.

quite often isn't there. In the South, they have some labor cost advantage, and they will produce a skirt there for $3.75 that might cost us $4.75 to make. At least, we will aim for a $4.75 figure and give it a finish and fit for that price that the Southern or Eastern skirts won't have. In the Midwest, we find a different type of competition. Many of them produce garments in a piecemeal production system that gives them high costs. Through manufacturing control, we are able to offer a garment for around $15 that competition will try to sell for as much as $25.

Mr. Seifert spends a lot of his time working between sales and production to be sure they are making the right thing at the right time. Mr. Seifert observed: "We watch our sales orders closely, and as we sense a good number, we will produce a quantity for stock. This is especially important in the early days of a season. Then there are some seasons when we just don't seem to 'hit.' This spring was one of them. Things just didn't seem to catch on, so we shut down our spring line early and moved into the fall items. And right now, although it's very early, we already have some reorders for some fall numbers. Someone has to watch these things and make the decisions of this sort."

Control of inventory and "feeling" the market are achieved largely through the use of a "Listing Book." Each day, orders for all of the different numbers in the line are accumulated and posted in this book. Then as a cutting is made, the size of which is based on the orders listed, it is posted in a column opposite the order total. Thus, a simple calculation gives the quantity which should be on hand at any given time.

Seifert Manufacturing Co. is set up with two divisions: the manufacturing division and the sales division. The manufacturing division produces the garments and after accumulating its costs, it adds a markup to cover its own overhead and general administrative expenses as well as a small amount for profit. This factory price becomes the sales division's cost, and it adds a markup to determine Seifert's selling price. The manufacturing division commonly takes a 20 percent markup, although certain garments, such as blue jeans which are very competitive, do not permit more than a 12 percent markup. The sales division usually tries to obtain a 25 percent markup.

All salesmen are paid a 6 percent commission on all items sold with the exception of blue jeans, close-outs, and "chain store items." These latter items are produced to meet low-price competition and are sold primarily to chain stores. Only a 3 percent commission is paid on these. These commission rates are competitive with other manufacturers.

Varying degrees of control are exercised over the salesmen. Those who sell full-time for Seifert are expected to turn in a route list and a daily call report indicating firm name, location, and remarks about each call made. The manufacturers' agents, however, generally have not supplied this information.

Occasionally, but not regularly, the home office sends out bulletins. These consist of mimeographed sheets listing close-outs, new items, or special price changes. Occasionally, the sales manager or Mr. Seifert himself will add a personal note of counsel or encouragement for an individual salesman.

Some control is achieved by personal contact. Salesmen selling in the areas near Denver come into the office several times a year. In addition, Mr. Seifert makes an annual trip to California, at which time he talks to the salesmen in that area. Finally, the annual Midwest Trade Show provides a point of contact, not only with the trade, but with the salesmen. All salesmen are expected to attend at their own expense.

Mr. Seifert is concerned about the quality of his salesmen. Some are good men, but he feels that improvement can be made in this area. Some men seem to be good in certain lines and not in others, or perhaps take a greater interest in certain products because of the nature of their territories, or the demands of their other lines, in the case of manufacturers' agents. The salesman in the Oklahoma and Texas area, for example, had a monthly sales range from approximately $6,000 to $52,000 in a recent year. Not all the salesmen had such extremes but their patterns vary so that it makes it very difficult for the plant to plan its production.

From the 25 percent markup the sales division usually tries to get, several major items of expense must be paid or deducted. It is customary to grant an 8 percent cash discount to all customers who pay their bill within 10 days after the end of the month. In addition, the salesman's commission, the sales manager's salary, general administrative salary allocation, sales office expense, and advertising expense must be deducted. Advertising expense usually runs about ½ of 1 percent of sales and consists primarily of selective advertising in Western wear magazines, the Midwest Trade Show, and advertising allowances to retailers. These allowances range from 25 to 50 percent of the cost of the advertisement and in most cases are for local newspaper advertising in which various Seifert brand names are prominently displayed.

Salesmen are permitted to make decisions regarding the cooperative advertising allowances made in their territory, but a control is placed on this by charging their personal commission account with 7 percent of the amount of Seifert's allowance. For example, if a salesman approves cooperative advertising in the amount of $100, Seifert might pay as much as 50 percent of this amount. The salesman's commission account would then be charged 7 percent of $50, or $3.50.

Evaluate the marketing strategy being used here. What changes would you want to make if you were the sales manager of this company?

29

AAA Plastics Co.

Bob McMahon is currently employed as a sales representative for a plastics goods manufacturer. He calls primarily on large industrial accounts, such as refrigerator manufacturers, who might need large quantities of custom-made products. He is on a straight salary of $8,000 per year, plus expenses and a company car. He expects some salary increases but does not see a great long-run opportunity with this

734

company. As a result, he is seriously considering changing jobs and investing $10,000 in the AAA Plastics Co., an established midwestern thermoplastic molder and manufacturer. Harry Mack, the present owner is nearing retirement age and has not developed anyone to run the business for him. He has agreed to sell the business to John O'Gorman, a lawyer-entrepreneur, who has invited Bob McMahon to invest and become the sales manager. Mr. O'Gorman has agreed to give Bob McMahon his current salary plus expenses, plus a bonus of 1 percent of profits. However, Bob must invest to become part of the new company. He will obtain a 5 percent interest in the business for his $10,000 investment.

The AAA Plastics Co. is well established and last year had sales of $1,500,000, but no profits. In terms of sales, cost of materials was 46 percent; direct labor, 13 percent; indirect factory labor, 15 percent; factory overhead, 13 percent; and sales overhead and general expenses, 13 percent. The company has not been making any profit for several years, but has been continually adding new machines to replace those obsoleted by technological developments. The machinery is well maintained and modern, but most of it is similar to that owned by competitors. Most of the machines of the industry are standard. Special products are then made by using dies in conjunction with these machines.

Sales historically have been approximately two thirds custom-molded products (that is, to order for other producers or merchandising concerns) and the balance proprietary items such as housewares and game items such as poker chips and cribbage sets. The housewares are copies of articles initiated by others and indicate neither originality nor style. Harry Mack is in charge of the proprietary items distributed through any available wholesale channels. The custom-molded products are sold through three full-time sales engineers who receive a 5 percent commission on sales up to $10,000 and then 3 percent above that level, as well as three independent representatives working part time on a similar commission plan.

Financially, the company seems to be in fairly good condition, at least as far as book value is concerned, as the $10,000 investment would buy approximately $30,000 in assets.

Mr. O'Gorman feels that, with new management, the company offers great opportunity for profit. He expects to make some economies in the production process and hold custom-molding sales to approximately the present $1 million level. The other major expectation is that he will be able to develop the proprietary line from a sales volume of about $500,000 to $2 million a year. Bob McMahon is expected to be a real asset here because of his sales experience. This will bring the firm up to about capacity level, but of course it will entail adding additional employees. The major advantage of expanding sales would be spreading overhead. Some of the products proposed by the lawyer for the expansion of the proprietary line are listed below.

New Products for Consideration

Women's tool kit—molded housewares
Six-bottle soft drink case

Laminating printed film on housewares—molded
Short legs for furniture—molded $0.5 million minimum market
Home storage box for milk bottles $0.5 million minimum market
Step-on garbage can without liner
Importing and distributing foreign housewares
Black-nylon-handled table utensils
Extruded and embossed or formed wall coverings
Extruded and formed wall decorations—nursery rhyme figures, etc.
Formed butyrate outside house shutters
Formed inside shutters in lieu of venetian blinds
School and toy blackboards
Translucent bird houses
Formed holder for vacuum cleaner attachments
Formed household door liners
Formed "train terrain" table topography for model trains
Formed skylights
Perforated extruded sheet for industrial sale as grilles
Formed drawers for houseware sale with supports for under-furniture
    storage
Formed drawers for industrial sales
Formed children's furniture, including chest of formed drawers and
    metal angles
Extruded corrugated butyrate sheet for outdoor patio and storage covers
Extruded corrugated translucent styrene sheet for indoor room dividers
Formed restaurant tray, with surface grain
Formed lap board for studying, serving
Formed washboard
Extruded and formed traffic and street signs

There is a great deal of competition in these markets and most retailers expect a wide margin, sometimes 40 to 50 percent, but even so manufacturing costs are such that there is some room for promotion while still keeping the price competitive. Apparently many consumers are willing to pay for the novelty of new products.

How would you advise Bob McMahon? Explain your reasoning.

30

**A. C. Gilbert
Company**

In the days before television became a toy-advertising medium and children's pastime, few toys were as sought as A. C. Gilbert's American Flyer trains and its chemistry and Erector sets—all first quality, high-ticket items. In 1966, however, company management was faced with the problem of reversing a downward trend in sales and profits in an industry that had grown to a record $2.4 billion in 1965. In 1961, Gilbert's profits had shrunk to $20,011 followed by losses of $281,000 in 1962, $5.7 million in 1963, $1.9 million in 1964, and $2.9 million in 1965—a total loss of almost $11 million.

Upon graduation from Yale in 1909, Alfred Carlton Gilbert set up the Mystro Manufacturing Company to produce the Erector set which he had perfected. In 1916, the name became the A. C. Gilbert Company. This same year, Gilbert founded and became the first president of the Toy Manufacturers Association. A son, A. C. Jr., who graduated with honors from Yale in 1951, became assistant to his father in 1946 and president of the company in 1954. In 1961, upon the death of his father, the younger Gilbert became chairman also.

A. C. Gilbert Co., with a reputation as a quality toymaker, was firmly among the top ten toymakers in the 1950's with sales topping $17 million. During this period, science achieved national attention and Gilbert's sales of chemistry, biology, and other scientific sets dominated its sales. These sets were neatly packaged in easy-to-store metal boxes.

Gilbert toys were sold directly by the company's own sales force to hobby and toy shops and department stores. The principal advertising medium was company catalogs and window displays.

In the late 1950's profits and sales slowly declined. But Gilbert retained its same product line and traditional marketing mix, assuming that the decline was merely temporary. In early 1961, Gilbert experienced serious financial difficulty and John Wrather, Jr., president of Wrather Holding Company, acquired ownership of about 51 percent of Gilbert's stock. In addition to Gilbert, Wrather had among its properties real estate, hotels, oil wells, Muzak, and the rights to "Lassie," "The Lone Ranger," and "Sgt. Preston of the Yukon." A. C. Gilbert, Jr., retained the board chairmanship, but his power was clearly reduced.

Mr. Wrather named former Wrather vice president, William Quilan, president of Gilbert. In an effort to rejuvenate sales, the sales staff was increased by half and a new marketing manager and director of international sales was hired. Despite these personnel changes, sales declined in 1962 and Gilbert experienced a loss of $281,000, attributed mostly to lower sales, the cost of preparing the 1963 line, and scrapping obsolete materials.

In 1963, the product line was expanded by 50 new toys, boosting the line to 307 items. For the first time, Gilbert offered toys for preschool children and for girls in the 6–14-year-old bracket as well as for boys, Gilbert's traditional market segment. Sales continued to fall and losses in 1963 amounted to $5.7 million, stemming mostly from huge returns of low-priced toys shipped on a guaranteed-sale basis to traditional outlets (nearly $3.5 million in unsold toys were in Gilbert's inventory after Christmas).

In 1964, losses were reduced as cuts in factory personnel and departments reduced administrative and operating expenses from $10 million to $4.7 million a year. Gilbert's sales force was scrapped and manufacturers' representatives were employed to distribute its products.

In 1965, Gilbert realized that television had become the primary advertising medium and invested $2 million in sponsoring a 52-week schedule of Saturday morning cartoon shows. Sales increased to $14.9 million, the best since the 1950's, but losses were $2.9 million. The immediate cause seemed to be heavy returns of the 007 racing auto set and other racing sets. Dealer complaints stated the cars were poorly engineered, burned out after a short time, and were poorly made—looking more like toys than models. The see-through cardboard box showed only the cars, and dealers had to explain that the track was also included.

Other comments from dealers were: "Gilbert had a natural in its Erector set. Instead they neglected it. They used to offer sets up to $75, packaged in metal boxes. Now the most expensive is only $20, the parts are flimsy, and it's in an oversize box. They did the same thing to their chemistry sets. You can't store anything in those oversize see-through packages.

"Manufacturers' representatives increase dealer coverage without increasing the cost of selling but they are not liked by dealers. It used to be that you could call a Gilbert salesman and get service on a problem. Now the reps just want to get the order!"

"Gilbert timing is late. It introduced spy figures (Man from UNCLE, James Bond, etc.) on Christmas Day in 1965—obviously too late for the selling season in which spy items were popular."

Evaluate what has been going on at Gilbert and in the toy industry. What should A. C. Gilbert Co. management do?

31

Modern Shirt Company (A)

As part of its research to find uses for by-products of meat packing, the Tasty Meat Company, a national manufacturer and distributor of canned and processed meats, discovered a new process for making synthetic fibers. After considerable experimentation it was discovered that this fiber was ideal for use in white dress shirts. Without blending with any other fibers, it made excellent wash-and-wear shirts which were highly spot and crease resistant, exceptionally soft and static free, and also could be woven so that the shirts would be porous (that is, they would "breathe"). Unfortunately, the cost of producing this material was relatively high so there was no hope of competing with the large cotton shirt market strictly on a price basis. These cotton shirts sell in the range of $2 to $5 and enjoy a large market, as the total adult male market for shirts is estimated at 50 million. The product was more directly competitive with the synthetic and synthetic blend shirts which retailed from $7 up.

The executives of Tasty Meat Company were quite enthusiastic about their find but felt that it really ought to obtain wider distribution than would be obtained at the $7 or above price. Their experience with selling meat products in low-margin outlets had convinced them that it was possible to sell almost anything in grocery stores and make a profit on large volume, even though margins were low. Therefore, rather than turning the basic patent for their fiber over to established shirt manufacturers, they set up the Modern Shirt Company to distribute high-quality shirts on a low-margin basis.

The Modern Shirt Company was set up as a sales subsidiary with its own president and vice president. Both of these men were strongly sales minded, as this subsidiary was to do no manufacturing, shipping, warehousing, or bookkeeping. Production was to be subcontracted to specialists in shirt manufacturing. All of the other physical handling and bookkeeping activities were to be handled by Tasty Meat Company with a charge made to Modern Shirt Company.

Modern Shirt Company planned to offer top-quality synthetic white dress shirts in popular styles at low prices (approximately $5 at retail). Order-getting salesmen were to be used to open up new accounts among the almost 300,000 grocery and meat markets, including supermarkets. These salesmen would explain the nature of the company's offering and install, at no charge to the retailer, a wire and plastic display rack in a suitable place. After the initial placement, Tasty Meat Company salesmen would continue to check the display racks and handle any necessary details. Tasty Meat Company already had salesmen calling regularly on the grocery trade. These men were basically supporting salesmen as the company sold exclusively through wholesalers. They were necessary, however, because the meat business is exceptionally competitive and the wholesalers did not give any special promotion to Tasty Meat Company's products. All orders for the meat products were filled by these wholesalers. They would handle the shirts too.

The grocery retailers were to be allowed a fairly attractive 25 percent markup plus the free use of display racks. Wholesalers would be allowed a 10 percent markup.

In addition to personal solicitation, Modern Shirt Company planned to use national advertising in magazines, newspapers, and on the radio. In fact, it was planned that the advertising for the shirts could tie in with the advertising for the meat products. The company executives were quite sure that this plan would work and therefore were budgeting only $50,000 a year for advertising.

All things considered, the company executives were certain they had a high-quality product and that their usual methods of promotion would enable them to secure good dealer support, especially with good margins on an item which would appear to be attractive price-wise. Their major concern was with the approximate size of the market. There were already a substantial number of well-known manufacturer's brands on the market, including Manhattan, Arrow, and Van Heusen brands. But the many dealer brands and nondescript brands led the executives to believe that brands were not too significant in the shirt market. Also, although the total shirt market was quite large, they were not completely certain about the size of the synthetic shirt market and especially the desire for synthetics at a lower price.

It was especially important to obtain a fairly accurate measure of demand as Modern Shirt Company wished to make arrangements with a shirt producer and to complete plans which would require other expenditures. It planned to buy shirts at $2.80 each already sealed in a plastic package which would be especially suitable for self-service selling. This plastic covering was transparent but of an especially heavy material, so that it would not easily rip or tear under handling; thus retailers would not have to be concerned about soiling through handling. In addition to the basic $2.80 per shirt cost, Modern Shirt Company planned an expenditure of $50,000 per year for national tie-in

advertising with the meat company advertising, and $150,000 for sala-
ries and expenses for eight men and a secretary. In addition, $300,000
was budgeted for the purchase of wire and plastic display racks which
were to be loaned to retailers. Also, an arrangement was made with
Tasty Meat Company whereby a charge of 5 percent of the shirt
company's selling price (based on a $5 retail price) would be made for
the cost of shipping, billing, collection, and sales assistance from the
Tasty Meat Company's retail salesmen.

In view of all these expenditures and the relatively low price being
considered, it appeared the plan would be profitable only if Modern
Shirt Company were able to operate on a high-volume basis. Accordingly, Tasty Meat Company's market research department conducted
an extensive study of the possible market for the shirts. Mail questionnaires were sent to 30,000 persons; 1,980 forms were returned. To the
question "What influences your choice of white dress shirts *most?*" the
replies were: well-known brand, 38 percent; style, 5 percent; material,
32 percent; and price, 25 percent. (No other alternatives were presented
on the questionnaire.) To the question "Who buys white shirts in your
family?" the answers were: men, 10 percent; women, 80 percent; and
both together, 10 percent. To the question "Do you or does someone in
your family buy white shirts for regular (daily) use?" the answers
were: 40 percent "yes," and 60 percent "no." Those who answered the
previous question "yes," were then asked: "Would you (they) be
interested in buying a new miracle fiber dress shirt at a budget price
(about $5)?" The replies to this question were considered especially
important; 30 percent said "yes," 60 percent "no," and 10 percent "don't
know."

In order to discover any significant differences between the questionnaire respondents and nonrespondents, the staff personally interviewed a random sample of 100 consumers who did not reply to the
questionnaire. Their findings revealed that, generally, those who did
not answer were much less interested in buying white shirts than were
those who did reply.

In addition to the questionnaires and the nonresponse interviews, the
research staff conducted a limited number of depth interviews. These
interviews consisted in probing more deeply than does the ordinary
interview into the buying motivations and habits of consumers. The
results of these interviews suggested that consumers were primarily
interested in price and convenience as long as the product seemed
acceptable. Most consumers seemed to feel that "white shirts were
white shirts"; a few, however, seemed especially interested in any kind
of a new product. Others, however, suggested that they would be
somewhat leery of buying a shirt of unknown quality—someone would
have to stand behind it, either a well-known manufacturer, or the
retailer.

A more detailed analysis of other data obtained during a situation
analysis indicated that education, occupation, and economic status had
a distinct bearing on white shirt consumption. Additional computation
led the researchers to conclude that, although the shirt market was very
large, the market for this type shirt was much smaller. They felt that

the survey results could be used (after adjusting for nonresponse), and that those who expressed interest in buying could be thought of as representative of buyers for the total adult male population and could be expected to buy one shirt per year.

In an effort to appraise the effectiveness of the meat channel of distribution, additional points were considered. It was decided that many consumers think of white dress shirts as convenience goods and will buy them at the most convenient store. For some consumers, however, these goods are definitely shopping goods. These consumers wish to feel the quality of the material in comparison with others and receive some assurance from the retail clerk. Especially on new type wash-and-wear clothes, some consumers seemed especially skeptical of the claims of producers and wished additional assurance before buying. When pushed further, many consumers felt that not being able to feel the material would be a distinct handicap. Further, many of them doubted very much whether a grocery store was the place to sell a shirt. They didn't quite see what a grocery store owner should know about selling shirts. Also, many survey respondents were surprised to find a meat packer in the shirt-making business and were somewhat skeptical of the quality of the product.

Knowing that consumer responses must be interpreted with a great deal of care, Modern Shirt Company executives interviewed a considerable number of grocery retailers to determine their response to the proposed plan. Much value was attached to their responses as Tasty Meat Company's market research department had found them extremely reliable in predicting expected consumer response to various new meat products which they had introduced.

Modern Shirt Company executives were somewhat surprised to find that the majority of small grocery store operators were not interested in the plan. Even when the free display rack was mentioned, little interest was aroused. The operators felt that the turnover would be rather low, the rack was too large for their store, and also their customers would not like to spend $5 for a shirt in a grocery store. The majority of their customers complained about spending $5 for groceries.

As the stores got larger, however, the interest of the retail merchants seemed to increase. Many superette operators showed some interest and almost all supermarket operators were quite enthusiastic, especially in view of the free display rack. Many of the larger operators visualized selling at least 200 to 300 shirts a year, but some were not nearly as enthusiastic. On the average, the larger superette operators and the supermarket operators felt that they would be able to sell approximately 150 shirts per year at the $5 price. Overall, Modern Shirt Company executives were relatively enthusiastic, as they felt sure that they should be able to obtain the cooperation of about two thirds of the supermarket and larger superette operators who numbered approximately 30,000.

Evaluate the management analysis. Should they have been so enthusiastic?

The Modern Shirt Company was convinced that the general market for their new type synthetic dress shirt was more than adequate for profitable operation, even on a relatively low-margin basis. They were also satisfied that they would obtain an enthusiastic response from about two thirds of the supermarket and larger superette operators and planned to market the product through grocery channels.

The basic plan called for a $50,000 expenditure on advertising to be tied in with the Tasty Meat Company's national advertising. The executives were convinced that this promotion, in conjunction with the sales assistance of Tasty Meat Company's retail salesmen and Modern Shirt Company's own salesmen, would be more than adequate.

Their advertising agency pointed out, however, that additional sales could be obtained by an additional investment in advertising. Accordingly, the agency developed four plans which it thought the company ought to consider. The basic philosophy guiding the development of these plans was to reach new consumers not yet covered by the planned promotion.

Table 1 *Summary of analysis of four media plans*

Plan	Effective Messages	Cost per 100 Effective Messages
1	33,000,000	$0.55
2	10,000,000	0.80
3	20,000,000	0.60
4	20,000,000	0.50

In evaluating the plans, Modern Shirt Company executives were particularly interested in aggressive, well-directed advertising campaigns. They were interested in the maximum profit per advertising dollar. However, they were also guided by a rule of thumb which had long been accepted by Tasty Meat Company, that total advertising expenditures should never exceed $1\frac{1}{2}$ percent of total expected sales. Since the product was new, the company did not feel that it necessarily should be bound by the $1\frac{1}{2}$ percent requirement, but in the absence of any other guide, had accepted this limit as a maximum above which it did not feel it could go. Modern Shirt Company was desirous of saturating its market to the greatest extent possible with its advertising, while keeping in view the ratio of advertising cost to sales dictated by company policy. With these restrictions in mind, the company executives studied four proposed advertising media plans submitted by their advertising agency (Table 1).

* See Modern Shirt Company (A) for more details.

The plans included only advertising in magazines, on radio, and in newspapers—the media thought to be most effective by the agency. The agency's and the company's research suggested that there would be roughly a direct relationship between effective messages and the extra sales to be obtained due to this additional advertising. Every 100 effective messages were expected to increase sales by three shirts at any reasonable price. Effective advertising messages were measured as messages which reached possible consumers, not just anyone. It was assumed that the messages in each of the four submitted plans would have about equal effectiveness.

Finally, Modern Shirt Company executives were faced with a definite decision on price. They had been thinking of a penetration, low-margin retail price of $5, but decided that long-run profit was their most important goal. They wished to maintain a stable price policy for at least three years, in order to establish buyer confidence. The Modern Shirt Company was to exist as a separate entity, therefore a low price

Table 2 Demand schedule for Modern Shirt Company shirts

Retail Selling Price	Quantity Demanded per Year for Next Three Years
$7.00	1,000,000
6.50	1,500,000
6.00	2,500,000
5.50	2,750,000
5.00	3,000,000
4.50	3,500,000
4.00	5,000,000

on this product was not to be used as a promotional leader for the meat products. The company had a relatively accurate knowledge of its costs and markups. However, rather than simply adding the markups and some allowance for profit (to obtain a price which might have to be subjected to many changes later in view of market demand) they decided that the demand should be considered at the outset.

With these facts in mind, the marketing research department began an intensive study of how many shirts people would buy at various prices (assuming, of course, that all other conditions would remain constant). Their findings are shown in Table 2. It should be noted that while Modern Shirt Company recognized the limitations in attempting to forecast demand, they felt they did so with reasonable accuracy. In addition to their own surveying and studying of all conditions (such as who buyers are and their incomes, habits, preferences, and prejudices) they relied on their dealers' opinions, which corresponded strikingly with the statistics gathered.

Evaluate the plans and proposal. What price should be used?

Index of names

746

Shaw, Steven J., 459
Sheeran, James J., 375
Shoaf, F. R., 186
Shycon, Harvey N., 411
Simon, Herbert A., 517
Simon, J. L., 616
Simon, L., 127, 253
Sissors, Jack Z., 606
Slater, Charles C., 587
Slichter, S. H., 649
Sloan, Alfred P., Jr., 20
Smith, Paul E., 348
Smith, Wendell R., 221
Smykay, E. W., 402, 409, 410
Snitzler, James R., 630
Stafford, James E., 473
Stanton, W. J., 472
Steinberg, Martin D., 428
Steiner, G., 152
Stern, Hawkins, 254
Stern, Louis L., 666
Stern, Louis W., 329, 586
Stevens, S. M., 473
Stewart, Charles F., 204, 586, 658
Stewart, W. M., 408
Stigler, George J., 660
Stolle, John F., 411
Stone, Gregory P., 174
Straits, Bruce C., 154
Sweet, Morris L., 319

T

Taff, C. A., 395
Tarpey, Lawrence X., 154, 588
Taylor, J. R., 77
Thompson, Joseph W., 459
Tull, D. S., 79, 616
Twedt, Dik W., 235, 249, 551

U

Udell, Jon G., 598, 616
Uhl, Kenneth P., 235

V

Vaile, R. S., 654
Van Cise, J. G., 598
Vincent, Clarence E., 644

W

Wagner, Louis C., 152
Wales, Hugh G., 75, 492
Warner, Lloyd, 162
Warshaw, Martin R., 313, 563
Wasson, Chester R., 292
Watt, Richard S., 558
Webster, F. E., Jr., 477
Wedding, Nugent, 336
Weigand, Robert E., 412, 421
Weilbacher, William M., 27
Weiss, E. B., 244, 349, 361, 362, 363,
    388, 459, 618
Weitz, Harold, 614
Wells, William D., 121
Werner, Ray O., 49
Westfall, Ralph, 5, 78, 144, 232, 404
Westing, J. Howard, 472, 598
White, I. S., 491
Whyte, William H., Jr., 167, 168, 440
Willett, Ronald P., 252
Williams, R. J., 416
Wilson, D. J., 476
Winer, Leon, 613
Winnick, Charles, 152
Wolf, Harold A., 596
Wolfe, Harry D., 496
Wolter, James H., 296
Wright, M. D., 458

Y

Yamey, B. S., 586
Yankelovich, Daniel, 606
Yoder, Wallace O., 509, 644

Z

Zaltman, Gerald, 153, 166, 437, 440,
    473

Index of subjects

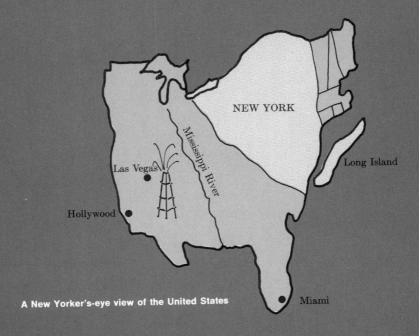

A New Yorker's-eye view of the United States

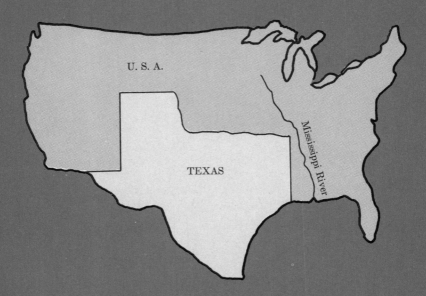

A Texan's-eye view of the United States